CODE NAMES DICTIONARY

OTHER GALE PUBLICATIONS

CONTEMPORARY AUTHORS—
A quarterly, hard-bound biographical reference offering detailed personal information concerning 4,000 current authors each year.

DIRECTORY OF SPECIAL LIBRARIES AND INFORMATION CENTERS—
Provides fourteen types of information for more than 10,000 units. Subject index.

NATIONAL DIRECTORY OF EMPLOYMENT SERVICES—
Gives essential details concerning more than 5,000 organization and university placement bureaus and private employment agencies.

ACRONYMS DICTIONARY—
A guide to the numerous bewildering alphabetic designations ranging from AA to ZTO which are common in modern life. Over 12,000 terms.

DIRECTORY OF UNIVERSITY RESEARCH BUREAUS AND INSTITUTES—
More than 1,300 university-related research units, with detailed information concerning staff, research, budget, etc. Four indexes.

STATISTICS SOURCES—
A dictionary-style guide to sources of statistics on more than 6,100 subjects from abrasives to zirconium. Compiled by leading librarians.

ENCYCLOPEDIA OF ASSOCIATIONS—
Volume 1: National Organizations of the U.S.—Details of membership, program, meeting schedules, etc., covering more than 11,400 groups.
Volume 2: Geographic and Executive Index—Names and addresses of organizations in Volume 1, arranged geographically, and an alphabetical list of their chief executive officers.

MANAGEMENT INFORMATION GUIDE SERIES—
Authoritative, detailed, carefully-indexed overviews of the literature in such major business and governmental areas as Real Estate, Taxation, Public Utilities, Atomic Energy, Communications, and similar fields.

CODE NAMES
DICTIONARY

**A GUIDE TO CODE NAMES, SLANG, NICKNAMES,
JOURNALESE, AND SIMILAR TERMS:**
*Aviation, Rockets and Missiles, Military,
Aerospace, Meteorology, Atomic Energy,
Communications, and Others*

Edited by

Frederick G. Ruffner, Jr.
Robert C. Thomas

Introduction by

Eric Partridge

Contributing Editors

CAPT. J. A. SKIERA
Office of the Secretary of the
Air Force

JAMES L. TRAINOR
National Aeronautics and
Space Administration

NORMAN A. MATSON
U. S. Weather Bureau
Department of Commerce

ROWLAND P. GILL
Office, Chief of Military History
Department of the Army

 GALE RESEARCH COMPANY · BOOK TOWER · DETROIT, MICHIGAN

LIBRARY OF CONGRESS
CATALOG CARD NUMBER
63-21847

Price $15.00

CONTENTS

MISCELLANEA

Editorial Objectives, Practices, and Acknowledgments

Eighteen or so years ago, following the dropping of the atomic bomb, the man who did not know the meaning of "Manhattan Project" (which undertaking, of course, had nothing to do with New York and was not adequately described by such a relatively puny word as project) would actually have been seriously handicapped in his understanding of the news of the day.

Today, there are thousands of topics in public affairs, space, aviation, defense, weather, and other areas of life in connection with which it is essential for the layman or the specialist to understand such cryptic names as "Plowshare," "Operation Mohole," "Friendship 7," "Apollo," "Donna," and "Telstar." Additionally, as details of World War II, the Korean Conflict, and other hot and cold war operations have become available, and as rocketry and space projects have developed, thousands of other code names have entered the contemporary vocabulary.

It has been the intention of the editors of CODE NAMES DICTIONARY to compile a guide to as many code names and related appellations as possible, for the assistance of the citizenry at large, and particularly for researchers, students, writers, historians, governmental agencies, defense contractors, scientists, and the military—in short, for all those to whom, like the citizen of eighteen years ago, an understanding of specialized but esoteric and exotic terms is essential.

Occasional "code name" types of words and phrases are encountered in nearly every area of modern life, including advertising, public relations, and even fund-raising. Unless they have achieved some substantial degree of public recognition, however, there has been no effort to include such transitory terms in this publication.

As the subtitle to this volume suggests, the editors have attempted to provide extensive coverage (while realizing that definitive coverage is not possible) of code names, nicknames, sobriquets, slang, journalistic jargon, etc., related to the following general subjects:

World War II, the Korean Conflict, and major peacetime exercises of the armed services since 1945, including names for military actions, locations, persons, and equipment.

Aviation and aircraft.

Military and scientific rocketry and space exploration, including satellites of all nations and activities of the International Geophysical Year.

Missile systems and equipment.

Weather phenomena, particularly named hurricanes, cyclones, and typhoons.

Data processing (with particular reference to acronyms and similar terms which have the appearance of code words).

Atomic energy projects and tests.

A very large proportion of the words in this volume come from the three areas of historic military actions, aviation, and space and missile activities, in the last two of which new code names appear daily. There also appears to be an increasing trend toward the use of code names in all kinds of activities, frequently for purposes of easy identification or for catching the imagination of the public.

Therefore, a revision of the CODE NAMES DICTIONARY is planned, and the editors hope that even broader coverage of the type of material included in this volume will be possible in the future. Suggestions from users as to specific names, sources, or areas of activity which should be covered in future editions will be welcome. Correspondence should be addressed as follows:

Editor
Code Names Dictionary
Post Office Box 1978
Detroit 31, Michigan

METHODS

Research for this volume has been underway for several years, in the sense that the Gale staff has been noting types of material which might be covered, sources (published or unpublished) for such material, and even a great many individual items.

Active compilation has been in process for about a year, during which time a special library of perhaps 450 volumes was assembled. This library was in turn made use of by an editorial and supporting staff which, altogether, involved a significant amount of effort by twenty-nine researchers, editors, and other personnel.

In addition, a number of field research trips (primarily to Washington and New York) were made by members of the staff. These trips were, of course, valuable in several positive ways, but were worthwhile also in bringing to light an important negative fact: Nowhere does there exist any research tool, published or private, similar to CODE NAMES DICTIONARY, and reactions in libraries, historical archives, military offices, and elsewhere to mention of the Gale project indicated beyond doubt the great usefulness of such a source.

The editorial library compiled for use of the CODE NAMES DICTIONARY staff consisted almost entirely of official publications of the governments of English-speaking countries throughout the world. A few private files and commercial publications were consulted, but these were generally less comprehensive than the official accounts of the same periods.

As examples of publications examined, the following

may be mentioned:

> The extensive series of historical volumes published by the United States Army under the series title, "United States Army in World War II," which includes detailed volumes on strategy, logistics, procurement, staff organization, etc., as well as volumes on specific campaigns; related volumes by individual services, such as the Corps of Engineers, the Ordnance Department, etc., were also used.

> The three British series, "The Strategic Air Offensive Against Germany," "Royal Air Force, 1939-1945," and "The War at Sea, 1939-1945," each of which ran to several volumes.

> Official multi-volume histories published by Canada and Australia.

> The U. S. Navy Office of Naval History "Glossary of U. S. Naval Code Words" (Second Edition).

> Progress reports and annual reports of the U. S. Atomic Energy Commission.

The individual contributing editors drew upon their own experience and files, of course, in addition to still other specialized resources (published and unpublished) in their fields.

In the Air Force, in particular, the phrase "code name" may designate a word which refers not only to matters which are classified for security reasons, but to a word which is itself likely to be classified. To eliminate any possible misunderstanding, it should be stated here that to the best of the editors' knowledge CODE NAMES DICTIONARY contains no material which is at present of a classified nature. As already explained, published sources and archival materials which are generally available to the public were used to a very great extent in compiling this work; in the case of material which has been prepared by persons having any official connection, such material has been approved prior to inclusion, wherever this is required by applicable regulations.

EDITORIAL PRACTICES

As material was being assembled and evaluated, a basic editorial problem had to be dealt with concurrently, namely: What should be included in this dictionary?

Military operations with distinctive names should be included, but what about military undertakings the names of which were acronyms, such as "PLUTO"? The decision here was to include acronyms which could be pronounced or which could be mistaken for a true code name or nickname, since the user would certainly not be helped by having such material omitted on a technicality.

Alpha-numeric equipment names, particularly aircraft names, presented another problem. Such designations are extremely numerous, and a considerable number of very similar designations are often used for what is essentially the same piece of equipment, with only minor technical modifications. It was felt that attempting to trace out and properly identify the various alpha-numeric designations would be unduly time consuming, and that the information which would often be required to discriminate between one model and another would usually be of a technical nature which is beyond the scope of this book. Therefore, with the exception of a very few cases such as the X-15 (where the aircraft is generally known by this designation, and has no widely-used popular name), alpha-numeric designations have not been used. (Anyone interested in the new designation system for U. S. military aircraft may find details in Air Force Regulation No. 66-11, 18 September 1962.)

Generic names or common names presented another problem. Sometimes, such a name, or a word having to all appearances a purely descriptive quality, was actually a word which warranted inclusion; an example of such a word is "Relay," as applied to a specific repeater satellite. Again, a word might clearly be a common or proper noun, but its application was such that its inclusion seemed appropriate; "Aero Code" is such an entry.

With certain limited exceptions, then, it can be said

that the common basis for all the terms in this dictionary is the fact that they are "cover" words, words used with some meaning other than their common one either for concealing details or to serve as a shorthand or popular designation for an object, person, place, etc., which probably is not otherwise identified.

In general, it has been the editors' purpose to furnish identifications rather than full explanations of the entry words, i.e., to place the words in contexts which would make clear their meaning in the material where found, or to indicate their primary reference, rather than to provide complete historic or technical details. (A description of the typical content and arrangement of an entry will be found inside the front cover.) A small amount of technical information has been given for some rockets and aircraft, particularly the former, because of the broad interest in the subject and because of the frequent value of such detail in distinguishing one item from another.

ACKNOWLEDGMENTS

The publisher's primary debt is, of course, to the contributing editors whose special skills helped assure an accurate and comprehensive book. These experts are named and identified on the title page, and need not be re-named here.

An equally basic contribution was made, however, by the research and editorial staff which provided much of the basic material for the entire book. Under Frederick G. Ruffner, Jr., head of the Gale Research Company, who conceived and developed the idea for this dictionary several years ago, Senior Editor Robert C. Thomas and Bibliographer Harold C. Young assembled and processed the materials necessary for the project, and Mr. Thomas wrote or reviewed the military operations entries, and provided informed and skillful direction to the work of the staff.

Special mention should be made of the contributions of

Gale staff editors Barbara Kopala, Bernard Harris, and Martha Leonard.

Valuable cooperation, materials, and suggestions were received from many sources.

Among libraries, particular mention should be made of the help given by the reference and/or social science staffs of The Library of Congress, Detroit Public Library, New York Public Library, and the University of Michigan and Wayne State University libraries.

In addition, significant assistance was received from the following:

> Office of the Assistant Secretary of Defense for Public Affairs (particularly Miss Edith Midgette, Chief, Magazine and Book Section)

> Department of the Air Force (numerous offices, but including especially Lieutenant Colonel Carroll V. Glines, Jr., head, Magazine and Book Branch, Office of Information; Mr. O. T. Albertini, Chief, Terminology Section, U.S.A.F. Headquarters; the staff of the Headquarters library; Colonel John H. Corcoran, Chief, Industrial Branch, Office of Information)

> Department of the Army Library, the Library of the Office of the Chief of Engineers, and the Office of the Chief of Information

> Department of the Navy (particularly the Naval Ordnance Laboratory Library and Mr. Robert Harmon, of the Naval Research Laboratory Library)

> National Aeronautics and Space Administration

> National Archives and Record Service

> Atomic Energy Commission Library and Office of Technical Information

> Civil Aeronautics Board

> Federal Aviation Agency

Cabinet Office Historical Section, London, England (particularly Miss Laura Cooper)

Royal Canadian Air Force Headquarters, Ottawa, Ont., Canada (particularly Flying Officer H. A. Halliday)

International Business Machines Corporation

Aerospace Industries, Inc.

Numerous other individuals and organizations made suggestions and provided leads which were helpful.

Sincere appreciation is extended to all who have participated in any way in the compilation of the CODE NAMES DICTIONARY. The editors feel confident that the result will be found worthy of the efforts of the many persons involved.

A MATTER OF HISTORY
AND LANGUAGE

The new "Webster" defines "code name" as "A word made to serve as a code designation"—here, "a secret designation" —"disguising single items in an otherwise intelligible discourse": in short, a secret word that, until the action concerned has taken place or the plan has been put into effect, bears a meaning unknown except to those persons who are directing the operation.

Usually I can make up my mind on a matter of language very quickly—if sometimes wrongly. Concerning these Code Names, I cannot decide whether the matter is predominantly historical or predominantly linguistic; probably it is both, and certainly these aspects are not in opposition, but complementary. I do, however, know that CODE NAMES DICTIONARY will be hardly less valuable to the philologist than to the historian and that it will prove invaluable to all who read history, whether world-scale or autobiographical, and delightful to all those curious people who "adore a reference book."

The history of code names goes back to prehistory—to the earliest forms of concerted efforts. By the time of Queen Elizabeth, codes and ciphers were relatively common (our Public Record Office, in London, has a record of nearly two hundred from this period) ; an example was the code-cipher employed by Lord Burghley in which signs of the Zodiac were used. In Burghley's scheme, "Cancer" referred to the Estates-General, and "Leo," the Council of State.

As in Burghley's, many of the early code names had a significant common element, and this characteristic has persisted in modern usage; this dictionary identifies many groups of words with common elements, as in the case of operation "Abigail," the subordinate parts of which were named after other Biblical women, "Jezebel," "Rachel," and "Delilah."

Nor is the history of code names entirely dissociated from acronyms, or words consisting of the initials of a group of words, as in "Defense of the Realm Act," which, by abbreviation, becomes "D.O.R.A.," which, by pronunciation as a word (the resultant acronym), becomes "Dora," which began as slang and has ended as a British government colloquialism and nickname. Occasionally an acronym can be mistaken—quite naturally and forgivably mistaken—for a code name, as in "Pluto," which equals "P.L.U.T.O." or "Pipe Line Under The Ocean" (strictly, the English Channel); if there be any connection with Pluto, the god of the underworld, it is purely subconscious.

Nicknames, also included in this compilation, are of course merely familiar names, whether slangy or colloquial, bestowed upon somebody or something whose real name is well known, at least in the circles or professions that coined it. But the editors of CODE NAMES DICTIONARY have displayed both commonsense and goodsense in their decision to include such nicknames as have corresponding code names, or might be inferred to be code names. Nicknames are not so numerous as to cause inconvenience; they are so human, a few are so humorous, as to add a spice of gaiety, an element of the picturesque, a hint of personality, to what might otherwise have become a rather solemn, inhuman collection of bureaucratic terms. And they would not be inappropriate even in such company, for even bureaucrats have been known to act with humanity.

A natural, unaffected humanity informs the private life and the public career of Sir Winston Churchill, who had a potent hand in forming the Fighting Services', as also the governmental (or High Policy), code names of the war years. In CLOSING THE RING, volume five of his monumental work, THE SECOND WORLD WAR, that indomitable statesman, who never lost the common touch, has, here as elsewhere, shown the warm certainty of his grasp on a subject vitally affecting the lives of human beings.

Writing to General Ismay on the 8th of August 1943, he remarks upon a list of proposed code names submitted to him: "Operations in which large numbers of men may lose their lives ought not to be described by code-words which imply a boastful and over-confident sentiment, such as 'Triumphant,' or, conversely, which are calculated to invest the plan with an air of despondency, such as 'Woebetide', 'Massacre,' 'Jumble'. . . . They ought not to be names of a frivolous character, such as 'Bunnyhug' . . . and 'Ballyhoo.' They should not be ordinary words often used in other connections, such as 'Flood,' 'Smooth,' 'Sudden'. . . .

"After all, the world is wide, and intelligent thought will readily supply an unlimited number of well-sounding names which do not suggest the character of the operation or disparage it in any way. . ."

World War I produced many code names; World War II, still more—at the very least 10,000. Among so many, a few had, for one good reason or another, to be changed. For instance, the Allied operation initiated against southern France on 15 August 1944, was at first called by the picturesque name "Anvil," but was changed to the picturesque but less appropriate "Dragoon." The tremendous main invasion of France, initiated on 6 June 1944, bore the distinctive and imaginative code name "Overlord," perhaps, at least among civilians, both British and American, and among journalists and historians, the best-known code name of the entire war.

My own favorites for the European theatre of war are "Fanfare," a very apt collective name that covered all operations in the Mediterranean area (1944-45); "Pantaloon," applied to Naples, a term with fascinating allusions to Italian costume and drama and opera; and "Soapsuds," the bombing of the oil wells at Ploesti in Rumania.

Closely rivalling "Overlord" in popular appeal, if not in importance, is a code name that designates a wonderful example of cloak-and-dagger imagination and bluff: "Operation Mincemeat." Many people think that the operation deserved a less grisly name: and a less grisly name it would have received had it not appealed to, and been promoted by, an important man very intimately concerned with the devising and execution of the plan. He himself has admitted that his imagination had "become somewhat macabre."

"Operation Mincemeat" was an Admiralty, not a War Office, code name, already used once for a very successful achievement and therefore prepossessing. (As too many knowledgeable persons forget, this was a British Intelligence Operation.)

In this scheme, the corpse of a fictitious Captain—Acting Major—William Martin of the Royal Marines, ostensibly the victim of an air crash, was to be washed up near Huelva in Spain. It was cast off from the submarine Seraph on the last day of April 1943. The Allies hoped thus to convince the Germans that this body of an, in the fact, unimportant man with no immediate family and no near relations, was that of an official messenger carrying, in a briefcase, some highly secret, highly classified, papers indicating that the real "Operation Husky"—it WAS put into effect—would take place in southern Greece instead of in Sicily, as was the real case. The bluff succeeded, despite a rigorous investigation by German intelligence. (The true facts of "Operation Mincemeat" have been admirably narrated by the Honourable Ewen Montagu in THE MAN WHO NEVER WAS, and in Lord Alfred Duff Cooper's OPERATION HEARTBREAK.)

Of all code names devised since World War II, the most picturesque, as also the most significant, are those concerning and employed in the exploration of aerospace. This dictionary contains hundreds of informative, but short, entries for names of this type, but among fuller treaments the best article I've seen on this fascinating subject is Professor T. M. Pearce's "The Names of Objects in Aerospace" (in NAMES, March, 1962); this concerns one facet only of aerospace terminology, it is true, but a very important facet.

Whatever the subject, it is clear that now, as in the dawn of this practice of code-naming, two factors have remained constant: mankind's unceasing and unweakened love of mystery and mankind's sporadic realization of the need for caution.

Eric Partridge

London
July, 1963

A

A, BASE -- U. S. naval base, Lough Erne, Ireland. WW-II.

ABC EXPRESS ROUTE -- See ABC HAUL

ABC HAUL -- Motor transport express system organized to move supplies from docks in port of Antwerp, Belgium, to advance depots. Initials in name stand for nationalities using system: Americans, British and Canadians. (Other references give Belgian cities of Antwerp, Brussels and Charleroi.) Also called ABC Express Route. 30 November 1944-26 March 1945, WW-II.

ABC-1 -- Agreements resulting from the Anglo-American military staff conversations held in Washington in January-March 1941. WW-II.

ABC-2 -- Second report of service staff committees of United States and Great Britain, recommended acceleration of aircraft production in both countries. March, 1941. WW-II.

A-BOMBERS -- Term originally applied to military aircraft capable of carrying atomic weapons but no longer apropos due to miniaturization of this type weapon.

A DAY -- Assault day for Allied invasion of Leyte, Philippines. 20 October 1944, WW-II.

A GO OPERATION -- Attack by Japanese Navy on U.S. Pacific Fleet in showdown battle; combined fleet's striking power organized into unit called 1st Task Force, which was assisted by 1st Air Fleet; power of attack reduced by redeployment for KON OPERATION; known to Allies as Battle of Philippine Sea, which occurred off Mariana Islands. Mid-June 1944. ("Go" in the name is roughly equivalent to English "number.") WW-II.

A.M.E.S. RIDGE -- Name for Hill 182 near Heraklion, Crete. May 1941, WW-II.

A, MISSILE -- One of the family of missiles evolved from 1959 Army study of tactical requirements. It is a tactical support missile with a relatively short range (up to 30 miles). The solid-fuel surface-to-surface missile is not being developed due to a 1962 Department of Defense decision to delay starting the program until the results of the MISSILE B development are clearer.

A OPERATION -- (1) See A GO OPERATION

(2) See TOENAILS

A PROJECT -- Proposal made in 1933 to construct plane with range of 5000 miles, speed of 200 miles per hour and bomb load of 2000 pounds; one plane, XB-15; completed in fall of 1937; contributed to development of B-17, B-24, and B-29 bombers.

A-SERIES -- Abbreviation for the Aggregate-Series of ten rocket vehicles designed and developed by the Germans from 1931-1945. Best known was the A-4 (more commonly called the V-2), first used against England in September, 1944. See also AMERIKA RAKETE.

AVT -- Abbreviation for Applications Vertical Test program to study the erection and inflation problems associated with the development of rigid erectable passive communications satellites. Using a THOR booster, the deployment and inflation of the spheres are photographed on ballistic trajectories; the reflectivity of the sphere is photographed by monitoring its radar cross section. One test successfully conducted in 1962.

AARON -- Bulawatan, New Britain. WW-II.

AARX -- A small, solid propellant, air-to-air rocket weapon with four folding fins. Developed and used by Japan.

ABACUS -- Kepler Point, Bawean Island, Netherlands, East Indies. WW-II.

ABATTOIR -- Code name for Dutch New Guinea. WW-II.

ABBEY AND SLOANE -- United States and British policy in event of Japanese occupation of Kra Isthmus, Thailand. WW-II.

ABBOTT -- Airagalpus, Bismarck Archipelago. WW-II.

ABBY -- Hurricane. 9-16 July 1960. Formed east of Windward Islands moved westward through Caribbean Sea and into Central America. Caused six deaths on St. Lucia, and damage in St. Lucia, Martinuque, and British Honduras.

ABDOMEN -- Salmaga Island, Aleutian Islands. WW-II.

ABDULLAH -- Royal Canadian Air Force equipment originally designed to enable a single seater aircraft to home to ground stations. Later a term for equipment which homed on enemy submarines. WW-II.

ABEL'S FIELD -- Allied airfield in central Papua, New Guinea, constructed voluntarily by Cecil Abel, a missionary, with assistance of native labor and equipment dropped by U.S. Fifth Air Force. Became operational October 1942, WW-II.

ABERDEEN -- Name for jungle clearing behind Japanese lines in northeast Burma; used as airstrip during Allied OPERATION THURSDAY. Spring 1944, WW-II.

ABERLOUR, OPERATION -- Planned British and Canadian operation against German salient north of Caen, France, to follow OPERATION EPSOM. Cancelled on 28 June 1944, WW-II.

ABERRATION -- Alexishaven, New Guinea. WW-II).

ABIGAIL -- (1) Mandock Island, Bismarch Archipelago. WW-II.

    (2) British plan for concentrated bombing of a selected German town by 235 aircraft. See also JEZEBEL, DELILAH, RACHEL. Night of 16 December 1940, WW-II.

ABLAZE -- Maradi, New Guinea. WW-II.

ABLE -- (1) Code word for letter "A" in a phonetic alphabet, used in transmitting messages to avoid possibility of a misunderstanding. See also ALFA.

    (2) Hurricane. 12-21 August 1950. Formed northeast of Leeward Islands. Moved northwestward, then turned northeastward off U.S. Atlantic coast and crossed Nova Scotia and Newfoundland back over Atlantic. Caused little damage.

    (3) Hurricane. 16-24 May 1951. Formed south of Bermuda, moved southwestward to Bahamas, looped back northeastward off U.S. Coast and out to sea.

    (4) Hurricane. 25 August - 2 September 1952. Formed in Atlantic 600 miles east of Puerto Rico, moved northwestward for 2000 miles and inland over South Carolina, then northeastward through Middle Atlantic States to New England. Caused two deaths and 2,750,000 dollars damage.

    (5) Name of monkey which, along with BAKER, was fired in a JUPITER nose cone, May 1959. Died after flight.

ABLE DAWGS -- U.S. Navy nickname for pilots of SKYRAIDER-Douglas dive-bomber. See also HAWGS. Korean Conflict.

ABLE, HILL -- Military name for topographic feature in PURPLE HEART RIDGE on Saipan. 1944, WW-II.

ABLE LINE -- U.S. Eighth Army defensive line north of Pyongyang, Korea; one of four lines drawn up for withdrawal in successive steps by Lieutenant General Walton H. Walker before his death. See also BAKER, CHARLIE and DOG LINES. December 1950, WW-II.

ABLE, PLAN -- Plan for building United States 1st Provisional Marine Brigade in Japan to war strength. July, 1950, Korean Conflict.

ABLE, POINT -- Military name for topographic feature on Attu, Aleutian Islands. May 1943, WW-II.

ABLUTION -- Nimrod Sound, China. WW-II.

ABNER -- Kaskas Island, Bismarck Archipelago. WW-II.

ABNORMAL -- (1) Maie River, New Britain. WW-II.

    (2) Advance to Yeu (Yey), Burma. WW-II.

ABOLITION -- Amoy, China. WW-II.

ABOUKIR -- Allied code name for highway between Pontecorvo and Aquino, Italy. May 1944, WW-II.

ABOVEBOARD -- Fort Randall, Alaska. WW-II.

ABRADE -- Langani, New Guinea. WW-II.

ABRAHAM -- U.S. code name for Ennugarret Island, Kwajalein Atoll, Marshall Group. WW-II.

ABROGATE -- Lupin, New Britain. WW-II.

ABSALOM -- Getmata, New Britain. WW-II.

ABSCONDER -- Cape Merkus (Mulus), New Britain. WW-II.

ABSENCE -- Nakagusukuwan, Okinawa Jima, Nansei Shoto Islands, Japan. WW-II.

ABSENTEE -- Cape Beechey, New Britain. WW-II.

ABSORPTION -- Atka Island, Aleutian Islands. WW-II.

ABSTRACT -- Hansa Bay, New Guinea. WW-II.

ABSURD -- Shinko (Sin-Kang), Formosa. WW-II.

ABU -- (English: Gadfly) Japanese nickname for Russian I-16 aircraft. See MOSCA.

ABUSE -- Miyako Shima, Japan. WW-II.

ABUSIVE -- (1) All remote-controlled expendable pilotless aircraft used as guided missiles. WW-II.

(2) Early Navy program to determine the effects of sea-launching on ships and missiles. In 1947, several such tests, including the deliberate tipping over of a V-2 on the carrier Midway's flight deck, were made. Corrosion and structural effects of sea launches were also studied.

ACACIA -- Sydney, Australia. WW-II.

ACAM - French surface-to-air, moderate range missile for use against aircraft at speeds up to 900 miles per hour.

ACAN - Army Command and Administrative Network, known until World War II as War Department Radio Net. See also WAR. WW-II.

ACCENT -- Balabac Island, Philippine Islands. WW-II.

ACCENTUATE -- (1) Adak Island, Aleutian Islands. WW-II.

(2) Canalasan Cove, Mindanao, Philippine Islands. WW-II.

ACCLAIM -- Fort Greely, Alaska. WW-II.

ACCOLADE -- (1) Kru, New Britain. WW-II.

    (2) Allied plan to occupy island of Rhodes on surrender of Italy. Not carried out. September 1943, WW-II.

ACCOMMODATION -- Kagi, Formosa. WW-II.

ACCOMPANY -- Sasebo, Japan. WW-II.

ACCORDIAN -- Malala, Marianas Islands. WW-II.

ACCOUTREMENT -- Sulu Sea, Philippine Islands. WW-II.

ACCUMULATION -- Leyte Island, Philippine Islands. WW-II.

ACCUSE -- Palembang, Sumatra, Netherlands East Indies. WW-II.

ACE -- Acronym for Aerospace Control Environment, a term used by the U.S. Air Force to denote the command and control requirements imposed by aerodynamic and space weapons.

ACE KNOB -- U.N. Military name for topographic feature in Korea near PORK CHOP HILL. See also KING-QUEEN-JACK FINGER. Spring 1953, Korean Conflict.

ACEPIECE -- Ngesebus Island, Palau Islands. WW-II.

ACES -- Acronym for Automatic Control Evaluation Simulator, an air-bearing platform capable of duplicating controls of a space vehicle. A man can sit on the platform and simulate the effects of space flight. Operational.

ACETATE -- Andru River, New Britain. WW-II.

ACETYLENE -- Pontangeras Island, Ulithi Atoll, Yap Islands. WW-II.

ACEY-DEUCEY -- Nickname for Royal Canadian Air Force aircraftsman, second class. Derived from the abbreviation AC2.

ACHING-BACK -- Nickname for supply drops to isolated Fifth Air Force radar stations and shoran beacon units conducted after beginning of truce talks, July 1951, to maintain proficiency. Korean Conflict.

ACHSE -- (English translation: Axis) German code word announcing surrender of Italians and measures to be taken by German forces, including disarming of Italian units no longer loyal to Axis, occupation of positions on peninsula, and evacuation of Sardinia. 8 September 1943, WW-II.

ACID -- Code name for beaches between Syracuse and Avola on east coast of Sicily, attacked by part of British 8th Army in invasion of Sicily, Operation HUSKY. See also BARK. 10 July 1943, WW-II.

ACIDITY -- Gavutu Island, Solomon Islands. WW-II.

ACIDORE -- Mamgak, New Guinea. (WW-II.

ACKCOL -- Name of column from British 50th Division during action near El Alamein, Egypt. July 1942, WW-II.

ACKNOWLEDGEMENT -- Nanshi, Formosa. WW-II.

ACORN -- Name for men and machines designated by U.S. Navy to construct advanced land and seaplane bases. See also CUB, LION. WW-II.

ACQUAINT -- Okino Erabue Jima, Nansei Shoto Islands, Japan. WW-II.

ACQUISITION -- Occupation by British of the Anglo-Persian Oil Companies areas in southern Iran. 23 July 1941, WW-II.

ACROBAT -- (1) Czech trainer aircraft. See AKROBAT and TRENER-MASTER.

   (2) Bonivat, Woodlark Island. WW-II.

   (3) Projected British westward advance in Libya from Cyrenaica into Tripolitania; planned to follow CRUSADER. Early 1942, WW-II.

ACTOR -- Acronym for Askania Cine-Theodolite Optical-tracking range

ACUMEN -- Wilwilan, New Guinea. WW-II.

ADAM -- (1) U.S. Air Force proposed vertical take-off and landing aircraft using lift fan, air deflector and modulation.

   (2) See FRIDA

ADDITION -- Evacuation of British troops from Bardia, Libya. 19-20 April, 1941, WW-II.

ADELAIDE -- U.S. Navy designation of zone in Manila Bay, Philippines, for mine sweeping operations. February 1945, WW-II.

ADELE -- Name reserved by meteorologists for tropical cyclone in eastern North Pacific.

ADELPHI -- Sandakan, British North Borneo. WW-II.

ADEQUATE -- Little Quemoy Island, Formosa Strait. WW-II.

ADHERENT -- Dublon Island, Truk Lagoon, Caroline Islands. WW-II.

ADIGE LINE -- See VENETIAN LINE

ADIPOSE -- Wotje Atoll, Marshall Islands. WW-II.

ADJECTIVE -- Ryuku-Sho, Lambai Island, Formosa Area. WW-II.

ADJOURN -- Tokuno Jima, Nansei Shoto Islands, Japan. WW-II.

ADJUTANT -- Miyako Jima, Nansei Shoto Islands, Japan. WW-II.

ADMEASURE -- Yawata, Japan. WW-II.

ADMIN BOX -- Headquarters of administrative troops of 7th Indian Division at Sinzweya, Burma. February 1944, WW-II.

ADMIRAL Q -- See Q, ADMIRAL

ADOAR -- Advanced DYNASOAR.

ADOBE -- Brisbane, Australia. WW-II.

ADOLF HITLER LINE -- Allied name for strongly fortified German defense line, backing up GUSTAV LINE in Italy; hinged on WINTER LINE at Mount Cairo, it reached west coast at Terracina after passing by Piedimonte, Aquino, Pontecorvo and Sant' Oliva. Called by Germans, at first, Führer Riegel (Führer Switchline) and later, Senger Riegel (after General Fridolin von Senger und Etterlin, commander of 14th Panzer Corps). See also DORA LINE. 1943-44, WW-II.

ADONIC -- Yawi River, Madang, New Guinea. WW-II.

ADULATE -- Yungo River, New Guinea. WW-II.

ADVANCED RELAY -- National Aeronautics and Space Administration medium altitude communications satellite launched by an ATLAS-AGENA into a 12,000 mile circular orbit. Capable of handling radio and television signals by way of a 600 pound active repeater satellite. In study stage, with program to be determined by results of RELAY program.

ADVANCED SYNCOM -- National Aeronautics and Space Administration high altitude (synchronous) communications satellite launched into 24-hour orbit by an ATLAS-AGENA. Capable of handling four television channels by way of a 500 pound active repeater satellite. Not under development. Program will be contingent on the results of the SYNCOM program. One six-month study contract let to determine satellite characteristics.

ADVENT -- U.S. Army program to develop and launch into synchronous orbit an instantaneous repeater satellite for military communications. ATLAS-CENTAUR launch vehicle was to have been used to place the 1000 pound satellite in a 24-hour orbit. However, technological improvements, delay in the Centaur program and increased weight of the Advent satellite itself forced essentially a cancellation of the program in May, 1962. Two systems, a low and high altitude system, will be developed under the "re-oriented" program. Outgrowth of COURIER, ATLAS-SCORE and other military communications experiments. See also CSAR, FLAG.

ADZUKI -- Selib Creek, New Guinea. WW-II.

AEOLUS -- A name used by both the U.S. and Australia for an atmospheric sounding rocket; Australian rocket can carry 30-130 pounds to a maximum altitude of 250,000 feet; U.S. name is used for a family of Navy rockets able to carry 6-9 pounds to varying altitudes from 60,000 - 200,000 feet.

AERIAL II -- See EMERAUDE

AERIAL DARTS -- Tow target with slim body and four triangular plywood fins. Later models were made of paper honeycomb and plastics which are designed to disintegrate when hit. In use in 1956.

AERIAL, OPERATION -- Evacuation of remainder of British Expeditionary Force in France after OPERATION DYNAMO: originally planned for ports in northwest, but extended to include ports to Spanish border and the Channel Islands; almost 200,000 British and Allied troops taken to United Kingdom. Also called OPERATION ARIEL. 15-23 June 1940, WW-II.

AERO -- Czech refinement and development of the C.Z.L. 45 light transport plane the 145. Flew in 1958.

AERO CODE -- International form of message in which observed meteorological elements of concern to aviation are encoded in groups of five numerical digits.

AERO COMMANDER -- See COMMANDER

AEROBEE -- A family of upper-atmosphere research rockets. First rocket of its type to be developed specifically to investigate the upper atmosphere. First fired in November, 1947, and still in wide use. Most advanced version can reach an altitude of 1300 miles with a 130 pound payload.

AEROBEE 75 -- See AEROBEE HAWK

AEROBEE 100 -- See AEROBEE, JR.

AEROBEE 150 -- See AEROBEE-HI

AEROBEE 300 -- See SPAEROBEE

AEROBEE HAWK -- Modified AEROBEE for Army use.

AEROBEE-HI -- Advanced version of AEROBEE, capable of reaching 160-mile altitude with a payload of 150 pounds. Now called Aerobee-150.

AEROBEE, JR. -- High-altitude sounding rocket designed for research at intermediate levels (between 50-100 miles). Short-range version of earlier Aerobee-Hi.

AEROFLOT -- A Soviet ministry responsible for all forms of civilian air transport, agricultural and other non-military flying in Russia. Sometimes referred to as the commercial airline.

AEROMITE -- An early U.S. air-to-air, small, solid propellant rocket, similar to the MIGHTY MOUSE and ZUNI. Never really developed; designed to fire 12 rockets in one quarter of a second from a standardized launcher.

AEROS -- National Aeronautics and Space Administration third-generation meteorological satellite to be launched into 24-hour stationary orbits for continuous observation of most of the earth's weather. Three or four satellites equally spaced about the equator are expected to form part of the National Operational Meteorological Satellite Network. Still in the planning stage, characteristics will depend on TIROS and NIMBUS programs. Launch vehicle will probably be the SATURN or ATLAS-CENTAUR. First flights expected in 1964 or 1965.

AESOP -- Acronym for Artificial Earth Satellite Observation Program. Sponsored by the U.S. Navy to automatically detect silent satellites using infra-red pre-selectors.

AFFABLE -- Sungum, New Guinea. WW-II.

AFFECTATION -- (1) Amchitka Island, Aleutian Islands. WW-II.

(2) Kabacan, Mindanao, Philippine Islands. WW-II.

AFFIRMATIVE -- Taihoku, Formosa. WW-II.

AFLOC -- British project for trans-Africa supply route for supply of vehicles and equipment to Middle East and east Africa. 1943, WW-II.

AFTERMATH -- Umnak, Alaska。 WW-II。

AG-CAT -- Grumman single-engine biplane cropduster. First flew 22 May 1957.

AG-2 -- Transland agricultural plane made in U.S. First flew in 1956.

AGATE -- (1) French vehicle for conducting space research and Intermediate Range Ballistic Missile flight testing. Six have been launched, and have carried half-ton payloads to altitudes of 30 miles. Operational in 1961. See also TOPAZE.

(2) Code name for Ascension Island, Atlantic Ocean; canceled. WW-II.

(3) Pulo Cecir De Mir, French Indo China. WW-II.

AGATHA -- Name reserved by meteorologists for tropical cyclone in eastern North Pacific.

AGENA -- Family of successively improved upper-stage satellites used in the Air Force's DISCOVERER, SAMOS and MIDAS space programs as well as various National Aeronautics and Space Administration programs such as MARINER, RANGER and ORBITING ASTRONAUTICAL OBSERVATORIES. Entire stage goes into orbit and has a restart engine capability. ATLAS and THOR used as Agena boosters. "A" model first used in 1959; "B" model in 1960 and "D" model in 1962. See also THOR-AGENA.

AGGRAVATE -- Fassarai Island, Ulithi Atoll, Yap Islands. WW-II.

AGGREGATE -- Celebes, Netherlands East Indies. WW-II.

AGHELIS -- Similar to autogyros of the period, this 1936 German effort by Focke-Wulf was considered the world's first successful helicopter.

AGILE -- Advanced Research Projects Agency program to develop techniques and equipment to meet the needs of counter-insurgency forces.

AGILITY -- Name for peacetime military exercise.

AGIP -- Operable ARGONAUT nuclear reactor in San Donato, Italy.

AGNES -- (1) Typhoon. 14-20 November 1948. First detected near Eniwetok Atoll, the Pacific. Moved west-northwestward through southern Marianas and over Philippine Sea. Recurved gradually to northeast, skirted southeast coast of Japan, and passed out over the North Pacific.

    (2) Typhoon. 30 October - 4 November 1952. Formed near northern Caroline Islands. Moved northwestward past Guam, across the Philippine Sea and recurved to the northeast, passing southeast of the Ryukus and Japan.

    (3) Typhoon. 12-21 August 1957. Formed in western Caroline Islands, Pacific. Moved northward through Philippine Sea, passing east of Okinawa and through Korea, then dissipated.

AGNOSTIC CHART -- Humorous term sometimes used among meteorologists to mean a prognostic meteorological chart which no one believes.

AGOUTI -- Bizerte, Tunisia. WW-II.

AGREEMENT, OPERATION -- British sea raid on Axis shipping and port facilities at Tobruk, Libya, involving landing and re-embarkment of marines and soldiers, and having overall purpose of relieving German pressure to the east on El Alamein front; failed, with three British war ships sunk and a number of troops made prisoner. Mid-September 1942, WW-II.

AGRICOLA -- British Auster B.8 agricultural aircraft first flown in 1955.

AGRICOLTA -- Czech agricultural version of the CZL 60 aircraft. See BRIGADYR.

AGRICULTURE -- Myitkyina, Burma. WW-II.

AGROUND -- Koto Sho (Antau Su), Formosa Area. WW-II.

AIBA 8 -- Pre-World War II Japanese biplane advanced trainer by Tokyo Koku.

AIDA -- German offensive operation against British in Libya and Egypt. Began 26 May 1942, WW-II.

AIGLET -- British Auster trainer/tourer aircraft. Flew in 1951.

AIKAROPPU -- See EGAROPPU

AINTREE, FORCE -- British naval convoy in eastern Australian waters, carrying Governor-General of Australia (Duke of Gloucester) and his staff. September 1945, WW-II.

AIR BRIDGE TO FREEDOM -- See SAFE HAVEN, OPERATION

AIR CIGAR -- See CIGAR

AIR COBRA, EXERCISE -- A week-long test of SEATO'S (Southeast Asia Treaty Organization) tactical airpower against a possible aggressor. Started 23 April 1962.

AIR COMMANDOS -- (1) U.S. Air Force guerrilla warfare fighters, trained after World War II. See also COIN.

(2) See TERRY AND THE PIRATES

AIR EXPRESS -- Lockheed single-engine, high-wing U.S. transport plane of 1928.

AIR FORCE SCOUT -- See BLUE SCOUT

AIR TOURER -- Australian Victa monoplane. First flew 1959.

AIR YACHT -- Bach tri-motor U.S. airliner of early 1930's.

AIRACOBRA -- Bell P-39 fighter ordered by the U.S. Army Air Corps in October 1937. First flew in 1939. Saw extensive combat service in WW-II. Called Caribou by British.

AIRACOMET -- First U.S. jet aircraft, the XP-59A; made its first flight, 1 October 1942.

AIRACUDA -- A twin-engine pusher, multi-seat pursuit plane built for the U.S. Army Air Corps by Bell as the XFM-1. First flight, 1 September 1937.

AIRBORNE CIGAR -- See CIGAR

AIRCAMPER -- Pietenpol amateur-built U.S. monoplane of early 1930's.

AIRCOMNET -- U.S. Air Force world-wide command communications network.

AIRCOUPE EXACTA -- See ERCOUPE

AIRCOUPE EXPEDITOR -- See ERCOUPE

AIRCOUPE EXPLORER -- See ERCOUPE

AIRCRUISER -- Bellanca transport plane, produced in U.S. in early 1930's.

AIREDALE -- (1) Beagle-Auster A.109 British cabin monoplane first flown in 1961.

(2) Kanigia Island, Solomon Islands. WW-II.

AIRONE -- (1) (English translation: Heron) Military version of Italian Cant Z.506 pre-WW-II transport plane.

(2) Italian air-to-air and surface-to-surface unguided, solid propelled rocket with a range of approximately seven miles. Operational, with considerable quantities purchased by Japan.

AIRSOLS -- Acronym for U.S. Air Solomons Command. WW-II.

AJAX -- (1) Name for a frequency dispersal radar.

(2) French radio operator of secret radio station, LINCOLN, in Casablanca, French Morocco which was used by U.S. consulate at time of Allied landings in North Africa. November 1942, WW-II.

AKIGUSA -- (English translation: Autumn Grass) Japanese MXY7 wooden glider used as trainer for World War II J8M1 rocket powered interceptor. See SHUSUI

AKROBAT -- (English translation: Acrobat) Single-seat version of Czech Z-326 TRENER-MASTER aircraft.

AKRON -- American-built dirigible which crashed at sea in a storm off the New Jersey coast in 1933. See also MACON.

AKWING -- Allied air unit formed on island of Akyab, Burma, during retreat from Japanese. Early 1942, WW-II.

AL KAHIRA -- (English translation: The Cairo) Egyptian-assembled Spanish Hispano HA-200 turbojet advanced trainer plane. See SAETA.

ALABAMA -- Obsolete U.S. battleship sunk by U.S. Air Service bombers in 1921 tests.

ALABASTER -- British troop convoy from Greenock, Scotland, to Iceland. May 1940, WW-II.

ALACRITY and OATMEAL -- Entry of Allied forces into the Azores. October 1943, WW-II.

ALADDIN -- Allied plan for possible measures to be taken on German withdrawal from northern Norway before total Allied victory in Europe. See also APOSTLE I and II. WW-II.

ALADIN -- Two operable Swiss nuclear reactors of the Aerojet-General Nucleonics-201 and 211 types. In Geneva and Basel, Switzerland.

ALAMO -- Code name for U.S. 6th Army while operating as special ground task force headquarters directly under general headquarters, Southwest Pacific Area. See also RECKLESS and PERSECUTION. Established in June 1943, WW-II.

ALARICH PLAN -- Plan devised by the Germans to deal with possible defeat of Italy after the North African campaign. 1943, WW-II.

ALARM -- Kasho To (Hoisho To), Formosa Area.

ALASKA -- Allied code name for divisional plan to protect road junctions between Ortona, Italy, and forward defense line of Indian troops. May 1944, WW-II.

ALBACORE -- (1) Pre-World War II British Fleet Air Arm biplane built by Fairey.

(2) Overall operational plan for Chinese Army in India to retake north Burma. See also ALBACORE ONE-THREE and LEDO STRIPTEASE. 8 August 1943, WW-II.

ALBACORE ONE -- Plan for Chinese defense of the Ledo Base, north Burma. WW-II.

ALBACORE TWO -- Plan providing for Chinese occupation of Shingbwiyang, north Burma, and for sending patrols to the lines of the Tarung and Tanai streams. WW-II.

ALBACORE THREE -- Plan for Chinese operation in north Burma in four phases -- Phase 3A: Seizure of Jambu Bum; 3B: Seizure of the Lonkin-Kamaing line; 3C: Seizure of Mogaung and Myitkyina: 3D: Seizure of Katha and Bhamo. WW-II.

ALBANY FLYER -- Glenn Curtiss airplane which he flew from Albany to New York City on 29 May 1910 to win a $10,000 prize offered by Joseph Pulitzer, publisher of the New York World.

ALBATROS D-5 -- German World War II biplane used as a scout-fighter.

ALBATROSS -- (1) Name for the huge, imaginary helicopter of Jules Verne's 1886 tale, "The Clipper of the Clouds."

(2) Bowlus 1930 high-performance U.S. sailplane.

(3) Early World War II British militarized version of DeHavilland D.H.91 airliner.

(4) Grumman triphibian used by the U.S. Air Force Air Rescue Service as the SA-16 and by the U.S. Navy as the UF-1. First flight in 1947 and still operational.

(5) U.S. Navy proposal for an ocean surveillance satellite to provide tactical intelligence data to fleet commanders. Not under development.

(6) Code name for Point 73, a hill near western end of gap between Hochwald and Balberger Wald, Germany. Objective of TIGER GROUP during Operation BLOCKBUSTER. Early 1945, WW-II.

ALBERT -- U.S. code name for Ennumennet Island, Kwajalein Atoll, Marshall Islands. WW-II.

ALBERT I and II -- Names of two rhesus monkeys used as test animals in two V-2 rocket flights from Holloman Air Force Base in June 1948 and June 1949. Neither monkey was recovered due to recovery parachute failures. Albert I reached an altitude of 37 miles and Albert II an altitude of 83 miles.

ALBERT-FRIEDA LINE -- German defense line across Italy, north of Rome; passed south of Lake Trasimene. Established after Allied entry into Rome to cover withdrawal to GOTHIC LINE. Called by Allies, Trasimene Line. Summer 1944, WW-II.

ALBREE MONOPLANE -- Albree-designed scout aircraft built by Pigeon-Fraser and delivered to U.S. Air Service in 1917. Also called Pigeon-Fraser Scout.

ALBUM LEAF -- Name for British OBOE Mark II radio guidance apparatus for aircraft. WW-II.

ALBUMOSE -- Hankow, China. WW-II.

ALCIONE -- (English translation: Kingfisher) Three-engine Italian bomber, Cant Z.1007, of WW-II.

ALCOTAN -- Twin-engine, light transport/trainer plane in service with the Spanish Air Force as the CASA 201.

ALCYON -- French basic trainer plane first flown in 1951.

ALDER -- Townsville, Queensland, Australia. WW-II.

ALDERPOINT -- Cape Rizzuto, Italy. WW-II.

ALDERSHOT -- Canadian recreational facility in MAPLE LEAF CITY (Campobasso, Italy). WW-II.

ALDON -- See TAIFUN

ALERT -- U.S. Atomic Mobilization Exercises conducted by Atomic Energy Commission and Office of Defense Mobilization. May 1958.

ALFA -- (1) (Pronounced: AL-FAH) International aviation phonetic alphabet for letter "A". See also $\overline{\text{ABLE}}$.

(2) U.S. surface-to-underwater, free-flight rocket for anti-submarine warfare. Operational in 1952 and deployed aboard cruisers and destroyers. Fired from turret-mounted guns to a maximum range of 900 yards; carries a conventional high explosive depth charge.

(3) See WEAPON ALFA

ALFALFA -- (1) Ottana, Sicily. WW-II.

(2) Purvis Bay, Florida-Tulagi Group, Solomon Islands. WW-II.

ALGOL -- First stage solid propellant booster for the SCOUT launch vehicle. Develops 115,000-pound thrust.

ALGONQUIN BRIDGE -- Canadian crossing of Kusten Canal, Germany. Names for Algonquin Regiment. 17-19 April 1945, WW-II.

ALIBABA -- Code name for the Russians. WW-II

ALICE -- (1) Tufi, New Guinea. WW-II.

   (2) Typhoon. October 1947. First detected near Truk, Caroline Islands. Moved northward into North Pacific.

   (3) Tropical storm. 25 May - 6 June 1953. Formed in western Caribbean. Moved erratically northward across western Cuba into Gulf of Mexico and inland near Panama City, Florida. Caused floods and several deaths in Cuba.

   (4) Hurricane. 24-26 June 1954. Formed in western Gulf of Mexico, moved inland south of Brownsville, Texas and dissipated over Rio Grande Valley. Caused floods and 17 deaths in Texas and 38 in Mexico.

   (5) Hurricane. 30 December 1954 - 5 January 1955. Formed in Atlantic northeast of Leeward Islands. Moved southwestward into eastern Caribbean Sea and dissipated. Caused property damage in Leeward Islands.

   (6) Typhoon. 14-23 July 1958. Formed south of Guam. Moved north-northwestward, then northward and crossed coast of Honshu, (Japan), causing 12 deaths and substantial damage, then died out.

   (7) Typhoon. 17-21 May 1961. Formed in South China Sea west of Luzon. Moved northward over Hong Kong into China mainland, then turned eastward back out to sea south of Japan. Caused 4 deaths in Hong Kong.

   (8) Name also applied to tropical cyclones in western Pacific which occurred prior to (2) through (7) above.

ALIZE -- (English translation: Tradewind) Brequet 1050 antisubmarine aircraft now operational with French Navy. First flew 1956.

ALIZE/RUBEOLE -- Operable French critical facility nuclear reactor in Saclay, France.

ALKALI -- Goose Bay, Lake Melville, Labrador, Canada. WW-II.

ALL-AMERICAN -- Name for peacetime military exercise.

ALL-AMERICAN DIVISION -- Nickname for U.S. 82nd Airborne Division.

ALL-ONE-PRICE -- German name for planned bombing attack on Wolverhampton, England; not carried out. November 1940, WW-II.

ALLEN -- U.S. code name for Ennubirr Kwajalein Atoll, Marshall Islands. WW-II.

ALLERGY -- Kiau Point, Soembawa, Netherlands East Indies. WW-II.

ALLEY CATS -- Nickname given by Rear Admiral Robert C. ("Ike") Giffen to U.S. Navy task group he commanded in Aleutians. WW-II.

ALLIGATOR -- (1) Name for U.S. Landing Vehicle, Tracked (LVT), Unarmored, Mark I. See also WATER BUFFALO. WW-II.

(2) Cape Muya, New Britain. WW-II.

(3) Royal Canadian Air Force convoy escort patrol. WW-II.

ALLIGATOR I -- Little Makin Island, Gilbert Islands. WW-II.

ALLIGATOR'S JAWS HILL -- U.N. military name for topographic feature in Yokko-kchon Valley, Korea. Scene of action during fighting on PORK CHOP HILL, Spring 1953. Korean Conflict.

ALLYN -- Typhoon. 16-23 November 1949. First detected in eastern Caroline Islands. Moved west-northwestward, passed south of Guam into Philippine Sea, then recurved northeastward, passed southeast of Japan and out over North Pacific.

ALMA -- (1) Typhoon. September 1946. First detected east of Philippines. Moved northwestward briefly, then recurved northeastward and passed southeast of Japan out over the North Pacific.

(2) Tropical storm. 14-16 June 1958. Formed in Bay of Campeche. Moved northwestward and inland south of Brownsville, Texas and dissipated over Rio Grande Valley. Caused 1 death.

(3) Hurricane. 27-30 August 1962. Formed off Georgia coast, moved northeast-ward, skirting Atlantic coast, and dissipated east of New England.

ALMA FORCE -- American Military units at Dobdura airfield in New Guinea, active in Buna campaign. 1942-43, WW-II.

ALMANAC -- Lakuk River, New Britain. WW-II.

ALMOND -- Tanambogo Island, Solomon Islands. WW-II.

ALOHA -- Bresse single-engine monoplane which finished second in the "Pineapple Derby" air race to Hawaii in 1927. See also WOOLAROC.

ALOUETTE -- (1) U.S. Canadian ionospheric investigation satellite launched by a THOR-GENA, 29 September 1962. The 275-pound satellite, part of the Topside-Sounder program, was built by Canada and launched by the U.S. to study the ionosphere from above, and over a wide range of frequencies, to determine the ionosphere's electron density and nature. Nicknamed Longlegs because it deploys 75-foot antennae once in orbit.

(2) Name for Royal Canadian Air Force Squadron Number 425.

ALOUETTE II -- French Sud-Aviation SE-3130 turbine-powered helicopter. First flew 1955.

ALOUETTE III -- Derived from the -II, the SE-3160 aircraft is a larger version and is being used world-wide.

ALPENVEILCHEN -- (English translation: Cyclamen) German operation to place one mountain division in Albania to aid Italians against Greece. Proposed January 1941, dropped February 1941, WW-II.

ALPHA -- (1) Northrop transport of 1930. First U.S. plane to have all-metal, stressed-skin monocoque fuselage.

    (2) Aruba, Netherlands West Indies. WW-II.

    (3) Code name for U.S. 3rd Division during landing between Bays of Cavalaire and Pampelonne, southern France, in Operation DRAGOON. 15 August 1944, WW-II.

    (4) Code word for tactical plans to concentrate Chinese troops for defense of Kunming and Chungking, China; later used for preparatory measure in taking major port on China coast. See also CARBONADO. Late 1944-1945, WW-II.

    (5) See WEAPON ALFA

ALPHA II -- Ice island established in Arctic by U.S. Project ICE SKATE.

ALPHA DRACO -- McDonnell Aircraft Company proposal for a two-stage solid propellant missile for air-to-surface application. The competition was won by Douglas with its SKYBOLT entry.

ALPHABET -- (1) Evacuation of British troops from Narvik, Norway 5 June 1940, WW-II.

    (2) British Operation against flying bomb carriers and E Boats. 3 December 1944, WW-II.

ALPHONSE -- Northeast Passage, Truk Lagoon, Caroline Islands. WW-II.

ALSAB -- Kano, Africa. WW-II.

ALSEAFRON -- U.S. Navy acronym for Alaskan Sea Frontier.

ALTAIR -- (1) U.S. Lockheed single-engine monoplane of 1933. Earlier model was the SIRIUS.

    (2) Name for the fourth stage of the SCOUT launch vehicle. Solid propellant, it develops a thrust of over 3000 pounds.

ALUMNUS -- Ballale, Bougainville Island, Solomon Islands. WW-II.

AMATEUR -- (1) Cotabato, Mindanao, Philippine Islands. WW-II.

(2) Kiska Island, Aleutian Islands. WW-II.

AMATORY -- Brisbane, Australia. WW-II.

AMAZEMENT -- Mangejang Island, Ulithi Atoll, Yap Islands. WW-II.

AMBASSADEUR -- French monoplane currently in production as the S.A.N. Jodel DR.100.

AMBASSADOR -- Airspeed A.S.57 British transport plane in civilian service and with the Royal Jordanian Air Force. First flew in 1947.

AMBIDEXTER -- Port Elizabeth, Union of South Africa. WW-II.

AMBIGUITY -- Astrolabe Bay, New Guinea. WW-II.

AMBROSE -- Hein Island, Bismarck Archipelago. WW-II.

AMBUSH ALLEY -- U.N. Name for road between Majon-ni and Wonsan, Korea; contained hairpin turns and deep gorges and was harassed by enemy guerrillas. Fall 1950, Korean Conflict.

AMELIORATE -- Falalop Island, Ulithi Atoll, Yap Islands. WW-II.

AMERI-CAN -- U.S. developed gasoline and water container similar to JERRY CAN, but having flexible nozzle attachment. WW-II.

AMERICA -- (1) Curtiss Twin-engine flying boat built in 1914.

(2) Fokker C-2 trimotor plane, piloted by Bert Acosta and Bernt Balchen, with Commander Richard E. Byrd aboard, attempted a flight across the Atlantic 29 June 1927 and ended up short of their goal, Paris, when they ditched off the Normandy coast.

(3) Italian Aeromere F8L single-engine monoplane of the mid-1950's. Also see FALCO.

AMERICAL DIVISION -- Not a nickname; actual name of U.S. Army's only un-numbered division. Formed from Task Force 6814 sent to New Caledonia at beginning of World War II. Name derived from combination of America and New Caledonia.

AMERICAN CLIPPER -- Sikorsky S-40 aircraft launched on South American routes in October 1931 by Pan American.

AMERICAN LEGION -- Plane flown by Commander Noel Davis and Lieutenant Stanton H. Wooster U.S. Navy, which crashed in Virginia in April 1927, while in preparation for New York to Paris flight. Make of aircraft unknown.

AMERICAN RANGERS -- Popular name for U.S. Army Amphibious Training Command. WW-II.

AMERIKA RAKETE -- Nickname for the German A-9/A-10 rocket. See A-SERIES.

AMGOT -- Acronym for Allied Military Government.

AMHERST, OPERATION -- Allied advance to North Sea, with the task of preserving canal and river bridges as well as two airfields at Steenwijk, north-eastern Netherlands. April 1945, WW-II.

AMI -- Acronym for Advanced Manned Interceptor, a U.S. Air Force-Artillery Spotting Division interceptor having a hypersonic speed range.

AMIGOS AIRLIFT -- American aid of food, clothing and medical supplies airlifted to Chile, by the U.S. Air Force, after the country was rocked by earthquakes and tidal waves in 1960.

AMIRAL NORD -- See NORD, AMIRAL

AMITY -- Goropio, New Britain. WW-II.

AMMUNITION -- Hozan (Hozan-Gai), Formosa. WW-II.

AMNESIA -- Attu Island, Aleutian Islands. WW-II.

AMOEBA -- Goodenough Island, New Guinea. WW-II.

AMOROUS -- Makassar Straits, Netherlands East Indies. WW-II.

AMOS -- Acronym for Automatic Meteorological Observing Station, an automatic system developed by the U.S. Weather Bureau for sensing, recording, and transmitting meteorological information. Operational 1962.

AMOUNT -- Kyushito, Formosa. WW-II.

AMOUR -- Murien, New Britain. WW-II.

AMPERSAND -- Espiritu Santo Island, New Hebrides Islands. WW-II.

AMPUTATION -- Bone, Algeria. WW-II.

AMSAC -- Rectangular canvas container used by U.S. to air-drop supplies. WW-II.

AMULET -- Tanaga Island, Aleutian Islands. WW-II.

AMY -- (1) Typhoon. 30 November - 19 December 1951. Formed in Caroline Islands. Moved westward across Philippine Sea and southern Philippines and weakened over South China Sea. Caused heavy damage and 991 casualties in Philippines.

(2) Typhoon. 3-5 August 1956. Formed southeast of Iwo Jima. Moved west-northwestward and dissipated south of Japan.

(3) Typhoon. 5-6 October 1959. Formed east of Luzon, Philippines, moved northward and lost intensity in Ryukyu Islands area.

(4) Typhoon. 29 August - 9 September 1962. Formed northeast of Guam. Moved westward over Philippine Sea, then northwestward across Taiwan into mainland China. Recurved northeastward across Yellow Sea, Korea, and Sea of Japan to Sakhalin Island. Caused damage and 4 deaths on Taiwan and floods in southeastern Siberia.

(5) Name also applied to tropical cyclones in western Pacific which occurred prior to (1) through (4) above.

ANACONDA -- Truk Island, Caroline Islands. WW-II.

ANAKIM -- Allied operation for the reopening of the Burma Road and recapture of Rangoon. Planned for November 1943, but abandoned. See also RAVENOUS, SAUCY. WW-II.

ANATHEMA -- Moen Island, Truk Lagoon, Caroline Islands. WW-II.

ANCHOR HILL -- U.S. military name for topographic feature on eastern front line in Korea. Called Anchor Valley by U.S. Navy pilots after heavy attack by their aircraft on 15 June 1943. Korean Conflict.

ANCHOR VALLEY -- See ANCHOR HILL

ANDERSON'S GULCH -- U.S. military name for topographic feature on Okinawa. 1945, WW-II.

ANDIRON -- Balangori Bay, New Britain. WW-II.

ANDREW -- U.S. code name for Obella Island, Kwajalein Atoll, Marshall Islands. WW-II.

ANDUS -- Acronym for Anglo-Dutch-United States. WW-II.

ANEMONE -- Navy Landing Beach Three, Torokina, Solomon Islands. WW-II.

ANFA -- See SYMBOL

ANGEL -- (1) Reflecting material dropped from an attacking aircraft as a radar countermeasure. Similar to WINDOW, Chaff, ROPE, Flack Paper, Maiden's Hair.

(2) Olutanga Island, Philippine Islands. WW-II.

ANGEL MOVE, OPERATION -- Proposed operation to send Canadian troops to reinforce Allied forces in the Dunkirk area, France. May 1940, WW-II.

ANGELIC -- Nanking-Pukow, China. WW-II.

ANGELO -- U.S. Air Force radio control station at Taejon, Korea, which directed fighter pilots to support targets as well as employment of airborne tactual air coordinators. Evacuated 19 July 1950, See also MELLOW CONTROL. Korean Conflict.

ANGELS, THE -- Nickname for U.S. 11th Airborne Division.

ANGER -- Operation in Netherlands by Canadian I Corps to cross IJssel River in vicinity of Westervoort and capture Arnhem. Originally crossing of Neder Rijn River planned. Also called Quick Anger. See also WALLSTREET. Began 12 April 1945, WW-II.

ANGLEFISH -- Code name for Adriatic Sea. WW-II.

ANGLICO -- Acronym for Air and Naval Gunfire Liaison Company, evolved in 1949, and split up into teams, composed of both U.S. Navy and Marine Corps personnel, to assist Army units lacking the forward air control and naval gunfire control units which are integral in Marine divisions.

ANGLO -- Bastia, Corsica. WW-II.

ANGUS -- Operation by Black Watch of Canada to capture objectives along railway embankment at base of South Beveland isthmus, west of Korteven, Netherlands. 13 October 1944, WW-II.

ANILINE -- Libya, Africa. WW-II.

ANISEED -- Planned amphibious raid by unit of special boat service on Lussin Piccolo, Adriatic Sea. WW-II.

ANITA -- (1) Tropical storm. 29 October 1950. Formed and dissipated west of Bonin Islands, the Pacific.

(2) Typhoon. 17-26 April 1955. Formed over western Caroline Islands. Moved west-northwestward through Philippine Sea and dissipated east of Ryukyu Islands.

(3) Tropical depression. 5-6 July 1959. Formed and dissipated between Truk and Ponape Islands in the Pacific.

(4) Tropical storm. 19-20 October 1961. Formed in South China Sea and moved westward into central Viet Nam.

(5) Name also applied to tropical cyclones in western Pacific which occurred prior to (1) through (4) above.

ANJOU -- French Sipavia S.261 twin-engine monoplane. First flight 1959.

ANKLET -- Combined Allied raid on the Lofoten Islands, Norway. 26 December 1941, WW-II.

ANN -- Tropical storm. 19-26 April 1945. Formed in Marshall Islands, the Pacific. Moved west-northwestward at first, then curved northward and weakened east of Mariana Islands.

ANNA -- (1) Acronym for Army, Navy, National Aeronautics and Space Administration and Air Force Geodetic Satellite. Weighing 355 pounds, and launched by a THOR-ABLE-STAR rocket into a 600-mile orbit, it is designed to provide a triangulation point in space for determining distances and positions on earth. Managed by the Navy, it is a tri-service program with the Army contributing a radio-ranging unit and the Air Force a high intensity flashing light for visible earth measurements. Sometimes called the Flashing Light Satellite. Successfully launched in November 1962. Also called Firefly. See also SECOR.

(2) Hurricane. 25-26 July 1956. Formed in Bay of Campeche and moved westward into Mexico south of Tampico, causing minor damage.

(3) Hurricane. 19-24 July 1961. Developed just east of Windward Islands, moved westward through Caribbean Sea into British Honduras, causing minor damage.

ANNETTE -- Tropical storm. 8-13 June 1960. Developed over Pacific Ocean 180 miles south of Tehauntepec, Mexico. Moved northwestward parallel to Mexican coast, then westward over the Pacific and dissipated.

ANNIVERSARY -- Shoko, Formosa. WW-II.

ANNUITY -- New Guinea operation subsequent to HOTPLATE. WW-II.

ANSON -- Avro Type 652 twin-engine British transport first flown in 1935. Over 11,000 built and many still in service.

ANSWER -- Dairimpo, Formosa. WW-II.

ANT -- Designation for Russian airplanes designed by A.N. Tupolev.

ANTARES -- (1) Name for third stage of the SCOUT launch vehicle. Essentially an improved VANGUARD third stage, the solid propellant motor develops more than a 13,600 pound thrust.

(2) French four-stage solid propellant Intermediate Range Ballistic Missile development vehicle for re-entry tests at speeds up to Mach 8. Operational since 1960.

ANTELOPE -- Vingora Islet, Bismarck Archipelago. WW-II.

ANTHONY -- Cerisy Peak, Long Island, Bismarck Archipelago. WW-II.

ANTHRACITE -- Code name for Newfoundland. WW-II.

ANTICS -- Tawai Point, Trobriand Island. WW-II.

ANTIPATHY -- Senorbi, Sicily. WW-II.

ANTIQUE -- Code name for West Africa. WW-II.

ANTITOXIN -- Milazzo, Sicily. WW-II.

ANTJE'S HURRICANE -- Hurricane. 30 August - 8 September 1842. So named because it dismasted the schooner, Antje, northeast of Puerto Rico. Moved westward into Mexico.

ANTON -- German occupation of southern part of France after Allied landings in North Africa. 10-11 November 1942, WW-II.

ANVIL -- See DRAGOON

ANZAC -- (1) Acronym for Australia-New Zealand Army Corps.

(2) Allied naval task force for protection of South Pacific route. February - March 1942, WW-II.

ANZIO ANNIE -- German 280-mm. railway gun, used in Italy in support of the infantry. WW-II.

ANZIO EXPRESS -- Nickname for German long range railway guns used against Anzio beachhead, Italy. 1944, WW-II.

AOBA DETACHMENT -- Japanese reinforced 4th Infantry Division. WW-II.

APACHE -- (1) Nickname for the World War II P-51 MUSTANG fighter bomber.

(2) Twin-engine Piper PA-23 "160". Originally known as the Twin-Stinson. First flew 1952.

(3) Solid propellant sounding rocket capable of carrying 35 pounds of scientific instruments to an altitude of 40 miles. Operational. See also NIKE-APACHE.

APARTMENT -- Medinilla Island, Marianas Islands. WW-II.

APARTMENT HOUSE -- U.S. nickname for large concrete school building, used as barracks, near Nakama, Okinawa; center of Japanese strength. 1945, WW-II.

APENNINE POSITION -- See GOTHIC LINE

APERIENT -- New Georgia Island, Solomon Islands. WW-II.

APEX BOATS -- Landing craft which towed two others loaded with high explosives, called Drones, released and directed them by radio control into obstructions to be exploded; used by U.S. Navy during landing operations. WW-II.

APEX HILL -- Military name for Hill 296 near Heraklion, Crete. May 1941, WW-II.

APHORISM -- Nauru Island, Gilbert Islands. WW-II.

APHRODITE -- (1) German radar decoy consisting of balloon, trailing plates covered with tin foil; launched from submarine. WW-II.

(2) Code name of experiment, initiated by U.S. General Carl Spaatz, for developing and using radar-controlled conventional bomber aircraft as guided missiles in CROSSBOW operation against German V-weapon sites. Also called BATTY, CASTOR, ORPHAN and WEARY-WILLIE. WW-II.

APOLLO -- Name for the three-man U.S. spacecraft to place two men on the moon before 1970. Consists of three modules (or sections): a Command module, a Service module and a Lunar Excursion Module. Earth orbital flights of Command module to take place in 1964-65; Lunar landing by two men from a lunar orbit perhaps as early as 1967, using the ADVANCED SATURN (C-5) launch vehicle. See also MAN-ON-MOON.

APOSTASY -- Manonuito Island, Caroline Islands. WW-II.

APOSTLE I -- Allied plan for return to Norway following unconditional surrender of Germany. See also ALADDIN. WW-II.

APOSTLE II -- Allied plan for return to Norway in case of German surrender there before total Allied victory in Europe. See also ALADDIN. WW-II.

APOSTROPHE -- Nice, France. WW-II.

APOTHECARY -- Code name for Samoa. WW-II.

APPAREL -- Massawa, Eritrea. WW-II.

APPARITION -- Nadzab, New Guinea. WW-II.

APPEARANCE -- British Landings east and west of Berbora, British Somaliland. 16 March 1941, WW-II.

APPEASE -- Talasea, New Britain. WW-II.

APPELLATION -- Churchill, Canada. WW-II.

APPENDAGE -- Minto Reef, Truk Lagoon, Caroline Islands. WW-II.

APPIAN -- U.S. Navy code word for arrangements for transfer of naval amphibious forces. WW-II.

APPLE -- (1) Avuavu, Guadalcanal, Solomon Islands. WW-II.

(2) Ponum, New Britain. WW-II.

APPLE BLOSSOM -- Allied position to the right of the Villa Grande-Tollo road where it began its sharp descent to the Arielli River, Italy. January 1944, WW-II.

APPLE JACK -- Name for peacetime military maneuver stressing combat training for chemical, biological and radiological warfare.

APPLE PIE -- Allied term for counter-flak fire by artillery. WW-II.

APPLES -- Area, west of Cap Sidi Ferruch, Algeria, where Allied landing was made in assault on Algiers. Name conforms with British phonetic usage. See also BEER, CHARLIE. November 1942, WW-II.

APPRAISE -- Duvuluk, New Britain. WW-II.

APPREHEND -- Dagupan, Luzon, Philippine Islands. WW-II.

APRICOT -- Ndeni Island, Santa Cruz Islands. WW-II.

APPROPRIATE -- Boryo (Horyo), Formosa. WW-II.

AQUASKIT -- Allied device used to deceive enemy during battle; was dropped from air and on striking water fired Verey lights. WW-II.

AQUILA, FORCE -- U.S. Tenth Air Force advanced bombing detachment; intended for bombing of Japan from Chinese bases. Early 1942, WW-II.

AQUILON -- (1) French license-built version of the British DeHavilland SEA VENOM aircraft.

(2) Operable French research nuclear reactor in Saclay, France.

ARABELLA -- Dodecanese Islands, Mediterranean Sea. WW-II.

ARABIC -- New Britain, Bismarck Archipelago. WW-II.

ARBALEST -- Bukama, Belgian Congo, Africa. WW-II.

ARBOR -- Acronym for proposed U.S. Argonne Boiling Reactor facility at Argonne National Laboratory, Illinois. Announced in 1956, the project was dropped when expenditures proved too great.

ARBUTUS -- U.S. code name for Muzinbaarikku Island, Eniwetok Atoll, Marshall Group. WW-II.

ARC -- U.S. research program to study manueverable re-entry vehicle concepts.

ARCADE -- One of the subdivisions of Advanced Research Projects Agency's SUNRISE program. Deals primarily with basic research studies. Continuing.

ARCADIA - First of major U.S. - British staff conferences following U.S. entry into the war, held in Washington in 20 December 1941 - 14 January 1942, WW-II.

ARCAS -- Acronym for All Purpose Rocket for Collecting Atmospheric Soundings; developed by U.S. Navy to collect meteorological data at altitudes up to 40 miles, and so aid in making routine weather forecasts. First tested 1958. See also ARCAS, BOOSTED, ROBIN.

ARCAS, BOOSTED -- U.S. sounding rocket to carry scientific payloads of 12 pounds to altitudes up to 60 miles. Basically, an ARCAS rocket with a solid propellant booster. Used by the military services and National Aeronautics and Space Administration. First fired in 1959.

ARCAS ROBIN -- See ARCAS

ARCHBISHOP -- Jaluit Island, Marshall Islands. WW-II.

ARCHDALE -- Kolom, New Guinea. WW-II.

ARCHER -- (1) A solid propellant rocket, used by the military services and National Aeronautics and Space Administration for atmospheric studies at altitudes up to 90 miles with 40 pounds of instruments. See also ARCHER 35KS 1490, NIKE-ARCHER.

(2) See SAGITTARIO

ARCHER 35KS 1490 -- Similar to ARCHER, but with greater thrust and altitude capabilities.

ARCHERY -- Combined British raid on the Vaagao Area of the Norwegian coast to destroy enemy shipping and shore batteries. 27 December 1941, WW-II.

ARCHIBALD -- Code name for South Greece. WW-II.

ARCHIVE -- Code name for Moses Point, Alaska. WW-II.

ARCLIGHT -- Code name for Yumyello, New Britain. WW-II.

ARCON -- An upper-air research rocket developed for the U.S. Navy by the Atlantic Research Corporation to carry instrumented payloads of 40 pounds to an altitude of 70 miles, or, with a NIKE booster, the same payload to 250 miles. First tested in 1958; operational since 1960.

ARCTIC BEAR -- U.S. Air Force high-altitude air refueling area off the coast of North Carolina.

ARCTIC NIGHT -- Name for peacetime military exercise.

ARDENT -- Name for peacetime military exercise.

ARENA -- Proposed airborne operation in the Kassel-Fritzlau-Hofgeisar area, Germany. WW-II.

ARENTS -- Acronym for Advanced Research Projects Agency Environmental Test Satellite designed to gather data on the space environment and radiation at the 24-hour, 22,000 mile orbit. Part of the Vela-Hotel program to detect nuclear explosions in space; three payloads were to have been launched by the ATLAS-CENTAUR in 1962, piggy-back on a National Aeronautics and Space Administration payload. However, with Centaur delay, another booster will have to be selected.

AREZZO LINE -- German defense line in Italy about seven miles south of main road from Arezzo to Florence. Summer 1944, WW-II.

ARFOR -- International code word used to indicate an area weather forecast for aviation.

ARFOT -- International code word used to indicate an area weather forecast for aviation in which values are given in units of the English system.

ARGENT -- Code name for Ghinda, Eritrea. WW-II.

ARGO SERIES -- Family of solid propellant, hypersonic test vehicles, developed by National Advisory Committee For Aeronautics (now National Aeronautics and Space Administration) with U.S. Air Force and Navy support, which has been converted into series of high-altitude test and research rockets. D-4 (JAVELIN) and D-8 (JOURNEYMAN) still in use by the Air Force to measure the natural radiation around the earth at altitudes up to 1000 and 30,000 miles, respectively. Most famous of the family is the E-5 used in JASON to measure the effects of nuclear explosion outside the earth's atmosphere during the 1958 HARDTACK and ARGUS test series. First fired in 1958. See also ARGO B-1, D-4, D-8, E-5.

ARGO B-1 -- See NIKE-CAJUN

ARGO D-4 -- See JAVELIN

ARGO D-8 -- See JOURNEYMAN

ARGO E-5 -- See JASON

ARGONAUT -- (1) U.S. low power, low cost nuclear training reactor. Introduced at Argonne National Laboratory, Lemont, Illinois, where it was studied by industrial representatives, March 1957.

    (2) Code name for international conferences held at Malta (CRICKET) between President Roosevelt and Prime Minister Churchill and at Yalta, Russia (MAGNETO), between Roosevelt, Churchill and Premier Stalin. 30 January - 9 February 1945, WW-II.

ARGOSY -- (1) British Armstrong-Whitworth biplane airliner of the 1920's.

    (2) British Armstrong-Whitworth four-engine turboprop commercial transport. First flew in 1959.

ARGUMENT, OPERATION -- Concentrated attack, by all available U.S. Army Air Forces and Royal Air Force bombers, on German aircraft production facilities. In six days, starting 19 February 1944, 3800 sorties were flown. Popularly called Big Week.

ARGUS -- (1) British nickname for Fairchild C-61 aircraft. See FORWARDER.

(2) Canadair CL-28 reconnaissance aircraft. First flew in 1957 and is operational with the Royal Canadian Air Force.

(3) Babo, New Guinea. WW-II.

(4) Code name for a series of three nuclear explosions in the South Atlantic in August and September 1958. Launched by rockets from the fantail of a ship. Nuclear explosions were designed to provide scientific and military information on the geomagnetic effects of the particles released. Information gathered had a profound effect on scientific thinking about the Van Allen belts and on military thinking on using nuclear explosions to disrupt communications. These ideas were again tested by the U.S. and Russia during the 1962 test series. See also JASON.

ARGUS II -- Code name for U.S. Navy Base Defense Warning Group. WW-II.

ARIEL -- (1) Aerial Steam Carriage designed by William Samuel Henson in 1841. It did not fly.

(2) First international satellite launched as a joint United Kingdom-U.S. effort on 26 April 1962. The 132 pound satellite was designed to acquire increased knowledge of the ionosphere and how it is affected by solar radiations, and to obtain data on primary cosmic radiations. Launched by a THOR-DELTA booster, the satellite was damaged by the 9 July 1962 U.S. high altitude nuclear explosion in the Pacific.

ARIEL, OPERATION -- See AERIAL, OPERATION

ARIES -- Acronym for Authentic Reproduction of an Independent Earth Satellite, a scale model of an orbiting space station presented to the American Museum of Natural History by the Martin Company in 1961.

ARIETE -- (English translation: Ram) World War II Italian Reggiane Re.2002 fighter-bomber which entered service in 1942.

ARITHMETIC -- Agattu Island, Aleutian Islands. WW-II.

ARIZONA -- Military name for phase line in Korea, comprising string of five hills north of Hoengsong. 1951, Korean Conflict.

ARK -- Bridge used for spanning narrow water passages with deeply cut banks; made by driving turretless Churchill tank into stream bed and opening two attached American treadway tracks to either bank. WW-II.

ARKANSAS, POINT -- Check point in East China Sea for convoys enroute to invasion of Inchon, Korea. September 1950, Korean Conflict.

ARKIE -- Nick name given to battleship USS Arkansas. WW-II.

ARLENE -- Tropical storm. 28 May - 2 June 1959. Formed in central Gulf of Mexico and moved into Louisiana. Caused 1 death and 500,000 dollars damage.

ARLINGTON -- Tacloban, Philippine Islands. WW-II.

ARM -- See SHRIKE

ARMAGEDDON -- Dutch Harbor, Alaska. WW-II.

ARMAMENT -- Tsugado-Iwa (Gadd Rock), Formosa Area. WW-II.

ARMCHAIR -- Wickham Anchorage, New Georgia Island, Solomon Islands. WW-II.

ARME, OPERATION -- U.S. aerial radiological monitoring exercise. Conducted at Nevada Test Site by Atomic Energy Commission for Federal Civil Defense Administration - sponsored personnel. Week of 17 October 1955.

ARMET -- International code word used to indicate an area weather forecast for aviation, with units in the metric system.

ARMLOCK -- Agattu Island, Aleutian Islands. WW-II.

ARMS -- Acronym for U.S. Aerial Radiological Measurements and Survey Program.

ARMS-II -- Aerial Radiometric system introduced by ARMS and calibrated with U.S. Geological Survey Radiation measuring equipment. 1961.

ARMY MULE -- See RETRIEVER

ARMY OF TERRIFIED CIVILIANS -- Name derived from initialism, ATC given to U.S. Air Transport Command personnel by combat airmen. Also called Association of Terrified Civilians. WW-II.

ARNO -- Name for peacetime military project to test equipment for night combat.

ARNOLD LINE -- Air service route across Atlantic from Washington to Ayr, Scotland, via Montreal, Canada, and Gander Lake, Newfoundland; opened summer 1941 to carry diplomatic mail and military and diplomatic officials of U.S. and Great Britain. Named by British in tribute to U.S. General H.H. Arnold. WW-II.

ARPA 162-61 -- Designation for an Advanced Research Projects Agency program to study techniques and equipment to be used in early warning satellites. Infra-red and/or ultra-violet sensing devices were studied as a means of detecting missile launchings. Feeding technology into, but not a part of, the Air Force MIDAS program.

ARPAT -- Acronym for Advanced Research Projects Agency Terminal. ARPA denotes the Defense Department agency involved and Terminal denotes the destruction of Intercontinental Ballistic Missiles during their re-entry (or terminal phase). Concept is similar to ZEUS, but differs in that non-nuclear kill mechanisms, such as stell pellets injected into the path of the warhead, are the prime avenues of investigation. System development has not been authorized, although some industrial contracts for advanced components have been let.

ARROGANT -- (1) Guasopa Plantation, Woodlark Island. WW-II.

    (2) Whittier, Alaska. WW-II.

ARROW -- (1) Italian World War II fighter monoplane. See FRECCIA.

    (2) German World War II fighter-bomber aircraft. See PFIEL.

    (3) Avro of Canada twin-jet, delta-wing all-weather interceptor, designated
        CF-105 by the Royal Canadian Air Force. Tested in 1950's but did not
        enter production.

    (4) Atomic Energy Commission-Sandia Corporation sounding rocket upper-stage
        used with a DEACON first stage to carry chaff for radar tracking to altitudes
        of 300,000 feet. In use.

    (5) Allied code name for route to GOTHIC LINE in British XIII Corps sector,
        central Italy. Summer 1944, WW-II.

ARROWROOT -- Termini, Sicily. WW-II.

ARSENAL 5.501 -- French target drone based on the German V-1. Launched from
a ramp or air-dropped, the drone is boosted to speed by jet assisted take-off
units before the pulsejet engine is started. With radio guidance it had a range
of 31 miles; guided by the mother plane it could reach out to 200 miles. Under
development in 1948.

ARSENAL HILL -- Military name for topographic feature in Yokkokchon Valley,
Korea, northeast of PORK CHOP HILL. Korean Conflict.

ARSENIC -- Marien Harbor, New Britain. WW-II.

ARSON -- Balabac Strait, Philippine Islands. WW-II.

ARTEMIS -- U.S. Office of Naval Research project designed to determine the
feasibility of using transducer and high-gain receivers, along with advanced data
processing equipment, for locating submarines at very long range in large ocean
areas. 1960's.

ARTERIAL -- Western Caroline Islands (Palau, Yap, Ulithi). WW-II.

ARTERY -- Yoloplo, New Britain. WW-II.

ARTHRITIS -- Solomon Islands. WW-II.

ARTICHOKE -- Barakoma A, Vella Lavella Island, Solomon Islands. WW-II.

ARTIFICIAL MOONLIGHT -- Illumination from searchlights used during combat.
WW-II.

ARTILLERY HILL -- Military name for topographic feature on central Bougainville, Solomon Islands. Captured by Australians in December 1944. WW-II.

ARTILLERY VALLEY -- U.N. name for enemy sector of front at Kumwha, Korea. So named because of frequent heavy shelling of U.N. lines from there. 1952, Korean Conflict.

ARTIST -- Ponape Island, Caroline Islands. WW-II.

ARTISTIC -- London, England. WW-II.

ASCENDER -- Experimental Canard (tail-first) fighter, designated XP-55 by U.S. Army Air Forces. First flight July 1943.

ASCOT -- Guimere Lagoon, New Britain. WW-II.

ASDIC -- Acronym for Anti-Submarine Detection Investigation Committee; used by British as name for under-water echo-sounding and direction-finding device for submarine detection. Corresponds to SONAR.

ASH -- Vella Lavella Island, Solomon Islands. WW-II.

ASH WEDNESDAY -- Nickname given to day on which documents were burned at British headquarter in Cairo after Axis advance to Egyptian border. Summer 1942, WW-II.

ASHCAN -- U.S. Navy slang for anti-submarine depth charge.

ASHPLANT -- The Hump, China-Burma-India Theater. WW-II.

ASP -- (1) Abbreviation for Airborne Support Platform, a U.S. Army project for a flying platform patterned after aerial jeep. Currently not under active development.

(2) Abbreviation for Aerospace Plane, a concept currently under study by National Aeronautics and Space Administration and U.S. Air Force for a recoverable booster which could take-off from earth go into orbit, de-orbit and land. Possibly operational in 1970. Research program to begin in 1964.

ASP I -- Rail-launched sounding rocket capable of carrying 50 pound payload to altitude of 35 miles.

ASP IV -- Solid propellant rocket capable of carrying 50 pound payload to altitude of 50 miles.

ASP SERIES -- Acronym for Atmosphere Sounding Projectile, a family of research rockets developed by the U.S. Navy to serve a variety of scientific purposes. Can carry a 25 pound payload up to altitudes of 35 miles; using a NIKE booster, the same payload can be carried to 425 miles. First tested in 1956. See also NIKE-ASP.

ASPAN -- See NIKE-ASP

ASPBITE -- Bugi Island, New Guinea. WW-II.

ASPEN -- (1) Airborne component of OBOE. Also known as Aspex when using another receiver. British designations include Album Leaf, Fountain Pen, Pen Wiper Receiver, Pepper Box Receiver.

(2) Cape Honslow, Guadalcanal, Solomon Islands. WW-II.

ASPERITY -- Code name for Asiatic Theater. WW-II.

ASPHYXIA -- Chinha Point, Amoy, China. WW-II.

ASPIDISTRA -- Large medium-wave radio transmitter, capable of changing its wavelength very quickly; broadcast secretly from United Kingdom to Germany, sometimes interrupting Deutschlandsender and sometimes taking over frequencies of German home stations. WW-II.

ASPIRIN -- Dumaguete, Philippine Islands. WW-II.

ASROC -- Acronym for Anti-Submarine Rocket; developed by U.S. Navy for surface ships. A surface-to-underwater solid propellant weapon with range of over 10 miles, its warhead is an acoustic homing torpedo or depth charge. Operational in 1960.

ASSEMBLE -- Laikang Bay, Celebes Island, Netherlands East Indies. WW-II.

ASSESSOR -- Nassau Bay, New Guinea. WW-II.

ASSET -- U.S. Air Force acronym for Aerothermodynamic Structural Systems Evaluation Test. Will use 600 pound spacecraft to be launched in late 1963 by a THOR booster to study the thermal and structural effects of a glide re-entry from orbit (DYNA-SOAR type landing). Program initiated in 1962.

ASSISTANCE -- Garan-Bi (Goaram), Formosa. WW-II.

ASSOCIATION OF TERRIFIED CIVILIANS -- See ARMY OF TERRIFIED CIVILIANS.

ASTER -- (1) Acronym for Anti-submarine Terrier, an adaptation of the ship-to-air missile to the anti-submarine warfare role. Equipped with a depth-charge type warhead. Not implemented.

(2) Bau Island (Naval Base), Rendova Island, Solomon Islands. WW-II.

(3) Port Darwin, Australia. WW-II.

ASTEROID -- Asmara, Eritrea. WW-II.

ASTONIA -- British operation to capture port of Le Havre, France. 10-12 September 1944, WW-II.

ASTOR -- U.S. Navy acronym for Anti-Submarine Torpedo Ordnance Rocket, a missile launched from submerged sub-marines into the air and back into the water. It carries a nuclear warhead and has a range of 10-12 miles. Under development.

ASTORIA -- Toulon, France. WW-II.

ASTRA -- Operable Austrian pool nuclear reactor in Seibersdorf, Austria.

ASTRO-TELESCOPE -- An early name for National Aeronautics and Space Administration's Orbiting Astronomical Observatory.

ASTROBEE SERIES -- Family of research rockets, developed by the Aerojet-General Corporation for the U.S. Air Force to explore atmospheric phenomena at altitudes up to 1500 miles. Two versions tested in 1961; five other versions being designed. Series begins where Aerobee ends. See also ASTROBEE 200 and 500.

ASTROBEE 200 -- Two-stage solid propellant sounding rocket designed for atmospheric exploration at nominal 200-mile altitude. See also ASTROBEE SERIES.

ASTROBEE 500 -- Three-stage solid propellant sounding rocket designed for exploration of upper atmosphere. See also ASTROBEE SERIES.

ASTRONOMY -- Schouten Islands, New Guinea. WW-II.

ASWORG -- Acronym for Anti-submarine Warfare Operational Research Group, composed of U.S. civilian scientists who rendered invaluable operational research service for improving tactics and following up new ideas on devices and weapons for detecting enemy submarines during World War II.

ATLANTIC -- Breguet 1150 twin-turboprop patrol aircraft built in France. First flew 21 October 1961; will enter NATO service in 1963.

ATLANTIC BRIDGE -- Service of ferrying aircraft from North America to Great Britain. Began July 1940, WW-II.

ATLANTIC CLIPPER -- Boeing super-clipper which Pan-American first flew to Southhampton, England, via the Northern Route, from New York in 1939.

ATLANTIC, OPERATION -- Second Canadian Corps portion of larger Operation GOODWOOD across Orne River, south of Caen, France. 18-21 July 1944, WW-II.

ATLANTIS -- (1) Former name of Intercontinental Ballistic Missile version of POLARIS.

(2) U.S. Navy's generic term for group of Anti-Submarine Warfare surveillance systems. Program includes Research and Development for ballistic missiles.

ATLAS -- (1) First U.S. Intercontinental Ballistic Missile; 13 squadrons, with 126 of the liquid-propelled, 6300-mile range missiles are expected to be operational by the end of 1962. Used in many space programs as a booster, it has also been test-flown four times, over distance of 9000 miles. First begun in 1945; did

CODE NAMES DICTIONARY

not really get underway until 1955. Using command is the Air Force's Strategic Air Command. D, E and F models being deployed. See also ATLAS-ABLE, ATLAS-AGENA, ATLAS BOOSTER, ATLAS-CENTAUR, ATLAS-HUSTLER, ATLAS MERCURY, ATLAS-SCORE, BIG JOE.

(2) Pinip Island, Solomon Sea. WW-II.

(3) Shipping Control Officer, Forward Area, Central Pacific. WW-II.

ATLAS-ABLE -- U.S. space booster using an Atlas D first stage, a specially adapted liquid propellant second stage and a solid propellant third stage. All three launches, designed to place PIONEER spacecraft in the vicinity of the moon, failed in November 1959 and September and December 1960 due to booster mal-functions. No longer used.

ATLAS-AGENA -- Space booster used by both Air Force and National Aeronautics and Space Administration consisting of ATLAS BOOSTER with AGENA upper stage. Can put approximately 5000 pounds (including Agena) into a 345-mile orbit. Combination first used in 1960. See also ATLAS. See also DISCOVERER, EGO, MARINER, NIMBUS, OAO.

ATLAS- AGENA A -- Liquid propellant rocket booster consisting of ATLAS first stage and AGENA A second stage. Designed to launch SAMOS and MIDAS.

ATLAS-AGENA B -- Liquid propellant rocket booster consisting of ATLAS first stage and AGENA B second stage. Launched MIDAS II, April 1960; scheduled to launch RANGER.

ATLAS BOOSTER -- Essentially an ATLAS Intercontinental Ballistic Missile modified for use in military and civilian space programs either by itself, in the MERCURY program, or with various upper stages. Develops approximately 390,000 pound thrust at liftoff using uprated engines. First used as a space booster in PROJECT SCORE in 1958.

ATLAS-CENTAUR -- First U.S. high-energy launch vehicle. "D" model of the ATLAS serves as booster for Centaur stage which uses two liquid-hydrogen, re-startable engines. Development began by military in 1958; transferred to National Aeronautics and Space Administration in 1959. Only Flight to date failed May, 1962. See also ARENTS.

ATLAS E -- Intercontinental Ballistic Missile designed to place thermonuclear war-head on target over 9000 miles away. See ATLAS.

ATLAS-HUSTLER -- An early name for the ATLAS-AGENA space booster.

ATLAS-MERCURY -- Booster-spacecraft combination for the first U.S. space flights. Consists of a "D" model ATLAS booster modified to launch the manned MERCURY capsule. First manned orbital flight 20 February 1962 by Lieutenant-Colonel John Glenn.

ATLAS-SCORE -- Rocket vehicle used in launching ATLAS satellite under PROJECT SCORE, 18 December 1958. See also COURIER.

54

ATMOSPHERE -- Capture by British of Massawa, Eritrea, Red Sea. 8 April 1941. WW-II.

ATO -- British acronym for Assisted Take-Off, an aviation and rocket term. U.S. equivalent is JATO.

ATOM -- Wallis Island, Samoan Islands. WW-II.

ATOMIC CLOCK -- National Aeronautics and Space Administration project to test Einstein's theory of relativity by placing an atomic clock in an orbiting satellite and measuring it against one on earth. Two different clocks are being built, one with ammonia and the other with cesium. Experiment will probably be conducted in 1963.

ATRAN -- Acronym for Automatic Terrain Recognition and Navigation system. Guidance technique used with MACE tactical missile in which a series of radar comparison photographs are utilized to guide the missile to its target. Self-contained system, difficult to jam. Operational with Mace missile squadrons in Germany.

ATROCITY -- Pilelo Island, Solomon Sea. WW-II.

ATROPHY -- Magier River, New Britain. WW-II.

ATTENDANCE -- Ghisonaccia, Corsica. WW-II.

ATTENTION -- Yoron Shima Island, Japan. WW-II.

ATTILA, OPERATION -- German plan for occupation of French territories not under German control. Proposed late 1940, WW-II.

ATTLEBOROUGH -- Dunkirk, France. WW-II.

AUBURN -- Gurinati, New Britain. WW-II.

AUCTION -- Tagbilaran, Philippine Islands. WW-II.

AUDAX -- British Hawker biplane used before World War II as an advanced trainer. Later used as tow for gliders.

AUDREY -- (1) U.S. Navy designation of zone in Manila Bay, Philippines, for mine sweeping operations. February 1945, WW-II.

(2) Hurricane. Formed in southwestern Gulf of Mexico, moved inland near Louisiana-Texas border and eventually dissipated near Lake Ontario. Caused 390 deaths and 150,000,000 dollars damage, mostly from tidal flooding in southwestern Louisiana.

AUGMENTATION -- Okayama, Japan. WW-II.

AUNT POLLY -- Study of cold criticals for U.S. ROVER project reactors at Los Alamos Scientific Laboratory, Los Alamos, New Mexico.

AURORA -- (1) Japanese World War II night-fighter bomber. See FRANCES.

(2) Swedish ship-to-underwater anti-submarine rocket launched by an eight-rocket launcher. Operational on Navy ships, the rocket has a range of 850 meters and carries a high explosive warhead. Advanced versions are under development.

AURORA 7 -- Name selected by U.S. Lieutenant Commander Malcolm Scott Carpenter for the MERCURY capsule in which he achieved three orbits, 24 May 1962.

AUSLADUNG -- German secondary attack, part of Operation OCHSENKOFF, designed to extend Tunis bridgehead in the north. February 1943, WW-II.

AUSTIN - (1) Hefele Point, New Britain. WW-II.

(2) Tulagi, Solomon Islands. WW-II.

AUTHENTIC -- Karenko (Hoirenkau) (Karendo-Gai) Formosa. WW-II.

AUTOCAR -- Casablanda, Corsica. WW-II.

AUTOMAT -- Aomo River, New Britain. WW-II.

AUTOMET -- Acronym for Automatic Meteorological corrections. A guidance technique in which a restartable engine is used to correct deviations from a given trajectory in flight, as sensed by inertial components in the guidance system. To be used with the Army's new LANCE missile.

AUTOMOBILE -- Nadzab, New Guinea. WW-II.

AUTONOMOUS -- Gander Bay, Newfoundland. WW-II.

AUTONYM -- Leopoldville, Belgian Congo, Africa. WW-II.

AUTUMN FOG -- See HERBSTNEBEL

AUTUMN GRASS -- World War II Japanese MXY7 AKIGUSA trainer for the J8M1 rocket-powered interceptor aircraft. See SHUSUI.

AUTUMN JOURNEY -- See HERBSTREISE

AVA -- Tropical storm. 16-20 August 1962. Formed 700 miles west of Acapulco, Mexico. Moved northwestward at first, then southwestward, and dissipated over Pacific between Mexico and Hawaii.

AVALANCHE -- Allied amphibious assault on Salerno, Italy, with objective to capture Naples and nearby airfields. Involved first landing of U.S. troops on European continent in World War II. Name early in planning stage was TOPHAT. 9 September 1943.

AVALANCHE DROP -- See GIANT I-IV

AVARICE -- Sitka, Alaska. WW-II.

AVENGER -- (1) British fighter called the fastest in the world when produced by Avro in 1925.

(2) U.S. Grumman World War II TBF aircraft now in second-line service with various foreign air arms.

AVIAN -- (1) British Avron sport/racing plane produced in 1930.

(2) Canadian gyroplane first flown in 1960 and under-going developmental testing.

AVIAVNITO -- Early Russian research rocket. Used a combination of alcohol and liquid oxygen as propellants to reach an altitude of three and one half miles. First fired in 1936.

AVION III -- Bat-wing, steam-powered machine by French electrical engineer, Clement Ader, which failed in its attempt to fly in 1897.

AVOCADO -- Lyons Point, Florida-Tulagi Group, Solomon Islands. WW-II.

AVONMORE -- Calais, France. WW-II.

AVONMOUTH -- Planned Allied military expedition to carry out landing at Narvik, Norway, if justified by German reactions to laying of mines off Norway, Operation WILFRED. Early April 1940, WW-II.

AVRE -- British acronym for Assault Vehicle, Royal Engineers; an adapted CHURCHILL Tank. WW-II.

AVROCAR -- Great Britain's three-engine jet VZ-9 vertical takeoff and landing "flying saucer" developed by Avro in the 1950's.

AWKWARD -- Cape Masas, New Britain. WW-II.

AXEHEAD -- Allied 21 Army Group plan, which emphasized the administrative importance of capture of French Seine ports, Le Havre and Rouen, after Normandy landings, but also suggested eastward and southwestward thrusts in order to deceive Germans, disperse their forces, and determine most favorable direction for advance. Followed by LUCKY STRIKE plan. WW-II.

AXIOM -- Mission sent by Allied Southeast Asia Command to London and Washington to urge CULVERIN attack on northern Sumatra. Early 1944, WW-II.

AXIS SALLY -- American woman, Mildred E. Gillars, who broadcast Nazi propaganda to Allied troops. Convicted for treason by U.S. jury in 1949; released in 1961. WW-II.

AZALEA -- Cape Torokina, Torokina, Solomon Islands. WW-II.

AZON -- Acronym for Azimuth Only. Type of bomb having movable control surfaces in tail adjusted by radio signals which controlled bomb in azimuth only. Employed in China and Burma during World War II. See also RAZON, TARZON, TRIZON.

AZOR -- Largest native-designed aircraft yet built in Spain and in service with the air arm.

AZTEC -- (1) Piper PA-23 monoplane, a development of the APACHE, delivered to the U.S. Navy in 1960 as the UO-1.

(2) Norfolk Island, Pacific Ocean. WW-II.

AZUSA -- Missile tracking and impact prediction system in operation at the Atlantic Missile Range. The extremely accurate system is used not only to predict impact areas, but also to provide, in the early phases of a flight, quick-look trajectory data to the range safety officer. Operational.

B

BB -- See BASEBALL

B.B. ROUTE -- See RED LION EXPRESS ROUTE

B, BASE -- U.S. naval base, Loch Ryan, Scotland. WW-II.

B-C KIT -- Abbreviation for Battle-Casualty or Bouillon-Cigarette ration kit containing cigarettes, bouillon cubes, and matches. 1944.

B-CANYON -- U.S. fuel element processing plant at Hanford, Washington. Reac-
tivated in 1961 to provide quantities of strontium 90 and cesium 137 by recovering
long-lived isotopes from waste streams.

B DAY -- Date for executing MIKE VII landing near San Antonio, Philippines.
29 January 1945, WW-II.

B, MESSAGE -- Message broadcast by British Broadcasting Corporation to French
Resistance forces confirming that invasion of Continent was imminent. 1944, WW-
II.

B, MISSILE -- One of the family of missiles based on Army tactical requirements.
Early name for the Army's LANCE missile now under development. Uses solid
propellant or prepackaged storable liquids and carries conventional or nuclear
warhead.

BR TASK FORCE -- Name given in January 1942 by U.S. Air Staff to projected bomber
force in United Kingdom. WW-II.

BABACOOTE -- Eniwetok Island, Marshall Islands. WW-II.

BABE -- Tropical storm. 14-16 September 1962. Formed in South China Sea, moved
northwestward into Viet Nam and dissipated.

BABS -- (1) Acronym for Blind-Approach Beacon System, a British pulse-type, ground-
based navigational guidance system used for runway approach.

(2) Typhoon. 11-15 December 1951. Formed over western Caroline Islands. Moved
west-northwestward into Philippine Sea, then recurved northeastward and lost
force over the North Pacific.

(3) Typhoon. 12-17 August 1956. Formed northeast of Luzon, the Philippines. Moved northward, then northeastward and dissipated over Sea of Japan.

(4) Tropical storm. 5-10 October 1959. Formed off west coast of Luzon, Philippines. Moved erratically northward and northeastward and dissipated east of Taiwan.

(5) Name also applied to tropical cyclones in western Pacific which occurred prior to (1) through (3) above.

BABY SERIES -- Family of Japanese test rockets used to obtain basic data on solid fuels, engine performance, telemetry and recovery equipment. Three versions: Baby S: used to train personnel in handling, launching and tracking (first fired in 1955); Baby T: used to gather telemetry data on speed, temperature, pressure and acceleration (six fired in 1955); and Baby R: used to investigate ocean recovery techniques (two successfully recovered in 1955).

BABY R -- See BABY SERIES

BABY S -- See BABY SERIES

BABY T -- See BABY SERIES

BABY TORTOISE TACTICS -- Japanese term for first time supplies were air dropped in Burma--to units of Indian Army on Arakan Front, early 1944. Also called BEEHIVE TACTICS. WW-II.

BABY-WAC -- A one-fifth scale model of the WAC-CORPORAL, built and fired under U.S. Army contract at Goldstone, California in July 1945. Proved the validity of the booster design and the feasibility of 3-fin control. As a consequence, the Army approved development of full-scale WAC-CORPORAL sounding rocket.

BABYDOLL -- Dagi River, New Britain. WW-II.

BACCHUS -- Crown Island, New Guinea. WW-II.

BACHELOR -- Mt. Reamur, Bismarck Archipelago. WW-II.

BACK-DOOR COLD FRONT -- Leading edge of cold air mass moving toward the south and southwest along the Atlantic seaboard of the U.S.

BACK ROOM BOYS -- Term first used by Lord Beaverbrook to refer to Allied scientists who worked to improve bombs and bombing instruments. WW-II.

BACKBITER -- Midway Island. WW-II.

BACKBONE -- Allied plan to attack Spanish-held Tangier-Ceuta area in North Africa if required by strategic situation after TORCH landings. Project active until 6 February 1943, WW-II.

BACKBONE II -- Revision of BACKBONE Plan. January 1943, WW-II.

BACKFALL -- Konn, New Guinea. WW-II.

BACKFIN -- Yakovlev Yak-42, supersonic tactical bomber, operational with the Soviet Air Force. First flew in 1956.

BACKGROUND -- Amur River, Union of Soviet Socialist Republic. WW-II.

BACKHANDER --Allied task force under ALAMO which carried out Operation DEXTERITY against Cape Gloucester, New Britain. 26 December 1943-10 February 1944, WW-II.

BACKSHEESH -- Kerama Retto, Nansei Shoto Islands, Japan. WW-II.

BAD -- Acronym for Berlin Airlift Device (Military).

BADEWANNE -- (English: Bathtub) German air force slang for airplane. WW-II.

BADGER -- (l) Weapon developed by Canadians consisting of WASP flame-thrower, Mark II, fitted to RAM personnel carrier. WW-II.

(2) Rescinded nickname for a Beech aircraft. See TRAVEL AIR.

(3) NATO designation for sweptback, twin-jet Russian bomber first observed in 1954.

BADMINTON -- Kassia, New Britain. WW-II.

BAEDEKER RAIDS -- German "terror" air raids on British Isles beginning in March 1940. WW-II.

BAETA -- Chemical agent, tested at Argonne National Laboratory, Lemont, Illinois, for treatment of persons exposed to plutonium.

BAGASSE -- Garua Harbor, New Britain. WW-II.

BAGGY -- Ceram, Netherlands East Indies. WW-II.

BAGWORN -- Massibang, New Guinea. WW-II.

BAILEY PIPER -- Military name for concrete pier extending into lagoon on Ebeye Island (BURTON), Kwajalein Atoll. February 1944, WW-II.

BAILEY'S BEACH -- One of two groups of beaches in U.S. CENT landing area near Scoglitti, Sicily, July 1943. Named after Captain W.O. Bailey, commanding transports there. WW-II.

BAIZE -- Wiwai, New Guinea. WW-II.

BAKA BOMB -- Japanese manned-missile airplane. Carried underneath BETTY medium bomber, equipped with 1200 pounds of high explosive, propelled by three solid rocket motors, guided into target by human suicide pilot, called Jinrai Butai (English: Divine Thunderbolt). Achieved some success as anti-ship weapon, but presented relatively easy target. Known as Oka Bomb to Japanese, meaning cherry blossom, and as Baka to Americans, meaning foolish. Also called MXY 7, Marudai. First used in Pacific on 12 April 1945, WW-II.

BAKER -- (1) Code word for letter "B" in a phonetic alphabet, used to avoid possibility to avoid possibility of a misunderstanding in transmitting messages. See also BRAVO.

(2) Tropical storm. 2-5 August 1951. Formed in mid-Atlantic and moved northward and northeastward over the open ocean.

(3) Hurricane. 1-8 September 1952. First detected in Atlantic, 400 miles east of Puerto Rico. Moved northwestward at first, then turned northward between Bermuda and Hatteras, and then northeastward over Atlantic.

(4) Name of a one-pound rhesus monkey which, with its partner Able, was fired down the Atlantic Missile Range in a JUPITER nose cone in May 1959.

BAKER BOARD -- U.S. special committee, directed by Newton D. Baker; recommended appropriations for research and development program for the air force and plans for modernizing the army. July 1934.

BAKER FERRY -- Military name for ferry site at Han River near Seoul, Korea; maintained by Baker Company, 1st Shore Party Battalion, U.S. Marine Corps. September 1950, Korean Conflict.

BAKER HILL -- See DICK BAKER

BAKER LINE -- U.S. Eighth Army defensive line along Imjin River and 38th Parallel in Korea; one of four lines drawn up for withdrawal in successive steps by Lieutenant General Walton H. Walker before his death. See also ABLE, CHARLIE and DOG LINES. December 1950, WW-II.

BAKER, PLAN -- Plan for bringing U.S. 1st Marine Division up to full war strength by calling reservist to active duty. July 1950, Korean Conflict.

BAKER ROGER -- Plan for interception and sinking of three enemy blockade runners by American task groups in conjunction with air patrols from Natal and Ascension Island. January 1944, WW-II.

BAKER-SIXTY -- Allied plan to use transport aircraft to land U.S. 11th Airborne Division, possibly U.S. 27th Infantry Division, and other military personnel in a critical portion of Tokyo Plain; part of BLACKLIST plan for occupation of Japan in event of early surrender. See also MISSION 75. August 1945, WW-II.

BAKER TEST -- First underwater test of a nuclear weapon; conducted at Bikini. 1946.

BALADOU -- Version of French Wassmer Super IV monoplane. See PARIOU.

BALANCE -- Almirante, Panama. WW-II.

BALBO -- Not-common nickname for a large formation of aircraft. Named in honor of General Italo Balbo who led a mass flight of Italian aircraft to the U.S. in 1933.

BALCONY -- Turbo, Colombia. WW-II.

BALD HILL -- Military name for Djebel Adjred or Hill 556, west of Djefna, Tunisia. 1942-43, WW-II.

BALDHEAD -- Masibang, New Guinea. WW-II.

BALDNESS -- Gura, Eritrea. WW-II.

BALDPLATE -- Grand Cayman Island, British West Indies. WW-II.

BALDWIN -- U.S. Air Force code name for critical items of various types intended for emergency supply by air drop of one infantry battalion for one day. First considered, July 1950; eventually abandoned. See also LIBERTY. Korean Conflict.

BALDY RIDGE -- U.S. Military name for topographic feature on Peleliu Island. Fall 1944, WW-II.

BALEFUL -- Cartagena, Colombia. WW-II.

BALIWICK -- Kogil River, New Britain. WW-II.

BALL POINT -- U.S. Air Force high-altitude air refueling area over California.

BALL PROJECT -- Program for dropping supplies and food to Norwegian underground for sabotage work and secret agents and radio equipment behind enemy lines in northern Norway. July-September 1944, WW-II.

BALLCOCK -- Yaimas, New Guinea. WW-II.

BALLINTOY -- Siracusa, Sicily. WW-II.

BALLIOL -- (1) British Boulton Paul advanced trainer plane delivered to Royal Ceylonese Air Force in 1953 after duty with the Royal Air Force.

(2) Sub-port of embarkation, Excursion Inlet, Alaska. WW-II.

BALMY -- Old Providence Island, Caribbean Sea. WW-II.

BALSA -- Midway Island. WW-II.

BALSAM -- Landing craft, tank (LCT) landing inside Onorisi Pass, New Georgia-Munda Area, Solomon Islands. WW-II.

BALTIMORE -- (1) Martin twin-engine bomber designed in 1940 to meet Royal Air Force requirements. First flew 14 June 1941. Designated A-30 by U.S. Army Air Forces, but all aircraft delivered to Britain.

(2) Ilia River, New Guinea. WW-II.

BALUSTRADE -- Sililaling, New Guinea. WW-II.

BALUT -- Cape San Jacques, French Indo China. WW-II.

BAMBI -- (1) Acronym for Ballistic Missile Boost Intercept, a U.S. Air Force proposal to destroy enemy Intercontinental Ballistic Missiles during their boost phase using interceptors aboard a large number of orbiting platforms. Some study work by industry has been done, but program is not under active development.

(2) Negros Island, Philippine Islands. WW-II.

BAMBOO -- British plan for operations against Hastings Harbor-Victoria Point area, Kra Isthmus, Burma. See also CLINCH. Fall 1944, WW-II.

BAMBOO HILL -- U.S. military name for topographic feature on Okinawa. 1945, WW-II.

BAMBOO ROAD -- Military name for topographic feature near Rabaul, New Britain. WW-II.

BAMBOOZLE -- Sibog, New Guinea. WW-II.

BAN -- Plans of Japanese Burma Area Army to meet anticipated attack of British 14th Army along Irrawaddy in front of Mandalay, Burma. Fall 1944, WW-II.

BANANA -- Doke Doke, New Georgia, Solomon Islands. WW-II.

BANANA FLEET -- Popular name for U.S. ships which maintained neutrality patrol of sub-infested waters between West Indies, Cape Verde Islands and "hump" of Brazil during summer and fall, 1941. WW-II.

BANANA RIDGE -- Military name for topographic feature on Negros Island, Philippines. Spring 1945, WW-II.

BANDAGE -- Negros Island, Philippine Islands. WW-II.

BANDBOX -- Casablanca, French Morocco. WW-II.

BANDITS -- U.S. Navy radar slang for unidentified aircraft. Also called Bastards. WW-II.

BANDYCOOT -- Sindama, New Guinea. WW-II.

BANG -- Shipping designator, used in World War II, for cargo to be received in United Kingdom, Zone III, which consisted of Northern Ireland. See also SOXO, GLUE, UGLY. Instituted 1943.

BANJO -- Gozo Island, Mediterranean Sea. WW-II.

BANK -- Nickname for the U.S. B-25's sent to Russia during World War II under Lend-Lease.

BANK GROUP -- Allied military organization which controlled assault crossings of rivers, ensuring that they were made according to priorities and that undue congestion was avoided at points of embarkation. WW-II.

BANKNIGHT -- Arimegi Plantation, New Britain. WW-II.

BANKNOTE -- Code name for Allied Rhine River crossing. 24 March 1945, WW-II.

BANNERET -- St. Croix, Virgin Islands. WW-II.

BANNISTER -- Eten Island, Truk Lagoon, Caroline Islands. WW-II.

BANQUET -- Macclesfield Bank, South China Sea. WW-II.

BANSHEE -- (1) McDonnell F2H U.S. Navy fighter plane of early 1950's, now in service with the Royal Canadian Navy.

    (2) U.S. Army-Atomic Energy Commission program to determine the propagation of blast waves in air using small charges of high explosives carried aloft by a balloon. Simulating nuclear blasts, the charges would be detonated at varying altitudes, and the blast propagation measured by ground, air, and balloon-borne instrumentation. Program conducted at White Sands Missile Range, New Mexico.

BANTAM -- (1) Swedish, wire-guided, solid-propelled, anti-tank missile. Launched from its transporter container; has a range of one and one-quarter miles. In operational use.

    (2) Arawe Harbor, New Britain. WW-II.

    (3) See JEEP

BANYAN -- Leru Island, Florida Group, Solomon Islands. WW-II.

BANYAN TREE I-II -- U.S. joint Army-Air Force training exercises held in Panama. 1959, 1960.

BANYAN TREE III -- Exercise designed to coordinate defense against a simulated aggressor in Panama by elements of U.S. Strike Command. Also called Operation Solidarity. 22 February 1962.

BANZAI -- Cebu, Philippine Islands. WW-II.

BAPTISM -- Air reconnaissance from North Russia, apparently for German Battleship Tirpitz. May-June 1944, WW-II.

BARBARA -- (1) Typhoon. March 1946. First detected over north-central Caroline Islands. Moved west-northwestward, passed south of Guam, across Philippine Sea and northern Luzon, and then turned northeastward through the Bashi Channel and dissipated southeast of the Ryukyu Islands.

    (2) Hurricane. 11-15 August 1953. Formed northeast of Bahama Islands. Moved northward and swept eastern North Carolina causing 2 deaths and 1.1 million dollars damage, then turned northeastward offshore to Gulf of Saint Lawrence.

    (3) Tropical storm. 28-29 July 1954. Formed near Louisiana coast, then moved inland in southwestern Louisiana. Caused little damage.

BARBARA LINE -- German defensive line in Italy south of WINTER LINE. November 1943, WW-II.

BARBARITY FORCE -- Detachment of British Royal Air Force and Army sent to Greece. Arrived November 1940, WW-II.

BARBAROSSA -- Code name for German invasion of the U.S.S.R. 22 June 1941, WW-II.

BARBERRY -- Nasubata Channel, Palawan Island, Philippine Islands. WW-II.

BARC -- U.S. Army 60-ton amphibious resupply cargo barge.

BARDIA BILL -- Australian nickname, used collectively for Italian medium guns during action in Libya. 1940-41, WW-II.

BARE PATCH -- Military name for area south of M. Veruca, near German GOTHIC LINE in Italy. Fall 1944, WW-II.

BARFLY -- Moljo, India. WW-II.

BARGAIN -- Kabib, New Britain. WW-II.

BARGE -- NATO designation for four-engine, turboprop long-range Russian strategic bomber.

BARK -- (l) Russian Ilyushin IL-2. First flew in 1938.

(2) Code name for beaches around southeasternmost tip of Sicily, attacked by part of British 8th Army with Pachino and its airfield as immediate objective, during invasion, Operation HUSKY. See also ACID. 10 July 1943, WW-II.

BARLEY -- Lua Point, Treasury Island. WW-II.

BARLEYCORN -- Capetown, Union of South Africa. WW-II.

BARLING BOMBER -- One-of-a-kind triplane, six-engine bomber, flown by the U.S. Air Service in 1923.

BARNEY -- Groups of U.S. submarines which penetrated the minefields in the Tsushima Strait, Japan Sea, and carried out three-week offensive patrol against enemy shipping. 27 May-30 June 1945, WW-II.

BARNYARD -- Rooke Island, Bismarck Archipelago. WW-II.

BARON -- Beechcraft Model 55 aircraft. First available in 1961.

BAROUDEUR -- (English translation: Fighter) French S.E. 5000 shoulderwing jet of late 1950's.

BARRACUDA -- (l) British Fairey-built torpedo/dive-bomber of World War II. First flown in 1940. Entered service in 1944.

(2) Undaga Island, Bismarck Archipelago. WW-II.

(3) Projected Post-HUSKY invasion by U.S. Fifth Army in Naples area, Italy. Not carried out. Fall 1943, WW-II.

BARRACUDA I -- Name for peacetime military exercise.

BARRAGE -- British code name for combined sea and air operation to intercept Japanese submarines carrying important officials from Germany to Singapore. 11-13 November 1943, WW-II.

BARREL -- Swedish SAAB J-29, first European swept-wing jet fighter. Currently operational.

BARRISTER -- Early U.S. plan for occupation of Dakar, French West Africa. Developed before Pearl Harbor under code name, Black; also briefly known as Picador. WW-II.

BARTS ROCK -- U.S. Air Force high-altitude air refueling area over Montana.

BASALT -- Malangas, Mindanao, Philippine Islands. WW-II.

BASEBALL -- England to Russia air shuttle. Also called BB. WW-II.

BASHFUL -- Code name for Moscow, U.S.S.R. WW-II.

BASIC -- Acronym for Battle Area Surveillance and Integrated Communications system. U.S. Marine Corps.

BASKETBALL PROJECT -- Half-facetious, half-disparaging nickname for the U.S. International Geophysical Year satellite project announced by the White House on 29 July 1955.

BASRA -- Code name for Headquarters, 1st Canadian Corps, used in deception Operation PENKNIFE, during movement of Canadian troops from Italy to north-western Europe. February-March 1945, WW-II.

BASTARDS -- See BANDITS

BASTION -- Mount Kabat, Solomon Sea. WW-II.

BAT -- (1) U.S. Navy winged anti-ship weapon carrying a high explosive payload of 1000 pounds. Using active radar homing, this glide bomb had a range of 15-20 miles. Used in April 1945 in the Pacific; in one action sank a destroyer at a maximum range. Launched by Navy Privateer patrol bombers.

(2) Pre-World War II Italian aircraft. See PIPISTRELLO.

(3) Russian World War II Tu-2 twin-engine attack bomber.

(4) McDonnell XP-67 aircraft delivered to the U.S. Army Air Forces in June 1945. Only one was built.

BATCH -- Foochow, China. WW-II.

BATHTUB -- (I) First U.S. Naval Training Base, British Isles. WW-II.

(2) See BADEWANNE

BATTER UP -- (I) Signal used by Allied Western Naval Task Force indicating that
local French resistance to landings in Morocco had been encountered. See also
PLAY BALL. November 1942, WW-II.

(2) Seward, Alaska. WW-II.

BATTERY -- Jitsugetsutan, Formosa. WW-II.

BATTING -- Port Sudan, Sudan. WW-II.

BATTLE -- British Fairey Mark II advanced trainer plane of early World War II.

BATTLE MOUNTAIN -- Military name for Hill 665, a bald peak in Sobuk-san
mountain mass, Korea. Also called Napalm Hill, Old Baldy, Bloody Knob.
Scene of fighting in summer, 1950. Korean Conflict.

BATTLE OF THE EASTERN SOLOMONS -- See KA, OPERATION

BATTLE ROYAL -- Name for NATO peacetime military exercise.

BATTLEAXE -- Unsuccessful British land offensive to relieve besieged Tobruk, Libya.
15-17 June 1941, WW-II.

BATTLE-AXE DIVISION -- Nickname for U.S. 65th Infantry Division.

BATTLER -- Curtiss CB biplane which crashed on test flight in U.S., 1918.

BATTY -- Code name of experiment, initiated by U.S. General Carl Spaatz, for
developing and using radar-controlled conventional bomber aircraft as guided
missiles in CROSSBOW operation against German V-weapon sites. Also called
APHRODITE, CASTOR, ORPHAN and WEARY-WILLIE. WW-II.

BAUS AU, OPERATION -- Large-scale movement of goods, supplies and weapons
into interior of Philippines for use later in guerrila warfare. Baus Au means
"get it back" in Visayan language. Spring 1942, WW-II.

BAWBEE -- Yakutsk, Siberia. WW-II.

BAYTOWN -- British Eighth Army invasion of southern Italy at Reggio di Calabria,
mounted from Sicily. 3 September 1943, WW-II.

BAZAAR -- Plan for U.S. air support of U.S.S.R. in event of Japanese attack
upon her. Also covered projected U.S. survey of air facilities in eastern
Siberia, which was abandoned in January 1943, WW-II.

BAZOOKA - U.S. recoilless anti-tank rocket launcher, hand carried. So named because of resemblance to improvised musical contraption of radio comedian, Bob Burns. See also British counterpart, PIAT. First produced in 1942.

BAZOOKA PANTS -- Nickname for additional armor used to protect tank tracks from anti-tank fire. WW-II.

BEACH BRICK -- Allied army organization set up to assist in unloading and loading supplies over open beaches. Later called Beach Group. WW-II.

BEACH GROUP -- See BEACH BRICK

BEACH JUMPERS -- Nickname of small U.S. Navy demonstration group operating in small boats to give Axis troops false impression that full-scale assault was being prepared in western Sicily. 10-11 July, 1943, WW-II.

BEACON -- Name given to two satellites launched in October 1958 and August 1959 to study atmospheric density at various levels for about two weeks by means of a thin inflated mylar plastic sphere. Both satellites failed to orbit. The first launch was with JUPITER-C, the second with a JUNO II.

BEADLE -- Thule, Greenland. WW-II.

BEADSMAN -- Samarai, New Guinea. WW-II.

BEAGLE -- NATO designation for the Russian IL-28, first light jet bomber to enter Soviet service. First flight in 1948. Involved in Cuban Crisis.

BEAN PATCH -- Name for U.S. 1st Provisional Marine Brigade bivouac area near Masan, Korea; actually was a bean patch. Summer 1950, Korean Conflict.

BEAR -- Russian Tupolev-design turbo-prop strategic bomber, only one of its kind in the world today. In service since 1954. Transport version called Cleat.

BEAR POINT -- Military name for topographic feature on Manus, Admiralty Islands. Spring 1944, WW-II.

BEAR TRAIL -- U.S. Air Force high-altitude air refueling area in the Pacific, off coast of California.

BEARCAT -- (I) Grumman F8F World War II U.S. Navy shipboard fighter. First flew 1944. In service with Thai and Vietnamese air arms.

(2) Flores Strait, Netherlands East Indies. WW-II.

BEARDLESS BARBARA -- Nickname for woman from New Jersey, Mrs. Barbara Ines Collins, whose English-language radio broadcasts from Havana, Cuba, beginning in May 1961, have been highly critical of U.S. and in favor of Castro regime.

BEARSKIN -- Release of certain information to Marshal Tito to coordinate peak of Partisan activity in Yugoslavia. WW-II.

BEAST -- (1) Russian IL-10 aircraft developed in 1943 as a follow-on to the IL-2 BARK.

(2) Dungun, Malaya. WW-II.

BEATRICE -- Tropical storm. October 1947. First detected in western Caroline Islands. Moved north-northeastward through Valcano Islands into North Pacific.

BEAUFIGHTER -- Versatile Bristol-built aircraft first used in World War II against German night intruders and, later, against Axis shipping. Torpedo version called TORBEAU.

BEAUFORT -- British twin-engine torpedo bomber of World War II. Developed by Bristol in the late 1930's.

BEAUTY -- Russian World War II KRASAVEC fighter plane. See MARK.

BEAVER -- (1) Canadian DeHavilland liaison plane designated the L-20 by the U.S. Air Force and Army. First flight 1947.

(2) Name for Royal Canadian Air Force Squadron Number 440.

(3) Major exercise, employing elements of U.S. VII Corps, held in Slapton Sands area, England and simulating later assault on UTAH Beach. See also DUCK I-III, FOX. 27-30 March 1944, WW-II.

(4) See BIBER

BEAVER I-IV -- Canadian First Corps training exercises in United Kingdom; first two were for headquarters staffs; last two were on divisional level. Spring 1942. WW-II.

BEAVER CLUB -- (1) British and Canadian rest and recreation facility for war-weary troops at Ortona, Italy. WW-II.

(2) Canadian enlisted men's recreational facility in MAPLE LEAF CITY (Campobasso, Italy); established in former local Fascist Youth Headquarters. WW-II.

BEAVER TAIL -- Medium-range, height-finding radar. Also called Big Abner. Smaller height-finder called Little Abner.

BEBE -- French light monoplane by Joly and Delemontez. First flew 1948.

BECKY -- (1) Awio, New Britain. WW-II.

(2) Tropical storm. 8-17 August 1958. Formed near Cape Verde Islands. Moved westward across Atlantic, passed north of Antilles and northeast of Bahamas, then turned northeastward between Bermuda and Hatteras and out over the Atlantic.

(3) Tropical storm. 27 August - I September 1962. Formed between Cape Verde Islands and Africa. Moved northward over eastern North Atlantic, but did not reach land.

BEDCHECK CHARLIES -- Nickname for low-flying small antique Communist aircraft which made nuisance raids over Seoul or front lines in Korea, sometimes dropping small bombs; their wood and fabric construction complicated radar detection and slow speed made interception difficult. Korean Conflict.

BEDFORD -- Kembul, New Britain. WW-II.

BEDMAKER -- Code name for Union of Soviet Socialist Republics. WW-II.

BEDPOST -- Pulap Island, Caroline Islands. WW-II.

BEDROCK -- Nusam Island, Solomon Sea. WW-II.

BEDSACK -- Koma Creek, New Guinea. WW-II.

BEDSIDE -- La Perouse Strait, Santa Cruz Islands. WW-II.

BEEFSTEAK -- Emirau Island, Admiralty Islands. WW-II.

BEEHIVE HILL -- U.S. military name for topographic feature on Okinawa. 1945, WW-II.

BEEHIVE ONE -- Name for peacetime military exercise to test allied defenses in Europe.

BEEHIVE TACTICS -- Japanese term for first time supplies were air dropped in Burma -- to units of Indian Army on Arakan Front, early 1944. Also called BABY TORTOISE TACTICS. WW-II.

BEEMAN -- Makari, Bougainville, Solomon Islands. WW-II.

BEER -- Area, east of Cap Sidi Ferruch, Algeria, where Allied landing was made in assault on Algiers. Name conforms with British phonetic usage. See also APPLES, CHARLIE. November 1942, WW-II.

BEERGROUP -- Composite battalion from 1st South African Division, in action south of Tobruk, Libya. Named after its commanding officer, Lieutenant-Colonel J.M. de Beer. June 1942, WW-II.

BEERHOUSE -- Jenkins Bay, Sideia Island. WW-II.

BEESWING -- Keflavik, Iceland. WW-II.

BEETHOVEN -- (1) German remote controlled bomber carrying a ME 109 fighter, which after release directs the larger aircraft. The JU-88 bomber filled with explosives is guided to a ground collision with its target. Under development in 1943.

(2) Richthofen Bay, New Britain. WW-II.

BEETLE -- U.S. Air Force armored vehicle for nuclear weapons.

BEETLES -- Allied nickname for concrete and steel pontons on which rested WHALES, pier roadways. 1944, WW-II.

BEFRIEND -- Taroa Island, Maloelap Atoll, Marshall Islands. WW-II.

BEGONIA -- Siota, Florida-Tulagi Group, Solomon Islands. WW-II.

BEGRUDGE -- Eniwetok Atoll, Marshall Islands. WW-II.

BEGUILE -- Operations against Hokkaido, Japan. WW-II.

BEHEAD -- Seydisfjorjur, Iceland. WW-II.

BEIJA-FLOR -- (English translation: Humming Bird) Brazilian CTA utility helicopter which began trials in 1959.

BELABOR -- Cape Croisilles, New Guinea. WW-II.

BELGIAN GATES -- Sections of steel anti-tank obstacle erected by Belgium, in pre-war days, along frontier with Germany; later used by Germans in coastal defenses. Also known as Element C. WW-II.

BELIER -- French solid propellant sounding rocket used to carry payloads of 67 pounds to an altitude of 62 miles. Mobile launcher used for flight tests. In operational use.

BELINDA -- Royal Canadian Air Force barrage ballon. WW-II.

BELL TELEPHONE DIVISION -- Nickname for U.S. 76th Infantry Division. Named after design of shoulder patch. Also called LIBERTY BELL DIVISION.

BELLOWS -- Babuyan Channel, Philippine Islands. WW-II.

BELLTENT -- Ladd Field, Alaska. WW-II.

BELSHAZZER -- Sumatra, Netherlands East Indies. WW-II.

BELVEDERE -- British Westland, previously known as the Bristol 192, now in Royal Air Force service. First flew 1958.

BENCH CHECK -- Name for peacetime military project involving a supply lift.

BENCH MARK HILLS -- Military name for several hills on Luzon, Philippines. 1945, WW-II.

BENCOL -- Name for British 22nd Guards Brigade Group in Operation CRUSADER against Germans south of Bengasi, Libya. December 1941. WW-II.

BENEDICTINE CROSSROADS -- Allied code name for track junction, 500 yards short of Melfa River, and southwest of Roccasecca Station, Italy. Named after alcholic beverage. May 1944. WW-II.

BENEFICE -- Anatahan Island, Marianas Islands. WW-II.

BENEFICIARY -- Allied plan to capture St. Malo, France, by combined airborne and amphibious operation if complete stalemate occurred in Normandy bridgehead area in summer 1944. WW-II.

BENEFIT -- Man Le, Burma. WW-II.

BENETO -- Continuous-wave navigation system, similar to CONDOR, in which a phase differential measurement of an audio signal taken on the ground determines the distance to an aircraft.

BENEVOLENT -- Milne Bay, New Guinea. WW-II.

BENITO -- Anti-invasion exercise conducted by Canadian 2nd Division in United Kingdom. 16-19 April 1941, WW-II.

BENREP -- Acronym for BIG BEN Report, a daily statement of latest information received from armed reconnaissance of German rocket-firing areas. WW-II.

BEQUEST -- Yap Island, Caroline Islands. WW-II.

BERENICE -- French research rocket for Intermediate Range Ballistic Missile development tests of re-entry systems. Speeds of Mach 12 attained by firing third and fourth stages during descent. One flight test reported.

BERLIN (1) Awab Point, New Britain. WW-II.

(2) North Gugegwe, Kwajalein Atoll. Early 1944, WW-II.

(3) Military name for outpost in Korea. Summer 1953, Korean Conflict.

BERLIN AIRLIFT -- Aerial resupply of West Berlin by U.S. Air Force, British Royal Air Force, and some U.S. Navy aircraft, when Russians closed surface transport to the city. From its start in June 1948 until its completion in May 1949, 196,031 flights delivered 1,588,293 tons of supplies in a major Allied Cold War victory. Also called Operation Vittles.

BERLIN BETTY -- Woman radio propagandist broadcasting for Germans. WW-II.

BERMUDA -- British naval version of Brewster light bomber used by U.S. Army Air Forces as the A-34 and by the U.S. Navy as the SB2A. See BUCCANEER.

BERNHARD LINE -- See WINTER LINE

BERNHARD, OPERATION -- German counterfeiting plot in which more than 100 million pounds of fake British bank notes, good enough to escape detection by Bank of England, were produced. After failure to disrupt British economy, this false currency was used to buy arms, pay secret agents, and in other activities. WW-II.

BERNICE -- Tropical storm. 1-5 September 1962. Formed near Mexican west coast south of Mazatlan. Moved northwestward off coast of Baja California, Mexico, and dissipated.

BERRY -- Wake Island; canceled. WW-II.

BERTHA -- (1) Tropical storm. August 1948. First detected west of Bonin Islands, the Pacific. Moved northeastward and passed southeast of Japan, out over ocean.

    (2) Tropical storm. 8-11 August 1957. Formed in northern Gulf of Mexico. Moved northwestward into southwestern Louisiana and dissipated over Arkansas and Oklahoma. Caused minor damage.

BESS -- (1) Typhoon. 9-13 November 1952. Formed over eastern Caroline Islands. Moved west-northwestward through Marianas, across Philippine Sea, passed between Taiwan and Luzon, recurved northeastward through the Formosa Strait, and dissipated over the Ryukyus.

    (2) Typhoon. 27 August - 7 September 1957. Formed northeast of Guam, Mariana Islands. Moved northwestward, passed just west of Iwo Jima, reached the Ryukus, then recurved northeastward over Japan and lost force.

    (3) Typhoon. 16-25 August 1960. Formed northeast of Iwo Jima. Moved northwestward at first, then turned northeastward short of the Japan coast, curved east-southeastward, looped back, but dissipated before reaching Japan.

    (4) Name also applied to tropical cyclones in western Pacific which occurred prior to (1) through (3) above.

BESTMANN -- Pre-World War II Nazi sportplane; later a Luftwaffe trainer and designated the Bucker 181.

BESTRIDE -- Faisi, Bougainville, Solomon Islands. WW-II.

BETA -- (1) South Seymour Island, Galapagos Islands. WW-II.

    (2) See CARBONADO

BETA I -- British rocket-assisted take-off device with a thrust of 900 pounds in each of two rocket chambers (1800 pounds of thrust per unit). Thrust duration is 44 seconds, and the fuel is a combination of 80 per cent solution of peroxide plus a mixture of 30 per cent hydrazine, 57 per cent methanol and 13 per cent water. In use during the early 1950's. See also BETA II.

BETA II -- British liquid propellant jet assisted take-off device with almost three times the thrust of BETA I: 2500 pounds for 40 seconds. In use, 1952-54; now obsolete.

BETHESDA -- Luxor, Egypt. WW-II.

BETSY -- (I) Hurricane. 9-19 August 1956. Formed in Atlantic, 800 miles east of Leeward Islands. Moved westward through Leeward Islands, northwestward across Puerto Rico, skirted the Bahamas, then turned northeastward between Bermuda and Hatteras out over the Atlantic. Caused 27 deaths and 35.6 million dollars damage in the Antilles.

(2) Hurricane. 2-11 September 1961. Formed in mid-Atlantic east of Antilles. Moved northwestward to position northeast of Bermuda, then turned northeastward and dissipated over the Atlantic west of Ireland.

BETTY -- (I) U.S. Navy nuclear depth charge capable of being adapted to missile or bomb application. Operational, it is an advancement over the LULU. Type classified as the Mark 90.

(2) Allied name for World War II Japanese Mitsubishi OB-01 twin-engine naval bomber.

(3) Porlock Harbor, New Guinea. WW-II.

(4) Tropical storm. 13-16 May 1945. First detected in central Philippine Sea. Moved northeastward through Bonin Islands and out over North Pacific.

(5) Typhoon. 4-9 November 1946. First detected east of central Philippines. Moved northward at first, then northeastward and passed southeast of Japan out over the North Pacific.

(6) Typhoon. 29 November - 7 December 1949. First detected over southern Philippine Sea. Moved west-northwestward through the Island of Mindanao, across the northern Sulu Sea, and over the South China Sea, where it dissipated.

(7) Typhoon. 27-30 October 1953. Formed over southern Philippine Sea. Moved northwestward across central Philippines and South China Sea to Hainan Island. Caused considerable damage in Philippines.

(8) Tropical storm. 13-16 July 1958. Formed and dissipated over South China Sea west of Luzon, Philippines.

(9) Typhoon. 22-28 May 1961. Formed near Koror Island. Moved northwestward through Philippine Sea and across Taiwan, then northward along China coast to Korea. Caused flooding on Taiwan.

(10) Name also applied to tropical cyclones in western Pacific which occurred prior to (4) through (9) above.

BEULAH -- (I) Mairi Creek, New Guinea. WW-II.

(2) Tropical storm. 15-18 June 1959. Formed in Bay of Campeche and moved into Mexico near Tampico. Caused no reported damage.

BEVERLEY -- British Blackburn transport plane. Entered Royal Air Force service in 1955 and is still operational.

BEVERLY -- (I) South Gugegwe, Kwajalein Atoll. Early 1944, WW-II.

(2) Typhoon. 3-9 December 1948. First detected in eastern Caroline Islands. Moved west-northwestward, passed south of Guam, crossed the Philippine Sea and northern Luzon and entered South China Sea.

BEVY -- Guadalcanal Island, Solomon Islands. WW-II.

BEWILDER -- Annenberg, New Guinea. WW-II.

BEWITCH -- Hollandia, New Guinea. WW-II.

BIAS -- Nteni, New Britain. WW-II.

BIB -- Acronym for Baby Incendiary Bomb.

BIBER -- (English translation: Beaver) German one-man midget submarine which carried two torpedoes. First used in August 1944, WW-II.

BIBLICAL -- Kolomi, New Britain. WW-II.

BICARBONATE -- Seeadler Harbor, Manus Island, Bismarck Archipelago. WW-II.

BICYCLE -- Pambukan Sur, Samar, Philippine Islands. WW-II.

BICYCLE CAMP -- Former Dutch barracks near Batavia, Java, used by Japanese as prisoner of war camp for Allied Troops. WW-II.

BIDDIE -- Bongomal, New Britain. WW-II.

BIES -- (English translation: Dare Devil) Polish basic trainer first flown in 1955.

BIF -- U.S. Air Force acronym for Bombardier's Information File.

BIG ABNER -- See BEAVER TAIL

BIG APPLE PEAK -- U.S. military name for topographic feature in Yaeju-Dake hill mass, Okinawa. 1945, WW-II.

BIG-B -- Large solid propellant rocket engine manufactured by the Thiokol Chemical Corporation in the 1950's. At the time, the largest ever made.

BIG BASTARD -- Nickname for battleship, USS South Dakota. Also called OLD NAMELESS, BATTLESHIP X. WW-II.

BIG BEN -- (I) Nickname for aircraft carrier, USS Franklin. WW-II.

(2) British Royal Air Force nickname for German V-2 rocket. WW-II.

BIG BLAST --- Name for series of peacetime military exercises.

BIG BROTHER -- Early name for the U.S. Air Force SENTRY program.

BIG DIPPER ROAD -- Military name for topographic feature near Rabaul, New Britain. WW-II.

BIG E -- Nickname for aircraft carrier, USS Enterprise. WW-II.

BIG ESCARPMENT -- See HACKSAW RIDGE

BIG GAME -- Cover plan to insure surprise for modified PIANORO, U.S. 5th Army offensive south of Bologna. Involved creating illusion that large units were moving from U.S. 5th Army front to that of British 8th Army. 1945, WW-II.

BIG HAUL -- Name for peacetime military operation.

BIG HILL -- Military name for topographic feature in North Korea. Its capture by U.S. Marines on 9 December 1950 permitted U.N. troops to pass southward through Funchilin Pass, which was commanded by hill, and out of Chinese entrapment.

BIG HOOK -- Device used by Germans in retreats; consisted of hook carried on a flat car and towed behind a train; while hook tore up ties, TNT charges were dropped to damage rails. Also known as Track Ripper or Rooter Plow. See also RAIL ROOTER. WW-II.

BIG INCH -- Pipeline laid from Texas oilfields to East Coast of U.S. during World War II. See also LITTLE BIG INCH.

BIG JAY -- Nickname for battleship USS New Jersey.

BIG JOE -- Single ATLAS-boosted full-scale "boiler plate" MERCURY capsule similar to the operational capsule in both size and weight. Fired from Cape Canaveral, 9 September 1959, on a 1500 mile suborbital flight to test capsule, re-entry and re-covery techniques. Fully successful.

BIG PHOTO -- A U.S. Strategic Air Command aircraft participating in AIR Defense Command training missions.

BIG POCKET -- Military name for Japanese position on Bataan Peninsula, Philippine Islands. Early 1942, WW-II.

BIG RAID, THE -- Japanese aerial attack by over 100 planes on Guadalcanal. 16 June 1943, WW-II.

BIG SCHEME -- Plan of Resistance in Poland for national uprising against Germans; led to abortive Warsaw uprising of August-September 1944. First considered in 1942, WW-II.

BIG SAM/PUERTO PINE, OPERATION -- Test of U.S. capability in brush-fire wars--principally, of the adequacy of U.S. Military Air Transport Service military airlift, in March 1960.

BIG SQUEEZE PLAY -- Unsuccessful attempt to have all units under command of General Stilwell converge on Japanese 18th Division in north Burma and crush it. March 1944, WW-II.

BIG STICK -- Name for Convair proposal for a nuclear ramjet missile. Proposal not accepted, but nuclear ramjet missile being developed in SLAM program.

BIG SWITCH, OPERATION -- Exchange of prisoners at Panmunjom, Korea, after Armistice. 5 August - 6 September 1953, Korean Conflict.

BIG T -- A not-commonly-used nickname for the TITAN.

BIG THRUST -- Name for U.S. peacetime military exercise at Fort Hood, Texas.

BIG WEEK -- Nickname for concentrated air attacks on German aircraft production facilities in World War II. See ARGUMENT OPERATION.

BIG WILLIE -- Collective name given by Allies to 340-mm. naval guns taken from French battleship, Provence, and mounted in turrets of fortress on Island of Saint Mandrier in the harbor of Toulon, France. August 1944, WW-II.

BIGCLUB -- Khartoum, Sudan. WW-II.

BIGELOW -- Igashik, Alaska. WW-II.

BIGHEART -- Pointe Noire, French Africa. WW-II.

BIGHUSKY -- American Mission, Fortaleza, Brazil. WW-II.

BIGOT -- Special procedure by which all papers relating to OVERLORD operations which disclosed target area or precise dates of assault were limited in circulation and subjected to stringent safeguards. Adopted September 1943, WW-II.

BIGTOP -- Accra, Gold Coast, Africa. WW-II.

BIGWIG -- Luya, New Guinea. WW-II.

BILGE -- Mission Pier, Trobriand Island, New Guinea. WW-II.

BILIOUS -- Code name for Central Pacific. WW-II.

BILLFISH -- Mave (Rahe) River, New Guinea. WW-II.

BILLIE -- (I) Typhoon. 4-13 November 1950. Formed northeast of Guam. Moved northwestward briefly, then recurved northeastward out over the North Pacific.

    (2) Typhoon. 2-5 June 1955. Formed in northern portion of South China Sea. Moved northward and dissipated in vicinity of Hong Kong.

    (3) Typhoon. 13-16 July 1959. Formed between Yap and Koror Islands. Moved northwestward across Taiwan to China mainland, then curved northeastward across Korea and merged with another storm. Caused 1 death on Taiwan.

    (4) Typhoon. 23-28 October 1961. Formed south of Guam. Moved northwestward, then northward, passing west of the Mariana Islands and east of the Volcano Islands, and merged with another storm east of Japan. Sank one Freighter near Guam.

    (5) Name also applied to tropical cyclones in western Pacific which occurred prior to (1) through (4) above.

BILLSTICKING -- Huon Peninsula, New Guinea. WW-II.

BILLYCAN -- Alexandria, Egypt. WW-II.

BINDWEED -- Boeroe Island, Netherlands East Indies. WW-II.

BINGHAM -- Sorrento, Italy. WW-II.

BINGHAM, OPERATION -- Establishment of Allied air forces at Zara, Yugoslavia, to increase air support to Marshal Tito's forces. April 1945, WW-II.

BINGHAMPTON -- U.S. code word for Munda on New Georgia Island. WW-II.

BINGO -- (I) Nome, Alaska. WW-II.

    (2) Allied air attacks on transformer stations between Verona and Brenner Pass to cut off electricity for trains supplying German forces in Italy. 1944-45, WW-II.

BINOCULAR -- Lae, New Guinea (canceled). WW-II.

BIOCELATE -- Yakot, New Guinea. WW-II.

BIOS -- Acronym for Biological Investigation of Space. Space probe packages used to study the effects of space radiation on various types of biological specimens. Part of the NERV program: first launched in 1961.

BIPED -- (I) Code name for Ivigtut, Greenland. WW-II.

    (2) Code name for the British. WW-II.

BIRCH -- (I) Christmas Island, Pacific Ocean. WW-II.

(2) Doma Cove, Solomon Islands. WW-II.

BIRD, THE -- See LIBERTY EAGLE

BIRD DOG -- (I) Cessna L-19 aircraft used by the U.S. Army in Korea in 1950 and recently returned to production.

(2) An early name for the GENIE (MB-1) air-to-air missile.

BIRD OF PARADISE -- Fokker C-2 trimotor which made a remarkable flight in 1927 by flying from Oakland, California to Honolulu, Hawaii. Piloted by two U.S. Army fliers, Lieutenants Maitland and Hegenberger.

BIRDIE -- Acronym for Battery Integration and Radar Display Equipment, a mobile, air-transportable air defense system for U.S. Army and Marine Corps use. Operational in 1961, it is scheduled to be deployed at 17 sites within the U.S. to control missile batteries.

BIRKE -- Plan for withdrawal of German 20th Mountain Army into northern Lapland. 1944, WW-II.

BIRTHDAY -- Trobriand Island, New Guinea. WW-II.

BISHOP -- Allied covering operation for DRACULA. 27 April-6 May 1945, WW-II.

BISLEY -- Mark V version of Bristol BLENHEIM, used as a bomber and fighter-bomber during World War II.

BISON -- (1) NATO designation for four-engine turbojet Russian long-range heavy bomber. First flew 1954.

(2) Kumbum Village, New Guinea. WW-II.

(3) Name for Royal Canadian Air Force Squadron Number 429.

BITING -- British paratroop raid on German WÜRZBURG radar installation at Bruneval, France, to collect intelligence. 27/28 February 1942, WW-II.

BITTER ENDERS -- Exclusive group of U.S. Navy Armed Guard personnel who had survived a torpedoing by an enemy submarine. WW-II.

BIVALVE -- Ceuta, Spanish Morocco, Africa. WW-II.

BLACK -- See BARRISTER

BLACK BOOK, THE -- U.S. Army study entitled, "Report on Certain Features of the Organization Problems Involved in Developing Resources to Meet Strategic Requirements." Named after color of cover in which it was bound. Completed 15 May 1942, WW-II.

BLACK BRANT -- Family of Canadian sounding rockets for scientific research up to altitudes of 600 miles. Several II A versions were used by U.S. Air Force in 1961. National Aeronautics and Space Administration will also fire an advanced version in 1963. Early name was SNOW GOOSE.

BLACK BULLET -- Unorthodox Northrop N2B flying wing delivered to U.S. Army Air Forces in 1943. Only two built.

BLACK CATS -- (I) Nickname for U.S. Navy amphibian patrol aircraft, CATALINA PBY-5A's; first used on Guadalcanal, December 1942. Also called Cats. See also DUMBO. WW-II.

(2) Nickname for U.S 13th Armored Division.

BLACK HAWK DIVISION -- Nickname for U.S. 86th Infantry Division.

BLACK JACK -- (I) Nickname for U.S. General of the Armies John J. Pershing.

(2) Name for peacetime military exercise.

BLACK KNIGHT -- British rocket test vehicle, at one time expected to develop into a long-range strategic weapon; later canceled in economy effort. Fired at Woomera Test Range in Australia to gather data on re-entry effects. First flight 7 September 1958.

BLACK LABEL -- U.S. Air Force high-altitude air refueling area over Minnesota-Michigan.

BLACK LINE -- German defense line in northern Italy. 1945, WW-II.

BLACK MONOCLE -- Nickname for Andre Canal, who was in charge of Secret Army Organization (OAS) operations in France, 1961-62; named for black monocle worn over left eye, which he lost in World War II.

BLACK PANTHER DIVISION -- Nickname for U.S. 66th Infantry Division.

BLACK PANTHERS -- Nickname for U.S. Marine Corps dive bombing squadron operating from air bases on Lingayen Gulf, Philippines. 1945. WW-II.

BLACK PIT -- Nickname given by Allied seamen to area in mid-Atlantic, not covered by anti-submarine aircraft patrols, where German submarines attacked in packs. 1941-43, WW-II.

BLACK SATURDAY -- Name given by Allies to Saturday, June 13, 1942, when British Eighth Army was forced by German Africa Corps to retreat after tremendous tank battle. WW-II.

BLACK SHEEP -- Name for U.S. Marine Corps air squadron of "misfit" pilots commanded by Colonel Gregory "Pappy" Boyington, who entitled his autobiography Baa Baa Black Sheep. WW-II.

BLACK SUNDAY -- Name given Sunday, 16 April 1944, by men of U.S. 5th Air Force when heavy losses in personnel and aircraft were incurred in raid on Hollandia, New Guinea, on account of bad weather conditions. WW-II.

BLACK WIDOW -- Northrop P-61 first ordered by the U.S. Army Air Forces in January 1941. Apart from the PN-1 of 1921, this was the first U.S. aircraft specifically designed as a night fighter.

BLACKBERRY -- Enogai, New Georgia, Solomon Islands. WW-II.

BLACKBIRD -- Polish monoplane. See KOS.

BLACKBOY -- (1) Segi Village, New Georgia Island, Solomon Islands. WW-II.

(2) Small anti-invation exercise conducted by Canadian First Division on south English coast to prepare for possible minor German raids. November 1942, WW-II.

BLACKCOCK -- British XII Corps operation to clear enemy from Roermond Triangle, north of Aachen, Germany, between the Roer and Meuse Rivers. January 1945, WW-II.

BLACKFRIARS BRIDGE -- Bailey pontoon bridge constructed by Royal Canadian Engineers across Rhine River in British area at Rees, Germany. 26-28 March 1945, WW-II.

BLACKHAWK -- Curtiss XF-87A aircraft. See NIGHTHAWK.

BLACKLIST -- General Douglas MacArthur's plan for occupation of Japan and Korea in event of early surrender. Published 25 July 1945, became operative on 15 August 1945 when Japan accepted terms of Potsdam Ultimatum, WW-II.

BLACKMAIL -- Operations in which French workers, in return for Allied promise not to bomb their factory, would themselves put it out of action. WW-II.

BLACKMARI -- British air-to air identification system.

BLACKPOOL -- Name for jungle clearing behind Japanese lines in northeast Burma; used as airstrip during Allied OPERATION THURSDAY. Spring 1944, WW-II.

BLACKSMITH -- Wewak Airdrome, New Guinea. WW-II.

BLACKSTONE SUB-TASK FORCE -- Unit of WESTERN TASK FORCE which landed at Safi, French Morocco. Also called Force X. November 1942, WW-II.

BLADE FORCE -- British armored unit which was landed at Bone, Algeria, to operate eastward into Tunisia. 13 November 1942, WW-II.

BLAIR PACKING COMPANY -- Fictious fish cannery equipment company created to mask operations of U.S. Army engineers in construction of air base on Umnak Island in the Aleutians, early 1942. Directed by Alaska Defense Command through dummy CONSOLIDATED PACKING COMPANY. WW-II.

BLAKESLEEWAFFE -- Sobriquet given to the famous World War II U.S. Army Air Forces 4th Fighter Group, based in England, when commanded by Colonel D.M. Blakeslee, who had been a member of the Royal Canadian Air Force and the

Eagle Squadron.

BLANCA -- Explosion site of underground nuclear weapons development tests at Nevada Test Site. 1958.

BLANCHMANGE -- Safi, French Morocco, Africa. WW-II.

BLANKENSHIP -- U.S. code name for Loi Island, Kwajalein Atoll. Early 1944, WW-II.

BLAST -- U. N. phychological warfare plan involving leaflet drops on Pyongyang, North Korea, warning civilians to stay away from military installations before impending air attack and telling them after attack that they had been so warned. Similar to STRIKE. 1952, Korean Conflict.

BLAZEUP -- Davao, Philippine Islands. WW-II.

BLAZING -- Projected and partially mounted allied raid on Alderney, Channel Islands. Cancelled 6 May 1942, WW-II.

BLEACHER -- Tongatabu, Tonga Islands. WW-II.

BLENHEIM -- Pre-World War II Bristol medium-range bomber for the British Royal Air Force. Later used as a night fighter and fighter and fighter-bomber. Canadian-built version, with U.S. engines, was called BOLINGBROKE. Mark V series called Bisley.

BLENNY -- Yembokau, New Guinea. WW-II.

BLISSFUL -- Choiseul Island, Solomon Islands. WW-II.

BLITZ CAN -- See JERRY CAN

BLITZBUGGY -- See JEEP

BLOCK BUSTER -- (1) Name for British 8000-pound double unit high-explosive bomb; first used against Karlsruhe, Germany, 2 September 1942. WW-II.

(2) Canadian II Corps offensive in Calcar-Üdem-Xanten area of Germany east of Rhine River. 22 February-10 March 1945, WW-II.

BLOCKING GROUP BODE -- Independent German infantry group formed to guard center of line in Italy south of Rome. Named after its commander. Winter 1944, WW-II.

BLONDIE -- Sand Island, New Guinea. WW-II.

BLOOD CHARIOTS -- Nickname for ambulance aircraft of Air Commandos in China-Burma-India Theater. See also TERRY AND THE PIRATES. WW-II.

BLOOD AND FIRE DIVISION -- Nickname for U.S. 63rd Infantry Division.

BLOOD AND GUTS -- See OLD BLOOD AND GUTS

BLOOD AND GUTS, USS -- Nickname, simulating name of ship, given by U.S naval unit to bombed-out cavalry school, Adolf Hitler Kaserne, near Toul, France, when it was billeted there while serving on land duty. November 1944, WW-II.

BLOOD AND IRON FOR THE EMPEROR DUTY UNITS -- About 750 male students of middle schools, fourteen years of age and over, trained by Japanese for Guerilla warfare in Okinawa. 1945, WW-II.

BLOODHOUND -- British surface-to-air missile. Guided to target by semi-active radar homing. Four solid rocket motors boost missile to speed of about 2200 miles per hour, at which point two kerosene-burning ramjet sustainer engines take over. First became fully operational in 1958. Deployed in Britain, Australia and Sweden. An advanced version with greater range and a ceiling of 60,000 feet is under development.

BLOODHOUND II -- British surface-to-air missile. Has 60,000-foot ceiling, and 70,000-yard range. Under development.

BLOODSUCKER -- Code name for Roumania. WW-II.

BLOODY BAMBOO THICKET -- Military name for topographic feature on Leyte, Philippine Islands. November 1944, WW-II.

BLOODY BUCKET -- Nickname for U.S. 28th Infantry Division. Reputedly so named after Normandy landings in World War II, by Germans for shoulder patch, a red keystone for parent state, Pennsylvania. Also called KEYSTONE DIVISION.

BLOODY GULCH -- Military name for topographic feature near Pongam-ni, Korea; scene of North Korean attack on U.S. artillery units. 12 August 1950, Korean Conflict.

BLOODY HILL -- (1) Military name for topographic feature on New Georgia. July 1943, WW-II.

(2) U.S. military name for Rougemont ridge line near Morhange, France. Scene of bitter fighting between Americans and Germans. Early November 1944, WW-II.

BLOODY KNOB -- See BATTLE MOUNTAIN

BLOODY NOSE RIDGE -- (1) U.S. Marine Corps nickname for topographic feature near Henderson Field, Guadalcanal. Also called Raider's Ridge. Scene of bitter fighting, 13-14 September 1942, WW-II.

(2) Topographical feature on Peleliu Island, western Pacific. Name is favorite U.S. Marine nickname for any costly objective. Scene of fighting, September 1944, WW-II.

BLOODY RIDGE -- Military name for topographic feature on Sicily. 1943, WW-II.

(2) Military name for topographic feature west of Dagami, Leyte, Philippine Islands. 1944, WW-II.

(3) U.S military name for topographic feature south of THE PINNACLE on Ie Shima, Ryukyu Islands. See also GOVERNMENT HOUSE HILL. 1945, WW-II.

(4) U.N. name for topographic feature in PUNCHBOWL area, eastern Korea; scene of heavy fighting in September–October 1951. Korean Conflict.

(5) See EDSON'S RIDGE

BLOODY SUNDAY -- Name given by U.S 182nd Infantry Regiment to heavy military action outside THE PERIMETER on Bougainville. 12 March 1944, WW-II.

BLOOMERS -- Detachable accordion-pleated screens made of canvas; when raised were capable of floating Allied DD TANKS. WW-II.

BLOSSOM -- Madu Island, Flores Sea, Netherlands East Indies. WW-II.

BLOWLAMP -- Supersonic Soviet light bomber. First seen in 1956 but not reported since.

BLOWTORCH AND CORKSCREW METHOD -- U.S. method of assaulting Japanese defenses in Okinawa by coordinated action of tank-infantry team using liquid flame (Blowtorch) from newly developed armored flame throwers and explosives (Corkscrew). 1945, WW-II.

BLUE -- Code name for United States in pre-World War II planning.

BLUE BEETLE -- Nickname for destroyers, USS Drayton; so given because she was once painted a peculiar experimental color. WW-II.

BLUE BELL -- U.S. Air Force high-altitude air refueling area over Michigan.

BLUE BOLT -- Name for peacetime military exercise.

BLUE CANOE -- Pilot's nickname for the Cessna 310 aircraft in use by the U.S. Air Force as the U-3.

BLUE AND GRAY -- Nickname for the U.S. 29th Infantry Division.

BLUE RIDGE DIVISION -- Nickname for U.S. 80th Infantry Division.

BLUE SCOUT -- U.S. Air Force family of special research support vehicles derived from, and closely related to, National Aeronautics and Space Administration's SCOUT research rocket. Used to gather scientific data, test equipment and evaluate re-entry techniques for ballistic missiles. Can reach an altitude of more than 6000 miles. Four stage, solid propellant vehicle. Also known as HETS (Hyper-Environment Test System). See also BLUE SCOUT, JR., BLUE SCOUT I AND II AND SEA SCOUT. First flight tested in 1960.

BLUE SCOUT I -- U.S. Air Force space probe rocket. First flew 7 January 1961. See also BLUE SCOUT.

BLUE SCOUT II -- U.S. Air Force space probe rocket. See also BLUE SCOUT.

BLUE SCOUT, JUNIOR -- U.S. Air Force space probe rocket. First flew 21 September 1960. See also BLUE SCOUT, RAM.

BLUE STEEL -- British air-to-surface stand-off missile designed to increase the strike and range of the VULCAN and VICTOR strategic bombers. Initial version is liquid propelled and has a range of 400-600 miles; improved version will have a solid motor. Also referred to as the "Avro Standoff Bomb," after the developer A.V. Roe, Limited. In operational use.

BLUE STREAK -- Initially, the name for a British Intermediate Range Ballistic Missile on which development was begun in 1954. Using liquid propellants, the two-engine vehicle was test fired several times before it was cancelled in 1960. It has been revived, however, as the first stage of the European Launch Vechicle under development by the European Launcher Development Organization, part of the European Space Research program.

BLUE WATER -- British surface-to-surface tactical missile comparable to the U.S. SERGEANT missile. It was developed to meet a NATO requirement for a 100-mile, solid propellant missile to replace U.S CORPORAL. Cancelled in 1962 in British defense cut-back.

BLUEBEARD -- Lama, Ceram, Netherlands East Indies. WW-II.

BLUEBELL -- Kaylan Point, Florida-Tulagi Group, Solomon Islands. WW-II.

BLUEBERRY -- Daly Rock, Treasury Island. WW-II.

BLUECOAT -- British 2nd Army offensive operation south from Caumont, France, during breakout from Normandy beachhead. Began 30 July 1944, WW-II.

BLUEGRASS -- (1) U.S. communications project for emergency communications in the event of nuclear attack. Sounding rockets would be used for communications between two points when all other links have been destroyed. Under development.

(2) Hate Tabako Airdrome, Halmahera Island Netherlands East Indies. WW-II.

BLUEHEARTS -- Early plan for amphibious operation to drive North Koreans back across 38th Parallel. Proposed for 22 July 1950, but canceled. Followed by CHROMITE. Korean Conflict.

BLUENOSE -- Name for Royal Canadian Air Force Squadron Number 434.

BLUFF -- Code name for Iran. WW-II.

BLUIE -- U.S. Army code name for Greenland. WW-II.

BLUIE EAST -- U.S. Army code name for eastern Greenland. See also BLUIE EAST 1-5. WW-II.

BLUIE EAST 1 -- U.S. Army code name for base at Torgilsbu, Greenland, near Cape Farewell. WW-II.

BLUIE EAST 2 -- U.S. Army code name for radio and meteorological station on Angmagsalik Island, opposite Iceland. WW-II.

BLUIE EAST 3 -- U.S. Army code name for Gurreholm on Scoresby Sound, Greenland. WW-II.

BLUIE EAST 4 -- U.S. army code name for Ella Island on Davy Sound at latitude 73 degrees north in Greenland. WW II.

BLUIE EAST 5 -- U.S. Army code name for radio station at Eskimonaes, Greenland, latitude 74 degrees north; seized by Germans on 23 March 1943; when re-established, located at Myggbukta. WW-II.

BLUIE WEST -- U.S. Army code name for western Greenland. See also BLUIE WEST 1-8. WW-II.

BLUIE WEST 1 -- U.S. Army code name for main Army and Navy base and airfield at Narsarssuak, Greenland, WW-II.

BLUIE WEST 2 -- U.S. Army code name for Kipisako, Greenland. WW-II.

BLUIE WEST 3 -- U.S. Army code name for high-frequency direction-finding station at Simiutak, at mouth of Skovfjord, Greenland. WW-II.

BLUIE WEST 4 -- U.S. Army code name for Faeringerhavnen, at latitude 63 degrees 40 minutes north, Greenland. WW-II.

BLUIE WEST 5 -- U.S. code name for Godhavn, on South Disko Island, Greenland. WW-II.

BLUIE WEST 6 -- U.S. Army code name for Thule, Greenland, at 76 degrees 30 minutes latitude north. WW-II.

BLUIE WEST 7 -- U.S. Army code name for Grondal, Greenland, base for protection of cryolite mine at Ivigtut. WW-II.

BLUE WEST 8 -- U.S. Army code name for emergency landing field at Sondrestromfjord, Greenland, at latitude 67 degrees north. WW-II.

BLUNDERBUSS -- Code name for Japan Sea. WW-II.

BOA -- U.S. sounding rocket designed to carry 500 pounds of scientific experiments to altitudes of 75 miles. Three-stage, solid propellant. Used by the Air Force.

BOAR -- Proposal to use an unguided rocket to carry a nuclear weapon to its target after release from a low-flying supersonic plane. Bomb would be released in an "over-the-shoulder" toss and carried by the rocket into the target. No active development.

BOARSHEAD -- Sourabaya, Java. WW-II.

BOB -- Russian World War II IL-4 bomber. Developed from TsKB-26 which first flew in 1935.

BOBBIN -- British ramjet test vehicle. Forerunner and test vehicle for the Blood-hound surface-to-air missile; also used to check out vehicle recovery at supersonic speeds. First fired at Australia's Woomera test range in 1956.

BOBCAT -- (1) Cessna T-50 aircraft of 1939. Used by the U.S. Army Air Forces as the AT-17 trainer and UC-78 transport. British model called Crane.

(2) U.S. Navy fueling station on Bora-Bora, Society Islands; first advance base to be established in Pacific after Pearl Harbor attack. Early 1942, WW-II.

BOCK'S CAR -- Crew's name for U.S. B-29 aircraft which dropped atomic bomb on Nagasaki, Japan, 9 August 1945. Named for Captain Frederick C. Bock, its regular pilot, who had for the mission exchanged planes with Major Charles W. Sweeney, apparently to avoid transferring scientific instruments. See also THE GREAT ARTISTE. WW-II.

BODE, BLOCKING GROUP -- See BLOCKING GROUP BODE

BODKIN -- Sondrestromfjord, Greenland. WW-II.

BODYGUARD -- Allied strategic plan of deception to persuade Germans before OVERLORD that invasion was to be in Pas de Calais area, France, and after OVERLORD that main blow was yet to come. Name taken from remark by Prime Minister Winston Churchill, "Truth deserves a bodyguard of lies." 1944, WW-II.

BODYLINE -- See CROSSBOW

BOEITAI -- Okinawa Home Guards, used as labor and service troops by Japanese, in defense of Okinawa. Spring 1945, WW-II.

BOFORCE -- Heavily armed motorized battalion group from 3rd Canadian Brigade which lead advance from Villapiana to Potenza, Italy. Named after its commander, then Lieutenant-Colonel M.P. Bogert. 17-21 September 1943, WW-II.

BOGGY -- Port Sufaga, Egypt. WW-II.

BOILINGPOINT -- Vitiaz Strait, New Guinea. WW-II.

BOISTEROUS -- Operations for the capture of Malaya. WW-II.

BOLD ORION -- U.S. Air Force test vehicle which led to the development of the SKYBOLT air-to-surface missile. Tested feasibility of air-launching ballistic missiles to ranges of 1000 miles. On 13 October 1959, the two-state solid propellant missile was launched from a B-47, 146 miles into space and passed within four miles of the EXPLORER VI satellite.

BOLERO -- Build-up of U.S. troops and supplies in United Kingdom in preparation for cross-Channel invasion, OVERLORD. See also SICKLE, RHUMBA. WW-II.

BOLINGBROKE -- Canadian-built version of Bristol BLENHEIM aircraft. Equipped with U.S. engines.

BOLO -- (1) Late 1930's military version of DOUGLAS DC-series aircraft. Designated B-18 by the U.S. Army Air Forces.

(2) Nickname for NORTH AMERICAN AVIATION proposal for the development of a nuclear-ramjet missile. Proposal was not accepted, but the missile is being developed by the U.S. Air Force in the SLAM program.

BOLT -- An uncommon nickname for the Army's M-55 multiple rocket launcher which can fire 45 four-inch chemical rockets. Operational in 1960.

BOMARC -- Surface-to-air missile developed and deployed by the U.S. Air force. Provides air defense against supersonic aircraft up to altitudes of 70,000 feet, and ranges of 200-400 miles. Delta-winged missile is an outgrowth of efforts in World War II and following, in ground-to-air pilotless aircraft. Two versions (A & B) produced. Operational in 1960, and deployed in U.S. and Canada. See also GAPA, METHUSELAH.

BOMARC A -- U. .S. Air Force surface-to-air missile with 200-nautical-mile range, and a ceiling of 68,000 feet. See also BOMARC.

BOMARC-B -- U.S. Air Force surface-to-air missile with over 400-mile range, and a ceiling of over 70,000 feet. See also BOMARC.

BOMB ALLEY -- British name for area of Mediterranean between island of Crete and Cyrenaica, North Africa. 1942, WW-II.

BOMBARDMENT -- Proposed U.S. air-to-air missile designed to enable jet bombers to stand-off from their targets and fire the nuclear weapon to the target. An industry proposal, it was not developed. See SKYBOLT.

BOMBARDONS -- Allied code name for floating units with steel cruciform super-structure, moored end to end in deep water, designed to act as breakwaters in artificial harbors, MULBERRIES. Also called Lilos after trade name of inflated rubber mattress used on bathing beaches in England. 1944, WW-II.

BOMBAY -- British Bristol twin-engine, fixed landing gear bomber of 1930's.

BOMBING BANSHEES -- Nickname for U.S. Marine Corps dive-bombing squadron operating from air bases on Lingayen Gulf, Philippines. 1945. WW-II.

BOMBRINI -- Italian two and three-quarter inch air-to-air rocket test program.

BOMI -- Nickname for Bell Aircraft proposal for a boost-glide orbital vehicle. Being developed by the U.S. Air Force as the DYNA-SOAR (X-20). Another name used in an earlier proposal was Brass Bell.

BONANZA -- Beechercraft plane, first flown in 1945.

BONNY -- Tropical storm. 21-26 June 1960. First detected 250 miles southwest of Acapulco, Mexico. Moved northwestward, then westward out over the Pacific and dissipated.

BONUS -- (I) Acronym for Boiling Nuclear Superheat Reactor under construction at Punta Higuera, Puerto Rico. Will demonstrate practicality of nuclear superheat utilizing a superheater region located peripherally to the boiling region on small reactors.

(2) Tui Island, Bismarck Archipelago. WW-II.

(3) See IRONCLAD

BOODLE -- (I) Kiska Island, Aleutian Islands. WW-II.

(2) Seuri, New Guinea. WW-II.

BOOKIE -- Fort Chimo, Province of Quebec, Canada. WW-II.

BOOKWORM -- Dilli, Timor, Netherlands East Indies. WW-II.

BOOMERANG -- (I) Australian Commonwealth CA-12 fighter aircraft. First flew in 1942.

(2) Code name for night attack by B-29 aircraft of U.S. XX Bomber Command, based on Ceylon against oil refinery at Palembang and other targets on island of Sumatra; 5th mission of MATTERHORN. 10-11 August 1944, WW-II.

BOOSTED ARCAS -- See ARCAS, BOOSTED

BOOTLEG -- Name for peacetime military exercise held in Germany to test combat building capacity of 37th Engineer Group. September 1961.

BOOTS, OPERATION -- See HAMMER, OPERATION

BORAX -- (I) Code name for Military Attache, Haiti, West Indies. WW-II.

(2) Series of five U.S. experiments which demonstrated feasibility of boiling water reactors. Conducted by Argonne National Laboratory at Idaho Testing Station, beginning 1953. See also BORAX 1-5.

BORAX-1 -- First of U.S. BORAX Experiments by Argonne National Laboratory at Idaho Testing Station. Tested stability and inherent safety characteristics of boiling water reactors. 1953.

BORAX-2 -- Second of U.S. BORAX experiments by Argonne National Laboratory at Idaho Testing Station. Tested new core combinations using enrichments of uranium 235 in the metal fuel plates. 1954.

BORAX-3 — Third of U.S. BORAX experiments by Argonne National Laboratory at Idaho Testing Station. Borax-3 reactor served as exclusive source of electricity for town of Arco, Idaho for about one hour, the first such event in history. July 17, 1955.

BORAX-4 -- Fourth of U.S. BORAX experiments by Argonne National Laboratory at Idaho Testing Station. Tested fuel elements made from mixed oxides of uranium and thorium. 1956.

BORAX-5 -- Fifth of U.S. BORAX experiments by Argonne National Laboratory at Idaho Testing Station. Demonstrated the feasibility of an integral boiling-super-heating reactor. Completed March 1961.

BOREALIS -- Alaskan-Siberian Air Ferry Project. WW-II.

BOSCARI -- Italian Army anti-tank weapon. Fired from a bazooka-type launcher.

BOSCO -- Telephone directory of American and British delegations at QUADRANT conference. August 1943, WW-II.

BOSS -- Acronym for Biological Orbiting Space Station. U.S. Air Force program to provide bioastronautical data on long-term (up to two weeks) effects of weight-lessness and radiation on primates. Not approved for development. See also SNOWBALL.

BOSTON -- (1) Nickname for one of the four Douglas World Cruisers of 1924 around-the-world fame. This particular plane did not finish the trip, being abandoned in the North Atlantic during the final phase. See WORLD CRUISER.

(2) Douglas DB-7, designed for the French in 1937. First flight in 1938. Later joined the U.S. Army Air Forces as the A-20/P-70. Also called HAVOC.

(3) Abau-Mullins Harbor area in southeast New Guinea. WW-II.

BOSUN -- Russian Tupolev-designed twin-jet light bomber which entered service in the early 1950's.

BOTANICAL -- Kawasaki, Kaga Hara. WW-II.

BOTANY -- Rome, Italy. WW-II.

BOTHA I -- Early World War II twin-engine bomber built by Great Britain's Black-burn Company.

BOOTCHER'S CORNER -- Name for position on beach near Buna, New Guinea, held by platoon under U.S. Staff Sergeant Herman J.F. Bottcher. December 1942, WW-II.

CODE NAMES DICTIONARY

BOTTLE -- Yulinkan, French Indo China. WW-II.

BOTTLENECKS -- See PANACEA TARGETS

BOTTOMSIDE -- Military name for low area on Corregidor Island, Philippine Islands.
Early 1942. WW-II.

BOULDER -- Saidia, Algeria. WW-II.

BOULEVARD, THE -- Name for Hodo Pando-Hungnam-Chaho sea route off eastern
Korean coast used by ships in U.N. blockade. Korean Conflict.

BOUNCING BETTY -- Nickname for German antipersonnel S MINE; so named
because when stepped on it would bounce a few feet in the air before a secondary
fuse set off the main explosive charge, scattering some three hundred steel balls
in all directions. WW-II.

BOUNDER -- NATO designation for Russian multi-jet medium bomber now in service
with Soviet Air Force.

BOURGEOIS -- Reykjavik, Iceland. WW-II.

BOUT-ONE -- Composite unit of U.S. and South Korean airmen, using Mustang
fighter-bomber aircraft, stationed at Taegu, Korea. Organized 27 June 1950,
Korean Conflict.

BOVEY -- Code name for road junction southwest of Rimini, Italy; captured by
Canadian troops. September 1944, WW-II.

BOWERY -- Aircraft for Malta from USS Wasp and HMS Eagle. 8-15 May 1942,
WW-II.

BOWL, THE -- Military name for bay near Heraklion, Crete. May 1941, WW-II.

BOWLER -- (1) Dar Es Salaam, Tanganyika, Africa. WW-II.

(2) British Royal Air Force attack on shipping in harbor of Venice. Name
chosen by Air Vice-Marshal R.M. Foster to signify type of hat threatened
for pilots if Venetian monuments were destroyed through inaccuracy. 21 March
1945, WW-II.

BOWLING ALLEY -- Nickname for western section of Taegu-Sangji road, Korea.
Probably named by men of F Company, U.S. 27th Regiment, during night battle
of 21-22 August 1950, when enemy tanks fired armor-piercing shells straight up
road toward American positions. Korean Conflict.

BOWSPRIT -- Code word devised to notify U.S. troops of 24-hour delay in OVER-
LORD. See also HORNPIPE.

BOWSTRING -- Petropavlovsk, Union of Soviet Socialist Republics. WW-II.

BOX -- Code name for Douglas A-20 aircraft delivered to Russia during World War-II.

BOXCAR -- (I) Originally the nickname for the Fairchild C-82 cargo plane which first flew in May 1945, but later shared by its successor, the C-119. See also FLYING BOXCAR.

(2) Belem, Brazil. WW-II.

(3) Moemi Airdrome, New Guinea. WW-II.

BOXCLOTH -- Apamama, Gilbert Islands. WW-II.

BOXER -- Tawi Tawi Bay, Philippine Islands. WW-II.

BOXWOOD -- Norupena Point, Torokina Island, Solomon Islands. WW-II.

BOYD RIDGE -- Military name for topographic feature on Peleliu Island. Fall 1944, WW-II.

BOYLE -- Capua, Italy. WW-II.

BRACKER -- Fotuna Point, Treasury Island. WW-II.

BRADDOCK II -- Dropping of small fuse incendiaries to European workers for use in sabotage operations against Germans. WW-II.

BRADLEY PLAN -- Study and recommendations concerning personnel needs and organization of U.S. 8th Air Force in United Kingdom; prepared by Major General Follett Bradley. May 1943, WW-II.

BRADMAN -- Heavy air bombardment of Cassino, Italy. A phase of Operation DICKENS. Morning of 15 March 1944, WW-II.

BRAID -- Cover name for General George C. Marshall during Casablanca Conference. January 1943, WW-II.

BRANCHPIPE -- Menado, Celebes, Netherlands East Indies. WW-II.

BRANGLE -- Singor, New Guinea. WW-II.

BRASENOSE -- Haiti, West Indies. WW-II.

BRASS -- Alesani, Corsica. WW-II.

BRASS BELL -- See BOMI, DYNA-SOAR

BRASS DONKEY -- German air force slang name for an all-metal aircraft. WW-II.

BRASS HAT -- Code name for Yo Do, largest island in Wonsan harbor, North Korea, occupied by U.N. forces during naval siege. 16 February 1951-27 July 1953, Korean Conflict.

BRASSARD -- French operation to liberate island of Elba. 17 June 1944, WW-II.

BRASSHAT -- Amphibious Training Group, Southwest Pacific. WW-II.

BRASSIERE -- Ulamaingi, New Britain. WW-II.

BRASSIERE BOYS -- Nickname for U.S. 6th Armored Division. Also called SUPER 6TH.

BRAVES -- Perth, Australia. WW-II.

BRAVO -- (I) Code word for letter "B" in a phonetic alphabet, used to avoid possibility of a misunderstanding in transmitting messages. See also BAKER.

(2) Part of the contemplated Air Force-Lockheed Biological Orbiting Space Station in which a 50-pound primate would be put into an orbit passing through the Van Allen belts to study the effects of space radiation. Funding difficulties prevented the Air Force from carrying through on the program. It may be re-proposed by Lockheed to National Aeronautics and Space Administration as part of its expanded BIOS program.

(3) Ice island established in Arctic by U.S. Project ICE SKATE.

BRAWN -- British operation to deliver a second heavy air strike on the German battleship Tirpitz in Altenfiord and incapacitate her for the rest of the war. 19 May 1944, WW-II.

BRAWNY -- Port Say, Algeria. WW-II.

BREACH -- British operation to deny enemy use of Mogadishu, Italian Somaliland, and reception base through destruction of shipping and harbor facilities and mining of approaches. 2 February 1941, WW-II.

BREAKDOWN -- Markham River Valley, New Guinea. WW-II.

BREAKFAST -- Arafura Sea, Australia. WW-II.

BREAKNECK RIDGE -- Military name for topographic feature near Carigara Bay on Leyte, Philippine Islands. November 1944, WW-II.

BREAKTHROUGH DIVISION -- Nickname for U.S. 4th Armored Division.

BREASTPLATE -- Planned Allied seaborne attack on Sousse, Tunisia, to be made simultaneously with attack from west. Not carried out. November 1942, WW-II.

BRED -- Missana Island, Celebes, Netherlands East Indies. WW-II.

BREECH BLOCK ABLE -- Name for peacetime military exercise.

BREN -- Acronym for U.S. Bare Reactor Experiment at Nevada Test Site. Program attempts to relate radiation exposure and medical data for Japanese survivors of Hiroshima and Nagasaki.

BRENDA -- (1) Typhoon. 12-16 May 1947. First detected over central Philippine Sea. Moved northeastward through Volcano and Bonin Islands and out over the North Pacific.

 (2) Tropical storm. 31 July-2 August 1955. Formed over north-central Gulf of Mexico, moved northwestward through Louisiana, and dissipated in northeast Texas. Caused 2 deaths.

 (3) Tropical storm. 28-31 July 1960. Formed in northeastern Gulf of Mexico. Moved northeastward across northern Florida and up the Atlantic coast through New England. Dissipated in Quebec. Caused minor damage.

BREQUET 910 -- French missile which was to be released from an airplane at 15,000 feet and glide unpowered to a target at 500 miles per hour. Guided to the target by the pilot. Unique in that its wings were pre-stressed concrete. Development started in 1953, but the program has been discontinued.

BRETAGNE -- Twin-engine transport plane, the S.O. 30 P, designed in unoccupied France in World War II.

BRETHREN -- Trinidad, British West Indies. WW-II.

BREVITY -- Unsuccessful British probing attack in Western Desert near Sollum, Egypt. Began 15 May 1941, WW-II.

BREWER -- Allied operation under ALAMO against Admiralty Islands, Bismarck Archipelago. 29 February-18 May 1944, WW-II.

BREWER'S HILL -- U.S. Military name for topographic feature near Gusu Kuma, Okinawa. 1945, WW-II.

BRIAR -- Laiana Beach, New Georgia-Munda Area, Solomon Islands. WW-II.

BRICABRAC -- Ndeni Island, Santa Cruz Islands. WW-II.

BRICKLAYER -- Removal of General Kreipe and party from Crete, 14 May 1944, WW-II.

BRIDE -- Western Entrance to Gulf Bone, Celebes, Netherlands East Indies. WW-II.

BRIDESMAID -- Code name for Greece. WW-II.

BRIDGE BUSTERS -- Name given to 490th Bombardment Squadron of U.S. 10th Air Force for their destruction of railroad bridges in North Burma campaign. WW-II.

BRIDGET -- Name reserved by meteorologists for trophical cyclone in eastern North Pacific.

BRIGADIERS HILL -- Military name for topographic feature near Giarabub, eastern Libya. 1940-41, WW-II.

BRIGADYR -- Czech multi-purpose aircraft developed in 1952. Another version is the AGRICOLTA.

BRIGAND -- Post-World War II twin-engine Bristol aircraft developed for Great Britain's Royal Air Force.

BRIGANTINE -- Borneo, Netherlands East Indies.   WW-II.

BRIGHT STAR/PINE CONE III, EXERCISE -- Largest peacetime maneuver on record, up to its start on 13 August 1960.   Involved U.S. Airforce Reserve as well as Regular troops.

BRIMSTONE -- Projected Allied invasion of island of Sardinia.   Not carried out. 1943, WW-II.

BRINDLE -- Kra Peninsula, Thailand.   WW-II.

BRISFIT -- Curtiss-built Bristol fighter for the U.S. Air Service, adapted for the Liberty engine, and delivered in May 1918.

BRISK -- Projected British occupation of Azores.   Late 1940, WW-II.

BRISTLE CONE, OPERATION -- Combined Army-U.S. Air Force exercise to test, under emergency conditions, the military strategic airlift capability.   2 March 1962.

BRITTANIA -- Bristol four-engine turboprop aircraft in British civilian and military service.   First flew 29 December 1958 in the C.1 military version.

BROADBEAN -- Dry Sand Cove, Florida-Tulagi Group, Solomon Islands.   WW-II.

BROADJUMP -- Code name for Africa.   WW-II.

BROADSWORD -- Operations to liberate Malaya and to open the Straits of Malacca. WW-II.

BROADWAY -- (1) Code word for jungle clearing behind Japanese lines in northeast Burma; used as main airstrip during Allied OPERATION THURSDAY.   Spring 1944, WW-II.

(2) Military name for portion of Wonsan harbor, North Korea, during U.N. naval siege.   16 February 1951-27 July 1953, Korean Conflict.

BROCADE -- Puluwat Island, Truk Lagoon, Caroline Islands.   WW-II.

BROCCOLI -- Olson's Landing, New Georgia-Munda Area, Solomon Islands.   WW-II.

BROCKTON -- Aghione, Corsica.   WW-II.

BRONCHITIS -- Kahili Airfield, Bougainville, Solomon Islands.   WW-II.

BRONX -- Sindangan, Philippine Islands.   WW-II.

BRONZE -- Code name for Alaska. WW-II.

BROOKFIELD -- Gizarum, New Britain. WW-II.

BROOM -- Subsidiary of HUSKY. WW-II.

BROOMSTICK -- (I) Nankina River, New Guinea. WW-II.

(2) Operation to counter an enemy breakout, either through the English Channel or through the Northern Passage, with the object of attacks on shipping. March 1945, WW-II.

BROTHER -- Naha, Okinawa Jima, Nansei Shoto Islands, Japan. WW-II.

BROUSSARD -- French Max Holste 1521M utility transport plane, operational with military air arms. First flew 1952.

BROWN -- (I) Japanese Navy name for Eniwetok Atoll, Marshall Islands; taken from name, Brown's Range, given to Atoll by Captain Thomas Butler when he discovered it in 1794. WW-II.

(2) British Guiana, South America. WW-II.

BROWN BRIDGE -- Bridge, designed in Italy by Canadian Army Captain B.S. Brown, to span 80-foot gap under assault conditions; constructed from Bailey bridge span put into place by tanks. 1944, WW-II.

BROWN LINE -- Defense line in north central Italy, used by Germans, preparatory to falling back on GOTHIC LINE. August 1944, WW-II.

BROWNJUG -- Name for NATO peacetime military exercise.

BRUSH -- Palmyra Island, Line Islands. WW-II.

BRUSHWOOD -- Fedala, French Morocco. WW-II.

BRUSHWOOD SUB-TASK FORCE -- Unit of WESTERN TASK FORCE which made main attack at Fedala, French Morocco. Also called Force Y. November 1942, WW-II.

BU, OPERATION -- Japanese plan for advance across Chindwin River, south of Homalin, Burma, and occupation of line of hills between it and Yu River. Late WW-II.

BUCCANEER -- (I) Brewster U.S. Army Air Forces A-34 and U.S. Navy SB2A aircraft used during World War II. Smaller engine used in British naval version, the BERMUDA.

(2) British Blackburn shipboard strike aircraft which entered service with the Royal Navy in 1962.

(3) Allied operation planned against the Andaman Islands, Bay of Bengal. Cancelled 5 December 1943. See also UTOPIA. WW-II.

BUCHAN -- Geographical location in connection with ARGONAUT. WW-II.

BUCHON -- Last Spanish version of the German World War II Messerschmitt Bf109 aircraft. Currently equips two Spanish wings.

BUCK -- Russian Petlyakov Pe-2 twin-engine close support bomber of World War II.

BUCKBOARD -- U.S. cratering study in basalt intended to provide knowledge for peaceful nuclear excavations. Conducted at Nevada Test Site by Sandia Laboratory of the Sandia Corporation, Albuquerque, New Mexico.

BUCKET BRIGADE -- Partial convoy system used along U.S. Atlantic coast whereby ships would move during day, escorted by such local craft as were available, and would stop overnight in protected anchorages. Early 1942, WW-II.

BUCKEYE -- North American T2J shipboard jet trainer which first flew in 1958.

BUCKEYES -- Nickname for U.S. 37th Infantry Division from Ohio.

BUCKNER BAY -- Military name for Nakagusuku Bay in southern Okinawa. Named for U.S. Lieutenant General Simon B. Buckner, Jr., commander of 10th Army. 1945, WW-II.

BUCKSHOT -- See COMPOSITE I

BUCO -- Acronym for Build-Up Control Organization, which was set up in United Kingdom to supervise the flow of personnel and vehicles from the concentration and marshalling areas and of ships and craft to the Continent in period immediately following Normandy landings, 6 June 1944. WW-II.

BUDDY -- Mount Lambe, Solomon Islands. WW-II.

BUDDY SYSTEM -- Nickname for project attaching Republic of Korea troops to battle-depleted U.S. Army units; they were paired off with American "buddies" for on the spot training, sometimes during battle. 1950. Korean Conflict.

BUEFFEL -- German operation for the relief of Narvik. June 1940, WW-II.

BUFFALO -- (1) Brewster F2A U.S Navy fighter used prior to, and during World War II. It was also the first plane flown by the American Volunteer Group with the Royal Air Force in England.

(2) Name for Royal Canadian Air Force Squadron Number 404.

(3) The plan selected from three others for U.S. VI Corps breakout from Anzio beachhead in Italy involving attack in direction of Cisterna-Cori-Valmontone. See also GRASSHOPPER, TURTLE, CRAWDAD, CHESTERFIELD. Began 23 May 1944, WW-II.

BUFFALO DIVISION -- Nickname for U.S. 92nd Infantry Division.

BUFFALO GUNS -- Nickname for 14.5-caliber anti-tank rifles used by North Koreans. Korean Conflict.

BUFFALOES -- Nickname used in North-West Europe for Landing Vehicles, Tracked. Called FANTAILS in Italy. WW-II.

BUG -- America's first pilotless bomber, a biplane flying bomb which took-off from tracks on a releasable four-wheel carriage in 1917. See LIBERTY EAGLE.

BUGHOUSE PATROL -- Nickname for Australian destroyer patrol of Boghaz Pass which led through shoals into Western Harbor of Alexandria, Egypt. WW-II.

BUGLE -- Allied air attack against communications in Ruhr, Germany, immediately prior to Allied crossing of Rhine, Operation PLUNDER. Beginning of March 1945, WW-II.

BUGLE HILL -- Name for topographic feature near TURTLE HEAD BEND of Kuryong River, Korea, where U.S. 5th Cavalry Regiment first encountered Chinese Communist Forces who attacked using bugles, horns and whistles as signaling devices. 2 November 1950. Korean Conflict.

BUIC -- Acronym for Backup Interceptor Control, a U.S. Air Force emergency system.

BUICK -- (1) Ablingi, New Britain. WW-II.

(2) Nura Island, Solomon Islands. WW-II.

BULKHEAD -- Hai K'au (Kaiko), Formosa. WW-II.

BULL -- Code name for Russian copy, designated Tu-4, of U.S. Army Air Forces of World War II B-29. See also CART.

BULL GOOSE -- See GOOSE

BULLDOG -- Nickname for an advanced version of the U.S. Navy's BULLPUP. Name is no longer used; missile now referred to as the Bullpup B or GAM-83B (Navy designation, ASM-7B).

BULLDOG III -- Name for peacetime military exercise.

BULLDOZER -- Allied plan for amphibious assault on Akyab, Burma, should favorable opportunity arise during CUDGEL Operation. See also BULLFROG. Cancelled February 1944, WW-II.

BULLET -- (1) Gallaudet single-engine pusher monoplane. Flown at Mineola, Long Island, in 1912.

(2) See CHRISTMAS BULLET

BULLFROG -- First Allied plan for amphibious operation against Akyab, Burma. Not carried out. See also BULLDOZER. 1943-44, WW-II.

BULLION -- Ile Rousse, Sardinia. WW-II.

BULLPUP -- Nickname for an air-to-surface missile developed by the U.S. Navy and used by the Navy and Air Force. Has a slant range of about 15,000 feet and carries a conventional warhead. Advanced version under development will have extended range new propulsion system and a nuclear warhead. First version (A) operational in April 1959. See also BULLDOG, WHITE LANCE.

BULLPUP A -- U.S. Navy and Air Force air-to-surface missile used by light attack aircraft against ground targets. See also BULLPUP AND BULLPUP 7B.

BULLPUP 7B -- U.S. Navy and Air Force missile which provides larger warhead than BULLPUP A, making it possible to destroy well-defended targets. See BULLPUP.

BULL-RING -- Australian army training method. WW-II.

BULLSEYE -- Night practice flights by British bomber and aircraft to experiment with use of searchlights to expose targets. 1942, WW-II.

BULLY -- Marshall Islands. WW-II.

BULRUSH -- Amoy Island, Amoy, China. WW-II.

BUMBLE PROJECT -- See BUMBLEBEE PROJECT

BUMBLEBEE PROJECT -- Code name for a broad research and development contract by the U.S. Navy with Applied Physics Laboratory of Johns Hopkins University in 1945 to undertake guided missile research. The Navy-APL relationship is still in existence and has led to the development of the TALOS, TERRIER AND TARTAR missile systems, and development work on the TYPHON missile system and Navy space systems such as TRANSIT and ANNA. See also COBRA.

BUMBLEPUPPY -- Map Island,,Yap, Caroline Islands. WW-II.

BUMBOAT -- Kajartalik, Greenland. WW-II.

BUMPER -- (1) Composite two-stage research rocket consisting of a V-2 first stage and a WAC-CORPORAL second stage. Designed to check out the performance of a two-stage missile based on proven components and to learn more about the basic staging problem. Paved the way for the development of multi-stage space probes, Intermediate Range Ballistic Missiles, and Intercontinental Ballistic Missiles. Eight firings took place between 13 May 1948 and 24 July 1950.

(2) Large-scale Allied anti-invasion exercise conducted in Chiltern Hills area, northwest of London, England; involved two army headquarters, four corps, and twelve divisions. 29 September-3 October 1941, WW-II.

BUMPKIN -- Apamama, Gilbert Islands. WW-II.

BUNCHBERRY -- Omura, Japan. WW-II.

BUNDLE -- Na-Pi River, Formosa. WW-II.

BUNGALOW -- Projected U.S. Navy capture of Martinique and Guadaloupe, Caribbean Sea, from Vichy French Forces. WW-II.

BUNGHOLE -- Mission flown by U.S. 7th Troop Carrier Squadron to drop American meteorologists and supplies near Ticevo, Yugoslavia. 27 February 1944, WW-II.

BUNKER -- Establishment of allied officers at German Naval Headquarters at Trento and Trieste, Italy, on surrender. 30 April-1June 1945, WW-II.

BUNKER HILL -- Military name for topographic feature, Hill 800, in central Korea, east of Seoul. Spring 1951, Korean Conflict.

BUNKHOUSE -- Ryukyu Islands, Japan. WW-II.

BUNKUM -- Reconnaissance on the beaches of Sumatra by a British Naval party. 23-24 April 1944, WW-II.

BUNNY HUG -- U.N. code name for position in Wonsan harbor, North Korea. Korean Conflict.

BURLESQUE -- Roi Island, Kwajalein Atoll, Marshall Islands. WW-II.

BURNET -- U.S. military name for island in Kwajalein Atoll with no known native name. Captured by U.S. forces, 4 February 1944, WW-II.

BURNISHED -- Dilli, Timor, Netherlands East Indies. WW-II.

BURNSALL -- Special force operation mounted by Headquarters, Allied Armies in Italy. WW-II.

BURP GUN -- Colloquial term applied by American troops to German submachine guns of the MP (Mashinenpistole) 40 type. WW-II.

BURTON -- U.S. code name for Ebeye Island, Kwajalein Atoll, Marshall Islands. WW-II.

BURWING -- Allied air unit formed at Magwe, Burma, during retreat from Japanese. Formerly X Wing. Early 1942, WW-II.

BUSH TRANSPORT -- Lockheed Model 60 single-engine, monoplane currently in production in Mexico, Italy, and Argentina.

BUSHMASTERS -- Name given to U.S. 158th Regimental Combat Team during Southwest Pacific campaign. WW-II.

BUSTER -- U.S. military name for islet in Kwajalein Attoll with no known native name. Captured by U.S. forces, 3 February 1944. WW-II.

BUSTER JANGLE -- U.S. nuclear weapons test conducted at Nevada Test Site. Fall of 1951.

BUSTLE -- Djilolo Passage, Halmabera Island, Netherlands East Indies. WW-II.

BUSYBODY -- Winguru, New Britain. WW-II.

BUTCHER -- Oued Bou Reg, French Morocco. WW-II.

BUTCHER BIRD -- German World War II Fw-190A aircraft. See WURGER.

BUTCHERS, THE -- Nickname given by TOKYO ROSE to U.S. 41st Infantry Division. Also called JUNGLEERS.

BUTTERBALLS -- Code word for "attack at night expected." WW-II.

BUTTERCUP -- Woleai, Caroline Islands. WW-II.

BUTTERCUP FIELD -- Military name for topographic feature near Heraklion, Crete. May 1941, WW-II.

BUTTERFLIES -- Four-pound bombs, usually dropped in clusters. WW-II.

BUTTERFLY -- (I) Code name for South China Sea. WW-II.

    (2) See SCHMETTERLING

BUTTON -- Espiritu Santo Island, New Hebrides Islands. WW-II.

BUTTRESS -- Project for British invasion of toe of Italy at Gioja, mounted from North Africa. Not carried out. Fall 1943, WW-II.

BUZZ BOMB -- Early name for the German V-1 rocket of World War II. Also called Doodle Bug.

BUZZ BOMB BOWL -- U.S. military name for topographic feature on Okinawa. 1945, WW-II.

BUZZ SAW, BATTLE OF THE -- Heavy exchange of gunfire between North Korean shore batteries and U.N. besieging destroyers in Wonsan harbor, North Korea. 17 July 1951, Korean Conflict.

BUZZARD -- (I) Ballistics range computer assembly used with airborne radar search sets.

    (2) Arot, New Britain. WW-II.

BUZZARD MISSIONS -- Weather reconnaissance missions flown by the U.S. Air Force over Korea, East China Sea and Yellow Sea. Began 26 June 1950, Korean Conflict.

BUZZER -- Operations for the capture of Wake Island. WW-II.

BYNG -- Proposed operation by British Infantry Division to enlarge bridgehead across Orne River, north of Bois de Bavent, France. Not carried out. See also

RAWLINSON.   August 1944, WW-II.

BYPRODUCT -- (1) Code name for Trobriand Islands.   (Kirwina)   WW-II.

   (2) Allied task force under ALAMO which carried out Operation CHRONICLE against Kiriwina Island, northeast of New Guinea.   30 June-5 August 1943, WW-II.

BYRON -- (1) Unea Island, Bismarck Archipelago.   WW-II.

   (2) U.S. military name for islet in Kwajalein Atoll with no known native name. Captured by U.S. forces, 3 February 1944.   WW-II.

C

C, MISSILE -- One of the family of missiles based on Army tactical requirements. It is of the SERGEANT class: solid-fueled, mobile and with a nuclear warhead. Sergeant is presently designated to fill the Missile C requirement, but an improved version of the 90-mile missile may be developed in the future.

C, OPERATION -- Plan by Japanese High Command to invade India. 1944, WW-II.

C.3, OPERATION -- See HERKULES.

CAB -- Code name for the Russian Li-2 aircraft, version of the C-47, built under Douglas license prior to WW-II.

CABARET -- Saui Point, New Guinea. WW-II.

CABBAGE -- Pagadian, Mindanao, Philippine Islands. WW-II.

CABOOSE -- Krasnoyarsk, Siberia. WW-II.

CAB-RANK -- (1) Small formations of patrolling fighters and fighter bombers of British Royal Air Force; on immediate call for close tactical support of ground troops. See also ROVER DAVID. WW-II.

(2) Adaban, Iran. WW-II.

CACAPON -- Aisalmpius, New Britain. WW-II.

CACTUS -- Guadalcanal-Tulagi, Solomon Islands. WW-II.

CACTUS DIVISION -- Nickname for U.S. 103rd Infantry Division.

CACTUS RIDGE -- U.S. military name for topographic feature on Okinawa. 1945, WW-II.

CADAVEROUS -- Code name for Middle East. WW-II.

CADDIE -- Milli Atoll, Marshall Islands. WW-II.

CADET -- Interstate L-6, WW-II U.S. trainer plane.

CADET II -- 1930 Baker-McMillan aerobatic U.S. sailplane.

CADILLAC -- (1) Malai Island, Solomon Sea. WW-II.

   (2) Second mass drop after Normandy landings by U.S. 8th Air Force of supplies to MAQUIS for resistance operations inside France. See also CARPET-BAGGERS, ZEBRA. 14 July 1944, WW-II.

CAESAR -- Allied code word which signaled final stage of evacuation of Rangoon, Burma, before advancing Japanese. 7 March 1942, WW-II.

CAESAR LINE -- German defense line in Italy, which crossed the peninsula from the sea coast west of Velletri to the Saline River north-west of Pescara. Name taken from letter C in German phonetic alphabet. Spring 1944, WW-II.

CAFTAN -- Helmholtz Point, New Guinea. WW-II.

CAIMAN -- Proposed operation involving French air support for Resistance forces in central France. June 1944, WW-II.

CAIRN -- Raprap Creek, New Guinea. WW-II.

CAIRO, THE -- Egyptian-Spanish jet trainer. See AL KAHIRA.

CAIRO TASK FORCE -- Name given in January 1942 by U.S. Air Staff to air units to be based in Egypt. WW-II.

CAIRO THREE -- See EUREKA

CALCUTTA -- Short multi-engine British flying boat of 1928. See RANGOON.

CALEB -- See YO-YO

CALEFACTION -- Fefan Island, Truk Lagoon, Caroline Islands. WW-II.

CALENDER -- Aircraft for Malta from USS Wasp. 20 April 1942, WW-II.

CALIFORNIA, POINT -- Check point in Yellow Sea for convoys en route to invasion of Inchon, Korea. September 1950. Korean Conflict.

CALIPH -- Allied plan to land at Bordeaux, France, shortly after OVERLORD. Not carried out. 1944, WW-II.

CALL SHOT -- Nickname for U.S. Navy close air support missions along front lines. Korean Conflict.

CALLIOPE -- U.S. Army 60 rocket launcher which fired a 4.5-inch rocket. An area weapon, it was mounted on a jeep or an M4 tank turret and had a range of 550 yards.

CALLOUS -- Townsville, Australia. WW-II.

CALLOWAY -- Cape Ngogo, New Britain. WW-II.

CALM HILL -- Allied military name for topographic feature near Balikpapan, Netherlands Borneo. July 1945, WW-II.

CALUMET -- Vambu Island, Bismarck Archipelago. WW-II.

CALVERTVILLE -- PT boat base on Tulagi, Solomon Islands. WW-II.

CAMEL -- (1) British Sopwith F-1 aircraft used in WW-1 by Allies.

(2) First Russian jet transport, the Tu-104, to enter service. 1956.

(3) Mankode Island, New Guinea. WW-II.

(4) Naso Point, Panay Island, Philippine Islands. WW-II.

(5) Code name for U.S. 36th Division during landing east of St. Raphael, southern France, in Operation DRAGOON. 15 August 1944, WW-II.

CAMELBACK MOUNTAIN -- See KAMELBERG.

CAMELIA -- Tellosson Cove, Florida-Tulagi Group, Solomon Islands. WW-II.

CAMEL'S HEAD BEND -- Military name for topographic feature on Kuryong River southwest of Unsan, Korea. Korean Conflict.

CAMEO -- Good Passage, New Britain, Solomon Islands. WW-II.

CAMID -- U.S. Second Marine Division and second Marine Aircraft Wing exercise held in Little Creek, Virginia, just prior to the Korean Conflict.

CAMILLA -- Typhoon. 5-14 December 1949. First detected in southern Philippine Sea. Moved northwestward into Luzon, then recurved to northeast, passed east of Taiwan and up the Ryukyu Islands and lost its force.

CAMORRA -- Abadan, Iran. WW-II.

CAMOUFLAGE -- Namur Island, Gilbert Islands. WW-II.

CAMP -- Antonov AN-8 turboprop assault/passenger transport designed in 1953 and first seen publicly in Russia in 1956.

CAMPUS -- U.S. Navy Admiral Chester W. Nimitz' plan for occupation of Japan. WW-II.

CAMROSE -- Serragio, Corsica. WW-II.

CAM'S SADDLE -- Military name for topographic feature in SHAGGY RIDGE AREA, northeastern New Guinea. WW-II.

CAN OPENER -- Slang for British Hawker HURRICANE fighter plane equipped with 40mm guns.

CANARY -- Port Lamon, Mindanao, Philippine Islands. WW-II.

CANBERRA -- (1) English Electric P.R.9 twin-jet light bomber. First flew in 1955 in this version. Used by U.S. Air Force as the Martin B/RB-57.

(2) U.S. Martin B-57 license-built version of the English Electric model aircraft. Also called INTRUDER.

CANCAN -- Moewe Harbor, New Britain. WW-II.

CANCER -- Kieta, Bougainville, Solomon Islands. WW-II.

CANGURU -- (English translation: Kangaroo) Italian Savoia-Marchetti SM.82 tri-motor transport of pre-World War II.

CANINE -- Torgilsbu, Greenland. WW-II.

CANITE -- Commodore Bay, New Britain. WW-II.

CANLOAN -- Loan of approximately 700 Canadian junior officers to the British Army. Early 1944, WW-II.

CANMILITRY -- Address used in telegrams for Canadian Military Headquarters, London. WW-II.

CANNA -- U.S. code name for Rujiyoru Island, Eniwetok Atoll, Marshall Islands. WW-II.

CANNED BATTLE -- Allied device for reproducing the sounds of hand-to-hand combat. WW-II.

CANNIBAL -- Unsuccessful British offensive against Akyab, Burma. Early 1943, WW-II.

CANNIBAL BATTALION -- American nickname for native bearers who carried supplies on Guadalcanal. 1942-43, WW-II.

CANON -- See KANONE

CANNON HILL -- Military name for topographic feature outside THE PERIMETER on Bougainville Island. 1944, WW-II.

CANNONBALL -- Unsuccessful U.S. Navy-sponsored program to develop a short-range missile during the early 1950's. No details of the project have been revealed.

CANNON BALL, OPERATION -- Long-range trans-Pacific flight held in peacetime.

CANNONSHOT -- Operation in Netherlands of Canadian 1st Infantry Division to cross IJssel River from east, capture Apeldoorn and high ground between there and Arnhem. Began 11 April 1945, WW-II.

CANOE -- See KAHN

CANSO -- Another nickname for the Consolidated PBY. See CATALINA.

CANTALOUPE -- (1) U.S. Air Force nickname for a space simulator to be used to determine the effects of high-altitude nuclear explosions. The simulator is to be built at the Air Force Special Weapons Center, Kirkland Air Force Base, Texas.

(2) Accra, Gold Coast, Africa. WW-II.

CANTLE -- Wab, New Guinea. WW-II.

CANTONMENT -- Kulanghsu Island, Amoy, China. WW-II.

CANUCK -- (1) Canadian version of the famous post-World War One Curtiss JN-4D aircraft. See also JENNY.

(2) Avro of Canada CF-100 twin-jet, all-weather interceptor. Production ceased in 1956.

CANVAS -- British occupation of ports of Kismayu and Matadishu, Italian Somaliland. 25 February 1941, WW-II.

CAPACIOUS -- Bangkok, Thailand. WW-II.

CAPE COD COMMANDOS -- Nickname given to the U.S. Army 2nd Engineer Amphibian Brigade, which trained on Cape Cod, Massachusetts, in 1942; later extended to all U.S. Army engineer amphibian personnel. WW-II.

CAPILLARY -- Code name for Ocean Island. WW-II.

CAPITAL -- Allied operation across Chindwin River in northern Burma toward Mandalay. Changed from code name, Champion, when believed compomised. Began October 1944, WW-II.

CAPON -- Cape Calavite, Mindoro, Philippine Islands. WW-II.

CAPRI -- German attack against Medenine, Tunisia. Began 6 March 1943, WW-II.

CAPSTAN -- Guasopa Plantation, Woodlark Island. WW-II.

CAPUCHIN -- Code name for Argentina. WW-II.

CARAMEL -- Port Moresby, New Guinea. WW-II.

CARAVAN -- World War II Curtiss-Wright C-76 plywood transport plane.

CARAVELLE -- French Sud-Aviation S.E.210 jetliner first flown 18 May 1958.

CARAWAY -- Tentative operations against the Istrian Peninsula. WW-II.

CARBON BLACK -- U.S. Air Force high-altitude air refueling area over Oregon-Washington.

CARBONADO -- Projected Allied operation to take Canton-Hong Kong area and thus secure a coastal port in China. Revision of Beta and Rashness. See also ALPHA. Summer-fall, 1945, WW-II.

CARBORUNDUM -- Karachi, India. WW-II.

CARBUNCLE -- Sarigan Island, Marianas Islands. WW-II.

CARDBOARD -- Ponak, Borneo. WW-II.

CARDIAC -- New Ireland, Bismarck Archipelago. WW-II.

CARDINAL -- (1) Nickname for U.S. Army-Navy KDB-1 target drone. Used as a high-speed, high-altitude "out of sight" target for surface-to-air and air-to-air missiles. First free flight in 1957. Advanced version under development.

(2) Arupon Plantation, New Britain. WW-II.

CAREEN -- Adak Island, Aleutian Islands. WW-II.

CARGO -- Exercise held by U.S. engineer special brigades in preparation for OVERLORD; involved handling of supplies over beaches. See also TONNAGE. WW-II.

CARGOMASTER -- Douglas C-133 turboprop transport plane currently in U.S. Air Force service with the Military Air Transport Service.

CARIB -- Joint plan for U.S. Army-Navy amphibious combat training. WW-II.

CARIB-EX -- U.S. all-service peacetime military exercise, held in Panama.

CARIBBEAN -- 1958 variant of the Piper PA-22 TRI-PACER monoplane.

CARIBOU -- (1) British nickname for the World War II P-39 AIRA-COBRA fighter plane.

(2) Canadian DHC-4 twin-engine transport in service with the U.S. Army. First flew 1958.

(3) Name for Royal Canadian Air Force Squadron Number 442.

CARIBOU I -- U.S. Army twin-engine, short take-off and landing aircraft. Formerly AC-IA.

CARIBOU II -- U.S. Army twin turbo, short take-off and landing aircraft. Formerly AC-2.

CARIBOU CREEK -- Name for peacetime military exercise held in Alaska.

CARILLON -- Kwajalein Atoll, Marshall Islands. WW-II.

CARLA -- (1) Tropical storm. 5-11 September 1956. Formed in Bahamas. Moved northward, then northeastward between Bermuda and Hatteras and out over Atlantic.

(2) Hurricane. 3-15 September 1961. Formed in western Caribbean Sea. Moved northwestward into Gulf of Mexico and inland over Texas coast. As weakening storm then moved northeastward across Great Lakes into eastern Canada. Caused 46 deaths and 300 million dollars damage, mostly in Texas. About 350,000 people evacuated coastal areas ahead of hurricane.

(3) Typhoon. 19-22 September 1962. Formed in South China Sea west of Luzon. Moved west-northwestward across Hainan Island into north Viet Nam and dissipated.

CARLETON -- Widu Harbor, New Britain. WW-II.

CARLOS -- U.S. code name for Ennylabegan Island, Kwajalein Atoll, Marshall Islands. WW-II.

CARLOTTA -- Name reserved by meteorologists for tropical cyclone in eastern North Pacific.

CARLOW -- St. Laurent-sur-Mer, France. WW-II.

CARLSON -- U.S. code name for Enubuj Island, Kwajalein Atoll, Marshall Islands. WW-II.

CARLSON'S CANYON -- Military name for topographic feature south of Kilchu in northeast Korea; "Bridge of Toko-ri," title of book by James A. Michener, spanned canyon. Named after U.S. Navy Lieutenant Commander Harold G. Carlson, who lead first air attack on this bridge, 3 March 1951. Korean Conflict.

CARMEN -- (1) Typhoon. 13-25 January 1949. Formed over western Caroline Islands. Moved northwestward over Philippine Sea, described a clockwise loop, moved westward and dissipated near island of Luzon.

(2) Typhoon. 16-20 November 1952. Formed in central Caroline Islands. Moved west-northwestward over Philippine Sea, then recurved northeastward and passed southeast of Japan.

(3) Typhoon. 9-15 September 1957. Formed in northwestern Philippine Sea. Moved westward at first, then northwestward between Luzon and Taiwan into China mainland and dissipated.

(4) Typhoon. 16-24 August 1960. Formed in northern Philippine Sea. Moved erratically northward past Okinawa, across Korea, and into eastern Siberia. Caused 24 deaths and 2 million dollars damage in Korea.

(5) Name also applied to tropical cyclones in western Pacific which occurred prior to (1) through (4) above.

CARMET -- Broadcast of Caribbean meteorological information, primarily for aviation, made by U.S. Government radio station at Miami, Florida. 1962.

CAROL -- (1) Typhoon. 16-21 June 1947. First detected in central Philippine Sea. Moved northwestward between Luzon and Taiwan into China mainland.

(2) Hurricane. 1-7 September 1953. First detected in Atlantic 500 miles east of Puerto Rico. Moved northwestward between Hatteras and Bermuda, then northeastward to Canadian Maritime Provinces. Caused one million dollars damage in Maine.

(3) Hurricane. 26-31 August 1954. First of series of devastating east coast hurricanes of 1954-55. Formed near northern Bahamas, moved northward, skirted Cape Hatteras, crossed eastern Long Island, passed through New England and dissipated in eastern Canada. Caused 60 deaths and 439 million dollars damage, mostly in southern New England.

CARPET -- Radio countermeasure to jam German radar and prevent use of automatic gun laying equipment. First used by U.S. 8th Air Force, October 1943. Similar to WINDOW. WW-II.

CARPETBAG -- St. Matthias Island, Bismarck Archipelago. WW-II.

CARPETBAGGERS -- U.S. air operations from United Kingdom to drop supplies to underground patriot forces in Western Europe. See also ZEBRA, CADILLAC. January-September 1944, WW-II.

CARRIE -- Hurricane. 2-24 September 1957. Formed near Cape Verde Islands. Moved erratically westward and northwestward to position north of Bermuda, then turned eastward along 35th parallel to the Azores and northeastward to the British Isles, a 6000-mile track. Sank German sailing vessel, Pamir, near Azores.

CARRIER -- Fuko, Formosa. WW-II.

CARRION -- India-China Wing, U.S. Air Transport Command. WW-II.

CARROT -- Lamon Island, Florida-Tulagi Group, Solomon Islands. WW-II.

CARRYALL, EXERCISE -- Arctic test conducted by U.S. Army Quartermaster Corps at Fort Churchill, Canada, in the winter of 1951-52, to develop new food rations.

CARSON -- Military name for outpost in Korea. Spring 1953, Korean Conflict.

CARSON'S GUN -- Australian 25-pounder gun at Buna, New Guinea. Named after Sergeant R.G. Carson. Also called Freddie One. December 1942, WW-II.

CART -- Tu-70 transport version of the Russian Tu-4 BULL aircraft.

CART HILL -- Allied military name for topographic feature near Balikpapan, Netherlands Borneo. July 1945, WW-II.

CARTE BLANCHE -- Name for NATO peacetime military exercise.

CARTER -- (1) U.S. code name for Gea Island, Kwajalein Atoll, Marshall Islands. WW-II.

(2) Langu, New Britain. WW-II.

CARTRIDGE -- Borgo, Corsica. WW-II.

CARTWHEEL -- Code name for Allied operations in South and Southwest Pacific Areas, set forth in ELKTON III plan, involving mutually supporting advances along two axes, converging finally on Rabaul, New Britain. Opened on 30 June 1943 with amphibious operations against central Solomons, Trobriands, and New Guinea; concluded on 20 March 1944 with seizure of Emirau Island, Bismarck Archipelago. WW-II.

CARVAIR -- Interesting adaptation of the Douglas DC-4 by Aviation Traders of Great Britain. First flew 1961.

CARVEL -- Cuyo Pass, Philippine Islands. WW-II.

CASABA -- Buraku, Murray Island, Florida-Tulagi Group, Solomon Islands. WW-II.

CASANOVA -- U.S. 95th Division diversionary action during operations against Metz, France. Began 8 November 1944, WW-II.

CASCADE -- Buyueai Bay, Woodlark Island. WW-II.

CASE RICHARD -- German landing in the Rome, Italy, area. WW-II.

CASEY COOKIE -- Improvised grenade used against Japanese snipers in Philippines; consisted of joint of bamboo stuffed with nails, barbed wire, pieces of glass and dynamite. Also called Cookie Grenade. Early 1942, WW-II.

CASEY'S DYNAMITERS -- Civilian engineers in Philippines, who were given military status and performed demolition work to block Japanese advance. Named after Major General Hugh J. Casey. December 1941-Early 1942, WW-II.

CASHEW -- Nako Island, Florida-Tulagi Group, Solomon Islands. WW-II.

CASHMERE -- Mararamu, Long Island, New Guinea. WW-II.

CAST -- Code name for Iceland. WW-II.

CASTANETS -- Name for peacetime military exercise.

CASTAWAY -- Code name for Poland. WW-II.

CASTLE -- U.S. nuclear weapons test at Eniwetok Proving Ground, Eniwetok Atoll, Marshall Islands. Spring 1954.

CASTLE HILL -- (1) Military name for topographic feature near Merdjayoun, Lebanon. Spring 1941, WW-II.

(2) Military name for topographic feature near Cassino, Italy. Early 1944, WW-II.

CASTOR -- (1) Name for the second stage of the SCOUT launch vehicle. A modified solid propellant SERGEANT motor produces more than 50,000-pound thrust.

(2) Code name of experiment, initiated by U.S. General Carl Spaatz, for developing and using radar-controlled conventional bomber aircraft as guided missiles in CROSSBOW operation against German V-weapon sites. Also called APHRODITE, BATTY, ORPHAN, and WEARY-WILLIE. WW-II.

CASTOROIL -- Batavia, Java, Netherlands East Indies. WW-II.

CAT -- (1) Name for ground station used by OBOE target finding system in bombing operations; by measuring time taken to receive pulse from aircraft, was able to calculate its progress and send signal when it was over target. See also MOUSE. WW-II.

(2) Another nickname for the Consolidated PBY CATALINA bomber.

(3) Russian four-engine turboprop, AN-10A, put in service with Aeroflot in 1960. Also called Ukraina.

(4) U.S. missile reportedly under development. No other details available.

CAT-B -- Military version of the Russian AN-10A, CAT transport plane.

CATALINA -- Pre-World War II Consolidated PBY twin-engine flying boat used by U.S. Navy during and after the war. Also called Cat, Black Cat, and Canso.

CATALPA -- Sunlight Channel, Florida - Tulagi Group, Solomon Islands. WW-II.

CATAPULT, OPERATION -- British naval attack on units of French Navy in the harbor of Oran, Algeria, after indication was not received that they would be put permanently beyond enemy's reach. 3 July 1940, WW-II.

CATARACT -- Marshall Islands campaign. WW-II.

CATCHPOLE -- U.S. operations against Eniwetok and Ujelang Atolls, Marshall Islands. Began 17 February 1944, WW-II.

CATENARY -- Huhukierak, New Guinea. WW-II.

CATERHAM -- Piscini Mendola, Sardinia. WW-II.

CATERPILLAR CLUB -- Unofficial British flyers' club; membership was restricted to those who had to parachute from a plane in order to save their lives. WW-II.

CATHEDRAL -- Bona Vista, Newfoundland. WW-II.

CATHERINE -- Proposed British operation by surface ships in Baltic Sea. Winter 1939-40, WW-II.

CATHY -- Typhoon. 29 October - 2 November 1947. First detected in western Caroline Islands. Moved west-northwestward through central Philippines and across South China Sea into Indo China.

CATOR -- Acronym for Combined Air Transport Operations Room, set up by Allies at Stanmore, England, for screening requests from armies and army groups for air supply. WW-II.

CATS -- See BLACK CATS.

CATSMEAT -- Viru Harbor, New Georgia, Solomon Islands. WW-II.

CATTLE -- (1) Salerno, Italy. WW-II.

(2) Sumba Strait, Flores Sea, Netherlands East Indies. WW-II.

CAULDRON, THE -- Area south of Acroma, Libya; scene of battle between German and British forces. Spring 1942, WW-II.

CAULIFLOWER -- Upolu, Samoan Islands. WW-II.

CAUSEWAY -- U.S. operation against Amoy, China, and Formosa, proposed for 15 February 1945, in GRANITE II plan. WW-II.

CAUTION -- Ihiya Jima, Japan. WW-II.

CAVALIER -- Guguan Islands, Marianas Islands. WW-II.

CAVE -- Allied liquidation of the enemy garrison of Piscopi, Dodecanese Islands, Aegean Sea. 28 February-1 March 1945, WW-II.

CAVE IN -- U.S. Air Force high-altitude air refueling area over Iowa-Nebraska-Missouri.

CAVENDISH ROAD -- Maintenance route near Cassino, Italy, used by British Indian troops. Early 1944, WW-II.

CAVERN -- Atka Island, Aleutian Islands. WW-II.

CAVIARE -- Timor Islands, Netherlands East Indies. WW-II.

CAVITY -- U.S. study of physics measurements of thin enriched uranium foils in thick D_2O cold critical experiments, at Los Alomos Scientific Laboratory, California. Start up 1960.

CAVU -- Operational term no longer formally defined in meteorology, but still commonly used in aviation, which designates a condition wherein the ceiling is more than 10,000 feet and the visibility more than 10 miles. The term is a contraction of the phrase "ceiling and visibility unlimited" (and unrestricted).

CAYDET -- U.S. Air Corps biplane trainers officially-called KAYDET.

CECIL -- U.S. code name for Ninni Island, Kwajalein Atoll, Marshall Islands. WW-II.

CEDAR -- Basra, Iraq. WW-II.

CELEBRATION -- Buayan (Boayan), Mindanao, Philippine Islands. WW-II.

CELERY -- New Georgia Island, Solomon Islands. WW-II.

CELESTE -- Hurricane. 19-22 July 1960. Formed 170 miles west of Acapulco, Mexico. Moved west-northwestward out over Pacific and dissipated.

CELIA -- Tropical storm. 12-15 September 1962. Formed 800 miles east of Windward Islands. Moved erratically northwestward and dissipated northeast of Puerto Rico.

CELLOPHANE -- U.S. Services of Supply skid-loading exercise held in Oxwich Bay area, United Kingdom, in preparation for Operation OVERLORD. Late April 1944, WW-II.

CELLULOID -- Oro Bay, New Guinea. WW-II.

CEMETERY HILL -- (1) Military name for topographic feature near Canea, Crete. May 1941, WW-II.

(2) Military name for hill near Agira, Italy, with cemetery on summit. WW-II.

(3) Military name for topographic feature in Inchon, Korea; important objective seized by U.S. Marines during landings there. 15 September 1950, Korean Conflict.

CEMETERY RIDGE -- Military name for topographic feature near Heraklion, Crete. May 1941, WW-II.

CENSTOCK -- Extract point, located in St. Louis, Missouri, for processing overseas requisitions for U.S. Army, Corps of Engineers. WW-II.

CENT -- Code name for beaches on each side of fishing village of Scoglitti, Sicily, attacked by part of U.S. 7th Army with airfield north of Comiso as objective, during invasion, Operation HUSKY. See also DIME, JOSS. 10 July 1943, WW-II.

CENTAUR -- (1) WW-II Italian Fiat G.55 aircraft. See CENTAURO.

(2) Type of Allied tank. WW-II.

(3) High-energy, liquid hydrogen upper stage being developed by National Aeronautics and Space Administration for launching SURVEYOR and MARINER spacecraft on lunar and planetary missions. First launch vehicle to use liquid hydrogen as a propellant. To be used most commonly with the ATLAS BOOSTER. First flight in May 1962 failed. See also ATLAS-CENTAUR.

CENTAURE -- French research rocket designed to carry 70-135-pound payloads of scientific instruments up to altitudes of 125 miles. Two-stage solid propellant. In operational use.

CENTAURO -- (English translation: Centaur) First flown in 1942, the Italian Fiat G.55 fighter entered production in 1943.

CENTAURUS -- Executive conversion of the Lockheed PV-2 aircraft.

CENTER TASK FORCE -- Allied force, under command of U.S. Major General Lloyd R. Fredendall, which made landings in area of Oran, Algeria. November 1942, WW-II.

CENTERBOARD -- Monara, New Guinea. WW-II.

CENTIMETER -- Uman Island, Truk Lagoon, Caroline Islands. WW-II.

CENTRAL -- Code name for New Guinea. WW-II.

CENTURY DIVISION -- Nickname for U.S. 100th Infantry Division.

CERBERUS -- German name for operation involving escape of German battle-cruisers, Scharnhorst and Gneisenau, from port of Brest, France. February 1942, WW-II.

CEREAL -- Nubara Island, Solomon Sea. WW-II.

CERISE -- Antigua, Guatemala. WW-II.

CHAFF -- See WINDOW

CHAFF ROCKET -- U.S. sounding rocket used to carry payloads of 10-15 pounds of chaff into the lower regions of the F layer of the ionosphere. Chaff is then tracked by ground-based radars to obtain wind velocity and direction data. First fired in 1956.

CHAGFORD -- Code name for Sicily. WW-II.

CHAIKA -- (English translation: Gull) Nickname for Russian I-153 biplane which fought in Spain, Finland, and the WW-II Eastern Front. First flew 1935.

CHAIN LIGHTNING -- Enlarged Lockheed P-38 aircraft with power turret and two-man crew. One built in 1943 as the XP-58.

CHAINMAIL -- Sea of Okhotsk, U.S.S.R. WW-II.

CHAIR HILL -- Allied military name for topographic feature near Balikpapan, Netherlands Borneo. July 1945, WW-II.

CHALK PITS HILL -- Military name for topographic feature within bend of Seine River, south of Rouen, France, and west of MAISIE. Captured by Canadians, late August 1944, WW-II.

CHALLENGER -- Single-engine monoplane in production by Champion Aircraft.

CHAMPION -- (1) Aeronca L-16 in service with U.S. Army from 1946 to 1951.

   (2) See CAPITAL

CHANNEL STOP -- Operation of the British Fighter Command to attempt to close Dover Straits to enemy ships during daylight. Began April, 1941, WW-II.

CHAPEAU -- (1) Bangkok, Thailand. WW-II.

   (2) Nankina River, New Guinea. WW-II.

CHAPLAIN -- Johanna River, New Britain. WW-II.

CHAPLET -- Upper Frobisher Bay, Baffin. WW-II.

CHARIOT -- (1) Nickname for an Air Force high-energy upper stage of missile, utilizing liquid propellants. Originally, to be used with the TITAN II as a backup vehicle for Advent communications satellites. Not under active development.

   (2) British operation to ram lock gates at St. Nazaire harbor, France, by H.M.S. Campbelltown. 28 March-3 April 1942, WW-II.

   (3) Title of an Atomic Energy Commission proposal, under the Plowshare program for the peaceful uses of atomic energy, to use nuclear explosions to create an artificial harbor in Alaska.

CHARIOTS -- (1) (German torpedoes) by Trondheim. WW-II.

   (2) British human torpedoes. WW-II.

CHARITY -- Nushacek, Alaska. WW-II.

CHARLIE -- (1) Code word for letter "C" in a phonetic alphabet, used to avoid possibility of a misunderstanding in transmitting messages.

   (2) U.S. Air Force light-weight radar apparatus used for warning and fire control against surface craft.

(3) Area, east of Algiers, where Allied landing was made. November 1942, WW-II.

(4) Hurricane. 27 August-4 September 1950. Formed in mid-Atlantic and moved northwestward, but recurved northeastward, without reaching land.

(5) Hurricane. 14-22 August 1951. Formed east of Lesser Antilles and moved westward through Caribbean, across Jamaica, the Yucatan Peninsula, the Bay of Campeche, and into Mexico near Tampico. Caused great disaster in Jamaica, where 152 were killed and 50 million dollars in property was lost. Total losses in all areas were over 250 lives and 75 million dollars in property.

(6) Hurricane. 23-29 September 1952. Formed in Caribbean, moved northwestward across Hispaniola, skirted Bahamas, and then turned northeastward over the Atlantic. Caused little damage.

CHARLIE HILL -- U.S. military name for topographic feature on east coast of Okinawa. 1945, WW-II.

CHARLIE LINE -- U.S. Eighth Army defensive line from Seoul area to Hongchon on east coast of Korea; one of four lines drawn up for withdrawal in successive steps by Lieutenant General Walton H. Walker before his death. See also ABLE, BAKER, and DOG LINES. December 1950, WW-II.

CHARLIE RIDGE -- U.S. military name for topographic feature north of Gusukuma, Okinawa. 1945, WW-II.

CHARLIES, THE -- Name for smooth twin hills near Heraklion, Crete. Name taken from Australian slang term meaning breasts. May 1941, WW-II.

CHARLOTTE -- (1) Typhoon. 11-16 May 1946. First detected southeast of Guam. Moved northwestward over Philippine Sea at first, then recurved northeastward toward the Volcano Islands and weakened.

(2) Typhoon. 7-14 June 1952. Began to form over central Philippines. Moved northwestward across South China Sea and into China mainland west of Hong Kong.

(3) Typhoon. 24-30 August 1956. Formed in eastern Caroline Islands. Moved northwestward and intensified over Philippine Sea, then turned westward across northern Luzon and South China Sea. Entered northern Viet Nam and dissipated.

(4) Typhoon. 10-18 October 1959. Formed near Yap and Koror Islands. Moved northwestward across Philippine Sea, then recurved northeastward, swept Okinawa, causing heavy damage and 46 deaths, and moved out over the north Pacific.

(5) Name also applied to tropical cyclones in western Pacific which occurred prior to (1) through (4) above.

CODE NAMES DICTIONARY

CHARM -- Canadian three-stage solid propellant sounding rocket with the ability to carry a scientific payload to an altitude of 100,000 feet. Under development.

CHARNWOOD -- Allied capture of Caen, France, area. 9 July 1944, WW-II.

CHARTERHOUSE -- Code name for Dominican Republic. WW-II.

CHASE-ME-CHARLIE -- British nickname for German remote-controlled glider using an explosive load and rocket booster. WW-II.

CHASTITY -- Allied plan for construction of artificial harbor in Quiberon Bay area, on southern coast of Brittany, France. Summer 1944, WW-II.

CHATEAU LAURIER -- Nickname for the Canadian officers' hotel in Rome, Italy. WW-II.

CHATO -- (English translation: Flat-nosed One) Russian I-15 biplane which enjoyed success during the Spanish Civil War. Powered by Wright-Cyclone engine.

CHATSWORTH -- St. Malo, France. WW-II.

CHATTANOOGA CHOO CHOOS -- Allied Expeditionary Air Force missions by fighter aircraft over France and Germany to fire and bomb railroad trains, prior to Normandy landings. Began 21 May 1944 (Chattanooga Day), WW-II.

CHATTANOOGA DAY -- Allied Fighter-bomber attack on railroad facilities in France. See also CHATTANOOGA CHOO CHOOS. 21 May 1944, WW-II.

CHAUNCEY -- U.S. code name for Gehh Island, Kwajalein Atoll, Marshall Islands. WW-II.

CHECK MATE SYSTEM -- British system whereby a warship which intercepted a suspicious ship could call for verification from London; if verification was denied, ship was assumed hostile. Started in late 1942, WW-II.

CHECKERBOARD DIVISION -- Nickname for U.S. 99th Infantry Division.

CHECKMATE II -- Biggest and most complex NATO training maneuver. Thousands of American, Turkish, and Hellenic soldiers, sailors, airmen, and marines participated. 15-25 September 1961.

CHEEKPOINT -- Vernon Channel (Heachi Men), Chusan Archipelago. WW-II.

CHEEKSTRAP -- Code name for New Caledonia. WW-II.

CHEERFUL -- Operation by U.S. and French air and ground forces against Germans in Colmar pocket, Alsace. January-February 1945, WW-II.

CHEERUP SHIP -- Popular name for battleship, USS Nevada, one of first ships damaged by Japanese at Pearl Harbor to go back into action. WW-II.

CHEESE -- Balintang Channel, Philippine Islands. WW-II.

CHEETAH -- Bangkok, Thailand. WW-II.

CHEMIST -- Shortland Islands, Solomon Islands. WW-II.

CHENILLE -- Kasan, Sumatra, Netherlands East Indies. WW-II.

CHEROKEE -- (1) Thermonuclear experimental bomb dropped from U.S. Air Force B-52 plane in the Eniwetok Proving Ground, Eniwetok Atoll, Marshall Islands. Part of OPERATION REDWING. 20 May 1956.

    (2) Piper PA-28 4-place aircraft first announced in 1960.

    (3) U.S. missile designed to help determine flight characteristics of ejection seats at altitudes of four or more miles, and velocities in the supersonic region. After release from an airplane and a period of parachute descent, the missile's solid motor would ignite and an ejection seat would jettison to be observed by optical and radar ground tracking stations.

    (4) Karachi, India. WW-II.

    (5) Massed carrier air strikes by U.S. Navy Task Force 77 against enemy troop, supply, and artillery positions near front lines in Korea. So named because of Cherokee Indian ancestry of Vice Admiral J. J. Clark, commander of U.S. 7th Fleet. 9 October 1952 - July 1953, Korean Conflict.

CHERRY -- San Cristobal Island, Solomon Islands. WW-II.

CHERRY TREE, OPERATION -- Raid by U.S. Navy Carrier Task Force 58 on Saipan and Tinian in Marianas; so named because it took place on Washington's Birthday. 22 February 1944, WW-II.

CHERRYBLOSSOM -- Empress Augusta Bay, Bougainville, Solomon Islands. WW-II.

CHERUB -- Tolock River, New Britain. WW-II.

CHERVIL -- Code name for Fiji Islands. WW-II.

CHESAPEAKE -- British nickname for VINDICATOR.

CHESHUNT -- Code name for Jugoslavia. WW-II.

CHESTERFIELD -- (1) Sipul, New Britain. WW-II.

    (2) Canadian I Corps operation to break through ADOLF HITLER LINE in Italy between Pontecorvo and Aquino; coincided with U.S. breakout from Anzio beachhead, BUFFALO. Began 23 May 1944, WW-II.

CHESTNUT -- Watson Island, Treasury Group. WW-II.

CHESTNUT HILL -- U.S. military name for topographic feature near Yonabaru, Okinawa. 1945, WW-II.

CHESTNUT NO. 1-4 -- Four small British air missions intended to harrass enemy communication lines in northeastern Sicily; part of HUSKY Operation. 12-19 July 1943, WW-II.

CHEVROLET -- (1) Ulawa Island, Solomon Islands. WW-II.

(2) U.S. Army, Corps of Engineers, marshalling exercise, held in United Kingdom in preparation for OVERLORD. See also JEEP, JALOPY. February 1944, WW-II.

CHEVRON -- Chinak (Kodiak), Alaska. WW-II.

CHICAGO -- Nickname for one of four Douglas World Cruisers of 1924. This plane made the entire trip. See WORLD CRUISER.

CHICAGO III -- U.S. space probe rocket vehicle designed as a low-cost, off-the-shelf satellite launcher. The four-stage, solid propellant rocket is expected to be able to put a 100-pound payload into a 200-mile orbit with enough injection control to insure a one-year satellite lifetime. Under development.

CHICAGO PIANO -- Nickname for antiaircraft weapon using four automatic cannons mounted together.

CHICKASAW -- (1) Widely-used Sikorsky S-55 helicopter. In service with the U.S. Army and Air Force as the H-19, with the U.S. Navy and U.S. Coast Guard as the HO4S, the U.S. Marine Corps as the HRS-1, and commercial service.

(2) Colombo, Ceylon. WW-II.

(3) Mior, New Guinea. WW-II.

CHICKEN-STEALER -- Operation conducted near Hungnam, Korea, by destroyer USS Halsey Powell of U.N. Naval Task Force 95 which neutralized an enemy supply buildup; two whaleboats were used to detect targets and direct gunfire. January 1952, Korean Conflict.

CHICKWEED -- Bombardment of the enemy in the Vasto area, Italy, by British destroyers. 3 November 1943, WW-II.

CHICORY -- (1) Bonifacio, Corsica. WW-II.

(2) Tuam Island, Solomon Sea. WW-II.

CHIDING -- Mukden, Manchukuo. WW-II.

CHIGOE -- Nomab River, New Guinea. WW-II.

CHILDHOOD -- British attack by motor torpedo boats from Malta on the Moles at Tripoli, to interfere with demolition and blocking of harbor. 20 January 1943, WW-II.

CODE NAMES DICTIONARY

CHILL, BATTLE GROUP -- Name for German 85th Infantry Division commanded by Lieutenant-General Kurt Chill. WW-II.

CHIME -- Bun, New Britain. WW-II.

CHIMNEY CRAG -- U.S. military name for topographic feature in ridge near Kuhazu, Okinawa. 1945, WW-II.

CHIMNEY SWEEP -- Hong Kong, China. WW-II.

CHIMNEYS -- German narrow-beam radar scanning installations; reinforced FREYA, a German aircraft reporting device. WW-II.

CHIMPANZEE -- Tripoli, Libya. WW-II.

CHINA CLIPPER -- Martin M-130, four-engine flying boat. Opened Pan American service to the Orient 22 November 1935.

CHINA WALL -- Military name for two razor-back ridges on Peleliu Island. Fall 1944, WW-II.

CHINCOL -- Primary trainer for the Chilean Air Force produced by Fanaero-Chile. First flight 1955.

CHINK BALDY -- U.N. military name for hill in Yokkokchon Valley, Korea, south of PORK CHOP HILL. Korean Conflict.

CHINMUSIC -- Kaptimati, New Britain. WW-II.

CHINOOK -- U.S. Army version of the Boeing-Vertol 107-11 helicopter which began tests as the HC-1B in 1961. Similar to SEA KNIGHT.

CHINTHE -- Name for Royal Canadian Air Force Squadron Number 435.

CHIPMUNK -- Canadian DeHavilland DHC-I post-World War II primary trainer. Also built in the United Kingdom.

CHIROPTER -- Keelung, Formosa. WW-II.

CHITTLING -- Ampul Islet, Solomon Sea. WW-II.

CHIVALTY -- Buna, New Guinea. WW-II.

CHLORATE -- Alesani, Corsica. WW-II.

CHOCOLATE DROP HILL -- U.S. military name for topographic feature on Okinawa. Named for resemblance to chocolate drop resting on slightly tilted saucer. Also called The Drop. 1945, WW-II.

CHOCTAW -- (1) Sikorsky helicopter operational with U.S. Army, Navy, and Marine Corps. Similar to SEABAT and SEAHORSE.

(2) Code name for Madras, India. WW-II.

CHOKE -- Two-part supply-route interdiction plan involving fighter-bomber attacks on road bridges in North Korea and subsequent night-intruder bombing of vehicles stalled behind blown-out bridges. November 1952, Korean Conflict.

CHOKER I -- Airborne operation against the Siegfried Line in vicinity of Saarbrucken, Germany. WW-II.

CHOKER II -- Airborne operation for crossing the Rhine in vicinity of Frankfurt, Germany. WW-II.

CHOOCHOO -- Witnari, New Britain. WW-II.

CHOP DATE -- Acronym for Change Of Operational Control date, when control for progress of convoy in Atlantic would change from U.S. Navy in Washington to British Admiralty in London. WW-II.

CHOPPER JOHN -- Nickname for a technique of employment of the HONEST JOHN or LITTLE JOHN free rockets. Rocket and launcher are helicopter-lifted into firing site and then launched from the ground position. First tested in 1958 by U.S. Army at White Sands Missile Range, New Mexico.

CHOWRINGHEE -- Name for jungle clearing behind Japanese lines in northeast Burma; used as airstrip during Allied OPERATION THURSDAY. Spring 1944, WW-II.

CHRIS -- Tropical storm. August 1948. First detected in northeastern Philippine Sea. Moved west-northwestward but dissipated before reaching any land area.

CHRISTMAS -- Vassee Island, Solomon Sea. WW-II.

CHRISTMAS BULLET -- Pursuit plane built by Cantilever Aero Company, and test flown Armistice Day 1918. Also known as the Christmas Strutless Biplane.

CHRISTMAS HILL -- See LONGSTOP HILL

CHRISTMAS KIDLIFT, OPERATION -- Airlifting of 989 Korean orphans by U.S. planes from Kimpo airfiled to Cheju-do Island, off Korea's southern coast. 20 December 1950, Korean Conflict.

CHRISTMAS STRUTLESS BIPLANE -- See CHRISTMAS BULLET

CHRISTMAS TREE -- Small standard placed on plotting table map to show track of aircraft.

CHROME -- U.S. Coast Guard defense project. WW-II.

CHROMITE, OPERATION -- Proposals for U.N. amphibious operation, taking place in September 1950, against North Koreans; consisted of three plans: Plan 100-B, landing at Inchon, Korea; Plan 100-C, landing at Kunsan on west coast; Plan 100-D, landing near Chumunjin-up on east coast. Followed BLUEHEARTS. Issued 23 July 1950, Korean Conflict.

CHRONICLE -- Allied operation against Kiriwina and Woodlark Islands, northeast of New Guinea. See also BYPRODUCT and LEATHERBACK Task Forces. 30 June-5 August 1943, WW-II.

CHRONOMETER -- Capture by British of the port of Ascab, Eritrea, East Africa. 11 June 1941, WW-II.

CHRYSLER -- Kaskas Island, Solomon Sea. WW-II.

CHUCKLE -- (1) Palawan Passage, Philippine Islands. WW-II.

(2) Originally, Canadian plan to capture Ravenna, Italy, by encircling attack and amphibious landing. Abandoned; later used to designate Canadian part in British Eighth Army's offensive toward Bologna. November 1944, WW-II.

CHUGACH PROJECT -- Liquid sodium - cooled, heavy water-moderated reactor proposed to U.S. Atomic Energy Commission by Chugach Electric Association, Incorporated, Anchorage, Alaska, and Nuclear Development Corporation of America, White Plains, New York. 1956.

CHURCH -- Shark Bay, Australia. WW-II.

CHURCHILL -- British infantry tank. WW-II.

CHURCHTOWN -- Dieppe, France. WW-II.

CICERO -- Awrin Island, Solomon Sea. WW-II.

CICOGNA -- (English translation: Stork) Pre-World War II Italian all-metal bomber which participated in early raids against Great Britain. Japanese version was Nichii Type 98. MIKADO.

CIDER CROSSROADS -- Highway intersection southwest of Ortona, Italy; captured by Canadian troops on 19 December 1943 after two weeks of bitter fighting. WW-II.

CIFAX -- Method of coded communications in which key generator pulses are mixed to assure security.

CIGAR -- Type of electronic communications-jamming device, either airborne or ground-based, used by Allies against German communications. WW-II.

CIGARETTE -- U.S. Navy designation of area of sea north of Inchon, on west coast of Korea, for minesweeping. Korean Conflict.

CIGARS -- (1) German air force slang name for bombs. WW-II.

(2) Flores Sea, Netherlands East Indies. WW-II.

CIMARRON DRIVE -- Name for Fourth U.S. Army peacetime exercise at Fort Hood, Texas, 1960.

CINCUS -- See COMINCH

CINDY -- Hurricane. 5-12 July 1959. Formed in Atlantic east of Florida. Moved erratically northward and inland near Charleston, South Carolina. Then turned northeastward through Carolinas and back over the ocean near Norfolk, Virginia, skirted Cape Cod, and entered the Canadian Maritime Provinces. Caused one death and minor damage.

CINEMA, THE -- British and Canadian rest and recreation facility for war-weary troops in Ortona, Italy. WW-II.

CIRCLE 10 MISSIONS -- U.N. visual air reconnaissance over circle of ten-mile radius to locate concentrations of enemy vehicles for subsequent attack by fighter-bombers. Began March 1951, Korean Conflict.

CIRCUIT -- Daihanratsu, Formosa. WW-II.

CIRCUMSPECT -- Code name for Albania. WW-II.

CIRCUS -- British code name for fighter escorted daylight bombing attacks against short-range targets with aim of bringing enemy air force to battle. See also RHUBARBS. WW-II.

CISTERN -- Dampier Strait, New Guinea. WW-II.

CITADEL -- (1) Code name for Cairns, Australia. WW-II.

(2) See ZITADELLE

CITRUS -- Bau Island, Rendova Area, Solomon Islands. WW-II.

CLAM -- (1) First post-World War II Russian four-engine transport. Prototype first flew in 1947.

(2) Acronym for U.S. Air Force program for a Chemically-fueled Low Altitude Missile, which would substitute liquid engines for the nuclear engine for the SLAM. Range/payload capability would necessarily be reduced, but the development time would be shorter. Not under active development.

CLAM-UP, OPERATION -- Abandonment of outpost positions on front lines in Korea and canceling of air-support missions within 20,000 yards of front lines for one week in February 1952; conducted with expectation that enemy would increase patrolling and consequently fall into ambuscades. Korean Conflict.

CLANCY'S BOOM -- Nickname for aerial refueling flying boom used on the KB-29, KC-97, and KC-135 aircraft. Also called Flying Boom.

CLARA -- (1) Typhoon. 4-13 November 1950. Formed over central Philippine Sea. Moved northwestward to a position east of Taiwan, then turned northeastward across Okinawa, and then eastward and dissipated.

(2) Typhoon. 7-15 July 1955. Formed near Guam. Moved northwestward across Philippine Sea to a position east of Taiwan, then turned northward over East China Sea and dissipated.

(3) Typhoon. 26 October – 1 November 1961. Formed near Wake Island. Moved northeastward at first, then looped and traveled northwestward to vicinity of Marcus Island where it merged with another North Pacific storm system.

(4) Name also applied to tropical cyclones in western Pacific which occurred prior to (1) through (3) above.

CLARENCE -- Allied code name for Rouen, France. WW-II.

CLARIDGES -- Code name for Uruguay. WW-II.

CLARION -- Widespread air attacks on communications all over Germany by heavy, medium, and light bombers as well as by fighters. End of February 1945, WW-II.

CLAUDE -- Japanese Mitsubishi A5M4 fighter first flown in 1935 and operational until 1942.

CLAUDIA -- Tropical storm. 20-23 September 1962. Formed south of tip of Baja California, Mexico, and dissipated.

CLAWHAMMER, OPERATION -- Proposed Allied raid on radar stations and other installations in Cap de la Hague area of Cherbourg Peninsula, France. Canceled October 1942, WW-II.

CLAYMORE, OPERATION -- British Commando raid on Lofoten Islands off northern Norway to destroy fish oil factories which were of substantial benefit to Germans. 4 March 1941, WW-II.

CLEANSER -- Drive in Netherlands by Canadian Fifth Armoured Division from Arnhem northwestward to IJsselmeer (formerly, Zuider Zee). Began 15 April 1945, WW-II.

CLEANSLATE -- U.S. operation against Japanese in Southern Solomons. February 1943, WW-II.

CLEAR LAKE OPERATION -- Joint U.S. Air Force-Army exercise held 22 May – 3 June 1962 at Eglin Air Force Base, Florida; demonstrated the strike forces of both under simulated combat conditions.

CLEAR WATER -- Name for U.S. peacetime military exercise at Elgin Air Force Base, Florida, 1961.

CLEAT -- Russian Tupolev Tu-114 turboprop transport derived from the BEAR bomber. First flew 1957.

CLEAVER, OPERATION -- Single-day U.N. raid at eastern end of IRON TRIANGLE and in Kumsong area, which accounted for large number of enemy casualties. 21 September 1951, Korean Conflict.

CLEO -- (1) Hurricane. 11-21 August 1958. Formed near Cape Verde Islands. Moved westward to mid-Atlantic, then turned northward to latitude of Newfoundland, then eastward. Dissipated over ocean west of Portugal.

(2) Hurricane. 17-20 August 1960. Formed in southeastern Bahamas. Moved northeastward between Hatteras and Bermuda and dissipated south of Newfoundland. Caused little damage.

CLEVELAND -- Curtiss SBC-4 biplane which entered U.S. Navy service in 1939 as a dive bomber. Used by Great Britain, during early days of World War II, as the Cleveland I.

CLEVER -- Anping (Ampin, An-Pieng), Formosa. WW-II.

CLIFTON -- U.S. code name for Eller Island, Kwajalein Atoll, Marshall Islands. WW-II.

CLIMATE -- St. Paul Island, Pribilof Islands. WW-II.

CLINCH -- British plan for operations against Kra Isthmus, Burma, in area of Mergui-Tavoy. See also BAMBOO. Abandoned in November 1944, WW-II.

CLIPBOARD -- Hung, New Britain. WW-II.

CLIPPER -- (1) Boeing 314 flying boat which entered service in 1939.

(2) Piper PA-11 from which the TRI-PACER was developed in 1950.

(3) British XXX Corps offensive to reduce Geilenkirchen salient, north of Aachen, Germany. Began 18 November 1944, WW-II.

CLIVE -- A type of artificial harbor for use against the Japanese. See also CLUBHOUSE. WW-II.

CLOCK -- (1) Boagis Passage, Woodlark Island. WW-II.

(2) Bombardment of Durazzo Harbor and installation on coast of Albania by British destroyers. 2-3 November 1943, WW-II.

CLOD -- Russian Antonov AN-14 STOL transport plane. First flew in 1958.

CLOUDSTER -- First plane to lift its own weight in payload. Initial model built by Donald Douglas when he formed own company in 1920.

CLOVER -- Halvavo, Tulagi-Florida Islands, Solomon Islands. WW-II.

CLOVER LEAF IV -- Name for peacetime military exercise.

CLOVERLEAF DIVISION -- Nickname for U.S. 88th Infantry Division.

CLOVERLEAF HILL -- Name for Hill 165 near Hwayong-ni and Naktong River, Korea. So named because shaped like four-leaf clover with stem pointing north. Summer 1950, Korean Conflict.

CLUBHOUSE -- Artificial harbors for Southeast Asia Command. Canceled; CLIVE substituted. WW-II.

COACH -- Russian IL-12, first post-World War II production transport. First flew in 1946.

COACH PROJECT -- U.S. experiment involving detonation of specially designed, several-kiloton nuclear explosive with high neutron flux. Held at Livermore Laboratory, California, beginning 1961.

COAGAR -- Name for Royal Canadian Air Force Squadron Number 410.

COAST WATCHERS -- Australian bands of observers located at strategic points on northeast Australian coast, reported Japanese movements in area. WW-II.

COAT -- British operation to move troops from England to Malta; carriage from Gibraltar made in ships joining Eastern Mediterranean Fleet as reinforcements. November 1940, WW-II.

COBRA -- (1) Italian Procaer F.400 turbojet trainer/tourer first flown in 1960.

   (2) U.S. Navy ramjet test vehicle used in the BUMBLEBEE PROJECT in the late 1940's. Information contributed to development of TALOS family of ramjet missiles. Over 200 were reportedly fired before 1950.

   (3) German wire-guided, antitank missile which can be carried, set up and fired by one man. It is a solid propellant missile with a maximum range of 5940 feet and a maximum effective range of one mile. It was also evaluated for U.S. use by the U.S. Marine Corps, but not purchased for use. Essentially the same as the Swiss COBRA I, it is operational with the German army.

   (4) Operation by U.S. 1st Army to break out of Normandy lodgment by penetrating German defenses west of St. Lo and securing Coutances, France. Began 25 July 1944, WW-II.

COBRA I -- Swiss anti-tank weapon with essentially the same characteristics as the German COBRA. Advanced version, Cobra 4, has one-third greater range, a shaped warhead and an improved control system. Later model in use in Swiss army.

COBRA 4 -- See MOSQUITO.

COCACOLA -- Suloga Island, New Guinea. WW-II.

COCAINE -- Koepang, Timor, Netherlands East Indies. WW-II.

COCHRAN'S YOUNG LADIES -- See TERRY AND THE PIRATES

COCKADE -- Name given to the diversionary actions of the Allies towards the Continent which were meant to give the impression that an invasion was being planned for 1943; divided into three groups: WADHAM, TINDALL, AND STARKEY. WW-II.

COCKATOO -- Mur and Kieng Plantations, New Guinea. WW-II.

COCKER -- Eskimonaes, Greenland. WW-II.

COCKLE -- Short Aircraft ultra-light British flying boat of 1924.

COCKNEY -- Sasag, New Britain. WW-II.

COCKPIT -- British air strike against Sabang, Sumatra, with Eastern Fleet in support. 19 April 1944, WW-II.

COCKTAIL -- Marshall Bennett Islands, Solomon Sea. WW-II.

COCONUT -- Blancho Channel, New Georgia-Munda Area, Solomon Islands. WW-II.

COCONUT GROVE -- Japanese camouflaged field fortification in New Guinea during Buna campaign. 1942-43, WW-II.

COCOON -- Luscancay Groups, Solomon Sea. WW-II.

COD -- Acronym for Carrier-On-Deck, U.S. Navy carrier-based aircraft.

CODHEADS -- American nickname for people of Iceland. WW-II.

CODLING -- Param Island, Truk Lagoon, Caroline Islands. WW-II.

COFFEETREE -- Code name for U.S. Fleet Admiral William D. Leahy. WW-II.

COFFIN CORNER -- Name for topographic feature near Henderson Field, Guadalcanal. October 1942, WW-II.

COFFIN CORNER, BATTLE OF -- Name of military action by U.S. Marine Corps against Japanese on New Britain Island. December 1943, WW-II.

COHEN -- U.S. code name for Ennugenliggelap Island, Kwajalein Atoll, Marshall Islands. WW-II.

COIN -- Acronym for Counter-Insurgency. A post World War II term for guerrilla warfare used by U.S. Air Force. See also AIR COMMANDOS.

COKE -- Antonov AN-24 twin-turboprop transport for Russian short- and medium-haul trips. First flew 1960.

COKE SPUR -- Allied military name for topographic feature near Balikpapan, Netherlands Borneo. July 1945, WW-II.

COLABOR -- Awi River, New Guinea. WW-II.

COLD SPOT -- Name for peacetime military exercise.

COLD WATER -- British counter-operation to German attacks against Coventry and Birmingham; involved Bomber Command attacks on German bomber airfields and a selected German town. November 1940, WW-II.

COLDRIDGE -- Code name for Luxembourg. WW-II.

COLDSTREAM -- Move of the 3rd Army units into southern Austria to relieve units of the 5th British Corps in Lienz-Spittal-Tamsweg-Judenberg area. WW-II.

COLLAR -- (1) Saleier Island, Flores Sea, Netherlands East Indies. WW-II.

(2) British convoy of three fast merchant ships and two cruisers carrying reinforcements through the Straits of Gibraltar to Malta and Alexandria, Egypt. November 1940, WW-II.

COLLATE -- Fort Morrow, Alaska. WW-II.

COLLEEN -- Code name for U.S. Fleet Admiral Ernest J. King. WW-II.

COLLEGE -- Vahsel Harbor, New Britain. WW-II.

COLLEGE HILL -- Name of topographic feature in Naga Hills near Kohima, Assam; site of heavy fighting between British and Japanese troops. April 1944, WW-II.

COLLIE -- Bangka Strait, Netherlands East Indies. WW-II.

COLLINSFIELD -- Bari, Italy. WW-II.

COLLODION -- Code name for U.S. Secretary of State Edward R. Stettinius. WW-II.

COLONEL WARDEN -- See WARDEN, COLONEL

COLONIAL -- Italian Caproni CA.101 bomber and military transport of pre-World War II vintage.

COLONNA -- Paronga, New Britain. WW-II.

COLOSSUS -- British airborne raid on large aqueduct at Tragino, in Italian province of Campagna, to cut off water supply to surrounding region. 10 February 1941, WW-II.

COL'S KNOLL -- Southern end of COL'S RIDGE in Lebanon. Spring 1941, WW-II.

COL'S RIDGE -- Name for topographic feature near Merdjayoun, Lebanon. Named after Australian Captain Colin Morris, killed in action, 13 June 1941. WW-II.

COLT -- (1) Piper PA-22 two-place aircraft introduced in 1960.

(2) Russian Antonov AN-2 post-World War II biplane.

COLTER -- Code name for U.S. General of the Army Henry H. Arnold. WW-II.

COLUMBIA -- Bellanca monoplane in which Clarence Chamberlain set a world's endurance record of more than 51 hours 14 May 1927. He later flew it across the Atlantic.

COLUMBIA CLIFF -- Name for Sixth U.S. Army peacetime exercise at Fort Lewis, Washington, 1960.

COLUMBINE -- U.S. Air Force Lockheed VC-121 assigned as President Eisenhower's aircraft during his first term.

COLUMBUS -- General term for series of U.S. studies with linear pinch devices at Los Alamos, New Mexico.

COLUMBUS II -- U.S. high-power pinch apparatus under study at Los Alamos, New Mexico.

COLUMN -- Ishigaki Jima, Nansei Shoto Islands, Japan. WW-II.

COMANCHE 180 -- All-metal, Piper PA-24 business aircraft first flown in 1956.

COMANCHE 250 -- A refinement of the Piper PA-24 180.

COMBAR CODE -- Weather reporting code used by combat aircraft, reporting observable meteorological elements in terms of five digit numbers. 1962.

COMBINE -- U.S. training airdrop operation held in Germany by 12th Air Force and 1st Infantry Division. 9 October 1951.

COMET -- (1) DeHavilland D.H.88 twin-engine racer of 1934.

(2) Great Britain's DeHavilland C.2, the first jet transport to be placed in scheduled service (May 1952); also flying with the Royal Air Force and Royal Canadian Air Force.

(3) U.S. study of critical configuration safety tests at Los Alamos Scientific Laboratory, California.

(4) See MARKET-GARDEN

COMET I -- Soviet surface-to-surface missile originally designed as a test vehicle for COMET 2, but later produced as a weapon. An unboosted, single stage, solid propellant missile with a range of 100 miles. Operational on submarines and land-based mobile launchers. Also referred to as the CH-17. Alternate spelling: Komet I.

COMET 2 -- Soviet, inertially guided surface-to-surface missile, drawing heavily on German V-2 guidance technology. A solid propellant missile with a range of about 600 miles. Operational with the Army, and adapted for firing from surface ships and submarines. Also referred to as CH-18. Alternate spelling: Komet II.

COMET 3 -- Soviet air-to-surface standoff missile, roughly equivalent to the British BLUE STEEL, with a range of about 100 miles. Reportedly, it is a solid propelled, radar-guided missile launched from a plane. In operational use.

COMET D -- Russian air-to-surface standoff missile with a range of 55 miles. Turbo-jet powered, the winged missile probably employs a beam-riding guidance system and carries a nuclear warhead. Launched from the BEAR or BISON jet bombers.

COMINCH -- Acronym for Commander in Chief, United States Fleet. Formerly CINCUS, but changed because of unfavorable notion given by pronunciation of this acronym. WW-II.

COMMAND POST -- Name for peacetime military excercise conducted in 1956.

COMMAND TRANSPORT -- Beechcraft L-23F multi-purpose transport plane in use by U.S. Army since 1959.

COMMANDER -- Twin-engine, high-wing monoplane in continuous production by Aero Commander since 1951. Designated U-4, formerly L-26, by the U.S. Air Force.

COMMANDO -- (1) Curtiss-Wright C-46, still in service, but best known for "flying the hump" with Air Transport Command during WW-II.

(2) Operation in Korea carried on by four U.N. divisions and accounting for about 25,000 enemy casualties. October 1951, WW-II.

COMMODORE -- Civilian version of the first Consolidated patrol boat (aircraft) for the U.S. Navy, the 1929 XPY-I.

COMMON -- Suiteiryo, Formosa. WW-II.

COMMON KNOWLEDGE, OPERATION -- Nickname given by newsmen in Tokyo to U.N. Inchon invasion plan because of lack of security. September 1950, Korean Conflict.

COMMUNAUTE -- French Dassault MD 415 twin-turboprop light transport produced in the late 1950's. See also SPIRALE.

COMPANDER -- Electronic device which acts as both a compressor and an expander to reduce and restore volume range of signals.

COMPASS -- British offensive operation against Italians in western Egypt. December 1940, WW-II.

COMPEER -- Suva, Fiji Islands. WW-II.

COMPLAINT -- Ailinglapalal Atoll, Marshall Islands. WW-II.

COMPLEMENT -- Okayama (Akoateaniu), Okayama-Gai, Japan. WW-II.

COMPOSITE I -- Navy attempt to launch five satellites with one launch vehicle. Attempt made from Cape Canaveral on 24 January 1962, using a THOR-ABLE STAR booster. A malfunction in the second stage of the booster prevented a successful orbit. The five payloads were: GREB 4, INJUN 2, LOFTI 2, SECOR, and SURCAL. Also known as BUCKSHOT.

COMPOST -- Code name for British Foreign Secretary Anthony Eden. WW-II.

COMPOSURE -- Anzio, Italy. WW-II.

COMPOUND -- Linden Harbor, New South Wales, Australia. WW-II.

COMRAZ -- System which determines the air-to-air or ground-to-air range between stations equipped with communications and range/azimuth equipment.

CONCERTINA -- Code name for North Greece. WW-II.

CONCOURSE -- Angles River, New Britain. WW-II.

CONDENSER -- Cap Benat, France. WW-II.

CONDOR -- (1) Continuous-wave navigation system, similar to BENETO, in which phase comparisons and automatic direction findings at a single ground station determine distance and bearing of an aircraft.

(2) Curtiss twin-engine biplane which ushered in the "age of the big bomber" in the 1920's and called the best bomber of the period.

(3) Reportedly, a U.S. Navy nickname for a air-to-surface missile to be carried by the tri-service fighter (TFX); to be developed for Navy-Air Force use. Approval for development expected in 1962.

CONELRAD -- Acronym for Control of Electromagnetic Radiation, a plan for controlling such radiation during emergencies, and thereby denying to enemy aircraft the use of electromagnetic radiation for navigation purposes. May be accomplished by having all commercial radio stations broadcast the same material on the same frequency. Assigned frequencies are 640 kc and 1240 kc.

CONESTOGA -- Budd RB-1 twin-engine stainless steel transport, first flown October 1943, but contracts from U.S. Air Force - U.S. Navy cancelled.

CONEY - Alexandria, Egypt. WW-II.

CONFERENCE -- Fuki-Kaku (Puki-Kaku), Formosa. WW-II.

CONFORMIST -- Nicosia, Cyprus. WW-II.

CONGAREE -- Name for peace time military exercise conducted in 1956.

CONGO AIRLIFT -- See SAFARI OPERATION

CONGRATULATION -- See KOTOBUKI

CONICAL HILL -- U.S. military name for topographic feature on east coast of Okinawa. Also called Million Dollar Hill because of number of expensive shells poured into it by U.S. Navy. 1945, WW-II.

CONNIE -- (1) Popular nickname for the Lockheed L.049 to L.1049 series. See CONSTELLATION and SUPER CONSTELLATION.

(2) Typhoon. 1-6 June 1945. First detected over central Philippine Sea. Moved northwestward at first, then recurved northeastward and passed southeast of Japan and out over the North Pacific.

(3) Hurricane. 3-14 August 1955. Formed in Mid-Atlantic east of Antilles. Moved west-northwestward, entered eastern North Carolina, moved up Chesapeake Bay, over western New York and into Canada. Caused 25 deaths and 46 million dollars damage.

CONNIVANCE -- Hainan Island, China. WW-II.

CONQUER -- Code word for U.S. Ninth Army.

CONQUEROR -- Cape William, Celebes, Netherlands East Indies. WW-II.

CONSERVE -- Agattu Island, Aleutian Islands. WW-II.

CONSOLAN -- Low-frequency, long-range navigational aid used principally for transoceanic navigation by an aircraft.

CONSOL -- Long-range radio aid to navigation that uses audio-frequency modulation characteristics to provide bearing assistance.

CONSOLE -- Bangalore, Mysore, India. WW-II.

CONSOLIDATED PACKING COMPANY -- Fictitious holding company through which directives were issued by U.S. Alaska Defense Command to dummy corporations, BLAIR PACKING COMPANY and SAXTON AND COMPANY, for their masked operations in building air bases at Umnak Island and Cold Bay, Alaska, early 1942. WW-II.

CONSOMME -- Tewfik, Egypt. WW-II.

CONSTELLATION -- Lockheed Model L.049 converted to military use during World War II and designated C-69 by the U.S. Army Air Force. See also SUPER CONSTELLATION.

CONSUL -- World War II OXFORD airframes used by British after World War II for this Airspeed A.S.65 light transport.

CONTANGO -- Beakhead Channel, Chusan Archipelago, China. WW-II.

CONTIN -- Italian liquid propellant rocket for upper atmospheric research.

CONTOUR -- Tainan, Formosa. WW-II.

CONTRAIL -- Condensation trail. (Also called "vapor trail".) Cloud-like streamer frequently observed to form behind aircraft flying in clear, cold, humid air.

CONTRAVES -- An Italian liquid-propelled surface-to-air missile.

CONVERTIPLANE -- (1) McDonnell Aircraft rotary wing U.S. Air Force XV-I; made its first flight in 1955. No longer under development.

    (2) Bell XV-3 research V/STOL aircraft being tested by National Aeronautics and Space Administration and the U.S. Army.

CONVICTION -- Huon Gulf, New Guinea. WW-II.

CONVOY COLLEGE -- Nickname given by U.S. submarine crews to Luzon Strait, between Formosa and northern Luzon, Philippines. WW-II.

COOKER -- (1) Tu-110 aircraft, four-jet version of the Russian CAMEL.

    (2) Landing at beaches on South Crete. 19 April 1944, WW-II.

COOKHOUSE -- Shikoku Island, Japan. WW-II.

COOKIE GRENADE -- See CASEY COOKIE

COOKIES -- Name for British 4000-pound high-explosive bombs; first used on Naples, Italy, 16 October 1941. WW-II.

COOKSTOWN -- Four-way road junction between Covignano and Le Grazie, Italy. September 1944, WW-II.

COOLTIPT -- Ninigo Islands, Bismarck Archipelago. WW-II.

COOPER BOMB -- Small, streamlined bomb developed by British and used by Allies during World War I.

COOT -- Russian LL-18 transport plane which resembles the Lockheed Electra in both appearance and performance. First used by Aeroflot in 1958. Also called MOSKVA.

COOTIE -- Motor Products SX-6 monoplane delivered to U.S. Air Service in December 1918. Also called Stout Cootie.

COPPER -- Code name for Territory of Hawaii. WW-II.

COPPER MINE HILL -- Military name for topographic feature southwest of Seoul, Korea. September 1950, Korean Conflict.

COPPERHEAD -- Allied project for decreasing vigilance of enemy in northwestern Europe prior to OVERLORD. WW-II.

COPPERSMITH -- Efman Island, Admiralty Islands. WW-II.

COPYBOOK -- Allied invasion exercise held in North Africa in preparation for HUSKY, invasion of Sicily. Summer 1945, WW-II.

CORA -- (1) Typhoon. 13-18 November 1953. Formed over western Caroline Islands. Moved west-northwestward across Philippine Sea and Luzon and dissipated in Balintang Channel north of Luzon. Caused 19 deaths and considerable damage in Philippines.

    (2) Typhoon. 22-25 June 1961. Formed in South China Sea west of Manilla, Philippines. Moved west-northwestward into northern Viet Nam as weak storm.

    (3) Name also applied to tropical cyclones in western Pacific which occurred prior to (1) and (2) above.

CORDIAL -- Maloelap, Marshall Islands. WW-II.

CORGON -- Single, liquid propellant missile built by the U.S. Navy in 1944 for a test of a radio-controlled anti-aircraft missile for bomber defense. Most notable feature of the Corgon was the fact that it was built in a month and a half for this test.

CORK -- (1) Russian Yak-16 twin-engine transport used on short runs by Aeroflot.

    (2) Name for Allied air patrol engaged in anti-submarine operations off French Atlantic coast. WW-II.

CORKSCREW -- (1) Grote, New Guinea. WW-II.

    (2) Allied invasion of Italian held island of Pantelleria, southwest of Sicily, in preparation for Operation HUSKY. 11 June 1943, WW-II.

    (3) See BLOWTORCH AND CORKSCREW METHOD

CORKSCREW HILL -- See CORKSCREW RIDGE

CORKSCREW RIDGE -- U.S. military name for southeastern spur of BREAKNECK RIDGE, Leyte, Philippine Islands. Also called Corkscrew Hill. November 1944, WW-II.

CORNCOB, OPERATION -- Bombing by Mediterranean Allied Strategic Air Force of road bridges over Adige and Brenta Rivers in northeastern Italy to block German withdrawal. April 1945, WW-II.

CORNCOBS -- Blockships used to form partial breakwaters, GOOSEBERRIES. 1944, WW-II.

CODE NAMES DICTIONARY

CORNELL -- Fairchild PT-19 primary trainer used by U.S. Army Air Forces during WW-II.

CORNERSTONE -- Attu Island, Aleutian Islands. WW-II.

CORNFIELD -- Itne River, New Britain. WW-II.

CORNLOFT -- Oran, Algeria. WW-II.

CORONA -- Radio counter measures used by British Royal Air Force, designed to give misleading instructions to German fighter pilots. WW-II.

CORONACH -- Allied pier equipment for artificial harbors for use against the Japanese. WW-II.

CORONADO -- (1) Four-engine Consolidated flying boat used by the U.S. Navy during WW-II.

(2) Convair CV-990 four-engine turbofan long-range commercial transport first flown in 1961.

CORONET -- Projected Allied operation to invade island of Honshu, Japan, and occupy Tokyo Plain, in March 1946. See also MAJESTIC. WW-II.

CORPORAL -- U.S. Army surface-to-surface missile for tactical use. Liquid propelled, it has a range of about 75 miles. Deployed in Europe, it will be replaced by the solid-fueled SERGEANT beginning in 1963. One of the earliest U.S. operational missile systems, it was rushed into field use as a result of the Korean War, in 1954.

CORPORAL E -- Surface-to-surface test vehicle for the CORPORAL missile developed for the Army by the Jet Propulsion Laboratory; used to checkout various aspects of guidance, control, propulsion, and other technical unknowns. First test firings were made in May, 1947.

CORPUSCLE -- Cape Padaran, Annam, French Indo-China. WW-II.

CORROLLARY -- Shanghai, China. WW-II.

CORRUPT -- Oristano, Sicily. WW-II.

CORSAIR -- The prototype Chance-Vought XF4U shipboard fighter first flown in 1940. Over 12,000 were built; a few are still in service with foreign air arms.

CORSAIR FLEET -- Large sailing vessels of U.S. Coast Guard without auxiliary motors considered useful for submarine patrol because they were noiseless, had large cruising radius and could stand heavy weather. WW-II.

CORTICATED -- Applies to a control airplane for pilotless aircraft. WW-II.

137

CORVUS -- U.S. Navy air-to-surface, liquid propellant missile designed to be launched from carrier based aircraft and to home on enemy radar. First full flight of the missile was 14 July 1960. Program cancelled shortly afterwards.

COSMIC -- Allied dispositions in the event of a breakout from Altenfiord, Norway, by the German Battleship Tirpitz. March 1944, WW-II.

COSMO -- See COSMOPOLITAN

COSMOPOLITAN -- (1) Medium range transport derived from the Convair 440 but with Tyne engines. Flown by No. 412 Squadron, Royal Canadian Air Force.

(2) Blackwall Island, Chusan Archipelago, China. WW-II.

COSMOS -- Aolavbav, Guadalcanal, Solomon Islands. WW-II.

COSSAC -- Acronym for Chief Of Staff to Supreme Allied Commander (Europe), Designate. Title assumed by British Lieutenant-General Sir Frederick E. Morgan, April 1943. Also used to refer collectively to planning staff for Operation OVERLORD. WW-II.

COSTELLO -- Gomlongon, New Britain. WW-II.

COTAR -- Acronym for Correlated Orientation Tracking And Range system, a continuous-wave, phase-comparison system used for satellite and missile tracking.

COTTAGE -- U.S. and Canadian unopposed landing on Kiska, Aleutian Islands. 15 August 1943, WW-II.

COTTONGRASS -- Ground-controlled airplane used as a missile. WW-II.

COUGAR -- Swept-wing version of the Panther, this model first flew in 1956. Grumman made the last delivery to the U.S. Navy in 1960.

COUNCILLOR -- Molucca Passage, Netherlands East Indies. WW-II.

COUNTENANCE, OPERATION -- British landing operation at head of Persian Gulf in Iran with purpose of putting Iranian Navy out of action, capturing enemy merchant ships, and neutralizing German political influence. 25 August 1941, WW-II.

COUNTER -- Dodoma, Tanganyika, Africa. WW-II.

COUNTRY BASKETS -- Containers made of hessian cloth, bamboo and rope, used to air-drop supplies by the British (and later by the Americans) during 1942 in the Burma campaign, WW-II.

COURIER -- (1) Helio utility aircraft served with the U.S. Air Force as the L-24. First flight 1949. A new version, first flown in 1958, is called the U-10A (formerly L-28).

(2) U.S. satellite program to test the feasibility of a global military communications network using delayed-repeater satellites which receive and store information until commanded to transmit. An outgrowth of the ATLAS-SCORE experiment. Two satellites were launched 1-A on 18 August 1960 and 1-B on 4 October 1960 from Cape Canaveral using THOR-ABLE-STAR boosters. 1-A failed to go into orbit because of booster failure; 1-B successfully orbited and proved feasibility of system by receiving and transmitting signals from Army ground stations. 1-B international designation 1960 Mu. Part of ADVENT program.

COURIER 1-A -- See COURIER

COURIER 1-B (1960 MU) -- See COURIER

COURIER, OPERATION -- See EILBOTE, UNTERNEHMEN

COURLIS -- (English translation: Curlew) French SUC-11G twin-boom civil monoplane originated in the late 1940's.

COWARD -- Whasela Point, Woodlark Island, New Guinea. WW-II.

COWBOY -- Gasmata Airdrome, New Britain. WW-II.

COXCOMB -- Ormed Island, Wotje Atoll, Marshall Islands. WW-II.

COZI -- Acronym for Communications Zone Indicator, a device which indicates whether or not long-distance, high-frequency broadcasts are transmitting successfully.

CRAB TANKS -- Improved FLAIL tanks, with short lengths of chain attached to a revolving drum on the front of the vehicle which beat the ground and exploded mines. WW-II.

CRABS -- German armored steel pillboxes housing two men and machine-gun; capable of being towed on removable wheels to place of installation. WW-II.

CRACKERJACK -- Name for joint U.S.-Canada air defense test, 1955.

CRANBERRY -- Lever Point, Florida-Tulagi Group, Solomon Islands. WW-II.

CRANE -- Cessna T-50 monoplane adopted by the British in 1940. Also see BOBCAT.

CRASH, PROJECT -- Mission by representatives of U.S. 5th Air Force to Columbus General Depot, Ohio, to make emergency requisitions of replacement parts for prime earth-moving equipment so that airfield construction work in Korea would not be delayed. April 1953, Korean Conflict.

CRASHER -- Proposed operations against Luzon-Formosa-Southeast China Coast area. WW-II.

CRATE -- Ilyushin IL-14, the backbone of Russian and satellite nations air transportation. First flew 1953. See also SUPER.

CRAWDAD -- One of four plans for U.S. breakout from Anzio beachhead in Italy involving attack in direction Ardea-Rome. Not used. See also BUFFALO. May 1944, WW-II.

CRAWFISH -- (1) Code name for electronic bomb release by which leader of formation of aircraft may simultaneously release all bombs carried by the formation.

(2) Alto, Corsica. WW-II.

CRAYON -- Tanimbar Island, Netherlands East Indies. WW-II.

CRAZY MARY -- U.S. Air Force high-altitude air refueling area over Alabama-Louisiana-Mississippi.

CREE -- U.S. Air Force vehicle for testing parachute recovery systems to be used by manned space vehicles and high performance aircraft. Capable of testing parachute systems at altitudes of 5-28 miles at speeds from 1520-3000 miles per hour. A single solid booster carries a cluster of three Cree vehicles to altitude where the separate and the chutes deploy. In use about 1960.

CREEK-D -- Designed originally in 1944, the Yak-12 series is a single-engine, high-wing Russian monplane.

CREOSOTE -- Wotje Atoll, Marshall Islands. WW-II.

CRESCENT -- U.S. military air transport service from Wilmington, Delaware, via Newfoundland, Azores, and North Africa to India. Began February 1944, WW-II.

CRESCENT BLEND -- U.S. military air transport service between Casablanca, Morocco, and Calcutta, India, using C-46 aircraft. Began 6 June 1944, WW-II.

CRESCENT HILL -- U.S. military name for topographic feature near Naha, Okinawa. Also called HALF MOON HILL. 1945, WW-II.

CRETONNE -- Akyab, Burma. WW-II.

CREWMAKER -- Early World War II twin-engine trainer by Boeing. Designated AT-15 by U.S. Army Air Forces, and used for bomber crew training.

CRIBS -- General term for gravel-filled trenches from which radioactive wastes are discharged into the ground.

CRICKET -- (1) An industry meteorological sounding rocket capable of reaching an altitude of 3000 feet. Small, transportable and firable by one man, the storable propellant rocket has an extremely low cost and can easily be used for weather gathering under field conditions.

(2) Code name for international conference at Malta, attended by U.S. President Roosevelt and British Prime Minister Churchill. First phase of ARGONAUT. 30 January-2 February 1945, WW-II.

CRIME -- Acronym for Censorship Records and Information, Middle East (Military).

CRIMSON -- Canadian-U.S. project to set up in central and northeastern Canada a series of airfields situated along alternate routes to permit a choice of landing fields in the event of bad weather. 1942-43, WW-II.

CRINGLE -- Code name for Netherlands East Indies. WW-II.

CROCKER'S HILL -- U.S. military name for topographic feature in Kakuzu Ridge, Okinawa. Also called Kakuzu West. 1945, WW-II.

CROCKERY SHIPS -- Large concrete barges used by U.S. Navy to hold up to 300 tons of general naval stores including food, clothing, canteen, tools, materials. WW-II.

CROCKET -- Mareka, New Britain. WW-II.

CROCODILE -- (1) Allied flame-throwing tank, adapted from British Churchill Tank. WW-II.

(2) Au Bay, New Britain. WW-II.

CROCODILE, CAMP -- Name for U.S. military installation on Guadalcanal. WW-II.

CROMLECH -- Bora Bora Island, Society Group. WW-II.

CROMWELL -- British alarm word meaning "invasion imminent." 1940, WW-II.

CROOKED LEG -- See KNICKEBEIN

CROONER -- San Bernadino Straits, Philippine Islands. WW-II.

CROSBY -- Mount Munlulu, New Britain. WW-II.

CROSS FIRE -- Name for peacetime military exercise conducted in 1955.

CROSSBOW -- (1) U.S. Air Force winged, air-to-surface missile similar to CORVUS and SHRIKE in that it homes on enemy radar signals. Program began in 1956, but has since been cancelled.

(2) Allied code word covering German preparations for, and Allied measures against, attacks by rockets and pilotless aircraft. Originally called Bodyline. See also NOBALL. 1943-44, WW-II.

CROSSKEYS -- U.S. naval plan for entry in Denmark. WW-II.

CROSSOVER -- U.S. peacetime military training operation.

CROSSROADS -- U.S. nuclear weapons test which showed effects of atomic bursts on ships. Held on Bikini Atoll in Pacific. July 1946.

CROSSWORD -- Surrender of German and Italian land, sea and air forces under command of German Commander-in-Chief, Southwest Mediterranean. May 1945, WW-II.

CROTCHET -- Richmond Gulf, Canada. WW-II.

CROW -- (1) Low-wing, two-seater plane of wooden construction which was a parallel development of the Russian Yak-12. See CREEK-D.

(2) Warhead for ZUNI rocket.

(3) An advanced air-to-air missile being developed and reportedly flight tested by the U.S. Navy. However, no details have been released on the system.

CRUISAIR -- U.S. single-engine private plane developed by the pioneer Bellanca firm after World War II.

CRUMPET I -- Planned Allied air operation against enemy defenses and troop concentrations at Pesaro, Italy. Later called off. Fall, 1944.

CRUMPET II -- Allied medium bomber attack against enemy defenses near Rimini, Italy, September 1944. WW-II.

CRUSADE -- U.S. attempt to destroy a strong Japanese naval force moving from Singapore to Japan. February 1945, WW-II.

CRUSADER -- (1) Chance-Vought supersonic swept-wing fighter developed for the U.S. Navy as the F8U, and first flown in 1955.

(2) Major British desert offensive in North Africa which relieved garrison of Tobruk, Libya, and temporarily drove Axis forces from Cyrenaica. Called the Winter Battle. See also ACROBAT. November-January 1942, WW-II.

CRUSTACEAN -- Kendari, Celebes, Netherlands East Indies. WW-II.

CRYSTAL -- Three U.S. weather stations and airfields in northern Canada. See also CRYSTAL I-III. Established September 1941, WW-II.

CRYSTAL I -- U.S. weather station and airfield at Fort Chimo, Quebec, Canada. Established September 1941, WW-II.

CRYSTAL II -- U.S. weather station and airfield on Frobisher Bay, Baffin Island, Canada. Established September 1941, WW-II.

CRYSTAL III -- U.S. weather station and airfield on Padloping Island, south of Baffin Island, Canada. Established September 1941, WW-II.

CRYSTAL NIGHT -- Evening of raids in November 1938 that marked beginning of Hitler's campaign to annihilate Germany's Jews. So named because Nazis broke windows in thousands of Jewish shops and homes.

CSAR -- U.S. Air Force proposal for communications satellite advanced research involving a two-ton, synchronous satellite for long-range strategic communications. A follow-on to the ADVENT program; Air Force proposal was never approved for development. See also FLAG, ADVENT.

CUB -- Name for men and machines designated by U.S. Navy to construct medium-sized fuel and supply bases. See also ACORN, LION. WW-II.

CUB ONE -- U.S. Navy crew responsible for establishing CUB base on Espiritu Santo Island, New Hebrides. Started December 1942, WW-II.

CUBBYHOLE -- Rhone River, France. WW-II.

CUCKOLD -- Babelthuap Island, Palau Islands. WW-II.

CUCKOO -- Sopwith torpedo plane used by the British in World War I.

CUCUMBER -- British sweep to intercept enemy convoys off Dutch coast. August 1943-April 1944, WW-II.

CUDDY -- Code name for Ecuador. WW-II.

CUDGEL -- Limited land advance by Allies on Arakan coast, Burma. See also BULLDOZER. 1943-44, WW-II.

CULTURE -- Code name for Formosa Strait area. WW-II.

CULVERIN -- Allied Southeast Asia Command plan for attack on northern Sumatra, Netherlands East Indies, first proposed in 1943. Not carried out. See also FIRST CULVERIN, AXIOM. WW-II.

CULVERT -- Chungking, China. WW-II.

CUMBERLAND -- Fulleborn Harbor, New Britain. WW-II.

CURE -- U.S. computer with generalized alternating - direction - implicit scheme. Available early 1956.

CURE-BO -- Atomic Energy Commission burnout program restricted to fully enriched reactors with burnable poisons.

CURIO -- Angmagssalik, Greenland. WW-II.

CURIOUS -- Naples, Italy. WW-II.

CURLEW -- French monoplane. See COURLIS.

CURLY LOCKS -- Code name for Sin Do, island occupied by U.N. forces during naval siege of Wonsan harbor, North Korea. 16 February 1951-27 July 1953, Korean Conflict.

CURMUDGEON -- Mota Tau Island, Chusan Archipelago, China. WW-II.

CURRYCOMB -- Code name for Venezuela. WW-II.

CURTAIN -- Vesuvius Baai, Soela Island, Netherlands East Indies. WW-II.

CURTAINPOLE -- Nubia, New Guinea. WW-II.

CURTISS BATTLER -- See BATTLER

CUSPIDOR -- Genoa, Italy. WW-II.

CUSTER DIVISION -- Nickname for U.S. 85th Infantry Division. So called because its soldiers trained during World War One at Camp Custer, Michigan. Also called ELITE ASSAULT DIVISION.

CUSTODY -- Keishu, Formosa. WW-II.

CUSTOM -- Roi Island, Kwajalein Atoll, Marshall Islands. WW-II.

CUTAWAY HILL -- U.S. military name for topographic feature north of Yonabaru Okinawa. 1945, WW-II.

CUTLASS -- Chance-Vought F7U fighter for the U.S. Navy which became the first Navy production aircraft to fly at supersonic speeds. First flew in 1948.

CUTTHROAT -- Operation by U.S. Third Air Task Force against Japanese positions on SHAGGY RIDGE in northeastern New Guinea. 1944, WW-II.

CUTTING -- Cutting and picking up by British of cable between Dakar, Africa, and Pernambuco, Brazil, in order to clear American Neutrality Zone area. 19 August 1941, WW-II.

CUTTY SARK -- Saunders-Roe twin-engine British amphibian of 1930.

CYANIDE -- Santa Cruz Islands. WW-II.

CYCLAMEN -- See ALPENVEILCHEN

CYCLE, OPERATION -- Allied evacuation of troops from Le Havre, France. Early June 1940, WW-II.

CYCLONE -- (1) French Caudron C.713 prototype fighter. Flew first in 1937. Became the C.714 which saw some combat in 1940.

(2) Leyte, Philippine Islands. WW-II.

(3) Allied task force under HURRICANE Task Force which carried out operations off north coast of New Guinea against Biak Island, HORLICKS, and against Noemfoor Island, TABLETENNIS. May-August 1944, WW-II.

CYCLONE DIVISION -- Nickname for U.S. 38th Infantry Division. So named after storm hit its bivouac area at Camp Shelby, Mississippi, during World War One.

CYCLOPS -- Japanese airdrome in Hollandia area, New Guinea. Captured by U.S. troops, 26 April 1944. WW-II.

CYCLORAMA -- Kalaloa River, New Britain. WW-II.

CYGNET -- British ultra-light Hawker biplane of 1924.

CYNICAL -- Kau Island, Bismarck Archipelago. WW-II.

CYRIL -- Marseilles, France. WW-II.

CYTAC -- See LORAN

D

D DAY -- General military term, with specific applications, for day on which hostilities, an operation, or an exercise commences, or is planned to commence. Most famous D Day was 6 June 1944, beginning of Operation OVERLORD, Allied landings in Normandy. (See also Y Day in this connection and H HOUR which originated in World War One.)

D, MISSILE -- The fourth in the family of Army missiles to meet tactical requirements. The solid-fueled, mobile nuclear-armed missile was to have a range of up to 900 miles. However, it is not under active development. This gap could be filled by extending the range of PERSHING as proposed by the Army.

D, PLAN -- (1) Abbreviation for Allied Plan Dyle for dealing with German attack through Lowlands by advancing to Namur-Antwerp line with central sector along River Dyle, Belgium. Alternative to PLAN E. May 1940, WW-II.

(2) See DOG, PLAN

D RATION -- See LOGAN BAR

DD TANKS -- Allied Sherman Tanks modified for amphibious use. Name came from duplex-drive twin propellers for swimming and normal track drive for overland travel. See also BLOOMERS. WW-II.

DACHSHUND -- (1) Kakimar (Yakima), New Guinea. WW-II.

(2) See DACKEL

DACKEL -- (English translation: Dachshund) German long-range pattern-running torpedo, 33 feet in length. First used in June 1944, WW-II.

DAEDALUS -- An early and not commonly used nickname for the Air Force-Navy program to conduct astronomical and aeromedical research from manned balloons at extreme altitudes.

DAFFODIL -- Cape Anukur, New Britain. WW-II.

DAGGER -- Ainaha, New Guinea. WW-II.

DAGMAR -- System intended to synthesize the aircraft return-to-base procedures into a standard manual system.

DAGWOOD -- (1) Explosive creation, improvised by Canadian Lanark and Renfrew Scottish Regiment during lull on north Italian front, winter 1945; consisted of one No. 36 grenade sandwiched between two No. 75 Hawkins grenades in a sandbag. Said to have had a "bad effect on the morale of the enemy." WW-II.

(2) Sand Island (off northern coast of New Britain). WW-II.

DAHLIA -- Kasu, New Guinea. WW-II.

DAISY -- (1) Taiena Island, Solomon Islands. WW-II.

(2) Hurricane. 24-31 Agust 1958. Formed northeast of Bahamas. Moved northeastward, skirted the U.S. Atlantic coast, and moved out over the Atlantic, south of Nova Scotia.

(3) Hurricane. 30 September - 7 October 1962. Formed east of Leeward Islands. Moved erratically northwestward, then northward between Bermuda and Cape Hatteras into the Bay of Fundy and eastern Canada. Caused two deaths and several million dollars damage in New England.

DAISY CUTTERS -- Nickname for bombs used in World War II.

DAISYMAE -- Dorf Point, New Britain. WW-II.

DAKAR -- 1933 development of the French Breguet Bizerte for trans-Atlantic aerial crossings.

DAKOTA -- British nickname for U.S. C-47. See SKY TRAIN.

DALLAS SQUADRON -- Provisional fighter squadron, equipped with Mustang aircraft, formed from select personnel of the U.S. 13th Air Force, 12th Fighter-Bomber Squadron. Flew first combat mission from Taegu, Korea, 15 July 1950. Korean Conflict.

DALY HOUSE -- Italian outpost near Giarabub, in eastern Libya. Named after Australian Brigadier T. J. Daly. March 1941, WW-II.

DAMASCENE -- Nauru Island, Gilbert Islands. WW-II.

DAMASK -- Saui, New Guinea. WW-II.

DAMNATION BATTALION -- Nickname for U. S. Marine Corps composite battalion formed during breakout from Yudam-ni, Korea. 30 November 1950, Korean Conflict.

DAMOCLES -- Kiambaua, New Guinea. WW-II.

DAMON -- Barim, New Britain. WW-II.

DAMP -- Acronym for Downrange Anti-missile Measurements Program, an Advanced Research Projects Agency - Army program to gather data on the characteristics of re-entry vehicles during descent. Several specially instrumented tracking ships are positioned down-range from Cape Canaveral to record with as many types of sensors as possible the profile of a re-entering warhead. Operational.

DAMP FLAT -- U.S. military name for topographic feature on New Britain Island. 1943. WW-II.

DAN -- (1) Acronym for DEACON And NIKE, the boosters which make up this upper-atmospheric research rocket. Developed by National Advisory Committee for Aeronautics, University of Michigan and the Air Force, it can carry a 10-60 pound payload of instruments to altitudes of 60-80 miles. Used extensively during the Inter-national Geophysical Year for air density and solar flare investigations. First firings in April 1955.

(2) Japanese Burma Area Army plan to keep China blockaded. Fall 1944, WW-II.

DANIEL -- Aweleng Island, Solomon Sea. WW-II.

DANTE -- Kakaru, New Britain. WW-II.

DANTORP -- Danish version of Hawker biplane. See HORSLEY.

DAPPERDAN -- Mt. Tangi, New Britain. WW-II.

DARBY -- Arung Bay Post, New Britain. WW-II.

DARBY'S RANGERS -- U.S. task force composed of two battalions of Rangers with supporting units, active in Sicily and Italy. Commanded by Lieutenant Colonel William O. Darby. Also called Task Force X. WW-II.

DARDO -- (English translation: Dart) SAI 403 Italian World War II interceptor aircraft which did not achieve production due to the World War II Italian capitulation.

DARE DEVIL -- Polish training aircraft. See BIES.

DAREDEVIL -- Pitoe, Morotai Island. WW-II.

DARKEN -- Kigo, Formosa. WW-II.

DARKY -- Arigual, New Britain. WW-II.

DARKY SYSTEM -- Nickname for network of low-power radio stations in England; used to advise pilots of their approximate location. WW-II.

DART -- (1) 1924 torpedo bomber produced by Great Britain's Blackburn Company.

(2) Italian World War II interceptor aircraft. See DARDO.

(3) U.S. Navy sounding rocket fired from five-inch deck guns to gather meteorological information for fleet operational use. Developed by the Naval Ordnance Test Station, the inexpensive rocket transmits information back to ship during ascent.

(4) U.S. Army anti-tank missile. Wire-guided and solid-propelled it had a maximum effective range of 6,000 feet. Program was cancelled in September 1958.

DASA-TRIGA -- U.S. biomedical radiation research facility under construction at Bethesda, Maryland.

DASH -- Acronym for Destroyer Anti-submarine Helicopter, an anti-submarine warfare weapon system destroyer-drone.

DATA -- Acronym for Defense Air Transportation Administration (Military).

DATU -- Maceio, Brazil. WW-II.

DAUGHTER -- Taroa Island, Maloelap Atoll, Marshall Islands. WW-II.

DAUNTLESS -- (1) World War II Douglas SBD aircraft for the U.S. Navy and the A-24 for the U.S. Army Air Forces.

(2) British XXX Corps operation in Rauray area, west of Caen, France. Preliminary to Operation EPSOM. Began 25 June 1944, WW-II.

DAUNTLESS DOTTY -- First U.S. B-29 bomber to take off from Isley Field, Saipan, for raid on Tokyo, Japan, in SAN ANTONIO I mission; piloted by Brigadier General Emmett ("Rosie") O'Donnell. 24 November 1944, WW-II.

DAVIE -- Dinner Island, Bismarck Archipelago. WW-II.

DAVY CROCKETT -- U.S. Army tactical atomic weapon capable of being fired from two different caliber recoilless rifles in support of front line combat troops. Weapon fires sub-kiloton warheads and can be mounted on a one-quarter ton truck or dis-assembled and carried by the crew. Operational, and deployed in Europe.

DAWN BREEZE III -- Name for NATO peacetime naval exercise. Conducted in 1958.

DAY-BOY CENTRES -- Centers in Australian metropolitan areas where army recruits received part-time training. Early WW-II.

DAYBED -- Ablaugul Island, Solomon Sea. WW-II.

DAYDREAM -- See METCHTA

DAYFLY -- Saidor Airdrome, New Guinea. WW-II.

DEACON -- Versatile U. S. sounding rocket used by all three services and National Aeronautics and Space Administration for various research programs. Can carry a 20-40 pound payload to an altitude of 70 miles. Development began in 1945 and first rockets were fired in 1947. See also ROCKOON, ROCKAIRE and DAN.

CODE NAMES DICTIONARY

DEAD HORSE GULCH -- U.S. military name for topographic feature near Gusu Kuma, Okinawa. 1945, WW-II.

DEAD LINK -- U.S. Air Force high-altitude air refueling area over the Gulf of Mexico-Florida- Atlantic Ocean.

DEAD MAN'S GULCH -- Name for 7th Indian Infantry Brigade maintenance route northeast of Cassino, Italy. March 1944, WW-II.

DEADEND -- Larnaca, Cyprus. WW-II.

DEADEYE DIVISION -- Nickname for U.S. 96th Infantry Division.

DEADWOOD -- Jaluit Atoll, Marshall Islands. WW-II.

DEATH VALLEY -- (1) Name for topographic feature near Cassino, Italy. Early 1944, WW-II.

(2) Military name for topographic feature on Peleliu Island. Fall 1944, WW-II.

(3) U.N. pilots nickname for area along road between Wonsan and Pyongyang, Korea; contained a maze of well-defended antiaircraft positions. Korean Conflict.

DEATH'S-HEAD -- See TOTENKOPF

DEBACLE -- Maien Passage, New Britain. WW-II.

DEBBIE -- (1) Tropical Storm. 7-9 September 1957. Formed in central Gulf of Mexico. Moved northeastward and inland near Fort Walton, Florida. Caused minor damage.

(2) Hurricane. 6-16 September 1961. Formed between Cape Verde Islands and Africa. Moved northwestward to mid-Atlantic, then northeastward across Azores to British Isles and coast of Scandinavia. Caused damage and 11 deaths in Britain.

DEBONAIR -- (1) Single-engine, four-place Beechcraft A-33 aircraft. First flew in 1959.

(2) Takao, Formosa. WW-II.

DEBRA -- Hurricane. 22-26 July 1959. Formed in northwestern Gulf of Mexico. Moved inland near Galveston, Texas and dissipated over Oklahoma. Caused seven million dollars damage.

DEBRIS -- Cape Wido, New Britain. WW-II.

DEBUNK -- Axis radio station broadcasting in English to North Africa. WW-II.

DECANTER -- U.S. Navy plan for capture of French Guiana. WW-II.

150

DECCA -- British continuous-wave, differential-distance, hyperbolic radio aid to navigation. Uses signals from two or more synchronized ground stations. Similar to LORAN except it does not use pulses.

DECKER -- Code name for the larger of two versions of an American incendiary weapon designed to be dropped from planes on crops and forests. See also RAZZLE. WW-II.

DECOMPOSE -- Koror Island, Palau Islands. WW-II.

DECOY, OPERATION -- U.N. amphibious demonstration feigning landing at Kojo on eastern coast of Korea in attempt to draw enemy troops from their underground frontline positions. 15 October 1952, Korean Conflict.

DECREE -- (1) Early name for the Defense Department's 24-hour orbit communications satellite. It was later known as ADVENT, and now is known simply as the High Altitude Communications satellite program. No contracts have been let; reportedly the program will be turned over to National Aeronautics and Space Administration while Defense Department concentrates on the Medium Altitude Comsat. See also NOTUS.

(2) Suri, New Guinea. WW-II.

DEDIMUS -- Greyhound, Australia. WW-II.

DEEP FREEZE -- Name for peacetime military operations held in Antarctica.

DEEP WATER -- Name for NATO peacetime military exercise.

DEERSLAYER -- Chusan Island, China. WW-II.

DEFENDER -- A general term covering all research by the Defense Department's Advanced Research Projects Agency into the methods, systems, phenomenology and other aspects of ballistic missile defense. Any and all research in this area is handled under ARPA's Project Defender; systems development, such as the NIKE-ZEUS, is handled by the individual service with information being passed on to ARPA. Annually funded at about 100 million dollars.

DEFENSOR -- Address used in telegrams for Canadian National Defence Headquarters. WW-II.

DEFIANT -- British Boulton Paul monoplane, one of the earliest World War II night fighters. First flew in 1937.

DEFILE -- Ibu Creek, New Guinea. WW-II.

DELANO -- Galelum Island, New Britain. WW-II.

DELEASE -- Delegation from Italian Comando Supremo to German Panzerarmee in North Africa, responsible for dealing with non-operational matters. Established August 1942, WW-II.

DELILAH -- (1) Code name given to Dusseldorf, Germany, as one of three possible objectives for a concentrated British bombing. See also ABIGAIL, JEZEBEL, RACHEL. Night of 16 December 1940. WW-II.

(2) Tropical storm. 20-22 November 1950. First detected as it crossed east coast of Mindanao, the Philippines. Moved northwestward across Philippines and South China Sea to Asiatic mainland.

DELLA -- (1) Typhoon. 12-20 June 1949. First detected in central Philippine Sea. Moved northwestward at first, then turned northward through the Ryukyus, across Honshu, Japan and into Sea of Japan.

(2) Typhoon. 23-26 November 1952. Formed in central Caroline Islands. Moved westward at first, then northwestward across Luzon, the South China Sea, and west of Taiwan, into China mainland, where it dissipated.

(3) Hurricane. 2-18 September 1957. Formed south of Hawaii. Moved northwestward across French Frigate Shoals, then erratically westward. Eventually recurved northeastward over the Pacific and dissipated near the Aleutian Islands.

(4) Typhoon. 17-31 August 1960. Formed near Eniwetok Atoll. Moved westnorthwestward at first, then northwestward and northward across southern Japan, through Japan Sea into Gulf of Tatary. Caused 55 deaths in Japan.

(5) Name also applied to tropical cyclones in western Pacific which occurred prior to (1) through (4) above.

DELOUSING -- U.S. Navy term for weeding out Japanese KAMIKAZE aircraft which were apt to join American aircraft formations returning from missions in order to attack their carriers. WW-II.

DELRAC -- British radio-navigation system designed to provide world-wide coverage by using 21 pairs of master/slave stations.

DELTA -- (1) Code word for letter "D" in a phonetic alphabet, used to avoid possibility of a misunderstanding in transmitting messages. See also DOG.

(2) Passenger-carrying version of the 1933 Northrop single-engine Gamma monoplane.

(3) Supersonic British jet fighter developed by Fairey. Set speed record in 1956.

(4) National Aeronautics and Space Administration upper stage combination using the THOR as the booster. The first Delta stage is a liquid propellant vehicle producing 7500-pound thrust, while the second Delta stage is a solid propellant rocket (named ALTAIR) producing 2800-pound thrust. The THOR-DELTA combination has a remarkable launch success record and is considered one of the most reliable launch vehicles in NASA's inventory. Used in the TIROS, ECHO, EXPLORER, TELSTAR and other programs. Sometimes NASA drops the THOR designation and refers to both the booster and its upperstages as just "the Delta." First used 13 May 1960.

(5) Awio Bay, New Britain. WW-II.

(6) Davao, Mindanao, Philippine Islands. WW-II.

(7) Code name for U.S. 45th Division during landing near Sainte Maxime, southern France, in Operation DRAGOON. 15 August 1944, WW-II.

DELTA DAGGER -- Convair supersonic F-102 which first flew in October 1953; used by the U.S. Air Force as an all-weather interceptor.

DELTA DART -- Convair delta-wing F-102B redesignated the F-106. Operational with the U.S. Air Force Air Defense Command in 1959.

DELUXE -- (1) Single-seat Aeronca C-2, available as a land or seaplane in the U.S. in the early 1930's.

(2) U.S. Army Air Forces adaptation of the popular pre-World War II light sport plane, the Taylorcraft L-2B.

(3) St. Thomas Island, Puerto Rico. WW-II.

DELUXE DOLPHIN -- Plush-version of the twin-engine Douglas Dolphin amphibian, which appeared in 1933 for the use of high officials of the U.S. Army and Navy.

DEMIJOHN -- Andaman Islands, Bay of Bengal. WW-II.

DEMOCRAT -- Canton, China. WW-II.

DEMOISELLE -- Tiny Santos-Dumont plane of 1909. Two-cylinder engine and 18-foot wingspan earned it the waggish nickname, INFURIATED GRASSHOPPER.

DEMON -- (1) Two-seater fighter version of the Hawker Hart, adopted by Great Britain's Royal Air Force in 1933. See also HART.

(2) Curtiss-Wright CW-21 lightweight interceptor development of 1938. First flown in 1939 and sent to the governments of China and Netherlands East Indies.

(3) World War II Japanese Nakajima KI.44 Shoki fighter. See TOJO.

(4) McDonnell F3H all-weather U.S. Navy fighter. Last delivery made in 1959.

(5) Name for Royal Canadian Air Force Squadron Number 407.

(6) British operation for withdrawal of troops from Greece. See also LUSTRE. April 1941, WW-II.

(7) Occupation of Abadan, Persia, by British troops. 25 August 1941, WW-II.

DEMON III -- U.S. First Marine Division and Wing amphibious demonstration held at Fort Leavenworth, Kansas, as part of general expansion. May 1950.

DEMPSEY -- U.S. Task Force B, North Pacific. WW-II.

DENCOL -- Name of small Allied column near Tobruk, Libya. Spring 1942, WW-II.

DENISE -- Name reserved by meteorologists for tropical cyclone in eastern North Pacific.

DENTIST -- (1) U.S. tactical air-direction center in Seoul area, Korea. Korean Conflict.

(2) Mindoro Strait, Philippine Islands. WW-II.

DENTYNE -- Government Station, Gasmata, New Britain. WW-II.

DENUNCIATION -- Heito, Formosa. WW-II.

DENVER HILL -- Military name for topographic feature on Corregidor Island, Philippine Islands. WW-II.

DERAIL -- Code word used with phonetic letters (Able through King) to indicate eleven points along Songjin-Jungman railroad, eastern Korea, which were to be kept under continuous attack by gunfire from U. N. blockade ships with aid of air spot by carrier aircraft. See also PACKAGE. Instituted 11 January 1952, Korean Conflict.

DERELICT DEFENSE -- Series of articles published by the Vancouver Sun complaining that the Canadian General Staff was devoting too much energy and thought to intervention in Europe, and not nearly enough to the defense of the west coast. 13-16 March 1942, WW-II.

DEROGATORY -- Arasalpua, New Britain. WW-II.

DERRINGER -- U.S. Army multi-purpose tactical missile weapon system.

DERVISH -- Small, surface-to-air or air-to-air rocket, originally designed as a replacement for the MIGHTY MOUSE. The two and three-quarter inch, spin stabilized rocket used a solid propellant motor. Not under active development.

DESECRATE ONE -- U.S. Navy carrier task force attack on Japanese in western Caroline Islands. 30 March - 1 April 1944, WW-II.

DESECRATE TWO -- U.S. capture and occupation of Hollandia, New Guinea. 21-27 April 1944, WW-II.

DESERT FOX -- Nickname for German Field Marshall Erwin Rommel. WW-II.

DESERT RATS -- Popular name for veterans of British Eighth Army under command of Field Marshall Bernard L. Montgomery in North Africa; name taken from genuine desert rat picked up as mascot on route between Alexandria and Tripoli. WW-II.

DESERT ROCK -- Name for series of peacetime military exercises.

DESERTER -- Byobi To, Formosa. WW-II.

DESK TOP -- Name for peacetime military exercise.

DESOTO -- Garu, New Britain. WW-II.

DESSERT -- Gom, New Britain. WW-II.

DESTINY -- Code name for U.S. Army. WW-II.

DESTROYER -- (1) Douglas B/RB-66 twin-jet tactical bomber or reconnaissance aircraft which first flew in 1954.

(2) Canadian I Corps operation to clear Germans from floaded "island" between Waal and Neder Rijn Rivers, Netherlands, and dominate left bank of Neder Rijn. 2-3 April 1945, WW-II.

DETACHMENT -- U.S. amphibious assault on island of Iwo Jima. See also POINT. Began 19 February 1945, WW-II.

DETAINED I -- Allied operation to kill or capture the entire garrison of the German held Island of Solta, off Yugoslavia, by landing a small force. 18-19 March 1944, WW-II.

DETAINED II -- Landing of a large force of partisans on Solta, in vicinity of Vis Island, Yugoslavia, in five British LCI's (Landing Craft, Infantry) and withdrawal following night. 8-10 May 1944, WW-II.

DETROITER - Stinson single-engine biplane used for many years after its introduction in 1927 as a transport.

DEUX PONTS -- French transport plane. See PROVENCE.

DEVASTATOR -- Douglas TBD-1 carrier-based U.S. Navy torpedo-bomber of World War II.

DEVIL'S PEAK PENINSULA -- Topographic feature in the area of Hong Kong. 1941, WW-II.

DEVON -- (1) British military version of the commercial De Havilland DOVE. First supplied to the Royal Air Force in 1948. Naval version called Sea Devon.

(2) Allied capture of Termoli, Italy. 2-3 October 1943, WW-II.

DEVOTION -- Panay, Philippine Islands. WW-II.

DEW LINE -- Abbreviation for Distant Early Warning Line, a pattern of north-facing radars stretching from Alaska to Greenland near the 70th parallel, with picket ships and radar aircraft to fill in the sea gaps. Built and operational in the late

1950's, it provided several hours of warning of an enemy jet bomber attack. Supplemented by three giant Ballistic Missile Early Warning radars over the past several years. See also PINETREE LINE, McGILL FENCE.

DEWEY -- U.S. Navy floating drydock stationed at Mariveles, on Manila Bay, Philippines; destroyed on 9 April 1942 to prevent being taken by Japanese. WW-II.

DEWPOND -- Attaka, Egypt. WW-II.

DEXTERITY -- Allied operations against Cape Gloucester and Arawe, New Britain, and Saidor, northeast New Guinea. See also DIRECTOR, BACKHANDER, and MICHAELMAS Task Forces. 15 December - 10 February 1944, WW-II.

DIABOLIC -- Kyushu island, Japan. WW-II.

DIADEM -- Full-scale ground offensive launched by Allies in Italy to effect union between main front and Anzio beachhead and to drive beyond Rome. Began 12 May 1944, WW-II.

DIAL -- Lunga, Solomon Islands. WW-II.

DIAMANT -- French space booster consisting of three stages, one liquid and two solid, and capable of putting 176 pounds into a 250-mile orbit. In early development. First stage is expected to be fired during 1963 as part of the EMERALD program to establish technical characteristics of the Diamond.

DIAMOND -- See DIAMANT

DIAMONDBACK -- U.S. Navy air-to-air missile. Actually, an advanced version of the SIDEWINDER, with a longer range, greater accuracy and a higher velocity. Now known as the 1-C version of the Sidewinder, it will be solid propelled and have switchable infra-red and radar warheads. In production.

DIANA -- (1) Code name for German navigational system used for day bombing. WW-II.

(2) Hurricane. 16-19 August 1960. First detected 180 miles southwest of Tehauntepec, Mexico. Moved northwestward along coast and into Gulf of California, where it dissipated.

DIANA-A -- Industry proposal for a liquid hydrogen second stage for the THOR booster. In addition to development of high energy upper stage, the company proposed clustering three solid propellant boosters at the base of the Thor. The first part of the proposal was rejected, but the second was implemented, and the first thrust-augmented Thor was fired early in 1963.

DIANE -- Hurricane. 7-21 August 1955. Sometimes called the Billion Dollar Hurricane. Formed in mid-Atlantic east of Antilles. Moved west-northwestward into North Carolina, then turned northeastward through Virginia and eastern Pennsylvania and along the south New England coast into the Atlantic. Wind damage was slight, but torrential rains caused great floods in the northeast. Caused 184 deaths and more than 800 million dollars damage, mostly in New England.

DIANNE -- Typhoon. 13-19 November 1946. First detected in vicinity of Guam. Moved northwestward into Philippine Sea, then recurved northeastward through Volcano Islands and out over the Pacific.

DIAPER -- Bilihe Island, Bismarck Archipelago. WW-II.

DIAPER, OPERATION -- Tranportation to U.S. of war brides and other dependents of American military personnel. Began in January 1946, WW-II.

DIAPHRAGM -- Code name for Formosa Island. WW-II.

DIBBLER -- Calcutta, India. WW-II.

DICK ABLE -- U.S. military name for hill on Okinawa. 1945, WW-II.

DICK BAKER -- U.S. military name for hill on Okinawa. Also called Baker Hill. 1945, WW-II.

DICK HILL -- See DICK RIGHT

DICK LEFT -- U.S. military name for hill on Okinawa. 1945, WW-II.

DICK OBJECTIVE -- Hill objective two miles west of Arnara, Italy, assaulted by Canadian troops. May 1944, WW-II.

DICK RIGHT -- U.S. military name for hill on Okinawa. Also called Dick Hill. 1945, WW-II.

DICKENS -- Allied offensive against Germans in area of Cassino, Italy. Included bombing phase, BRADMAN. Began 15 March 1944, WW-II.

DICKIE -- Lombok Strait, Netherlands East Indies. (WW-II.

DIGBY -- British nickname for the Douglas B-18. See BOLO.

DIGNITARY -- Southeast China Coast. WW-II.

DILATORY -- Sep Sep, New Britain. WW-II.

DIME -- Code name for beaches in Gela area, Sicily, attacked by part of U.S. 7th Army, during invasion, Operation HUSKY. See also JOSS, CENT. 10 July 1943, WW-II.

DIMINISH -- Finschhafen, New Guinea. WW-II.

DIMWIT -- Meingi, New Britain. WW-II.

DINA -- Airborne radar-jamming transmitter used for spot or barrage jamming.

DINAH -- (1) Japan's first twin-engine reconnaissance plane. Designed by Mitsubishi in 1937 and flown in 1940.

(2) Tropical storm. 18-21 June 1945. First detected in central Philippine Sea. Moved northwestward and skirted Luzon, then turned northeastward through the Ryukyus, along the southeast coast of Japan, and out over the Pacific.

(3) Typhoon. 29 August - 3 September 1956. Formed over central Philippine Sea. Moved erratically northwestward across northern Taiwan into China mainland and dissipated.

(4) Typhoon. 15-21 October 1959. Formed southeast of Guam. Moved west-northwestward, passing south of Guam, then turned northward through Philippine Sea and northeastward over North Pacific east of Japan.

(5) Typhoon. 29 September - 3 October 1962. Formed northwest of Guam. Moved northward at first, then westward between Taiwan and Luzon into mainland northeast of Hong Kong and dissipated.

(6) Name also applied to tropical cyclones in western Pacific which occurred prior to (1) through (5) above.

DING DONG -- An early name for GENIE.

DINOCERAS -- Kangguiriri, New Guinea. WW-II.

DIOGENES -- Cape Raoult, New Britain. WW-II.

DIORIT -- Operable Swiss natural uranium nuclear reactor in Wurenlingen, Switzerland.

DIPLOMAT -- Allied operation to protect shipping on the Australian-Indian shipping routes. 19 March - 2 April 1944, WW-II.

DIPLOMATIC -- Discussions with Portuguese prior to Allied occupation of the Azores. July 1943, WW-II.

DIPPER -- Bougainville Island, Solomon Islands. WW-II.

DIPPER EXERCISE -- Canadian preliminary planning exercise carried on in southern England. August 1943, WW-II.

DIPSOMANIAC -- Wigim Island, Solomon Sea. WW-II.

DIPSYDOODLE -- Ayumete, New Britain. WW-II.

DIRECTOR -- Allied task force under ALAMO which carried out Operation DEXTERITY against Arawe, New Britain. 15 December 1943 - 10 February 1944, WW-II.

DIRTY DOZEN -- Nickname for British Royal Air Force, No. 12 Squadron. WW-II.

DIRTY TRICK DEPARTMENT -- Nickname for U.S. Navy Admiral William F. Halsey, Jr. and staff; refers to their operational planning against Japanese. WW-II.

DISCOVERER -- U.S. Air Force open-end space research program utilizing various payloads with the AGENA space vehicle to test materials, components, bioastronautical experiments or techniques in the space environment. Both the THOR-AGENA and the ATLAS-AGENA space boosters are used in program. Discoverer I was the first U.S. satellite to be put into polar orbit 28 February 1959 while Discoverer XIII was the first man-made object successfully recovered from space 11 August 1959. Program was classified in early 1962. At that time, 38 Discoverers had been launched. Record: 26 achieved orbit, 11 recovered (7 by air snatch, 4 from the sea). Program continuing.

DISCUS -- Gilnit, New Britain. WW-II.

DISDAIN -- Scoresbysund, Greenland. WW-II.

DISLOCATE -- Rongerik Atoll, Marshall Islands. WW-II.

DISPLAY -- Elizabethville, Belgian Congo. WW-II.

DISTAFF -- Mot River, New Guinea. WW-II.

DISTINCTIVE -- Greenwich Island, Caroline Islands. WW-II.

DISTORT -- (1) Luther Anchorage, New Guinea. WW-II.

(2) Milli Atoll, Marshall Islands. WW-II.

DIVER -- U.S. Navy radar-guided, air-to-surface torpedo weapon based on a 1000-pound bomb. Developed by the National Bureau of Standards, it was a member of the KINGFISHER family of winged torpedos which eventually led to the development of PETREL. A post-World War-II development.

DIVER FRINGE -- Belt of 152 heavy guns for defense against attacks by German V-weapons; extended from Skegness to Flamborough Head, England. WW-II.

DIVER STRIP -- Belt of heavy and light gun defenses against German V-weapons; stretched from Clacton to Great Yarmouth, England. WW-II.

DIVES -- Nampa, New Guinea. WW-II.

DIVINE THUNDERBOLT -- See BAKA BOMB

DIVINE WIND -- See KAMIKAZE

DIVING DEVILDOGS OF LUZON -- Popular name for flyers of U.S. Marine Aircraft Groups 24 and 32 in combined operations from air bases on Lingayen Gulf, Philippines. 1945. WW-II.

DIVORCE -- Amphibious training for U.S. Army and Marines on West Coast. WW-II.

DIXIE -- (1) Nickname for U.S. 31st Infantry Division, originally composed of men from the South.

(2) U.S. Army observer group sent to Communist Chinese forces. 1944, WW-II.

DIXIE AND PIXIE -- Code name for a bioastronautic program to orbit mice in a small satellite air-launched as part of the CALEB program. Never carried out under Caleb but might be part of the Navy's Hi-Hoe program, a successor to Caleb, with the missile being launched by F-4H fighters.

DIZZY -- Lingga Anchorage, Netherlands East Indies. WW-II.

DJINN -- World's first tip-jet helicopter. The Sud-Aviation SO-1221. First flew in 1953, and is in French service.

DOCTRINE -- Kaileuna, New Guines. WW-II.

DODGE -- (1) Cape Rula, New Britain. WW-II.

(2) Indispensable Strait, Solomon Islands. WW-II.

DODOS -- Eil River, New Britain. WW-II.

DOESKIN -- Poretta, Corsica. WW-II.

DOG -- (1) Code word for letter "D" in a phonetic alphabet, used to avoid possibility of a misunderstanding in transmitting messages. See also DELTA.

(2) Hurricane. 31 August - 14 September 1950. First detected near Leeward Islands, moved northwestward close to Antigua and Barbuda, where it took two lives and caused one million dollars damage, then turned northward off Middle Atlantic coast and eastward into Atlantic south of Newfoundland.

(3) Hurricane. 1-5 September 1951. Formed near Martinique, moved westward through Lesser Antilles, and dissipated over western Caribbean Sea. Caused seven deaths and three million dollars damage in Lesser Antilles.

(4) Hurricane. 25-30 September 1952. Formed and dissipated in the Atlantic about 900 miles east of Puerto Rico.

DOG, EXERCISE -- Major "anti-invasion" exercise in March 1941 for Canadian troops in England. WW-II.

DOG LINE -- U.S. Eighth Army defensive line across Korea through Pyongtaek, Wonju and Samchok; one of four lines drawn up for withdrawal in successive steps by Lieutenant General Walton H. Walker before his death. See also ABLE, BAKER and CHARLIE LINES. December 1950, WW-II.

DOG, PLAN -- One of the four plans for U.S. strategy, drawn up by Admiral Harold R. Stark in fall 1940; proposed taking offensive across Atlantic, defensive in Pacific. Also called Plan D. WW-II.

DOG, TASK FORCE -- U.S. Army units during action near Chinung-ni, North Korea. December 1950, WW-II.

DOGEARED -- Vella Lavella Island, Solomon Islands. WW-II.

DOGFACE -- Avialo, New Britain. WW-II.

DOGFISH -- Entry of allied military liaison forces into Greece after German withdrawal or surrender. WW-II.

DOGGED -- Lukunor Island, Caroline Islands. WW-II.

DOGMA -- Aiun Island, Solomon Islands. WW-II.

DOGMATIC -- Waigeo Island, New Guinea. WW-II.

DOGONE -- Isangan, New Guinea. WW-II.

DOGTROT -- Galimaruhi Island, Bismarck Archipelago. WW-II.

DOGWOOD -- Guadalcanal Island, Solomon Islands. WW-II.

DOLLY -- (1) U.S. Air Force sounding rocket. Reportedly operational. No other
details available.

(2) Typhoon. 17-24 June 1946. First detected in southern Philippine Sea.
Moved northward at first, then northwestward and north again, skirting Luzon
and Taiwan, then turned northwestward into China mainland north of Taiwan.

(3) Hurricane. 8-13 September 1953. Formed just northeast of Puerto Rico.
Moved northwestward at first and then curved northward and northeastward
close to Bermuda and over the Atlantic.

(4) Hurricane. 1-2 September 1954. Small hurricane, formed east of Bahamas,
moved northward between Hatteras and Bermuda, turned northeastward, and
dissipated over water east of Nova Scotia.

(5) -- See PUEPPCHEN

DOLMAN -- Hong Kong, China. WW-II.

DOLORES -- (1) Tropical storm. August 1948. First detected south of Marcus
Island, the Pacific. Moved northwestward and dissipated off the southeast
coast of Japan.

(2) Name also included in sequence prepared by meteorologists for future tropical
cyclones in eastern North Pacific.

DOLPHIN -- (1) Douglas twin-engine amphibian built for the U.S. Army and Navy
in 1931-32.

(2) U.S. Navy test vehicle for the POLARIS submarine-launched ballistic missile.
Used to test the compressed air "pop-up" launch mechanisms of the submarine.
Inert, "boiler-plate" model. First used to test USS George Washington Fleet
Ballistic Missile sub in 1960.

DOMESTIC -- Angaur Island, Palau Group, Caroline Islands.   WW-II.

DOMINATOR -- Consolidated Aircraft XB-32. A four-engine bomber development of World War II.

DOMINIC -- United States atmospheric testing of nuclear weapons, after a three-and-one-half-year moratorium, in the Central Pacific Ocean, 25 April 1962.

DOMINIE -- (1) DeHavilland twin-engine biplane used by the British Royal Air Force in the mid-1930's. Also see DRAGON RAPIDE.

(2) Mulumiana, New Guinea. (WW-II.

DOMINION -- Address used in telegrams for the High Commissioner for Canada in the United Kingdom.   WW-II.

DONATION -- Pescadores Islands, Formosa.   WW-II.

DONKEY -- Fulleborn Plantation, New Britain.   WW-II.

DONNA -- Hurricane. 29 August - 13 September 1960. Formed off west coast of Africa. Traveled westward across Atlantic, through southern Bahamas and Florida Keys, then turned northward through Florida and northeastward along Atlantic coast. Crossed eastern North Carolina, Long Island, and New England and dissipated in Davis Strait. Caused 50 deaths in U.S. and 115 in Antilles, as well as 300 million dollars in damage.

DOODLE-BUG -- British nickname for German flying bomb.   WW-II.

DOORKNOB -- U.S. sounding rocket developed for high ballistic accuracy in both a single-stage and a two-stage version. Latter model was able to carry 150 pounds of instruments to altitudes of 45 miles. Powered by two LaCrosse solid motors, the vehicle's nose cone was parachute-recoverable. Over 30 successful tests had been conducted by mid-1959.

DOORMAT -- Aomo River, New Britain.   WW-II.

DOORSTOP -- U.S. 5th Air Force plan for quick dispersal of F-86 Sabre jet fighter aircraft, based in Korea, to alternate airfields in event of surprise enemy air attack; replaced by similar plan FAST SHUFFLE.   January-April 1953, Korean Conflict.

DORA -- (1) Typhoon. 1-9 November 1947. First detected in western Caroline Islands. Moved northwestward across Philippine Sea and central Luzon, then out over South China Sea, where it recurved northeastward. Dissipated in the vicinity of Taiwan.

(2) Tropical storm. 10-12 September 1956. Formed in Bay of Campeche and moved westward into Mexico at Tuxpam. Caused minor damage.

DORA LINE -- (1) German name for portion of ADOLF HITLER LINE south of Sant'
Oliva, Italy; eventually became their name for entire line. 1943-44, WW-II.

(2) German defense line which crossed Italian peninsula about 40 miles north of
Rome, passing south of Lake Bolsena to merge into the Foro defenses on the
Adriatic Coast. June 1944, WW-II.

DOREEN -- Hurricane. 30 September - 4 October 1962. Formed about 200 miles
southwest of Acapulco, Mexico. Moved northwestward along Mexican coast, then
northward into Gulf of California, and inland in Sinaloa, Mexico.

DORIS -- (1) Typhoon. 7-14 May 1950. Formed near Truk, Caroline Islands.
Moved northwestward across Guam, recurved to the northeast over the Philippine
Sea, passed between Iwo Jima and Torishima and moved out over the Pacific.

(2) Tropical storm. 18-21 June 1954. First detected in central Philippine Sea.
Moved northeastward over North Pacific and lost force.

(3) Typhoon. 23-29 July 1958. Formed near Eniwetok Atoll. Moved northwestward, passing northeast of Guam and southwest of Iwo Jima, then turned
northeastward and weakened east of Japan.

(4) Tropical storm. 23 June - 2 July 1961. Formed in central Philippine Sea.
Moved northward, then westward and passed south of Taiwan into China mainland northeast of Hong Kong.

(5) Name also applied to tropical cyclones in western North Pacific which occurred
prior to (1) through (4) above.

DORMANT -- Amgoring, New Britain. WW-II.

DORNIER-FALKE -- Swiss single-engine pursuit plane of 1923.

DOROTHY HILL -- U.S. military name for topographic feature near Shuri, Okinawa.
1945, WW-II.

DOT -- (1) Typhoon. 13-16 July 1955. Formed in central Philippine Sea. Moved
northward at first, then northwestward and dissipated as it crossed the island of
Kyushu, Japan.

(2) Hurricane. 1-7 August 1959. First detected 1200 miles southeast of Honolulu.
Moved westward, passed south of large island of Hawaii, turned northwest and
passed across Kauai and dissipated. Caused six million dollars damage.

(3) Typhoon. 9-15 November 1961. Formed between Guam and Wake Island.
Moved westward through northern Mariana Islands, then northeastward and
passed south of Iwo Jima and out over the North Pacific. Caused damage
on Alamagan Island.

(4) Name also applied to tropical cyclones in western North Pacific which occurred prior to (1) through (3) above.

DOTTY -- Celebes, Netherlands East Indies. WW-II.

DOUBLE DATE -- U.S. Air Force high-altitude air refueling area over Idaho - Wyoming.

DOUBLET -- Salamaua, New Guinea. WW-II.

DOUBLOON -- S. Catherine, Corsica. WW-II.

DOVE -- (1) Heat-homing bomb. WW-II.

    (2) Basic version of the DeHavilland D.H.104 aircraft series. In continuous production since 1945. The latest model, SRS.8 first flew in 1960. See also DEVON.

    (3) U.S. Navy air-to-surface or air-to-underwater infra-red guided missile built around a 1000-pound general-purpose bomb. Never became operational; development initiated in April, 1944, but was cancelled in February, 1955.

    (4) Main Allied glider operation during invasion of Southern France, 15 August 1944, involving landing of 332 towed gliders and 2762 paratroopers. WW-II.

DOVETAIL -- Cape Gloucester, New Britain. WW-II.

DOWNBEAT -- Amalut Point, New Britain. WW-II.

DOWNFALL -- Allied strategic plan for occupation of home islands of Japanese Empire. WW-II.

DOWNPOUR -- Woleai Island, Caroline Islands. WW-II.

DOWNSIDE -- Eniwetok, Marshall Islands. WW-II.

DOWSER -- Rendova Island, Solomon Islands. WW-II.

DOXOLOGY -- Tsis Island, Truk Lagoon, Caroline Islands. WW-II.

DRACO -- Jask, Iran. WW-II.

DRACULA -- Allied airborne and amphibious assault on port of Rongoon, originally called Plan Z, then given code name Vanguard, which was changed when thought compromised. Carried out without opposition. 2 May 1945, WW-II.

DRAG RACE -- U.S. Air Force high-altitude air refueling area over Idaho-Montana-Wyoming.

DRAGNET -- Gasmata Island, New Britain. WW-II.

DRAGOMAN -- Palau Islands. WW-II.

DRAGON -- (1) British biplane first flown by DEHavilland as the D.H.84 in 1932. Still flying in Australia.

(2) French sounding rocket designed to carry scientific payloads of 70 to 440 pounds up to altitudes of 365 miles. Four-stage solid propellant research vehicle.

(3) Project to construct high-temperature gas-cooled nuclear reactor at Winfrith Heath, England. Joint undertaking of United Kingdom Atomic Energy Authority and Organization for European Economic Cooperation.

DRAGON FIREBALL -- Name for U.S. peacetime military exercise.

DRAGON HEAD -- Name for U.S. peacetime military exercise at Fort Bragg, North Carolina, 1959.

DRAGON KILLER -- World War II Japanese Kawasaki KI.45 Toryu fighter. See NICK.

DRAGON RAPIDE -- First flown in 1934, the DeHavilland DH.89 remained in continuous production until 1946. Used by the British Royal Air Force as the Dominie.

DRAGON TOOTH -- U.S. Air Force high-altitude air refueling area in Gulf of Mexico, off Louisiana-Texas.

DRAGONFLY -- (1) British-built, licensed version of the Sikorsky S-51 helicopter.

(2) Experimental twin-engine biplane built in the early 1930's by the Crouch-Bolas Aircraft Corporation in the U.S.

(3) DeHavilland D.H.90 twin-engine wooden British biplane. First flew 1935.

(4) Ryan Aircraft YO-51, two-place observation plane. World War II development for the U.S. Army Air Forces.

DRAGON'S TEETH -- Concrete pillars or iron posts erected as tank barriers. WW-II.

DRAGOON -- Allied invasion of southeastern Mediterranean coast of France. Name changed on 27 July 1944 from Anvil. Began 15 August 1944, WW-II.

DRAKE -- (1) Popular name for U.S. Army eight-ton amphibious truck.

(2) Plan offered by U.S. General Joseph W. Stilwell to bomb Japan by B-29 aircraft based in Calcutta, India, and staged through airfields along Kweilin-Changsha railroad in China. Alternative to earlier SETTING SUN and later MATTERHORN. Also called TWILIGHT. Fall 1943, WW-II.

DRAKEN -- Swedish SAAB-35 delta-wing, supersonic interceptor which first flew in 1955.

DRAMA -- American Mission, Fortaleza, Brazil. WW-II.

DRAWBRIDGE -- Taongi Atoll, Marshall Islands. WW-II.

DRAWL -- Pasuna Creek, New Guinea. WW-II.

DREAM -- Pearl Harbor, Territory of Hawaii. WW-II.

DREAMGIRL -- Kikivlai, New Britain. WW-II.

DREAMLAND -- Liang Airdrome, Solomon Islands. WW-II.

DREWS -- U.S. Navy parties for operating captured enemy ports. WW-II.

DROLLERY -- Frankfurt, Germany. WW-II.

DRONE -- Light single-engine sport monoplane produced in 1932 by B.A.C. Limited of Great Britain.

DRONES -- See APEX BOATS

DROP, THE -- See CHOCOLATE DROP HILL

DROVER 3 -- Australian DeHavilland DHA-3 tri-motor light utility transport. First flew in 1948.

DRUMFIRE -- Likiep Atoll, Marshall Islands. WW-II.

DRY HILLS -- Name for U.S. peacetime military exercise held at Yakima, Washington. 1959.

DRYGOODS -- U.S. code name for movement of supplies to Guadalcanal in preparation for invasion of New Georgia. February-June 1943, WW-II.

DRYSHOD -- British 1st Army large-scale amphibious landing exercise held in Scotland in preparation for Operation TORCH. August 1942, WW-II.

DUCHESS -- Jesselton, Borneo. WW-II.

DUCK -- (1) Grumman J2F amphibian used by the military after its introduction in the early 1930's.

    (2) German Focke-Wulf F-19a. See ENTE.

    (3) U.S. Air Force air-to-air missile designed as defensive armament for the B-58 HUSTLER jet bomber. Project paralleled GOOSE, and has been discontinued.

    (4) British bombardment of Stavanger, Norway. 17 April 1940, WW-II.

    (5) See DUKW

DUCK I-III -- Three major exercises covering all phases and aspects of an amphibious operation, held in Slapton Sands area, England, and involving mainly elements of U.S. V Corps, in preparation for Operation OVERLORD. See also FOX, BEAVER. Assault dates were January, 14 and 29 February 1944, WW-II.

DUCK BILL -- Nickname for piece of steel welded to end connectors of each track of a tank, reducing ground pressure by widening track, and thereby increasing traction in mud and soft terrain. WW-II.

DUCK HILL -- U.S. military name for topographic feature on Okinawa. 1945, WW-II.

DUCKPIN -- (1) U.N. code name for portion of Wonsan harbor, North Korea. Korean Conflict.

(2) Code name for U.S. General of the Army Dwight D. Eisenhower. WW-II.

DUCKPOND -- Tonkin Gulf, China. WW-II.

DUELLIST -- Erikub Atoll, Marshall Islands. WW-II.

DUENA -- Sel, New Guinea. WW-II.

DUGOUT SUNDAY -- Name given by veterans of Guadalcanal to Sunday, 25 October 1942, when Japanese artillery and aircraft were especially active. WW-II.

DUKE OF WONSAN -- Honorific title for Rear Admiral Allan E. Smith, commander of U.N. Naval Task Force 95, at beginning of naval siege of Wonsan, North Korea. Early 1951, Korean Conflict.

DUKW -- U.S. developed two and a half ton swimming truck capable of carrying fifty men or equivalent load of supplies from ship to shore. Was equipped with six driving wheels and conventional steering gear for use on land and marine propeller and rudder for use in water. Name given by engineers of General Motors Corporation: D for 1942, U for utility, K for front-wheel drive, and W for two rear driving axles. Frequently called Duck. WW-II.

DUMBDORA -- Sauren Hamlet, New Britain. WW-II.

DUMBO -- (1) Allied pipelines from England to Boulogne, France. See also PLUTO. Pumping started 26 October 1944, WW-II.

(2) Nickname for U.S. Navy patrol seaplane, Cataline PBY, specially equipped for rescue missions at sea. Named after Walt Disney cartoon character. See also BLACK CATS. WW-II.

(3) Early name for flight version of the KIWI nuclear rocket engine being developed in National Aeronautics and Space Administration's project ROVER. Flight version now called NERVA.

DUNKER -- Code name for Foreign Minister Vyacheslaff M. Molotov of U.S.S.R. WW-II.

DUNMORE -- Code name for Jersey. WW-II.

DUNN, OPERATION -- Evacuation by air of refugees from airstrip, PICCADILLY HOPE A, at Griblje, Yugoslavia. Late March 1945, WW-II.

DUPLICITY -- Nan Wan, Formosa. WW-II.

DURANDAL -- French mixed-powerplant rocket interceptor using a turbojet engine for take-off and landings and a liquid rocket to boost it to supersonic speeds at high altitude. Plane can reach a speed of Mach 1.5 and an altitude of 10-11 miles. First flown 20 April 1956, but was powered by its turbojet only.

DURBAR -- Code name for Gibraltar. WW-II.

DURBEX -- Name for peacetime military exercise.

DURBIN -- Aromot Island, Bismarck Archipelago. WW-II.

DUST-BINS -- Nickname for retractable under-turrets on British Wellington bombers. WW-II.

DUSTER -- Popular name for U.S. Army self-propelled, twin 40-mm. antiaircraft gun.

DUSTMAN -- Algiers, Algeria. WW-II.

DUSTPAN -- Sang Creek, New Guinea. WW-II.

DWARF -- Awit River, New Britain. WW-II.

DYLE, PLAN -- See D, PLAN

DYNASOAR -- U.S. Air Force, boost-glide, manned space-craft for demonstration of the feasibility to operate at near-orbital and orbital speeds, re-enter the atmosphere at hypersonic speeds and maneuver to a controlled landing. Name is a contraction of the words Dynamic Soaring. Booster will be the TITAN III, and the first flights are expected in late 1964 or early 1965. Air Force alternate designation for the spacecraft is the X-20. See also BOMI, X-15, STREAMLINE.

DYNAMO -- Ambon, Ceram, Netherlands East Indies. WW-II.

DYNAMO, OPERATION -- Allied evacuation of troops (officially given as 338,226 men) from Dunkirk, France perimeter to Dover, England. See also X,Y, and Z ROUTES. 26 May - 4 June 1940, WW-II.

DYNASTY -- Code name for U.S. Navy Task Force 39. WW-II.

E

EAGEES -- Port Ambon, Ceram, Netherlands East Indies. WW-II.

EAGLE -- (1) Fisher Body hybrid XP-75, first flown November 1943. Production model delivery started in 1944, but cancelled by U.S. Army Air Forces due to World War II's imminent end.

(2) U.S. Navy long-range, air-to-air missile designed to be mated with the A2F Navy fighter. With a fully active radar guidance system, the solid-propellant missile would have a range of about 100 nautical miles, and a speed of Mach 3. Program was cancelled in 1961. Could be revived under a different name for the TFX aircraft.

(3) Code word for U.S. Twelfth Army Group. WW-II.

(4) See WINJEEL

EAGLE BOATS -- U.S. Navy escort vessels. World War One.

EAGLE EYE -- U.S. Air Force high-altitude air refueling area over New Mexico-Oklahoma-Texas-Kansas.

EAGLEROCK -- Three-seat open cockpit biplane built by Alexander Aircraft in the U.S. in the late 1920's.

EAGLET -- (1) Two-seat light monoplane built in 1932 in the U.S. by Eagle-Lincoln Aircraft.

(2) U.S. Navy scaled-down version of the EAGLE. No development initiated on proposal.

EARLY SPRING -- U.S. Navy proposal for an anti-satellite weapon which could be launched from ships. Interceptor would be fired vertically to the vicinity of the unfriendly spacecraft, would scan it with optical equipment, and destroy it if a determination is made that it is a threat. Not under active development. See also SKIPPER.

EARPHONE -- Aiyou, New Guinea. WW-II.

EARTHENWARE -- Peleliu Island, Palau Group, Caroline Islands. WW-II.

EARTHNUT -- Ann Creek, New Guinea. WW-II.

EARTHPEA -- Nurnberg, Germany. WW-II.

EARTHQUAKE MAJOR -- Allied employment of Liberator B-24 heavy bombers in tactical attacks against enemy entrenchments on battle fields; developed in exercise Earthquake I and used in Burma. 1944-45, WW-II.

EARTHQUAKE MINOR -- Allied employment of Mitchell B-25 medium bombers in tactical attacks against enemy entrenchments on battle fields; developed in exercise Earthquake II and used in Burma. 1944-45, WW-II.

EARTHQUAKE I -- See EARTHQUAKE MAJOR

EARTHQUAKE II -- See EARTHQUAKE MINOR

EARTHWORKS -- Beyreuth, Syria. WW-II.

EARWAX -- Anglem, New Guinea. WW-II.

EAST -- See VOSTOK

EAST BERLIN -- Military name for outpost in Korea. Summer 1953, Korean Conflict.

EAST CAVES -- Military name for topographic feature and Japanese strong point on Biak Island off Netherlands New Guinea. May-June 1944, WW-II.

EAST HILL -- Military name for topographic feature near Heraklion, Crete. May 1941, WW-II.

EAST PINNACLE -- Military name for topographic feature in Urasoe-Mura Escarpment on Okinawa. See also BATTLE OF THE PINNACLES. April 1943, WW-II.

EAST WADI -- Military name for topographic feature near Heraklion, Crete. May 1941, WW-II.

EASTER -- Fangger, New Guinea. WW-II.

EASTERN ASSAULT FORCE -- Allied force, under command of U.S. Major General Charles W. Ryder, which made landings in area of Algiers, North Africa. November 1942, WW-II.

EASTERN TASK FORCE -- Allied force, under command of British Lieutenant General Kenneth A.N. Anderson, held in reserve during initial landings at Algiers, North Africa, by EASTERN ASSAULT FORCE; employed after landings for advance eastward into Tunisia. November 1942, WW-II.

EASY -- (1) Code word for letter "E" in a phonetic alphabet, used to avoid possibility of a misunderstanding in transmitting messages. See also ECHO.

(2) Hurricane. 1-7 September 1950. Formed near Isle of Pines, moved northward across Cuba into Gulf of Mexico and inland at Cedar Keys, Florida. Caused two deaths and 3.3 million dollars damage in Florida.

(3) Hurricane. 3-12 September 1951. First detected in Atlantic 1200 miles east of Puerto Rico. Moved northwestward then turned northeast and passed southeast of Bermuda without reaching land.

(4) Hurricane. 7-9 October 1952. Flared briefly to hurricane intensity and then rapidly dissipated over Atlantic 700 miles east of Antigua, British West Indies.

EASY FIT -- U.S. Air Force high-altitude air refueling area over Nevada-Utah.

EASY HILL -- U.S. military name for topographic feature near Yonabaru, Okinawa. 1945, WW-II.

EAVES -- Bunsen Point, New Guinea. WW-II.

EBAR -- Cayo Frances, West Indies. WW-II.

EBERHARD -- Aitaplok, Vitaz Strait, New Guinea. WW-II.

EBLIS -- Biding River, New Guinea. WW-II.

EBON -- Espiritu Santo, New Hebrides Islands. WW-II.

EBONY -- San Christobal Island, Solomon Islands. WW-II.

EBOSHI YAMA -- See RAZORBACK HILL

ECHO -- (1) Code word for letter "E" in a phonetic alphabet, used to avoid possibility of a misunderstanding in transmitting messages. See also EASY.

(2) National Aeronautics and Space Administration passive communications satellite, 135 feet in diameter, from which radio signals are reflected between ground stations. Boosted into a 645-mile orbit by a THOR-AGENA, the mylar plastic balloon is inflated after ejection from the booster. First launched 12 August 1960 and, although considerably wrinkled, it is still visible from the earth. Second shot failed to orbit. Additional launch planned in 1963. See also SHOT PUT, ECHO II.

(3) Code name for Sydney, Australia. WW-II.

ECHO II -- National Aeronautics and Space Administration 135-foot passive communications satellite launched from the Pacific Missile Range by a THOR-AGENA in January 1962. Failed to orbit. A further launch of the inflatable mylar satellite is expected in 1963, after which the program is to be cancelled. See also ECHO.

ECLIPSE -- Code name given in November 1944 to Allied posthostilities plans for Germany. Changed from Talisman after that code name was reported compromised. WW-II.

ECSTASY -- Malaita Island, Solomon Islands. WW-II.

EDENS -- Bada, New Guinea. WW-II.

EDGEL -- Bilieu Village, New Guinea. WW-II.

EDICT -- Kumaru Plantation, Solomon Islands. WW-II.

EDIT -- Tongatabu, Tonga Islands. WW-II.

EDITH -- (I) Hurricane. 21 August - 3 September 1955. Formed in mid-Atlantic east of Antilles. Moved northwestward at first, then turned northward and northeastward over Atlantic while still far from land.

    (2) Tropical storm. 17-19 August 1959. Formed east of Antilles. Moved westward into Caribbean Sea and dissipated. Caused no reported damage.

EDMONTON, CITY OF -- Name for Royal Canadian Air Force Squadron Number 418.

EDNA -- (1) Tropical storm. 27-30 July 1945. First detected near Marcus Island, the Pacific. Moved northward and dissipated over the Pacific.

    (2) Hurricane. 14-19 September 1953. Developed near Leeward Islands, moved northwestward at first, then northward and northeastward past Bermuda out over the Atlantic. Caused damage on Bermuda.

    (3) Hurricane. 6-11 September 1953. Formed near Turks Island, swept outer Bahamas as it moved northward. Passed near Cape Hatteras, across Cape Cod, and into eastern Maine and Canadian Maritimes. Caused 21 deaths and 42 million dollars damage.

EDSON'S RIDGE -- Military name for topographic feature near Henderson Field on Guadalcanal. Named for U.S. Marine Corps Colonel M.A. Edson. Also called Bloody Ridge. Scene of heavy fighting between U.S. Marines and Japanese, 12-14 September 1942, WW-II.

EDUCATOR -- Graphite/water teaching reactors in use at University of California at Los Angeles, College of Engineering, and University of Washington. Both became operational in 1960.

EELGRASS -- Bisi, New Guinea. WW-II.

EERIE, OUTPOST -- Military name for fortified hill about ten miles west of Chorwon, Korea. March 1952, Korean Conflict.

EFFECTIVE -- Proposed airborne operation by 1st Allied Airborne Army, to seize the airfield in the Bisingen, Germany, area. WW-II.

EFFETE -- Dagur, New Guinea. WW-II.

EFFICIENT -- Arakabesan Island, Palau Islands. WW-II.

EFFIGY -- Chungking, China. WW-II.

EGAROPPU -- Allied transliteration of Japanese version of place name on New Britain Island, headquarters of Major General Iwao Matsuda; also transliterated Aikaroppu; finally associated with Nakarop on Australian map. WW-II.

EGGS -- (1) Slang name, used by both Germans and Allies, for bombs. WW-II.

(2) Allied departure camps in England for paratroops and glider troops for operation OVERLORD. 1944. WW-II.

EGO -- Acronym for Eccentric Orbiting Geophysical Observatory, a specialized mission description for the OGO satellite program. Launched into a highly elliptical orbit at inclinations of 33° to the equator by an ATLAS-AGENA, the 1000-pound satellite will carry 150 pounds of instruments to measure the earth's environment. First launch planned in 1963 with about one launch per year for following five years.

EGOTIST -- Mirapo, New Guinea. WW-II.

EICHE -- German operation, under command of S.S. Hauptsturmfuehrer Count Otto Skorzeny, which rescued Mussolini from a resort hotel on Gran Sasso mountain in the Abruzzi, central Italy, after armistice with Allies. 12 September 1943, WW-II.

EIGHT BALLS -- Nickname for U.S. Army Air Forces 44th Heavy Bombardment Group. WW-II.

8, PROJECT -- Plan for air transport of materiel for constructing gasoline pipeline from Assam to China; on account of delay, aircraft assigned to it were used for augmented air transport to China and project eventually merged into normal Hump operations. December 1943, WW-II.

EILBOTE, UNTERNEHMEN -- (English translation: Operation Courier) German operation to capture Kebir River dam in central Tunisia and drive French off Eastern Dorsal. Began 18 January 1943, WW-II.

EILEEN -- Name reserved by meteorologists for tropical cyclone in eastern North Pacific.

EJECTIJET -- U.S. Army personnel transport.

EL KAHER -- Unit Arab Republic, V-2 type ballistic missile with a range of about 220 miles. First fired 21 July 1962. Uses single stage, liquid propellants. Believed to have been developed for the UAR by German rocket expert, Eugen Saenger.

EL ZAHIR -- United Arab Republic, V-2 type ballistic missile with a range of about 300 miles. First fired 21 July 1962. Uses single-stage, liquid propellants. Believed to have been developed for the UAR by German rocket expert, Eugen Saenger.

ELAINE -- (1) Modeng Island, Bismarck Archipelago. WW-II.

(2) Tropical storm. 30 June – 10 July 1949. Formed east of Manilla, Philippines. Moved northwestward across Philippines, South China Sea, and China Coast near Hong Kong.

(3) Typhoon. 4-19 December 1952. See FAYE.

(4) Typhoon. 14-19 September 1957. Formed over northern Mariana Islands. Moved northwestward, passed west of Iwo Jima, then recurved northeastward and passed southeast of Japan out over the Pacific.

(5) Typhoon. 19-25 August 1960. Formed in South China Sea southeast of Hong Kong. Moved northeastward at first, then turned westward across Taiwan to China mainland. Caused damage and five deaths on Taiwan.

(6) Name also applied to tropical cyclones in western North Pacific which occurred prior to (2) through (5) above.

ELDRITCH -- Guimaras Strait, Philippine Islands. WW-II.

ELEANOR -- (1) Melinglo Island, Bismarck Archipelago. WW-II.

(2) Name reserved by meteorologists for tropical cyclone in eastern North Pacific.

ELECTRA -- (1) German radio-navigation system for wartime bombing and navigation. Basically a multiple radio range with a large number (usually 24) of equal signal zones. System becomes SONNE when equal signal zones are periodically located in bearing.

(2) Lockheed all-metal, twin-engine air liner introduced in 1933.

(3) Lockheed four-engine turboprop transport which first flew in 1957.

ELECTRIC RED DEAN -- British air-to-air unguided missile for use with high-speed aircraft. Liquid propelled, with a range of up to five miles, it was never placed in production. Program cancelled in 1957.

ELECTROCUTE -- Kaven Island, Maloelap Atoll, Marshall Islands. WW-II.

ELEGIZE -- Wangore Bay, New Britain. WW-II.

ELEPHANT -- Name for Royal Canadian Air Force Squadron Number 436.

ELEPHANT, OPERATION -- Attack by 4th Canadian Armored Division which drove Germans from bridgehead at Kapelsche Veer, harbor on Maas River, Netherlands. See also OPERATION HORSE. 26-30 January 1945, WW-II.

ELEPHANT, TASK FORCE -- Units of U.S. 6th Medium Tank Battalion. October 1950, Korean Conflict.

ELEVATOR -- Keelung, Formosa. WW-II.

ELEVEN, MISSION -- Movement of U.S. Strategic Air Forces cargo and personnel from Great Britain via North Africa and Middle East (Tehran, Iran) to Poltava region in western Russia, where three bases were located for American shuttle bombing of Germany. Began 13 March 1944, WW-II.

ELITE ASSAULT DIVISION -- Name reputedly given in Italy during World War II by Germans to U.S. 85th Infantry Division. Also called CUSTER DIVISION.

ELK HORN -- Name for U.S. peacetime military exercise at Yakima, Washington, 1960.

ELKTON I-III -- Plans for Allied operations in both South and Southwest Pacific Areas in 1943 involving mutually supporting advances along two axes, converging finally on Rabaul, New Britain. See also CARTWHEEL. Final plan issued 26 April 1943, WW-II.

ELLA -- (1) Airborne propeller-modulation detector and indicator used with airborne radar gunsights.

   (2) Hurricane. 30 August - 6 September 1958. Formed east of Lesser Antilles. Moved west-northwestward through the northern Caribbean Sea, across Gulf of Mexico into south Texas where it dissipated. Caused heavy damage and some loss of life in Hispaniola, but only minor damage elsewhere.

   (3) Hurricane. 14-22 October 1962. Formed northeast of Bahamas. Moved northward at first, then northeastward between Bermuda and Cape Hatteras and crossed eastern Newfoundland into Atlantic south of Greenland. Caused two deaths and minor damage along Carolina coast.

ELLA HILL -- U.S. military name for topographic feature on Okinawa. 1945, WW-II.

ELLAIS -- Buota Island, Gilbert Islands. WW-II.

ELLEN -- (1) Typhoon. 15-22 July 1955. Formed west of Marcus Island, the Pacific. Moved northwestward to position south of Japan, then looped counterclockwise and moved northeastward out over the Pacific.

   (2) Typhoon. 3-8 August 1959. Formed northwest of Guam. Moved northwestward through Ryukyu Islands, then northeastward along southeastern coast of Japan, causing 11 deaths and considerable damage, and then out over the North Pacific.

   (3) Typhoon. 5-13 December 1961. Formed near Truk Island. Moved westward between Yap and Koror, then northwestward to Catanduanes Island, Philippines, then northeastward over northern Philippine Sea and dissipated. Caused some damage on Cataduanes Island.

   (4) Name also applied to tropical cyclones in western North Pacific which occurred prior to (1) through (3) above.

ELLINGTON -- Gurunati, Bismarck Archipelago. WW-II.

ELM -- (1) Tagoma Point, Solomon Islands. WW-II.

(2) Second phase objective of Canadian troops in Normandy landing; included crossings of Seulles and Mue Rivers and capture of high ground near villages of Colomby-sur Thaon, Anisy and Anguerny. See also YEW, OAK. June 1944, WW-II.

ELMWOOD -- Koratul, New Britain. WW-II.

ELNORA -- Tropical storm. November 1947. First detected in central Philippine Sea. Moved northward a short distance and dissipated.

ELSAS -- German code name for World War II German surface-to-air missile Rheintocher I. The system was a radio-controlled device with gyroscopes for roll control. It was built by Telefunken and Strassfurt Rundfunk. Missile was test fired over 80 times but was never used in combat.

ELSIE -- (1) Typhoon. 23-24 June 1950. First detected in northwestern Philippine Sea. Moved north-northeastward through East China Sea and into Sea of Japan.

(2) Typhoon. 5-9 May 1954. First detected in southern Philippine Sea. Moved west-northwestward through southern Philippines and over South China Sea. Caused damage and eight deaths in Philippines.

(3) Typhoon. 6-8 August 1958. Formed west of Marcus Island. Moved northeastward and died out over the northern North Pacific.

(4) Typhoon. 12-15 July 1961. Formed northeast of Truk, but moved west-northwestward 2300 miles to position northeast of Luzon, Philippines before reaching typhoon intensity. Continued across southern Taiwan and into China mainland northeast of Hong Kong, causing floods.

(5) Name also applied to tropical cyclones in western North Pacific which occurred prior to (1) through (4) above.

ELSTER -- (English translation: Magpie) German single-engine monoplane first delivered in 1960 for aero club use.

ELSTREE -- Taranto, Italy. WW-II.

ELUSIVE -- Cape Campbell, New Britain. WW-II.

ELYSIUM -- Little Mt. Gulu, New Britain. WW-II.

EMANATE -- Gaveira, Bismarck Archipelago. WW-II.

EMBALM -- Alaid Island, Aleutian Islands. WW-II.

EMBANKMENT -- Quemoy Island, Amoy, China. WW-II.

EMBER -- Matavulu Plantation, New Britain. WW-II.

EMBLEM -- Namur Island, Kwajalein Atoll, Marshall Islands. WW-II.

EMBRYO -- Mount Mululus, New Britain. WW-II.

EMERALD -- See EMERAUDE

EMERALDBEACH -- Soanotalu (Mono Island), Solomon Islands. WW-II.

EMERAUDE -- (1) French Scintex CP. 301 two-seat monoplane first flown in 1952. To be produced in England as the Linnet and in South America as the Genair Aerial 2.

    (2) French research vehicle designed to evaluate propulsion, design and airframe characteristics for SAPPHIRE and DIAMANT space launch vehicles. Liquid propellant first stage, dummy second and third stages. First flight expected in 1963. See also TOPAZE.

EMERGE -- Code name for Greece. WW-II.

EMERITUS -- Russell Islands, Solomon Islands. WW-II.

EMIL -- General slang name used by German air force for a pilot. WW-II.

EMMA -- (1) Typhoon. 28 June - 5 July 1952. Formed in Caroline Islands. Moved west-northwestward across central Philippines, then northwestward across South China Sea and into China west of Hong Kong.

    (2) Typhoon. 1-10 September 1956. Formed near Guam. Moved north-north-westward to vicinity of Iwo Jima, looped to southwest over Philippine Sea, turned northwestward through Ryukyus, northward over East China Sea and north-northeastward across Sea of Japan into Siberia near Vladivostok. Caused considerable damage in Ryukyus.

    (3) Typhoon. 10-13 November 1959. Formed south of Kwajalein Atoll. Moved westward to Philippine Sea, then turned northward and northeastward, passing near Okinawa and out over the North Pacific. Sank a number of ships. Caused damage on Okinawa.

    (4) Typhoon. 1-16 October 1962. Formed northeast of Guam. Moved to vicinity of Iwo Jima, then turned eastward and northeastward over the North Pacific, eventually reaching the Bering Sea and Alaska after losing its typhoon characteristics.

    (5) Name also applied to tropical cyclones in western North Pacific which occurred prior to (1) through (4) above.

EMPANEL -- Sawar River, New Guinea. WW-II.

EMPIRE -- (1) Four-engine flying boat built by Short Brothers of Great Britain. First flight July 1963.

(2) Acronym for Early Manned Planetary-Interplanetary Round Trip Experiment, a set of studies contracted for by National Aeronautics and Space Administration's Marshall Space Flight Center in June 1962. Each of three companies are making six-month studies of interplanetary missions: Fly-by missions of Mars and Venus, a single mission to both planets (flyby) and a Mars mission with a landing and stopover.

EMPIRE DIVISION -- Nickname for U.S. 27th Infantry. Originally composed of National Guardsmen from state of New York. Also called NEW YORK DIVISION, GALLA VANTERS, TOKYO EXPRESS.

EMPORIUM -- Gavuvu, Bismarck Archipelago. WW-II.

ENAMEL -- Buka Island, Solomon Islands. WW-II.

ENCLOSE -- Allied code name for air patrol seeking out German submarines in Bay of Biscay. Began in 1943, WW-II.

END RUN -- Task force for drive on Myitkyina, Burma, combining Chinese troops with Americans of depleted GALAHAD Force. Organized 21 April 1944, WW-II.

ENDICOTT -- Nup Island, New Guinea. WW-II.

ENDZONE -- Yakutat, Alaska. WW-II.

ENFILADE -- Wuhu Island, Bismarck Archipelago. WW-II.

ENGINE BLOCK -- Portion of naval blockade by units of U.N. Task Force 95 between Wonsan and Chaho off Korean east coast. Began early 1951, Korean Conflict.

ENGLEWOOD -- Calabria, Italy. WW-II.

ENKINDLE -- Nakajima, Musashino, Japan. WW-II.

ENOLA GAY -- Nickname for the B-29 which ushered in the age of atomic warfare by dropping a nuclear weapon on Hiroshima, Japan. 6 August 1945.

ENORMOUS -- Bombardment of Mersa Matruh harbor area, Egypt, by British ships. 12 July 1942, WW-II.

ENRICH -- Satawan (Nomoi) Island, Caroline Islands. WW-II.

ENSA -- Code name for U.S. 3rd Infantry Division with attached units during landings in Sicily. Summer 1943, WW-II.

ENSIGN -- Pre-World War II British commercial airliner by Armstrong-Whitworth.

ENSLAVEMENT -- Awar, New Guinea. WW-II.

ENTAC -- Acronym for Engin Tactique Anti-char, a French wire-guided, solid motor anti-tank missile with a range of 6,600 feet. Carries high explosive shaped-charge warhead, and can be launched from ground, jeep or helicopter. U.S. has procured the ENTAC as a replacement for the French SS-10 and SS-11 anti-tank missiles. See also TOMAHAWK.

ENTE -- (English translation: Duck) Focke-Wulf F-19a twin-engine, tail-first cabin monoplane built in Germany 1932-33.

ENTERPRIZE -- Strategic plan proposed by U.S. Joint Chiefs of Staff in February 1944 to build up and push forward air forces in China-Burma-India Theater for cooperation with Pacific-based moves into Luzon or Formosa. WW-II.

ENTERTAINMENT -- Dummy reconnaissance of beach on southeastern corner of Zante in Kieri Bay, Greece, as a diversion for operation HUSKY. 27 May 1943, WW-II.

ENTRANCE -- Alage Island, New Britain. WW-II.

ENVIOUS -- Apongwal, New Britain. WW-II.

ENVISAGED -- Mei Shan Island, Chusan Archipelago. WW-II.

ENVOY -- (1) Airspeed Convertible transport used as a light bomber and transport by Great Britain. Pre-World War II. See also OXFORD.

  (2) An industry proposal for a three-stage solid propellant launch vehicle capable putting a 230-pound payload in orbit. An alternative to SCOUT, it was never actually developed.

  (3) Ocean Island, Gilbert Island. WW-II.

ENZIAN -- German anti-aircraft rocket able to reach an altitude of 9 miles at ranges up to 18 miles. Solid propellant motor. Experimental models built in 1943 and early 1944. Of the 24 test firings, about 8 were successful. Program cancelled in January 1945. Two advanced versions were planned but never developed. Unusual in that it combined metal and wood in its construction.

EOLE-51 -- A French test rocket built to determine the performance of the liquid propellant motor and the control and recovery systems as well as to check out the tracking network of the Colomb-Bechar, Algeria, firing range. Two versions were built and tested. First fired on 22 and 24 November 1952.

EPERVIER -- (English translation: Hawk) French Morane-Saulnier MS1500 turboprop multi-purpose two-seater. First flight 1958.

EPIC -- Noumea, New Caledonia. WW-II.

EPIDERMIS -- Code name for El Salvador, Central America. WW-II.

EPISODE -- Pyramid Mountain, New Britain. WW-II.

EPSOM -- British VIII Corps offensive which established shallow bridgehead across River Odon, west of Caen, France. See also DAUNTLESS. Began 26 June 1944,

WW-II.

EQUILIBRIUM -- Madang, New Guinea. WW-II.

EQUINOX -- Code name for American Air Force, India. WW-II.

ERADICATE -- Mitsubishi engine plant, Nagoya, Japan. WW-II.

ERCOUPE -- Single-engine, two-seat monoplane which first flew in 1937. Present production models, built by the Air Products Company, are called the Aircoupe Exacta. When built by Fornaire from 1955-60, the various models were called Aircoupe Explorer, Aircoupe Expeditor and Aircoupe Exacta.

ERECTION -- Tavalo River, New Britain. WW-II.

ERIDAN -- French surface-to-air research vehicle to determine the propulsion, guidance, control characteristics of a solid-fueled surface-to-air missile. Research and development currently underway.

ERIE HILL -- Military name for topographic feature in Yokkokchon Valley, Korea, east of PORK CHOP HILL. Scene of action, Spring 1953, Korean Conflict.

ERIKA -- Swedish ship-to-underwater, solid-fueled missile designed for anti-submarine warfare. Presently under going evaluation tests with the Swedish Navy.

ERMA -- Acronym for Electronic Recording Machine Accounting.

ERMINE -- (1) Benin, New Britain. WW-II.

(2) The Pas, Manitoba. WW-II.

ERMITA SUPPORT GROUP -- Designation given to Boat Battalion, U.S. 534th Engineer Boat and Shore Regiment, on 2 June 1945, after arrival in Manila, Philippines. WW-II.

EROSION -- Exmouth Gulf, Western Australia. WW-II.

ERUPTION -- Task force operation in Kiel Canal, Germany. WW-II.

ESCALATOR -- New Britain force. WW-II.

ESCORT -- Mt. Bangum, New Britain. WW-II.

ESCUTCHEON -- Santa Maria, Azores. WW-II.

ESKIMO -- (1) Gamatua Island, Bismarck Archipelago. WW-II.

(2) Joint U.S.-Canadian training exercise involving a 150-mile move by a composite force in dry cold of central Saskatchewan. Winter 1944-45, WW-II.

ESME A -- Military diversion by British consisting of an advance from Ambilobe during capture of Majunga, Madagascar. 10 September 1942, WW-II.

ESME B -- British Capture of Nossi Bay, Madagascar. 11 September 1942, WW-II.

ESPLANADE -- Alor Strait, Lesser Sundas. WW-II.

ESQUITE -- Taunu Shoal, Guadalcanal. WW-II.

ESTATE -- Mokuai Island, Bismarck Archipelago. WW-II.

ESTELLE -- Hurricane. 28 August - 9 September 1960. First located 160 miles south-southwest of San Salvador, El Salvador. Moved northwestward along Mexican coast, across Isla Socorro, and out over the Pacific.

ESTHER -- (1) Military name for outpost in Korea. Summer 1953, Korean Conflict.

    (2) Tropical storm. 16-19 September 1957. Formed in southwestern Gulf of Mexico. Moved northward into southeastern Louisiana and dissipated in Arkansas. Caused crop damage of one million dollars.

    (3) Hurricane. 11-26 September 1961. First detected by TIROS III satellite in southeastern North Atlantic. Moved west-northwestward across ocean, turned northward east of Cape Hatteras, looped clockwise southeast of New England, moved northward through New England into Labrador. Caused five-ten million dollars damage on Long Island and in New England.

ETENDARD -- French G.A.M. Dassault turbojet shipboard strike fighter delivered to the Aeronavale in 1961.

ETHEL -- (1) Tropical storm. 11-13 September 1956. Formed in Bahamas, moved northeastward and dissipated over Atlantic between Bahamas and Bermuda. Caused no reported damage.

    (2) Hurricane. 14-17 September 1960. Formed in central Gulf of Mexico and moved northward into Mississippi. Dissipated over Tennessee. Caused minor damage.

ETNA -- Landing of Allied agents on Corsica. 6 May 1943, WW-II.

ETNA LINE -- Defensive position of the Germans in Sicily. July 1943, WW-II.

EU -- U.S. Navy task force of USS Tuscaloosa and 2 destroyers which sailed from Scapa Flow to north Russia with medical units and supplies. August 1942, WW-II.

EUCLID, EXERCISE -- Planning exercise for amphibious assault carried out by British 49th Division. August-September 1943, WW-II.

EUNICE -- Tropical storm. August 1948. Occurred in same area and about same time as tropical storm DOLORES. Because of lack of tracking data, identification uncertain; Dolores and Eunice may have been same storm.

EURATOM -- Acronym for European Community for Atomic Energy. Consists of Belgium, France, Federal Republic of Germany, Italy, Luxembourg, and The Netherlands. See also Euratom-Nukem.

EURATOM-NUKEM -- Uranium carbide experimental work at Wolfgang, near Hanan, Germany, See also EURATOM.

EUREKA -- (1) Code name for international conference at Teheran, Iran, attended by President Roosevelt, Prime Minister Churchill, and Premier Stalin. Held between sessions of SEXTANT Conference. Also called CAIRO THREE. Late November 1943, WW-II.

(2) See REBECCA-EUREKA

EVA -- Typhoon. 28 July - 4 August 1945. Formed over northern Philippine Sea. Moved southwestward at first, then northward through Ryukyu Islands and East China Sea into Korea.

EVANSTON -- Wanopo, New Britain. WW-II.

EVEREST CARRIER -- Pack worn by Allied troops in mountain climbing operations. WW-II.

EVERGREEN -- Siaua Island, Treasury Group. WW-II.

EVERGREEN DIVISION -- Nickname for U.S. 9lst Infantry Division; name taken from design on shoulder patch, symbolic of Far West origin of most of its personnel during World War I.

EVERMORE -- Kulu River (North Branch), New Britain. WW-II.

EVOLVE -- Mount du Faure, New Britain. WW-II.

EXCALIBUR -- Pre-World War II Lockheed Model 44 twin-engine transport with retractable tricycle gear.

EXCELSIOR -- (1) Code name for Philippine Islands. WW-II.

(2) Nickname for a U.S. Air Force study of the effects of ejection and parachuting from high altitudes on the human body.

EXCERPT -- Kaldedarnes, Iceland. WW-II.

EXCESS -- British convoy of four fast merchant ships carrying troops and supplies to Malta and Piraeus, Greece, from Gibraltar. January 1941, WW-II.

EXCHEQUER -- Markham River Valley, New Guinea. WW-II.

EXECUTIONER -- Code name for Mexico. WW-II.

EXECUTIVE -- Spartan Aircraft single-engine Model 7W cabin monoplane built in Oklahoma in 1940.

EXECUTIVE FULLER -- Code word signal to set British operation FULLER into motion. 3 February 1942, WW-II.

EXILIC -- Plan for reduction of U.S. Army forces in the Pacific. WW-II.

EXODUS -- Langu Plantation, New Britain. WW-II.

EXOS -- U.S. Air Force high altitude sounding rocket consisting of a solid propellant three-stage vehicle to carry scientific payloads of 80 pounds to altitudes up to 300 miles. First fired on 26 June 1958 to an altitude of 240 miles.

EXOTIC -- Nairobi, Kenya, Africa. WW-II.

EXPEDITOR -- Beech D18S, first flown in 1937, was used by the U.S. military and Allies as a transport and trainer plane. Operational with the U.S. Air Force as the C-45 until 1961. Still active with the U.S. Navy as the SNB/RC-45. Sometimes called VOYAGER, KANSAN, NAVIGATOR -- in various versions.

EXPLORATION -- Movement of air units eastward through Russia. WW-II.

EXPLORER -- (1) Air-survey single-engine pusher monoplane built by Abrams Aircraft in Michigan, 1940.

(2) Name given to a series of geophysical satellites and probes of various configurations designed to study the earth environment. Explorer I was the first U.S. satellite successfully orbited, and it discovered the van Allen radiation belts, confirmed by Explorer IV. Explorer VI took the first still television photograph of earth from a satellite, and also discovered earth's ring current. Explorer X marked the first major attempt to map cislunar magnetic fields. Launched by various boosters ranging from SCOUT to THOR-DELTA, program is designed for special purpose space experiments. Continuing.

EXPLORER II -- High-altitude balloon used by Captains Orvil Anderson and Albert Stevens of the U.S. Army Air Corps. They soared to 72,394 feet in its gondola 11 November 1935.

EXPORTER -- Allied operation sending expeditionary force into Syria. June 1941. WW-II.

EXPRESS -- 1932 Handley-Page bomber. See HEYFORD.

EXPURGATION -- Wawesi, Dutch New Guinea. WW-II.

EXTERNAL -- Address used in telegrams for Canadian Department of External Affairs. WW-II.

EXTORTION -- Ransiki River, New Guinea. WW-II.

EXTRAVERSION -- Project of furnishing Europe and Mediterranean Theaters of operation with YP-80A aircraft. WW-II.

EYELID -- Au River (East Branch), New Britain. WW-II.

EYESPLICE -- Java Sea, Netherlands East Indies. WW-II.

EYRIE -- Kwajalein Atoll, Marshall Islands. WW-II.

EZEKIEL -- Columbia, South America. WW-II.

F

FABER -- Potsaken River, New Britain. WW-II.

FABIAN -- Dekays Bay, New Guinea. WW-II.

FABIUS I-VI -- Six part full-dress rehearsal invasion exercise, held in southern England, in preparation for Normandy landings, Operation OVERLORD; included all Allied units involved except U.S. VII Corps which conducted its own TIGER Exercise. Began 3 May 1944, WW-II.

FABMIDS -- Acronym for Field Army Ballistic Missile Defense System, a mobile, anti-missile missile for defending the Field Army against ballistic missiles. Six feasibility contracts were let to study the super-classified program in 1961. No development has been initiated because of the unavailability of the necessary technology. Also fate of the system is contingent on the outcome of NIKE-ZEUS/ATLAS target tests in the Pacific. See also PLATO.

FABULOUS -- Kautaga Island, New Britain. WW-II.

FACEPLATE -- Soviet Mig-21 jet interceptor. First entered service in 1958.

FACOM -- Long-distance, baseline, radio-navigation system which uses phase-comparison technique.

FACTOR -- Ailinglapalap Atoll, Marshall Islands. WW-II.

FACTORIAL -- Umnak Island, Aleutian Islands. WW-II.

FACTORY BUSTER -- Name for British 12,000-pound triple unit high-explosive bomb; first used against Limoges, France, 8 February 1944. WW-II.

FACTOTUM -- Tongareva (Penrhyn) Island, Pacific Ocean. WW-II.

FADDY -- Damoin, New Guinea. WW-II.

FAGOT -- Flown for the first time in 1947, the Mig-15 jet aircraft was soundly trounced by U.S. Air Force F-86 pilots in Korea. See also MIDGET.

FAIL SAFE -- U.S. peacetime precautionary measure to prevent starting war because of false alarm of enemy attack; stipulates that bombers of Strategic Air Command are not to proceed beyond a certain line unless they receive positive, confirmed instructions to do so. Also called Positive Control.

FAIREY FIREFLY -- British radio controlled drone version of a two place fighter in use by the Navy in 1956. Official designation, Mk8.

FAIRFIELD -- Advance command post at Constantine, Algeria, of Commander in Chief, Allied Force. 1943, WW-II.

FAIRWAY -- Ritter Island, New Britain. WW-II.

FAIRY -- Kiambo, New Britain. WW-II.

FAITH -- (1) Sag Sag Anglican Mission, Philippine Islands. WW-II.

(2) Tropical storm. July 1947. Formed in central Philippine Sea. Moved northwestward briefly and dissipated.

FAITH, HOPE AND CHARITY -- Nicknames for three British Gladiator fighter aircraft operating from Malta with such success that the Italians estimated the island's fighter strength at 25 aircraft. June 1941, WW-II.

FAITH 7 -- Name selected by U.S. Air Force Major Leroy Gordon Cooper Jr. for the MERCURY capsule in which he achieved 22 orbits, 15-16 May 1963.

FAKE -- Bora Bora Island, Society Islands. WW-II.

FAKIR -- Code word for German anti-jamming radar system. WW-II.

FALCO -- (1) (English translation: Falcon) Italian Fiat C.R.42. First flew 1939. Remained in production until 1942. The last biplane to be manufactured by any of the World War II combatants.

(2) (English translation: Falcon) Italian Aviamilano monoplane. First flew in 1955. Also called America.

FALCO I -- Manufacturer's nickname for the Reggiane Re.2000 fighter. First flew in 1938.

FALCON -- (1) Airborne, range-only, fire-control radar with 12-centimeter wave length. Feeds range of waterborne targets to sights of fixed, forward-firing, 75-millimeter cannon of medium bombers.

(2) Curtiss A-3 biplane first appeared in late 1920's. Especially designed for support of ground troops.

(3) Curtiss-Wright 22 pre-World War II sport plane converted for use by the U.S. Navy as the SNC-1 trainer.

(4) Italian Fiat C.R. 42 aircraft. See FALCO.

(5) Italian monoplane. See AMERICA and FALCO.

(6) German Focke-Wulf A-43 aircraft of 1933. See FALKE.

(7) German World War II Fw-187 aircraft. See FALKE.

(8) Family of U.S. Air Force air-to-air missiles officially designated GAR-1, -2, -3,-4,-9,-11. Models 1 and 3 use active radar homing, 2 and 4 infra-red homing and 11 a combination of the two. All solid propelled with a range of about 5 miles and a high explosive warhead, except for 11 which has a nuclear warhead. GAR-9, only model not operational, is being developed at a stretched out pace for the still-to-be approved F-108 fighter interceptor. First fired in 1950 and became operational in 1956 as the first guided air-to-air missile in the Air Force arsenal.

(9) Name for Royal Canadian Air Force Squadron Number 412.

(10) Name for Russian cosmonaut, Major Andrian Nikolayev, during orbital flight. See also VOSTOK, GOLDEN EAGLE. 11-15 August 1962.

FALCON I -- Italian Re.2000 fighter plane. See FALCO I.

FALCONS -- Nickname for United States Air Force Academy athletic teams. Mascot of teams is a Falcon.

FALKE -- (1) Swiss 1923 monoplane. See DORNIER-FALKE.

(2) (English translation: Falcon) German Focke-Wulf A-43 three-seat monoplane of 1933.

(3) (English translation: Falcon) German Focke-Wulf Fw187. First flew in 1937. Did not enter production.

FALKEN -- Svenska-built advanced-training aircraft produced in Sweden 1932-33.

FALL GELB -- See GELB OPERATION

FALL WEISS -- See WEISS OPERATION

FALL WESERUBUNG -- See WESERUBUNG

FALLEX -- NATO peacetime military exercise, held in Europe. 1962.

FALLRIVER -- Milne Bay, New Guinea. WW-II.

FALSCHE PROPHETEN -- (English: False Prophets) German air force slang name for weather forecasters of the meteorological service. WW-II.

FALSE PROPHETS -- See FALSCHE PROPHETEN

FALSEHOOD -- Tinian, Marianas Islands. WW-II.

FALSTAFF -- Kambili, New Britain. WW-II.

FAMINE -- Volupai Point, New Britain. WW-II.

FAMOUS FOURTH -- Nickname for U.S. 4th Infantry Division. Also called IVY DIVISION.

FANCY -- Hela Point, New Britain. WW-II.

FANFARE -- (1) Armored Task Force, Middle East. WW-II.

(2) Generic term denoting all Allied operations in Mediterranean. WW-II.

FANG -- Lavochkin La-11 aircraft, developed during World War II. Was the last Soviet piston-engine fighter; phased out of service in 1950.

FANNY -- Nickname for radio device attached to airborne search receiver; used for homing on a jamming or radar signal.

FANTAIL -- Soviet La-15 aircraft, built in small quantities in 1947-48, and developed in parallel with Mig-15.

FANTAILS -- Nickname used in Italy for Landing Vehicles, Tracked. Called BUFFALOES in North-West Europe. WW-II.

FANTAN -- Code name for Fiji Islands. WW-II.

FANTAN ONE -- Nandi, Viti Levu, Fiji Islands. WW-II.

FANTAN TWO -- Suva, Viti Levu, Fiji Islands. WW-II.

FAR EX 62 -- Name for U.S. peacetime military exercise at Fort Dix, New Jersey, and Fort Devens, Massachusetts, 1961.

FARES -- Amchitka, Aleutian Islands. WW-II.

FARGO -- First operational jet fighter in the Soviet Union. The Mig-9 first flew in 1946 in prototype.

FARM HAND -- U.S. Air Force high-altitude air refueling area over Colorado-Utah.

FARMER -- Mig-19, the first Russian Mach 1 fighter, first flew in 1953.

FARMER BOY -- U.S. Air Force high-altitude air refueling area over New York-Vermont-New Hampshire-Maine.

FARMHAND -- Rano Plantation, New Britain. WW-II.

FARRAGO -- Ajaccio, Corsica. WW-II.

FARSIDE ROCKET -- U.S. Air Force four-stage solid propellant sounding rocket designed for firing from a balloon above the dense layers of the lower atmosphere. Objectives were to place a 3-5-pound payload out to 4,000 miles, approximately one earth radius, and to provide data for a longer-range vehicle capable of conducting research in the vicinity of the moon. Six tests, all at Eniwetok Atoll in the Pacific, were conducted in September-October 1957 and all failed. Four failures were of the telemetry transmitter after the vehicle had been successfully launched. Program discontinued.

FARTHERPOINT -- Magamo, Dutch New Guinea. WW-II.

FASCISM -- Sivia Gila, Viti Levu, Fiji Islands. WW-II.

FASCIST -- Oran, Algeria. WW-II.

FASHION -- House Fireman Beach, New Britain. WW-II.

FAST SHUFFLE -- U.S. 5th Air Force plan for quick dispersal of F-86 Sabre jet fighter aircraft, based in Korea, to alternate airfields in event of surprise enemy air attack. Similar to DOORSTOP, which it replaced on 12 April 1953. Korean Conflict.

FATSTUFF -- Au River, New Britain. WW-II.

FAYE -- (1) Typhoon. 11-15 July 1949. First detected over northern Philippine Sea. Moved northwestward and northward across Kyushu, Japan, into Sea of Japan, and lost force.

(2) Typhoon. 4-19 December 1952. Apparently formed northwest of Marshall Islands; may have been a continuation of typhoon ELAINE which was charted east of Wake Island on basis of sparse data. Moved westward across Philippines and over South China Sea.

(3) Typhoon. 17-27 September 1957. Formed in eastern Caroline Islands. Moved northwestward, passing south of Guam and across Philippine Sea. On approaching Taiwan, recurved to northeastward, passed over Okinawa, and moved southeast of Japan, out over the Pacific.

(4) Typhoon. 22 August - 1 September 1960. Formed between Guam and Wake Island. Moved northward at first, then southwestward, westward, northward, and eastward on a sweeping track southeast of Japan and out over the Pacific.

(5) Name also applied to tropical cyclones in western North Pacific which occurred prior to (1) through (4) above.

FEARSOME -- Halmahera Island, Netherlands East Indies. WW-II.

FEATHER -- (1) Russian Yak-17 aircraft, a development of the -15; entered Soviet service in 1948.

(2) Bawean Island, Netherlands East Indies. WW-II.

FEATHERWEIGHT -- Merauke, New Guinea. WW-II.

FEATURE -- Malalia, New Britain. WW-II.

FEB-EX -- Name for U.S. peacetime military exercise.

FEBRUARY -- Line of advance near Aquino, Italy; taken by Canadian troops, 23 May 1944. WW-II.

FEDERAL -- Mio, New Britain. WW-II.

FEDERATION -- Dampier Straits, New Guinea. WW-II.

FEDORA -- Kabamata, New Britain. WW-II.

FEEBLE -- Hainan Strait, China. WW-II.

FEEDBAG -- Cape Heussner, New Britain. WW-II.

FELIX -- German plan for an attack, after securing Spanish compliance, on Gibraltar to start 10 January 1941. Postponed and eventually abandoned. WW-II.

FELIX I -- Brazilian sounding rocket capable of reaching an altitude of 112 miles and a speed of 4470 miles per hour. Adapted from the French SS-10 anti-tank rocket.

FELIX - VB-6 -- U.S. Air Force air-to-ground, radio-guided bomb with a heat seeking warhead. Wingless, it had an octagonal tail configuration for control. Total weight was about 1000 pounds. WW-II.

FELSPAR -- Shemya Island, Aleutian Islands. WW-II.

FENDER -- Dabanma, New Guinea. WW-II.

FENNEC -- French modification of the North American T-28, as a close-support aircraft, undertaken by Sud-Aviation. See also TROJAN.

FEODARY -- Germalei, New Guinea. WW-II.

FERDINAND -- Australian coastwatching system conducted by bushmen in Bismarck and Solomon Islands to report Japanese land, air and naval movements and to organize the natives for resistance. WW-II.

FERDY -- Allied Landing made in the Vilo Valentia area, Italy. 8 September 1943, WW-II.

FERMENT -- Teller, Alaska. WW-II.

FERN -- Cape Esperance, Guadalcanal, Solomon Islands. WW-II.

FERNANDA -- Hurricane. 2-8 September 1960. First located 160 miles south-southwest of San Salvador, El Salvador. Moved west-northwestward along the Mexican coast and dissipated over the Pacific south of Baja California.

FERRET -- (1) U.S. Air Force monitoring satellite of SAMOS program.

(2) Name for peacetime military operation.

FERRY -- Ten-passenger trimotor biplane transport of 1932. First plane produced by the Airspeed Company of Great Britain.

FERVOUR -- Address used in telegrams for Canadian general commanding officer, Hong Kong. WW-II.

FESTER -- Koimumu, New Britain. WW-II.

FESTIVE -- Tukwauuka, Trobriand Island. WW-II.

FESTOON -- Suloga Peak, New Guinea. WW-II.

FESTOONERY -- Rangoon, Burma. WW-II.

FETLOCK -- Funafuti, Ellice Islands. WW-II.

FETTLE -- Building up India as a base. WW-II.

FEUDAL -- Guarak, New Guinea. WW-II.

FEUERLILIE F 25 -- German subsonic surface-to-air missile for anti-aircraft defense. A mid-wing monoplane, it could carry a high explosive warhead to an altitude of 1.8 miles and a range of three miles. First tested in April 1943, in a generally successful series of tests, but, by 1944, the program had been cancelled. See also HECHT.

FFAR 3.5-in. -- U.S. Navy, forward-firing barrage rocket designed to be carried by aircraft as an anti-ship and anti-submarine weapon as well as point targets such as anti-aircraft guns, storage dumps and parked planes. Initially carried a solid-steel warhead; later a high explosive warhead was developed. Became operational in late 1943 and recorded its first submarine kill in the Atlantic, 11 January 1944.

FICKLE -- British term describing weather condition, which was neither cloudy nor clear, calling for use of both anti-aircraft guns and fighter aircraft in defense against German V-weapon attacks. See also FLABBY, SPOUSE. WW-II.

FIDDLESTICK -- Vogelkop, New Guinea. WW-II.

FIDO -- (1) Homing torpedo developed by U.S. Navy for use by airplanes against submarines. WW-II.

(2) Acronym for Fog Investigation and Dispersal Operation; involved installing gasoline burners at intervals along airfield runways, which, when lit, dispersed fog so that aircraft could land. WW-II.

FIENDISH -- Emidj Island, Jaluit Atoll, Marshall Islands. WW-II.

FIFI -- Hurricane. 4-12 September 1958. Formed in mid-Atlantic east of Lesser Antilles, Moved northwestward at first, then turned northeastward and dissipated over Atlantic, east of Bermuda.

FIFOR -- International code word used to indicate a flight meteorological forecast.

50, PROJECT -- Program of U.S. Air Corps Ferrying Command (predecessor to Air Transport Command) for training about 90 reservists to man new C-54 and C-87 four-engine transport aircraft. 1942, WW-II.

54-GROUP PROGRAM -- See FIRST AVIATION OBJECTIVE

FIG -- Fulau Island, Solomon Islands. WW-II.

FIGHTER -- A study to improve the man-machine effectiveness of men under the conditions of prolonged isolation such as in nuclear submarines and prolonged space missions.

FIGHTING FIRST, THE -- Nickname for U.S. 1st Infantry Division. Also called THE RED ONE, THE FIRST.

FIGHTING GENERAL -- Post World War I popular reference to General Billy Mitchell, crusader and, later, martyr in the cause of airpower.

FIGHTING SIXTY-NINTH -- Nickname for U.S. 69th Infantry Division.

FIGHTING THIRD, THE -- Nickname for U.S. 3rd Infantry Division. Also called ROCK OF THE MARNE.

FILBERT -- Russell Islands, Solomon Islands. WW-II.

FILLET -- Maleolap, Marshall Islands. WW-II.

FIN, POINT -- Military name for position off entrance to Leyte Bay, Philippines. October 1944, WW-II.

FINANCIER -- Mapia Island, Pacific Ocean. WW-II.

FINCH -- Light biplane trainer plane built by Fleet Aircraft Limited in Canada for the Royal Canadian Air Force in 1940.

FINGER RIDGE -- Military name for topographic feature near Tugok and Naktong River, Korea. Summer 1950, WW-II.

FINGERPRINT -- Terceira, Azores. WW-II.

FINICULA -- Aima River, New Britain. WW-II.

FINKELSTEIN -- Kiwok Island, New Britain. WW-II.

FIRE CRACKER -- Name for peacetime military mobility exercise.

FIRE, PROJECT -- National Aeronautics and Space Administration program for flight investigation of re-entry problems at earth escape speeds and higher. Also will study the convective and radiant heating environment, audio attenuation and materials behavior. Special research vehicles will be launched using an ATLAS BOOSTER with solid upper stages. First launch proposed for 1963.

FIREARM -- Kiska Island, Aleutian Islands. WW-II.

FIREBALL -- (1) U.S. military air transport service from Miami, Florida, along southeastern route over Atlantic, across central Africa to Agra, India. Began September 1943, WW-II.

    (2) U.N. military operation in Korea. Completed 21 May 1951, Korean Conflict.

    (3) Name for peacetime military maneuver stressing combat training for chemical, biological and radiological warfare.

FIREBEE -- A family of high-speed jet drones used by the U.S. Air Force's Tactical Air Command and the Continental Air Defense Command for weapons proficiency tests. Latest version the Q-4B has a ceiling of 70,000 feet, a speed of Mach 2 and an endurance of about one hour. It is air-launched from a carrier plane and is parachute recoverable. First version flight tested in April 1951. Primary target in the William Tell Weapons Meets.

FIREBIRD -- U.S. Air Force, forward-firing, spin-stabilized air-to-air missile designed to be fired to a range of 5-8 miles at a maximum operational altitude of 11 miles. Guided to its target by an active radar homing device, its warhead was detonated by a proximity fuse. First flight tested on 6 October 1947, the program was terminated in 1950. Essentially, the first modern guided air-to-air missile.

FIREBRAND -- (1) Blackburn shipboard fighter. First proto-type flew 1942. Delivered to British Fleet Air Arm 1945.

    (2) Projected Allied invasion of island of Corsica. Not carried out. 1943, WW-II.

FIREBREAK -- Defense of U.S. West Coast against aircraft carrier raids. WW-II.

FIREFLASH -- British radar-guided, air-to-air missile boosted to about Mach 2 by two solid-propellant motors and detonated near its target by a proximity fuze. First Royal Air Force air-to-air missile, now replaced by the FIRESTREAK, and used only for training. Operational since 1957.

FIREFLY -- (1) U.S. Air Force C-47 transport aircraft modified for flare-dropping missions. Also called Lightning Bug, Old Lamplighter of the Korean Hills. Korean Conflict.

    (2) Fairey T.T.4 aircraft. World War II development now used as a target tug by British Fleet Air Arm and other nations.

    (3) Journalistic name for the ANNA satellite.

    (4) U.S. Air Force program of upper atmospheric and ionospheric research using sounding rockets launched from Eglin Air Force Base, Florida. Over 30 launches are planned. See also JANET, KATHY.

(5) An industry proposal for a missile with rotating blades at the base for pinpoint landings. Missile could be used for delivering supplies to isolated combat units or for fighting forest fires. Not under development.

FIREFLY, OPERATION -- Flare-dropping missions flown by U.S. Navy patrol squadrons in coordinated action with attack aircraft supporting ground operations in Korea. Korean Conflict.

FIREPLACE -- U.S. return to Adak, Aleutian Islands, after its occupation by Japanese, construction of airfield there. August 1942, WW-II.

FIREPOWER -- Army study program designed to increase the weapon effectiveness of armored vehicles. Included in the study is the application of missiles to tanks. For example, the combination of Shilleglah and the M-60 tank, now under development.

FIRESIDE -- Pearl Harbor, Territory of Hawaii. WW-II.

FIRESTREAK -- British air-to-air missile equipped with an infra-red homing device to kill aircraft at ranges up to four miles and at altitudes up to 10 miles. Has a solid propellant motor and is currently operational with the Royal Air Force and Navy. First fired in 1955; became operational in 1958. See also FIREFLASH.

FIREWORKS -- Oyamba, Solomon Islands. WW-II.

FIRMAMENT -- Karafuto Island, Japan. WW-II.

FIRST, THE -- Nickname for U.S. 1st Infantry Division. Also called THE FIGHTING FIRST, THE RED ONE.

FIRST AVIATION OBJECTIVE -- Plan recommending in June 1940 building up total U.S. Army airplane strength to 12,835 modern planes by April 1942, permitting establishment of 60 air groups, of which 54 would be combat groups. Also called 54-Group Program. WW-II.

FIRST CULVERIN -- Allied plan for attack on northern Sumatra, Netherlands East Indies; used interchangeably with CULVERIN. WW-II.

FISHBED -- Russian delta-wing, supersonic fighter plane. First appeared in 1956, but has not been reported since.

FISHNET -- Bismarck, Admiralty, north New Guinea operations. WW-II.

FISHPOT -- Similar in appearance to the FISHBED, the Sukhoi model aircraft was first seen in 1956 and is in service with the Soviet Air Force.

FISHTAIL -- Gig, New Guinea. WW-II.

FISHTRAP -- Cape Prince of Wales, Alaska. WW-II.

FISTULA -- Boagis Bay, Trobriand Island. WW-II.

FITTER -- Russian jet fighter, demonstrated at Tushino in 1956; has not been seen since.

FIVE BROTHERS -- Military name for ridge on Peleliu Island. Fall 1944, WW-II.

FIVE ISLANDS TASK FORCE -- Name given in January 1942 by U.S. Air Staff to air units to be based on following islands for defense of South Pacific ferry route; Fiji, Canton, Christmas, New Caledonia and Palmyra. (Some references include Tongatabu in place of Palmyra.) WW-II.

FIVE O LAST -- Nickname for U.S. Army Air Forces 501st Bomber Squadron. WW-II.

FIVE POINTS -- Military name for U.S. position on Highway 414, south of Moyen-vic, France. Early November 1944, WW-II.

FIVE SISTERS -- Military name for cluster of hill peaks on Peleliu Island. Fall 1944, WW-II.

FIVESOME CONFERENCE -- Meeting of representatives from Allied commands at MacArthurs' Hollandia, New Guinea headquarters. Plans for ICEBERG and de-cisions regarding air strikes against Hong Kong and Formosa were made. Novem-ber 1944, WW-II.

FIXED FREQUENCY TOPSIDE SOUNDER -- National Aeronautics and Space Admin-istration ionospheric investigation satellite to measure the electron density dis-tribution in the region above the maximum density of the F2 layer. The 110-pound satellite was launched into a 600-mile orbit in 1962 with a SCOUT vehicle.

FLABBY -- British term describing weather condition, when visibility was very good, which called for use of fighter aircraft only in defense against German V-weapon attacks. See also SPOUSE, FICKLE. WW-II.

FLACK PAPER -- See ANGEL

FLAG -- One of the Air Force's early names for a 24-hour communications satellite. Later became CSAR and then ADVENT. None of these concepts are under active development. First proposed in 1959.

FLAGMAN -- Tapiantana Passage, Philippine Islands. WW-II.

FLAGON -- Ogliuga Island, Aleutian Islands. WW-II.

FLAGRANT -- Mogadiscio Italian Somaliland. WW-II.

FLAIL TANKS -- Allied tanks for exploding mine fields. Also see CRAB TANKS. WW-II.

FLAIR -- 1000-Kilowatt reactor being built by General Dynamics Corporation, San Diego, California. Redesignated Triga Mark F.

FLAK --Acronym for German term, Fliegerabwehrkanone, for anti-aircraft gun. WW-II.

FLAMANT -- French Dassault MD-311 bombing and navigation trainer in service with the Armee de l'Air.

FLAMBO -- Allied Force Headquarters, Advanced Administrative Echelon, set up in Naples area in Italy, October 1943. WW-II.

FLAMINGO -- (1) Twin-engine DeHavilland D.H.95 commercial airliner. First flew 1938. Military version called Hertfordshire.

(2) Austrian twin-engine monoplane. First flew in 1959.

FLAPJACK -- Mt. Penga, Java, Netherlands East Indies. WW-II.

FLAPPER -- El Fasher, Sudan. WW-II.

FLASH BURN -- U.S. peacetime military exercise. April-May 1954.

FLASHLIGHT A -- Standard Soviet all-weather interceptor since 1955, the Yak-25 is a twin-jet, swept-wing fighter.

FLASHLIGHT B -- Light-bomber version of Yak-25. Has plexiglass nose.

FLASHLIGHT C -- Yet another of the Yak-25 series. This model has afterburning twin-jets and a pointed radome.

FLASHPOINT -- U.S. 9th Army crossing of Rhine River, south of Wesel, Germany, as part of Operation PLUNDER. 24 March 1945, WW-II.

FLASHY -- Egum Island, New Guinea. WW-II.

FLATBUSH -- Vila Airfield, Solomon Islands. WW-II.

FLATCATCHER -- Tarakan, Borneo. WW-II.

FLATFOOT -- Ruakana, New Britain. WW-II.

FLAT-NOSED ONE -- Spanish nickname for Russian I-15 biplane. See CHATO.

FLATTOP -- U.S. study of spherical metal cores in thick metal reflector at Los Alamos Scientific Laboratory, New Mexico. Began 1957.

FLATTOP HILL -- U.S. military name for topographic feature on Okinawa. 1945, WW-II.

FLAX -- Allied Air operation to disrupt flow of German air transports from Italy to Sicily and Tunisia. Began with large effort on 5 April 1943 and continued with smaller ones on succeeding days. WW-II.

FLEDGLING -- Proposal made in the early days of National Aeronautics and Space Administration; intended to conduct a program of research into the nature and composition of the sun by orbiting 12 small satellites at distrances from 5-15,000 miles from the earth. A VANGUARD booster with a solid-fuled modified SERGEANT booster as the second stage would have been used for each launch. The proposal was not adopted.

FLETCHER -- Avahain Island, New Britain. WW-II.

FLIEGENDES STACHELSCHWEIN -- (English translation: The Flying Porcupine) World War II German Luftwaffe nickname for British Short Sunderland flying boat. See SUNDERLAND.

FLIEGEREHE -- (English: Flying Family) German air force slang name for an air-craft crew. WW-II.

FLINTLOCK -- U.S. operations against Kwajalein and Majuro Atolls, Marshall Islands. Began 31 January 1944, WW-II.

FLINTLOCK, JR. -- U.S. campaign to neutralize and control the Lesser Marshalls consisting of those atolls and islands thought to be undefended or lightly held by Japanese. March-April 1944. WW-II.

FLIT, EXERCISE -- Exercise in coordination between headquarters of 1st Canadian Army and No. 84 Group, Royal Air Force, held in England. May 1944, WW-II.

FLIVER -- Fonseca, Nicaragua. WW-II.

FLIVVER -- Henry Ford's 1924 entry in the light-plane field.

FLO -- Tropical storm. August 1948. First detected in South China Sea west of Luzon. Moved westward across Hainan Island into northern Indo China.

FLOAT -- Plan of action to be taken by U.S. Office of Strategic Services and British Secret Operations Executive to hamper enemy troop movements to a depth of 200 miles from the south coast of France. WW-II.

FLOATING RESERVE -- See KOOL

FLOODED -- Shimpo, Formosa. WW-II.

FLOODTIDE -- Publir, New Britain. WW-II.

FLORA -- (1) Yak-23 Russian jet fighter plane, first flown in 1947. No longer in service.

(2) Swedish ship-to-underwater anti-submarine rocket. Similar to LAURA.

(3) Typhoon. 13-18 November 1947. First detected in western Caroline Islands. Moved west-northwestward across Philippine Sea and central Luzon. Recurved northeastward over South China Sea, crossed Tai.wan, and lost force south of Japan.

(4) Hurricane. 2-9 September 1955. Formed near Cape Verde Islands, moved westward at first, then turned gradually northward and northeastward in mid-Atlantic without reaching land.

(5) Hurricane. 9-13 September 1959. Formed in mid-Atlantic east of Puerto Rico. Moved northward and northeastward and dissipated north of Azores Islands.

FLORENCE -- (1) Hurricane. 23-26 September 1953. Formed near Jamaica and moved northwestward through Yucatan Channel into Gulf of Mexico, then northward and inland near Panama City, Florida. Caused three million dollars damage.

(2) Tropical storm. 11-12 September 1954. Formed in southwestern Gulf of Mexico and moved westward into Mexico near Tuxpan. Caused five deaths and 1.5 million dollars damage.

(3) Tropical storm. 17-26 September 1960. Formed northeast of Puerto Rico. Moved westward to Florida straits, then northward into Florida and northwestward to Alabama and Mississippi where it dissipated. Caused minor damage.

FLOSSIE -- (1) Typhoon. 15-21 July 1950. First detected over northeastern Philippine Sea. Moved erratically northwestward across Japan, into Sea of Japan, and lost force as it turned to northeast.

(2) Typhoon. 7-10 July 1954. Formed over southeastern Philippine Sea. Moved northwestward at first, then turned northward and dissipated over northern Philippine Sea.

(3) Typhoon. 22-25 August 1958. Formed in Philippine Sea and moved northward across Honshu, Japan, causing considerable damage.

(4) Tropical storm. 16-19 July 1961. Formed in Philippine Sea. Moved westward across Luzon, Philippines and northwestward into China mainland just northeast of Hong Kong.

(5) Name also applied to tropical cyclones in western North Pacific which occurred prior to (1) through (4) above.

FLOSSY -- Hurricane. 21-28 September 1956. Formed in western Caribbean Sea. Moved northwestward, across Yucatan Peninsula, into Gulf of Mexico, northeastward across Mississippi delta, and out into Atlantic Ocean north of Cape Hatteras. Caused 15 deaths and 25 million dollars damage.

FLOTSAM -- Kwiguk, Alaska. WW-II.

FLOUNCED -- Japen Island, New Guinea. WW-II.

FLOUNDER -- East Coast Surigao, Philippine Islands. WW-II.

FLOWER -- (1) Kakia Island, Solomon Islands. WW-II.

   (2) Allied air patrolling of enemy night fighter air fields. WW-II.

FLURRY -- Ormed Island, Wotje Atoll, Marshall Islands. WW-II.

FLUSHOUT, OPERATION -- Reassignment by U.S. units in Japan of part of their troops as replacements for use in Korean Conflict. Summer 1950.

FLUTTER DART -- British rocket test vehicle designed to investigate the aerodynamic characteristics of super-sonic vehicles. Under development in 1960, it still has not been flight tested.

FLUX -- Code name for New Zealand. WW-II.

FLY -- Russian 1-16 aircraft. See MOSCA.

FLYING BANANA -- Early nickname for H-21 helicopter. See WORKHORSE.

FLYING BOMB -- Nickname for the German V-2 rocket. Later applied to any remote-controlled bomb or missile developed in the latter phases of WW-II.

FLYING BOOM -- See CLANCY'S BOOM

FLYING BOXCAR -- C-119, a considerably improved modification of the C-82. The Fairchild aircraft first flew in 1947. Originally called PACKET. See also BOXCAR.

FLYING BRICK -- German air force slang for Messerschmitt fighter plane. WW-II.

FLYING CIRCUS -- Three C-47 aircraft from U.S. 5th Air Force carrying radio and radar equipment for use in fighter control in New Guinea and Biak Island. 1944, WW-II.

FLYING CLASSROOM -- See FLYING SCHOOLROOM

FLYING CRANE -- Type of U.S. military helicopter capable of transporting loads up to 50,000 pounds for distances under 100 miles.

FLYING DREADNAUGHT -- Amphibious Vought-Sikorsky PBS-1 patrol bomber built for the U.S. Navy before World War II.

FLYING DUCK -- U.S. Army amphibious aerial truck.

FLYING EGGBEATER -- Bell H-13 helicopter. See RANGER.

FLYING EGGBEATERS -- Nickname for U.S. Marine Corps dive bombing squadron operating from air bases on Lingayen Gulf, Philippines. 1945. WW-II.

FLYING FAMILY -- See FLIEGEREHE

FLYING FISH -- Tunis, Tunisia. WW-II.

FLYING FORTRESS -- The only aircraft in the U.S. inventory two years before World War II that flew as a first-line aircraft during the entire war. The Boeing B-17 was the backbone of the Allied bombing fleet. Many are still flying in various configurations.

FLYING GOLDBRICKS -- Nickname for U.S. Marine Corps dive bombing squadron operating from air bases on Lingayen Gulf, Philippines. 1945. WW-II.

FLYING JEEP -- Another nickname for the World Ward II L-5 SENTINEL aircraft.

FLYING PENCIL -- Popular name for German World War II Dornier aircraft of the Do.17 series.

FLYING PORCUPINE -- British World War II Short Sunderland aircraft. See FLIEGENDES STACHELSCHWEIN.

FLYING SAUCER -- Disc-shaped synthetic rubber gasoline container designed for free-dropping liquids from aircraft. Developed by U.S. Army Quartermaster Corps in 1951.

FLYING SCHOOLROOM -- Convair-40 series transports converted into navigator trainers for the U.S. Air Force and designated T-29. First flew 1949. Sometimes called Flying Classroom.

FLYING TEETH -- U.S. Marine Corps nickname for tiny, biting insects in Cuba. 1960's.

FLYING WING -- (1) Twin-engine fifteen-passenger monoplane, based on Burnelli concepts', built by Cunliffe-Owen of England in 1939.

(2) U.S. Air Force jet-powered experimental missile using preset guidance, and capable of carrying two tons of high explosives. Post World War II development; never put into production.

FLYING YACHTSMEN -- Name for Royal Canadian Air Force Squadron Number 422.

FODDER - Apo Island, New Guinea. WW-II.

FOGBOUND -- Biliku Island, New Britain. WW-II.

FOKKER SCOURGE -- 1915 Fokker E.IV, the first aircraft to be equipped with synchronous guns. WW-I.

FOLD -- Tulagi, Solomon Islands. WW-II.

FOLGORE -- (English translation; Lightning) Macchi C.202 fighter plane. First flew in 1940, and entered service with Italian Air Arm in 1941.

FOLLOW ME -- Name for joint U.S. Army-Air Force peacetime military exercise.

FOLLY -- Rawlings Point, New Guinea. WW-II.

FOMENT -- Point Hope, Alaska. WW-II.

FOOTLIGHTS -- Blockade of the French West Indies. WW-II.

FOOTMAN -- Cocos Island, Costa Rica. WW-II.

FORAGER -- U.S. operation to capture Mariana Islands. Part of GRANITE and GRANITE II. Began 15 June 1944 with landing on Saipan, WW-II.

FORCEFUL -- Aurapushekaru Island, Palau Islands. WW-II.

FORCEPS -- South Pass, Truk Lagoon, Caroline Islands. WW-II.

FORD I-III -- Three Canadian training exercises in England; actually were used for movement of units to embarkation ports for JUBILEE raid on Dieppe, France. August 1942, WW-II.

FOREARM -- Kavieng, New Ireland. WW-II.

FOREDOOM -- Kawasaki, Japan. WW-II.

FOREMOST -- Concentration of Allied submarines off Norwegian coast against the German battleship Tirpitz. 20 March 1944, WW-II.

FORERUNNER -- Zamboanga, Philippine Islands. WW-II.

FORFAR-HOW -- Attempted landing at Quend Plage, France. 3-4 August 1943, WW-II.

FORFAR-ITEM -- Landing in vicinity of Point d'Ailly, France. 2-3 September 1943, WW-II.

FORFAR-LOVE -- Landing north of Dunkirk, France. 4 August 1943, WW-II.

FORK -- Landing of battalion of British Marines in Iceland from Greenock, Scotland. 7-17 May 1940, WW-II.

FORK-TAIL DEVIL -- German nickname for the World War II Lockheed P-38 aircraft.

FORMER NAVAL PERSON -- Name for British Prime Minister Winston S. Churchill used by U.S. President Roosevelt in communications. WW-II.

FORMULA -- Amchitka Island, Aleutian Islands. WW-II.

FORMULATE -- Angup Island, New Britain. WW-II.

FORSOOTH -- Brisbane, Australia. WW-II.

FORT -- Small, single engined advanced trainer designed and built at the beginning of WW-II by Fleet Aircraft. Used in small numbers by Royal Canadian Air Force.

FORTITUDE -- (1) Analo, New Britain. WW-II.

(2) Allied deception operation in connection with OVERLORD; intended to convince German High Command before D DAY that invasion would be in Pas-de-Calais area, France, and after D DAY that Normandy landings were intended as preliminary and diversionary operation to draw German forces away from area north of Seine River where main Allied assault would come at later date. 1944, WW-II.

FORTRESS -- Boeing B-17. See FLYING FORTRESS.

FORTUNE -- Allied Planning Group Force located near Ecole Normale, Algiers, North Africa. WW-II.

FORTY-SECOND STREET -- Military name for north-south road through an old bivouac area between Suda and Canea, Crete. May 1941, WW-II.

FORWARDER -- Fairchild four-seat, single-engine light plane used by U.S. Army and Navy during World War II as the C-61 and GK. British version called ARGUS.

FOSDICK -- Kavieng, New Guinea. WW-II.

FOSSIL -- Leghorn, Italy. WW-II.

FOUNTAIN -- Aineman Island, Jaluit Atoll, Marshall Islands. WW-II.

FOUNTAIN PEN -- See ASPEN

FOUR WAYS -- Name for road junction near Rabaul, New Britain. WW-II.

FOURFOLD -- Code name for U.S. General of the Army George C. Marshall. WW-II.

FOURSQUARE -- Panama, Canal Zone. WW-II.

FOURTH OF JULY HILL -- Military name for portion of Hill 721 on Saipan Island. Captured by U.S. marines on 4 July 1944, WW-II.

FOX -- (1) Code word for letter "F" in a phonetic alphabet, used to avoid possibility of a misunderstanding in transmitting messages. See also FOXTROT.

(2) Fairey Aviation, Great Britain, single-engine biplane bomber of the early 1930's.

(3) Hurricane. 10-16 September 1950. First detected in mid-Atlantic 1000 miles east of Puerto Rico. Moved northwestward, then curved to northeastward and never reached land.

(4) Hurricane. 5-9 September 1951. Small, fast-moving storm first detected in Atlantic 600 miles east of Puerto Rico. Moved northwestward, then curved north and northeastward in mid-Atlantic without reaching land.

(5) Hurricane. 22-28 October 1952. Small, severe hurricane formed over western Caribbean Sea, moved northward across Cuba and northeastward through the Bahamas and over the Atlantic. Caused heavy damage, but no deaths, in Cuba and Bahamas.

(6) Exercise staged near Dover, England in which the 1st Canadian Division practiced anti-invasion tactics. March 1941, WW-II.

(7) One of four flights in U.S. KIT PROJECT to send A-20 aircraft from Florida to Oran, Algeria, for use in North African campaign. November 1942, WW-II.

(8) Last of major assault training exercises conducted by U.S. V Corps before final OVERLORD rehearsals, FABIUS I-VI and TIGER: held in Slapton Sands area, England. See also DUCK I-III and BEAVER. Assault date was 9 March 1944, WW-II.

FOX HILL -- (1) U.S. military name for topographic feature near Yonabaru, Oki--nawa. 1945, WW-II.

(2) Military name for height which commanded Toktong Pass in North Korea. Held by U.S. Marines while U.N. troops moved from Yudam-ni to Hagaru-ri. Late 1950, Korean Conflict.

FOX MOTH -- British DeHavilland D.H. 83 biplane. First flown in 1932 and produced in Canada as late as 1945.

FOX PINNACLE -- U.S. military name for topographic feature on FOX HILL, Okinawa. 1945, WW-II.

FOX RIDGE -- U.S. military name for topographic feature north of Gusukuma, Okinawa. 1945, WW-II.

FOX SCHEDULE -- Collective transmission of coded messages to individual or several ships of U.S. Navy on fixed schedule by powerful, long-range, very-low-frequency broadcasts from Washington, San Francisco, and Pearl Harbor. WW-II.

FOXER -- Device developed by U.S. National Defense Research Council to be installed on transatlantic escort vessels for use in anti-submarine warfare. Consisted of parallel rods which clacked together when towed, making a noise which attracted and detonated German acountic ZAUNKONIG torpedo. Also called FXR. Introduced September 1943, WW-II.

FOXHOLE CORNERS -- Nickname for road junction at Digahongan, Leyte, Philippine Islands. October 1944, WW-II.

FOXTON -- Code name for "heel" of Italy. WW-II.

FOXTROT -- (1) Code word for letter "F" in a phonetic alphabet, used to avoid possibility of a misunderstanding in transmitting messages. See also FOX.

(2) Takaradi, Africa. WW-II.

FRACTION -- Nakajima, Ota, Japan. WW-II.

FRAGILE -- Engebi Island, Eniwetok Atoll, Marshall Islands. WW-II.

FRAMATOME -- Group of seven French companies which, along with three Belgian firms and Westinghouse Electric International Company, would supply plant equipment for a proposed 210,000 electric kilowatt, pressurized water reactor station to be built near Givet, France.

FRAN -- (1) Typhoon. 29 December 1950 - 1 January 1951. First detected near east coast of central Philippines. Passed west-northwestward across Philippines and dissipated over South China Sea.

(2) Typhoon. 18-21 July 1955. Formed in northern Philippine Sea. Moved northeastward and passed southeast of Japan.

(3) Tropical depression. 11-12 August 1959. Formed near Guam, moved northwestward, and dissipated over Philippine Sea. Never attained typhoon intensity.

(4) Tropical storm. 2-6 February 1962. Formed east of Mindanao, Philippines. Moved slowly northward and dissipated.

(5) Name also applied to tropical cyclones in western North Pacific which occurred prior to (1) through (4) above.

FRANCENE -- Name reserved by meteorologists for tropical cyclone in eastern North Pacific.

FRANCES -- (1) Allied designation for World War II Japanese Kawanishi P1Y2 night fighter version of the P1Y1 bomber. Japanese name: Kyokko Aurora.

(2) Tropical storm. 9-13 August 1945. First detected west of Marcus Island, the Pacific. Moved northwestward at first, then recurved northeastward and out over North Pacific.

(3) Hurricane. 30 September - 10 October 1961. Formed east of Leeward Islands. Moved westward into Caribbean Sea, then northward over eastern Hispaniola, across western North Atlantic and dissipated in Nova Scotia. Caused floods in Puerto Rico.

FRANCESCA -- Name reserved by meteorologists for tropical cyclone in eastern North Pacific.

FRANCIS -- Poi Island, New Britain. WW-II.

FRANCISCAN -- Code name for Burma. WW-II.

FRANCO'S REVENGE -- Nickname for Spanish brandy which appeared in Allied officers' liquor rations late in 1945, WW-II.

FRANK -- (1) World War II Japanese Nakajima KI.84. First flight in 1944. Entered combat service 1944. The Japanese called this fighter-bomber Hayate Gale.

(2) Yak-9, late World War II Russian fighter plane, also used by the North Koreans in 1950-51.

FRANKFURTER - Agur Island, New Britain. WW-II.

FRANKTON -- Combined operation landing from canoes carried in British submarine, Tuna, at mouth of Gironde River, France, with object to destroy enemy shipping. December 1942, WW-II.

FRANTIC -- U.S. Army Air Forces shuttle bombing of enemy targets by aircraft operating between bases in England and Italy and at Poltava, Migorod, and Piryatin in Russia. Ended with supply mission to patriot uprising in Warsaw, Poland. See also FRANTIC JOE. 2 June - 11 September 1944, WW-II.

FRANTIC JOE -- Initial mission in shuttle bombing operation FRANTIC: bombing of strategic targets at Debrecen, Hungary, by U.S. Fifteenth Air Force planes taking off from Italy and landing in U.S.S.R. 2 June 1944, WW-II.

FRANZ -- General slang name used by German air force for an observer. WW-II.

FRECCIA -- (English translation: Arrow) Fiat G.50, first all-metal, single-seat fighter monoplane designed and flown in Italy. First flight 1937.

FRED -- Code name for the Bell P-63 Kingcobra aircraft sent to Russia under Lend-Lease during World War II.

FREDA -- (1) Typhoon. 13-18 September 1956. Formed in central Philippine Sea. Moved northwestward across Taiwan and into China mainland.

(2) Typhoon. 14-17 November 1959. Formed near Island of Yap. Moved northwestward over northern Philippines causing 58 deaths and 2.5 million dollars damage, then recurved to northeast over Okinawa and out over the North Pacific.

(3) Typhoon. 3-10 October 1962. Formed west of Wake Island. Moved northeastward over the Pacific and merged with another storm system which moved rapidly eastward to the Pacific Northwest on October 12, causing heavy damage.

(4) Name also applied to tropical cyclones in western North Pacific which occurred prior to (1) through (3) above.

FREDDIE ONE -- See CARSON'S GUN

FREE PLAY -- Name for peacetime military exercise.

FREEBORN -- Plans for occupation of Austria. WW-II.

FREECAR -- Allied cruiser and air patrols in the Atlantic Narrows. December 1943, WW-II.

FREEDOM -- (1) Allied code designation for radio station at Algiers. WW-II.

(2) Rescue of some 300 U.S. Prisoner of war in Bulgaria and their transportation to Italy by way of Turkey and Egypt. Fall 1944, WW-II.

FREEDOM FIGHTER -- Northrop N-156 first flew in 1959 and recently designated F-5 by the Department of Defense.

FREEDOM 7 -- Name selected by Commander Alan B. Shepard for the MERCURY capsule which carried him on the first U.S. suborbital flight on 5 May, 1961. After being shown in Paris and Rome, the capsule was given to the Smithsonian Institute in October, 1961.

FREEDOM VILLAGES -- U.N. processing center near Munsan, Korea for exchanged prisoners during operations LITTLE SWITCH and BIG SWITCH. April-May, August-September, 1953, Korean Conflict.

FREEKICK -- Nabire, New Guinea. WW-II.

FREEZE -- British Indian operation to keep Germans from crossing Senio River from Lugaccio to Tebano, northern Italy. January 1945, WW-II.

FREIGHT CARRIER -- Japanese transport. See SOYOKAZE.

FRELON -- French Sud-Aviation SE-3200 heavy transport and antisubmarine helicopter. First flew 1959.

FRENCHMAN -- Sigul River, New Britain. WW-II.

FRESCO -- Completely revamped Mig-15 aircraft, the Mig-17 entered service in 1954. Being built in Red China and other satellite nations.

FRETWORK -- Plan for reduction of United States Army forces in Japan and Korea.

FREW GROUP -- Artillery units supporting Australian 16th Infantry Brigade in action near Bardia, Libya; commanded by British Brigadier J.H. Frowen. 1940-41, WW-II.

FREYA -- German radar installation for long-range early warning of the approach of bombers. WW-II. See also HOARDINGS.

FRICTION -- Kikae (Kikaiga) Jima, Nansei Shoto Islands Japan. WW-II.

FRIDA -- One of a family of three Swedish air-to-air and air-to-surface rockets to be launched and subsequently controlled from an airplane. Other missiles are Gerda and Adam (the latter an air-to-surface weapon). All use solid propellants and are operational in the Swedish Air Force.

FRIEDA -- Hurricane. 20-27 September 1957. Formed near Bermuda. Moved southward, then westward, then northward and finally northeastward between Cape Hatteras and Bermuda, past Newfoundland and over the Atlantic south of Greenland where it dissipated. Caused no reported damage.

FRIEDA LINE -- See ALBERT-FRIEDA LINE

FRIEDENSEMIL -- (English: Peaceful Emil) German air force slang name for an old pilot. WW-II.

FRIENDSHIP -- Dutch Fokker F.27 twin-turboprop commercial transport plane in world-wide service.

FRIENDSHIP PROJECT -- Code name for U.S. Navy plan to establish network of weather-reporting stations across China. Began May 1942, WW-II.

FRIENDSHIP 7 -- Name selected by Lieutenant Colonel John H. Glenn Jr. for the MERCURY capsule which carried him on first U.S. orbital mission, 20 February 1962.

FRIGID FLUTTER -- Name for peacetime military exercise.

FRIGIDAIRE -- Bougainville Island, Solomon Islands. WW-II.

FRISKY -- Magipun Passage, New Britain. WW-II.

FRITZ -- Russian La-9 fighter plane of late World War II development.

FRITZ LINE -- See IRMGARD LINE

FRITZ X -- German air-to-surface armor-piercing bomb, radio-guided to its target. Unpowered, it was principally designed for use against surface ships. World War II development begun in 1939. Had a range of 4.5 miles when released from a three-mile altitude.

FROG -- Kukum, Solomon Islands. WW-II.

FRONTBUMMEL -- German air force slang term for a flight over enemy lines. Bummel means joy ride or spree. WW-II.

FROST -- An industry study of the means of storing and preserving food on long space voyages.

FROSTBITE -- United States Navy aircraft carrier operation to Arctic 1946, WW-II.

FRUEHLINGSWIND -- (English translation: Spring Breeze) German Fifth Panzer Army attack against U.S. forces at Sidi Bou Zid, followed by MORGENLUFT. Began 14 February 1943, WW-II.

FRUITCAKE -- Kawasaki, Kaga Hara, Japan. WW-II.

FRUITION -- Upmandung, New Britain. WW-II.

FRY -- British and Italian partisan occupation of four islands in Lake Comacchio, northern Italy. See also ROAST, LEVER. 4/5 April 1945, WW-II.

FUDDLE -- Followed by name of target (e.g. Fuddle Wake) denoted a hit and run strike on the designated target. WW-II.

FÜHRER RIEGEL -- See ADOLF HITLER LINE

FÜHRER SWITCHLINE -- See ADOLF HITLER LINE

FULCRUM -- Auckland, New Zealand. WW-II.

FULL HOUSE -- Allied air operation by fighter planes designed to interfere with enemy air and land movement in France during Normandy invasion, June 1944. Similar to STUD and ROYAL FLUSH, which followed it. WW-II.

FULL LOAD -- U.S. Air Force high-altitude air refueling area over Arizona - New Mexico - Utah.

FULLBACK -- Code name for Palestine. WW-II.

FULLCRY -- Palau Islands, Caroline Islands. WW-II.

FULLER -- British operation involving counter-measures to be taken against the escape of the German battle-cruisers, Scharnhorst and Gneisenau, from port of Brest, France. See also EXECUTIVE FULLER. February 1942, WW-II.

FULLSIZE -- Messina, Sicily. WW-II.

FULMAR -- British Fairey fighter of the Fleet Air Arm during early World War II activity.

FUME -- Canberra, Australia. WW-II.

FUNDAMENTAL -- Giran, Formosa. WW-II.

FUNERAL -- Wanri, Formosa. WW-II.

FUNNYBONE -- Kamiri, Noemfoor Island, New Guinea. WW-II.

FUNRYU SERIES -- A family of four Japanese surface-to-air research missiles using a command guidance system and, in three versions, a liquid propellant engine. Most advanced version had a range of 20 miles and could reach an altitude of 15 miles. Development began during World War II.

FURIOUS -- Nakajima Koizumi, Japan. WW-II.

FURNACE -- Cagayan Island, Philippine Islands. WW-II.

FURY -- (1) Hawker Aircraft single-seat interceptor fighter plane built in Great Britain in 1932. See also SUPER FURY.

(2) Lightweight British fighter plane developed by Hawker in 1944 for the Royal Air Force. Fleet Air Arm version, SEA FURY, built by Boulton Paul.

(3) North American NA 134 prototype aircraft ordered by the U.S. Navy in 1945 and designated the FJ-1. Later ordered by the U.S. Army Air Forces as the XP-86. See also SABRE.

FUSILADE -- Planned operation for heavy Allied attack on Dieppe, France. Not necessary; town evacuated by Germans and occupied by Second Canadian Infantry Division on 1 September 1944. WW-II.

FUSILLIER -- Sape Strait, Lesser Sundas. WW-II.

FUSTIAN -- British paratroop operation to seize Primasole bridge over Simeto River, north of Lentini, Sicily, and hold until arrival of ground forces. 13 July 1943, WW-II.

G

G, ASSAULT FORCE -- Naval unit which carried British troops to GOLD Beach. 6 June 1944, WW-II.

G DAY -- Target date for U.S. landings on Panay, Philippines. 18 March 1945, WW-II.

G, OPERATION -- Allied operation in Hollandia area, New Guinea. See also RECKLESS Task Force. 22 April - 25 August 1944, WW-II.

GABBLE -- Jolo Islands, Philippine Islands. WW-II.

GABERDINE -- Hall Islands, Line Islands. WW-II.

GABION -- Amun, New Guinea. WW-II.

GABLE -- Aumo, New Britain. WW-II.

GADABOUT -- Chittagong, Burma. WW-II.

GADFLY -- (1) Translation of Japanese nickname for Russian I-16 aircraft. See MOSCA.

(2) Cape Pasuwati, New Britain. WW-II.

GAIL -- Hurricane. 2-5 October 1953. Formed and dissipated in the Atlantic east of the Lesser Antilles.

GALAHAD -- 5307th Provisional Unit (Special) organized in India for long range penetration operations from volunteers obtained in U.S., Caribbean area and Southwest Pacific. Fought in Burma at Walawbum, Inkangahtawng, Nhpum Ga, and Myitkyina from March to August 1944. Given name, Merrill's Marauders, by American newspapermen after its commander, U.S. Major General Frank D. Merrill. Followed by MARS. See also NEW GALAHAD. WW-II.

GALE -- Japanese Nakajima KI.84 Hayate World War II fighter plane. See FRANK.

GALA VANTERS -- Nickname for U.S. 27th Infantry Division. Also called EMPIRE DIVISION, NEW YORK DIVISION, TOKYO EXPRESS.

GALLIVANT -- Salala, Oman. WW-II.

GALLOP -- See PUGILIST GALLOP

GALLOPER -- Code name for British force, Iceland. WW-II.

GALLOPING HORSE -- Group of hills west of Matanikau River and northwest of SEA HORSE on Guadalcanal. Named after resemblance in aerial photographs. January 1943, WW-II.

GALOOT -- Lapalam, New Britain. WW-II.

GALVANIC -- U.S. invasion of Gilbert Islands. Began 20 November 1943, WW-II.

GAMBIT -- An industry proposal for two-three man orbiting space station to study the effects of zero "G" on humans and other bioastronautic data. Proposal not adopted but, in effect, GEMINI and APOLLO programs will achieve the same objectives.

GAMEKEEPER -- Anchorage, Alaska. WW-II.

GAMMA -- (1) All-metal Northrop mailplane produced in U.S. in 1933.

(2) Raulili, New Britain. WW-II.

(3) Salinas, Ecuador. WW-II.

GANDER -- (1) Proposed advanced version of the U.S. Air Force GOOSE with a nuclear warhead. Development never initiated.

(2) Oum River, New Britain. WW-II.

(3) Landing by Allied party on Island of Casterlorizo in Aegean Sea to take advantage of Italian Armistice before Germans could take control. 9-10 August 1943, WW-II.

GANGRENE -- Thompson's Creek, Woodlark Island. WW-II.

GANGWAY -- Code name for U.S. 12th Air Liaison Party in Pacific Theater. WW-II.

GANNET -- Fairey A.S.4 turboprop aircraft now in service with Deutsche Kriegsmarine and Indonesian Navy. A later version, first flown in 1958, serves with Great Britain's Royal Navy as the AEW.3.

GAOLBIRD -- Code name for Red Sea. WW-II.

GAP, THE -- Narrow foot pass through Owen Stanley Mountains, south of Kokoda, New Guinea; captured by Japanese in attack on Port Moresby. 1942, WW-II.

GAPA -- Acronym for Ground-to-Air Pilotless Aircraft, a series of test vehicles which eventually led to the development of the operational BOMARC. Tested propulsion systems, guidance, warheads, accuracy and various aspects of aerodynamics for surface-to-air missiles. Developed as early as 1945, 111 were fired in all before 1950.

GAR-1 -- See FALCON

GAR-2 -- See FALCON

GAR-3 -- See FALCON

GAR-4 -- See FALCON

GAR-9 -- See FALCON

GAR-11 -- See FALCON

GARDEN -- (1) Jolo Passage (East), Philippine Islands. WW-II.

(2) See MARKET-GARDEN

GARDENING -- British code name for the laying by aircraft of magnetic and acoustic sea mines. WW-II.

GARGANTUAN -- Manam Island, New Guinea. WW-II.

GARGLE -- Makassar City, Celebes, Netherlands East Indies. WW-II.

GARGOYLE -- U.S. Navy radio-controlled, gyro-stabilized air-to-surface missile launched from carrier-based aircraft, tracked visually and radio-guided; incorporated either a general-purposed or a semi-armor-piercing warhead. Project initiated in November 1943 and tested in March-July 1945. After 1945 used to test components applicable to other missiles.

GARLAND -- Madau Plantation, Trobriand. WW-II.

GARLIC -- Ella Island, New Ireland. WW-II.

GARRISON HILL -- Military name for topographic feature near Mubo, northeastern New Guinea, inland from Huon Gulf. 1943, WW-II.

GARWAY -- Movement of Allied troops to and from Cyprus. July 1944, WW-II.

GASKET -- Sia Island, Trobriand. WW-II.

GASLIGHT, PROJECT -- U.S. Army program designed to solve the problem of re-entry heating of ballistic missiles, particularly that of the JUPITER. A modified REDSTONE missile was used to achieve the speeds necessary for the re-entry tests. First successful Gaslight experiment was conducted on 8 August 1957 proving the ablation principle of warhead shielding.

GASP -- (1) Early code name for the PUTT-PUTT series.

(2) U.S. Navy study of space vehicle launch sites and methods.

GASPER -- Allied striking force responsible for defense of Tinsukia-Nazira line of communication in India. April 1944, WW-II.

GASTON -- Modulator assembly which produces random-noise signal to provide countermeasures to impair enemy electronics.

GASTRONOMY -- Schouten Islands, New Guinea. WW-II.

GATE, THE -- U.S. military name for saddle in Nishibaru Ridge, Okinawa. 1945, WW-II.

GATE HILL -- Allied military name for topographic feature near Balikpapan, Netherlands Borneo. July 1945, WW-II.

GATEWAY -- Marianas Islands. WW-II.

GAUCHE -- Busaka, New Guinea. WW-II.

GAUCHO -- Pucio Point, Panay Island, Philippine Islands. WW-II.

GAUDY -- Port of Spain, British West Indies. WW-II.

GAUNTLET -- Destruction by British of facilities on Spitzbergen and removal of Russian inhabitants to Archangel, U.S.S.R., and Norwegians to United Kingdom. 27 August 1941, WW-II.

GAWRON -- (English translation: Rook) Polish 1958 agricultural development of Russian Yak-12 CREEK-D.

GEE -- British medium-range radar system by which the navigator could calculate the position of his aircraft by observing the time taken to receive pulse signals from three different ground stations -- one MASTER STATION and two SLAVE STATIONS. Development started in 1940, WW-II.

GEISHA -- Derby, Australia. WW-II.

GEKKO -- (English translation: Moonlight) Japanese Nakajima J1N1 World War II night fighter plane. See IRVING.

GELATIN -- Inungapun River, New Britain. WW-II.

GELB OPERATION -- (English translation: Yellow Operation) German plan for invasion of Low Countries and France, which began on 10 May 1940. Originated in Hitler's "Directive No. 6 for the Conduct of the War," issued 9 October 1939. Also called Fall Gelb. WW-II.

GEMINI -- (1) British Miles M.65 evolved from M.38 Messenger. Prototype flew 1945.

(2) U.S. two-man spacecraft to follow MERCURY to test components, techniques and man-machine relationships for the APOLLO lunar landing program. With 50 per cent more volume than Mercury, it will be able to carry men on

orbital flights lasting up to two weeks. Also will be used to test rendezvous techniques in space. Booster will be modified TITAN II; rendezvous target will be the AGENA spacecraft boosted by the ATLAS. Fourteen manned flights and one sub-orbital flight presently planned, but may be cut back for lack of funds. First flight: early 1964.

GENAIR AERIAL 2 -- See EMERAUDE

GENDER -- Kesamola, New Britain. WW-II.

GENERALSTRABBRILLE -- (English: Staff-Goggles) German air force slang name for an observer. WW-II.

GENEVIEVE -- Patnai, Normandy Island. WW-II.

GENIE -- First nuclear-armed, air-to-air missile in the U.S. Air Defense Command's arsenal. Solid propelled, it has a range of about six miles at a speed of Mach 3 and is carried as "special" armament aboard the F-101 and F-106 fighter-interceptors. Shorter range version was test fired from an F-89 in the Atomic Energy Commission's PLUMBOB tests in 1957, and became operational in the same year. Official designation is MB-1. During development it was known variously as Ding Dong, High Card, Bird Dog, Ting-A-Ling.

GENOA -- Nalvovo, New Britain. WW-II.

GENTLE -- Aviklo, New Britain. WW-II.

GENZAN -- One of three groups of Japanese 22nd Air Flotilla, which attacked and sank British battleship, Prince of Wales, and battlecruiser, Repulse, off east coast of Malaya. See also MIHORO, KANOYA. 10 December 1941, WW-II.

GEOFREY -- Umtingalu, New Britain. WW-II.

GEOLOGIST -- MacCluer Gulf, New Guinea. WW-II.

GEORGE -- (1) Code word for letter "G" in a phonetic alphabet, used to avoid possibility of a misunderstanding in transmitting messages. See also GOLF.

(2) British nickname for automatic pilot.

(3) World War II Japanese Kawanishi N1K1 fighter. One version was equipped with floats and called Kyofu (Mighty Wind); the landplane was called Shiden (Violet Lightning). First flew in 1942.

(4) Hurricane. 1-5 October 1950. Formed south of Bermuda, moved northwestward past Bermuda, then turned northeastward off New England and the Canadian Maritime Provinces.

(5) Tropical storm. 20-21 September 1951. Formed in Bay of Campeche and moved into Mexico south of Tampico. No damage reported

GEORGE-HOW, HILL -- Military name for topographic feature in PURPLE HEART RIDGE on Saipan. 1944, WW-II.

GEORGETTE -- Name reserved by meteorologists for tropical cyclone in eastern North Pacific.

GEORGIA -- (1) Typhoon. 23-29 July 1955. Originated in Marshall Islands, the Pacific. Moved westward at first, then northwestward across Ryukyu Islands. Dissipated in East China Sea.

(2) Typhoon. 12-14 August 1959. First detected near Iwo Jima. Moved northwestward at first, then northward, crossing the Island of Honshu, Japan, and causing 246 deaths and nearly 50 million dollars damage. Passed into Sea of Japan and dissipated.

(3) Typhoon. 16-25 April 1962. Formed in western Caroline Islands. Moved northward through eastern Philippine Sea, then turned northeastward to the east of Japan and the Kurile Islands and dissipated.

(4) Name also applied to tropical cyclones in western North Pacific which occurred prior to (1) through (3) above.

GERDA -- (1) Tropical storm. 13-15 September 1958. Formed near Lesser Antilles. Moved west-northwestward through northeastern Caribbean Sea, and dissipated between Jamaica and eastern Cuba. Caused three deaths in Puerto Rico.

(2) Tropical storm. 16-22 October 1961. Formed near Jamaica, moved northward across Cuba, passed between Cape Hatteras and Bermuda, and turned eastward over the Atlantic south of Newfoundland. Caused floods in Jamaica and Cuba.

(3) See FRIDA

GERMAN DUTY PILOT -- Nickname given to Axis agent who observed Allied flights taking off from Gibraltar with binoculars from roof tallest hotel in La Linea, Spain. WW-II.

GERMICIDE -- Code name for Central Africa. WW-II.

GERTRUDE -- Typhoon. 27 August - 2 September 1948. First detected west of Mariana Islands. Moved westward across Luzon, then northwestward across South China Sea to China mainland west of Hong Kong. Caused considerable damage in Philippine Sea.

GERUND -- Gusap River, New Guinea. WW-II.

GESTAPO -- Acronym for Geheime Staats Polizei, the German State Secret Police, during the Nazi period.

GET IT BACK, OPERATION -- See BAUS AU, OPERATION

GET REDY, OPERATION -- Project undertaken at Ashiya Air Base, Japan, to put C-119 Flying Boxcar military transports of U.S. 403rd Troop Carrier Wing back into operational condition. September 1952, Korean Conflict.

GETUP -- Digi Creek, New Guinea. WW-II.

GHENGIS KHAN LINE -- German defensive line in Italy which ran from Valli di Comacchio, across Reno River and its tributaries, over Apennies to merge with GOTHIC LINE. 1945, WW-II.

GHERKIN -- Asar, New Britain. WW-II.

GHETTO -- Melokopula, New Britain. WW-II.

GHIBLI -- Twin-engine monoplane built by Bergamaschi for the Italian Air Force before WW-II.

GHOST -- Name for Royal Canadian Air Force Squadron Number 428.

GHOST DIVISION -- Popular name for German 11th Panzer Division. WW-II.

GHOST MOUNTAIN -- Military name for Mount Suwemalla, Owen Stanley Range, New Guinea. WW-II.

GI JOE DINERS -- Places on YELLOW DIAMOND ROUTE in western Europe where Allied truck drivers could exchange cold rations for hot at any time. WW-II.

GIANT I-IV -- Three U.S. air drops of troops and equipment during invasion of Italy at Salerno, Operation AVALANCHE. Giant II, proposed for Rome area, was cancelled. Giant III was also called Avalanche Drop. 13-15 September 1943, WW-II.

GIBBON-SLAPSTICK -- British air and ground landings at Taranto, southern Italy, mounted from Bizerte, Tunisia. 9 September 1943, WW-II.

GIBRALTER -- Faiguruf, New Guinea. WW-II.

GIBSON GIRL -- SCR 578, a portable, watertight radio transmitter used by men adrift at sea; distress signals were automatically sent at the turn of a crank; nicknamed for its curvaceous shape. WW-II.

GIFT -- Johnston Island, Pacific Ocean. WW-II.

GIGGLE -- Omoi River, New Britain. WW-II.

GILBEY -- Davao Gulf, Philippine Islands. WW-II.

GILDA -- (1) Tropical storm. 25-27 September 1954. Formed in western Caribbean Sea and moved westward into British Honduras, causing damaging floods.

(2) Typhoon. 18-23 September 1956. Formed in southern Philippine Sea. Moved northwestward across Samar Island, Philippines, then turned northward, skirted east coast of Luzon, crossed Batan Island in Luzon Strait, then moved across Taiwan into China mainland.

(3) Typhoon. 13-21 December 1959. Formed near Truk Island. Moved westward across central Philippines, causing 23 deaths and considerable damage; continued on across the South China Sea, entered coast of Viet Nam, and dissipated.

(4) Typhoon. 19-30 October 1962. Formed in central Philippine Sea. Moved westward, but recurved northward before reaching the philippines and then northeastward before reaching Japan. Weakened over North Pacific. See also IVY.

(5) Name also applied to tropical cyclones in western North Pacific which occurred prior to (1) through (4) above.

GILLETTE -- Aden, Arabia. WW-II.

GIMLET -- (1) U.S. Navy, solid propellant, unguided air-to-surface missile to be used by fighter and attack aircraft program; not being actively developed.

(2) Tetling, Alaska. WW-II.

GINGER -- Goodenough, New Guinea. WW-II.

GINNY -- Name reserved by meteorologists for tropical cyclone in the North Atlantic.

GIPSY MOTH -- DeHavilland biplane trainer of the 1920's. Forerunner of the famed, widely-used TIGER MOTH.

GIRAFFE -- Marklo, New Britain. WW-II.

GIRDLE -- Peter Harbor, New Britain. WW-II.

GIRHEL -- French Helicop-Air L.50 light gyroplane which began trails in 1960.

GLACIER -- Air operation from the north against Japan. WW-II.

GLADE ROAD -- Military name for topographic feature near Rabaul, New Britain. WW-II.

GLADIATOR -- Gloster biplane, one of the last warplanes of its type to see operational service. First flew in 1934 and fought gallantly through 1940 with the British Royal Air Force, especially at Malta.

GLADYS -- Hurricane. 4-7 September 1955. Formed in Bay of Campeche. Moved into Mexico north of Tampico. Caused floods and loss of life in Mexico.

GLAMIS -- Deauville, France. WW-II.

GLAND -- Bagen, New Guinea. WW-II.

GLEASON -- Amgem River, New Britain. WW-II.

GLEECOL -- One of two columns from 5th Indian Division in action south of Matruh, Egypt, 26 June 1942. See also LEATHERCOL. WW-II.

GLENDA -- Name reserved by meteorologists for tropical cyclone in eastern North Pacific.

GLENDALE -- Code name for Bulgaria. WW-II.

GLIDE -- Missile trajectory concept in which a missile would be fired to an altitude of approximately 50 miles and then pitched horizontally and allowed to glide to its target at speeds up to 10,000 miles per hour.

GLOBEMASTER -- The C-74, largest land transport aircraft of its day. The Douglas U.S. Army Air Forces plane first flew in May 1945.

GLOBEMASTER II -- Douglas C-124, operational since 1950 with the U.S. Air Force. First flown in 1949.

GLOBEMASTER III -- Non-official nickname for the C-133 Douglas turboprop transport first flown in 1956. See CARGOMASTER.

GLOBETROTTER -- Allied operation against Sansapor area, Netherlands New Guinea, carried out by TYPHOON Task Force. 30 July-21 August 1944, WW-II.

GLOMB -- U.S. Navy/Army glide bomb designed to carry 3000 gallons of gasoline or 18,000 pounds of bombs, and be towed to the vicinity of its target by an airplane. Terminal guidance was provided by radio control from information furnished by a television unit. Development began in 1941 and was discontinued after some success in 1944.

GLORIA -- (1) El River, New Britain. WW-II.

(2) Typhoon. 16-23 July 1949. First detected in central Philippine Sea. Moved northward at first, then northwestward across Okinawa and into China mainland near Shanghai.

(3) Typhoon. 18-23 December 1952. Formed over central Caroline Islands. Moved westward through central Philippines across the South China Sea and into southern Viet Nam.

(4) Typhoon. 16-22 September 1957. Formed in southern Philippine Sea. Moved northwestward across northern Luzon, entered China coast near Hong Kong and dissipated.

GLOUCESTERIZING -- Term used by U.S. 5th Air Force to describe complete obliteration of a target and continuous isolation of battle area by pre-invasion bombing. Named after success of such an operation at Cape Gloucester, New Britain, in December 1943. WW-II.

GLOVE -- Pulo Cecie de Mir, French Indo China. WW-II.

GLOVER -- Runglo, New Britain. WW-II.

GLOW -- Rendova Island, Solomon Islands. WW-II.

GLOW WORMS -- German Air Force slang for searchlights. WW-II.

GLOWWORM -- Piaanu Pass, Truk, Caroline Islands. WW-II.

GLUE -- Shipping designator, used in World War II, for cargo to be received in Zone II of United Kingdom, comprising area south of line of county boundaries drawn through London and Banbury. See also SOXO, BANG, UGLY. Instituted 1943.

GLYPTIC -- Code name for Premier Joseph Stalin of U.S.S.R. WW-II.

GNAT -- (1) Folland F.O.141 lightweight fighter. This British jet first flew in 1955.

   (2) The Folland T.1 is an updated version of the British fighter plane, and first flew in 1959.

   (3) U.S. Navy surface-to-air missile reportedly under development.

   (4) See ZAUNKÖNIG

GNATS -- Sibutu Passage, Philippine Islands. WW-II.

GNOME PROJECT -- First of several peaceful nuclear detonations planned under U.S. PLOWSHARE program. Carried out near Carlsbad, New Mexico. 10 December 1961.

GNOSTIC -- Daril Creek, New Guinea. WW-II.

GOALPOST SUB-TASK FORCE -- Unit of WESTERN TASK FORCE which landed in Mehdia-Port Lyautey area, French Morocco. Also called Force Z. November 1942, WW-II.

GOBI -- U.S. Air Force air-to-surface missile. Development started in 1946, but the program was cancelled due to fund limitations in 1947.

GOBLET -- Project for British invasion of southern Italy at Crotone as post-HUSKY operation. Not carried out. Fall 1943, WW-II.

GOBLIN -- McDonnell XF-85 "parasite" escort fighter, with folding wings, designed to be carried by a B-36. First flew 23 August 1948.

GOCART -- Asiet, New Guinea. WW-II.

GODIVA I -- U.S. bare metal, prompt burst neutronics studies at Los Alamos Scientific Laboratory, New Mexico. Began 1951. Dismantled 1957.

GODIVA II -- U.S. study of super prompt critical bursts with plated bare enriched core at Los Alamos Scientific Laboratory, New Mexico. Began 1957.

GOELAND -- Peacetime Caudron C.440 transport plane used by the Luftwaffe after the Nazi occupation of France.

GOGMAGOG -- Waigeo Island, New Guinea. WW-II.

GOLD -- Beach assaulted by troops of British XXX Corps on D DAY, 6 June 1944, in Operation OVERLORD; located between Le Hamel and La Riviere, Normandy, France. See also ASSAULT FORCE G.

GOLD STONE -- Name for U.S. peacetime military exercise at Fort Irwin, California, 1963.

GOLDBERG -- Mount Langla, New Britain. WW-II.

GOLDBRICK -- Mount Talawe, New Britain. WW-II.

GOLDEN -- Pucio Point, Panay Island, Philippine Islands. WW-II.

GOLDEN ACORNS -- Nickname for U.S. 87th Infantry Division.

GOLDEN AGE -- Term applied during World War One to the era of individual aerial combat and glorification of the fighter ace.

GOLDEN ARROW DIVISION -- Nickname for U.S. 8th Infantry Division. A golden arrow bisects an Arabic numeral eight in shoulder patch design. Formerly called PATHFINDER DIVISION.

GOLDEN EAGLE -- Name for Russian cosmonaut, Lieutenant-Colonel Pavel Popovich, during orbital flight. See also VOSTOK, FALCON. 12-15 August 1962.

GOLDEN HAWKS -- Royal Canadian Air Force aerobatics team which flies Sabre Mk. VI's.

GOLDEN LION DIVISION -- Nickname for U.S. 106th Infantry Division.

GOLDEN RAIN -- Name for German pyrotechnic fired from anti-aircraft guns as navigational aid to aircraft. WW-II.

GOLDEN RAM -- Name of a U.S. Air Force program to tighten launch control procedures to eliminate problems causing partial failures of missile launches. First missile successfully launched under the program was an ATLAS from Vandenberg Air Force Base, California, on 16 December 1960.

GOLDEN SQUARE -- Nickname for four Iraqi generals who backed pro-German Rashid Ali during his temporary seizure of power in Baghdad. Spring 1941, WW-II.

GOLDEN STARIS -- Australian name for long series of ramshackle log steps cut into mountainside leading upwards from Uberi, New Guinea. August 1942, WW-II.

GOLDENBOUGH -- Sorong, New Guinea. WW-II.

GOLDFISH -- Code name for France. WW-II.

GOLDFLAKE -- Withdrawal of 1st Canadian Corps from Italy and movement to northwestern Europe via Marseilles, France, to rejoin remainder of First Canadian Army. See also PENKNIFE. February-March 1945, WW-II.

GOLDSTICK -- San Miguel, Azores. WW-II.

GOLDWIN -- Atua, New Britain. WW-II.

GOLEM 1. -- Soviet underwater-to-surface, approximately 400-mile range missile based on German V-2 technology. Carrying a nuclear warhead, two or three of these missiles can be towed behind a submarine, and, by flooding the base of the missile container, raised to the vertical and fired. Liquid-propelled, with a thrust of 120,000 pounds, it uses a radio-inertial guidance system. Operational with the Russian Navy. An advanced, two-stage version, called GOLEM 2, has also been developed.

GOLEM II -- Soviet underwater-to-surface missile with a range of 1200-1300 miles. Radio-inertial guided, with a nuclear capability, it is an advanced version of the GOLEM I. Both were adopted from German plans for an underwater V-2. The liquid-fueled missile is towed behind a submarine in a sealed fire tube. When ready to fire, the base of the tube is flooded, raising the missile to verticle position. Under development.

GOLEM 3 -- Soviet underwater-to-air and surface-to-air infrared guided missile which can be launched from submarines, surface ships or land based mobile carriers. Can reach an altitude of about 10 miles at ranges out to 30 miles. Operational with Navy units and under development for the Army.

GOLEM IV -- Soviet surface-to-air missile with a range of 45 miles. Operational on surface ships, the radar-guided solid fuel missile may also be converted for use aboard submarines.

GOLF -- Code word for letter "G" in a phonetic alphabet, used to avoid possibility of a misunderstanding in transmitting messages. See also GEORGE.

GOLIATH -- German remote-control explosive tank. WW-II.

GOLLIWOG -- Code name for Fighting French. WW-II.

GOMORRAH -- British Royal Air Force, Bomber Command's main offensive (four raids) on Hamburg, Germany. 24/25 July-2/3 August 1943, WW-II.

GONDOLA -- Allied code name for air patrol seeking out German submarines in Bay of Biscay. Began in 1943, WW-II.

GOOBER -- Dadbur River, New Guinea. WW-II.

GOOD LUCK -- Translation of Oklahoma Indian nickname for a 1927 Travelair. See WOOLAROC.

GOODGAME -- St. Helena Island, Atlantic Ocean. WW-II.

GOODMAN -- Lakei Island, New Britain. WW-II.

GOODRICH -- Garowe Island, Bismarck Archipelago. WW-II.

GOODTIME -- Treasury Island, Solomon Islands. WW-II.

GOODWILL, OPERATION -- Project to deliver clothing, collected on U.S. West
Coast, to Hope Hospital, Pusan, Korea. Korean Conflict.

GOODWOOD -- Allied Twenty-First Army Group offensive across Orne River, south
if Caen, France, to break out of Normandy lodgment. Coincided with U.S.
Operation COBRA. 18-21 July 1944, WW-II.

GOONEY BIRD -- C-47 aircraft. See SKY TRAIN.

GOOSE -- (1) Grumman G-21 aircraft, first flown in 1937, still serves with several
air arms and navies as well as in civil operations.

(2) Four-engine version of the Grumman G-21. Modified by McKinnon and
flown in 1958.

(3) U.S. Air Force turbojet-powered missile designed as a decoy to confuse
enemy radar and draw the fire of enemy surface-to-air missiles, thereby
aiding the penetration capability of Strategic Air Command bombers. Jet
assisted take-off launched, it had a range of over 2000 miles. First tested
in May 1958 and cancelled in December 1958.

(4) Cape Natoka, Viti Levu, Fiji Islands. WW-II.

(5) Name for Royal Canadian Air Force Squadron Number 408.

GOOSEBERRIES -- Five partial breakwaters formed in shallow water by sinking of
blockships, CORNCOBS, after Normandy landings. See also MULBERRIES. 1944,
WW-II.

GOOSEWING -- Code name for Alaska. WW-II.

GOOTCH -- Monga, New Britain. WW-II.

GORDON -- Single-engine biplane day bomber built by Great Britain's Fairey
Aviation in the early 1930's. Another version called SEAL.

GORGON DRONES -- Two parachute-recoverable drones developed from the
GORGON 5 and 2C for the U.S. Navy. The former was aircraft-launched
and could reach an altitude of 6-7 miles and a range of 20 miles at speeds up to
500 miles per hour. Turbojet-powered. The later used a pulsejet, and could
achieve speeds of 175-450 miles per hour. 18 flights of the Gorgon 5, and 8 of
the 2C model were conducted. Program ended in 1949. Drone designations
were KDN-1 and KD2N-1, respectively. See also PLOVER.

GORGON SERIES -- Family of eight U.S. Navy research test vehicles designed to test the feasibility of developing a radio-controlled, jet-powered air-to-air missile (some experiments were conducted on ship-to-shore and air-to-surface concepts). Two different air frames and various engines (including rocket) were tested with the first flight test in August 1945. Following World War II, various models were used as control test vehicles and drones. Last of the series was terminated in December 1949. Models developed were: 2A, 2B, 2C, 3A, 3B, 3C, 4 and 5.

GOSHAWK -- Single-seat shipboard fighter plane delivered to the U.S. Navy in 1933 by Curtiss as the F11C. See also SEA HAWK.

GOSSIPMONGER -- Talaud Island, Netherlands East Indies. WW-II.

GOTENSTELLUNG -- See GOTHIC LINE

GOTHA -- German World War One twin-engine biplane bomber.

GOTHIC LINE -- (German: Gotenstellung) German defense line across Italy from coastal plain south of Spezia to Foglia River and Pesaro on Adriatic. Originally called by Germans Apennine Position and finally called by them GREEN LINE. Also known as Pisa-Rimini Line. See also BROWN and RED LINES. 1944, WW-II.

GOVERNMENT HOUSE HILL -- U.S. military name for small rise on BLOODY RIDGE, le Shima, Ryukyu Islands; topped by large concrete building. 1945, WW-II.

GRACE -- (1) Cape Endaiadere, New Guinea. WW-II.

(2) Tropical storm. 15-22 August 1945. First detected west of Wake Island, the Pacific. Moved northwestward to Japan.

(3) Typhoon. 15-21 July 1950. First detected in northern Philippine Sea. Moved northwestward, passed just east of Okinawa through Korea, and along western shore of Sea of Japan, where it lost force.

(4) Typhoon. 12-14 August 1954. Formed southwest of Iwo Jima, the Pacific. Moved west-northwestward at first, then north-northwestward across Okinawa into East China Sea.

(5) Typhoon. 29 August - 4 September 1958. Formed south of Guam. Moved northwestward past northern tip of Taiwan and dissipated over mainland China.

(6) Tropical storm. 21-25 July 1961. Formed near Okinawa and moved northward to Korea and lost force.

(7) Name also applied to tropical cyclones in western North Pacific which occurred prior to (2) through (6) above.

GRACIE -- Hurricane. 20 September - 2 October 1959. Formed just north of Hispaniola. Moved erratically northward, then northwestward and into South Carolina near Beaufort. Turned northeastward through New England as weak storm and dissipated south of Nova Scotia. Caused 22 deaths and 14 million dollars damage.

GRAMMAR -- Urukthapel Island, Palau Islands. WW-II.

GRAND OLD LADY -- C-47 aircraft. See SKY TRAIN.

GRAND SLAM -- (1) Allied 22,000-pound penetrating earthquake bomb. First dropped on Bielefeld, Germany, 14 March 1944. WW-II.

(2) U.S. Army 24-tube rocket launcher for use with chemical or high explosive rockets. WW-II.

GRANDDAD -- Kropan, Wooklark Island. WW-II.

GRANDE -- Montevideo, Uruguay. WW-II.

GRANDPA -- Gurisau (Gurissu), New Britain. WW-II.

GRANDSTAND -- Papua Bay, New Guinea. WW-II.

GRANITE -- U.S. campaign plan outlining tentative operations to be conducted in Central Pacific in 1944 and timetable. Included following operations: HAILSTONE, CATCHPOLE, GYMKHANA-ROADMAKER, FORAGER, STALEMATE. See also GRANITE II. Published by Admiral Chester W. Nimitz, 13 January 1944. WW-II.

GRANITE II -- U.S. campaign plan outlining tentative operations to be conducted in Pacific Ocean areas and timetable. Included following operations: FORAGER, STALEMATE, INSURGENT, CAUSEWAY, INDUCTION. See also GRANITE. Issued by Admiral Chester W. Nimitz, early June 1944, WW-II.

GRANNY -- (1) Manila, Philippine Islands. WW-II.

(2) Moro Gulf, Philippine Islands. WW-II.

GRAPEFRUIT -- (1) Nickname disparagingly given to VANGUARD I by the Russians and later picked up by U.S. commentators and writers. Vanguard I weighed 3.25 pounds; Sputnik I weighed 184 pounds.

(2) Offensive in north Italy by U.S. 5th Army. Began 9 April 1945, WW-II.

GRAPES -- Military name for house in Kapelsche Veer, Netherlands, during OPERATION ELEPHANT. January 1945, WW-II.

GRAPESHOT -- Allied 15th Army Group spring offensive designed to destroy German forces in Italy. WW-II.

GRASS -- Berande Point, Guadalcanal, Solomon Islands. WW-II.

GRASSCUTTING -- Term applied to learning to fly a Curtiss airplane in 1911. Throttle was tied to limit speed to 15 miles per hour. Practice necessary due to plane being a single-seater.

GRASSHOPPER -- (1) L-2, -3, -4 light liaison planes built by Taylorcraft, Aeronca and Piper during World War II for the U.S. Army Air Forces.

    (2) Code name for the Azores. WW-II.

    (3) Simban, New Guinea. WW-II.

    (4) One of four plans for U.S. breakout from Anzio beachhead in Italy involving attack in direction Littoria-Sezze. Not used. See also BUFFALO. May 1944, WW-II.

GRATING -- Mombasa, Kenya, Africa. WW-II.

GRATITUDE -- U.S. Navy operation, planned by Admiral William F. Halsey, Jr., to sweep through South China Sea. Early 1945, WW-II.

GRAVEYARD -- Louisa Harbor, Trobriand. WW-II.

GRAY -- U.S. plan for occupation of Azores. Drafted in May 1941, suspended in June 1941, WW-II.

GREAT ARTISTE, THE -- Crew's name for U.S. B-29 aircraft which, because of error in official communique, was until 1946 considered to have dropped atomic bomb on Nagasaki, Japan, when actually it flew as observation plane under command of Captain Frederick C. Bock. BOCK'S CAR dropped the bomb. 9 August 1945, WW-II.

GREAT BEAR -- U.S. peacetime military exercise held in Alaska, 1962.

GREAT SHELF, OPERATION -- Joint U.S. Air Force-Army exercise, held during January-February 1962 at Clark Air Base, Philippine Islands, to test speed of deployment of ground and airborne troops and the ability of Military Air Transport Service to expedite this deployment.

GREAT SNOW -- U.S. Air Force high-altitude air refueling area off the coast of California.

GREB -- Acronym for Galactic Radiation Experiment Background satellite carried as a piggy-back passenger on U.S. Navy's transit satellite to measure solar activity in ultraviolet and X-ray wave lengths. First launched with TRANSIT IIA on a THOR-ABLE-STAR, 22 June 1960. Also called SUNRAY. See also COMPOSITE I.

GREBE -- U.S. Navy air-to-underwater torpedo equipped with aerodynamic surfaces and turbojet or pulsejet engine to enable it to glide or fly to its target. Guided by the launching aircraft until it hit the water's surface, and then it used on acoustical homing system to its target. Initiated in 1944; program cancelled in 1951.

GREEK -- San Bernardino, Philippine Islands. WW-II.

GREEN -- Code name for Mexico. WW-II.

GREEN BANK -- Strategic Army Command peacetime military test, 1962.

GREEN DIAMOND EXPRESS ROUTE -- Allied military trucking route for movement of supplies from dumps and depots in Cotentin area to rail loading points at Avranches and Dol-de-Bretagne, France. October 1944, WW-II.

GREEN DIAMOND ROUTE -- U.N. east coast military transportation route from Pusan to Taegu, Korea. See also RED DIAMOND ROUTE. Korean Conflict.

GREEN DRAGONS -- Nickname for Landing Ships, Tank (LST's); given by U.S. Marines in Pacific because of jungle camouflage. WW-II.

GREEN HILL -- (1) Military name for Djebel Azag or Hill 396, west of Djefna, Tunisia. 1942-43, WW-II.

  (2) Military name for topographic feature near Mubo, northeastern New Guinea, inland from Huon Gulf. 1943, WW-II.

GREEN HILLS -- Name for peacetime military maneuver stressing combat training for chemical, biological and radiological warfare.

GREEN HORNETS -- Nickname given by staff of U.S. Office of the Chief of Military History to green-bound volumes in series, "United States Army in World War II."

GREEN LINE -- New name given to German GOTHIC LINE across Italy in June 1944 when Allies began to threaten positions. WW-II.

GREEN LINE II -- Hastily executed German defense line about ten miles behind GOTHIC LINE in Italy. September 1944, WW-II.

GREEN MANIFEST PASSENGERS -- Passengers on U.S. Air Transport Command GREEN PROJECT flights from overseas to U.S. May-September 1945, WW-II.

GREEN, OPERATION -- German plan for military action against Czechoslovakia with 1 October 1938 as target date.

GREEN PEAK -- U.S. military name for eastern spur ridge of Sobuk-san mountain mass, Korea. Korean Conflict.

GREEN, PLAN -- See VERT, PLAN

GREEN PROJECT -- Movement by U.S. Air Transport Command from overseas to U.S. of military personnel for reassignment or discharge from service. May-September 1945, WW-II.

GREEN QUAIL -- An early name for QUAIL.

GREEN ROOM -- A name, current in the 1950's for the Command Center of the Cape Canaveral Central Control building.

GREEN, TASK FORCE -- Armored force, part of CENTER TASK FORCE, which landed at X BEACH near Oran, Algeria. See also TASK FORCE RED. November 1942, WW-II.

GREENE HORNETS -- Special U.S. Army intelligence and reconnaissance patrol of 12 men in action near Schmidt, Germany. Commanded by First Lieutenant Jack B. Greene. November 1944, WW-II.

GREENFLASH -- Name for peacetime military exercise.

GREENHOUSE -- U.S. nuclear weapons test at Eniwetok Proving Ground, Marshall Islands. Spring, 1951.

GREENLIGHT -- (1) Name given to Canadian force participating in landing on Kiska, Aleutian Islands, Operation COTTAGE, and its special preparatory training. Summer 1943, WW-II.

(2) Allied system of expedited shipment of ammunition and engineer construction materials from England to Normandy beachheads after OVERLORD. Ships carrying these supplies had large green disk painted on bow. 21 June-23 July 1944, WW-II.

GREENLINE -- Operation by British 12th Corps to seize high ground south of Evrecy, near Caen, France. Preliminary to Operation GOODWOOD. 15 July 1944, WW-II.

GREENSPRING -- Lulakuvi, New Britain. WW-II.

GREENWOOD -- Durazzo, Albania. WW-II.

GREIF, OPERATION -- German plan to spread confusion at beginning of their Ardennes offensive; involved using German officers and men, dressed in U.S. uniforms and driving U.S. vehicles, to issue false orders and seize key positions; also included air drop by 800 parachutists in Malmedy, Belgium, area. Directed by S.S. Colonel Count Otto Skorzeny. December 1944, WW-II.

GRENADE -- U.S. 9th Army northeastward drive across Roer River, Germany, to clear area west of Rhine River between Duesseldorf and Wesel; complementary to Canadian Operation VERITABLE. Postponed from 10 February to 23 February 1945 because Germans blew Roer dams and created formidable water barrier. WW-II.

GRENADIER HILL -- Military name for Djebel Bou Mouss or Hill 250 near Medjez el Bab, Tunisia. Attacked by 754th Grenadier Regiment of German 334th Infantry Division, 20-21 April 1943. WW-II.

GRETA -- Hurricane. 30 October - 6 November 1956. Developed near Jamaica, moved northward across Cuba and through southeastern Bahamas, looped southeastward over Atlantic, and finally turned northeastward and dissipated in mid-Atlantic. Caused several million dollars surf and tide damage along Florida and island coasts.

GREW -- Code name for Australia. WW-II.

GREYHOUND -- (1) Italian World War II Macchi C.205 aircraft. See VELTRO.

(2) Borgen Bay, New Britain. WW-II.

GRIDIRON -- U.N. code name for portion of Wonsan harbor, North Korea. Korean Conflict.

GRINDSTONE -- (1) Lolobata Airdrome, Halmabera Island, Netherlands East Indies. WW-II.

(2) Mokmer, New Guinea. WW-II.

GRIPFAST -- Allied plan for attack on north and central Burma. Modification of TARZAN. 1943-44, WW-II.

GRITS -- Kapuluk River, New Britain. WW-II.

GRIZZLEY BEARS -- Name for Royal Canadian Air Force Squadron Number 411.

GRIZZLY -- Canadian military name for ridge west of Agira, Sicily. July 1943, WW-II.

GRIZZLY II, EXERCISE -- Training exercise in England, directed by 2nd Canadian Corps; first time Canadian 4th Armored Division exercised as a unit with all arms and services participating. Fall 1943, WW-II.

GRIZZLY BEAR -- Nickname for German close-support weapon, mounting a short-barreled howitzer in a high, armored superstructure. WW-II.

GROSBEAK -- Shinchiku, Formosa. WW-II.

GROUNDHOG -- Nowra, New South Wales, Australia. WW-II.

GROUNDSMAN -- Cape Sudest, New Guinea. WW-II.

GRUBWORM -- Transfer by air of over 25,000 troops and equipment of Chinese 14th and 22nd Divisions and other units from Burma to China. Directed by Colonel S.D. Grubbs of U.S. 10th Air Force. 5 December 1944-5 January 1945, WW-II.

GRUMPY -- Balboa, Canal Zone. WW-II.

GUARDIAN ANGEL -- Type of early parachute used by British. 1917.

GUARDSMAN -- Dive bomber version of the Republic 2-PA Model 200 of 1940. Did not enter production.

GUAVA -- Daumie Island, Solomon Islands. WW-II.

GUILD -- Agulupella, New Britain. WW-II.

GUILDHALL -- Aikon Hamlet, New Britain. WW-II.

GUINEA PIG, USS -- Nickname for U.S. Navy LST 386 because she performed work during Sicilian operation never done before by Landing Ship, Tank (LST), such as serving as midget aircraft carrier, floating stable, and anchor for causeway. July 1943, WW-II.

GULFSTREAM -- (1) Grumman twin-turboprop executive transport. First delivery made in 1959.

(2) Name for U.S. Army peacetime military exercise.

GULL -- (1) Popular name for U.S. Army five-ton amphibious truck.

(2) Three-seat cabin monoplane by Percival Aircraft of England, 1933.

(3) Nickname for Russian I-153 during its Spanish Civil War service. See CHAIKA.

(4) U.S. market name for Piaggio P.136-L twin-pusher flying boat now in production.

(5) Allied exercise, held in United Kingdom, to test loading and landing of personnel and vehicles from Landing Ships, Tank (LST's). See also SNIPE, NUDGER. March 1944, WW-II.

GULL FORCE -- Australian troops sent to Amboina, Dutch East Indies. December 1941, WW-II.

GULLCRY -- Palau Island, Palau Islands. WW-II.

GULLIVER -- Plan for development of U.S. fighter air bases on Goodenough Island, and at Milne Bay and Buna during New Guinea campaign. WW-II.

GULLY, THE -- Canadian name for ravine south of Ortona, Italy. December 1943, WW-II.

GUMDROP -- Christmas Island, Line Islands. WW-II.

GUMTREE ROAD -- Military name for road from El Guettar to Mahares, Tunisia. Spring 1943, WW-II.

GUN BUS -- British two-seat fighter built by Vickers Aircraft early in World War II.

GUN LAZY BOYS -- Nickname U.S. gunfire liaison officers who worked with the Army in advanced, exposed observation posts on shore spotting targets for naval fire. WW-II.

GUN POST -- U.S. Air Force high-altitude air refueling area over North Carolina-South Carolina-Virginia.

GUN VAL PROJECT -- Combat tests in Korea of eight F-86F Sabrejet aircraft equipped with 20-mm. cannon. Spring 1953, Korean Conflict.

GUNMAN -- Galena, Alaska. WW-II.

GUNMETAL -- Messina, Sicily. WW-II.

GUNROOM -- Gander Lake, Newfoundland. WW-II.

GUNSMITH -- Torres Strait, Australia. WW-II.

GUSTAV LINE -- Strongly fortified southern portion of German WINTER LINE in Italy from Monte Cassino along west bank of Rapido-Gari-Garigliano River to Gulf of Gaeta. Name taken from letter G in German phonetic alphabet. 1943-44, WW-II.

GWEN -- (1) Typhoon. 2-7 August 1947. First detected in central Philippine Sea. Moved northward at first, then weakened as it turned northeastward and passed southeast of Japan out over the North Pacific.

(2) Hurricane. 4 October 1960. Detected by ship about 800 miles west of Acapulco, Mexico, but no further reports of the storm were obtained. Presumably dissipated between Mexico and Hawaii.

GYMKHANA-ROADMAKER -- U.S. Navy plan for capture of Mortlock and Truk, Caroline Islands, by 1 August 1944. Part of GRANITE. WW-II.

GYMNAST -- Early Allied plan for invasion of North Africa, referring to either the American idea of landing at Casablanca or the British plan for landing farther eastward on the Mediterranean coast. Often used interchangeably with SUPER-GYMNAST. See also TORCH. 1941-42, WW-II.

GYROSCOPE -- Name for U.S. peacetime military operation.

H

H DAY -- Day of U.S. landings on island of Palawan, Philippines. 28 February 1945, WW-II.

H, FORCE -- One of two major forces of British Navy in Mediterranean. Was to rendezvous in Ionian Sea under heel of Italy and feint toward Greece during HUSKY, the invasion of Sicily. See also Z, FORCE. July 1943, WW-II.

H HOUR -- General military term, with specific applications, for hour on which hostilities, an operation, or an exercise commences, or is planned to commence. Along with term, D DAY, originated in World War I.

H, OPERATION -- See STICKATNAUGHT

H-WATER -- Name for peacetime military operation.

HA GO OPERATION -- Japanese offensive in Arakan, Burma, designed to mislead British and make them contain forces in area, as a preliminary to U GO OPERA-TION. Began 4 February 1944, WW-II.

HAAW -- Acronym for U.S. Army Heavy Antitank/Assault Weapon proposed by the Army in its fiscal year 1963 budget to Congress; development delayed. No de-tails are available beyond the name of the weapon.

HABAKKUKS -- Proposed artificial landing fields made out of reinforced ice for use in ocean or English Channel; a British conception. WW-II.

HABFORCE -- British troops sent from Trans-Jordan across desert to relieve Habban-iya, besieged by rebels in Iraq, May 1941. See also GOLDEN SQUARE. Later active in Syria. WW-II.

HABO -- British Coastal Command night air patrol covering English Channel from point near Cherbourg to point near Boulogne, France. WW-II.

HACKBUT -- Calek, New Guinea. WW-II.

HACKNEY -- Lubang Island, Philippine Islands. WW-II.

HACKSAW -- McGrath, Alaska. WW-II.

CODE NAMES DICTIONARY

HACKSAW RIDGE -- U.S. military name for eastern end of Urasoe-Mura Escarpment on Okinawa. Also called Maeda Escarpment and Big Escarpment. 1945, WW-II.

HADDOCK -- (1) Agaris River, New Britain. WW-II.

(2) British operation to bomb northern Italy from airfields in Marseilles area, France. June 1940, WW-II.

HADES -- Makassar Strait, Netherlands East Indies. WW-II.

HADRIAN -- Nickname for the Waco CG-4 combat glider. Nearly 14,000 built during World War II.

HAEMATITE -- Funafuti Island, Ellice Islands. WW-II.

HAIFA -- Code name for Canadian 5th Armoured Division, used in deception operation PENKNIFE, during movement of Canadian troops from Italy to northwestern Europe. February - March 1945, WW-II.

HAIL STORM -- Name for peacetime military maneuver stressing combat training for chemical, biological and radiological warfare.

HAILSTONE -- U.S. aircraft carrier raid on Truk, Caroline Islands. Part of GRANITE. 17-18 February 1944, WW-II.

HAIRBRUSH -- Puruata Harbor, Bougainville, Solomon Islands. WW-II.

HAIRLESS -- Middleburg Island Airdrome, New Guinea. WW-II.

HAIRLESS JOE -- U.N. code name for Kalma Pando on Wonsan harbor, North Korea. See also SQUARE HEAD. Korean Conflict.

HAIRPIN HILL -- Military name for topographic feature west of Monglo, Luzon, Philippine Islands. Taken by U.S. 148th Infantry Regiment on 15 April 1945, WW-II.

HALB-SOLDATEN -- (English: Half-soldiers) German Wehrmacht slang for over-age and poorly trained troops. WW-II.

HALBERD -- (1) Concrete caissons serving as breakwaters in artificial harbors used by Allies against Japan. WW-II.

(2) British supply convoy from Gibraltar to island of Malta. September 1941, WW-II.

HALBERSTADT -- Two-place German fighter/observation scout biplane of World War One.

HALCON -- Spanish CASA 202 light transport. First flew 1952.

HALF MOON HILL -- See CRESCENT HILL

HALF-SOLDIERS -- See HALB-SOLDATEN

HALFTERM -- Code name for Manchukuo. WW-II.

HALFWAY -- Georgetown, British Guiana. WW-II.

HALIBUT -- West Coast Surigao, Philippine Islands. WW-II.

HALIFAX -- (1) Handley-Page British bomber developed for the Royal Air Force in 1940. Flew night missions against key Nazi targets during World War II.

(2) Canadian military name for objective on ROYAL CANADIAN AVENUE near San Leonardo, Italy. See also TORONTO. December 1945, WW-II.

HALITUS -- Gulrol Creek, New Guinea. WW-II.

HALLAM -- U.S. reactor under construction by Consumers Public Power District of Nebraska.

HALLIE -- Name reserved by meteorologists for tropical cyclone in the North Atlantic.

HALLUCINATION -- Meningo, New Guinea. WW-II.

HALPRO -- Acronym for Halverson Project to send group of 23 B-24 bombers from U.S. to China for bombing Japan; under command of U.S. Colonel Harry A. Halverson; detained in Middle East for service against Germans and Italians. June 1942, WW-II.

HALTER -- Kwaiapan Bay, New Britain. WW-II.

HALVERSON PROJECT -- See HALPRO

HAM -- Nickname for Animal Number 65, a 37-pound chimpanzee who rode in REDSTONE rocket during first U.S. suborbital flight, 31 January 1961. So named because his behavior was described as being "half ham, half human."

HAMILCAR -- British heavy-cargo glider of World War II built by General Aircraft Limited. Also a twin-engine powered model.

HAMILTON -- Natamo, Solomon Islands. WW-II.

HAMMER -- Bombardment of Reggio, South Italy. 31 August 1943, WW-II.

HAMMER, OPERATION -- Proposed Allied frontal attack on Trondheim, Norway. Also known as Operation Boots. Revived as OPERATION HAMMER 2. Canceled 19 April 1940, WW-II.

HAMMER 2, OPERATION -- Plan to capture or neutralize forts at mouth of Trondhemsfiord, Norway. See also HAMMER. Canceled 26 April 1940, WW-II.

HAMMOCK -- Molopun, New Britain. WW-II.

HAMP -- Allied code name for clipped-wing version of World War II Mitsubishi Navy Zero Mark II. Also called Hap. See ZEKE.

HAMPDEN -- Handley-Page twin-engine medium bomber ordered by the Air Ministry of Great Britain in 1936 and used in World War II.

HAMPER -- Lamogai, New Britain. WW-II.

HAMSTRING -- Membe Reef, New Britain. WW-II.

HANDCUFF -- Operation for capture of Rhodes Aegean Sea. WW-II.

HANDI-TALKIE -- See HANDY TALKIE

HANDICAP -- Fairbanks, Alaska. WW-II.

HANDIE-TALKIE -- See HANDY TALKIE

HANDKERCHIEF -- Eil Malk Island, Palau Islands. WW-II.

HANDLE -- Mt. Gulu, New Britain. WW-II.

HANDS UP -- Allied plan to capture Quiberon Bay, France, by combined airborne and amphibious operation if complete stalemate occurred in Normandy bridgehead area in summer 1944. WW-II.

HANDSOME -- Gulkana, Alaska. WW-II.

HANDSPRING -- Gumbi, New Guinea. WW-II.

HANDY TALKIE -- U.S. two-way voice radio set, SCR 536; battery-powered, weighed 6 pounds, and had range of one and a half miles. Also spelled Handi-Talkie, Handie-Talkie. WW-II.

HANDYMAN -- Kalapiai Island, New Britain. WW-II.

HANGDOG -- Babo, New Guinea. WW-II.

HANGMAN'S HILL -- British military name for topographic feature southeast of Monte Cassino, Italy. So called from gibbet-like appearance of concrete stanchion for aerial ropeway on summit. Captured by Indian troops, 16 March 1944; abandoned, 24 March 1944. WW-II.

HANGNAIL -- Kumarau Bay, New Guinea. WW-II.

HANGOVER -- Vakuta Island, New Guinea. WW-II.

HANNAH -- (1) Typhoon. November 1947. First detected in northern Philippine Sea. Moved northeastward through Bonin Islands and out over North Pacific.

(2) Hurricane. 27 September - 8 October 1959. Formed over Atlantic 600 miles

southeast of Bermuda. Moved westward, then northward between Cape Hatteras and Bermuda, then eastward to mid-Atlantic. Dissipated south of Greenland.

HANNIBAL -- Handley-Page 42 four-engine airliner of 1932. Designed to operate on the Eastern section -- Egypt to India -- of Great Britain's Imperial Airways. See also HERACLES.

HANWOOD -- Bizerte, Tunisia. WW-II.

HAP -- See HAMP and ZEKE

HAPHAZARD -- Kapo Island, New Britain. WW-II.

HAPPY HOME -- U.S. Air Force high-altitude air refueling area over Montana-South Dakota - Wyoming.

HAPPY VALLEY -- Headquarters, about 10 miles from Chungking, China, of SACO, where men received training for guerrilla and intelligency activities behind Japanese lines. WW-II.

HAPPYLARK -- Umnak, Alaska. WW-II.

HARAKIRI GULCH - Name given by U.S. 27th Infantry Division to canyon between steep, cave-studded cliffs in northwest Saipan, south of PARADISE VALLEY. Scene of fighting 5-7 July 1944, WW-II.

HARD-LUCK-I -- Nickname for aircraft carrier, USS Intrepid. WW-II.

HARDGATE, OPERATION -- British 8th Army's part of Allied army group offensive in Sicily. Began 29 July 1943, WW-II.

HARDIHOOD AGREEMENT -- Anglo-Turkish agreement signed April 1943, in which Britain would provide air and ground forces to assist in Turkey's defense if Turkey entered World War II. See also SATURN.

HARDS -- Beaches in southern England paved with concrete slabs and connected with main highways; landing craft could lower ramps and take on men and vehicles for Normandy landings. 1944, WW-II.

HARDTACK -- (1) Rauto, New Britain. WW-II.

(2) U.S. nuclear test series at Eniwetok Proving Ground, Marshall Islands. See also ORANGE and JASON. Summer 1958.

HARDTACK II -- Last series of U.S. nuclear weapons tests held at Nevada Test Site. Fall 1958.

HARDTACK 4 -- Allied landing and reconnaissance on French Coast in vicinity of Le Treport. 26-27 December 1943, WW-II.

HARDTACK 7 -- British landing for purposes of reconnaissance in vicinity of Point Terrible, Channel Island of Sark. December 1943, WW-II.

HARDTACK 21 -- Landing and reconnaissance in vicinity of St. Marcouf Isles, in English Channel. 27 December 1943, WW-II.

HARDTACK 28 -- Allied landing for reconnaissance purposes in vicinity of Gifford Bay Channel Island of Jersey. 25-26 December 1943, WW-II.

HARDWARE -- Tanuan, Philippine Islands. WW-II.

HARE -- (1) Russian Mil Mi-1 helicopter in continuous production since 1950. Latest variant is called Moskvich.

   (2) German air force slang name for a young airman. WW-II.

   (3) U.S. Air Force proposal to power a missile by breaking down the oxygen of the atmosphere into atoms through the action of ultraviolet radiation and subsequently burning the atomic oxygen for propulsive power. No development program initiated, although some Advanced Technology Funds may be allocated to the study.

HARE, EXERCISE -- Anti-invasion exercise involving Canadian 1st Division and 1st Corps troops. April 1941, WW-II.

HARLEM -- Chiling Island, New Britain. WW-II.

HARLEQUIN -- British and Canadian exercise, held in southern England, representing embarkation program for invasion of Continent. August - September 1943, WW-II.

HARLOT -- Au River, New Britain. WW-II.

HARMLESS - Nuvure Island, New Britain. WW-II.

HARMONICA -- Code name for British Guiana. WW-II.

HAROLD, EXERCISE -- Training exercise under direction of 12th British Corps, in which Canadian troops simulated an invasion force attacking the 46th British Division. July 1942, WW-II.

HARP -- Acronym for Australian High Altitude Research Project designed to carry a 750 pound payload to altitudes of 57 miles. Rocket carried to about seven mile altitude by balloon, and then fired by radio command. Also known as ROCKOON because of balloon launch.

HARPOON -- (1) Lockheed PV-2, derived from PV-1 Ventura, served with U.S. Navy during World War II; still flying in various countries.

   (2) Code name for 2nd Australian Corps, Cairns, Australia. WW-II.

(3) British convoy of six merchant ships under powerful escort including one battleship and two aircraft carriers, sailing from United Kingdom to Malta, coinciding with west bound VIGOROUS convoy; two merchantmen reached Malta after heavy air attacks and encounter with Italian fleet; four were sunk. June 1942, WW-II.

HARPSICHORD -- Gulf of Salerno, Italy. WW-II.

HARPUNE -- German cover operations to divert attention from attack on Russia. Divided into two phases: Nord (Norway) and Sued (France and Denmark). Directed at leading Allies to believe that projected attack on England was imminent. May-August 1941, WW-II.

HARPY -- (1) U.S. Army surface-to-air missile designed to be bazooka-fired by the individual soldier against low-flying aircraft. Not under development; concept used by REDEYE.

(2) Takotna, Alaska. WW-II.

HARRIET -- (1) Typhoon. 26-29 July 1952. Formed in Philippine Sea east of Luzon. Moved northwestward through Luzon Strait and into China just east of Hong Kong.

(2) Typhoon. 19-27 September 1956. Formed over central Philippine Sea. Moved northwestward for a time, then recurved northeastward across Ryukyu Islands, skirted southeast coast of Japan and lost force. See also IVY.

(3) Typhoon. 25-31 December 1959. Formed between islands of Truk and Ponape. Moved northwestward, passed south of Guam, and turned westward across central Philippines, causing five deaths and extensive damage. Dissipated over South China Sea.

(4) Tropical storm. 25-26 October 1962. Formed near coast of Thailand and moved inland into that country causing severe flooding, nearly 800 deaths, and 20 million dollars damage.

(5) Name also applied to tropical cyclones in western North Pacific which occurred prior to (1) through (4) above.

HARROW -- Twin-engine heavy bomber built by Handley-Page on a 1936 order from Great Britain's Air Ministry. Production ceased in 1937.

HARRY -- British Eighth Army operation to cross Cosina River, near Faenza, northern Italy, and establish bridgehead. 21-22 November 1944, WW-II.

HARRY OBJECTIVE -- Hill objective for Canadian troops, two and a half miles northwest of Arnara, Italy. May 1944, WW-II.

HART -- Single-engine biplane day bomber built by Great Britain's Hawker Aircraft and in Swedish service in 1933. Another version was the OSPREY. See also DEMON.

CODE NAMES DICTIONARY

HARTFORD -- Meitzen Point, New Britain. WW-II.

HARTMUT -- German submarine operation in support of occupation of Denmark and Norway. April 1940, WW-II.

HARVARD -- (1) British World War II nickname for the North American AT-6 TEXAN aircraft.

(2) Namuramunga, New Britain. WW-II.

HASHISH -- Cape Iris, New Britain. WW-II.

HASP -- Acronym for U.S. Navy High Altitude Sounding Program designed to carry a radar instrument package to altitudes of 20 miles and, by tracking it, to gather atmospheric data during its parachute descent. Used the DART sounding rocket.

HASP, PROJECT -- Series of flights in 1957 to 1961 by the U.S. Air Force to gather upper-air samples after nuclear tests. Used specially-equipped U-2's.

HASTINGS -- Handley-Page transport plane in British service with Royal Air Force in various versions.

HASTY -- Small Allied paratroop mission against German-held bridges in Italy. Part of DIADEM Operation. June 1944, WW-II.

HAT -- Russian Ka-10 experimental one-man helicopter.

HAT IN THE RING -- First American-trained pursuit squadron to fight at the front in World War One, the 94th. Later commanded by Capt. Eddie Rickenbacker.

HATCHERY -- U.N. code name for portion of Wonsan harbor, North Korea. Korean Conflict.

HATCHET -- Mass Mass Island, New Britain. WW-II.

HATHOR -- Goriong, New Guinea.

HATCHET MEN -- Nickname reputedly given during World War II by Germans to U.S. 84th Infantry Division; taken from design on shoulder patch. Also called LINCOLN DIVISION, RAILSPLITTERS.

HATO -- (English translation; Pigeon) Mitsubishi single-engine photo monoplane built in Japan in the mid-1930's.

HATPIN -- U.S. Naval 5th Training Base, British Isles. WW-II.

HATRACK -- Tidal Creek, New Guinea. WW-II.

HATS -- British operation by naval force, starting at Gibraltar, to land supplies at Malta, pass reinforcements to Eastern Mediterranean Fleet, based at Alexandria, Egypt, and attack Italian bases on the way. August-September 1940, WW-II.

HATTIE -- Hurricane. 27-31 October 1961. Formed in southwestern Caribbean Sea. Moved northward at first, then turned westward into British Honduras and Guatemala. Winds over 150 miles per hour and tides 10-11 feet high destroyed 75 per cent of Belize. Caused 274 deaths and 60 million dollars damage.

HAUL -- Name for peacetime military exercise.

HAVOC -- (1) Douglas DB-7/A-20/P-70 aircraft of World War II fame with American, British and French forces. Called Boston by British.

(2) Witat, New Britain. WW-II

HAW-HAW, LORD -- See LORD HAW-HAW

HAWGS -- U.S. Navy nickname for pilots of Vought CORSAIR fighter aircraft. See also ABLE DAWGS. Korean Conflict.

HAWK -- (1) U.S. Air Force acronym for Homing All the Way Killer.

(2) Basic nickname applied to Curtiss P-1, -6, -36 series aircraft starting with the P-1 in 1925. P-36/Hawk 75 used 1939-40 by British and French. Later earned dubious distinction of having been the only American fighter to serve both sides during World War II, when Vichy French used them at Dakar and Rabat.

(3) Light monoplane of miles design and built by the British aircraft firm of Phillips and Powis in 1933.

(4) French turboprop. See EPERVIER.

(5) Polish PZL P.50 pre-World War II fighter plane. See JASTRZAB.

(6) Italian SM.79 tri-motor plane. See SPARVIERO.

(7) U.S. Army surface-to-air, semi-active radar homing missile designed to destroy high-speed aircraft at altitudes from 100-38,000 feet out to ranges of 22 miles. Solid-fueled the missile is deployed in Europe, the U.S. and the Far East. Marine Corps also uses system. Proposal being considered to extend the capability of Hawk to destruction of tactical ballistic missiles.

(8) Name used by Russian cosmonaut Lieutenant Colonel Valery Feodorovich Bykovsky during his orbital flight in VOSTOK V. 14-19 June 1963.

(9) See WARHAWK

HAWKER -- British aircraft.

HAWKEYE -- (1) Grumman W2F shipboard early warning aircraft for U.S. Navy. First flight in 1960.

(2) An early name for the Air Force's SAINT program.

HAWKINS -- Lagore, New Britian. WW-II.

HAWKINS GRENADE -- Allied No. 75 grenade, weighing two and a quarter pounds which could be buried like anti-tank mine, thrown at moving vehicle, or used as portable demolition charge. WW-II.

HAWSER -- Avungai Island, Solomon Sea. WW-II.

HAYABUSA -- (1) Single-engine commercial monoplane built by the Manchuria Airplane Company in the late 1930's.

(2) (English translation: Peregrine Falcon) World War II Japanese fighter. See OSCAR.

HAYATE -- (English translation: Gale) World War II Japanese Nakajima KI.84 fighter plane. See FRANK.

HAYFEVER -- Aloester Island, Louisiade Archipelago. WW-II.

HAYFIELD -- See HUTTON and HAYFIELD

HAYMAKER -- Northern advance in Germany by Canadian II Corps. April 1945, WW-II.

HAZARD -- Naveilpur, New Britain. WW-II.

HAZEL -- (1) Tropical storm. 8-10 October 1953. Formed in Yucatan Channel. Moved northeastward across central Florida and out over the Atlantic. Caused 250,000 dollars damage in Florida.

(2) Hurricane. 5-16 October 1954. Formed near Windward Islands, moved westward into Caribbean, then northward across Haiti and through the Bahamas. Entered the Carolina coast, continued northward through the eastern U.S., and crossed Lake Ontario into Canada. Losses included 95 lives and 252 million dollars in property in the U.S., 78 lives and 100 million dollars in property in Canada, and 400-1000 lives in Haiti.

HEADACHE -- British code name for counter-measures taken against use by Germans of their navigational beams in night bombing operations. Early WW-II.

HEADLAND -- Lashio, China. WW-II.

HEADLINE -- Code name for stevedoring concern of G. Heyn and Son Limited, which controlled port labor in Northern Ireland. WW-II.

HEADSHED -- Royal Canadian Air Force headquarters in Ottawa.

HEADSTRONG -- Kumbum Passage, New Britain. WW-II.

HEADWAY -- Maffin Airdrome, New Guinea. WW-II.

HEAT BREAK, OPERATION -- See MINCEMEAT

HEATBREAK RIDGE -- U.N. name for topographic feature in PUNCHBOWL area, eastern Korea; scene of heavy fighting in September - October 1951.   Korean Conflict.

HEARTH -- Sunda Strait, Java, Netherlands East Indies.   WW-II.

HEARTSTRINGS -- Parry Island, Eniwetok Atoll, Marshall Islands.   WW-II.

HEATH -- Cairo, Egypt.   WW-II.

HEATHER -- Sisigal, New Guinea.   WW-II.

HEATWAVE -- Antigua, West Indies.   WW-II.

HEAVENLY THUNDER -- World War II Japanese Nakajima J5N1 fighter plane. See TENRAI.

HEAVNER -- Tikan, New Britain.   WW-II.

HECHT -- (1) (English translation: Pike) German two-man midget submarine.   WW-II.

(2) One of Germany's earliest attempts to develop a surface-to-air missile; was powered by a hydrogen peroxide engine and designed to carry a high explosive warhead to an altitude of three-four miles at a speed of 650 miles per hour.   One flight test was conducted before the program was abandoned for the FEUERLILIE.

HECTOR HILL -- U.S. military name for topographic feature northwest of Shuri on Okinawa.   1945, WW-II.

HEDGE -- Faielau Island, Solomon Islands.   WW-II.

HEDGEHOG -- U.S. Navy ahead-thrown anti-submarine weapon, Mark-10 and 11, firing 24 contact-fuzed projectiles; adapted from a British design.   See also MOUSETRAP.   Adopted 1942, WW-II.

HEDGEHOGS -- Obstacles used in German beach defenses; made of three lengths of heavy angle-iron bolted together at centers to form large double tripod. WW-II.

HEDONISM -- Tarik Island, Truk Lagoon, Caroline Islands.   WW-II.

HEEZE -- Tamata River, New Guinea.   WW-II.

HELEN -- (1) Nakajima-designed bomber of 1939.   First went into production for Japanese forces in 1941.   Used throughout World War II.

(2) Mitre, New Guinea.   WW-II.

(3) Typhoon. 29 August - 4 September 1945. First detected in southeastern Philippine Sea. Moved northwestward across Taiwan and into China mainland, then turned northeastward to Manchuria.

(4) Typhoon. 9-18 September 1958. Formed southwest of Guam. Moved north-westward over Philippine Sea, then recurved northeastward along southeast coast of Honshu, Japan, and died out northeast of Japan.

(5) Typhoon. 27 July - 3 August 1961. Formed in Philippine Sea. Moved northward through Ryukyus, skirted west coast of island of Honshu, Japan, crossed Korea and dissipated in western Sea of Japan. Caused floods and two deaths in Ryukyus. See also IDA.

(6) Name also applied to tropical cyclones in western North Pacific which occur-red prior to (3) through (5) above.

HELENE -- (1) Typhoon. August 1947. First detected in northern portion of South China Sea. Moved northward into China mainland west of Hong Kong.

(2) Typhoon. 27-28 July 1950. First detected near Iwo Jima, the Pacific. Moved northwestward and dissipated in Tsushima Strait area between Japan and Korea.

(3) Hurricane. 21-29 September 1958. First detected in southern North Atlantic 800 miles east of Puerto Rico. Moved northwestward and approached Caro-lina coast, but recurved northeastward and swept extreme eastern North Carolina, causing eleven million dollars in damage. Remained at sea past Nova Scotia. Crossed Newfoundland and moved eastward across the Atlantic.

HELI-BABY -- Ultra-light Czech helicopter currently under development.

HELICAR -- Italian Agusta A.104 light helicopter. First flight in 1960.

HELIGUN -- U.S. Army 7.62-mm. rapid-fire gun.

HELIOS -- Acronym for an industry-proposed Hetropowered Earth-Launched Inter-Orbital Spacecraft, a combined chemical-nuclear space vehicle for small plan-etary expeditions. The two-stage vehicle could put 60,000 pounds on the moon and lesser amounts on Mars and Venus. Proposed in 1960, it is not under active development.

HELL FIRE PASS -- Name of pass on Burma-Thailand DEATH RAILWAY cut by prisoners of war of Japanese. 1943, WW-II.

HELL FOR LEATHER DIVISION -- Nickname for U.S. 1st Calvalry Division.

HELL ON WHEELS -- Nickname for U.S. 2nd Armored Division

HELL VALLEY -- See PARADISE VALLEY

HELLCAT -- (1) Grumman World Ward II F6F carrier-based U.S. Navy fighter of World War II Pacific fame.

(2) Port Said, Egypt. WW-II.

HELLCATS -- Nickname for U.S. 12th Armored Division.

HELLDIVER -- (1) Curtiss F8C two-seat shipboard biplane fighter of 1932-33. Used by the U.S. Navy.

(2) Curtiss-Wright SB2C dive bomber which made its first flight in 1940 and was used by the U.S. Navy in the Pacific during World War II. U.S. Army Air Forces version was the A-25.

(3) Canadian objective on Ausa River, Italy. September 1944, WW-II.

HELLER -- Canadian anti-tank rocket under development. Reportedly, tested by the U.S. Army.

HELLHOUND -- British plan to bomb Hitler's sanctuary at Berchtesgaden, Germany. Abandoned June 1944, WW-II.

HELL'S POCKET -- Military name for a strongpoint, a cove in mountain wall, south of Mount Tapotchau, central Saipan. Scene of fighting, June 1944, WW-II.

HELL'S POINT -- Military name for topographic feature on New Britain Island. Later renamed TERZI POINT. December 1943, WW-II.

HELLZAPOPPIN RIDGE -- Military name for topographic feature outside THE PERIMETER on Bougainville Island. December 1943, WW-II.

HELMET -- (1) Kaimana, New Guinea. WW-II.

(2) Advanced Research Projects Agency program to investigate a terminal defense system against ballistic missiles.

HELMSMAN -- Calvi, Corsica. WW-II.

HEMISPHERE -- Emuya, New Britain. WW-II.

HEMLOCK -- Gavutu Island, Solomon Islands. WW-II.

HEMLOCK HILL -- U.S. military name for topographic feature south of Yonabaru Okinawa. 1945, WW-II.

HEMSTITCH -- Serragio, Corsica. WW-II.

HEN -- (1) Russian Kamov Ka-15 helicopter in service with Russian Navy since it first appeared in 1956.

(2) Sueng, New Guinea. WW-II.

HEN HILL -- U.S. military name for topographic feature northeast of Shuri, Okinawa. 1945, WW-II.

HENBIT -- Sueng, New Guinea. WW-II.

HENCHMAN -- Mipolok, New Britain. WW-II.

HENLEY -- Hawker light bomber used by Great Britain early in World War II.
Later used as a target-tower.

HENRY, OPERATION -- Preliminary landing of British forces near Namsos, Norway.
See also OPERATION MAURICE. 14 April 140, WW-II.

HEPCAT -- Alau Passage, New Britain. WW-II.

HERACLES -- Handley-Page 42 four-engine airliner designed for England to Egypt
section of Great Britain's Imperial Airways route to India. See also HANNIBAL.

HERALD -- (1) Handley-Page twin-turboprop British commercial transport. First
flown in 1958.

(2) Talmiro, New Guinea. WW-II.

HERALDS -- Acronym for Harbor Echo Ranging and Listening Devices.

HERBERT -- Sigrilo, New Britain. WW-II.

HERBSTNEBEL -- (1) (English translation: Autumn Fog) Proposed German plan to
withdraw behind Po River in Italy. Rejected by Hitler in October 1944. WW-II.

(2) (English translation: Autumn Fog) German code name for their Ardennes offensive. First called Wacht am Rhein (English: Watch on the Rhine).
December 1944, WW-II.

HERBSTREISE -- (English translation: Autumn Journey) Deception measure planned by
Germans to feign landing on northeast coast of Great Britain between Aberdeen
and Newcastle before SEELOEWE landings in the south. Fall 1940, WW-II.

HERCULES -- (1) Lockheed four-engine turboprop troop carrier first delivered to the
U.S. Air Force in December 1956 as the C-130. Also in use by the U.S. Navy,
U.S. Marine Corps, U.S. Coast Guard.

(2) Allied plan to capture island of Rhodes in early 1944. Canceled December
1943, WW-II.

(3) See HERKULES

(4) See NIKE-HERCULES

HEREFORD -- Built by Short-Harland in Belfast from the Handley-Page Hampden
design. This World War II aircraft differed from the original in that it was
powered by inline engines.

HEREFORD POINT -- Ukiangong Point, Gilbert Islands. WW-II.

HERKULES -- (English: Hercules) Planned German operation to capture Malta in summer of 1942. Not carried out. Called by Italians Operation C.3. WW-II.

HERMANN -- Code name for air raid by German Luftwaffe against British 2nd Tactical Air Force bases in Holland and Belgium. 1 January 1945, WW-II.

HERMES -- (1) British post World War II commercial version of the Handley-Page HASTINGS.

(2) Kikiviai, New Britain. WW-II.

HERMES SERIES -- U.S. Army surface-to-surface missile research test program based on the technology of the German V-2, and designed to develop viable weapons of 75 and 150-mile ranges. Over 103 various models of the missile were fired (including component-carrying V-2s and composite BUMPERS) from January 1947 to the end of 1954. Much of present propulsion and guidance technology stems from this test program. Both liquid and solid motors, and inertial and radio-intertial guidance systems, were developed and flight tested.

HERMIT -- Auckland, New Zealand. WW-II.

HERO -- United Kingdom zero energy, gas-cooled reactor experiment at Windscale, England. Part of cooperative gas-cooled reactor exchange program with U.S. Established 1957.

HERON -- (1) Italian World War II Cant Z.506 aircraft. See AIRONE.

(2) British DeHavilland D.H. 114 light transport/executive aircraft now in service.

(3) Small Australian military detachment, installed on Ocean Island in the western Pacific, in February 1941 to serve against attacks by German raiders. WW-II.

HERRINGBONE -- Eskimo Bay, Canada. WW-II.

HERTFORDSHIRE -- Military version of the DeHavilland FLAMINGO.

HESTER -- (1) Kalapiai Island, New Britain. WW-II.

(2) Typhoon. July 1949. First detected in vicinity of Mariana Islands. Moved north-northwestward across Honshu, Japan, into Sea of Japan.

(3) Typhoon. 28 December 1952 - 2 January 1953. Formed in Marshall Islands. Moved westward and passed south of Mariana Islands into Philippine Sea then recurved northeastward and passed out over central North Pacific.

(4) Typhoon. 3-9 October 1957. Formed central Caroline Islands. Moved northwestward at first, then northward passing just east of Guam and near Iwo Jima. Dissipated northeast of Japan.

HETTY HILL -- U.S. military name for topographic feature on Okinawa. 1945, WW-II.

HEXAMETER -- Shimushu Island, Kurile Islands. WW-II.

HEXOSE -- Souaivinda Creek, New Guinea. WW-II.

HEYFORD -- Twin-engine, long-range "Express" night-bomber developed by Great Britain's Handley-Page Limited in the early 1930's.

HI-FI -- Proposed two-megacurie cobalt 60 High Intensity Food Irradiator for U.S. Army Quartermaster Corps' radiation preservation of food. To be located at Sharpe General Depot, Lathrop, California.

HIBISCUS -- Tulagi Island, Solomon Islands. WW-II.

HICKOK -- Laut, New Britain. WW-II.

HICKORY -- Lanau Island, Solomon Islands. WW-II.

HIDROSIS -- Dingalan Bay, Philippine Islands. WW-II.

HIDYNE -- A hydrazine propellant used in place of alcohol in the Army's JUPITER-C space launchings. Its use boosted the missile's thrust by about 12 per cent. Nickname is also spelled Hydyne.

HIEN -- (English translation: Swallow) World War II Japanese fighter. See TONY.

HIFOR -- International code word used to abbreviate "high-level flight weather forecast".

HIGGINS BOATS -- Name for Allied LCVP's (Landing Craft, Vehicle and Personnel). WW-II.

HIGH CARD -- An early name for GENIE.

HIGH LIFE -- U.S. Air Force high-altitude air refueling area over Nebraska-South Dakota-Wyoming.

HIGH POWER -- Cornell University study sponsored by U.S. Defense Department, of extremely high energy (megawatt range) and of microwave radar techniques which could be used to detect and track ballistic missiles. Particularly applicable to NIKE-ZEUS and NIKE-X programs.

HIGH SEAS SPECIAL -- Name for U.S. peacetime military exercise.

HIGH TIDE -- Name for U.S. peacetime military maneuver stressing combat training for chemical, biological and radiological warfare.

HIGHBALL -- (1) U.S. Army two-stage, solid propellant rocket used in tests of the NIKE-ZEUS system in the Pacific. Part of the SPEEDBALL series from Roi-Namur Island.

(2) Gingoog Bay, Mindanao Island, Philippine Islands. WW-II.

HIGHBOY -- Cristobal, Panama. WW-II.

HIGHFLYER -- Damascus, Syria. WW-II.

HIGHJUMP -- U.S. Navy Antarctic Developments Project. 1947.

HIGHSTEP -- Freetown, Sierra Leone, Africa. WW-II.

HIGHWAY -- Caroline Islands. WW-II.

HIGHWAYMAN -- Putu Island, Chusan Archipelago, China. WW-II.

HILDA -- Hurricane. 10-19 September 1955. Formed near Leeward Islands. Moved northwestward at first, then westward, passing north of Puerto Rico and Hispaniola, across southeastern Cuba, the Yucatan Peninsula, the Bay of Campeche and into Mexico near Tampico. Caused 300 deaths and 120 million dollars damage in Tampico area.

HILL TOP -- Name for peacetime military exercise.

HILLBILLIES -- Nickname for U.S. 102nd Infantry Division. Also called OZARKS.

HILLOCK -- Kunming, China. WW-II.

HILLSIDE -- Code name for Ceylon. WW-II.

HINAZURU -- (English translation: Young Crane) Japanese commercial monoplane version of the British Airspeed ENVOY built under pre-World War II license, in Japan, by Mitsubishi.

HINDSIGHT -- Somek, New Guinea. WW-II.

HINKLE -- Runglo River, Serang Island, Netherlands East Indies. WW-II.

HINTERLAND -- Bitokara, New Britain. WW-II.

HIPPODROME -- Fatu Channel, Chusan Archipelago, China. WW-II.

HISS -- Acronym for High-Intensity Sound Simulator.

HITLER LINE -- See ADOLF HITLER LINE

HO HO CRY -- Special dog-barking sound used by Australian 9th Infantry Division as battle cry from El Alamein onwards. WW-II.

HOARDINGS -- German wide-beam radar scanning installations; used to reinforce FREYA, a German aircraft reporting device. Also called MAMMUT. WW-II.

HOBBLE -- Mt. Karberg, New Britain. WW-II.

HOBGOBLIN -- Pantelleria Island, Mediterranean Sea. WW-II.

HOBNOB -- Tactical air-direction post supporting U.S. X Corps in Korea. Korean Conflict.

HOCKSHAW -- Annen Point, New Britain. WW-II.

HOG -- Ka-18 four-seat development of the HEN: first appeared 1957 and is used in a variety of roles by the Soviet Union.

HOGAN'S GOAT, OPERATION -- Name given to attack on Nasipit area, Mindanao, Phillipine Islands. April 1945, WW-II.

HOGCALLER -- Lombok Strait, Java Island, Netherlands East Indies. WW-II.

HOLBEIN -- Code name for Norway. WW-II.

HOLD FAST -- Name for NATO peacetime military exercise.

HOLE, THE -- Excavation costing 23,000,000 million dollars under pineapple fields near Schofield Barracks, Hawaii, intended for under-ground airplane assembly. WW-II.

HOLE-IN-THE-WALL -- British and Canadian rest and recreation facility for war-weary troops in Ortona, Italy. Named after London pub near Waterloo Station. WW-II.

HOLIDAY -- Miligui Point, Solomon Islands. WW-II.

HOLLY -- (1) Canton Island, Phoenix Islands. WW-II.

(2) Point Cruz Signal Tower, Guadalcanal, Solomon Islands. WW-II.

HOLLYHOCK -- Beaufort Bay, Guadalcanal, Solomon Islands. WW-II.

HOLY MOSES -- Nickname for high velocity aircraft rocket designed as an air-to-surface, 950-miles per hour Navy bomb. Patterned after British and Russian developments, and introduced in the Pacific in July 1944. See also RAM. WW-II.

HOME RUN PROJECT -- See WHITE PROJECT

HOME SWEET HOME -- Nickname for British developed radar apparatus, H2S, completely self-contained within an aircraft, which scanned territory over which it passed and presented rough picture on a cathode ray screen. WW-II.

HOMECOMING, OPERATION -- Release by U.N. Command of 27,000 Korean prisoners of war who had been reclassified according to Geneva Convention as civilian internees. June-August 1952, Korean Conflict.

HOMEFRONT -- Name for peacetime military operation.

HOMER -- U.S. code name for Boggerik Island, Marshall Group. WW-II.

HOMERUN -- Valdez, Alaska. WW-II.

HOMETOWN TACTICS -- U.S. attack procedure in which stream of individual aircraft crossed target at one minute intervals, bombing individually by radar. Korean Conflict.

HOMINY -- Potnangara River, New Britain. WW-II.

HONCHOS -- Nickname for experienced and able Communist pilots of MIG jet fighter aircraft in Korea; probably instructor pilots. Honcho means boss in Japanese. See also STUDENTS. Korean Conflict.

HONDURAS -- Combined Western Hemisphere defensive exercise, 1962.

HONEST JOHN -- U.S. Army unguided, solid propellant, free rocket capable of carrying a nuclear warhead to a range of about 12 miles. Deployed with U.S. troops for close support of combat operations. Military designation M31. Improved version with approximately 30-mile range just entering inventory. Designation: M50. Advanced model called Slim John. See also CHOPPER JOHN and LANCE.

HONEY -- Ulawa Island, Solomon Islands. WW-II.

HONEYCOMB -- (1) Kaurokabin Point, New Britain. WW-II.

   (2) U.S. study of cold criticals for ROVER reactors at Los Alamos Scientific Laboratory, New Mexico.

HONEYDEW -- Olevuga Island, Solomon Islands. WW-II.

HOOK -- Soviet Mi-6, called the world's largest helicopter; powered by twin-turbines; entered service in 1961.

HOOK, BATTLE OF THE -- Name for military action in Korea by U.S. Marine Corps. October 1952, Korean Conflict.

HOOKER -- British brigade landing in Italy north of Pizzo during Operation BAYTOWN. 8 September 1943. WW-II.

HOPE -- (1) Typhoon. 4-12 August 1955. Formed in east-central Philippine Sea. Moved northeastward and passed southeast of Japan out over the Pacific.

   (2) Tropical depression. 18-19 August 1959. Formed and dissipated in South China Sea west of Luzon.

   (3) Typhoon. 16-24 May 1962. First detected northeast of Mindanao, Philippines. Moved northwestward and northward across Philippines, then northeastward and merged with other storm system south of Japan. Brought beneficial rains to Japan.

(4) Name also applied to tropical cyclones in western North Pacific which occurred prior to (1) through (3) above.

HOPE, MR. -- Assumed name used by a Colonel Peresitch of Yugoslav General Staff during talks in Athens with Field Marshal Lord Wilson, commander of British troops in Greece, who used name, MR. WATT. March 1941, WW-II.

HOPEFUL -- Roebourne, Australia. WW-II.

HOPGARDEN -- Baler Bay, Luzon, Philippine Islands. WW-II.

HOPI -- U.S. Navy air-to-surface missile for use by carrier-based aircraft. Not under active development as a weapon, but has been used with instrumented payloads as a sounding rocket (Hop-Dart, Hopi-Plus and Hopi-Pima) capable of carrying 10 pounds to altitudes of 60 miles. All the HOPI vehicles are essentially the same, differing only in the second stage.

HOPI-DART -- See HOPI

HOPI-PIMA -- See HOPI

HOPI-PLUS -- See HOPI

HOPKINS -- North Cape, New Ireland. WW-II.

HORACE -- Higgins Point, New Britain. WW-II.

HORIZON -- 1959 U.S. Army study of the techniques, equipment, scheduling, costs and other requirements for a manned lunar landing before 1965.

HORLICKS -- Allied operation against Biak Island, off north coast of Netherlands New Guinea, carried out by CYCLONE Task Force. 27 May - 30 August 1944, WW-II.

HORNBLOWER -- German preparation for demolition of Alexandria Harbor, Egypt, Stage Two; not brought into force. Depth charges and explosives were ready but not placed in positions in order that plan should not be disclosed to Egyptians. 29 June 1942, WW-II.

HORNET -- (1) German 88-mm. tank-destroyer gun. WW-II.

(2) Curtiss 18B biplane follow-on to the 18T tri-plane. Delivered in 1919.

(3) DeHavilland D.H. 103, first flown in 1944, but too late to see World War II operational service for Great Britain. Joined Royal Air Force 1946. Second version was the SEA HORNET.

(4) Yugoslav aircraft. See STRSLJEN.

(5) German Me-410 aircraft. See HORNISE.

(6) Name for Royal Canadian Air Force Squadron Number 443.

HORNISE -- (English translation: Hornet) Messerschmitt 410, initially ordered into production in 1942 as a light bomber for the Luftwaffe.

HORNPIPE -- Allied code word used in place of OVERLORD in message of 4 June 1944 notifying troops of postponement of cross-channel invasion from 5 to 6 June. HORNPIPE BOWSPRIT meant "OVERLORD delayed". WW-II.

HORRIFIED -- Code name for Sicily. WW-II.

HORROR -- Ulithi Island, Caroline Islands. WW-II.

HORSA -- Huge troop-carrying glider built by Airspeed for Great Britain in World War II.

HORSE -- (1) Russian Yak-24 dual-rotor transport helicopter. Entered production in 1954.

(2) Alice Channel, British North Borneo. WW-II.

HORSE ISLAND -- Butaritari Island, Gilbert Islands. WW-II.

HORSE, OPERATION -- Unsuccessful attack by British 47th Royal Marine Commando on German bridgehead at Kapelsche Veer, harbor on Maas River, Netherlands. See also OPERATION ELEPHANT. 13-14 January 1945, WW-II.

HORSEFLIES -- Allied name used in Italy for liaison pilots who directed fighter-bombers to obscure close support targets. WW-II.

HORSEPLAY -- Cagayen River Valley, Mindanao, Philippine Islands. WW-II.

HORSERADISH -- U.S. tactical air-direction center at Pyongtaek, Korea. Korean Conflict.

HORSESHOE, THE -- Name for deep curve in Masan road, four miles east of Koman-ni, Korea. Korean Conflict.

HORSESHOE HILL -- Military name for topographic feature on New Georgia. Summer 1943, WW-II.

HORSESHOE RIDGE -- (1) Military name for topographic feature on Cebu, Philippine Islands. Taken by U.S. 182nd Infantry Regiment on 4 April 1944, WW-II.

(2) U.S. military name for topographic feature near Kochi, Okinawa. 1945, WW-II.

HORSESHOE ROUTE -- British air transport route from Durban, Natal, north up east coast of Africa, down Persian Gulf to India; passage between Durban and United Kingdom was by ship. WW-II.

HORSESHOE VALLEY -- See MORTIMER VALLEY

HORSESHOE WOODS -- Small irregular-shaped patch of woods across from Dornot, France on east bank of Moselle River, apparently named because of U.S. horseshoe-shaped defense set-up there. WW-II.

HORSESHOES -- Chukea Island, Chusan Archipelago, China. WW-II.

HORSLEY -- Torpedo bomber built by England's Hawker Aircraft in 1933. Also used by Denmark and called Dantorp.

HOSPITABLE -- Melbourne, Australia. WW-II.

HOST -- Tutuila, Samoan Islands. WW-II.

HOT POINT -- U.S. Navy proposal for an air-to-surface missile with a nuclear warhead for use against aircraft on the ground. Not approved for development.

HOT ROCKS -- Nickname for Mount Suribachi, Iwo Jima. Also called Mount Plasma. 1945, WW-II.

HOT SHOT -- Early name for U.S. Navy SPARROW.

HOTEL -- Code word for letter "H" in a phonetic alphabet, used to avoid possibility of a misunderstanding in transmitting messages. See also HOW.

HOTFOOT -- Proposed U.S. Navy aircraft carrier strike against Tokyo, Japan, immediately prior to SAN ANTONIO I. Indefinitely postponed. 12 November 1944, WW-II.

HOTHOUSE -- Kotzebue, Alaska. WW-II.

HOTPLATE -- Operations against New Guinea. WW-II.

HOTSHOT -- Dauli, New Britain. WW-II.

HOTSPUR II -- Glider developed for Great Britain by General Aircraft. Used to expedite pilot-transition from powered flight to gliders during World War II.

HOUND -- Russian Mi-4 helicopter. More than a thousand have entered service since 1952.

HOUND DOG -- U.S. Air Force, air-launched, aerodynamic missile for use by Strategic Air Command for suppressive fire of enemy air defenses. Two, and later four, missiles will be carried under the wings of the B-52G jet bomber. Missile carries nuclear warhead to a range of more than 500 miles, and was initially an interim system for the SKYBOLT missile. However, it now appears it will be retained in the U.S. inventory. Military Designation: GAM-77. See also RISE.

HOUR -- Upolu, Samoan Islands. WW-II.

HOURGLASS -- Anambas Islands, Malay Peninsula. WW-II.

HOURGLASS DIVISION -- Nickname for U.S. 7th Infantry Division; taken from design of shoulder insignia.

HOUSE FIREMAN BEACH -- Military name for topographic feature in Arawe Peninsula, New Britain. Site of Allied landing, 15 December 1943, WW-II.

HOUSEHOLD -- Hollandia Airdrome, New Guinea. WW-II.

HOUSTON -- Matenai Island, New Britain. WW-II.

HOW -- (1) Code word for letter "H" in a phonetic alphabet, used to avoid possibility of a misunderstanding in transmitting messages. See also HOTEL.

    (2) Tropical storm. 1-4 October 1950. Formed in Gulf of Mexico and moved into Mexico north of Tampico. Caused little damage.

    (3) Hurricane. 1-7 October 1951. Formed in Yucatan Channel moved northward into Gulf of Mexico, then turned eastward across southern Florida as weak storm. After leaving Florida, storm intensified to hurrican force as it moved northeastward into Atlantic.

HOW HILL -- (1) U.S. military name for topographic feature on Okinawa. 1945, WW-II.

    (2) Name for hill 750 near Chinhung-ni, Korea. Korean Conflict.

HOWARD -- Misambral, New Britain. WW-II.

HOWLIN' MAD -- Nickname for Lieutenant General Holland M. Smith, U.S. Marine Corps. WW-II.

HOYDEN -- Kwaiapan Plantation, New Britain. WW-II.

HUBBLE -- Wabula, Celebes, Netherlands East Indies. WW-II.

HUBERT -- U.S. code name for Boggerlapp Island, Marshall Group. WW-II.

HUCKLEBERRY -- Tassafaronga, Guadalcanal, Solomon. WW-II.

HUDDLE -- U.S. code name for occupation of Ndeni, Santa Cruz Islands; proposed for fall 1942, but never carried out. WW-II.

HUDDLE, EXERCISE -- Peacetime maneuver for U.S. airborne troops which preceded Exercise SWARMER in 1950.

HUDSON -- (1) World War II British designation, and, later, U.S. Army Air Forces, for the Lockheed Model 14 1937 airliner. Used as the A-29, C-63 and AT-18 by the Army Air Forces. British slang was Old Boomerang.

(2) Munda Bar, Solomon Islands. WW-II.

(3) Santiago, Chile. WW-II.

HUGHESLIERS -- Volunteer force consisting of men of 55 years of age and older, formed by Colonel A.W. Hughes for defense of Hong Kong. December 1941, WW-II.

HUGO -- U.S. Navy/Weather Bureau program to study techniques for photographing meteorological phenomena from sounding rockets. Using the NIKE-CAJUN booster, a 38 pound camera has photographed cloud cover over an area of 500,000 square miles. Firings are conducted from Wallops Station, Virginia.

HUMMING BIRD -- (1) U.S. Army surveillance aircraft to replace OV-1.

(2) Brazilian helicopter. See BEIJA-FLOR.

(3) Dutch helicopter. See KOLIBRIE.

HUMPBACK -- La Fe, Cuba. WW-II.

HUNDRED METER HILL -- U.S. military name for eastern extension of Wana Ridge on Okinawa. Also called Knob Hill. 1945, WW-II.

HUNTER -- Hawker swept-wing aircraft of many versions; serving with a host of foreign countries. The latest variant, F.G.A.9, first flew in 1959.

HUNTER GROUPS -- Name for volunteers from Chinese 4th Field Army, who were promised "hero" decorations and furloughs for the destruction of three U.N. aircraft in any 90-day period. Began 4 January 1951, Korean Conflict.

HUNTER-KILLER OPERATIONS -- Procedure used by U.S. Air Force in Korea whereby a "Hunter" B-26 medium bomber would select site for roadblock and establish it with fire, general purpose, and Butterfly bombs; then, another B-26, the "Killer" would be called in to attack enemy vehicles backed up behind roadblock. Devised September 1952, Korean Conflict.

HURL -- Funafuti, Ellice Islands. WW-II.

HURRIBOMBER -- British Hawker. See HURRICANE.

HURRICANE -- (1) Britain's most versatile fighter, the Hawker F36 prototype first flew in 1935. Destroyed more German aircraft during the World War II Battle of Britain than all other aircraft combined. Other versions were: SEA HURRI-CANE, Hurribomber, CAN OPENER.

(2) Japanese World War II Mitsubishi A7M1 Reppu shipboard fighter. See SAM.

(3) Allied task force under ALAMO assigned to Operations STICKATNAUGHT, HORLICKS, and TABLETENNIS along northern coast of Netherlands New Guinea for which it was split into TORNADO and CYCLONE Task Forces. May- September 1944, WW-II.

HURRICANE I -- Operation, proposed by British, to concentrate power of all Allied air forces in Europe, strategic and tactical, in crushing attack on the Ruhr, Germany. Planned to begin 15 October 1944; canceled. WW-II.

HURRY -- Transport of 12 Hurricane aircraft on British aircraft carrier, H.M.S. Argus, from which they were flown off to Malta. Early August 1940, WW-II.

HUSKIE -- (1) U.S. Army one and one-half ton cargo carrier for arctic use.

(2) Kaman H-43 crash-rescue helicopter in service at nearly every Air Force base in the world. First rolled out in 1958.

HUSKY -- (1) Name for Royal Canadian Air Force Squadron Number 437.

(2) Invasion of southeastern Sicily by British 8th and U.S. 7th Armies. See also ACID, BARK, CENT, DIME, JOSS. Began 10 July 1943, WW-II.

HUSKY NOS. 1-2 -- U.S. paratroop missions in vicinity of Gela, Sicily. 9 and 11 July 1943, WW-II.

HUSTLER -- (1) The world's first supersonic bomber, the delta-wing B-58; U.S. Air Force strategic bomber which made its first flight in November 1956.

(2) Name of the engine used in the AGENA upper stage. Uses liquid propellants to develop 15,000 pound thrust, and has a restart capability. Word is not generally used since the generic term, Agena, is considered to include the engine.

HUTTON and HAYFIELD -- Subplans of TORCH. WW-II.

HYACINTH -- Hurricane. 21-23 October 1960. First located 70 miles south-southeast of Manzanillo, Mexico. Moved northwestward, then turned northward and entered Mexican coast north of Mazatlan.

HYDRA -- U.S. Navy program to determine the feasibility of launching missiles and space boosters from the sea. Basic idea is to tow the missile to the launch site, right it and fire. Some feasibility studies have been conducted. Program is a low-funding effort, in-house project.

HYDRA-1 -- U.S. Navy program which proved the feasibility of sea-launch of rockets and led to the expanded HYDRA II program.

HYDRA II -- U.S. Navy project to study the handling, erection, acceleration, effects and checkout concepts of water launch of missiles and space vehicles. Initiated in 1960 at the U.S. Naval Missile Center, Point Mugu, California. A successful launch was conducted off San Clemente Island in 1961. Further tests are underway.

HYDRANGEA -- Kavin Island, New Britain. WW-II.

HYDRO -- U.S. experiment on jocketed enriched core lateral and base reflector of water studies, used as neutron sources for exponential column. At Los Alamos Scientific Laboratory, New Mexico. Began 1956.

HYDROGEN -- Batangas Bay, Luzon, Philippine Islands. WW-II.

HYDYNE -- See HIDYNE

HYOSCINE -- Adelaide, Australia. WW-II.

HYPO -- Homogeneous water-boiler reactor at Los Alamos Scientific Laboratory, New Mexico. Startup 1944; dismantled 1950.

HYPOCRITE -- Code name for Japan. WW-II.

HYSTERIA -- Pilandimi, New Britain. WW-II.

I

I, BASE -- U.S. naval base, Londonderry, Ireland. WW-II.

I BOATS -- Japanese transport submarines, capable of carrying tiny scout planes. WW-II.

I-GO SERIES -- Japanese series of air-to-surface missiles of mono-plane construction with much wood being used in manufacture. Radio-guided from launch aircraft, it used a hydrogen peroxide engine and had a range of five-seven miles. Developed during World War II; tests were successfully conducted during 1944-45, but it was never used in combat. Three versions, 1A, 1B and 1C, were built.

I OPERATION -- Abortive Japanese air offensive attempting to win air supremacy over the Southern Solomons and Eastern New Guinea. April 1943, WW-II.

ICARUS -- (1) Code name for Honduras. WW-II.

(2) Royal Canadian Air Force practice ground attack on defense of aerodrome. WW-II.

ICE CUBE -- Joint U.S. Army-Air Force and Royal Canadian Air Force peacetime project in the Arctic.

ICE SKATE -- U.S. peacetime project connected with International Geophysical Year research.

ICEBERG -- Allied invasion of Ryukyu Islands. Began 26 March 1945. WW-II.

ICEBERG VII -- Attacks on Sakishima Gunto Island, Japan, by U.S. Naval Air Squadron 4-5 May 1945, WW-II.

ICEBLINK -- Code name for U.S. Secretary of State James F. Byrnes. WW-II.

ICEWAY, PROJECT -- Tests conducted by the U.S. Air Force in 1960-61 to determine the feasibility of using iced-surfaces for air operations.

ICHIGO -- Over-all Japanese operations for east China in 1944. Divided into KOGO and TOGO. WW-II.

ICHOR -- Talifai, New Guinea. WW-II.

ICONIC -- Tetere, Solomon Islands. WW-II.

IDA -- (1) Typhoon. 12-18 September 1945. First detected southeast of Guam. Moved west-northwestward out over Philippine Sea, curved gradually northward through Ryukyu Islands and northeastward through Japan and out over North Pacific.

(2) Typhoon. 10-19 August 1950. Formed in northern Philippine Sea. Moved east-northeastward past Iwo Jima, then southeastward for a time, and finally northeastward out over the Pacific.

(3) Typhoon. 25-28 August 1954. First detected south of Guam. Moved west-northwestward across Philippine Sea, through Balintang Channel and to China mainland near Hong Kong.

(4) Typhoon. 20-26 September 1958. One of the most intense ever experienced, with winds estimated over 250 miles per hour and central pressure about 25.78 inches of mercury. Formed near Guam, moved westward at first, then northward to Honshu, Japan, and dissipated. Caused at least 241 deaths and heavy damage on Honshu.

(5) Typhoon. 28-31 July 1961. Formed southeast of Iwo Jima. Moved northwestward past Iwo Jima and across Ryukyu Islands and merged with typhoon HELEN. Caused little damage.

(6) Name also applied to tropical cyclones in western North Pacific which occurred prior to (1) through (5) above.

IDENTICAL -- Asor, Ulithi Atoll, Yap Islands. WW-II.

IDIOT -- (1) Acronym for Instrumentation Digital On-Line Transcriber.

(2) Surigao Strait, Philippine Islands. WW-II.

IDLEAGE -- Wab Bay, New Guinea. WW-II.

IEGUSUGU PINNACLE -- See PINNACLE, THE

IFF -- Acronym for Identification Friend or Foe; radar instrument enabling aircraft bearing it to pass unmolested through Allied gunbelts and night fighters; absence of it brought these defenses into action. First used in World War II.

IGOR -- See ME

IKARUS -- Proposed German occupation of Iceland. June 1940, WW-II.

ILLEGITIMATE -- Gagil-Tomil Area, Yap Islands. WW-II.

ILLOGICAL -- Hiroshima, Japan. WW-II.

ILSA -- Hurricane. 24-29 September 1958. Formed in Atlantic 800 miles east of Puerto Rico. Moved west-northwestward briefly, then turned northward and northeastward over the open Atlantic.

IMAGINATIVE -- Frederik Hendrik Island, New Guinea. WW-II.

IMI -- Acronym for Improved Manned Interceptor having range of Mach 3.

IMP -- Acronym for Interplanetary Monitoring Probe designed to support the APOLLO project by collecting data on the cislunar radiation environment, interplanetary magnetic field and its relationship with particle fluxes from the sun, to provide help in solar flare prediction. Weighing 125 pounds, and launched by a modified THOR-DELTA, the spacecraft will have a highly elliptical trajectory (apogee 150,000 miles) and will carry eight experiments. First launch proposed for 1963-64.

IMPERATOR -- Proposed large-scale Allied raid on European Continent to last two or three days; inland objectives never set, but armored attack on German Headquarters in Paris discussed. Cancelled through intervention of Prime Minister Winston Churchill June 1942, WW-II.

IMPERIALS -- Name for Royal Canadian Air Force Squadron Number 414.

IMPERSONAL -- Allied occupation of Batavia, Java, Netherlands East Indies. 28-30 September 1945, WW-II.

IMPOSSIBLE BRIDGE -- Bailey bridge, constructed by engineers of 8th Indian Division under difficult conditions, across Moro River south of Rogatti, Italy. December 1943, WW-II.

IMPROMPTU -- Chusan Archipelago, China. WW-II.

IMPROVED HONEST JOHN -- See Honest John

IMPROVER -- Amami O Shima, Japan. WW-II.

INCANTATION -- Labi, Goodenough Island. WW-II.

INCENTIVE -- Tansui (Tainsui), Formosa. WW-II.

INCESSANT -- Kaven Island, Maloelap Atoll, Marshall Islands. WW-II.

INCISOR -- Reggio di Calabria, Italy. WW-II.

INCOME -- Koryu, Formosa. WW-II.

INCREDIBLE -- Tarawa Island, Gilbert Islands. WW-II.

INCUBUS -- Dutch Harbor, Alaska. WW-II.

INDEPENDENCE -- (1) French First Corps offensive against Germans Belfort Gap, western France. Began 14 November 1944, WW-II.

(2) Plan for first French Army offensive against German garrisons on French south-

western coast.   December 1944, WW-II.

INDIA -- Code word for letter "I" in a phonetic alphabet, used to avoid possibility of a misunderstanding in transmitting messages.   See also ITEM.

INDIAN RIVER -- Name for joint U.S. Army-Tactical Air Command peacetime military exercise held on west coast.

INDIAN SUMMER -- Name for U.S. peacetime military exercise.

INDIANHEAD, TASK FORCE -- Special U.S. task force which entered North Korean capital of P'yongyang with advance units of 1st Cavalry Division; had mission to secure and protect specially selected government buildings and foreign compounds until they could be searched for enemy intelligence materials.   October 1950, Korean Conflict.

INDICTMENT -- Pakin Island, Caroline Islands.   WW-II.

INDIGENCE -- San Fernando, Luzon, Philippine Islands.   WW-II.

INDIGO-1 -- Plan for U.S. reinforcement of defenses of Iceland.   1941, WW-II.

INDISPENSABLE -- Ie (Iye) Shima, Nansei Shoto Islands, Japan.   WW-II.

INDUCTION -- U.S. operation against Luzon, Philippines, to be carried out if one against Formosa and Amoy, China, CAUSEWAY, proved impracticable.   Proposed for 15 February 1945 in GRANITE II plan.   WW-II.

INEBRIATE -- Kagi, New Guinea.   WW-II.

INEZ -- (1) Typhoon.   August 1947.   First detected over central Philippine Sea. Moved northwestward over Taiwan and into China mainland.

(2) Name reserved by meteorologists for tropical cyclone in North Atlantic.

INFANTRY -- Ihiya Jima, Nansei Shoto Islands, Japan.   WW-II.

INFATUATE I -- Allied amphibious attack on Flushing, Walcheren Island, southwest Netherlands.   1 November 1944, WW-II.

INFATUATE II -- Seaborn assault by British 4th Special Service Brigade on Westkapelle, Walcheren Island, southwest Netherlands.   See also NELSON.   Began 1 November 1944, WW-II.

INFERNO -- Code name for United States.   WW-II.

INFURIATED GRASSHOPPER -- A wag's nickname for the Santos-Dumont Demoiselle when he first saw the tiny 1909 airplane.

INGA -- Tropical storm.   4-8 November 1961.   Formed and dissipated in southwestern Gulf of Mexico.

INGRAIN -- Buin, Bougainville, Solomon Islands. WW-II.

INGRID -- Typhoon. 11-19 July 1946. First detected in eastern Philippine Sea. Moved west-northwestward across northern Luzon and into China near Hong Kong.

INHERITANCE -- Dadjangas, Mindanao, Philippine Islands. WW-II.

INJUN -- Navy satellite to measure the intensity of radiation in the lower regions of the Van Allen belt. Launched 29 June 1961 as a piggy-back payload on TRAN-SIT IV-A. GREB was also launched and the two secondary satellites failed to separate. Experiments on both functioned normally, however. THOR-ABLE-STAR was used to launch combination payload. See also COMPOSITE I.

INK SPOTS -- North Korean heavy gun batteries on Wonsan harbor, North Korea. Korean Conflict.

INKLING -- Vancouver, British Columbia. WW-II.

INKSPOT -- Lafuai River, Woodlark Island. WW-II.

INKSTAND -- Cherchel, Algeria. WW-II.

INMATE -- Allied neutralization of air installations in Truk Atoll, Caroline Islands. 12-16 June 1945, WW-II.

INNER -- Sharyo (Sharyo-To, Sia-Liau-To), Formosa. WW-II.

INSECT -- (1) Tanimaiki Village, Gilbert Islands. WW-II.

(2) British ship, H.M.S. Eagle flying off Spitfires to Malta. 21 July 1942. WW-II.

INSERTION -- Surigao, Mindanao, Philippine Islands. WW-II.

INSOLENCE -- Frederikshaab, Greenland. WW-II.

INSOMNIA -- U.S. Navy night operations by carrier-based planes against rail communications and truck movements in North Korea; used irregular launching schedules to catch enemy unawares. Spring, 1952, Korean Conflict.

INSPIRATION -- Allied round-up of French tunny vessels which were brought into Penzance, Cornwell. September 1942, WW-II.

INSTITUTION -- Aroe Island, New Guinea. WW-II.

INSTRUCTOR -- Dutch Fokker S.11 trainer aircraft first flown in 1947. In service with Israel, Italy, Brazil and the Netherlands.

INSURGENT -- U.S. operation against Mindanao, Philippines, proposed 15 November 1944, in GRANITE II plan. WW-II.

INTEGER -- Visayan Group, Philippine Islands. WW-II.

INTERCEPTION -- Iromote Jima, Japan. WW-II.

INTERDICT -- Acronym for Interference Detection and Interdiction Countermeasures, a program to determine the type, source and effect of electromagnetic radiations at missile sites. All three services have electromagnetic compatibility programs, of which Interdict was just one industry study.

INTERLOCK -- New Hanover Island, New Ireland, Bismarck Archipelago. WW-II.

INTERLUDE -- Allied operation against Morotai Island, Netherlands East Indies, carried out by TRADEWIND Task Force. 15 September-4 October 1944, WW-II.

INTERRUPTION -- Lagonoy Gulf, Luzon, Philippine Islands. WW-II.

INTRACTABLE -- Elato Island, Caroline Islands. WW-II.

INTREPID -- A captive balloon used by the Union Balloon Corps during the Civil War.

INTRUDER -- (1) Another nickname for the Martin-built version of the English Electric twin-jet light bomber used by the U.S. Air Force in the 1950's. Also called CANBERRA.

   (2) Navy attack fighter of the Mach .9 class, launched from aircraft carriers. Carries a two-man crew and up to 18,000 pounds of weapons. Its designation is A-6A (old designation A2F-1). An electronic counter-measures version of the two-engine fighter is to be procured.

   (3) Code name for British night patrols over enemy territory intended to destroy hostile aircraft and dislocate enemy flying organization. Began 1940, WW-II.

INVADER -- Douglas B-26, originally designated the A-26 when it first flew in 1942. Still operational with the U.S. Air Force.

INVENTION -- Salebaboe Island, Talaud Islands, Netherlands East Indies. WW-II.

INWALL -- Code name for U.S. Army General Joseph W. Stilwell. WW-II.

IODINE -- Losey Field, Ponce, Puerto Rico. WW-II.

IONE -- (1) Typhoon. 12-15 September 1948. First detected east of Guam. Moved northwestward through Mariana Islands and recurved northeastward over southeastern Japan and out over the Pacific.

   (2) Hurricane. 10-23 September 1955. Formed in mid-Atlantic east of the Antilles. Moved westward and northwestward into eastern North Carolina, then turned northeastward out to sea and across Newfoundland into the northern Atlantic. Caused seven deaths and 88 million dollars damage in North Carolina.

IOWA, POINT -- Check point in East China Sea for convoys en route to invasion of Inchon, Korea. September 1950, Korean Conflict.

IRAH -- Name reserved by meteorologists for tropical cyclone in eastern North Pacific.

CODE NAMES DICTIONARY

IRENE -- (1) Douglas Harbor, New Guinea. WW-II.

    (2) Tropical storm. 6-8 October 1959. Formed in central Gulf of Mexico, moved into northwest Florida, and dissipated over Georgia. Caused minor damage.

    (3) Tropical storm. November 1947. First detected over central Philippines. Moved northward through Luzon and curved northeastward over northern portion of Philippine Sea, where it lost force.

IRET -- New Caledonia. WW-II.

IRIDIUM -- Sagan, New Guinea. WW-II.

IRIS -- (1) U.S. sounding rocket capable of carrying a 100-pound payload to altitudes of 200 miles. Solid propellant, single stage; fired from an AEROBEE tower, and has been successfully flight tested at National Aeronautics and Space Administration's Wallops Station, Virginia.

    (2) Typhoon. 29 April - 9 May 1951. Formed in Caroline Islands. Moved west-northwestward across Philippine Sea and island of Samar, passed just south of Manila and into South China Sea, then recurved northeastward between Taiwan and Luzon and passed southeast of Japan out over the Pacific. Caused damage and 156 casualties in Philippines.

    (3) Typhoon. 22-24 August 1955. Formed east of northern Philippines. Moved north-northwestward across Taiwan and into China mainland.

    (4) Typhoon. 20-22 August 1959. Formed in central Philippine Sea. Moved northwestward, swept the Batan Islands off northern Luzon and the south end of Taiwan and moved into the China mainland, then dissipated. Caused sinking of several ships.

    (5) Typhoon. 26-30 May 1962. Formed northeast of Mindanao, Philippines. Moved north-northwestward offshore and dissipated northeast of Luzon.

    (6) Name also applied to tropical cyclones in western North Pacific which occurred prior to (2) through (5) above.

IRMA -- (1) Tropical storm. 26-29 July 1949. First detected west of Luzon in South China Sea. Moved northeastward across Taiwan into Yellow Sea.

    (2) Typhoon. 20-26 February 1953. Formed west of Truk, Caroline Islands. Moved westward across Philippine Sea and dissipated over central Philippines, causing minor damage.

    (3) Typhoon. 8-12 October 1957. Formed in South China Sea west of Luzon. Moved westward into Viet Nam and dissipated.

IRMGARD LINE -- Phase line held by Germans on rocky ridge west of Montevarchi, Italy, during northward withdrawal to Arno River. Also called Fritz Line. Summer 1944, WW-II.

IRON CIGAR -- Nickname for B-26 aircraft. WW-II.

IRON SNAKE -- Nickname for U.S. 8th Armored Division. Earlier name was SHOW HORSE DIVISION.

IRON TRIANGLE -- Area bounded by Chorwon, Kumhwa and Pyonggang, Korea; central anchor of North Korean line north of 38th Parallel, protecting, by log, rock, and concrete reinforcements, the hub of communication and supply network. Korean Conflict.

IRONBOTTOM SOUND -- Body of water between Guadalcanal, Savo and Florida Islands. So named for large number of sunken ships there. WW-II.

IRONCLAD -- British operation to seize and hold Vichy French naval and air base at Diego Suarey, northern Madagascar. Originally called Bonus. May 1942, WW-II.

IRONGREY -- Allied South Pacific Forces in Southwest Pacific Area. WW-II.

IRONHORSE -- Artificial harbor in connection with CORONET, projected Allied invasion of Japan. WW-II.

IRONMONGER -- Wotje Islands, Marshall Islands. WW-II.

IRONSTONE -- Sakhalin, Japan. WW-II.

IROQUOIS -- (1) Bell Model 204 helicopter currently in production for the U.S. Army as the HU-1A.

(2) Allied code name for road junction south of Ortona, Italy, in area to be defended by British Indian troops. May 1944, WW-II.

(3) Name for Royal Canadian Air Force Squadron Number 431.

IROQUOIS DIVISION -- Nickname for U.S. 98th Infantry Division.

IRRITANT -- Paramushiru, Kurile Islands. WW-II.

IRVING -- Allied code name for Japanese Nakajima J1N1, night fighter of 1943, which first flew in 1941. Japanese name: Gekko (Moonlight).

ISABELLA -- German code word for proposed operation to expel British from Spain. 1941, WW-II.

ISKRA -- (English translation: Spark) TS-11 jet basic trainer in service with Polish air arm. First flew 1960.

ISLAND -- Tactical air-direction post supporting U.S. I Corps in Korea. Korean Conflict.

ISOLATOR -- Operations against the southeast coast of China. WW-II.

ISOSCELES -- Amboina, Ceram, Netherlands East Indies. WW-II.

ISTHMUS FORCE -- British and New Zealand troops sent to Corinth, Greece for demolition work and to keep roads open. April 1941, WW-II.

ITALUFT -- Liaison staff set up in Rome in 1940 to coordinate action of Italian and German air forces. WW-II.

ITEM -- (1) Code word for letter "I" in a phonetic alphabet, used to avoid possibility of misunderstanding in transmitting messages. See also INDIA.

    (2) Hurricane. 8-10 October 1950. Small storm which formed in Gulf of Mexico northwest of Yucatan and entered Mexico south of Vera Cruz. Heavy losses reported.

    (3) Hurricane. 12-16 October 1951. Small hurricane which formed in western Caribbean Sea and dissipated near Isle of Pines, south of Cuba.

ITEM HILL -- U.S. military name for topographic feature on Okinawa. 1945, WW-II.

ITEM POCKET -- U.S. military name for center of Japanese resistance north of Gusukuma, Okinawa. 1945, WW-II.

IVA -- Hurricane. 9-10 June 1961. Formed about 200 miles south of Acapulco, Mexico and moved northward into Mexico.

IVAN -- U.S. code name for Mellu Island, Kwajalein Atoll, Marshall Group. WW-II.

IVORY SNOW -- U.S. Air Force high-altitude air refueling area over New Mexico-Texas.

IVY -- (1) Typhoon. 23-27 September 1956. Formed near Iwo Jima, the Pacific. Moved northeastward, then made large clockwise loop between Iwo Jima and Marcus Island, moved northward and was absorbed by typhoon HARRIET southeast of Japan.

    (2) Typhoon. 28-29 October 1962. Formed northwest of Guam and merged with the circulation of typhoon GILDA over the Philippine Sea.

    (3) U.S. nuclear weapons test at Eniwetok Proving Ground, Marshall Islands. Fall, 1952.

    (4) Name for peacetime military operation.

IVY DIVISION -- Nickname for U.S. 4th Infantry Division. Named after shoulder insignia, which was rebus (I-vy) for Roman numeral IV. Also called FAMOUS FOURTH.

J

J, ASSAULT FORCE -- Naval unit which carried British troops to JUNO Beach. 6 June 1944, WW-II.

J DAY -- (1) Beginning date of U.S. assault on Zamboanga, island of Mindanao, Philippines. 10 March 1945, WW-II.

(2) Date for U.S. landings in Tawitawi Group, Sulu Archipelago, Philippines. 2 April 1945, WW-II.

J, FORCE -- Canadian naval force which participated in raid on Dieppe, France, in July 1942, and was kept intact afterwards. J stood for Dieppe code name JUBILEE. Officially constituted 12 October 1942, WW-II.

J PROGRAMS -- Three ordnance training programs originated for use in war plants by the Training Within Industry Service of War Manpower Commission. 1942-43, WW-II.

J SERVICE -- British monitoring of friendly radio nets to provide commanders with immediate and accurate information upon progress of their own troops. Also known as PHANTOM SERVICE. WW-II.

JABBER -- Klagen, New Britain. WW-II.

JACK -- Code name for the Mitsubishi J2M2 interceptor which first flew in 1942. Japanese: Raiden (Thunderbolt).

JACK KNOB -- See KING-QUEEN-JACK FINGER.

JACK PATROLS -- Patrols of U.S. Navy anti-snooper fighter planes, called Jacks, stationed at each of four cardinal points of compass around a task group as a defense against low-flying enemy planes. WW-II.

JACKAROO -- (1) Four-seat cabin conversion of the British TIGER MOTH aircraft.

(2) Sape Strait, Sea, Netherlands East Indies. WW-II.

JACKASS -- Bla River, New Britain. WW-II.

JACKBOOT -- Attu Island, Aleutian Islands. WW-II.

JACKFROST -- Code name for Canada. WW-II.

JACKIE -- Typhoon. 13-17 September 1948. First detected in central Philippine Sea. Moved northwestward across northern Taiwan and into mainland of China.

JACKKNIFE -- Johnson Island, Pacific Ocean. WW-II.

JACKPOT FLIGHTS -- Name given by U.S. Sabre Jet pilots in Korea to high-flying enemy formations that could easily be destroyed if Sabres could reach their altitudes. Early 1952, Korean Conflict.

JACKS -- See JACK PATROLS.

JACKSTAY -- Code name for Sardinia. WW-II.

JACOB -- U.S. code name for Ennuebing Island, Kwajalein Atoll, Marshall Group. WW-II.

JACOBITE -- Kauai, Hawaii. WW-II.

JACONET -- Munda, New Georgia Island, Solomon Islands. WW-II.

JADE -- Perth, Australia. WW-II.

JAEGER DIVISIONS -- German mobile light infantry divisions. WW-II.

JAGBOMBER -- German fighter-bomber (Jagdbomber). WW-II.

JAGUAR -- (1) Bomber version of the World War II German ME.110 aircraft.

(2) U.S. Air Force, three-stage solid propellant sounding rocket designed to be air-launched from B-47 jet bombers and to carry a 35-pound payload to an altitude of 500 miles. Used to gather data on the natural radiation belts, as well as to measure corona and auroral discharges. Test firings from White Sands Missile Range, New Mexico, conducted in 1958. No longer active.

(3) Alas Strait, Java, Netherlands East Indies. WW-II.

(4) British air reinforcement of Malta. 1941, WW-II.

JAILBAIT -- Pirau River, New Britain. WW-II.

JAKAL -- Series of airborne barrage jammers which are frequency modulated and operate unattended during flight.

JAKE -- Allied name for the World War II Japanese Aichi EI3AI aircraft.

JAKEY -- Cape Kamao, French Indo China. WW-II.

JAKTFALK -- Swedish fighter biplane of the early 1930's built by the Aktiebolaget Svenska Company.

CODE NAMES DICTIONARY

JAKTROBOT -- Swedish tactical, air-to-surface missile with a range of less than three miles. Boosted by a solid propellant motor, and radio guided to the target; two of these missiles can be carried by the Saab 32 Lansing aircraft. Now operational, the development was started in 1949 with the first missile being fired in 1955. Also called Robot 304.

JALOPY -- U.S. exercise, held in Northern Ireland, for training in mounting of build-up forces in preparation for OVERLORD. See also CHEVROLET, JEEP. Spring 1944, WW-II.

JAM JARS -- Royal Canadian Air Force term for armoured cars. WW-II.

JAM PACK -- U.S. Air Force high-altitude air refueling area over Texas.

JAMBOREE -- Sep Sep Island, New Britain. WW-II.

JAMES -- (1) Cocos Island, Solomon Islands. WW-II.

(2) Kabanaki Village, Gilbert Islands. WW-II.

JAMJAR -- Naknek, Alaska. WW-II.

JAMLEX -- Joint U.S. Army-Marine Corps peacetime amphibious exercise at Camp LeJeune, North Carolina, 1961.

JAMORE -- Makassar City, Celebes, Netherlands East Indies. WW-II.

JAMPUFF -- Nandi, Fiji Islands. WW-II.

JANE -- (1) Typhoon. 30 August - 4 September 1950. First detected west of Bonin Islands, the Pacific. Moved northeastward across Honshu, Japan, into Sea of Japan and over Hokkaido. Caused considerable damage in Kobe-Osaka area of Japan.

(2) British assault landing from seaward to capture Tamatave, Madagascar. 18 September 1942, WW-II.

JANE HILL -- U.S. military name for topographic feature near Shuri on Okinawa. Also called Three Sisters. 1945, WW-II.

JANE RUSSELL HILL -- Military name for topographic feature in Korea. Korean Conflict.

JANES AND JOES -- Allied female and male secret agents dropped by planes behind enemy lines in Europe during World War II.

JANET -- (1) U.S. Air Force multi-stage sounding rocket in use at Eglin Air Force Base, Florida, to launch FIREFLY payloads.

(2) Kuching, Borneo, Netherlands East Indies. WW-II.

    (3) Hurricane. 21-29 September 1955. One of "great hurricanes" of twentieth century. Formed east of Windward Islands. Moved westward through Caribbean Sea, across Yucatan Peninsula, and into Mexico near Tampico. Winds reached 200 miles per hour. Caused at least 700 deaths and 50 million dollars damage. Floods in Tampico resulted in one of greatest natural disasters in Mexican history.

JANGLE -- Taruk Mission, New Britain. WW-II.

JANICE -- Hurricane. 5-12 October 1958. Formed south of Cuba. Moved northeastward across Cuba, through Bahamas, between Cape Hatteras and Bermuda, and out over North Atlantic. Caused heavy flood damage in Jamaica.

JANITOR -- Code name for Corsica. WW-II.

JANTZEN -- British exercise for administrative and supply troops to practice maintenance of a corps and supporting troops over beaches for period of two weeks. Planning phase held in April-May 1943, landing phase in July 1943 on beaches near Tenby, Wales. WW-II.

JANUS -- U.S. biological research reactor under construction, 1962, at Argonne National Laboratory, Lemont, Illinois.

JAPONICA -- Tinghai, Chusan Islands, China. WW-II.

JARGON -- Bena Bena, New Guinea. WW-II.

JARRAH -- Onslow, Australia. WW-II.

JASMINE -- Kaub Island, New Guinea. WW-II.

JASON -- U.S. sounding rocket designed to carry a 50-pound payload to an altitude of 500 miles. Five-stage solid propellant vehicle; used to measure the effect of high-altitude nuclear tests during both the ARGUS and HARDTACK series in 1958. Also known as the Argo E-5. See also ARGO SERIES.

JASPER -- Aikon, New Britain. WW-II.

JASTRZAB -- (English translation: Hawk) Polish PZL P.50 fighter. First flew in 1939.

JATO -- U.S. acronym for Jet-Assisted Take-Off, an aviation and rocket term. British equivalent is ATO.

JAVELIN -- (1) Gloster FAW.8, world's first delta-wing twin-jet all-weather interceptor. Ceased production in 1960. A mainstay of the British Royal Air Force Fighter Command.

    (2) U.S. Air Force name for the Argo D-4 sounding rocket designed to carry a 50-pound payload to altitudes of 1000 miles. Four-stage solid propellant rocket, first fired in July 1959. See also ARGO SERIES.

    (3) Bali Plantation, New Britain. WW-II.

JAZZ HORN -- U.S. Air Force high-altitude air refueling area over Alabama-Florida-Georgia.

JEAN -- (1) Typhoon. 25 September - 2 October 1945. First detected over western Caroline Islands. Moved northwestward across Philippine Sea, passed between Luzon and Taiwan, turned northeastward through Formosa Strait and dissipated.

(2) Typhoon. December 1947. First detected in western Caroline Islands. Moved west-northwestward across Philippine Sea and central Philippines to South China Sea. Recurved northeastward between Luzon and Taiwan and lost force southeast of Japan.

(3) Typhoon. 15-25 October 1956. Formed in central Philippine Sea. Moved erratically westward across northern Luzon and South China Sea. Dissipated in vicinity of Hainan Island.

(4) Typhoon. 6-12 November 1962. Formed in western Philippine Sea. Moved west-northwestward across central Philippines and the South China Sea, dissipated off the coast of Viet Nam.

(5) Name also applied to tropical cyclones in western North Pacific which occurred prior to (1) through (4) above.

JEDBURGHS -- Three-man teams, consisting of one French and one U.S. or British officer and a radio operator, which were parachuted in uniform behind enemy lines shortly before Normandy landings to provide communication links with FFI (Forces Francaises de l'Interieur; English: French Forces of the Interior). 1944, WW-II.

JEDDAH -- Port Prince Ruper, British Columbia. WW-II.

JEEP -- (1) One-quarter ton, four-wheel drive, utility vehicle. First built for U.S. Army by American Bantam Car Company of Butler, Pennsylvania, in 1940. Originally called Peep, with name, Jeep, applied to a one-half-ton truck, which was discontinued. Also called Bantam, Blitzbuggy. Two theories of origin of name: 1. From slurring of letters GP, standing for General Purpose. 2. From name of character in comic strip, "Popeye," created by E. C. Segar. See also VEEP.

(2) Allied exercise to give training in mounting of build-up forces; involved movement of elements of U.S. 2nd Infantry Division from their stations to Belfast, Northern Ireland. See also CHEVROLET, JALOPY. March 1944, WW-II.

JELLO -- Opol, Philippine Islands. WW-II.

JELLY -- Tablos Strait, Philippine Islands. WW-II.

JELLYFISH -- Umbolding, New Guinea. WW-II.

JEMMY -- U.S. force in southwest Scotland. WW-II.

JEN-1 -- Operable Spanish pool nuclear reactor in Moncloa, Spain.

JENER -- Acronym for Joint Establishment for Nuclear Energy Research. See also NORA.

JENNIFER -- Name reserved by meteorologists for tropical cyclone in eastern North Pacific.

JENNY -- (1) Curtiss JN-1 biplane trainer first ordered by the U.S. Army in 1914. In use for years after.

(2) Hurricane. 1-9 November 1961. Formed in Windward Islands, moved erratically northeastward and dissipated in mid-Atlantic. Caused little damage.

JERBOA -- Foggia, Italy. WW-II.

JEREMIAD -- Code name for Crete. WW-II.

JEREMIAH -- Mt. Bola, New Britain. WW-II.

JERK -- Wellington, New Zealand. WW-II.

JEROBOAM -- Code name for Wake Island. WW-II.

JERRICAN -- See JERRY CAN.

JERRY CAN -- Five-gallon, flat-sided gasoline and water container, copied by Allies from German model. Also called Jerrican (by French) and Blitz Can. See also AMERI-CAN. WW-II.

JET PROVOST -- Hunting Percival jet trainer aircraft entered British Royal Air Force service in 1959. An armed version serves with the Royal Ceylon Air Force. A newer version now in Royal Air Force.

JET STREAM -- U.S. project involving hurricane research.

JETSTAR -- Lockheed C-140, four-engine jet transport, became operational with the U.S. Air Force late in 1961.

JEWEL -- Name reserved by meteorologists for tropical cyclone in eastern North Pacific.

JEWESS -- Sandakan, Borneo, Netherlands East Indies. WW-II.

JEZEBEL -- (1) Code name given to Bremen, Germany, as one of three possible objectives for a concentrated British bombing. See also ABIGAIL, DELILAH, RACHEL. Night of 16 December 1940, WW-II.

(2) U.S. plated bare uranium 233 sphere studies at Los Alamos Scientific Laboratory, New Mexico. Startup 1954.

JIBBOOM -- U.S. Navy force in Jamaica. WW-II.

JIBDOOR -- Rumung, Yap Island. WW-II.

JIFFY- -- Waiwi Creek, New Guinea. WW-II.

JIG -- (1) Code word for letter "J" in a phonetic alphabet, used to avoid possibility of a misunderstanding in transmitting messages. See also JULIET.

   (2) Hurricane. 13-16 October 1950. First detected in mid-Atlantic. Moved northwestward, then curved northeastward 300 miles southeast of Bermuda, and over North Atlantic.

   (3) Hurricane. 15-20 October 1951. Formed and dissipated in Atlantic between Bermuda and Bahamas.

JIG DAY -- Date for starting U.S. 4th Marine Division invasion of Tinian Island, Mariana group. 24 July 1944, WW-II.

JIGSAW -- Waren Airdrome, New Guinea. WW-II.

JILL LAKE -- Military name for topographic feature on Butaritari Island, Makin Atoll. November 1943, WW-II.

JIM CROW -- British Fighter Command reconnaissance patrol in English Channel. WW-II.

JIMJAM -- 2nd U.S. Naval Training Base, British Isles. WW-II.

JINDIVIK -- British liquid propelled target drone used to check out guided missile performance, as well as serving as a gunnery target. Can operate at an altitude of ten miles for about an hour, but achieves maximum 575 miles per hour speed at an altitude of seven and one half miles. Several versions built, all essentially the same. First flight took place in 1952. Australia and Sweden have also used vehicle as a gunnery target.

JINRAI BUTAI -- See BAKA BOMB.

JIVELAND -- San Remo Point, France. WW-II.

JOAN -- (1) Typhoon. 30 August - 3 September 1955. Formed north of Mariana Islands and moved northward, then northeastward, passing southeast of Japan and the Kurile Islands.

   (2) Typhoon. 26-30 August 1959. Formed near Guam. Moved northwestward, passed across Taiwan, entered China mainland, and dissipated. Caused eleven deaths and substantial damage on Taiwan.

   (3) Typhoon. 7-11 July 1962. First detected in northern Philippine Sea. Moved northwestward at first, but recurved northeastward off China coast near Shanghai, weakened, and crossed Korea into Sea of Japan.

   (4) Name also applied to tropical cyclones in western North Pacific which occurred prior to (1) through (3) above.

JOAN LAKE -- Military name for topographic feature on Butaritari Island, Makin Atoll. November 1943, WW-II.

JOANNE -- Tropical storm. 10-12 July 1961. First detected in Pacific 500 miles south of Baja, California. Moved westward over ocean and dissipated.

JOB 5 -- Austrian Oberlerchner monoplane. In production.

JOBLOT -- Code name for Nicaragua. WW-II.

JOCK COLUMNS -- Special battle-groups, usually mobile artillery, used by British in North Africa in raiding, harassing, covering, delaying, support and pursuit operations; named after Major-General J. C. ("Jock") Campbell. WW-II.

JOCKEY -- Misamis Occidental, Mindanao, Philippine Islands. WW-II.

JOE-HOLE -- Cargo hatch made by removing ball turret and placing metal shroud inside opening on planes engaged in CARPETBAGGER operation; used to drop secret agents (nicknamed JOES) and supplies to resistance forces behind enemy lines in Europe during World War II.

JOEBLOW -- Kulu River, New Britain. WW-II.

JOES -- See JANES AND JOES.

JOGALONG -- Magdalene River, New Britain. WW-II.

JOHANNES -- Talasea Island, Netherlands East Indies. WW-II.

JOHNNIAC -- Acronym for Johns (Von Neumann) Integrator and Automatic Computer.

JOHNNY WALKER -- British anti-shipping bomb. WW-II.

JOHNSON -- Sauren, New Britain. WW-II.

JOLLY -- Italian Partenavia P.59 single-engine monoplane first flown in 1960.

JOLLYBOAT -- Hoji Island, Chusan Archipelago, China. WW-II.

JOLTIN' JOSIE, THE PACIFIC PIONEER -- First B-29 aircraft to arrive at Saipan, Marianas, for eventual bombing of Japan; piloted by Brigadier General Haywood S. ("Possum") Hansell, commander of U.S. XXI Bomber Command. 12 October 1944, WW-II.

JOMINI -- Pilelo Passage, New Britain. WW-II.

JOSHUA -- (1) Waru, New Guinea. WW-II.

(2) U.S. Air Force propellant research program to develop high-energy, storable liquid propellants for a light weight Intercontinental Ballistic Missile.

JOSS -- Code name for beaches in Licata area, Sicily, attacked by part of U.S. 7th Army, during invasion, Operation HUSKY. See also CENT, DIME. 10 July 1943, WW-II.

JOURNALBOY -- Java, Netherlands East Indies. WW-II.

JOURNEYMAN -- U.S. Air Force name for Argo D-8 sounding rocket capable of lifting a 20-pound payload to 2800 miles. A four-stage solid propellant vehicle, used to measure radiation around the earth as part of National Aeronautics and Space Administration's NERV program during 1960. See also ARGO SERIES, RAM.

JOYCE -- Name reserved by meteorologists for tropical cyclone in eastern North Pacific.

JUBILANT -- Airborne operations by 1st Allied Airborne Army, under ECLIPSE conditions, to safeguard and supply prisoner-of-war camps. WW-II.

JUBILEE -- Combined Allied raid on Dieppe, France; five-sixths of assault force were Canadian troops. Originally planned, mounted in July 1942, and then canceled, under code name Rutter. 18-19 August 1942, WW-II.

JUDITH -- (1) Typhoon. 5-14 August 1949. Formed in central Caroline Islands. Moved west-northwestward, then northwestward through Philippine Sea. Recurved northeastward off northern Luzon and passed southeast of the Ryuku Islands.

(2) Hurricane. 17-21 October 1951. Formed near western Cuba. Moved northeastward across southern Florida and northern Bahamas. Dissipated in mid-Atlantic. Caused minor damage.

JUDY -- (1) Name for Japanese Navy Aichi torpedo-bomber aircraft. WW-II.

(2) Typhoon. 29 May – 6 June 1953. Formed in western Caroline Islands. Moved west-northwestward across Philippine Sea and northern Luzon, then recurved northeastward, passed east of Taiwan and lost force. Caused 13 deaths in Philippines.

(3) Typhoon. 18-26 October 1957. Formed north of Eniwetok Atoll, the Pacific. Moved westward through Mariana Islands. Recurved northeastward over Philippine Sea and lost force southeast of Japan.

JUG -- Pilot's nickname for the World War II Republic P-47. See THUNDERBOLT.

JUGGERNAUT -- U.S. Argonne Low Power Research Reactor under construction, 1962, at Argonne National Laboratory, Lemont, Illinois.

JUGGLE -- Waterlood, Sierra Leone, Africa. WW-II.

JUGGLER -- Projected long-range coordinated attacks by United Kingdom-based U.S. 8th Air Force and Africa-based U.S. 9th Air Force against Messerschmitt fighter aircraft production complexes at Regensburg, Germany, and Wiener Neustadt, Austria. Planned for 7 August 1943, but abandoned because of weather. WW-II.

JUGULATED -- Strategic positions selected for occupation upon Japanese withdrawal, collapse or surrender. WW-II.

JUICE -- Allied code name for North Sea. WW-II.

JUICYFRUIT -- Baru, New Guinea. WW-II.

JULIET -- (1) Code word for letter "J" in a phonetic alphabet, used to avoid possibility of a misunderstanding in transmitting messages. See also JIG.

    (2) Baronga Island, Burma. WW-II.

JULIUS CAESAR, PLAN -- Scheme for defense of United Kingdom. 1939-40, WW-II.

JUMBLE -- (1) El Obeid, Sudan. WW-II.

    (2) Taraua, New Britain. WW-II.

JUMP LIGHT -- U.S. peacetime military troop test.

JUNAK -- Polish primary trainer first flown in 1948.

JUNCTION SPRING -- Name for U.S. 5th Army peacetime exercise at Fort Riley, Kansas, 1960.

JUNE -- (1) Typhoon. 9-12 September 1954. Developed 500 miles northeast of Guam. Moved westward at first, then northwestward. Turned northeast, skirted southeast coast of Japan and passed out into the Pacific.

    (2) Typhoon. 1-8 August 1961. Formed near island of Ulithi, West Caroline Islands. Moved northwestward through Philippine Sea, across Taiwan, and into China mainland, where it dissipated. Caused flooding, landslides, and 20 deaths on Taiwan.

    (3) Name also applied to tropical cyclones in western North Pacific which occurred prior to (1) and (2) above.

JUNE HILL -- U.S. military name for topographic feature on Okinawa. 1945, WW-II.

JUNGLE JIM -- Name for peacetime military maneuver stressing combat training for chemical, biological, and radiological warfare.

JUNGLE JIM, OPERATION -- Training of Latin American forces in counter-infiltration and guerrilla activities by U.S. Air Force Commandos in Panama 1962.

JUNGLE KING -- Name for British Royal Air Force Bomber Command's peacetime military exercise.

JUNGLEERS -- Nickname for U.S. 41st Infantry Division. So called because involved in more jungle combat than any other American outfit. Also called THE BUTCHERS.

JUNGMANN -- Bucker Bu 131, designed in 1933, and built in considerable numbers for the Luftwaffe and German private owners.

JUNGMEISTER -- Bucker Bu. 133, German acrobatic trainer plane, first produced in 1935, and still flying in Spain and Switzerland.

JUNIOR -- (1) Light monoplane built by Rearwin Airplanes of Kansas in 1933. See also KEN ROYCE.

(2) Swedish MFI-9 cabin monoplane first flown in 1958.

(3) Name given to newly created U.S. 12th Air Force during preparations for landings in North Africa. 1942, WW-II.

JUNIPER HILL -- U.S. military name for topographic feature south of Yonabaru, Okinawa. 1945, WW-II.

JUNK -- See KLAMOTTE.

JUNKET -- Operation of U.N. naval blockade Task Force 95 which placed emphasis on capturing enemy junks in order to get intelligence information rather than sinking them. Began January 1952, Korean Conflict.

JUNO -- Beach assaulted by troops of 3rd Canadian Infantry Division on D Day, 6 June 1944, in Operation OVERLORD; located between GOLD and SWORD Beaches in Normandy, France. See also ASSAULT FORCE J.

JUNO I -- Early name, not widely used, for JUPITER C.

JUNO II -- U.S. Army four-stage launch vehicle capable of putting 95 pounds in a 600-mile orbit and 13 pounds into an escape orbit. Basically a modified JUPITER Intermediate Range Ballistic Missile with three upper stages; was used to launch PIONEERS III and IV and EXPLORER VI-VIII. First launch (Pioneer III) took place from Cape Canaveral 6 December 1958. Phased out by National Aeronautics and Space Administration in 1961. See also JUPITER, BEACON.

JUNO V -- Early name for the SATURN.

JUNO, OPERATION -- German naval operation by force including two battle cruisers to divert British warships from Norwegian inshore shipping routes and threaten base in area of Vestfiord, Norway; resulted in sinking of British aircraft carrier, H.M.S. Glorious, and two British destroyers. Early June 1940, WW-II.

JUPITER -- (1) U.S. Army-developed, Air Force-operated, 1500-mile Intermediate Range Ballistic missile. A single-stage, liquid-propelled vehicle, it is deployed in Italy and Turkey with two, 15-missile squadrons in each country. It was the first Intermediate Range Ballistic Missile successfully fired by the U.S. and also the first to have its nose cone recovered. First full-range firing 31 May 1957. Also used as space booster in JUNO II program. Official Air Force designation SM-78. See also JUPITER A and C.

(2) Panguil Bay, Philippine Islands. WW-II.

(3) Projected Allied operation in northern Norway. 1942, WW-II.

JUPITER A -- A not-commonly-used name for the U.S. Army's REDSTONE missile when used to test components of the JUPITER.

JUPITER C -- U.S. Army research vehicle initially designed to test re-entry and stability characteristics of JUPITER nose cones. Essentially a modified REDSTONE with two solid upper stages. It also tested various Jupiter components. With the addition of a single, small solid motor, it was used to launch EXPLORER I, the first U.S. satellite, in January 1958. The vehicle bears little relation to the Jupiter, and was given this name for funding and priority purposes only. First firing of three-stage version was in September 1956, with an altitude of 600 miles and a range of 3400 miles being attained. Early name was Juno I. See also BEACON.

JURIST -- Allied occupation of Malaya, after Japanese surrender. 18 August 1945, WW-II.

JURYMAST -- Selaru Island, Netherlands East Indies. WW-II.

JUVENILE -- Dobodura, New Guinea. WW-II.

K

K DAY -- General term used by U.S. Navy for day set for strike or assault by a carrier's aircraft.

K-GUN -- U.S. Navy anti-submarine depth-charge projector, Mark-6; replaced Y-GUN. Early WW-II.

KA, OPERATION -- Japanese plan to transport 1500 troop reinforcements to Guadalcanal with support of powerful combined fleet; ended up in large-scale naval engagement between U.S. and Japanese forces called Battle of the Eastern Solomons. 23-25 August 1942, WW-II.

KADETT -- Heinkel H.D.72 open-cockpit biplane German trainer of the early 1930's.

KAHER, EL -- See EL KAHER

KAHN -- (English: Canoe) German Air Force slang for airplane. WW-II.

KAKUZU WEST -- See CROCKER'S HILL

KALAMAZOO -- Nickname for advanced U.S. Army base near Kalikodobu in Papua, New Guinea. 1942, WW-II.

KALEIDOSCOPE -- Cape Nelson Area, New Guinea. WW-II.

KAMELBERG -- (English: Camelback Mountain) German military name for Djebel Bou Keurnine or Hill 396 near Sebkret el Kourzia, Tunisia. Named for characteristic silhouette. April 1943, WW-II.

KAMIKAZE -- (1) (English translation: Divine Wind) Single-engine Japanese monoplane which flew from Tokyo to Croydon Airport, London, England, in 1937.

(2) (English translation: Divine Wind) Japanese suicide plane of WW-II.

KAN -- Japanese Burma Area Army plan to defend the Burma Coast. Fall 1944, WW-II.

KANGAROO -- (1) Allied nickname for modified tank or self-propelled gun, used as armored personnel carrier. WW-II.

(2) Italian tri-motor transport plane. See CANGURU.

(3) German World War II Fw-190B aircraft. See KANGURUH.

KANGURUH -- (English translation: Kangaroo) German World War II Fw-190B.
First built in 1942. Received its name and distinction from its large belly-mounted
turbo-supercharger.

KANOA -- Hurricane. 14-26 July 1957. Hawaiian name meaning "the free one".
Formed 750 miles southwest of Manzanillo, Mexico. Moved west-northwestward
but dissipated shortly before reaching Hawaii.

KANONE -- (English: Cannon) German air force slang name for an ace pilot.
WW-II.

KANOYA -- One of three groups of Japanese 22nd Air Flotilla, which attacked
and sank British battleship, Prince of Wales, and battlecruiser, Repulse, off east
coast of Malaya. See also GENZAN, MIHORO. 10 December 1941, WW-II.

KANSAN -- World War II Beech monoplane used by the U.S. Army Air Forces as
the AT-11, by the U.S. Navy as the SNB. See EXPEDITOR.

KANSAS -- Military name for U.N. main defense line in Korea from point slightly
north of Inchon to Pannam-ni on east coast. 1951, Korean Conflict.

KANSAS BLITZ -- Nickname for project, involving team of civilian and military
personnel, to investigate delays and speed up production and modification of
B-29 bombers in Kansas for overseas flight and combat. Winter 1944, WW-II.

KAPPA -- Curacao, Netherlands West Indies. WW II.

KAPPA SERIES -- Family of seven Japanese sounding rockets designed to fulfill Japan's
commitments to the International Geophysical Year. All are solid propelled and
rail-launched with four being single-stage vehicles, two one-stage and one three-
stages. Capable of carrying 13-100-pound payloads to altitudes from 20 to 200
miles. Yugoslavia bought 6 Kappa VI vehicles. Kappa IX may be used as
satellite launch vehicle. The first single-stage vehicle was fired in September
1956.

KARA -- Name reserved by meteorologists for tropical cyclone in the North Atlantic.

KAREN -- (1) Typhoon. 11-17 January 1948. First detected in central Caroline
Islands. Moved erratically westward into Philippine Sea, then turned northeastward across Mariana Islands and out over Pacific.

(2) Typhoon. 12-17 August 1952. Formed in southern Philippine Sea. Moved
west-northwestward at first, then north through East China Sea and northeastward across Korea and Japan Sea to Hokkaido.

(3) Typhoon. 10-21 November 1956. Because of uncertainties in tracking also
called Lucille and Mary at various stages. Formed south of Guam. Moved
west-northwestward to central Philippine Sea, then westward across Luzon.
Dissipated over South China Sea.

(4) Typhoon. 22-25 April 1960. Formed southwest of Philippines. Moved northwestward through Philippines as weak storm, dissipating north of Luzon. Caused 56 deaths and two million dollars damage in Philippines.

(5) Typhoon. 7-13 November 1962. Formed near Truk Island. Moved northward at first, then west-northwestward, passing directly over Guam and into Philippine Sea, where it dissipated. Devastated Guam. Caused 11 deaths and 200 million dollars damage.

(6) Name also applied to tropical cyclones in western North Pacific which occurred prior to (1) through (5) above.

(7) U.S. Navy designation of zone in Manila Bay, Philippines, for mine sweeping operations. February 1945, WW-II.

KARIGANE -- (English translation: Wild Goose) Japanese World War II Mitsubishi light bomber.

KARIN -- Code name of one of series of rearguard action on phase line fought by Germans during northward withdrawal to Arno River, Italy. Summer 1944, WW-II.

KARO PLANS -- Code name for U.S. Army letter plans reducing supply operations in Persian Corridor. 1945, WW-II.

KATE -- (1) Nakajima World War II carrier-based torpedo bomber which took part in the Japanese attack on Pearl Harbor. Also responsible for the sinking of the U.S. aircraft carriers Wasp, Lexington and Yorktown.

(2) Tropical storm. 1-5 October 1945. First detected in vicinity of Saipan, Mariana Islands. Moved northwestward across Philippine Sea, then turned northeastward, skirted southern Japan, and moved out over the Pacific.

(3) Typhoon. 24-29 June 1951. Formed south of Guam. Moved westward into Philippine Sea, recurved gradually to the northeast, passed southeast of Okinawa, and lost force.

(4) Typhoon. 16-25 September 1955. Formed northeast of Truk, Caroline Islands. Moved west-northwestward across Philippine Sea, northern Luzon, and South China Sea to vicinity of Hainan Island. Caused some damage on Luzon.

(5) Typhoon. 18-24 July 1962. Formed northeast of Luzon, Philippines. Moved northward across Taiwan, causing widespread flooding, passed into China mainland north of Foochow, and dissipated.

(6) Name also applied to tropical cyclones in western North Pacific which occurred prior to (2) through (5) above.

KATE, EXERCISE -- Canadian practice exercise in assault crossings of tidal estuaries in preparation for OVERLORD. Held on River Trent in Yorkshire, England. April-May 1944, WW-II.

KATHLEEN -- (1) Typhoon. 10-15 September 1947. First detected in eastern Philippine Sea. Moved west-northwestward at first, then recurved to northeast, skirted southeastern Japan, and moved out into North Pacific.

(2) Tropical storm. 14-16 July 1961. First detected 300 miles west of Acapulco, Mexico. Moved westward over the Pacific and dissipated.

KATHY -- (1) U.S. Air Force sounding rocket capable of carrying an 8-35-pound payload of scientific instruments. Being used in the FIREFLY program.

(2) Typhoon. 23-25 October 1958. Formed east of Samar, Philippines. Moved westward across Philippines before reaching typhoon intensity, then moved across South China Sea into Viet Nam.

(3) Typhoon. 15-18 August 1961. Formed near Iwo Jima and moved northwestward over Kyushu, Japan, where it dissipated. Caused minor damage on Iwo Jima.

(4) Name also applied to tropical cyclones in western North Pacific which occurred prior to (2) and (3) above.

KATIE -- U.S. Navy surface-to-surface and surface-to-underwater missile reportedly under development.

KATRINA -- Name reserved by meteorologist for tropical cyclone in eastern North Pacific.

KATY -- Name reserved by meteorologists for tropical cyclone in North Atlantic.

KATY MINE -- German anti-shipping mine, usually planted in growth on floor of harbors. WW-II.

KATYDID -- U.S. Navy target drone capable of flying for about 40 minutes at a speed of 250 miles per hour, and being parachute recovered. Although capable of surface launch, it was generally carried on the bomb racks of CATALINA aircraft. Pulsejet powered. World War II development.

KATYUSHA -- Russian solid propellant barrage rocket fired from the ground or from truck-mounted assemblies. Generally the firing racks were arranged in two rows of eight each. First version had a range of three miles, while a lighter model could be fired to ranges of six miles. Used against the Germans in WW-II.

KAUZ II -- (English translation: Screech Owl II) Dornier Do. 17z night fighter and intruder plane which entered Luftwaffe service in 1940. Also called Flying Pencil.

KAYDET -- Early World War II U.S. Army Air Corps primary training biplane built by Stearman/Boeing and designated the PT-13. PT-17, -18, -27 modifications were also called Caydet. Also Known as the Yellow Peril.

KE, OPERATION -- (1) Japanese evacuation from Guadalcanal. February 1943, WW-II.

(2) Japanese evacuation from Kiska, Aleutian Islands. July 1943, WW-II.

KEE BIRD -- U.S. Army ski-mounted, propeller-driven vehicle for arctic use.

KEENSET -- Sorlen Island, Ulithi Atoll, Yap Islands. WW-II.

KELLY GANG -- Popular name for Australian troop of 40 horsed men, active on patrol duty in Syria. 1941, WW-II.

KELVINATOR -- Lulua River, Belgian Congo. WW-II.

KEN ROYCE -- Three-seat version of JUNIOR.

KENTUCKY -- Gingoog, New Guinea. WW-II.

KERBSTONE -- Code name for Arabia. WW-II.

KEROSENE -- Luschan Harbor, New Britain. WW-II.

KESTREL -- Calcutta, India. WW-II.

KETTERING AERIAL TORPEDO -- See LIBERTY EAGLE

KUTZU -- (English translation: Decisive) Japanese plan for defense of home islands of Kyushu and Shikoku. 1945, WW-II.

KEYRING -- Wellington, New Zealand. WW-II.

KEYSTONE -- (1) Nickname for U.S. 28th Infantry Division. Named after parent state, Pennsylvania.

(2) Proposed Allied airborne operation west of IJssel River, Netherlands, to assist Operation CANNONSHOT. Cancelled 14 April 1945 on account of unsuitability of planned drop zone. WW-II.

(3) Name for peacetime military operation.

KEYWAY -- Yokosuka, Japan. WW-II.

KEZIA -- Typhoon. 7-14 September 1950. First detected near Eniwetok Atoll, Pacific. Moved west-northwestward, passed north of Guam, turned northward and crossed Kyushu, Japan, into Sea of Japan, where it lost force.

KICK-OFF, OPERATION -- Intensified bombardment of known and suspected positions of enemy harbor defense guns at Wonsan, North Korea. Began 18 July 1951, Korean Conflict.

KICKERS -- Popular name for U.S. 3841st QM Truck Company who, under hazardous conditions flew and dropped (kicked) supplies from air transports to Chinese Army in Burma. 1943.

KICKSHAW -- Code name for Canada. WW-II.

KIDLIFT, OPERATION -- Airlifting of 139 children by U.S. planes from advanced bases near front lines in Korea to Kangnung field so that they could receive assistance in the south. January- February 1952. Korean Conflict.

KIDNEY RIDGE -- Military name for topographic feature west of El Alamein, Egypt. 1942, WW-II.

KIDNEYBEAN -- Aichi, Japan. WW-II.

KIKKA -- Japanese World War II piloted bomb project.

KIKU -- Code name for Japanese 18th Division, active in Burma. WW-II.

KILKENNY -- Dulag, Leyte Island, Philippine Islands. WW-II.

KILLER -- U.S. offensive operation in vicinity of Hoengsong, Korea. 21 February- 4 March 1951. Korean Conflict.

KILLJOY -- Timika, New Guinea. WW-II.

KILO -- Code word for letter "K" in a phonetic alphabet, used to avoid possibility of a misunderstanding in transmitting messages. See also KING.

KILTING -- Code name for U.S. President Harry S. Truman. WW-II.

KIM IL SUNG -- U.N. name for mountain ridge in Korea; scene of heavy fighting in Fall, 1951. Nicknamed after North Korean premier. Korean Conflict.

KINDLE -- U.S. force in southeast England. WW-II.

KINDRED -- Omarakan A, Trobriand Island. WW-II.

KING -- (1) Code word for letter "K" in a phonetic alphabet, used to avoid possibility of a misunderstanding in transmitting messages. See also KILO.

(2) Hurricane. 15-19 October 1950. Small but violent storm which formed in northwestern Caribbean Sea, moved northward across Cuba, directly across Miami, Florida, and up the Florida Peninsula into Georgia where it dissipated. Caused three deaths and 28 million dollars damage.

(3) Plans for U.S. operations to secure initial lodgment in southern and central Philippines and establish bases to support subsequent operations. For specific parts see KING I-III. Late 1944, WW-II.

KING I -- Plan for U.S. operation in Saragani Bay, Mindanao, Philippines. Cancelled in November 1944, WW-II.

KING II -- U.S. landing in Leyte Gulf, Philippines, to establish major air, naval and logistic bases. 20 October 1944, WW-II.

KING III -- Project for airborne invasion of Misamis Occidental Province, western Mindanao, Philippines, to set up fighter air fields. Late 1944, WW-II.

KING COBRA -- U.S. sounding rocket designed to carry a 100-pound payload to an altitude of 300 miles or a 25-pound payload to 500 miles. Launched from a zero-length launcher, the four-stage vehicle is solid propelled. Under development.

KING COLE -- Name for peacetime military exercise.

KING HILL -- (1) U.S. military name for topographic feature on Okinawa. 1945, WW-II.

(2) Military name for topographic feature in PURPLE HEART RIDGE on Saipan. 1944, WW-II.

KING KNOB -- See KING-QUEEN-JACK FINGER

KING I -- U.S. code name for rocky ledge extending from P'il-bong south toward Sobuk-san, Korea. Also known as Rocky Crags. Korean Conflict.

KING-QUEEN-JACK FINGER -- U.N. military name for three bald limestone knobs in Korea near PORK CHOP HILL. See also ACE KNOB. Spring 1953, WW-II.

KINGCOBRA -- Bell P-63, developed from the XP-39E. Many, called FRED, sent to Russia during WW-II.

KINGCOL -- Detachment of troops from British HABFORCE which advanced on Baghdad, Iraq, held by pro-German rebels. May 1941, WW-II.

KINGCRAFT -- Tau Hwa Island, Chusan Archipelago, China. WW-II.

KINGFISHER -- (1) Vought-Sikorsky/Chance-Vought OS2U. Land plane and float-equipped catapult-launched seaplane for the U.S. Navy. Flown during WW-II.

(2) Italian World War II bomber. See ALCIONE.

(3) U.S. Army target drone ramjet-powered and designed as a target from anti-aircraft missiles. Capable of reaching a speed of Mach 2, the drone is controlled by command signals from its autopilot and is equipped with a parachute and nose spike for recovery. Based on the Lockheed X-7 ramjet test vehicle, the drone became operational in 1958. Army designation is the Q-5. See also DIVER, PUFFIN.

KING GRAB -- Operations against Wewak, New Guinea. WW-II.

KINGPIN -- Gulf of Boni, Celebes, Netherlands East Indies. WW-II.

KING'S JOKER -- British peacetime training exercise.

KIPPER KITE -- Aircraft of Royal Canadian Air Force Coastal Command which escorted fishing boats in the North and Irish Seas. WW-II.

KIRA -- Aratu, Brazil. WW-II.

KIRKDALE -- Monserrato, Sicily. WW-II.

KIRSTEN -- Name reserved by meteorologists for tropical cyclone in eastern North Pacific.

KISHAN -- Operation by one company, Indian Gurkha Rifles, against Germans on road between Ricci and Arielli Rivers, near Ortona, Italy. May 1944, WW-II.

KISSING -- Name for the facility at Sonthofen, Germany, where the German ENZIAN surface-to-air missile was built during WW-II.

KISTE -- (English translation: Trunk) German air force slang for airplane. WW-II.

KIT -- (1) Typhoon. 24-27 July 1948. First detected in southern Philippine Sea. Moved northwestward across Luzon and South China Sea and entered mainland of China near Hong Kong. Caused considerable damage on Luzon.

   (2) Typhoon. 26 June - 4 July 1953. First detected 500 miles south-southeast of Guam. Moved northwestward across Philippine Sea and Taiwan and into China mainland.

   (3) Typhoon. 6-16 November 1957. Formed in Marshall Islands, the Pacific. Moved westward through Trust Territories and across Philippine Sea, turned northward over Luzon, then northeast out to sea and dissipated.

   (4) Typhoon. 2-13 October 1960. Formed west of Guam. Moved westward across central Philippines, the south China Sea, and Hainan Island. Caused 149 deaths and great damage in Philippines; also caused damage on Hainan Island and China mainland.

   (5) Name also applied to tropical cyclones in western Pacific which occurred prior to (1) through (4) above.

KIT PROJECT -- Ferrying by U.S. Air Transport Command of 36 A-20 aircraft in four flights from Morrison Field, Florida, across South Atlantic route to Oran, Algeria, via Natal and Accra, for use in North African campaign. See also TIGER, SHARK, PANTHER, FOX. November 1942, WW-II.

KITCHEN -- Ablingi Harbor, New Britain. WW-II.

KITCHENMAID -- Manado, Celebes, Netherlands East Indies. WW-II.

KITE -- Italian monoplane. See NIBBIO.

KITTEN -- Martin K-III which incorporated many advanced features for 1918 airplane. On display at the Smithsonian Institute in Washington.

KITTY -- Typhoon. 27 August - 2 September 1949. Formed near Marcus Island, moved over Tokyo and into northern Japan, with loss of over 100 lives and 40 million dollars in property.

KITTY CAT -- U.S. Air Force high-altitude air refueling area over Colorado-Kansas-New Mexico.

KITTYBOMBER -- Curtiss Kittyhawk modified as a fighter bomber. See WARHAWK.

KITTYHAWK -- (1) Single-engine biplane built in Connecticut in 1933 by Viking Flying Boat Company.

(2) See WARHAWK

KIWI -- U.S. program for assembly, test, disassembly, and post-mortem examination of experimental nonflyable reactors at Nevada Test Site in preparation for Project ROVER. Named after flightless Australian bird.

KIWI-A -- First of series of reactor experiments in Project ROVER at Nevada Test Site. Reactor operated at high power at a predetermined temperature level and a duration representative of an operational cycle. Completed July 1959.

KIWI-A3 -- Improved version of U.S. KIWI-A reactor experiment at Nevada Test Site. Completed 1960.

KIWI-B -- Continuation of U.S. KIWI reactor experiments at Nevada Test Site. Will substitute liquid for gaseous hydrogen as coolant-propellant.

KIWI-B1 -- Scheduled further experiments in U.S. KIWI reactors at Nevada Test Site.

KIWI-B1A -- Continuation of U.S. KIWI reactor experiments at Nevada Test Site. Employed gaseous hydrogen. December 1961.

KIWI-B2A -- Planned continuation of U.S. KIWI reactor experiments at Nevada Test Site. Will use liquid hydrogen.

KIWI-C -- Scheduled further experiments in U.S. KIWI reactors at Nevada Test Site.

KLABUTERMANN -- German PT boat operations on Lake Ladoga, Finland. Summer 1942, WW-II.

KLAMOTTE -- (English translation: Junk) German air force slang name for a worn out aircraft. WW-II.

KLAXON I and II -- British evacuation of Namsos and Narvik, Norway. 2-3 May 1940, WW-II.

KLONDIKE I -- Code name for supposed Allied training exercise in England; actually was a cover for operation to embark troops on infantry landing ships for raid on Dieppe, France, 2-3 July 1942. Raid was not carried out at this time and troops left ships on 8 July 1942. See also JUBILEE. WW-II.

KNAPWEED -- Toshien, Formosa. WW-II.

KNEE MORTAR -- Nickname for Japanese 50-mm. grenade discharger. WW-II.

KNEECAP -- Albany, Western Australia. WW-II.

KNICKEBEIN -- (English translation: Crooked Leg) German radio-beam navigational system; used to direct bombers to target area. Superseded by X GERÄT. WW-II.

KNIFEREST -- Occidental Province, Mindanao, Philippine Islands. WW-II.

KNIGHT'S MOVE -- See ROESSELSPRUNG

KNIGHTSBRIDGE -- British military name for track junction south of Acroma, Libya, 1941-42. WW-II.

KNOB HILL -- See HUNDRED METER HILL

KNOTTY -- Manipa Strait, Moluccas, Netherlands East Indies. WW-II.

KNOWLEDGE -- Kume Jima, Luchu Islands, Japan. WW-II.

KNUTE -- Omo Island, New Guinea. WW-II.

KODAK -- Aikuvuri, New Britain. WW-II.

KOGEKIKI -- Carrier-based torpedo bomber developed as the Type 97 by Nakajima for the World War II Japanese Navy.

KOGO -- Japanese operation designed to clear Chinese off railroad lines running north to Yellow River from Hankow, China. First part of ICHIGO. Began 19 April 1944, WW-II.

KOHINOOR -- Code name for Chile. WW-II.

KOKEN -- Pre-World War II Tokyo Gasu Denki commercial aircraft which established several international aviation records for non-stop endurance flying.

KOLIBRIE -- (English translation: Humming Bird) Ramjet light utility helicopter in production in the Netherlands. First flew in 1956.

KOMET -- German Me-163, the world's first operational rocket-powered fighter plane. Designed in 1941, first entered combat in 1944.

KOMET I -- See COMET I

KOMET II -- See COMET II

KOMET D -- See COMET D

KON OPERATION -- Three attempts by units of 1st Task Force, Japanese Navy, detached from A-GO OPERATION, to move reinforcement troops to Biak Island off north coast of Netherlands, New Guinea. May-June 1944, WW-II.

KONDOR -- Focke-Wulf Fw.200 transport plane of pre-World War II German design and development. See also KURIER.

KOOL -- Name for reserve force of two combat teams, U.S. 2nd Armored Division, and one combat team, U.S. 1st Division, during landings in Sicily, July 1943 Operated with DIME Force. Also called Floating Reserve. WW-II.

KOPJE -- Borinquen Field, Puerto Rico. WW-II.

KOS -- (English translation: Blackbird) Polish PZL-102B monoplane first flown in 1958.

KOSONG TURKEY SHOOT -- U.S. Marine Corps fighter aircraft attack on North Korean Peoples Army 83rd Motorcycle Regiment forced out of Kosong, Korea, by artillery shelling. 11 August 1950, Korean Conflict.

KOTOBUKI -- (English translation: Congratulation) Japanese radial, air-cooled engine rated at 550 horsepower. First used in 1935.

KOURBASH -- Makin Island, Gilbert Islands. WW-II.

KRASAVEC -- (English translation: Beauty) Russian I-26/Yak-1/7 aircraft. See MARK.

KRISHAK -- More powerful, roomier version of the Hindustan PUSHPAK.

KRISTY -- Name reserved by meteorologists for tropical cyclone in North Atlantic.

KROMUSKITS -- A name tentatively given in 1944 to 57-mm. and 75-mm. recoilless rifles in honor of their Frankford Arsenal inventors, William J. Kroeger and C. Walton Musser; the name did not stick. WW-II.

KRONE -- Suit, New Guinea. WW-II.

KRUSCHEN -- Planning exercise conducted by British 163rd Infantry Brigade to find means of driving Germans out of their concrete defenses in coastal areas of northwestern Europe. April 1943, WW-II.

KRYPTON -- Aden, Arabia. WW-II.

KUDOS -- U.S. Army bomber force, east England. WW-II.

KUMQUAT -- Ugi Island, Solomon Islands. WW-II.

KUNKELKOMMANDO -- Group of nine German night fighter Junkers 88 aircraft stationed at Nantes, France, and engaged in operations against Allied air patrols in Bay of Biscay. Named after their leader, Hauptmann F. Kunkel. WW-II.

KURIER -- Mine-laying and commerce-raiding military version of pre-World War II Focke-Wulf Fw.200 aircraft. Civilian version called Kondor.

KYOFU -- (English translation: Mighty Wind) World War II Japanese Kawanishi N1K1 fighter plane. See GEORGE.

KYOKKO -- (English translation: Aurora) World War II Japanese Kawanishi P1Y2 night fighter bomber. See FRANCES.

KYTOON -- Captive balloon used to maintain meteorological equipment aloft at approximately a constant height. Kytoon is streamlined, and combines the aerodynamic properties of a balloon and kite.

KYUSHU GYPSY SQUADRON -- Nickname given to U.S. 21st Troop Carrier Squadron until its incorporation into 6461st Troop Carrier Squadron on 1 December 1952. Korean Conflict.

L

L DAY -- (1) Day of landing, 30 June 1943, in U.S. TOENAILS operation in Central Solomons. WW-II.

(2) Landing Day in assault on Okinawa. April 1, 1945, WW-II.

L HOUR -- Time, 0630 hours, 15 September 1950, set for landing by U.S. Marines on Wolmi-do, an island guarding inner harbor of Inchon, Korea; term used to distinguish this from H Hour of main Inchon landing, 1730 hours, 15 September 1950. Korean Conflict.

L PLANE -- U.S. Army Liaison aircraft.

LABOR DAY HURRICANE -- Most intense hurricane observed in western hemisphere. Crossed Florida Keys 2 September 1935. Caused over 400 deaths and extensive damage. Wind estimated over 200 miles per hour and central pressure 26.35 inches of mercury.

LABORATORY -- Hokkaido Island, Japan. WW-II.

LACE -- Acronym for Liquid Air Cycle Engine, a power plant concept for possible use with Aerospace Plane in which liquid hydrogen is used to cool and liquefy atmospheric air through which the plane is flying. The liquefied air is then injected into the combustion chamber and burned with liquid hydrogen to propel the plane. Concept is being funded by the Air Force as an advanced technology project.

LACHSFANG -- Proposed German and Finnish operations against Kandalaksha and Belomorsk. Summer and fall 1942, WW-II.

LACROSSE -- U.S. Army tactical, all-weather, surface-to-surface missile for use against hard enemy point targets such as pillboxes. Mounted on a mobile launcher, the missile is solid propelled and command-guided to its target by a forward acquisition unit in sight of the target. Having a range of less than 20 miles, the missile is scheduled to be replaced by LANCE (Missile B). Development began in 1947, and the missile entered field service in 1958. Deployed in U.S. and Europe.

LACUNA -- San Juanico Strait, Samar Island, Philippine Islands. WW-II.

LADBROKE -- British glider mission in area of Syracuse, Sicily. Began 9 July 1943, WW-II.

LADEN -- Choshu (Choshu-Gai), Formosa. WW-II.

LADIES MILE -- Peacetime name for footpath in Naga Hills near Kohima, Assam; site of heavy fighting between British and Japanese troops. April 1944, WW-II.

LADY BE GOOD -- Crew's name for a B-24 bomber lost when returning from a World War II combat mission to Italy. Recently found, nearly intact, in North Africa.

LADYBIRD -- Nakajima Tama, Japan. WW-II.

LADYLOVE -- Code name for New Zealand. WW-II.

LADYSLIPPER -- U.S. code name for Japtan Island, Eniwetok Atoll, Marshall Group. WW-II.

LADYSMANTLE -- Ant Island, Caroline Islands. WW-II.

LAGER TRACK -- Canadian name for narrow trail leading westward from San Leonardo, Italy, to Ortona road. Named for familiar beverage; sometimes erroneously called Laager (a park for armored vehicles). December 1943, WW-II.

LAIKA -- Name of the dog orbited by the Russians in SPUTNIK II from 3-11 November 1957. The first animal to be placed in orbit, the husky-class female dog was reported alive by the Soviets on the 10th and dead on the 11th.

LAINDON -- Tunis, Africa. WW-II.

LAKACOOKIE -- U.S. Navy crew-name for PT Boat 152, operating in Pacific Theater. WW-II.

LAKERS -- U.S. ships of moderate draft with large hatches. So named because they were built mainly under World War One contracts in Great Lakes shipyards. Used in Pacific during World War II.

LAMBDA 3S -- Japanese three-stage, solid propellant research test vehicle designed to carry 22-pound payload to altitudes of 1000 miles. Fired from a mobile launcher. Earlier versions were basically the same, but with less performance. Nearly operational, it will be fired from the Kagoshima Space Center on Kyushu Island.

LAMBERT -- Aimola, New Britain. WW-II.

LAMBSKIN -- Niigata, Japan. WW-II.

LAMEDUCK -- Wallis Island, New Hebrides. WW-II.

LAMENT -- Awang Island, Solomon Sea. WW-II.

LAMOUR -- Balangori Bay, New Britain. WW-II.

LAMP -- Acronym for Lunar Analysis and Mapping Program, a U.S. Army Corps of Engineers study of the lunar surface. Maps of various scales and types will be produced. Under agreement with National Aeronautics and Space Administration. Information from SURVEYOR orbiter missions will be utilized.

LAMPLIGHTER -- Deir-ez-zor, Syria. WW-II.

LAMP LIGHTERS -- U.S. Navy P4Y2 Privateer aircraft modified for flare-dropping missions. Korean Conflict.

LAMPOON -- Fanning Island, Line Islands. WW-II.

LAMPPOST -- 4th U.S. Naval Training Base, British Isles. WW-II.

LAMPRE -- Acronym for U.S. series of Los Alamos Molten Plutonium Experiments. Achieved criticality 1961 at Los Alamos Scientific Laboratory, New Mexico.

LAMPREY -- Algiers, Algeria. WW-II.

LANCASTER -- Avro-built four-engine bomber of World War II night-bombing fame. A few are still in service in other roles. Later versions called LINCOLN.

LANCASTRIAN -- Long-range transport conversion of the Lancaster bomber. In service in Argentina.

LANCE -- (1) Swedish J-32 aircraft. See LANSEN.

(2) U.S. Air Force air-to-surface missile with an advanced guidance system (perhaps television) and storable propellant motor. Based on the Navy's BULLPUP, it would carry a nuclear warhead and would be used by Tactical Air Forces. Work discontinued. Air Force designation GAM-79. Also called White Lance.

(3) U.S. Army storable-propellant, Division support, surface-to-surface missile using AUTOMET guidance. With a range of 3-30 miles, the fully mobile missile is expected to replace the HONEST JOHN and LaCROSSE in about 1965-66. Under development. Formerly known as Missile B.

LANCER -- As the Republic YP-43, this was a development of the Seversky XP-41, and a forerunner of the fabulous P-47 of World War II fame.

LANCEWOOD -- Toko (Tankan, Toko-Gai), Formosa. WW-II.

LANCRABEU -- Acronym for Landing Craft and Bases, Europe; U.S. Navy command for build-up operations prior to landings in western Europe. Established 15 July 1943, WW-II.

LAND MATTRESS -- Code name for experimental rocket battery armed with 12 projectors; developed in United Kingdom as a Canadian project. First fired on enemy at Flushing, Holland, 1 November 1944. WW-II.

LANDCRAB -- U.S. invasion of Japanese-occupied Attu Island, Aleutians. Began 11 May 1943, WW-II.

LANDLINK -- Name for peacetime military exercise.

LANDLOCKED -- U.S. Navy Advanced Base, Corinto, Nicaragua. WW-II.

LANDSHARK -- Code name for Cuba. WW-II.

LANDWIRT SUBMARINES -- German submarines of Group Landwirt, a special anti-invasion force of thirty-six small U-boats, active against Allies during Normandy landings, Operation OVERLORD. June 1944, WW-II.

LANESBOROUGH -- Aghione, Corsica. WW-II.

LANGTREE -- Algiers, Algeria. WW-II.

LANGUEDOC -- French Sud-Est SE.161 transport/trainer first flown in 1939. A few are still in service.

LANKY -- Molokai, Hawaii. WW-II.

LANO -- Walker Cay, Bahama Islands. WW-II.

LANOLIN -- Northwestern Pacific Area. WW-II.

LANSEN -- (English translation: Lance) Swedish SAAB J-32 all-weather aircraft first flown in 1952.

LANTANA -- Florida Island, Solomon Islands. WW-II.

LANTPHIBEX -- Joint U.S. Navy-Air Force-Marine Corps peacetime military training exercise.

LAPICIDE -- Pulo Anna Island, Caroline Islands. WW-II.

LAPOVER -- Savaii, Samoa. WW-II.

LAPRE-1 -- Acronym for U.S. Los Alamos Power Reactor Experiment. Utilized circulating pump. Completed 1956 at Los Alamos Scientific Laboratory, New Mexico.

LAPRE-2 -- Second in series of U.S. Los Alamos Power Reactor Experiments. Used natural connection to circulate fuel. Completed 1959 at Los Alamos Scientific Laboratory, New Mexico.

LARBOARD -- Winslow, Alaska. WW-II.

LARDYDARDY -- Cairns, Australia. WW-II.

LARGE SLOW TARGET -- Nickname derived from initialism, LST (Landing Ship, Tank). See also GREEN DRAGONS. WW-II.

LARGESSE -- Landing of Allied force near Sfax, east Tunisian coast, to destroy Italian lines of communication and to coincide with Allied advance from west Tunisia. 5 January 1943, WW-II.

LARK -- U.S. Navy, solid-boosted, liquid sustained, surface-to-air subsonic missile for use as an anti-KAMIKAZE weapon. It had a range of about 38 miles and could reach an altitude of a little under five miles. Used command mid-course guidance and semi-active homing guidance. Development began in late 1944; became operational in 1946 as a research test vehicle to solve radar guidance, stability, control and launching problems. The program ended in December 1950.

LARKSPUR -- (1) Lagos, Nigeria, Africa. WW-II.

(2) Savo Island, Guadalcanal, Solomon Islands. WW-II.

LARYNX -- Earliest British guided weapon, basically a flying bomb which carries a bomb load of 250 pounds at speeds up to 200 miles per hour to a distance of 100 miles. Radio-controlled. Development began in 1927.

LASSIS -- Marcus Island, Pacific Ocean. WW-II.

LASSO -- Tioro Strait, Celebes, Netherlands East Indies. WW-II.

LAST -- Canadian II Corps signals exercise held in United Kingdom in preparation for OVERLORD. Intended to give all unit levels practice in passing information and conducting operations involved in breaking out of a bridgehead. Mid-April 1944, WW-II.

LATEST -- Tatto (Taito-Gai, Taito-Shi), Formosa. WW-II.

LAUNDRESS -- Code word for Vichy French. WW-II.

LAURA -- (1) Swedish ship-to-underwater anti-submarine rocket to be deployed on destroyer-class ships. Has range of about 1.6 kilometers. Under evaluation. See also FLORA.

(2) U.S. code name for Majuro Island, Marshall Group. WW-II.

(3) Typhoon. 11-17 September 1947. First detected near Marcus Island, Pacific. Moved westward at first, then recurved to north and northeastward and out over the Pacific.

(4) Name also included in sequence prepared by meteorologists for future tropical cyclones in North Atlantic.

LAURENCETOWN -- Bastia, Corsica. WW-II.

LAURIE -- Name reserved by meteorologists for tropical cyclone in North Atlantic.

LAVA PLAINS -- Name for U.S. peacetime military exercise at Yakima, Washington; designed to provide combined unit training for infantry division. 1961.

CODE NAMES DICTIONARY

LAW -- Acronym for Light Anti-tank Weapon, which is carried and fired by one man from its disposable carrying case; has a solid propellant rocket motor and fires a shaped charge which can penetrate armor to ranges of 500 yards. Launcher and weapon weigh only 4.5 pounds. Army designation M-72. Operational.

LAWLORD -- Jaluit Island, Marshall Islands. WW-II.

LAWMAKER -- Tipaza, Algeria. WW-II.

LAWMAKING -- Karafuto, Japan. WW-II.

LAWNMOWER -- North Loloda Islands, Halmahera, Netherlands East Indies. WW-II.

LAWYER -- Ascension Island, Atlantic Ocean. WW-II.

LAYFORCE -- Commando force under British Major-General (then Colonel) Sir Robert Edward Laycock in action on Crete. Spring 1941, WW-II.

LAYMAN -- Ramu River Valley, New Guinea. WW-II.

LAZAR -- Maui, Hawaii. WW-II.

LAZARETTO -- Gasmata, New Britain. WW-II.

LAZY DOG -- U.S. Air Force anti-personnel air-to-surface missile designed to be dropped from low-flying aircraft. Only two inches long. Tested at Eglin Air Force Base, Florida. Not under active development.

LEADER, OPERATION -- Air strike by combined U.S. and British naval force against German shipping in northern waters and port of Bordo, Norway. October 1943, WW-II.

LEADMINE -- Singapore, Malaya. WW-II.

LEAP -- Allied destruction of enemy heavy ships attempting to enter the Mediterranean. 20-31 December 1942, WW-II.

LEAP-FROG -- Nickname for procedure by which aircraft are advanced from base to forward base, usually with a tanker aircraft refueling the bomber enroute. See also YO-YO.

LEAPYEAR -- Mostaghanem, Algeria. WW-II.

LEARNTOWER -- North Loloda Islands, Halmahera, Netherlands East Indies. WW-II.

LEARSTAR -- PACAERO modification of the Lockheed 18-56 Lodestar. It first flew in 1954.

LEASIDE -- Name for Royal Canadian Air Force Squadron Number 432.

LEATHERBACK -- Allied task force which carried out Operation CHRONICLE against Woodlark Island, northeast of New Guinea, under ALAMO. 30 June - 5 August 1943, WW-II.

LEATHERCOL -- One of two columns from the 5th Indian Division in action south of Matruh, Egypt. See also GLEECOL. 26 June 1942, WW-II.

LEATHERNECK -- Fortaleza, Brazil. WW-II.

LEAVENWORTH -- Cape Bach, New Britain. WW-II.

LECTERN -- Noumea, New Caledonia. WW-II.

LEDO ROAD -- Military road constructed by Allies; began at Ledo in Assam, intersected Burma Road, and ended in Kunming, China. Also called PICK'S PEAK, STILWELL ROAD. WW-II.

LEDO STRIPTEASE -- Plan for Chinese 22nd Division to move into Shingbwiyang area, North Burma, when Nambyu-Tawang river lines were secured. One regiment would protect Chinese 38th Division's right flank; other would fly to Fort Hertz. See also ALBACORE. 1943, WW-II.

LEECH -- Sunda Strait, Java, Netherlands East Indies. WW-II.

LEFT -- Brisbane, Australia. WW-II.

LEGREST -- Mussan Island, Bismarck Archipelago. WW-II.

LEGSTUMP -- Lesser Sunda Islands. WW-II.

LEGUMINOUS -- (1) Okinawa-Jima Islands, Japan. WW-II.

(2) U.S. plan for base development of Okinawa. 10 February 1945, WW-II.

LEHRGANG -- German operation to evacuate forces from Sicily. August 1943, WW-II.

LEIBSTANDARTE ADOLF HITLER -- Name of German Schutzstaffel (S.S.) division. WW-II.

LEMMING -- Joint U.S.-Canadian exercise, carried out near Churchill, Manitoba, to test operation of various types of over-snow vehicles. Spring 1945, WW-II.

LEMON -- Wonai Bay, Woodlark Island. WW-II.

LENADERG -- Bonifacio, Corsica. WW-II.

LENNONS -- Bambak, New Britain. WW-II.

LENTIL -- (1) Second Allied attack on Pangkalang Brandan Sumatra, preliminary to MERIDIAN. WW-II.

(2) See LINSE

LENTON -- Code name for Gibraltar. WW-II.

LEOPARD -- Bukum, New Guinea. WW-II.

LEOPARD MOTH -- Light cabin monoplane by DeHavilland and introduced in Great Britain in 1933.

LERWICK -- Twin-engine Saunders-Roe flying boat used by Great Britain early in World War II.

LETTERBOX -- Dobodura, New Guinea. WW-II.

LETTERPRESS -- Allied landing force under RECKLESS Task Force which carried out operation against Humboldt Bay, Hollandia area, New Guinea. Began 22 April 1944, WW-II.

LEVER -- British operation to clear area between Reno River and southwest shore of Lake Comacchio, northern Italy. See also FRY, ROAST. April 1945, WW-II.

LEVIATHAN -- System Development Corporation research project to dynamically simulate large social groups by using real-time operation of large digital computer.

LIBECCIO -- Italian Bergamaschi airplane, similar in appearance to the pre-World War II Lockheed Electra. Used in the late 1930's as a transport.

LIBEL -- Cordova, Alaska. WW-II.

LIBELLE -- German Dornier high-wing monoplane flying boats.

LIBERANDOS -- Nickname for U.S. Army Air Forces 376th Heavy Bombardment Group. WW-II.

LIBERATOR -- Consolidated-built heavy bomber which reached higher production than any other U.S. World War II aircraft. Over 18,000 were built. The B-24 was used mainly in the Mediterranean and Pacific due to its longer range.

LIBERATOR DIVISION -- Nickname for U.S. 14th Armored Division.

LIBERATOR EXPRESS -- Cargo conversion of the B-24 aircraft during World War II as the C-87.

LIBERATOR II -- Designation assigned to B-24 aircraft by Great Britain.

LIBERTY -- U.S. developed packet, containing clothing, medical supplies, and personal items, intended primarily for air drop to prisoners of war. See also BALDWIN. Korean Conflict.

LIBERTY BELL DIVISION -- Nickname for U.S. 76th Infantry Division. Also called BELL TELEPHONE DIVISION.

LIBERTY BELL 7 -- Name given by Captain Virgil P. Grissom to his MERCURY capsule in which he made the second U.S. suborbital flight, July 1961. Premature blowout of the escape hatch caused the capsule to flood and eventually sink in 18,000 feet of water.

LIBERTY EAGLE -- U.S. small, pilotless World War One biplane powered by a 2-cycle, 40-horse power engine and guided by a gyro and a highly sensitive aneroid barometer. Capable of carrying 300 pounds of TNT, it was not used operationally, but was flight tested in October 1918 and was in production when the armistice was signed. Made of papier-mache and wood. Also called The Bird, The Bug and the Kettering Aerial Torpedo.

LIBRETTO -- Code name for Bermuda. WW-II.

LICORICE -- Button Passage, Halmahera, Netherlands East Indies. WW-II.

LIDLESS -- Suri, New Guinea. WW-II.

LIEGE -- See LÜTTICH

LIFEBELT -- Operations against Portuguese Atlantic Islands. WW-II.

LIFEBLOOD -- Balboa, Canal Zone. WW-II.

LIFEBOAT -- Code name for Mediterranean Sea. WW-II.

LIFEBUOY -- Panama Railroad Company. WW-II.

LIFEGUARD -- Satawal Island, Caroline Islands. WW-II.

LIFELINE -- Rayak, Syria. WW-II.

LIFEPRESERVER -- Code name for South Atlantic. WW-II.

LIFTMASTER -- Douglas C-118. Military version of the DC-6 which first flew in 1949.

LIFTON -- Code name for target north of La Spezia, Italy, where supplies were air-dropped to Partisans. Winter 1944-45, WW-II.

LIGHTFOOT -- British offensive operations in Libyan Desert, launched westward from El Alamein, Egypt. October 1942, WW-II.

LIGHTHOUSE -- Kowanshi Bay, Formosa. WW-II.

LIGHTHOUSE HILL -- Military name for topographic feature on western Angaur Island, Palau Group. Fall 1944, WW-II.

LIGHTNING -- (1) U.S. Navy program to develop high speed computers and data processing systems with nano-second (10-6 second) speeds. Such processors would have immediate application in missile, space, and command and control systems.

(2) Lockheed P-38 fighter plane. Outstanding combat record in all World War II combat theaters. A YP-38, an XP-38 with an engine change and outward rotating propellors, was called Yippee. Also called CHAIN LIGHTNING.

(3) English Electric P.1 twin-jet presently entering service with Royal Air Force Fighter Command.

(4) Spanish trainer plane. See SAETA.

(5) Italian Macchi C.200 aircraft. See SAETTA.

(6) World War II Italian Macchi C.202 aircraft. See FOLGORE.

LIGHTNING BUG -- See FIREFLY

LIGHTNING DIVISION -- Nickname for U.S. 78th Infantry Division.

LIL -- Acronym for Lunar International Laboratory, a lunar scientific station proposed by Dr. Theodore Von Karman in 1961. He predicted the station would be in operation within 25 years. Other scientists have proposed a similar approach to utilizing the moon.

LILA -- Name reserved by meteorologists for tropical cyclone in North Atlantic.

LILAC -- Plan to concentrate U.S. forces in Belem-Natal-Recife area of Brazil. Late 1941, WW-II.

LILLIAN -- Name reserved by meteorologists for tropical cyclone in eastern North Pacific.

LILLIPUT -- Allied plan for supplying and defending Buna, New Guinea, after its capture.

LILLY -- Typhoon. 11-20 August 1946. First detected between Marianas and Marcus Island. Moved northwestward through Bonin Islands and Ryukyus and turned northward into Korea.

LILOS -- See BOMBARDONS

LILY -- (1) Allied code name for Japanese Kawasaki bomber of World War II.

(2) Ufa Island, Solomon Islands. WW-II.

(3) Name reserved by meteorologists for tropical cyclone in eastern North Pacific.

LIMA -- Code word for letter "L" in a phonetic alphabet, used to avoid possibility of a misunderstanding in transmitting messages. See also LOVE.

LIMABEAN -- (1) Ketchikan, Alaska. WW-II.

(2) Visale, Guadalcanal, Solomon Islands. WW-II.

LIME SODA -- U.S. Air Force high-altitude air refueling area over Minnesota.

LIMEJUICE -- Kodiak, Alaska. WW-II.

LIMEPIT -- South Atlantic Command. WW-II.

LIMERICK -- Ausak Island, Solomon Sea. WW-II.

LIMESTONE -- Thursday Island, Solomon Islands. WW-II.

LINCE -- (English translation: Lynx) Italian Breda 88 World War II twin-engine high-wing fighter and light bomber.

LINCOLN -- (1) Original term for semiautomatic system for data processing in weapon control and air defense operations. Named for Lincoln Laboratories of Massachusetts Institute of Technology which were largely responsible for its development. Now known as SAGE.

(2) Clandestine radio station in Casablanca, French Morocco, used by U.S. consulate at time of Allied landings. See also AJAX.. November 1942, WW-II.

(3) World War II development of the LANCASTER. Last piston-engine bomber to serve with the British Royal Air Force. Remained with first line units until 1955.

(4) Oquaia Point, Trobriand Island. WW-II.

LINCOLN DIVISION -- Nickname for U.S. 84th Infantry Division. Also called RAILSPLITTERS, HATCHET MEN.

LINEOUT -- Aitutaki Island, Cook Islands. WW-II.

LINER -- Code word used to instruct pilots to adjust power for maximum range versus fuel consumption.

LINK, EXERCISE -- Large training exercise involving 61st British Infantry Division and 1st Polish Armoured Division. September 1943, WW-II.

LINK TRAINING PLAN -- Canadian plan for linking of basic and advanced training centres on a corps basis to lessen administrative burden and increase efficiency. Introduced August 1943, WW-II.

LINNET -- French monoplane. See EMERAUDE.

LINNET I -- Allied plan for air drop on Tournai, Belgium; canceled on account of weather. September 1944, WW-II.

LINNETT II -- Allied airborne operation at Aachen-Maastricht Gap in western Europe, planned for 4 September 1944; cancelled. WW-II.

LINSE -- (English translation: Lentil) German radio-controlled motor boat. Operated in units of one control and two explosive motor boats; the latter were steered near target by human pilots, who then jumped overboard and were picked up by control boat, which also directed explosive boats into target by radio. WW-II.

LINTEL -- Matadi, Belgian Congo. WW-II.

LION -- (1) Canadian military name for ridge east of Nissoria, Sicily. July 1943, WW-II.

(2) Name for men and machines designated by U.S. Navy to construct full-sized advanced naval operating bases. See also ACORN, CUB. WW-II.

(3) Name for Royal Canadian Air Force Squadron Number 427.

LION GROUP -- Canadian force active during Operation BLOCKBUSTER in fighting for ALBATROSS objective, a hill at western end of gap between Hochwald and Balberger Wald, Germany. See also TIGER GROUP. Late February, early March 1945, WW-II.

LION ISLAND -- Nabuni Island, Gilbert Islands. WW-II.

LION NOIR -- Name for NATO peacetime military exercise.

LION ONE -- U.S. Navy crew responsible for establishing LION base at Espiritu Santo, New Hebrides. WW-II.

LION SQUADRON -- Popular name for German bomber squadron. Name derived from its crest, a sitting lion, and motto, Vestigium Leonis (the track of the lion). WW-II.

LIONHEARTED -- Los Negros Island, Admiralty Islands. WW-II.

LIPSCOMB -- Bopeenbeen River, New Britain. WW-II.

LIPSTICK -- Great Sitkin Island, Alaska. WW-II.

LIQUIDATOR -- Campaign in China. WW-II.

LIQUORICE -- Code name for Rumania. WW-II.

LISACUL -- Calvi, Corsica. WW-II.

LISE -- Typhoon. 31 August - 4 September 1949. First detected in northern Mariana Islands. Moved westward over Philippine Sea but recurved sharply northeastward and out over North Pacific.

LITERARY -- Ataig, New Britain. WW-II.

LITHARGE -- Mogmog, Ulithi Atoll, Yap Islands. WW-II.

LITIGANT -- Gulf of Tartary, Japan. WW-II.

LITTLE ABNER -- See BEAVER TAIL

LITTLE BEAR -- Name for U.S. peacetime military exercise in Alaska, 1960.

LITTLE BEAVERS -- Nickname for U.S. Navy Destroyer Squadron 23, commanded by Captain Arleigh A. Burke, during operations in Pacific. WW-II.

LITTLE BIG INCH -- Pipeline laid from Texas oilfields to East Coast of U.S. during World War II. See also BIG INCH.

LITTLE BLITZ -- Series of German retaliatory air raids against England. January - March 1944, WW-II.

LITTLE BURMA ROAD -- Nickname for topographic feature on New Caledonia. 1942, WW-II.

LITTLE EVA -- (1) U.N. code name for Umi Do area on Wonsan harbor, North Korea. Korean Conflict.

  (2) U.S. enriched metal experiment at Los Alamos Scientific Laboratory, New Mexico. Began 1951.

LITTLE GEORGE HILL -- Military name for topographic feature on central Bougainville, Solomon Islands. Captured by Australians, November 1944, WW-II.

LITTLE ITALY -- Military name for wadi near Bardia, Libya. 1940-41, WW-II.

LITTLE JOE -- (1) U.S. Navy air-to-air or ship-to-air missile launched by a 1000-pound booster. Sustained by four solid motors and radio-controlled, the winged missile carried a high explosive warhead of 100 pounds. Used operationally in the Pacific, 1944.

LITTLE JOE -- National Aeronautics and Space Administration solid propellant rocket test vehicle designed to flight test "boiler plate" models of the MERCURY capsule and its emergency abort system over short-range, low-altitude trajectories. Between August 1959 and April 1961, seven flight tests were conducted proving the validity of the Mercury design. A more advanced, Little Joe II, is being developed to conduct essentially the same tests on boiler plate models of the APOLLO Command module. Tests are scheduled to begin at White Sands Missile Range, New Mexico, in 1963-64 time period.

LITTLE JOHN -- U.S. Army, unguided solid propelled artillery rocket for use by airborne troops. A smaller version of the HONEST JOHN, the missile is both air and helicopter transportable, and capable of being fired to ranges of over 10 miles from a simple, highly mobile launcher. Will be replaced by LANCE. First fired in 1956, it became operational in 1961 and is integral to units of the 101st Airborne Division. See also CHOPPER JOHN.

LITTLE MAGINOT LINE -- French defense line on the Riviera along Italian border. WW-II.

LITTLE MAROON -- Patos Island, British West Indies. WW-II.

LITTLE ONE -- Russian rocket-powered fighter plane prototype. See MALYUTKA.

LITTLE POCKET -- Military name for Japanese position on Bataan Peninsula, Philippine Islands. Early 1942, WW-II.

LITTLE PROFESSOR -- Nickname for U.N. 155-mm. howitzer emplacement at Komam-ni, Korea, which fired at enemy on THE NOTCH. 1950, Korean Conflict.

LITTLE RED BALL EXPRESS ROUTE -- Allied military trucking route for fast delivery of high-priority items from Carentan, France, to Paris. Replaced by TOOT SWEET EXPRESS. 15 December 1944 - 18 January 1945, WW-II.

LITTLE SWITCH, OPERATION -- Exchange of prisoners at Panmumjam, Korea. 20 April - 3 May 1953, Korean Conflict.

LITTLE TOBRUK -- Nickname for formidable German strongpoint east of Knocke-sur-Mer, Belgium. Cleared by Highland Light Infantry of Canada on 1 November 1944, WW-II.

LITTLE WADI -- Military name for topographic feature near Bardia, Libya; named after Major M.C.D. Little of Australian Army. Winter 1940-41, WW-II.

LITTLE WOLVES -- U.S. code word for destroyer escorts during naval battle with Japanese off Samar, Philippines. See also WOLVES. October 1944, WW-II.

LITTLEJOE -- Code name for Liberia. WW-II.

LITTLEJOHN -- Allied two-pounder anti-tank gun, highly mobile. WW-II.

LITTORAL -- Kato, Formosa. WW-II.

LIVEOAK -- Kanaga Island, Aleutian Islands. WW-II.

LIVESTOCK -- Sangie Island, Netherlands East Indies. WW-II.

LIZA -- Tropical storm. 14-19 July 1961. Formed 300 miles southeast of Acapulco, Mexico. Moved west-northwestward offshore for four days, then northwestward, and dissipated over the Pacific.

LOBBER -- Proposal to the U.S. Army to develop a short range cargo missile to deliver supplies to troops in isolated positions and under emergency conditions. Could carry a 50-pound payload to a range of 50 miles. Never actively developed.

LOBWORN -- Arno Atoll, Marshall Islands. WW-II.

LOCKET -- Kema River, Guadalcanal, Solomon Islands. WW-II.

LOCKJAW -- Allied plans for operations against Kavieng, New Ireland. WW-II.

LOCKSMAN -- Mille Island, Mille Atoll. WW-II.

LOCKSTITCH -- Battle Harbor, Labrador. WW-II.

LOCUST -- Kablumgu Point, New Britain. WW-II.

LOCUST HILL -- U.S. Military name for topographic feature south of Yonabaru, Okinawa. 1945, WW-II.

LODESTAR -- (1) Lockheed Model 18 World War II transport used by the U.S. Army Air Forces as the C-56,-57,-60, and by the U.S. Navy as the R50. Now in civil use. See also SUPER LODESTAR.

(2) Name for peacetime military exercise.

LOEW'S THEATRE -- British and Canadian rest and recreation facility for war-weary troops at Ortona, Italy. WW-II.

LOFTER -- U.S. Advanced Research Projects Agency proposal for a satellite surveillance and warning system to detect ballistic missiles, during their boost phase, with infra-red and ultra-violet sensors. Cancelled in 1962, but sensor research continuing under TABSTONE and TRUMP programs.

LOFTI -- U.S. Navy low frequency experimental communications satellite to measure the intensity of very low frequency (VLF) signals through the ionosphere. Launched piggy-back with TRANSIT III-B on a THOR-ABLE STAR, 21 February 1961. Although payloads did not separate, enough data was collected to indicate feasibility of VLF use in spacecraft guidance and submarine communication via a satellite relay. A second satellite has been launched and the program is continuing. See also COMPOSITE I.

LOGAN -- U.S. explosion site of underground nuclear weapons development test. Nevada Test Site, 1958.

LOGAN BAR -- Nickname for supplementary field ration, mainly chocolate, intended to sustain men in emergency situations for a very short time; named for Captain Paul P. Logan, who developed it in 1934-36. Officially called D RATION.

LOGARITHM -- Surigao Strait, Philippine Islands. WW-II.

LOGBOOK -- Tenes, Algeria. WW-II.

LOGEX -- Joint U.S. Army-Navy-Air Force annual peacetime military exercises.

LOGLINE -- Code name for Paraguay. WW-II.

LOKI -- Originally developed for the U.S. Army as an anti-aircraft barrage rocket, the solid propelled rocket was used to carry research payloads of 6.6 pounds to altitudes of nine miles. Principally used as first stage for the Loki-Dart sounding rocket. Developed between 1949 and 1955, it is still in use as a sounding rocket.

LOLA -- (1) Typhoon. 7-20 November 1957. Formed in Marshall Islands. Moved west-northwestward, passed just south of Guam and over Philippine Sea, then recurved northeastward, passed north of Iwo Jima, and lost force woutheast of Japan.

(2) Typhoon. 8-17 October 1960. Formed east of Taiwan. Moved southwest-ward, then westward across Luzon, Philippines and the South China Sea into northern Viet Nam. Caused 58 deaths and 15 million dollars damage in Philippines.

LONDON -- Saro of England twin-engine flying boat built in the early 1930's and used by Great Britain during the early days of World War II.

LONE TREE HILL -- (1) Military name for topographic feature near Maffin, Netherlands New Guinea. Spring 1944, WW-II.

(2) Military name for topographic feature on Luzon, Philippine Islands. Spring 1945, WW-II.

LONEWOLF -- Plan establishing South Pacific Amphibious Force. WW-II.

LONG BASE -- Name for U.S. peacetime military exercise at Fort Jackson, South Carolina, 1962.

LONG PASS -- Name for U.S. peacetime military exercise in Pacific, 1961.

LONG THRUST II, EXERCISE -- Trans-Atlantic airlift of 5723 American troops from the U.S. to Germany under the U.S. Strike Command. 22 January 1962.

LONG TOM -- (1) A 155-mm gun, believed in 1940 to be the largest needed by the U.S. ground forces. WW-II.

(2) Australian research and test missile designed to check out the Woomera test range tracking equipment and to assist in the development of airborne instrumentation. A three-stage solid propellant missile, it is capable of carrying an instrument payload of 180 pounds to an altitude of about 100 miles and a range of 120 miles. In operational use.

LONGBOW -- Wellington, New Zealand. WW-II.

LONGFACE -- U.S. military attaché, Caracas, Venezuela. WW-II.

LONGHOP -- Plans for operations against Manus Island. WW-II.

LONGHORN -- Name for peacetime military exercise.

LONGLEG -- Kornasoren, Noemfoor Island, New Guinea. WW-II.

LONGLEGS -- See ALOUETTE

LONGSHORE -- Emidj Island, Jaluit Atoll, Marshall Islands. WW-II.

LONGSHOT -- British air-to-air and air-to-surface missile test vehicle designed to check out controls, stability and "g" loading. Beam guided with a homing device for terminal guidance, it was boosted by three clustered jet assisted take-off units. Development began in 1944.

LONGSIGHT -- Advanced Research Projects Agency program for studies of technology which, at some future date, may have application to military requirements. Unorthodox or under-explored applications of technology are emphasized.

LONGSTEP -- Name for peacetime military operation.

LONGSTOP HILL -- Allied name for Djebel el Ahmera or Hill 290 in Tunisia. Called Christmas Hill by Germans because they held on to it through 25 December 1942. WW-II.

LONGSTRIDE -- Name for peacetime military operation.

LONGSUIT -- Tarawa Island, Gilbert Islands. WW-II.

LONGTOM, OPERATION -- Allied occupation of Chusan Archipelago off coast of Chekiang Province, China. 1945, WW-II.

LONGVIEW -- Adak Island, Aleutian Islands. WW-II.

LOOKOUT HILL -- U.S. military name for topographic feature west of Yongdung-po, Korea. September 1950, Korean Conflict.

LOON -- U.S. produced version of German V-1 for use as either a surface-to-surface or air-to-surface missile. Over 300 were built, but the end of World War II precluded their operational use. All three services used the vehicle for several years as a training missile. First American V-1 was fired from Eglin Air Force Base, Florida, in October 1944. Other designations included: JB-2, KUW-1, LTV-N-2.

LOP-GAP -- Acronym for Liquid Oxygen Petrol, Guided Aircraft Projectile, an early post-World War II British attempt to develop a surface-to-air missile using liquid oxygen and gasoline as propellant. At least two versions were tested before the program was discontinued.

LOPSIDED -- Tutuila, Samoa Islands. WW-II.

LOQUAT -- Bungana Island, Tulagi-Florida Group, Solomon Islands. WW-II.

LORAC -- Hyperbolic radio-navigation system which uses intersection of lines to determine position of vehicle. Similar to RADIST.

LORAN -- Acronym for Long-Range Radio Aid to Navigation. Previously called Cytac. See also DECCA.

LORD HAW-HAW -- Nickname for radio propagandist, William Joyce, reputely born in Ireland, who broadcast to England from Germany during World War II. Hanged for treason in London, 3 January 1946.

LORENZ -- German radio-beam blind-landing system. WW-II.

LORNA -- (1) Typhoon. 24 October - 2 November 1958. Formed near Truk Island. Moved westward nearly to Philippines, then turned northeastward and dissipated southeast of Japan.

(2) Typhoon. 20-26 August 1961. Formed Philippine Sea. Moved northwestward across Taiwan and into mainland China. Caused three deaths and floods in Taiwan.

(3) Name also applied to tropical cyclones in western North Pacific which occurred prior to (1) and (2) above.

LORRAINE -- Name reserved by meteorologists for tropical cyclone in eastern North Pacific.

LOS ANGELES -- Name given to hurricane which struck Puerto Rico on 2 August 1837. Named after day in Liturgical calendar on which it occurred.

LOS ANGELES, BATTLE OF -- State of alert in Los Angeles, California, during which a blackout was ordered and anti-aircraft batteries fired on enemy planes, probably falsely, believed to be over area. 25 February 1942, WW-II.

LOST BATTALION -- Nickname for 2nd Battalion, U.S. 19th Infantry Regiment. So named because it held out for 13 days behind Japanese lines in vicinity of Ormoc, Leyte, Philippines. Late 1944, WW-II.

LOSWORM -- Arno Atoll, Marshall Islands. WW-II.

LOTUS -- Doma Reef, Guadalcanal, Solomon Islands. WW-II.

LOUIS -- (1) Typhoon. 24-27 August 1952. Formed in western Caroline Islands. Moved west-northwestward across northern Philippines and South China Sea, and into northern Viet Nam.

(2) Name also included in sequence prepared by meteorologists for future tropical cyclones in North Atlantic.

LOUIS THE LOUSE -- Nickname for Japanese plane which made nightly nuisance raids over Henderson Field, Guadalcanal. See also MAYTAG CHARLIE, WASHING-MACHINE CHARLIE. October 1942, WW-II.

LOUISE -- (1) Typhoon. 3-11 October 1945. First detected in central Caroline Islands. Moved northwestward through Marianas, then curved gradually to the northeast and passed through southwestern Japan into the Sea of Japan.

(2) Typhoon. 25 July - 1 August 1951. Formed south of Guam. Moved west-northwestward across Philippine Sea, the island of Luzon, and the South China Sea to northern Indo China. Caused 38 casualties in Philippines.

(3) Typhoon. 20-30 September 1955. Formed east of Guam. Moved northward first, then northwestward across Iwo Jima, causing heavy damage, then to a position south of Kyushu, Japan. Moved northward across Kyushu causing heavy damage and northeastward across Sea of Japan to Hokkaido.

(4) Typhoon. 1-4 September 1959. Formed near Guam. Moved northwestward across northern Taiwan, entered China coast, then turned north-northeast and merged with another storm system. Caused damage and six deaths on Taiwan.

(5) Typhoon. 20-27 July 1962. Formed between Wake Island and Marianas. Moved northward at first, then westward, then northward into southern Honshu, Japan, curved northeastward and dissipated. Caused landslides and some flooding in Japan.

(6) Name also applied to tropical cyclones in western North Pacific which occurred prior to (1) through (5) above.

LOVE -- (1) Code word for letter "L" in a phonetic alphabet, used to avoid possibility of a misunderstanding in transmitting messages. See also LIMA.

(2) Hurricane. 18-21 October 1950. Formed in Gulf of Mexico off Louisiana coast, moved erratically southward and eastward and weakened before entering upper west Florida coast. Caused little damage.

(3) U.S. plan for series of campaigns designed to seize favorable line of departure and to provide air and naval bases for operations against central Luzon, Philippines. See LOVE I-V. Early 1945, WW-II.

LOVE I -- U.S. landing at Legaspi on Bicol Peninsula of southeastern Luzon, Philippines. 1 April 1945, WW-II.

LOVE II -- U.S. operation to establish air bases at Aparri on northern coast of Luzon, Philippines, in order to cover convoy movements through Luzon Strait. Planned for early 1945, WW-II.

LOVE III -- U.S. occupation and development of airfields in southwestern Mindoro, Philippines. 15 December 1944, WW-II.

LOVE IV -- Unopposed U.S. landing on Marinduque Island, northeast of Mindoro, Philippines. 3 January 1945, WW-II.

LOVE V -- Small unopposed U.S. landing at Bongabong on east coast of Mindoro, Philippines. 1 January 1945, WW-II.

LOVE HILL -- (1) U.S. military name for topographic feature on Okinawa. 1945, WW-II.

(2) Military name for topographic feature in PURPLE HEART RIDGE on Saipan. 1944, WW-II.

LOVE, OPERATION -- Project by chaplains of U.S. 1st Marine Division in Korea to distribute clothing collected in U.S. Korean Conflict.

LOW BLOW -- U.S. Navy surface-to-air ramjet missile, under development.

LOW CARD -- U.S. Air Force program designed to evaluate infra-red sensors as a means of detecting missile launchings at high altitudes. Directly applicable to the now-reoriented MIDAS program; some sensors were evaluated in U-2 flights during missile launches.

LOWBOY -- Okha, Sakhalin Island, U.S.S.R. WW-II.

LOWER BROADWAY -- Military name for portion Wonsan harbor, North Korea, during U.N. naval siege. 16 February 1951 - 27 July 1953, Korean Conflict.

LOYALIST -- Proposed operations to liberate Burma at the earliest possible date. WW-II.

LUBRICATE -- Leyte Gulf, Philippine Islands. WW-II.

LUCERNE -- Umm Qaar, Iraq. WW-II.

LUCERO -- British device, similar to an inquisitor or interrogator, used as auxiliary with radar sets which interrogate radar beacons. Name alludes to member of Spanish Inquisition.

LUCID -- Acronym for Language for Utility Checkout and Instrumentation Development.

LUCIFER -- Blae Harbor, New Britain. WW-II.

LUCILLE -- (1) U.S. code name for Eroj Island, Majuro Atoll, Marshall Group. WW-II.

(2) Tropical storm. 25 May - 1 June 1960. Formed west of Koror Island. Moved northwestward to northern Philippines, joined another storm circulation, and turned northeastward over the Pacific. Caused floods that killed nearly 300 in Philippines.

(3) Typhoon. See KAREN.

LUCIOLE -- C-232 light biplane by Avions Caudron of France in 1933.

LUCK -- Turkish Trainer plane. See UGUR.

LUCKY -- Code word for U.S. Third Army. WW-II.

LUCKY BRAVO -- Name for peacetime military exercise.

LUCKY GOLF -- Name for U.S. peacetime military exercise at Fort Gordon, Georgia, 1962.

LUCKY LADY II -- U.S. Air Force B-50 which made the first nonstop round-the-world flight in 1949. The flight covered 23,452 miles in one minute over ninety-four hours, and the Strategic Air Command bomber was refueled in the air four times.

LUCKY 7TH -- Nickname for U.S. 7th Armored Division.

LUCKY STRIKE -- (1) One of five camps of RED HORSE STAGING AREA in region of Le Havre-Rouen, France. Established November 1944, WW-II.

(2) Allied plan which called for eastward drive with maximum strength after Normandy landings in an effort to defeat German forces west of Seine, followed by a crossing and capture of Seine ports. Followed AXEHEAD plan. Considered early July 1944, WW-II.

LUCKYBAG -- Natal, Brazil. WW-II.

LUCRATIVE -- Bentoni Isthmus, Netherlands East Indies. WW-II.

LUCRETIA -- Tropical storm. 17-19 September 1950. First detected in northern Philippine Sea. Moved northeastward past Japan. See also MISSATHA.

LUCY -- Typhoon. 25 November - 1 December 1962. Formed in western Caroline Islands. Moved westward across southern Philippines, the northern Sulu Sea, the South China Sea, and southern Viet Nam (causing eight deaths), and dissipated in the Gulf of Siam.

LUELLA -- U.S. code name for Calalin Island, Majuro Atoll, Marshall Group. WW-II.

LUGSAIL -- Tulagi Island, Solomon Islands. WW-II.

LULU -- U.S. Navy air-to-surface or ship-to-surface missile carrying a nuclear warhead for use against enemy submarines. Essentially, the 500-pound, two-three mile range weapon is a nuclear depth charge. Tested by the Navy but discontinued in favor of ASROC and SUBROC. Early name was Betsy. See also BETTY.

LULUBELLE -- Surface-to-surface missile under development by the U.S. Navy.

LUMBERJACK -- Allied 12th Army Group advance on Rhine River between Cologne and Coblenz, Germany; resulted in capture of Cologne and seizure intact of Ludendorff Bridge at Remagen. Began 1 March 1945, WW-II.

LUMINOSITY -- Macalajar Bay, Mindanao, Philippine Islands. WW-II.

LUMPSUGAR -- Timor, Netherlands East Indies. WW-II.

LUNA -- An industry proposal for large chemical booster for lunar missions. Has take-off thrust of 10 million pounds. Not under development.

LUNGPOWER -- Mokil Island, Caroline Islands. WW-II.

LUNIK SERIES -- Soviet Lunar and space research vehicles designed to study components of interplanetary matter, corpuscular solar radiation and magnetic fields of the earth and moon. Three flights, January, September and October, 1959, were undertaken with Lunik I passing by the moon and going into solar orbit; Lunik II impacted the moon and Lunik III photographed and transmitted back to earth pictures of 70 per cent of the back side of the moon. Instrumented weights of the Luniks varied from 800 to 959 pounds. Lunik I was also called Mechta (Dream).

LURE OF THE STREAMLINED BAIT -- Ruse, devised by Admiral William F. Halsey, Jr., to bring Japanese naval forces into trap; two damaged U.S. cruisers would send messages in clear asking for assistance while two task forces would remain in hiding off Formosa to sweep in for kill should Japanese appear. Plan uncovered by Japanese. October 1944, WW-II.

LURK DEEP -- Name for peacetime military operation.

LUSAC 11 -- Packard-built, Le Pere-designed biplane. The only American-built fighter to arrive in France before the end of World War One but it did not get into combat.

LUSAC 21 -- Differed from the -11 only in power plant.

LUSTRE -- Movement of British troops and supplies in convoys from Egypt to Greece. See also DEMON. March-April 1941, WW-II.

LUTIN -- Early French rocket-boosted, ramjet-sustained missile; part of series of short and moderate range surface-to-surface test vehicles. Weighing a little over 30 pounds, it had a speed of about 280 miles per hour and a range of three miles. Post World War II development, it was never produced in quantity.

LUTINE -- Bandar Shahpur, Iran. WW-II.

LÜTTICH -- (English translation: Liège) German armored counter-offensive against U.S. line of communication running down western coast of Normandy through Avranches. 6-7 August 1944, WW-II.

LUX -- (1) Ground flare used by German pathfinders. WW-II.

(2) First convoy in TIGAR 26B project from Persian Gulf to China. Arrived in China, March 1945, via LEDO ROAD instead of from Sinkiang Province where an uprising was taking place.

LUXURIANT -- Kai Islands, New Guinea. WW-II.

LYDIA -- Code name of one of series of rearguard actions on phase lines fought by Germans during northward withdrawal to Arno River, Italy. Summer 1944, WW-II.

LYNX -- (1) Italian Breda 88 aircraft. See LINCE.

(2) Name for Royal Canadian Air Force Squadron Number 406.

LYNYE -- Subura, Schouten Islands, New Guinea. WW-II.

LYRICAL -- Singorkai, New Guinea. WW-II.

LYSANDER -- British Westland single-engine aircraft of the late 1930's.

M

M BALLOONS -- Small leaflet-carrying balloons sent by British over Germany; M, which stands for Meteorological, was used to disguise purpose; initially called P BALLOONS. First dispatched October 1939, WW-II.

M DAY -- General military term, with specific applications, for day on which mobilization begins or is postulated to begin.

M-DEFENSE -- Standard E-1 trainer plane, with an engine change, used as a trainer only after delivery in November 1918 to the U.S. Air Service.

MABLE -- (1) U.S. Navy designation of zone in Manila Bay, Philippines, for mine sweeping operations. February 1945, WW-11.

(2) Aisega, Lottin Island, Dampier Strait, New Guinea. WW-II.

MABEL HILL -- U.S. military name for topographic feature on Okinawa. 1945, WW-II.

Mac ARTHUR'S NAVY -- Nickname for U.S. 7th Fleet because of support it gave to the land operations in Pacific commanded by General Douglas MacArthur. WW-II.

MACE -- (1) U.S. Air Force air-breathing, turbo-jet powered, tactical cruise missile with an original 500-mile range, or 1000 miles in the more advanced versions. Uses an unique ATRAN guidance package which allows it to "recognize" the ground it is flying over, and thereby avoid obstacles; an alternative inertial guidance package is also available. An outgrowth of the MATADOR which it replaced, the missile was deployed in Germany in 1958. See also ATRAN, PINPOINT.

(2) See MACZUGA.

MACH TRAINER -- Fokker S.14 jet trainer for the Royal Netherlands Air Force. First flew in 1951; production ceased in 1955.

MacLEAN BRIDGE -- High-level Bailey pontoon bridge constructed across Rhine River at Emmerich, Germany. Named in honor of Brigadier A.T. MacLean, former Chief Engineer of 1st Canadian Army. Spring 1945, WW-II.

MACON -- Sister ship of the early-1930's dirigible, the AKRON. Wrecked off the coast of California in 1935.

MACZUGA -- (English translation: Mace) Military name for topographic feature formed by Hills 252 and 262 above Coudehard, France. So called by Polish troops because of its shape on map. Summer 1944, WW-II.

MAD -- Acronym for Maintenance Assembly and Disassembly, an Atomic Energy Commission program to develop remote control procedures for handling nuclear reactors for ROVER and other nuclear programs. Due to residual radioactivity after a reactor test, the engine must be taken out of the test stand and transported to a safe area by remote control. Program is being actively pursued.

MADAM -- Wolwol, New Britain. WW-II.

MADCAP -- Au (north of Cape Anukur), New Britain. WW-II.

MADELINE -- (1) Typhoon. September 1949. First detected southwest of Marcus Island, the Pacific. Moved northward; when east of Japan turned northeastward out over Pacific.

   (2) Tropical storm. 19-20 July 1961. Formed 400 miles west-southwest of Acapulco, Mexico, moved westward over the Pacific and dissipated.

MADGE -- The only Russian military post-World War II flying boat to be built in quantity. The Beriev Be-6 entered service in 1951.

MADISON -- Offensive operation by General Patton's U.S. Third Army against German positions in the vicinity of Metz, France, and eastward. November-December 1944, WW-II.

MADONNA -- Dumagerette, Negros Island, Philippine Islands. WW-II.

MADRAS CIRCUS -- Name for 7th Indian Infantry Brigade tank maintenance supply head, northeast of Cassino, Italy. March 1944, WW-II.

MADRE -- (1) Acronym for Magnetic Drum Receiving Equipment, a search radar system which uses magnetic drum signal storage principles.

   (2) Name for peacetime military project.

MAE WEST -- Nickname for inflatable lifesaving jackets worn by air crews when flying over water. So named because of their busty appearance when blown up and worn. Term originally used by British Royal Air Force. WW-II.

MAEDA ESCARPMENT -- See HACKSAW RIDGE.

MAEDCHEN -- Code name of one of series of rearguard actions on phase lines, fought by Germans during northward withdrawal to Arno River, Italy. Summer 1944, WW-II.

MAELSTROM -- Okur, New Britain. WW-II.

MAESTRO -- Oahu, Territory of Hawaii. WW-II.

MAGDELINA -- Didmop, New Britain. WW-II.

MAGGIE -- (1) Typhoon. 22-27 August 1946. First detected in central Philippine Sea. Moved northeastward through Volcano Islands and out over North Pacific.

(2) Name also included in sequence prepared by meteorologists for future tropical cyclones in eastern North Pacific.

MAGGOT -- Cape Bolinao, Luzon, Philippine Islands. WW-II.

MAGIC -- (1) Acronym for Modified Action Generated Input Control.

(2) Means by which messages from Tokyo to Japanese agents and officials in Honolulu, Washington, Berlin, and Panama were intercepted and decoded by the U.S. before attack on Pearl Harbor in 1941. WW-II.

MAGIC CARPET -- U.S. Navy name for operation to bring servicemen home to U.S. from overseas after formal Japanese surrender in World War II. Involved convert- ing suitable combatant ships into temporary transports. Began in September 1945.

MAGINOT LINE -- Line of defensive fortifications built, 1927-36, by France along eastern frontier from south of Belfort to Belgian border; overrun by Germans in 1940. Named after André Maginot, 1877-1932, French minister of war in 1920's and 1930's.

MAGISTER -- Potez-Air Fouga CM.170 twin-jet trainer plane in service with many air forces.

MAGNET -- (1) Code name for the two-place trainer version of the Russian Yak-17 jet. Entered service in 1948.

(2) Movement of U.S. troops to Northern Ireland to replace British troops. Began in January 1942, WW-II.

(3) Name for peacetime military project.

MAGNETO -- Code name for international conference held at Yalta, U.S.S.R., attended by U.S. President Roosevelt, British Prime Minister Churchill, and Soviet Premier Stalin. Second phase of ARGONAUT. 4-9 February 1945, WW-II.

MAGNIFICENT LIGHTNING -- Japanese Kyushu J7W1 World War II "canard" fighter. See SHINDEN.

MAGPIE -- (1) German monoplane. See ELSTER.

(2) Bombay, India. WW-II.

MAHATMA -- Haha Jima, Bonin Islands, Japan. WW-II.

MAICE -- Plan to seize French Somaliland by a Free French coup d'etat. WW-II.

CODE NAMES DICTIONARY

MAID -- Acronym for Maintenance Automatic Integration Director, a computer term.

MAIDEN'S HAIR -- See ANGEL.

MAIL RUN -- Routine night attacks by British Wellington bombers on port facilities of Bengasi, Libya, 1941-42. Inspired popular squadron song, to tune of "Clementine." WW-II.

MAILCAN -- Canadian forces air-mail service from Montreal to Prestwick, Scotland, and from there to Naples and Foggia, Italy. Inaugurated late 1943, WW-II.

MAILFIST -- (1) Code name for East Indies. WW-II.

(2) British plan to capture Singapore. Late 1945 or early 1946, WW-II.

MAIN -- Acronym for Medical Automation Intelligence System.

MAINBRACE -- Name for NATO peacetime military exercise. 1952.

MAINE -- Kwalakessi, New Britain. WW-II.

MAINLAND -- Rokko (Rokan, Rokko-Gai), Formosa. WW-II.

MAINSHEET -- Brunei Bay, Northwest Borneo. WW-II.

MAINSPRING -- (1) Code name for Germany or German. WW-II.

(2) Mt. Namur, Lottin Island, Dampier Strait, New Guinea. WW-II.

MAINSTREET -- Wadi Halfa, Sudan. WW-II.

MAINYARD -- Guadalcanal, Solomon Islands. WW-II.

MAISIE -- Military name for area of high ground within bend of Seine River, south of Rouen, France. See also CHALK PITS HILL. Captured by Canadians, late August 1944, WW-II.

MAJESTIC -- (1) Taliwaga, New Britain. WW-II.

(2) Code word substituted in August 1945 for OLYMPIC, projected Allied operation to invade Kyushu, Japan, after that code word had been compromised by being published in a Restricted memorandum. See also CORONET. WW-II.

MALACANAN -- Cape St. Augustin, Mindanao, Philippine Islands. WW-II.

MALACCA -- Godthaab, Greenland. WW-II.

MALAFACE -- French surface-to-surface missile for use against small ships in support of landing craft. Missile weighs 1545 pounds, and has a range of 25 miles. Installed aboard one missile ship and scheduled for more. Solid propelled and command-guided, the missile carries a conventional warhead.

MALAFON -- French ship-to-underwater rocket-boosted homing torpedo for use against submarines at ranges up to 16,500 yards. Missile is programmed to its target, and final guidance is provided by an acoustical homing device. Operational, and installed aboard the Anti-Submarine Warfare Command ship, La Galissoniere.

MALICIOUS -- Palermo, Sicily. WW-II.

MALKARA -- Australian two-stage solid propellant missile used against tanks and field fortifications. Wire-guided to its target at ranges up to two miles; carries a 55-60-pound conventional-shaped charge warhead. Successfully passed field tests against earth and log-stone bunkers in 1961. Operational. Also used by British.

MALLARD -- (1) Grumman's first post-World War II flying boat. The G-73 commercial amphibian is currently in service.

(2) Hyderbad, India. WW-II.

(3) Operation sending gliders bearing reinforcements and supplies into British 6th Airborne Division area, Normandy, toward end of D DAY, Operation OVER-LORD. 6 June 1944, WW-II.

MALLEABLE -- Pingelap Island, Caroline Islands. WW-II.

MALLET -- Marilinan, New Guinea. WW-II.

MALLORY MAJOR -- Allied air offensive against rail and road bridges over Po River to disrupt enemy's flow of supplies into northern Italy. 12-15 July 1944, WW-II.

MALVERN -- Brest, France. WW-II.

MALYUTKA -- (English translation: Little One) Polikarpov Ti-302 rocket-powered fighter plane which underwent powered tests in 1942.

MAMIE -- (1) Nickname for battleship, USS Massachusetts. WW-II.

(2) Typhoon. 12-23 November 1957. Formed in Marshall Islands area. Moved west-northwestward, but recurved northeastward before reaching Mariana Islands and Bonin Islands, and moved past Marcus Island out into Pacific.

(3) Typhoon. 13-21 October 1960. Formed near Kwajelein Atoll. Moved west-northwestward through northern Mariana Islands, then northward past Iwo Jima and northeastward past Japan and out over the Pacific.

(4) Name also applied to tropical cyclones in western North Pacific which occurred prior to (2) and (3) above.

MAMMUT -- See HOARDINGS.

MAMMY -- Broome, Australia. WW-II.

MAMOS -- Acronym for Marine Automatic Meteorological Observing Station, an automatic system for sensing, recording, and transmitting meteorological information mounted in a buoy or small unmanned vessel. Under development, 1960-63.

MAN-ON-MOON -- A not-generally-used term to denote National Aeronautics and Space Administration programs beyond the manned lunar landing, particularly denoting a manned scientific base. Various studies have been, and are being, made of APOLLO follow-on programs.

MANASSAS -- Wogwog Island, New Britain. WW-II.

MANCHESTER -- Britain's Avro 679; largest, and one of the fastest, twin-engine bombers of early 1940's.

MANCHU LAW -- Popular name for an Army regulation, circa 1909, which limited a line officer to four consecutive years of detached duty--a category which included the early Army pilots.

MANCHU, OPERATION -- Planned U.S. company-sized combat patrol raid on suspected enemy command post across Naktong River at Paekchin ferry, Korea. Canceled after North Koreans crossed river in force, 31 August 1950. Korean Conflict.

MANDIBLES -- Proposed British occupation of Dodecanese Islands. 1940-41, WW-II.

MANDRAKE -- Kavilpo River, New Britain. WW-II.

MANDREL -- Allied device for jamming German FREYA radar installations, which gave early warning of approach of bomber aircraft. WW-II.

MANHATTAN DISTRICT -- See MANHATTAN PROJECT.

MANHATTAN PROJECT -- Manhattan District project that developed atomic-energy program, especially the atomic bomb. August 1942-August 1946.

MANHIGH -- U.S. project involving manned, sealed-cabin balloon flight. Reached 101,000 feet. Safely landed 9 October 1958.

MANHOLE -- Code name for Hawaii. WW-II.

MANHOLE, OPERATION -- Allied infiltration by glider of Russian military mission from Italy into Yugoslavia. 23 February 1944, WW-II.

MANIAC -- Acronym for Mathematical Analyzer, Numerical Integrator and Computer.

MANIAC II -- U.S. high-speed electronic computer made by Los Alamos Scientific Laboratory, New Mexico.

MANILA BAY TURTLE SHOOT -- Name for U.S. Navy mine sweeping operation in Manila Bay, Philippines. February 1945, WW-II.

MANILA-TO-LEYTE EXPRESS -- Nickname for Japanese convoy carrying reinforcements bound for island of Leyte, Philippines. November 1944, WW-II.

MANNA -- (1) British occupation of Greece on German withdrawal to pave way for establishment by Allies of a Greek government. See also NOAH'S ARK. October 1944, WW-II.

(2) British air transportation of supplies and food to citizens of western Holland. 29 April-8 May 1945, WW-II.

MANNER -- Shimchiku (Shinteku), Formosa. WW-II.

MANTELSHELF -- Woodlark Island. WW-II.

MANURE -- Walinda River, New Britain. WW-II.

MAORI -- Visayan, Philippine Islands. WW-II.

MAPLE -- (1) Port Moresby, New Guinea. WW-II.

(2) Special minelaying operations in connection with OVERLORD. WW-II.

MAPLE LEAF CITY -- Canadian administrative and recreational center at Campobasso, Italy. WW-II.

MAPLE LEAF HOSTELS -- Canadian hostels in London staffed by the Canadian Red Cross. Used by troops on leave for rest and recuperation. WW-II.

MAQUIS -- An individual or group of individuals engaged in underground activities during World War II; specifically, young men who fled to mountains of Haute-Savoie, France, to avoid German forced labor drafts. Word comes through French from Corsican dialect word, makis, meaning a wild place abounding in bushes and shrubs, and once used to refer to Corsican outlaws who had taken to the wilds.

MARACAIBOS -- Three shallow-draft ships, designed for use as oilers on Lake Maracaibo, Venezuela; converted by British for landing light tanks during attack on Oran, Algeria, November 1942; later did ferry work in Mediterranean. WW-II.

MARAUDER -- Martin B-26, designed in 1939 and first flown in 1940; first U.S. bomber built with a gun turret. Originally called Martian.

MARBLE -- Carnarvon, Australia. WW-II.

MARCO POLO -- Nickname for the VIKING during its development.

MARDER -- (English translation: Marten) German electrically propelled torpedo which was steered by human pilot who released it from its carrier body at short range of target; designed to be used from beach against enemy landing. WW-II.

MARDIGRAS -- Kimbe Bay, New Britain. WW-II.

MARFA -- Code word for U.S. plans for occupation of western New Britain Island to include the general line Gasmata-Talasea. Issued 15 July and 26 August 1943. WW-II.

MARFAK NO. 2 -- Nickname, given by U.S. troops, to preserved butter in combat rations. Named after well-known brand of motor oil. WW-II.

MARGE -- (1) Surabaya, Java, Netherlands East Indies. WW-II.

    (2) Tropical storm. 31 October - 4 November 1945. First detected in western Caroline Islands. Moved west-northwestward across Philippine Sea and southern Luzon into South China Sea.

    (3) Typhoon. 10-18 August 1951. Formed between Truk and Guam. Moved northwestward, passing south of Guam, across Philippine Sea and east of Okinawa into Yellow Sea and Manchuria.

    (4) Typhoon. 27 September - 3 October 1955. Formed near Guam. Moved northwestward to island of Kyushu, Japan, and lost force.

MARGERINE -- Gulei, New Britain. WW-II.

MARGIE -- (1) Tropical depression. 2-3 September 1959. Formed over northern part of South China Sea and moved northwestward into China mainland west of Hong Kong.

    (2) Tropical storm. 28-29 July 1962. Formed and dissipated short distance east of Guam, Mariana Islands, the Pacific.

    (3) Name also included in sequence prepared by meteorologists for future tropical cyclones in western North Pacific.

MARGO -- Name reserved by meteorologists for tropical cyclone in North Atlantic area.

MARIANAS TURKEY SHOOT -- Nickname for U.S. naval air victory on 19 June 1944, during Battle of Philippine Sea; 402 Japanese planes were destroyed. WW-II.

MARIE -- (1) Typhoon. 19-25 September 1954. Formed over eastern Caroline Islands. Moved northwestward over Philippine Sea, then turned northeastward, passed east of Taiwan and west of Okinawa into East China Sea.

    (2) Typhoon. 26 October - 3 November 1958. Formed near Kwajalein Atoll. Moved erratically northwestward, then recurved northeastward, passed south of Japan and weakened over the North Pacific. Sank two Japanese fishing vessels. Caused 35 deaths.

    (3) Tropical storm. 29 August - 3 September 1961. Formed near Marcus Island, the Pacific. Moved northward briefly, then westward and dissipated west of the Bonin Islands.

(4) Name also applied to tropical cyclones in western North Pacific which occurred prior to (1) through (3) above.

(5) Free French plan to seize Jibuti, French Somaliland, by a bloodless coup d'etat. Proposed November 1940, WW-II.

MARIGOLD -- British operation to land military personnel along east coast of Sardinia. 30 May-1 June 1943, WW-II.

MARINE TRAIL -- U.S. military name for topographic feature on Guadalcanal. 1942-43, WW-II.

MARINER -- (1) Martin twin-engine PBM flying boat used by the U.S. Navy during World War II.

(2) Name for NATO peacetime military exercise. 1950's.

(3) National Aeronautics and Space Administration planetary space probe program to study interplanetary space between earth and Mars and Venus, and to obtain data on the planets' temperature distribution, atmospheric composition, geo-magnetically trapped particles and interplanetary and planetary magnetic fields. Launched by ATLAS-AGENA, the initial Mariners will fly-by planets and scan electronically to collect data. Later versions will eject a capsule to planetary surface. First Mariner launch failed, but second was successful in summer of 1962; reached Venus 14 December 1962 and furnished first close-up data on Venus. See also CENTAUR, VOYAGER.

MARITA -- German operation for occupation of Grecian Macedonia and, possibly, Greek mainland to prevent British from establishing air bases in Balkans. Spring 1941, WW-II.

MARK -- Designation for Soviet Yak-7, first flown in 1940 as the I-26. Later versions escorted American bombers on the famed shuttle raids of World War II. Called Krasavec (Beauty) by the Russians.

MARK 20 -- Forerunner of the Mooney Mark 21, the 20A air frame was of laminated spruce; first flown in 1953.

MARK 21 -- Single-engine, all-metal monoplane in production by Mooney Aircraft since 1961.

MARKET-GARDEN -- Allied operation to establish a bridgehead across the Rhine in the Netherlands. Operation Market, the airborne phase, involved seizure of bridges between Eindhoven and Arnhem; Operation Garden, the ground phase by British XXX Corps, was to open a corridor from Eindhoven northward toward Germany. Originally conceived as smaller Operation Comet. Began 17 September 1944, WW-II.

MARKET II -- Name for U.S. peacetime airborne exercise.

MARKSMAN -- On Mark Aircraft Corporation executive conversion of the Douglas B-26 INVADER.

MARLIN -- Martin P5M twin-engine flying boat developed for the U.S. Navy; first flown in 1951.

MARLOW -- Capri, Italy. WW-II.

MARMALADE -- Santa Lucia, Cuba. WW-II.

MAROON -- Trinidad, British West Indies. WW-II.

MAROUBRA FORCE -- Australian units charged with mission of holding Kokoda, Papua, New Guinea. Summer 1942, WW-II.

MARQUEE -- Hobart, Tasmania. WW-II.

MARQUIS -- Cooperative development of the Beech Model 95 in France. First flown 1960.

MARROW -- Maika, New Britain. WW-II.

MARROWBONE -- Code name for Eastern Siberia. WW-II.

MARS -- (1) Acronym for Military Affiliated Radio System, a world-wide network of amateur-operated radio stations sponsored by U.S. Air Force-Army in order to provide an alternate communications system in times of emergency. Formerly known as Military Amateur Radio System.

(2) Acronym for Multi-Aperature Reluctance Switch, a random access data storage unit to be used in the Orbiting Astonomical Observatory. Memory storage capacity is the largest available in space vehicle-size unit.

(3) Acronym for Mobile Atlantic Range Ships, converted liberty ships which can be positioned in the South Atlantic or Indian Oceans to track missile and space vehicle launchings. Fleet now numbers four, and will grow to about nine within the next several years to meet the requirements of U.S. Air Force-National Aeronautics and Space Administration launch rates.

(4) Martin JRM World War II U.S. Navy flying boat now used in Canada as a water tanker to "bomb" forest fires.

(5) Acronym for an industry proposal for a Manned Astronautical Research Station, a three-man space laboratory for the development of long-term (up to two weeks) biological data, equipment and techniques for space missions. This particular proposal is not under development, but objectives will be achieved in the GEMINI and APOLLO programs.

(6) U.S. 5332nd Brigade (Provisional) organized for long-range penetration operations in Burma. Contained many survivors of GALAHAD. Originally planned by General Joseph W. Stilwell to be Sino-American combined unit. Activated 26 July 1944, WW-II.

MARSA -- Acronym for Military authority Assumes Responsibility for Separation of Aircraft in flight.

MARSH BUGGY -- U.S. Army off-road transportation test vehicle.

MARSHA -- Name reserved by meteorologists for tropical cyclone in North Atlantic area.

MARSHALL MEMORANDUM -- Name given by British to informal plans U.S. General George C. Marshall and MODICUM party took to London for British consideration; outlined objective, timing, combat strength and strategic advantages of operations in western Europe. April 1942, WW-II.

MARSHMALLOW -- (1) Mokmer, Biak Island, New Guinea. WW-II.

(2) Code word for "torpedo track sighted." WW-II.

MARSUPIAL -- See MARSUPIALE.

MARSUPIALE -- (English translation: Marsupial) S.M.75 Italian commerical aircraft prototype of the World War II tri-motor Savoia-Marchetti S.M.79 transport. See also SPARVIERO.

MARTEN -- See MARDER

MARTHA -- (1) Typhoon. October 1948. First detected south of Marcus Island, the Pacific. Moved northward at first, then turned westward but recurved northeastward before reaching land. Passed out over the North Pacific.

(2) Name also included in sequence prepared by meteorologists for future tropical cyclones in North Atlantic.

MARTIAN -- Original nickname for Martin B-26 of World War II. See Marauder.

MARTIN, MAJOR WILLIAM -- See MINCEMEAT

MARTINI -- Dodecanese Islands, Mediterranean Sea. WW-II.

MARTLET -- British nickname for the World War II Grumman F4F WILDCAT aircraft.

MARU BOATS -- Small Japanese boats, similar in construction and operation to Q BOATS. WW-II.

MARUCA -- French Navy surface-to-air missile used to checkout components and systems for the MASURCA missiles and to train personnel in the handling of ship-launched missiles. Solid propellant motors are used to boost missile, and liquid motors used as sustainer. Has a range of 11 miles, and can reach altitudes of about 10 miles. Operational since 1957. Now used for training.

MARUDAI -- See BAKA BOMB.

MARUEL -- U.S. Army short take-off and landing aircraft under study by Mississipi State University.

MARY -- (1) Typhoon. 29-31 August 1952. Formed over southern Philippine Sea. Moved northwestward across northern Luzon, then northward through Formosa Strait and eastern China, then northeastward across Korea into Sea of Japan.

(2) Typhoon. 3-12 June 1960. Formed in South China Sea. Moved northward, entered China mainland near Hong Kong, turned eastward back out to sea, passed north of Okinawa and South of Japan and out over the Pacific. Caused great destruction in Hong Kong.

(3) Typhoon. See KAREN

(4) Name also applied to tropical cyclones in western North Pacific which occurred prior to (1) through (3) above.

MARYLAND -- Bulu-Murli, New Britain. WW-II.

MASALCA -- French Navy surface-to-air ship-launched missile. Solid propelled, employs semiactive radar homing guidance, and has a range of approximately 60 miles. Became operational on cruisers in 1961.

MASCOT -- Training version of the Russian IL-28 BEAGLE aircraft.

MASER -- Acronym for Microwave Amplification by Stimulated Emmission of Radiation.

MASHIE -- Navalapua, New Britain. WW-II.

MASONITE -- Koskins Peninsula, New Britain. WW-II.

MARQUERADE -- Cape Reilnitz, Manning Strait, Solomon Islands. WW-II.

MASS -- U.S. Army peacetime project involving supply system.

MASSACRE VALLEY -- Name for topographic feature north of Wonju, Korea. Scene of entrapment of U.N. troops. Early 1951, Korean Conflict.

MASTER -- Code word for U.S. First Army. WW-II.

MASTER STATION -- Center station of GEE medium-range radar system, situated on east coast of Great Britain; time-lag in reception of signals transmitted by it and SLAVE STATIONS to north and south enabled navigator to plot position of his aircraft. WW-II.

MASTHEAD -- Numundo Point, New Britain. WW-II.

MASTIFF -- Air transportation of medical supplies and evacuation of Allied prisoners of war in Far East after surrender of Japan. 1945, WW-II.

MASURCA -- French Navy surface-to-air ship-launched missile with a range of 18 miles. Solid propelled; uses a beam rider guidance system and a high explosive warhead. Mark I version is in limited production and is operational on cruisers and squadron escorts; Mark II version is undergoing flight tests.

MAT I -- Japanese tactical anti-tank weapon being developed for the Japan Army Self Defense Forces. Wire-guided and solid-propelled, it reportedly has a range of 5000 feet. First firing took place in March 1961.

MATADOR -- (1) U.S. Air Force air-breathing, turbojet-powered, tactical cruise missile with a range of 600 miles. Using a solid booster, it is essentially a pilotless bomber. First missile operationally deployed by the Air Force in 1951. Squadrons deployed in Germany, Korea, and Taiwan. Two squadrons in Germany being turned over to the West Germans. Replaced in U.S. arsenal by MACE.

(2) British plan to occupy Singora area on Malay Peninsula in Siam to forestall the Japanese. First formulated in August 1941; canceled on 8 December 1941 after Japanese landings there. WW-II.

MATADOR MACE -- Early name for MACE.

MATAJUR -- Yugoslav KB-6 monoplane. First flown 1952.

MATCHABLE -- Panaon Strait, Philippine Islands. WW-II.

MATCHWOOD -- Talasea Airdrome, New Britain. WW-II.

MATICA -- (English translation: Queen Bee) Yugoslav twin-jet basic trainer which first flew in 1960.

MATILDA -- British infantry tank. WW-II.

MATRA -- French air-to-air missiles for MIRAGE aircraft and other Air Force and Navy planes. Matra R.511 is already operational while Matra R.530, a more advanced version is undergoing final flight testing preparatory to production. Both are solid fueled and employ high explosive warheads. R.511 has an auto-pilot guidance system and the R.530 has an infra-red homing unit.

MATT I -- Abatiku Island, Gilbert Islands. WW-II.

MATTERHORN -- Bombing of targets in Japan by B-29 aircraft of U.S. XX Bomber Command based in Bengal, India, and staged through airfields at Chengtu, China. First mission flown against Yawata, Japan, 15 June 1944. See also DRAKE. WW-II.

MATTERHORN PROJECT -- U.S. study on controlled thermonuclear problem; conducted at Princeton University. 1951.

MATTRESS -- U.S. Air Force radio and telephone communications code word signifying "am flying below clouds."

MATURE -- Kabunikau Point, Lusancay Island. WW-II.

MAUDE -- Acronym for Morse Automatic Decoder.

MAULER -- U.S. Army surface-to-air missile for mobile defense against supersonic aircraft, short-range ballistic missiles and rockets in combat areas. Air and helicopter transportable, the system is normally mounted on a fully-tracked armored vehicle. A single-stage solid-propellant missile, it uses infra-red acquisition for guidance. Undergoing firing tests, it should become operational in 1963. Navy is considering use of the system on landing craft. NATO countries are also considering buying the system.

MAURICE, OPERATION -- Allied plan for attack from north on Trondheim, Norway, by force landed at Namsos. Successor to RUPERT. See also OPERATION HENRY. Not carried out. April 1940, WW-II.

MAUSI -- Royal Canadian Air Force Junkers 52, equipped for minelaying. WW-II.

MAVIS -- Name for Japanese Kawansishi 97 flying boat patrol bomber. WW-II.

MAWSEED -- Tanamerah, New Guinea. WW-II.

MAX -- Russian Yak-18 trainer plane introduced in 1946 and progressively developed since.

MAXWELL -- Siwat Island, New Britain. WW-II.

MAY DAY -- Radio distress signal originating from the French m'aider, meaning to help me.

MAYFLOWER -- Gilva, Lottin Island, Dampier Strait, New Guinea. WW-II.

MAYFLY -- U.S. base, Midlands, England. WW-II.

MAYNOOTH -- Allied code name for Asnelles, France. WW-II.

MAYOR OF WONSAN -- Honorific title which passed from one commander of U.N. naval Task Unit 95.2.1 to another, along with "Key to the City," during duty in siege of Wonsan, North Korea. Probably originated May 1952, Korean Conflict.

MAYTAG CHARLIE -- Nickname for Japanese plane which made nightly nuisance raids over Henderson Field, Guadalcanal. See also LOUIS THE LOUSE, WASHING-MACHINE CHARLIE. October 1942, WW-II.

MAZE -- Melbourne, Australia. WW-II.

McDUFF -- Boeroe Island, Netherlands East Indies. WW-II.

McGILL FENCE -- Radar warning fence across Canada, mainly equipped with devices developed by McGill University. Gives warning of approaching aircraft. See also PINETREE LINE and DEW LINE.

McGOWAN, LIEUTENANT COLONEL -- Name used by U.S. diplomat, Robert Murphy, when he traveled in disguise from Washington to London to discuss plans for North African landings with General Dwight D. Eisenhower. September 1942, WW-II.

ME -- Soviet solid-propelled anti-tank missile with a range of over two miles. Fired from a bazooka-type launcher, the 10.5-pound missile has a high explosive warhead. Operational in Eastern Europe and the Middle East, it is believed that the missile, in production since 1946, is being replaced with more modern weapons. Also known as IGOR.

MEACONING -- Counter-measure used by British to falsify German radio direction-finding transmissions. WW-II.

MEADOWS -- Code word for "dangerous ground." WW-II.

MEASLES -- German air force slang for anti-aircraft fire. WW-II.

MEAT BALL EXPRESS -- Special military railway service delivering perishables, mostly meat, from Namur, Belgium, to U.S. 1st and 9th Armies. Began March 1945, WW-II.

MEAT BALLS -- U.S. Navy nickname for Japanese planes. WW-II.

MECCA AIRLIFT -- One of the most dramatic airlifts in history; U.S. Air Force airlifted to Mecca nearly 4000 pilgrims who would have otherwise been stranded in Beirut, Lebanon. 1952.

MECHANICAL MULE -- Popular name for quarter-ton U.S. Infantry carrier.

MECHANISM -- Gosei, Formosa. WW-II.

MECHTÁ -- (English translation: Daydream) Russian lunar probe fired 2 January 1959. Missed moon by 4600 miles, but achieved solar orbit. See also LUNIK SERIES.

MEDFLEX B -- Name for peacetime military exercise.

MEDICO -- Anurio Island, New Britain. WW-II.

MEDLAND EX -- Name for peacetime military exercise.

MEETINGHOUSE -- Tokyo, Japan. WW-II.

MEGAPHONE -- American Mission, Salinas, Ecuador. WW-II.

MELINITE -- Argentia, Newfoundland. WW-II.

MELL, MR. -- See MR. MELL

MELLOW -- U.S. Air Force tactical radio control station at Taegu, Korea. Established 20 July 1950 after evacuation from Taejon, Korea. See also ANGELO. Korean Conflict.

MELODEON -- Broadband, panoramic receiving set generally used for counter-measures reception.

MELUSINE -- Operable French pool nuclear reactor in Grenoble, France.

MELVILLE BRIDGE -- Low-level Bailey pontoon bridge constructed by Allies across Rhine River at Emmerich, Germany. Named in honor of Brigadier J. L. Melville, former Chief Engineer of 1st Canadian Army. Opened to traffic, 1 April 1945, WW-II.

MEMBER -- Sao, Formosa. WW-II.

MEMSAHIB -- Raboul, New Britain. WW-II.

MENACE -- Unsuccessful Allied naval expedition to establish Free French forces under General de Gaulle in Vichy controlled Dakar, French West Africa. Originally planned under code name Scipio. September 1940, WW-II.

MENDICANT -- Malakal Island, Palau Islands. WW-II.

MENTONE -- Code name for Peru. WW-II.

MENTOR -- Beech T-34 trainer plane delivered to the U.S. Air Force in 1952; formerly used as a primary trainer by the Air Force, Navy, and foreign countries.

MERCANTILE -- Manus Island, Bismarck Archipelago. WW-II.

MERCAST -- Radio broadcast system for delivery of messages originated by government agencies and addressed to merchant ships, including storm warnings.

MERCATOR -- Martin P4M patrol and search plane in limited service with the U.S. Navy.

MERCEDES -- Sealark, Santa Isabel Island, Solomon Islands. WW-II.

MERCENARY -- Honshu Island, Japan. WW-II.

MERCHANT OF VENICE -- Code signal indicating that process of supply and reinforcement could begin after U.S. capture of airstrip west of Myitkyina, Burma. 17 May 1944, WW-II.

MERCURY -- (1) U.S. National Aeronautics and Space Administration one-man spacecraft project designed for earth orbital missions. Launched by ATLAS D into a low earth orbit. First manned suborbital flight was that of Lieutenant Commander Alan Shepherd, 5 May 1961. First orbital flight was that of Lieutenant Colonel John Glenn, 20 February 1962. Program's flights completed with that of Major Gordon Cooper. Program officially ended 12 June 1963. See also LITTLE JOE, GEMINI, APOLLO.

(2) Code name for Panama. WW-II.

(3) See MERKUR

MERCURY-ATLAS -- See ATLAS-MERCURY

MERCURY-REDSTONE -- Combination of the MERCURY capsule and a modified REDSTONE missile used for suborbital flights to test capsule and astronauts. Developing 78,000-pound thrust, the· liquid-propelled Redstone was used for the 5 May 1961 successful sub-orbital flight of Commander Alan B. Shepherd and the 21 July 1961 flight of Captain Virgil Grissom. After these flights, Redstone was discarded for ATLAS for orbital flights.

MERCURY SCOUT -- National Aeronautics and Space Administration program to use SCOUT launch vehicle to place a 100-pound satellite in approximately the same orbit that would be followed by the MERCURY capsule in order to test the world-wide tracking network. Also designed to test communications. Launch on 1 November 1961 from Cape Canaveral failed after 30 seconds.

MERCY MISSION NO. 1 -- Unsuccessful attempt by U.S. Air Force to use L-5 liaison planes for air rescue in Korea. July 1950, Korean Conflict.

MERIDIAN -- Allied attack on refineries at Palembang, Sumatra, by carrier-borne aircraft. January 1945, WW-II.

MERILL'S MARAUDERS -- See GALAHAD.

MERITORIOUS -- Aineman Island, Jaluit Atoll, Marshall Islands. WW-II.

MERKUR -- (English translation: Mercury) German operation to capture Island of Crete. May 1941, WW-II.

MERLIN -- Allied operation to advance to and capture Faenza, Italy. Began 21 November 1944, WW-II.

MERRY-GO-ROUND V-BEAM -- Radar system used for early-warning and height-finding.

MERRYMAID -- Bohol, Philippine Islands. WW-II.

MERRYMAKER -- Petropavlovsk, U.S.S.R. WW-II.

MESA DRIVE -- Name for U.S. peacetime military exercise at Yakima Firing Center, Washington, 1962.

MESPOT -- Cover and deception policy for western Europe from 1 January 1944 until NEPTUNE plus 21 days. WW-II.

MESQUITE DUNE -- Name for U.S. peacetime military exercise at Camp Irwin, California.

MESSENGER -- The British Miles M.38, produced in small numbers during World War II for the Royal Air Force.

META-SOKOL -- Czech monoplane which first flew in 1954.

METAL -- Code name for Newfoundland. WW-II.

METAPHOR -- Cold Bay, Unimak, Alaska. WW-II.

METEO -- (1) Soviet sounding rocket for upper atmospheric research during the International Geophysical Year. Parachute-recoverable 159-pound payload could be launched to altitudes of 60 miles by the solid booster and liquid sustainer engines. First fired in 1950.

    (2) Family of three Italian sounding rockets capable of carrying scientific payloads of 12 pounds to altitudes of 43 miles in early versions, and 25-pound loads to 95 miles in the most advanced version. All are solid propelled, two-stage vehicles. Meteo I has been flight tested. Meteo II and III are under development.

METEOR -- British Gloster twin-turbojet fighter; no longer first-line equipment with the Royal Air Force. In its earliest version, saw limited service during World War II.

METEOR II -- (1) U.S. twin-engine monoplane built by Saturn Aircraft. First flew in 1960.

    (2) Israeli surface-to-surface and surface-to-air unguided research rocket. Reportedly weighs between 550 and 660 pounds, and is solid propelled. First firing in 1961.

METFIELD -- Code name for Bulgaria. WW-II.

METHUSELAH -- U.S. Air Force air-launched supersonic ramjet test vehicle for the BOMARC program. Boosted to the supersonic flight regime after drop, the test vehicle was recovered by parachute. Used between 1951 and 1960. Was also known as the X-7 and, in the drone version, the Q-5.

METRO -- Sarhe, New Britain. WW-II.

METROC -- Acronym for Meteorological Rocket, a U.S. sounding rocket used to gather weather data at altitudes up to 20 miles. A two-pound instrument package, recoverable by parachute; launched to altitude by a single small solid motor producing 130-pound thrust. Entire rocket weighs only 18 pounds. In operational use.

METROPOLITAN -- Nickname for the Convair 440 twin-engine aircraft in commercial and military use in large numbers since it first flew in 1955. See SAMARITAN.

METTLE -- Grass Point, New Britain. WW-II.

MEW -- Military acronym for Microwave Early Warning.

MIA -- Acronym for the U.S. Air Force "Mouse in Able" program, in which mice were carried aboard THOR-ABLE boosters. The first flight test with mice was in 1958. Also, reportedly, the name of one of the mice used in the experiments.

MICHAEL -- U.S. tactical air-direction center at Taegu, Korea, Korean Conflict.

MICHAELMAS -- Allied task force under ALAMO which carried out Operation DEXTERITY against Saidor, northeast New Guinea. 2 January-10 February 1944, WW-II.

MICHIGAN -- Puspun, New Britain. WW-II.

MICKEY -- Series name for 3-centimeter, airborne radar equipment used in high-altitude bombing, search and navigation.

MICKEY FINN, OPERATION -- Company-size raid by Black Watch of Canada on Knapheide, south of Groesbeek, Netherlands. 7 December 1944, WW-II.

MICKEY MOUSE -- Early U.S. Army microwave radar, the SCR 547, used with anti-aircraft gun batteries in range finding; nicknamed for its two-dish antennas which were shaped like mouse ears. WW-II.

MICKEY MOUSE BATTLE FLEET -- Popular name for three 40-foot motor launches equipped with light armament active against Japanese on Bataan cliffs opposite Corregidor in Philippines. Early 1942, WW-II.

MICROCOSM -- Goodenough Island, New Guinea. WW-II.

MICROSCOPE -- Nagoya, Japan. WW-II.

MICROWEX 50 -- U.S. peacetime military training exercise. 1950.

MIDAS -- Acronym for Missile Defense Alarm System, a U.S. Air Force program to detect ballistic missile launches, during the launch phase, through infra-red sensors in orbiting satellites. ATLAS-AGENA booster is used with the AGENA, providing on-orbit stabilization and control once payload is injected into orbit. Technical difficulties have forced the re-orientation of the program back into the development stage. At least six Midas satellites have been launched, but since Department of Defense space secrecy directive, it is impossible to determine the exact number.

MIDDLE WEST DIVISION -- Nickname for U.S. 89th Infantry Division. Also called ROLLING W DIVISION.

MIDDLESEX HILL -- British name for topographic feature near Songju, Korea; captured by 1st Battalion, Middlesex Regiment on 22 September 1950. Also called Point 325 and Hill 341. Korean Conflict.

MIDGET -- Mig-15 UTI two-seater trainer version of the FAGOT fighter aircraft. In service in Russia, her satellites and "neutral" nations.

MIDGETMAN -- U.S. Air Force study of a small solid propellant intercontinental ballistic missile beyond MINUTEMAN. Never approved for development.

MIDWIFE -- Salier Strait, Celebes, Netherlands East Indies. WW-II.

MIG -- Acronym for Russian aircraft named for designers Mikoyan and Gurevich.

MIG ALLEY -- Name given by U.N. aviators to air space in northwest Korea from Yalu River south to Pyongyang. Korean Conflict.

MIGHTY A -- Nickname for light cruiser, USS Atlanta. WW-II.

MIGHTY B -- See OLD FAITHFUL

MIGHTY MINE DODGERS CERTIFICATE -- Unofficial award given to group of U.S. submarines which penetrated heavily-mined Tsushima Strait, between Korea and Japan, and entered Sea of Japan. 1945, WW-II.

MIGHTY MOUSE -- U.S. Navy and Air Force, unguided, folding fin aircraft rocket capable of being fired in salvos of more than 100 from fighter-interceptors of the two services. Small (2.75-inch diameter) and inexpensive (less than 100 dollars per copy), the solid propellant rocket was developed shortly before and during the Korean War. Its high explosive warhead has the power of a 75-mm. artillery shell. In production in 1951.

MIGHTY WIND -- Kawanishi N1K1 World War II Japanese Kyofu fighter. See GEORGE.

MIHORO -- One of three groups of Japanese 22nd Air Flotilla, which attacked and sank British battleship, Prince of Wales, and battlecruiser, Repulse, off east coast of Malaya. See also GENZAN, KANOYA. 10 December 1941, WW-II.

MIKADO -- Japanese-built Italian Fiat B.R.20 twin-engine bomber. Also see CICOGNA.

MIKE -- (1) Code word for letter "M" in a phonetic alphabet, used to avoid possibility of a misunderstanding in transmitting messages.

(2) U.S. thermonuclear explosion in Pacific Proving Grounds. In the debris of explosion, elements 99 and 100 were discovered. November 1952.

MIKE, HILL -- (1) U.S. military name for topographic feature on Leyte, Philippine Islands. October 1944, WW-II.

(2) U.S. military name for topographic feature on Okinawa. 1945, WW-II.

MIKE OPERATIONS -- Series of U.S. operations and planned operations on island of Luzon, Philippines. See MIKE I-VII. 1945, WW-II.

MIKE I -- U.S. invasion of Lingayen Gulf, Luzon, Philippines. 9 January 1945, WW-II.

MIKE II -- Plan for U.S. invasion of Baler-Atimonan area on eastern coast of Luzon, Philippines. Early 1945, WW-II.

MIKE III -- Plan for U.S. invasion of Batangas area of southwestern Luzon, Philippines; later changed to area around Vigan in northern Luzon. Early 1945, WW-II.

MIKE IV -- U.S. plan to strike west coast of Luzon, Philippines, in Zambales Province. Early 1945, WW-II.

MIKE V -- U.S. plan to consolidate operations in Luzon, Philippines. 1945, WW-II.

MIKE VI -- U.S. amphibious and airborne landing in Nasugbu-Pagbilao area south of Manila, Philippines. 31 January 1945, WW-II.

MIKE VII -- U.S. landing near San Antonio, west-central Luzon, Philippines. 29 January 1945, WW-II.

MIKI -- U.S. peacetime military exercise held in Hawaii. Fall 1949.

MILCH COWS -- Name used by German Navy for their U-tankers in supply and fueling operations for submarines. WW-II.

MILD -- Canton Island, Phoenix Islands. WW-II.

MILDRED -- Typhoon. 22-25 September 1947. First detected in the Philippine Sea east of Luzon. Moved west-northwestward across Luzon and into China west of Hong Kong.

MILEPOST -- Agreement, made at Moscow Conference in October 1944, to have U.S. build up stocks in Far East in preparation for Russian entry into war against Japan. WW-II.

MILES MAGISTER -- One of the earliest monoplanes to be selected as a trainer by the British Royal Air Force. Built by Phillips-Powis prior to World War II.

MILES MASTER -- World War II British Phillips-Powis advanced trainer for the Royal Air Force.

MILLENNIUM -- British air raid on Cologne, Germany; first 1000 bomber attack of war. 30-31 May 1942, WW-II.

MILLET -- Diversionary operation by British in the form of an air strike within the Southeast Asia Command to coincide with major operations by United States Forces in the Philippines. 15-21 October 1944, WW-II.

MILLION DOLLAR GUARD -- Nickname applied to American flying cadets, who, while waiting for planes and instructors at Issoudon during World War I, were receiving $100 a month pay for performing menial chores.

MILLION DOLLAR HILL -- (1) Military name for topographic feature in central Korea, northeast of Seoul. August 1951, Korean Conflict.

(2) See CONICAL HILL.

MILLRACE -- Pulusuk Island, Caroline Islands. WW-II.

MILWAUKEE RAILROAD -- Military name for short rail line in central Angaur Island, Palau Group. Fall 1944, WW-II.

MIMIC -- Linguistic compiler for grammar structure work.

MINCEMEAT -- Allied deception operation in which cadaver of a man in his early thirties was deposited on 30 April 1943 by British submarine Seraph so as to wash up near Huelva, Spain. Object was to convince Germans that this fictitious Captain (Acting Major) William Martin, Royal Marines, had been a victim of an air crash and that the false highly classified papers he carried in a briefcase indicated that Operation HUSKY would take place in Peloponnesus and not in Sicily as actually planned and later executed. Subject of novel, Operation Heartbreak, by Lord Alfred Duff Cooper. WW-II.

MINERAL -- Code name for Caucasus. WW-II.

MINERVA -- Escape of General Henri Giraud from southern France. 6 November 1942, WW-II.

MINERVE -- Operable French nuclear pool reactor in Fontenay, France.

MINICAB -- French C.A.B. GY-20 monoplane. First flight in 1949.

MINIGUN -- U.S. Army 7.62-mm. lightweight aircraft machine gun.

MINITRACK -- Continuous-wave, trajectory-measuring system used to track satellites.

MINIVER -- Djailolo Pass, Halmahera, Netherlands East Indies. WW-II.

MINK -- Device for optical display of radar data.

MINK I-II -- U.S. battalion landing team tests held in Slapton Sands area, Great Britain, in preparation for OVERLORD. See also OTTER I-II. March 1944, WW-II.

MINNIE MOUSE -- U.S. Navy anti-submarine rocket launched from rails mounted on submarine chasers and cutters. Equipped with a hydrostatic fuse, the 2.5-inch rocket was launched in clusters, providing a straight-line pattern upon striking the water. Widely used in the latter stages of World War II, it was designed and developed in 1943.

MINOTAUR -- One of several studies of advanced intercontinental ballistic missiles with particular emphasis on reduction of missile size without consequent reductions in range-payload. Conducted by industry for U.S. Air Force.

MINT JULEP -- Name for peacetime military project in Greenland.

MINUTEMAN -- (1) Second generation U.S. intercontinental ballistic missile stored and fired from hardened and dispersed silos. The three-stage, solid propellant missile has a range of over 6000 miles, and can carry a thermonuclear warhead. Expected to become, along with POLARIS, the backbone of the U.S. strategic retaliatory force. Over 950 missiles will be deployed in the U.S., and will be capable of being fired individually, salvoed or fired en masse. An advanced version with greater range-payload under development and expected to be operational in 1966. First 20 missiles operational in December 1962.

(2) Name for peacetime military operations.

MINUTEMAN, ADVANCED -- See MUSCLEMAN

MIRACLE -- Namatutu, New Britain. WW-II.

MIRAGE -- G.A.M. Dassault single-engine turbojet serving with the French air arm in a variety of versions ranging from trainer to interceptor. Earliest version flown in 1951. See also MATRA.

MIRAGE IV -- Twin-jet, scaled-up version of the basic Dassault programmed to enter the French Armee de l'Air in 1964 as a light bomber.

MIRAK -- Acronym for German phrase, minimum rocket. A series of rocket models, developed by members of the German Society for Space Travel, to test various theories which they intended to use in larger rockets. None were really successful, although much experimental data was obtained. A program of the early 1930's.

MISAWA FUEL TANK -- Fuel tank for F-80C fighter-bomber aircraft improvised at Misawa Air Base, Japan; provided fuel for extra hour of flight. Used in Korean Conflict.

MISHAP -- An automatic coding system used in data processing.

MISS -- Acronym for Man In Space Soonest, a U.S. Air Force proposal to orbit a MERCURY type vehicle by 1960. Booster would have been the ATLAS-AGENA A. Permission to proceed was not given; the program was implemented by National Aeronautics and Space Administration in Project Mercury. First proposed in 1958.

MISSATHA -- Tropical storm. 18-19 September 1950. First detected west of Chichi Jima, Bonin Islands. Apparently moved northward briefly and dissipated. Tracking data scarce; possibility this may have been same storm as LUCRETIA.

MISSILE MASTER -- U.S. Army early warning system for tactical control of air defense units. The semi-automatic electronic system also provides readiness data of air defense units and co-ordinates their firing. Operational.

MR. MELL -- Code name under which General George C. Marshall traveled with MODICUM party to London. April 1942, WW-II.

MR. WHITE -- Code name under which Colonel Albert C. Wedemeyer traveled in MODICUM party to London. April 1942, WW-II.

MISTRAL -- Development of the DeHavilland Vampire built under license in France. The Sud-Est version flew in 1951.

MITCHELL -- North American-U.S. Army Air Forces B-25 aircraft, built without prototype; entered production in 1941 and a year later made the famous Doolittle Tokyo Raid. Has had an illustrious career in air arms of the world.

MITTELMEER -- German operation basing Luftwaffe units in southern Italy and Sicily to attack British Shipping in Mediterranean. Began December 1940, WW-II.

MO OPERATION -- Japanese plan for occupation of Port Moresby, important positions on Tulagi and in southeastern New Guinea to establish air bases for operations in Australian area; also included attack on Nauru and Ocean Islands to secure phosphorus resources. Early 1942, WW-II.

MOANING MINNIE -- Nickname for German NEBELWERFER. WW-II.

MOBFOOT -- Name for peacetime military exercise.

MOBIDIC -- Acronym for Mobile Digital Computer, a part of U.S. Army's Fieldata program.

MOBILE -- Onagaia, New Britain. WW-II.

MOBILE YOKE -- U.S. Air Force Tactical Air Command peacetime military exercise. 1960.

MOBILE ZEBRA -- U.S. Air Force peacetime mission flown from Cannon Air Force Base, New Mexico, to George Air Force Base, California. 1958.

MOBILITY -- U.S. Army exercise in which the experimental rocket lift device was demonstrated. Device consists of twin hydrogen peroxide jets which provide lift and enable a man to propel himself up to 50 feet and over obstacles. Still being tested.

MOCCASIN -- Wake Island. WW-II.

MODEM -- Acronym for Modulator-Demodulator, a data-processing term.

MODEST -- Kukurio, New Britain. WW-II.

MODICUM -- U.S. group that went to England to present the Marshall Memorandum to the British. April 1942, WW-II.

MODS -- Acronym for Manned Orbiting Development Station, an Air Force proposal for a manned space station. Two versions have been proposed: an enlarged or converted GEMINI capsule or a 20,000-pound TITAN III launched station. Also known as MOSS (Manned Orbiting Space Station) and MTSS (Military Test Space Station). The station designed for one-year life would be used to develop the equipment and techniques required for potential military space missions. Not approved for development.

MOHAWK -- (1) Popular name for the 1937 Curtiss Hawk 75/P-36 aircraft used by France early in World War II. Later used by U.S. as a trainer.

(2) Grumman AO-1 STOL front-line observation turboprop aircraft first service-tested by the U.S. Army in 1959.

(3) Allied code name for road junction at Santa Apollinare, near Ortona, Italy, in area to be defended by British Indian troops. May 1944, WW-II.

MOHAWK ARROW -- Name for U.S. peacetime military exercise at Camp Drum, New York; designed to provide combined unit training for infantry brigade. 1961.

MOHOLE, OPERATION -- U.S. oceanographic research program to drill through earth's crust under ocean to determine composition and physical properties of crust and underlying mantle. Eventually may be conducted in water up to 18,000 feet deep into thickness of about 15,000 feet of crustal rock. Intended to provide information on history of ocean, its currents, temperatures, life and chemistry. Name taken from boundary between crust and denser mantle which is called Mohorovic discontinuity after a Yugoslav seismologist. Began in 1959.

MOJAVE -- Twin-engine Sikorsky S-56 helicopter in service with the U.S. Marine Corps as the HR2S and the Army as the H-37A. New Department of Defense designation CH-37.

MOLAR -- Dabanu Village, Woodlark Island. WW-II.

MOLCH -- (English translation: Salamander) Early German one-man submarine intended for offensive use near coast. WW-II.

MOLEHILL -- Ellice Islands. WW-II.

MOLLE -- German air force slang for airplane. Named after large glass found in Berlin cafes. WW-II.

MOLOTOV -- Soviet surface-to-air rocket adapted right after World War II from the German TAIFUN missile. Most likely the first rockets deployed on surface ships, being installed on at least two aircraft carriers and one battleship right after the war.

MOLLY -- Name reserved by meteorologists for tropical cyclone in North Atlantic area.

MOMP -- Acronym for Mid-Ocean Meeting Place, usually near Iceland, where U.S. Navy exchanged responsibility for escorting convoys in Atlantic with British and Canadian naval forces. WW-II.

MONA -- Name reserved by meteorologists for tropical cyclone in eastern North Pacific.

MONA LISA -- Name for peacetime military project involving the re-supplying of radar sites.

MONARCH -- Spratly Island, South China Sea. WW-II.

MONASTERY, THE -- Australian objective in Miyeoumiye, Lebanon. Thought to be a monastery, but was actually a military barracks and French headquarters. June 1941, WW-II.

MONASTERY HILL -- Allied military name for Monte Cassino, Italy (Hill 516), where a Benedictine abbey was situated. 1944, WW-II.

MONASTERY INN -- British and Canadian rest and recreation facility for war-weary troops at Ortona, Italy. WW-II.

MONEY DIVISION -- Nickname for U.S. 33rd Infantry Division, which, while attacking in Philippines during World War II, unearthed trove of silver pesos buried by Japanese and, then, soon after, recaptured some of richest gold mines in world. Also called PRAIRIE DIVISION.

MONICA -- (1) Family of five French sounding rockets for upper atmospheric research; particulary studies cosmic ray and exo-atmospheric physics. All are three-stage solid propellant rockets, carrying payloads ranging from 15 pounds to 33 pounds to altitudes of 33 to 100 miles. First fired in 1957.

(2) Name reserved by meteorologists for tropical cyclone in eastern North Pacific.

MONKEY POINT -- Military name for topographic feature on Corregidor Island, Philippines. WW-II.

MONKEYPUZZLE -- Code name for Japan. WW-II.

MONKEY'S SEAT -- Name for Mount Vina Roni near Munda Point, New Georgia Island. WW-II.

MONOCLE -- Code name for Siberia. WW-II.

MONSOON -- Otta Pass, Truk Lagoon, Caroline Islands. WW-II.

MONSTERS -- Nickname for large Allied passenger liners employed, under British control, as troopships during World War II.

MONSTROUS -- Operation which set World War II time record for hunting and sinking submarines; involved U.S. ships and British aircraft in swamp operation against German U-616 in Mediterranean off Algeria. 13-17 May 1944, WW-II.

MONT CODE -- Form of meteorological message in which observations of clouds at and below the elevation of mountain observing stations are encoded and trans-mitted.

MONTCLAIR -- Allied operations in southern Philippines (VICTOR OPERATIONS, which were originally part of MUSKETEER) and in Borneo and Netherlands East Indies (OBOE OPERATIONS). 1945, WW-II.

MONTE CARLO -- U.N. code name for Commander, Task Group 95.2, during naval siege of Wonsan harbor, North Korea. 16 February 1951 - 27 July 1953, Korean Conflict.

MOOLAH, PROJECT -- Offer by U.N. Command in Korea to give 50,000 dollars and political asylum to enemy pilot who delivered MIG-15 jet aircraft to Kimpo Airfield; publicized by leaflet drops and radio broadcasts in Chinese, Russian, and Korean. Began 26 April 1953, Korean Conflict.

MOONBEAM -- An industry proposal for a chemical-nuclear space booster capable of landing a large payload on the moon. Proposal no longer active; was similar to the Saturn V proposal now under development.

MOONLIGHT -- Japanese Nakajima night fighter plane of World War II. See GEKKO.

MOONLIGHT SONATA -- (1) German name for bombing attack against Coventy, England. November 1940, WW-II.

(2) U.S. Navy heckling operation by carrier-based planes against rail communications in North Korea; carried out on moonlight nights with snow on ground. Winter 1952, Korean Conflict.

MOONMAN -- Skagway, Alaska. WW-II.

MOONSHINE -- Kulumadau, Woodlark Island. WW-II.

MOONSHOT -- Nickname for a lunar-orbiting satellite equipped with a 100-meter resolution photographic system. Would use the ATLAS-CENTAUR booster. Study contracts were let to industry, but the program will not be implemented. A similar capsule with finer resolution cameras will be used in SURVEYOR orbiter missions planned for 1965.

MOONSTRUCK -- Vogelkop Peninsula, New Guinea. WW-II.

MOOSE -- (1) Yakovlev Yak-11 trainer which entered Soviet service in 1947. Used extensively by satellite countries.

(2) Name for Royal Canadian Air Force Squadron Number 419.

MOOSE HORN -- U.S. peacetime military exercise held in Arctic. 1956.

MOOSEJAW -- Allied code name for defense of Ortona, Italy. Originally planned for Canadian forces; carried out by 10th Indian Division. May 1944, WW-II.

MOOSETRAP EXERCISES -- Large-scale U.S. Navy task force training exercises simulating enemy tactics in order to show up weak spots in air defense. WW-II.

MOP -- PBY Catalina built under license in Russia since 1938, and still used there.

MORAVA -- Twin-engine Czech monoplane in use by Aeroflot as a taxi aircraft. First flown 1957. A turbo-prop version is under development.

MORGENLUFT -- German Africa Corps attack against Gafsa, Tunisia, after Operation FRUEHLINGSWIND. February 1943, WW-II.

MORINO -- Code name for Singapore. WW-II.

MORNING GLORY, OPERATION -- Canadian drive into German defense line southwest of Ortona, Italy. Originally code name for artillery barrage opening operation. Began 18 December 1943, WW-II.

MORNING MIST -- Name for peacetime military exercise.

MORNING STAR -- Name for peacetime military exercise.

MOROCCO -- Sunpanam, Umboi Island, Bismarck Archipelago. WW-II.

MORTIMER VALLEY -- U.S. military name for topographic feature on Peleliu Island. Also called Horseshoe Valley. Fall 1944, WW-II.

MOSCA -- (English translation: Fly) Nickname gained during the Spanish Civil War by the Russian I-16, which first flew in 1933 and remained in first-line service until 1943. Called RATA (Rat) by opponents in Spain and Abu (Gadfly) by the Japanese in China in 1937.

MOSCOW -- (1) Reilly's Creek, Woodlark Island. WW-II.

(2) See MOSKVA and COOT

MOSKITO -- (1) Comte A.C. 12 light cabin monoplane built in Switzerland in 1933.

(2) (English translation: Mosquito) Unofficial designation for the German Focke-Wulf TA-154A night fighter plane. First flown in 1943.

MOSKVA -- (English translation: Moscow) Russian nickname for the Ilyushin IL-18 turpo-prop transport plane. First flown 1957. Called COOT by NATO.

MOSKVICH -- Russian helicopter. See HARE.

MOSQUITO -- (1) Versatile British DeHavilland twin-engine aircraft built entirely of wood. First used by the Royal Air Force in a raid on Oslo in 1942.

(2) German World War II fighter. See MOSKITO.

(3) Swiss anti-tank wire-guided missile with a shaped charge warhead. The solid propellant missile has a range of about 6000 feet and can be carried and fired by one man. Also known as Cobra 4; in operational use.

MOSQUITO MELLOW -- Plane which relayed radio messages to tactical air-control center MELLOW at Taegu, Korea, from MOSQUITOES (airborne control aircraft) too far distant to communicate directly. Korean Conflict.

MOSQUITOES -- (1) Name, popular during Korean Conflict, for U.S. Air Force airborne controllers and their planes; initially pinpointed targets for attack planes, later also communicated with ground patrols. Name originated in radio call signs, such as Mosquito Able, given to airborne controllers operating out of Taegu in July 1950.

(2) See RHUBARBS

MOSS -- See MODS

MOSSBANK -- Code name for Pierre Laval. WW-II.

MOTH -- A variation of the PELICAN, designed to home on enemy radar.

MOTH MINOR -- DeHavilland light training monoplane built in Australia in 1940 after all equipment moved there from England.

MOTHER -- Cape Selatan, Borneo. WW-II.

MOTHER, THE -- Military name for mountain height near Rabaul, New Britain. WW-II.

MOTOROLA -- Cape Mensing, New Britain. WW-II.

MOTTLED -- Limassol, Cyprus. WW-II.

MOUNT PLASMA -- Nickname for Mount Suribachi, Iwo Jima. Also called Hot Rocks. 1945, WW-II.

MOUNTAINEERS -- Nickname for U.S. 10th Mountain Division.

MOUSE -- (1) Name for ground station used by OBOE target finding system in bombing operations; transmitted signals to aircraft consisting of continuous note for correct course and dots and dashes for deviation from course. See also CAT. WW-II.

(2) Comper monoplane of 1932 for Britain's private pilots.

(3) Acronym for Minimum Orbital Unmanned Satellite, a 100-pound satellite first proposed by Dr. S. Fred Singer, in 1954. It was never developed, although EXPLORER and VANGUARD achieved its objectives.

MOUSE HILL -- U.S. military name for topographic feature west of Yonabaru, Okinawa. 1945, WW-II.

MOUSETRAP -- (1) U.S. Navy ahead-thrown anti-submarine weapon, Mark-20 and 22, firing four or eight small rocket projectiles; developed for use where HEDGEHOG was too large or powerful. Adopted 1942, WW-II.

(2) Name for valley surrounded by hills on upper Tine River, Tunisia. Spring 1943, WW-II.

MOUSQUETAIRE -- D.140, a development of the French S.A.N. Model DR.100 aircraft. First flown in 1958.

MOWE -- (English translation: Seagull) Focke-Wulf A-38 monoplane of the early 1930's in Germany.

MOZART -- Code name for Union of Soviet Socialist Republics. WW-II.

MUD PACK -- U.S. Air Force high-altitude air refueling area over the coast of California.

MUDBANK -- Allied operations against Ponape, Caroline Islands. WW-II.

MUDBATH -- U.S. Army occupation of Martinique, Guadaloupe and French Guina. WW-II.

MUFFLER -- U.N. code name for portion of Wonsan harbor, North Korea. Korean Conflict.

MUG -- First program in two-space-dimension multi-group calculation. Widely used 1953-56.

MULBERRIES -- Two artificial harbors, built by Allies off Normandy beachheads. See also MULBERRY A and B, WHALES, PHOENIXES, BOMBARDONS, CORNCOBS, GOOSEBERRIES. 1944, WW-II.

MULBERRY A -- Artificial harbor built in American sector at OMAHA (St. Laurent-sur-Mer, France) after Normandy landings. 1944, WW-II.

MULBERRY B -- Artificial port built in British sector at Arromanches-les-Bains, France, after Normandy landings. 1944, WW-II.

MULBERRY, FORCE -- U.S. Naval Task Force 127.1 in charge of MULBERRY A artificial harbor at OMAHA Beach. 1944, WW-II.

MULE -- (1) Polikarpov Po-2 biplane. First flown in 1927 as the U-2 and is still used as a glider tug and flying club trainer.

(2) Suva, Fiji Islands. WW-II.

MULTI-PRO -- Light cabin monoplane built by the Pander Company of Holland in 1933.

MULTITUDE -- Ngargol Island, Palau Islands. WW-II.

MUMMY -- Sibuyan Island, Philippine Islands. WW-II.

MUNSTER -- Le Havre, France. WW-II.

MURDER -- (1) Esaihi, New Britain. WW-II.

(2) Allied term for a pin point concentration of all available guns. WW-II.

MURSLEY -- Loire River, France. WW-II.

MUSCATEL -- Katurai, New Britain. WW-II.

MUSCLEMAN -- U.S. Air Force program for an intercontinental ballistic missile with increased payload and range over the MINUTEMAN. Program may be under full-scale development as the Advanced (Wing 6) Minuteman. No details available because of restrictive defense security regulations.

MUSH -- British Royal Air Force training exercise in preparation for Operation OVERLORD. April 1944, WW-II.

MUSICAL NEWHAVEN -- British method of ground marking a target by flares or target indicators dropped blindly from aircraft using OBOE radar equipment, followed, if possible, by visual identification. See also NEWHAVEN. WW-II.

MUSICAL PARAMATTA -- British method of ground marking a target by colored markers dropped blindly from aircraft using OBOE radar equipment. See also PARAMATTA. WW-II.

MUSICAL WANGANUI -- British method of sky marking a target by colored markers dropped blindly from aircraft using OBOE radar equipment. See also WANGANUI. WW-II.

MUSKET -- Projected invasion of southern Italy by U.S. Fifth Army at Taranto. Canceled. Fall 1943, WW-II.

MUSKETEER -- (1) Beechcraft Model 23 business plane of 1962.

(2) Plan issued by Southwest Pacific Area command on 10 July 1944 for Allied advance to and landings on Luzon, Philippines; contained four major phases of operations: KING, LOVE, MIKE, VICTOR (VICTOR later became part of MONTCLAIR operations.). WW-II.

MUSKETEER II -- Revision of MUSKETEER plan. Issued on 29 August 1944, WW-II.

MUSKETEER III -- Revision of MUSKETEER plan. Issued on 26 September 1944, WW-II.

MUSKETRY -- Allied code name for air patrol seeking out German submarines in Bay of Biscay. Began in 1943, WW-II.

MUSKRAT -- U.S. Army three-quarter ton cargo and personnel carrier.

MUSKRAT I-II -- U.S. battalion level exercises involving combat teams and engineer detachments, held in Firth of Clyde, Scotland, in preparation for OVERLORD. 1944, WW-II.

MUSTANG -- Fighter bomber originally designed by North American for the British in 1940 as a replacement for the P-40. U.S. Army Air Forces ordered it in 1942 as the P-51. Over 15,000 were built before production ceased in 1946. Sometimes called Apache.

MUTT AND JEFF -- Nickname for British Overseas Service Medal and the Allied Victory Medal, 1914-18; so called because the two were always worn adjacent to each other.

MUTTON -- British long aerial mine, consisting of 2000 feet of piano wire with parachute at top and small bomb at top and small bomb at bottom; intended to be unspooled by patrolling aircraft, struck by and pulled into enemy raider. Abandoned early in World War II.

MUTUAL -- Nus Nus, New Britain. WW-II.

MYRSKY -- (English translation: Storm) Finnish MY-1 fighter plane. First flown in 1942.

MYSTERE -- French Dassault M.D.452 jet fighter. First flown in 1951. First French aircraft to exceed the speed of sound. See also SUPER MYSTERE.

MYSTERY -- Ren Island, Solomon Sea. WW-II.

MYSTIC -- U.S. Air Force missile test center automatic coder.

MYTHOLOGY -- Canton Island, Phoenix Islands. WW-II.

N

NNK -- Abbreviation for Notify Next of Kin, adopted by U.S. Navy PBY patrol aircraft as radio sign-off call. Derived from radio message sent by pilot, "Sighted enemy carrier. Please notify next of kin." WW-II.

NABOB -- Code name for Northern Ireland. WW-II.

NABS -- U.S. satellite under development.

NACCAM -- Acronym for National Coordinating Committee for Aviation Meteorology. Consists of representatives of Departments of Commerce, Air Force, Army, and Navy; Civil Aeronautics Board, Federal Aviation Agency, National Aeronautics and Space Administration.

NADINE -- Typhoon. 24-25 November 1956. Formed east of Luzon, Philippines. Moved little before being absorbed by typhoon OLIVE.

    (2) Tropical storm. 3-10 June 1960. Formed in Philippine Sea. Moved northeastward and passed southeast of Japan out over North Pacific.

    (3) Name also applied to tropical cyclones in western North Pacific which occurred prior to (1) and (2) above.

NAKAROP -- See EGAROPPU

NAMELESS HILL -- U.S. military name for topographic feature on New Britain Island. December 1943, WW-II.

NAN -- Code word for letter "N" in a phonetic alphabet, used to avoid possibility of a misunderstanding in transmitting messages. See also NOVEMBER.

NAN, HILL -- (1) U.S. military name for topographic feature on Leyte, Philippine Islands. October 1944, WW-II.

    (2) U.S. military name for topographic feature on Okinawa. 1945, WW-II.

NANCY -- (1) Tropical storm. 6-7 July 1945. First detected in South China Sea west of Luzon. Moved northwestward into China mainland near Hong Kong.

    (2) Tropical storm. 19 September 1950. Formed and dissipated in area west of Valcano Islands, the Pacific.

(3) Typhoon. 4-10 October 1954. Formed in eastern Philippine Sea. Moved westward across Philippine Sea, Luzon, and South China Sea to Hainan Island.

(4) Typhoon. 22-26 November 1958. Formed near Yap Island. Moved north-westward over Philippine Sea, then recurved northeastward and dissipated southeast of Japan.

(5) Typhoon. 7-17 September 1961. Prolonged and devastating storm, formed near Kwajalein Atool, moved westward, passed just south of Guam, turned northwestward across Philippine Sea, turned northward, passed just east of Okinawa, turned northeastward through Japan and dissipated over Sea of Okhotsk. Caused at least 172 deaths, made 650,000 homeless, sank over 300 ships, and caused other damage, mostly in Japan.

(6) Name also applied to tropical cyclones in western North Pacific which occurred prior to (1) through (5) above.

NANETTE -- Name reserved by meteorologists for tropical cyclone in eastern North Pacific.

NANNIE MISSIONS -- Three strikes (Able, Baker, Charlie) by B-29 bombers of Far Eastern Air Force against factories of Communist chemical combine at Hungnan, North Korea. 31 July-3 August 1950, Korean Conflict.

NANTYDERRY -- Bordeaux, France. WW-II.

NAOMI -- Tropical storm. 3-5 August 1961. Discovered 800 miles west of Acapulco, Mexico. Moved westward and dissipated over Pacific Ocean.

NAPALM HILL -- See BATTLE MOUNTAIN

NAPKIN -- Keuea Village, Gilbert Islands. WW-II.

NAPOLEON -- Counter-invasion measures taken at Dover by British. 30 June 1940, WW-II.

NARCISSUS -- Palix River, New Britain. WW-II.

NARCOTIC -- Rumut Passage, New Britain. WW-II.

NASAL -- Burma Road, Burma-China. WW-II.

NASTY -- Air-to-air missile developed for the Air Force by North American Aviation as a bomber defense weapon. Program was canceled without explanation in early 1950's.

NATALIE -- Name reserved by meteorologists for tropical cyclone in eastern North Pacific.

NATCHEZ -- Senla, New Britain. WW-II.

NATE -- World War II Japanese Nakajima KI.27 fighter/fighter-bomber. In continuous production from 1937 to 1940.

NATIV -- Acronym for North American Test Instrument Vehicle, U.S. Air Force test rocket designed to check out systems and techniques of guided missile flight. Using liquid hypergolic propellants, the missile had a range of 40-60 miles and could reach altitudes of 12 miles. A large number of the tower-launched vehicles were fired at Holloman Air Force Base, New Mexico, beginning in the summer of 1948. Test vehicle for NAVAHO.

NATIVE -- New Guinea Force. WW II.

NATO -- Acronym for North Atlantic Treaty Organization. See also OTAN.

NATTER -- (English translation: VIPER) German piloted rocket plane developed in latter stages of World War II for use against Allied bomber formations. Launched vertically by solid boosters, the plane would come within 250 feet of the bombers before launching 24-48 electrically fired air-to-air missiles. Pilot would bail out after bringing the plane down to an altitude of two miles, and the costly liquid sustainer would be recovered by parachute. Three models were developed, but none were used in combat. First unsuccessful manned flight was attempted in February 1945.

NAUGHTY -- Alimbit River, New Britain. WW-II.

NAUMBURG -- Proposed German landing in Lyngen Fiord to relieve Narvik, Norway. June 1940, WW-II.

NAUSEATE -- Kapoli River, New Britain. WW-II.

NAVAHO -- U.S. Air Force ramjet-powered missile initially planned as a 6300-mile intercontinental ballistic missile before the program was cancelled in July 1957. Information from the development program contributed significantly to the development of propulsion systems for REDSTONE, JUPITER, THOR and ATLAS. Also, it was the principal participant in the RISE (Research in Supersonic Environment) program which provided data on the Mach 3 temperature and pressure flight regime, useful in the development of HOUND DOG, the B-70 and the F-108. Eight flight tests were conducted, the first on 6 November 1956.

NAVAJO -- Cape Aulop, New Britain. WW-II.

NAVAR -- Acronym for Navigation Radar.

NAVARHO -- Acronym for Navigation and Radio Homing.

NAVIGATOR -- Beechcraft AT-7. Development of AT-11 KANSAN. Used by U.S. Army Air Force during World War II.

NAXOS -- German radar device enabling fighter aircraft to home on H2S transmission of Allied bombers. WW-II.

NEAR -- Acronym for National Emergency Alarm Repeater, a U.S. Air Force-Civil Defense system.

NEARHAND -- Mangrove Island, New Britain. WW-II.

NEBELWERFERS -- German artillery piece designed to launch smoke shells, but modified to launch rockets, including 15, 21 and 32 cm. surface-to-surface rockets. As many as six launchers were mounted on one vehicle. First used on the Russian front in 1941.

NEBUL CODE -- International form of message in which data on cloud systems are encoded and transmitted.

NECKERCHIEF -- Kaka River, New Georgia, Solomon Islands. WW-II.

NECROMANCER -- Sepik River, New Guinea. WW-II.

NECTAR -- Paligmete, New Britain. WW-II.

NEEDLE ROCK -- U.S. military name for topographic feature at eastern end of Urasoe-Mura Escarpment on Okinawa. 1945, WW-II.

NEEDLES -- See WEST FORD

NEES -- Acronym for Naval Engineering Experiment Station.

NEIGHBOR -- Natal, Brazil. WW-II.

NELL -- Name used for some of the early rockets fired by Dr. Robert Goddard in launchings between 1914 and 1945. Rockets were first fired in Massachusetts and later at Goddard's experimental center at Roswell, New Mexico.

NELLY -- Typhoon. 7-15 September 1949. First detected in northern Mariana Islands. Moved west-northwestward across Taiwan into China mainland.

NELSON -- Code word signal from frigate, H.M.S. Kingsmill, indicating that British 4th Special Service Brigade had decided to proceed with assault Operation INFATUATE II, on Westkapelle, Walcheren Island, southwest Netherlands. 1 November 1944, WW-II.

NEMESIS -- Kumbun Island, New Britain. WW-II.

NEOPHYTE -- Molua, New Britain. WW-II.

NEPA -- Acronym for Nuclear Energy Propulsion of Aircraft.

NEPTUNE -- (1) U.S. Navy P2V. In continuous production by Lockheed from 1944 to 1961. the -7 was built under license in Japan; a few flew with the U.S. Air Force as the RB-69.

(2) An early name for the VIKING.

(3) Embarkation of members of French General Giraud's staff from River Var, near Nice, south France. 7-8 November 1942, WW-II.

(4) Allied code word for the seaborne cross-Channel operation within OVERLORD. 6 June 1944, WW-II.

NERV -- Acronym for Nuclear Emulsion Recovery Vehicle, a National Aeronautics and Space Administration space probe carrying a thick pad of space radiation sensitive film to gather environmental data for the development of methods of spacecraft protection. First launch 19 September 1960 using an ARGO D-8 sounding rocket. Also see BIOS.

NERVA -- Acronym for Nuclear Engine for Rocket Vehicle Application. U.S. rocket engine whose initial in-flight test period anticipated 1966-67. See also DUMBO.

NERVOUS -- Arowak Island, New Britain. WW-II.

NEST EGG -- (1) Pru River, New Britain. WW-II.

(2) Allied plan for occupation of Channel Islands, off west coast of France, in case of German collapse or surrender there. Not carried out, September 1944-May 1945, WW-II.

NETTY -- Name reserved by meteorologists for tropical cyclone in North Atlantic area.

NEUROTIC -- Olapum, New Britain. WW-II.

NEW -- Acronym for (U.S.) Navy Early Warning.

NEW BROOM -- Name for series of peacetime military exercises.

NEW DEAL -- British decision involving reduction of number of pilots in bomber aircraft from two to one and other changes in bomber personnel and equipment in order to increase length of training courses for Royal Air Force bomber crews. Spring 1942, WW-II.

NEW GALAHAD -- Two battalions organized from replacements for GALAHAD and some survivors of Galahad. Late May 1944, WW-II.

NEW HAVEN -- Yamai, New Guinea. WW-II.

NEW JERSEY -- Obsolete U.S. battleship sunk in September 1923 tests by Air Service bombers.

NEW ORLEANS -- Nickname for one of the Douglas World Cruisers of 1924. Along with the Chicago, this plane made the entire trip. See WORLD CRUISER.

NEW YORK -- Allied phase line in Ringenberg-Krudenberg area, Germany. Late March 1945, WW-II.

NEW YORK DIVISION -- Nickname for U.S. 27th Infantry Division. Originally composed of National Guardsmen from state of New York. Also called EMPIRE DIVISION, GALLA VANTERS, TOKYO EXPRESS.

NEWBIGGIN -- Guernsey Island, English Channel. WW-II.

NEWCOMBER -- Sorong, New Guinea. WW-II.

NEWHAVEN -- British method of ground marking a target by flares or target indicators dropped blindly from aircraft using H2S radar equipment, followed, if possible, by visual identification. See also MUSICAL NEWHAVEN. WW-II.

NEWINGTON -- Brittany, France. WW-II.

NEWLANDS -- Cherbourg-Querqueville, France. WW-II.

NEWS -- Acronym for (U.S.) Naval Electronic Warfare Simulator.

NEWSPAPER -- Gaho River, New Britain. WW-II.

NIBBIO -- (English translation: Kite) Four-seat version of the Italian Falco, the Aviamilano F.14 first flew in 1958.

NIBLICK -- Oran, Algeria. WW-II.

NICETY -- Riff Point, New Britain. WW-II.

NICK -- World War II Japanese Kawasaki KI.45, first flown in 1940 as a long-range escort fighter; converted to the night fighter role. Japanese name: Toryu (Dragon Killer).

NICK ISLAND -- Entrance Island, Solomon Islands. WW-II.

NICKELING -- British military slang for process of dropping leaflets (NICKELS) from aircraft over enemy-occupied areas. WW-II.

NICKELS -- British military slang for propaganda and information leaflets dropped by Allied aircraft over enemy-occupied areas. WW-II.

NICKFORCE -- Provisional organization of British, American and French units assembled for the defense of Thala, Tunisia; commanded by British Brigadier Cameron Nicholson. February 1943, WW-II.

NIEUPORT -- French biplane in use during World War One.

NIGHTHAWK -- (1) Curtis XP-87, jet-powered aircraft, first flown 15 February 1948. Large U.S. Air Force order cancelled and only two built. Later version, XF-87A, called Blackhawk.

(2) Name for Royal Canadian Air Force Squadron Number 409.

NIGHTINGALE -- Vessi Islet, New Britain. WW-II.

NIGHTLIGHT -- Task force planned for the occupation of Norway in the event of a German withdrawal from that country or against light German resistance. WW-II.

NIGHTMARE -- South Coast, Mindanao, Philippine Islands. WW-II.

NIGHTOUT -- Latakia, Syria. WW-II.

NIGHTSTICKER -- Khabarovsk, U.S.S.R. WW-II.

NIKE -- Generic name for a family of U.S. Army surface-to-air missiles used to provide continental air defense against ever increasing levels of enemy attack. The Nike family consists of the NIKE-AJAX, NIKE-APPACHE, NIKE-ARCHER, NIKE-ASP, NIKE-CAJUN, NIKE-HURCULES, and NIKE-ZEUS.

NIKE-AJAX -- U.S. Army surface-to-air missile deployed in the U.S. with National Guard units, and also in Europe and the Far East with active Army units. The first operational air defense missiles in the U.S., Ajax has a range of 25 nautical miles, and a ceiling of 60,000 feet. Solid boosted and liquid sustained, it uses a radio command guidance system and conventional warhead. Now obsolete, the last Ajax units in the U.S. are being phased out and replaced by HERCULES. First operational in 1953.

NIKE-APACHE -- National Aeronautics and Space Administration two-stage sounding rocket consisting of a NIKE booster first stage and an APACHE (improved version of the CAJUN) solid motor. Combination can lift a 50-pound payload to an altitude of 150 miles. A total of 10 of these vehicles will be launched by NASA during fiscal year 1963.

NIKE-ARCHER -- U.S. two-stage sounding rocket consisting of NIKE first stage and an ARCHER second. It is capable of launching a 40-pound payload to an altitude of 230 miles. In use by all military services and National Aeronautics and Space Administration.

NIKE-ASP -- National Aeronautics and Space Administration two-stage solid propellant rocket consisting of a NIKE booster first stage and an ASP second stage. Combination is capable of launching a 25-pound payload to an altitude of 150 miles. Also known as Aspan. In operational use.

NIKE-CAJUN -- National Aeronautics and Space Administration two-stage sounding rocket consisting of a NIKE solid motor as the first stage and a Cajun solid second stage. Combination is capable of launching a payload of 50 pounds to an altitude of 150 miles. NASA will fire a total of 45 during fiscal year 1963. Also called Argo B-1. See also ARGO SERIES.

NIKE-HERCULES -- Second in the family of U.S. Army surface-to-air continental air defense missiles. Hercules, boosted by four clustered NIKE solid motors, and utilizing a solid propellant sustainer, has a range of 75 miles, and an operational ceiling of over 150,000 feet. Also radio command guided. Deployed in the U.S. in 1958, Hercules units are being taken over by Army National Guard units. It has also been used to intercept tactical missiles in controlled tests at White Sands Missile Range, New Mexico.

NIKE-X -- U.S. Army anti-intercontinental ballistic missile. See also SPRINT, NIKE-ZEUS, HIGH-POWER.

NIKE-ZEUS -- Newest in the U.S. Army's family of surface-to-air continental air defense missiles. Zeus is designed to provide defense against Intercontinental Ballistic Missiles, Intermediate Range Ballistic Missiles and cruise missles. The three-stage solid propellant missile has a range of over 200 nautical miles, and an estimated speed of Mach 4. An extremely complex and expensive system; is being withheld from production because of questions of its cost and effectiveness. Test against special ATLAS target vehicles are being conducted in the Pacific to determine some answers to these questions. First successful intercept took place 19 July after at least one "partial success." In December 1962 Zeus intercepted a decoy-carrying target. Tests will continue through most of 1963. See also HIGHBALL.

NIKKO -- Japanese Fuji LM-1 adaptation of the Beech T-34, U.S. Air Force Mentor, as a four/five-seat liaison monoplane.

NILE -- American Mission, Salinas, Ecuador. WW-II.

NIMBUS -- (1) National Aeronautics and Space Administration meteorological satellite, a second generation weather sattellite to replace TIROS. Weighing 650 pounds, with improved television cameras and infra-red scanners, it will be launched into polar orbit by an ATLAS-AGENA and will be earth-stabilized to provide continuous coverage of the earth. First launching scheduled for late 1963 or early 1964.

(2) Nukuoro Island, Caroline Islands. WW-II.

(3) British I Corps exercise involving landing by an infantry battalion and field battery covered by attacks by light and fighter bombers; held at Kilbride Bay, Scotland. September 1943, WW-II.

NIMROD -- Early Hawker fighter in limited service as a British trainer plane at the outbreak of WW-II.

NINA -- (1) Typhoon. 9-16 August 1953. Formed in Caroline Islands. Moved northwestward across Guam and Philippine Sea, passed between Okinawa and Taiwan and entered China mainland.

(2) Hurricane. 30 November - 6 December 1957. First detected near Palmyra Island about 1000 miles south-southwest of Honolulu. Moved northward at first, then northwestward, passing close to the island of Kauai, then turned westward and dissipated west of Hawaii. Caused minor damage.

(3) Typhoon. 23-27 October 1960. Formed between Guam and Philippines. Moved rapidly northeastward. Passed southeast of Japan and into the northern North Pacific.

(4) Name also applied to tropical cyclones in western North Pacific which occurred prior to (1) through (3) above.

NIPPER -- Belgian Tipsy T.66 kit-form or ready-to-fly single-engine monoplane. First flown in 1957.

NIPPLE -- (1) Magulato Point, Trobriand Island. WW-II.

(2) Schaumann Island, New Britain. WW-II.

NIRVANA -- Manila, Philippine Islands. WW-II.

NISI -- Camocim, Brazil. WW-II.

NITA -- Name reserved by meteorologists for tropical cyclone in North Atlantic area.

NO DOZE -- U.S. Navy plan, proposed at end of Korean conflict, to use aircraft carriers which would operate exclusively at night.

NO JOY -- U.S. Air Force radio and telephone communications code word signifying "cannot find the raid assigned to me."

NO NAME RIDGE -- See RED SLASH HILL

NOAH -- (1) Joint U.S. Army-Navy directive for the defense of Iceland and Greenland. WW-II.

(2) Canadian evacuation operation in "island" between Waal and Neder Rijn Rivers, Netherlands, after Germans blew dykes to cause a flood. Early December 1944, WW-II.

NOAH'S ARK -- (1) Operations against retreating German forces in Greece by guerrillas aided by Allied Balkans Air Forces. See also MANNA. Fall 1944, WW-II.

(2) Liapo, New Britain. WW-II.

NOBALL -- Allied air forces code name for various types of sites connected with German V-weapon operations. WW-II.

NODEX 17 -- Name for U.S. peacetime military offshore discharge exercise.

NOGGIN -- Dulu-Daba, New Britain. WW-II.

NOISELESS -- Allied landing force under RECKLESS Task Force which carried out operation against Tanahmerah Bay, Hollandia area, New Guinea. Began 22 April 1944, WW-II.

NOMAD -- Upper stage liquid fluorine engine for use with the ATLAS space booster. The toxic high energy propellant engine would be able to substantially improve the performance of present boosters. National Aeronautics and Space Administration is funding several fluorine engine programs but none is in full-scale development.

NONA -- (1) Typhoon. 1-5 September 1952. Formed over western Caroline Islands. Moved west-northwestward across Philippine Sea, northern Luzon, northern part of South China Sea, and Hainan Island into northern Viet Nam.

(2) Name also included in sequence prepared by meteorologists for future tropical cyclones in North Atlantic.

NONAKA PARACHUTE -- Japanese seamless-panelled cargo parachute developed for use by U.N. troops in Korean Conflict.

NONAME LINE -- U.N. defensive line in Korea situated along crest of hill mass separating two rivers, Hongchon and Soyang. Scene of action during North Korean and Chinese drive for Seoul. May 1951, Korean Conflict.

NONAME RIDGE -- Military name for finger ridge near northwestern rim of PUNCH-BOWL in eastern Korea. Spring 1952, Korean Conflict.

NONCONFORMIST -- Buna, New Guinea. WW-II.

NON-PARENT -- SAGE Direction Center or Combat Center to which the PARENT CC by reallocation action, has given control over the use of a weapon not based within Centers' areas of responsibility.

NONSTOP -- (1) Ruango, New Britain. WW-II.

(2) Redeployment of U.S. forces following the defeat of Germany. WW-II.

NOONTIDE -- Waisisi, New Britain. WW-II.

NORA -- (1) Operable Norwegian natural uranium pool reactor in Kjeller, Norway. Used jointly by Norway and International Atomic Agency. U.S. - supplied fuel core.

(2) Typhoon. 22-29 November 1945. First detected in western Caroline Islands. Moved west-northwestward into Philippine Sea but recurved northeastward and moved past the northern Marianas toward the North Pacific.

(3) Typhoon. 27 August - 2 September 1951. Formed in western Caroline Islands. Moved west-northwestward across Philippine Sea and northern Luzon. Dissipated over South China Sea.

(4) Typhoon. 4-11 October 1955. Formed in central Philippine Sea. Moved north-northeastward, skirted the southeast coast of Japan, and lost force.

(5) Tropical storm. 5-12 September 1959. Formed in central Philippine Sea. Moved northwestward between Philippines and Taiwan, then turned northeastward along China coast into East China Sea.

(6) Typhoon. 26 July - 3 August 1962. Formed in southern Philippine Sea. Moved north-northwestward, passed southwest of Okinawa into Yellow Sea near Shanghai, recurved northeastward across Korea and merged with another storm system over Hokkaido.

(7) Name also applied to tropical cyclones in western North Pacific which occurred prior to (2) through (6) above.

NORALPHA -- French Nord 1101 development of the World War II German occupation Me.208 aircraft. Originally planned for civilian use but joined the military as the Ramier.

NORD, AMIRAL -- Code name for French Vice Admiral Abrial when he was responsible for naval operation off Belgian coast. May-June 1940, WW-II.

NORD 5.401 -- French air-to-surface missile launched from aircraft in level flight or dive against tactical ground targets. Both the booster and sustainer are solid propellant and a high frequency radio guidance system is used. In operational use.

NORDLIGHT -- (1) Projected German operation against Leningrad, U.S.S.R. Fall 1942, WW-II.

(2) Withdrawal of German 20th Mountain Army from Finland. October 1944-January 1945, WW-II.

NORDWIND -- German counteroffensive against U.S.7th Army in Alsace, France. Began 1 January 1945, WW-II.

NORECRIN -- French single-engine monoplane first flown by Nord in 1948.

NOREEN -- Name reserved by meteorologists for tropical cyclone in North Atlantic area.

NORGROUP -- Force of three British and one Australian air squadrons, formed to take part in operation MATADOR. 1941, WW-II.

NORMA -- (1) Tropical storm. October 1948. First detected in vicinity of Volcano Island; moved northeastward out into the Pacific.

(2) Name also included in sequence prepared by meteorologists for future tropical cyclones in eastern North Pacific.

NORMAN -- Allied capture of Corsica and Sardinia. September 1943, WW-II.

NORMAN FORCE -- Allied composite force of various formations. June 1940, WW-II.

NORSEMAN -- Noorduyn single-engine transport built in Canada and first flown in 1935; remained in production for a quarter of a century. Used by the U.S. Army Air Forces as the C-64.

NORTH DAUGHTER -- Military name for mountain height near Rabaul, New Britain. WW-II.

NORTH KNOB -- Part of hill 260 outside THE PERIMETER on Bougainville. WW-II.

NORTH STAR -- Canadair C-54-GM, Canadian version of the Douglas DC-4 aircraft, powered by inline engines.

NORTH STAR, OPERATION -- Joint U.S. Air Force-Army Alaskan Theater winter maneuver held near Nenana, Alaska, about 75 miles south of Fairbanks; held in 40-degree-below-zero weather. 1954.

NORTHERN PATROL -- Portion of naval blockade by units of U.N. Task Force 95 between Yang Do and 41 degrees 50 minutes North latitude. Began early 1951, Korean Conflict.

NORTHERN TIER, PROJECT -- Proposed joint use of selected U.S. Air Force Air Defense SAGE Centers for air-traffic control by moving in certain Federal Aviation Agency Centers in 1962.

NORTHPOLE -- Vitu Islands, Bismarck Archipelago. WW-II.

NORVEGIE -- French Nord N.C. 856A single-engine monoplane. First flown in 1951.

NOSEBAG -- Geraldton, Australia. WW-II.

NOSERING -- Sarmi, New Guinea. WW-II.

NOTCH, THE -- Military name for mountain pass northwest of Chungam-ni, Korea. 1950, Korean Conflict.

NOTEBOOK -- Buildup of air transport route to China. WW-II.

NOTS -- (1) Abbreviation for Naval Ordnance Test Station, located at China Lake, California, one of the U.S. Navy's principal research and development facilities. Among the projects at NOTS are Caleb and Sidewinder.

(2) U.S. Navy low-cost supersonic satellite launcher aircraft. See also NOTSNIK, YO-YO.

NOTSNIK -- U.S. Navy project for launching small satellites from aircraft. 1958 orbit failed. Program continued under YO-YO and NOTS.

NOTUS -- Advanced Research Projects Agency title for all Defense communications satellite programs. Included under the blanket title are COURIER, STEER, TACKLE, and DECREE. A 1959 grouping, neither Notus nor any of the other nicknames are now in use although the concepts they embodied are under development in the re-oriented ADVENT program.

NOUGAT -- Haiphong, China. WW-II.

NOVA -- National Aeronautics and Space Administration launch vehicle for more advanced space exploration beyond the initial manned lunar landing. Originally, Nova was the name for a 12 million-pound first stage thrust vehicle which would be able to orbit 400,000 pounds. However, due to re-study and evaluation of future space missions, Nova is now a generic name for a vehicle with significant capability beyond the ADVANCED SATURN. Thrust is expected to be between 20-30 million pounds in the first stage. Probably will not be operational until the latter 1960's or early 1970's.

NOVEMBER -- Code word for letter "N" in a phonetic alphabet, used to avoid possibility of a misunderstanding in transmitting messages. See also NAN.

NOVUS -- An industry proposal for a space booster with a clustered thrust of 14 million pounds achieved by 2.4 million-pound thrust, solid motors strapped together. Booster could put a payload of 150,000 pounds into a 300-mile orbit. Proposal is not under active development.

NUBBIN -- Sul River, New Britain. WW-II.

NUCLEAR BULLPUP -- An early name for the GAM-83B advanced BULLPUP.

NUCLEAR FALCON -- An early name for the GAR-11, latest member of the FALCON family.

NUCLEUS -- Boimagi Island, Trobriand Island. WW-II.

NUDETS -- Nuclear detonation detection and reporting system deployed to provide surveillance coverage of critical, friendly target areas and automatically indicate place, height of burst, yield and ground zero of nuclear detonations. Information would be relayed to the NORAD Combat Operations Center in Colorado for display and evaluation. To be in limited operation in 1963.

NUDGER -- U.S. Canadian loading exercise, held at Southampton, England, December 1943, in preparation for OVERLORD. See also GULL, SNIPE. WW-II.

NULACE -- Acronym for Nuclear Liquid Air Collection Engine, an engine designed to use a nuclear reactor in conjunction with an air collection system which would scoop up and liquify air during flight. The liquid would then be heated by the reactor and expanded through a nozzle to provide thrust for an aerospace plane. Under study.

NUMBSKULL -- Kapiura River, New Britain. WW-II.

NUSSKNACKER -- Nickname for the MF-5 underwater-to-air missile under development for the German Navy during World War II. The two-stage solid-propellant missile was designed to be used against aircraft at low altitudes. Development was halted in 1944.

NUTCRACKER -- (1) Sosoli, New Britain. WW-II.

(2) Code name for Panama Canal. WW-II.

NUTMEG -- Heavy bombing operation by Mediterranean Allied Air Forces on enemy coastal defense batteries and radar stations from Genoa, Italy, to Sète, France, 10-15 August 1944, in preparation for DRAGOON. WW-II.

NUTPINE -- Corregidor, Philippine Islands. WW-II.

O

O, PLAN -- See Y, PLAN

OAK -- Third phase objective of Canadian troops in Normandy landing; included capture of area on Bayeux road, five miles west of Caen, and areas of Putot-en Bessin, Secqueville-en-Bessin and Norrey-en-Bessin. See also YEW, ELM. June 1944, WW-II.

OAK HILL -- U.S. military name for topographic feature on Okinawa. 1945, WW-II.

OAKTREE -- Forrester Island, Alaska. WW-II.

OAO -- Acronym for Orbiting Astronomical Observatory, National Aeronautics and Space Administration program for astronomical studies of the sky with a 36-inch optical telescope, and ultra violet and radiation density sensors. Weighing 3300 pounds, and launched by a ATLAS-AGENA, it will be orbited for the first time in 1964, with two more orbits in 1965.

OATMEAL -- (1) Labuan Island, North Borneo. WW-II.

(2) See ALACRITY and OATMEAL

OBELISK -- U.S. Navy code for coast watcher sighting. WW-II.

OBEN -- Paramaribo, Dutch Guiana. WW-II.

OBERON -- Davao Gulf, Mindanao, Philippine Islands. WW-II.

OBESE -- Deepwater Passage, Philippine Islands. WW-II.

OBLIQUE -- Tsushima Strait, Japan. WW-II.

OBOE -- (1) Code word for letter "O" in a phonetic alphabet, used to avoid possibility of a misunderstanding in transmitting messages. See also OSCAR.

(2) British radio system used for guiding aircraft to target; consisted of two ground stations transmitting signals: the MOUSE, which set the course to be flown and the CAT, which calculated plan's progress along course up to target. Named for oboe-like quality of pulse from MOUSE. Developed in 1941, WW-II. See also ASPEN.

OBOE OPERATIONS -- Allied landings and planned landings in Borneo and Netherlands East Indies; part of MONTCLAIR. See OBOE 1-6. 1945, WW-II.

OBOE 1 -- Australian landing on Tarakan Island off northeastern Borneo. Began 1 May 1945, WW-II.

OBOE 2 -- Australian landing at Balikpapan, Netherlands Borneo. Began 1 July 1945, WW-II.

OBOE 3 -- Proposed Allied plan to take Bandjermasin, Netherlands Borneo. Suspended 8 April 1945, WW-II.

OBOE 4 -- Proposed Allied plan to reoccupy either Surabaya or Batavia, Java. Suspended 8 April 1945, WW-II.

OBOE 5 -- Proposed Allied plan to reoccupy eastern part of Netherlands East Indies. Suspended 8 April 1945, WW-II.

OBOE 6 -- Australian landing in Lubuan-Brunei Bay area, British North Borneo. Actually followed OBOE 1. Began 10 June 1945, WW-II.

OBOE, HILL -- (1) Military name for topographic feature in PURPLE HEART RIDGE on Saipan. 1944, WW-II.

(2) U.S. military name for topographic feature on Okinawa. 1945, WW-II.

OBSERVATION HILL -- (1) Military name for topographic feature near Mubo, northeastern New Guinea, inland from Huon Gulf. 1943, WW-II.

(2) Millitary name for topographic feature near Obong-ni and Naktong River, Korea. Summer 1950, Korean Conflict.

OBSERVATORY HILL -- Military name for topographic feature in Inchon, Korea; important objective seized by U.S. Marines during landings there. 15 September 1950, Korean Conflict.

OBTRUSIVE -- Aparri, Philippine Islands. WW-II.

OCCIDENTAL -- St. Johns, Newfoundland. WW-II.

OCEANBLUE -- Kodiak, Alaska. WW-II.

OCELOT -- Recife, Brazil. WW-II.

OCHSENKOPF -- German operation to extend Tunis bridgehead by capturing Bedja and Medjez el Bab. See also AUSLADUNG. 26 February 1943, WW-II.

OCTAGON -- Second Anglo-American conference at Quebec, Canada, attended by President Roosevelt and Prime Minister Churchill. See also QUADRANT. 12-16 September 1944, WW-II.

OCTOPUS -- (1) Marklo Island, New Britain. WW-II.

(2) Mompog Pass, Philippine Islands. WW-II.

OCTOROON -- Palau Harbor, Palau Islands. WW-II.

ODETTE -- Name reserved by meteorologists for tropical cyclone in North Atlantic area.

ODIOUS -- Suez, Egypt. WW-II.

ODOP -- Cienfuegos, Cuba. WW-II.

OERLIKON -- Extensive series of missiles manufactured and marketed by the Oerlikon Company of Switzerland, ranging from small folding fin aircraft rockets to the OERLIKON 54, with a launch weight of over 700 pounds, and a range of 15.5 miles. Missiles include air-to-air rockets, anti-tank and surface-to-surface weapons, and anti-aircraft missiles. The Oerlikon 54 was tested for use by the U.S. Army. All were developed in the early 1950's or before; none are currently in use.

OGO -- Acronym for Orbiting Geophysical Observatory, National Aeronautics and Space Administration program for geophysical measurement of the earth and its environment from a 1000-pound earth-stabilized satellite. One of three boosters, ATLAS-AGENA, THOR-AGENA and CENTAUR, will be used to launch the spacecraft. Also see EGO and POGO. First flight scheduled in 1964, with two more in 1965.

OGRE 1 -- French ramjet-sustained photo reconnaissance missile launched by a liquid booster. The 720-pound vehicle had a range of 50 miles, and carried a television camera and radio transmitter. A post World War II development.

O'HARA'S KNOB -- U.S. military name for topographic feature on east coast of Okinawa. 1945, WW-II.

OHKA -- Japanese name for BAKA BOMB.

OIL PLAN -- Allied plan to bomb German oil industry, with secondary attacks on aircraft, ball bearing and rubber production plants, in support of OVERLORD. Spring 1944, WW-II.

OKA BOMB -- See BAKA BOMB

OKEMAN -- Kabasalan, Philippine Islands. WW-II.

OKLAHOMA FILE -- U.S. General Joseph W. Stilwell's personal file of messages about his recall from China. WW-II.

OKRA -- Townsville, Queensland, Australia. WW-II.

OLAFSON BRIDGE -- Lightweight portable footbridge, used in Italy; invented by Canadian Captain E.A. Olafson. WW-II.

OLD BALDY -- (1) U.S. military name for Hill 300 on Peleliu Island. Fall 1944, WW-II.

(2) See BATTLE MOUNTAIN

(3) Military name for hill in Yokkokthon Valley, Korea, south of PORK CHOP HILL. Korean Conflict.

OLD BLOOD AND GUTS -- Nickname for U.S. Lieutenant General George S. Patton, Jr. WW-II.

OLD BOOMERANG -- British Royal Air Force airmen's nickname for the Lockheed HUDSON.

OLD FAITHFUL -- (1) Nickname for light cruiser, USS Birmingham. Named from geysers which spouted from trunk leading up to main deck devised to relieve pressure in water-filled compartments damaged in Japanese air attack on 8 November 1943. Also nicknamed Mighty B. WW-II.

(2) U.S. 4.5-inch beach barrage rocket for close support of troops in amphibious operations. Mounted on landing craft and surface ships, it proved extremely effective between the time naval and air bombardment ceased and troops actually landed. Used in the Casablanca campaign on 8 November 1942, it was normally a ship-to-shore weapon; but in December 1944, completely destroyed a Japanese ship, probably the first ever sunk by an all rocket attack. It was also used as a surface-to-surface weapon by the Marines in October 1943. Some 1,600,000 were delivered to the armed services between 1942 and the end of the war.

OLD GOLD -- One of five camps of RED HORSE STAGING AREA in region of Le Havre-Rouen, France. Established November 1944, WW-II.

OLD HICKORY -- Nickname for U.S. 30th Infantry Division. So named after World War One National Guardsmen from Carolinas, Georgia, and Tennessee, the region of Andrew Jackson.

OLD HOUSE -- U.S. Air Force high-altitude air refueling area over Louisiana-Texas.

OLD IRONSIDES DIVISION -- Nickname for U.S. 1st Armored Division.

OLD LADY -- Nickname for submarine tender, USS Canopus, built in 1919 and active in Philippines during siege of Corregidor. December 1941 - April 1942, WW-II.

OLD LAMPLIGHTER OF THE KOREAN HILLS -- See FIREFLY

OLD NAMELESS -- Nickname for battleship, USS South Dakota. Also called BIG BASTARD, BATTLESHIP X. WW-II.

OLD RELIABLE -- Name of a nine-month-old monkey fired down the Atlantic Missile Range in a JUPITER nose cone, December 1958. During the eight and one half minutes of zero gravity, the monkey experienced no ill effects. However, during re-entry the monkey's pulse rate went up to 280 and he sustained

40 g's. Telemetry indicated a return to normal before the water impact. The nose cone sank after impact and the monkey was not recovered.

OLEANDER -- (1) Code name for Akyab, Burma. WW-II.

(2) Munda Island, Solomon Islands. WW-II.

OLGA -- (1) Typhoon. 2-7 December 1958. Formed in Marshall Islands. Moved northwestward into Philippine Sea, then turned northeastward and eastward, passing south of Marcus Island into central North Pacific.

(2) Typhoon. 8-10 September 1961. Formed northeast of Luzon, Philippines. Moved westward, reached typhoon intensity in South China Sea, and entered China mainland northeast of Hong Kong. Reported to have caused five deaths and some damage.

(3) Name also applied to tropical cyclones in western North Pacific which occurred prior to (1) and (2) above.

(4) Code name of one of series of rearguard actions on phase lines fought by Germans during northward withdrawal to Arno River, Italy. Summer 1944, WW-II.

OLIVE -- (1) Taivu Point, Guadalcanal, Solomon Islands. WW-II.

(2) Typhoon. 13-18 October 1947. First detected between Eniwetok Atoll and Guam. Moved northward at first, then northeastward into North Pacific.

(3) Typhoon. 15-18 September 1952. Formed east of Wake Island. Moved westward across Wake Island, turned gradually northwestward, northward, and northeastward and dissipated over central North Pacific.

(4) Typhoon. 24-29 November 1956. Formed in western Caroline Islands. Moved northwestward across Philippine Sea and absorbed typhoon NADINE east of Luzon. Crossed central Luzon and dissipated over South China Sea.

(5) Typhoon. 23-30 June 1960. Formed in western Caroline Islands. Moved west-northwestward across central Philippines and South China Sea into China mainland, 200 miles west of Hong Kong. Caused 104 deaths in Philippines, and floods there and in Hong Kong.

(6) Name also applied to tropical cyclones in western North Pacific which occurred prior to (2) through (5) above.

(7) Allied attack on German GOTHIC LINE in Italy. Began 25 August 1944, WW-II.

OLIVENERNTE -- German planned operation to capture Medjez el Bab, Tunisia. Not executed. January 1943, WW-II.

OLYMPIC -- Projected Allied operation to invade island of Kyushu, Japan, in fall of 1945. Code name changed to MAJESTIC for security reasons. See also CORONET. WW-II.

OLYMPUS -- Cape Padaran, French Indo China. WW-II.

OMAHA -- Beach assaulted by troops of U.S. V Corps on D DAY, 6 June 1944, in Operation OVERLORD; located on both sides of Vire River at Saint-Laurent-sur-Mer, Normandy, France. Originally called Y, but name changed in March 1944. See also ASSAULT FORCE O. WW-II.

OMAR -- U.S. Navy air-to-surface high velocity rocket program never carried beyond the development stage. Optically guided, it reportedly weighed several hundred pounds. Development took place in the early 1950's.

OMELIA -- Typhoon. 28 September - 4 October 1949. First detected in western Caroline Islands. Moved northwestward between Luzon and Taiwan into China mainland, where it dissipated.

OMET 1-7 -- Seven U.S. Army supply depots in Middle East. WW-II.

OMIS -- Acronym for Operational Management Information System; OMIS Project designed to investigate relationship between system operational management needs and the manner in which they may be satisfied by data processing.

ON THE DECK -- U.S. Air Force radio and telephone communications code word signifying "at minimum altitude."

ON TOP -- U.S. Air Force radio and telephone communications code word signi-fying "above the overcast."

ONCEOVER -- Aqaba, Palestine. WW-II.

ONE HUNDRED METER HILL -- See HUNDRED METER HILL

ONE SHOT II, OPERATION -- U.S. Strike Command drop of paratroopers 1,000 miles from home in a test of quick-reaction capabilities.

ONOTO -- Narsarssuak, Greenland. WW-II.

ONTOS -- U.S. Marine Corps multiple 106-mm. rifle.

OP HILL -- Military name for topographic feature near Carigara Bay on Leyte, Philippine Islands. November 1944, WW-II.

OP TREE -- Platform on 150 foot-high tree on SOUTH KNOB, Bougainville; used by mortar and artillery forward observers. WW-II.

OPAL -- (1) Tropical storm. 15-21 July 1945. First detected in southern Philippine Sea. Moved northwestward at first, then curved northeastward through Ryukyus and Japan.

(2) Typhoon. 7-11 September 1946. First detected south of Guam. Moved westward across Philippine Sea, then northwestward across Luzon and South China Sea into mainland China, west of Hong Kong.

(3) Typhoon. 11-20 October 1955. Formed in western Caroline Islands. Moved northwestward to position east of Taiwan, then turned northeastward along Ryukyu Island and into Japan as weakening storm.

(4) Tropical storm. 5-6 September 1959. Formed and dissipated in vicinity of Ponape, Caroline Islands, the Pacific.

(5) Typhoon. 30 July - 9 August 1962. Formed near Truk Island. Moved northwestward through Philippine Sea, across Taiwan, and into mainland China, then recurved northeastward over Shantung Peninsula, Korea, and Hokkaido. Caused at least eighty-seven deaths and heavy damage on Taiwan.

(6) Name also applied to tropical cyclones in western North Pacific which occurred prior to (1) through (5) above.

OPERA -- U.S. Army acronym for Ordnance Pulses Experimental Research Assembly, a nuclear reactor at Aberdeen Proving Ground, Maryland; designed to study the characteristics and effects of pulsed nuclear radiation.

OPHELIA -- (1) Tropical storm. June 1948. First detected in South China Sea off Hong Kong. Moved northwestward into China mainland.

(2) Typhoon. 11-13 August 1953. Formed east of Luzon. Moved west-north-westward, skirting north coast of Luzon, and across South China Sea to Asiatic mainland.

(3) Typhoon. 6-17 January 1958. Formed near Majuro, Marshall Islands. Moved westward through the U.S. Trust Territory, causing sixteen deaths and considerable damage en route, and into the Philippine Sea, where it dissipated.

(4) Typhoon. 21 November - 6 December 1960. Formed near Kwajalein Atoll. Moved westward across Ulithi Atoll into Philippine Sea, then turned northward and northeastward over North Pacific. Caused two deaths and severe damage on Ulithi.

(5) Name also applied to tropical cyclones in western North Pacific which occurred prior to (1) through (4) above.

OPIUM -- Transfer of 3rd U.S. Marine Regiment to Samoa. WW-II.

OPTOMETRIST -- Lula Lagoon, Choiseul Island, Solomon Islands. WW-II.

ORA -- (1) Typhoon. 13-21 September 1951. Formed in southeastern Philippine Sea. Moved west-northwestward, passed between Luzon and Taiwan, and weakened over South China Sea.

(2) Name also included in sequence prepared by meteorologists for future tropical cyclones in eastern North Pacific.

ORACLE -- Acronym for Oak Ridge Automatic Computer and Logical Engine, a high-speed digital computer.

ORANGE -- (1) Joint U.S. Army-Navy basic plan for possibility of war with Japan. First approved in 1924, revised, and finally replaced by RAINBOW in 1939.

(2) U.S. high-altitude nuclear weapon detonation. Part of Operation HARTACK at Eniwetok Proving Ground, Marshall Islands. Summer 1958.

ORANGE BLOSSOM -- Second artillery barrage on 18 December 1943 in Canadian OPERATION MORNING GLORY near Ortona, Italy. Named for cocktail because it "carried a tremendous wallop." WW-II.

ORANGEADE -- Moemi Airfield, New Guinea. WW-II.

ORANGES SOUR -- U.S. Air Force radio and telephone communications code word signifying "weather unsuitable for aircraft mission."

ORANGES SWEET -- U.S. Air Force radio and telephone communications code word signifying "weather suitable for aircraft mission."

ORATION -- Infiltration operation of Royal Air Force to drop supplies to British liaison mission at Marshal Tito's headquarters in Yugoslavia. January 1944, WW-II.

ORATOR -- Kaibola, Lusancay Island, Trobriand Islands. WW-II.

ORBITER PROJECT -- U.S. Army proposal to use a three-stage launch vehicle to put a satellite in orbit. The proposal was based on a REDSTONE first stage, a cluster of LOKI rockets for the second and the third a single Loki. Proposed in 1954, the idea lost out to the VANGUARD proposal. Revived in 1958.

ORBY -- Allied code word for ground control interception. WW-II.

ORCHID -- (1) Tenaru Signal Tower, Guadalcanal, Solomon Islands. WW-II.

(2) Name reserved by meteorologists for tropical cyclone in North Atlantic area.

ORCON -- U.S. Navy acronym for Organic Control, a program which would employ pigeons sealed inside a missile to guide the missile to its target. A re-inforcing reward mechanism would be used so that the pigeon would peck at a particular spot on a glass plate. An electrode on the bird's beak would complete an electrical circuit and furnish correction signals. Abandoned.

ORDEAL -- Code name for Okhotsk Sea. WW-II.

ORELOB -- See RHUMBA

ORENCO B -- The first American pursuit aircraft designed as such. Designed by Walter Phipps and delivered to the Air Service in March 1918.

ORENCO D -- Improvement of the B model was delivered to the U.S. Air Service in 1919 and later designated the PW-3. Curtiss delivered another revision in 1920.

ORENDA -- Engine designed and built in Canada f'or CF-100.

OREX -- Seeadler Harbor, Manus Island, Admiralty Islands. WW-II.

ORGANGRINDER -- Kaiapit, New Guinea. WW-II.

ORIENE -- Name reserved by meteorologists for tropical cyclone in Eastern North Pacific.

ORIENT PROJECT -- Proposal, depending on American air forces remaining in China for long term after World War II, to establish series of airlines radiating out from Shanghai to Vladivostok, Harbin, Mukden, Peiping, Lanchow, Hanoi, and Colombo; not carried out.

ORIENTAL -- Komebail Lagoon, Palau Islands. WW-II.

ORIGIN -- 3rd U.S. Naval Training Base, British Isles. WW-II.

ORIOLE -- (1) U.S. Navy air-to-air test missile with a range of about 20 miles and a speed of Mach 2 to 3. Powered by a ramjet engine, it was radar-guided and intended for fleet use. Development began in May 1948 and was cancelled January 1954 in favor of the SPARROW.

(2) Naso Point, Kandavu Island, Fiji Islands. WW-II.

ORION -- (1) Lockheed 9D six-passenger cabin monoplane of early 1930's.

(2) Long-range reconnaissance version of the Lockheed Electra aircraft. In the U.S. Navy as the P3V.

(3) World War II Macchi C.205N aircraft. See ORIONE.

(4) U.S. Air Force program to propel space vehicles, weighing up to one million pounds, by a continuing series of small nuclear explosions. Feasibility studies have been conducted since 1959 and, in the PUT-PUTT series of high explosive tests, the feasibility was proven on a small scale. However, program is not under active development and may be cancelled or transfered to National Aeronautics and Space Administration in the fiscal year 1964 budget.

ORIONE -- (English translation: Orion) Macchi C.205 N interceptor which made its first flight in 1942. Italian capitulation prevented production.

ORINE SAR -- Italian surface-to-air or surface-to-surface missile available in 2.25 or 3.4-inch diameter. Unguided Post World War II development.

ORKAN -- Yugoslavian twin-engine monoplane built by Ikarus for the military before World War II.

ORLA -- Tropical storm. 6-11 September 1961. First detected near Isla Socorro 500 miles west of Acapulco, Mexico. Moved north-northwestward to the west of Baja California and dissipated near Punta Eugenia.

ORNATE -- Puerto Castillo, Honduras. WW-II.

ORPHA -- Name reserved by meteorologists for tropical cyclone in North Atlantic area.

ORPHAN -- (1) U.N. code name for Hodo Pando on Wonsan Harbor, North Korea. Korean Conflict.

(2) Code name of experiment, initiated by U.S. General Carl Spaatz, for developing and using radar-controlled conventional bomber aircraft as guided missiles in CROSSBOW operation against German V-weapon sites. Also called APHRODITE, BATTY, CASTOR and WEARY-WILLIE. WW-II.

ORSCHOLZ SWITCH LINE -- German line of field works, antitank barriers and reinforced concrete pillboxes and bunkers, constructed as east-west extension, at right angles, to WESTWALL; extended from Orscholz on Saar River to Moselle River. Known to Americans as Siegfried Switch. Scene of heavy fighting. November-December 1944, WW-II.

ORTHODOX -- Code name for Aleutian Islands. WW-II.

ORVA -- Name reserved by meteorologists for tropical cyclone North Atlantic area.

OSCAR -- (1) Code word for letter "O" in a phonetic alphabet, used to avoid possibility of a misunderstanding in transmitting messages. See also OBOE.

(2) Nakajima KI.43, first flown in 1939; became, numerically, the most important Japanese Army Air Force fighter of the war. Japanese: Hayabusa Peregrine Falcon).

(3) U.S. Navy acronym for Optimal Survival Containment and Recover, an integrated pilot escape capsule.

(4) Acronym for Orbiting Satellite Carrying Amateur Radio, a 10-pound satellite launched piggyback aboard DISCOVERER XXXVI on 12 December 1961. The satellite transmits a signal which can be picked up by ham radio operators. Developed and put together by members of Lockheed Missiles & Space Company.

(5) Molucca Passage, Netherlands East Indies. WW-II.

OSHAWA, CITY OF -- Name for Royal Canadian Air Force Squadron Number 416.

OSLO REPORT -- Anonymous report on German technical developments, obtained by British naval attache in Oslo, Norway. November 1939, WW-II.

OSO -- Acronym for Orbiting Solar Observation, National Aeronautics and Space Administration program to measure the sun's ultraviolet radiation, gamma radiation and solar X-rays. Weighing 440 pounds, the first was launched 7 March, 1963 by a THOR-DELTA. Second planned for 1963, with 10 more through 1967. Advanced version being studied.

OSO-I -- First of National Aeronautics and Space Administration's Orbiting Solar Observatories. Launched 7 March, 1962, the 485-pound satellite carried 13 experiments to measure the ultra-violet, x-ray and gamma ray characteristics of the sun. No longer transmitting; improved and advanced versions planned.

OSPREY -- (1) Military version of the Curtiss-Wright A14D Speedwing aircraft of 1933, designed C-14r and -b in U.S.

(2) British Fleet Air Arm adaptation of Hawker day bomber. See HART.

OSSIA -- Typhoon. 1-5 October 1950. First detected east of central Philippines. Moved west-northwestward across central Luzon and the South China Sea into Indo China.

OSTENTATION -- Makar, Mindanao, Philippine Islands. WW-II.

OSTFRIESLAND -- "Unsinkable" German battleship sent to the bottom by Mitchell's bombers in restrictive 1921 tests.

OSTLER -- Tongareva (Penrhyn) Island, Cook Islands. WW-II.

OTAN -- Acronym for Organisation du Traite de l'Atlantique Nord; the French equivalent of NATO.

OTORI -- (English translation: Phoenix) Bomber version of the Mitsubishi Type 96 twin-engine pre-World War II Japanese commercial transport.

OTTAWA -- Planned Canadian attack from north on Carpiquet village near Caen, France. Replaced by Operation WINDSOR. June 1944, WW-II.

OTTER -- Canadian DeHavilland DHC-3 which first flew in 1951. In service with the U.S. Army and U.S. Navy as the U-1, as well as with many other countries.

OTTER I-II -- U.S. battalion landing team tests held in Slapton Sands area, Great Britain, in preparation for OVERLORD. See also MINK I-II. March 1944, WW-II.

OTVAZHNAYA -- (English translation: Daring) Name of dog used by the Russians for a space shot in 1959. The dog was recovered with apparently no ill effects. See also ZNEZHINKA.

OURAGAN -- Dassault MD-450. First French jet fighter of national design to be manufactured in quantity. First flown in 1949. Called Toofani in India.

OUTBUILDING -- Code word for South Pacific Theater. WW-II.

OUTCROP -- Tripolia, Syria. WW-II.

OUTDOORS, OPERATION -- Two-part program by U.S. Forest Service for development of recreational facilities in forests.

OUTER GONDOLA -- Name given by Allied air patrols to Bay of Biscay. WW-II.

OUTGENERAL -- Engebi Island, Eniwetok, Marshall Islands. WW-II.

OUTGOING -- Komsomoesk-Nilolaevsh Area, U.S.S.R. WW-II.

OUTJOCKEY -- Ulejang Atoll, Marshall Islands. WW-II.

OUTPOST I, II -- An industry proposal for twin four-man space vehicles to be put into 300-mile orbits at a 300-mile altitude. Empty vehicles would be orbited and then manned transport vehicles would rendezvous with the stations to transfer the crew. Not under development.

OUTRANGE -- Keelung, Formosa. WW-II.

OUTRIGHT -- Ngatik Island, Caroline Islands. WW-II.

OUTSPOKEN -- Borokoe, Netherlands East Indies. WW-II.

OUTSTEP -- Curacao, Netherlands West Indies. WW-II.

OVERBOARD -- Sovetskaya Gavan, U.S.S.R. WW-II.

OVERBOARD, OPERATION -- Term parodying Normandy invasion plan, Operation OVERLORD, given by an Allied staff officer who explained, "The general principle is that the number of divisions required to capture the number of ports required to maintain those divisions is always greater than the number of divisions those ports can maintain."

OVERBUILD -- Parry Island, Eniwetok, Marshall Islands. WW-II.

OVERCAST -- Project of exploiting German civilian scientists. WW-II.

OVERCOAT -- Staines, British Isles (Central Spare Parts Depot). WW-II.

OVERDOSE -- Kepler Point, New Guinea. WW-II.

OVERFEED -- Gilbert Islands. WW-II.

OVERFLOW -- Code name for Transjordania. WW-II.

OVERHEAD -- Tokyo Area, Japan. WW-II.

OVERLAND TRAIN -- U.S. Army logistic vehicle for rough terrain.

OVERLORD -- Allied cross-Channel invasion of continent of Europe on Normandy coast of France. Commenced on D DAY, 6 June 1944. Code name first used in planning, July 1943. Previous invasion projects: RUDGE, SLEDGEHAMMER, ROUNDUP, SUPER-ROUNDUP, ROUNDHAMMER, SKYSCRAPER, RANKIN. Landing beaches: UTAH, OMAHA, GOLD, JUNO, SWORD. See also BOLERO, COSSAC, COCKADE, BIGOT, FORTITUDE, NEPTUNE, RHUMBA, Y DAY, BOWSPRIT, HORNPIPE. WW-II.

OVERLORD DIVER -- British plan for defensive measures against German V-weapon attacks; involved use of fighters, guns, searchlights and balloons. See also DIVER. 1943, WW-II.

OVERPAY -- Rhodes, Mediterranean Sea. WW-II.

OVERPITCH -- Code name for South Africa. WW-II.

OVERSCENTED -- Bandjermasin, Dutch Borneo. WW-II.

OVERSTRESS -- Camotes Sea, Philippine Islands. WW-II.

OVERTRUMP -- Rongelap, Marshall Islands. WW-II.

OWL -- (1) Curtiss O-52 monoplane used by the U.S. Army Air Forces early in WW-II.

(2) World War II German He-219 aircraft. See UHU.

(3) U.S. Air Force solid propellant sounding rocket designed to carry radar-reflective material to altitudes of 50 miles so that ground stations can track the material and determine wind velocity and direction. Essentially a small DART, the rocket is launched to obtain meteorological data prior to launch of ballistic missiles. In operational use.

OWLET -- Open-cockpit monoplane trainer made by General Aircraft of Great Britain. Development of their pre-World War II CYGNET.

OWLSCLOVER -- Dipalog, Mindanao, Philippine Islands. WW-II.

OXEYE -- Heliopolis, Egypt. WW-II.

OXFORD -- Later version of the ENVOY. Used as an advanced trainer plane by Britain's Royal Air Force.

OXFORD BRIDGE -- Bailey bridge built across Gari River south of Sant'Angelo, Italy, by Indian army engineers. May 1944, WW-II.

OXIDIZE -- Crete, Mediterranean Sea. WW-II.

OXYGEN -- Cebu, Philippine Islands. WW-II.

OYSTER -- (1) Name for type of German sea mine laid by aircraft. WW-II.

(2) Busai, Woodlark Island. WW-II.

OZARK RUN -- Name for U.S. peacetime military exercise at Fort Riley, Kansas, 1959.

OZARKS -- Nickname for U.S. 102nd Infantry Division. Design on shoulder patch includes O and Z. Also called HILLBILLIES.

OZMA -- Research program to try to detect signals reaching earth from outer space. The National Radio Astronomy Observatory in West Virginia has made one tentative attempt to detect these signals with no results. Another attempt may be made in 1963.

OZONE -- Guimaras Strait, Philippine Islands. WW-II.

P

P BALLOONS -- British propaganda balloons carrying leaflets over Germany; name changed to M BALLOONS to disguise purpose. First dispatched October 1939, WW-II.

P DAY -- (1) General military term, with specific applications, for earliest day on which rate of production for any given item equals or exceeds rate at which item is required by armed forces.

(2) Date for beginning of Australian landing on Tarakan Island off northeastern Borneo. 1 May 1945, WW-II.

P, PLAN -- See W, PLAN

PAC-AID -- U.S. code name for missions flown by XX Bomber Command, based in China, in direct support of operations in Pacific. 1944-45, WW-II.

PACK OF CARDS BRIDGE -- Wooden bridge on Burma-Thailand DEATH RAILWAY built by prisoners of war of Japanese in 17 days. So named because it fell down three times during construction. 1943, WW-II.

PACKAGE -- Code word used with numbers to indicate five points along Sonjin-Hungnam railroad, eastern Korea, suitable for continuous cooperative attacks by U.N. naval aircraft and ships. See also DERAIL. Instituted 11 January 1952, Korean Conflict.

PACKARD -- (1) Alaro, New Britain. WW-II.

(2) Tetere, New Georgia, Solomon Islands. WW-II.

PACKET -- Originally applied to the U.S. Army Air Forces C-82 Fairchild twin-boom, twin-engine freighter plane, now in civil and foreign service. Popular name later given to C-119, but changed to FLYING BOXCAR.

PACT -- Acronym for Project for the Advancement of Coding Techniques.

PACT DOC -- Allied guerrilla medical unit west of Hangchow, China, behind Japanese lines, where Chinese doctors and medical assistants were trained. See also SACO. Originally established in western Hunan, November 1943, WW-II.

PADDLEWHEEL -- Nickname applied to EXPLORER VI (Able III) satellite. So called because the four solar paddles which extended on arms from the satellite looked like paddlewheels. Launched 7 August 1959, the 142-pound satellite was the first to detect the earth's ring current.

PADLOCK -- Buriwadi Island, Trobriand Islands. WW-II.

PADRE RUIZ HURRICANE -- Hurricane, 20-23 September 1834, which struck Dominica and Santo Domingo, the latter during funeral services for a priest, Father Ruiz.

PAGE -- Fanning Island, Central Pacific. WW-II.

PAGODA -- Nickname for Japanese built tower on Henderson Field, Guadalcanal, which was used by U.S. forces as observation post for air attacks. 1942, WW-II.

PAINTBOX -- U.S. Navy Base II, Rosneath, British Isles. WW-II.

PAINTBRUSH -- Lunga Signal Tower, Guadalcanal, Solomon Islands. WW-II.

PALEFACE -- Udot Island, Truk Lagoon, Caroline Islands. WW-II.

PALISADE -- Taboga Island, Canal Zone. WW-II.

PALLIASSE -- Wau-Bulolo Valley,,New Guinea. WW-II.

PALL MALL -- One of five camps of RED HORSE STAGING AREA in region of Le Havre-Rouen, France. Extablished April 1945, WW-II.

PALM -- Vatilau Island, Solomon Islands. WW-II.

PALMAR -- Kudat, British North Borneo. WW-II.

PALMOIL -- Code name for U.S. Army in Ireland. WW-II.

PALMOLIVE -- Lagoon Point, New Britain. WW-II.

PAMELA -- (1) Typhoon. 28 October - 6 November 1954. Formed over western Caroline Islands. Moved northwestward over Philippine Sea, then west-north-westward through Balintang Channel toward China mainland.

    (2) Tropical storm. 30 November - 4 December 1958. Formed northwest of Guam. Moved erratically westward over Philippine Sea and died out.

    (3) Typhoon. 8-12 September 1961. Formed northeast of Guam and moved westward across Taiwan and dissipated over China mainland. Caused 98 deaths and four million dollars damage on Taiwan.

    (4) Name also applied to tropical cyclones in western North Pacific which occurred prior to (1) through (3) above.

PAN PAN -- U.S. Air Force radio and telephone communications code word signi-fying "urgent message."

PANACEA TARGET -- Opprobrious term, defined by British Air Chief Marshal

Sir Arthur Harris as "targets which were supposed by economic experts to be such a vital bottle-neck in the German industry that when they were destroyed the enemy would have to pack up." Ball-bearing factories were an example. Also called Bottlenecks. WW-II.

PANAY FORCE -- Garrison of VISAYAN FORCE for defense of Philippines. Spring 1942, WW-II.

PANCAKE -- Allied bombing assault against enemy supplies, equipment and troop concentrations in area of Bologna, Italy. October 1944, WW-II.

PANCAKE HILL -- Military name for topographic feature south of Hollandia, Netherlands New Guinea. April 1944, WW-II.

PANDA BEAR -- U.S. Air Force high-altitude air refueling area over Illinois-Missouri.

PANDEMONIUM -- Aleppo, Syria. WW-II.

PANDORA -- British air-to-surface missile reportedly under development for the TRS-2 supersonic fighter bomber. Would be launched against ground targets at very low altitudes.

PANGLOSS -- U.S. Navy program designed to develop secure communications between nuclear submarines (particularly Polaris) and other subs, surface ships, shore-based stations and aircraft. Several industrial contracts have been let.

PANHANDLE -- Truk, Caroline Islands. WW-II.

PANPUS -- Hui Island, Solomon Islands. WW-II.

PANTALOON -- Naples, Italy. WW-II.

PANTECHNICON -- German air force slang name for a heavy bomber. WW-II.

PANTHEON -- Code name for Alaska. WW-II.

PANTHER -- (1) German Mark V medium tank with heavy armor and high velocity gun. See also TIGER. WW-II.

(2) Keystone B-6A twin-engine biplane bomber built for the U.S. Army Air Corps starting in 1931.

(3) Grumman F9F U.S. Navy jet fighter of the early 1950's.

(4) One of four flights in U.S. KIT PROJECT to send A-20 aircraft from Florida to Oran, Algeria, for use in North African campaign. November 1942, WW-II.

(5) British X Corps drive across the Garigliano River, Italy. Began 17 January 1944, WW-II.

(6) Projected U.S. limited objective attack to reduce Carroceto salient of Anzio beachhead, Italy, Cancelled 18 March 1944, WW-II.

PANTHER, POSITION -- Narva River-Lake Peipus, Estonia, field fortifications, constructed in Fall 1943. WW-II.

PANTOBASE -- YC-123 J version of the PROVIDER, built by Stroukoff Aircraft for arctic operations, but never put into production.

PAPA -- Code word for letter "P" in a phonetic alphabet, used to avoid possibility of a misunderstanding in transmitting messages. See also PETER.

PAPERCLIP -- Bali Strait, Java, Netherland East Indies. WW-II.

PAPERCLIP PROJECT -- Operation in which Colonel C. Toftoy rounded up German rocket experts after World War II and brought them to the U.S. Over 150 of Germany's top rocket experts were thus prevented from falling into Russian hands. Brought into U.S. through Mexico and they lived around El Paso, Texas, and White Sands, New Mexico, until their move in 1950 to Redstone Arsenal, Alabama.

PAPOOSE PROJECT -- U.S. program to include biological and scientific experiments in the unused portions of experimental missiles and space vehicles. Basic idea is to fill the empty and ballast space in nose cones and rockets with useful payloads. Program being actively pursued.

PAR -- Acronym for Precision Approach Radar, a rapid scanning airport radar system.

PARADE DIVISION -- Popular name for Panzer Lehr Division, German armored unit. WW-II.

PARADISE VALLEY -- U.S. military name for topographic feature on Saipan. Called Hell Valley by Japanese. 1944, WW-II.

PARAFFIN -- Namu Atoll, Marshall Islands. WW-II.

PARAMATTA -- British method of ground marking a target by colored markers dropped blindly from aircraft using H2S radar equipment. See also MUSICAL PARAMATTA. WW-II.

PARAPET -- Dumanquilas Bay, Philippine Islands. WW-II.

PARASITE -- Code name for Italy (Italian). WW-II.

PARASOL -- Single-engine light monoplane built by Heath Aircraft Company of Michigan in 1933.

PARCA -- French surface-to-air liquid propelled missile with a range of 21 miles; able to reach altitudes of 15 miles. Boosted by four wrap-around solid motors, the system uses a radar command guidance system. In production in the early 1950's, it was the first French surface-to-air missile to become operational.

PARDON -- Ras Al Hadd, Oman. WW-II.

PARENT CC -- SAGE Combat Center to which PARENT DC reports. See also NON-PARENT.

PARENT DC -- SAGE Direction Center. See also PARENT CC.

PARIOU -- Basic model of French Wassmer Super IV monoplane first delivered in 1960. Deluxe model called Baladou. Fully-instrumented version is the Sancy.

PARIS -- (1) Morane-Saulnier M.S.760 twin-jet aircraft, first flown in 1954. In military use with French and in other countries.

(2) Allied phase line west of Erle, Germany. Late March 1945, WW-II.

PARKPLATZ -- Proposed German operation against Leningrad, U.S.S.R. Spring 1943, WW-II.

PARROT -- Radiophone terminology for the radar beacon, IFF, (Identification, Friend or Foe) set, installed in some aircraft.

PARROT STANDBY -- Radiophone terminology for turning the radar beacon (IFF) to the Standby position.

PASADENA -- Bogadjim, New Guinea. WW-II.

PASQUINADE -- Atka Island, Aleutian Islands. WW-II.

PASS, THE -- Name for quarter-mile-long mountain defile along Kunu-ri to Sunchon road, Korea; site of Chinese ambuscade of U.S. 2nd Infantry Division. 2 December 1950, Korean Conflict.

PASSAGE TO FREEDOM OPERATION -- Evacuation of Vietnamese in 1950's.

PASSION -- Sinku Rai River, Woodlark Island. WW-II.

PASTURAGE -- Okiduse Mountain Range, Woodlark Island. WW-II.

PAT -- (1) Acronym for Plenum Air Tread, U.S. Army one and one-quarter ton amphibian vehicle.

(2) Mangrove Island, Bismarck Archipelago. WW-II.

(3) Tropical storm. October 1948. First detected between Guam and Wake Island, the Pacific. Moved westward through Mariana Islands, then recurved gradually to the northeast and passed southeast of Japan, out over Pacific.

(4) Typhoon. 22-26 September 1951. Formed over central Philippine Sea. Moved west-northwestward across northern Luzon as weak storm, but intensified over South China Sea. Recurved northeastward across Taiwan and weakened over East China Sea.

PAT-1 -- Argentine, air-to-surface glide bomb based on German World War II developments. Weighing approximately one ton, the bomb is air-dropped and guided to its target by the mother aircraft. Maximum range is 12 miles.

PATCH -- Foochow, China. WW-II.

PATCHWORK -- Fala-Beguets Island, Truk, Caroline Islands. WW-II.

PATERNITY -- Kusaie Island, Caroline Islands. WW-II.

PATHFINDER DIVISION -- Former nickname for U.S. 8th Infantry Division, GOLDEN ARROW DIVISION.

PATHFINDER PLANT -- Northern States power reactor at Sioux Falls, South Dakota.

PATHFINDERS -- Lead planes which would locate and mark target to guide bomber aircraft which followed, Consisted of: finders, which dropped flares over general area; illuminators, which laid a close pattern of flares around actual target; markers which dropped incendaries. Originally British. WW-II.

PATRICIA -- (1) Typhoon. 18-27 October 1949. First detected south of Guam. Moved northwestward at first, then recurved northeastward and passed southeast of Japan, and out over the Pacific.

(2) Name also included in sequence prepared by meteorologist for future tropical cyclones in eastern North Pacific.

PATRICIAS -- Princess Patricia's Canadian Light Infantry.

PAT'S NOSE -- Military name for topographic feature on Hill 700 outside THE PERIMETER on Bougainville Island. 1944, WW-II.

PATSY -- (1) Typhoon. 29 November - 3 December 1955. Formed near east coast of central Philippines. Moved northeastward, passed southeast of Japan, and lost force over the North Pacific.

(2) Typhoon. 6-10 September 1959. Formed near the 180th meridian between Hawaii and Wake Island, moved erratically northward, and lost its typhoon characteristics over the North Pacific.

(3) Typhoon. 6-11 August 1962. Formed in Philippine Sea. Moved west-northwestward across central Philippines, the South China Sea, and Hainan Island. Dissipated in Gulf of Tonkin.

(4) Name also applied to tropical cyclones in western North Pacific which occurred prior to (1) through (3) above.

PATTY -- Name reserved by meteorologists for tropical cyclone in North Atlantic area.

PAULA -- (1) Name reserved by meteorologists for tropical cyclone in North Atlantic area.

(2) Code name of one of a series of rearguard actions on phase lines fought by Germans during northward withdrawal to Arno River, Italy. Summer 1944, WW-II.

PAULETTE -- Leu Island, New Britain. WW-II.

PAULINE -- (1) Typhoon. 3-7 October 1947. First detected in central Philippine Sea. Moved west-northwestward across northern Luzon and into China mainland east of Hong Kong.

(2) Tropical storm. 2-4 October 1961. First detected by ship about midway between Hawaii and Baja, California. Moved westward and dissipated, though weak circulation persisted past Honolulu..

PAVILION -- Ngajangel Island, Palau Islands. WW-II.

PAWNEE -- Piper PA-25 agricultural aircraft first delivered in 1959.

PAX -- Acronym for Private Automatic Exchange.

PAXTON -- Tunis, Tunisia. WW-II.

PE -- General arrangement for British naval ships in the event of invasion of England. 5 July 1940, WW-II.

PEACEFUL EMIL -- See FRIENDENSEMIL

PEACEMAKER -- Convair B-36, the only U.S. Air Force aircraft ever capable of attacking a target on another continent and returning to friendly bases without aerial refueling. First delivery made in 1947; retired on 12 February 1959.

PEACH BOTTOM -- Nuclear reactor under construction by Philadelphia Electric Company.

PEACHBLOW -- Osaka, Japan. WW-II.

PEANUT -- Code name used in U.S. radio messages for Generalissimo Chiang Kai-shek. Also used by General Joseph W. Stilwell in his papers. WW-II.

PEARL -- Typhoon. 1-5 July 1948. First detected south of Guam. Moved north-westward across Philippine Sea and the northeastern tip of Taiwan, then north along the China coast and northeastward across Yellow Sea to Korea.

PEARL RIDGE -- Military name for topographic feature on central Bougainville, Solomon Islands. Captured by Australians in December 1944, WW-II.

PEASHOOTER, OPERATION -- U.S. Navy program in which a special test vehicle was used to develop techniques for ejecting POLARIS from its container. A dry-land program conducted at San Francisco Naval shipyard in 1958. See also OPERATION POP-UP.

PECAN -- United States coast defense of Peru. WW-II.

PECON -- Lanalau Island, Solomon Islands. WW-II.

PECULIAR -- Ulul (Namonuito), Caroline Islands. WW-II.

PEDAGOGUE -- Northwest River, Labrador, WW-II.

PEDESTAL -- Most powerfully enforced Allied convoy to Malta and last to be seriously opposed; composed of 14 merchant ships sailing from United Kingdom by way of Gibraltar, with escort including two battleships and three aircraft carriers; after enemy air attacks and threats by Italian fleet, five merchantmen reached Malta; one British aircraft carrier was sunk. August 1942, WW-II.

PEDLAR -- Jaffa, Palestine. WW-II.

PEEP --See JEEP

PEEPHOLE -- Kuop Island, Caroline Islands. WW-II.

PEEPING TOM -- See SNOOPER

PEEPSHOW -- Suez Canal. WW-II.

PEERAGE -- Nikolaevsk, U.S.S.R. WW-II.

PEEWIT -- Swedish monoplane. See VIPAN.

PEG O' MY HEART -- Nickname for 105-mm. howitzer protecting VICKERY'S BRIDGE (Namji-ri Bridge) over Naktong River, Korea. 1950, Korean Conflict.

PEGASUS -- U.S. research vehicle based on the X-17, and used to test components and systems of SAMOS. Vehicle is launched from Pt. Mugu, California. Five versions, all solid propelled, are available; 1) a single-stage vehicle to carry 250 pounds to 250 miles; 2) two-stage, with a payload of 400-700 pounds to 370-490 miles; 3) three-stage with 35-pound payload to 2000 miles; 4) four-stage with 700 pounds to 650 miles, and 5) five-stage with 150 pounds to 3700 miles.

PEGASUS C -- Name for an advanced version of the X-17 sounding rocket proposed by the developer, Lockheed, in 1958. Proposal was not adopted.

PEGGY -- (1) Operable French pool nuclear reactor in Saclay, France.

(2) Cape Killerton, New Guinea. WW-II.

(3) Tropical storm. 21-23 July 1945. First detected east of Philippines. Moved northwestward across central Philippines and South China Sea into China mainland near Hong Kong.

(4) Name also included in sequence prepared by meteorologists for future tropical cyclones in North Atlantic area.

PEKINESE -- Doroeba, Morotai Island, Halmahera, Netherlands East Indies. WW-II.

PELICAN -- U.S. Navy glide bomb which was used as a test vehicle for the BAT program. Designed for firing against enemy shipping; went into production in early 1944. There were two versions; one with 500-pound warhead and the other with a 1000-pound warhead. Not used operationally.

PELLET -- Port Heiden, Alaska. WW-II.

PEMBROKE -- Hunting Percival P.66 first flew in 1952. Operational with Great Britain's Royal Air Force and various foreign air arms. Commercial version called President.

PEMMICAN -- Milne Bay, New Guinea. WW-II.

PEN WIPER RECEIVER -- See ASPEN

PENCIL -- Japanese rocket, probably the smallest ever produced, used to obtain test data; designed to study the relationship between center of gravity location and dispersion, launcher length and dispersion, nozzles and propellants and tail configurations. The rocket was 0.7 inches in diameter and 9-12 inches long, with a solid rocket motor. Over 200 were fired in 1955, with the first firing in April.

PENDULUM -- Kaurakuba Beach, Lusancay Island, Trobriand Islands. WW-II.

PENGUIN -- Snowmobile developed by Canadians for use in OPERATION PLOUGH; later modified. WW-II.

PENITENT -- Operations against Dalmation Coast, Yugoslavia. WW-II.

PENKNIFE -- Code name for measures taken to deceive enemy into believing that movement of all Canadian formations from Italy to northwestern Europe in GOLD-FLAKE operation was merely a regrouping in rear areas. See also BASRA, HAIFA, POONA, and SIMLA. February-March 1945, WW-II.

PENMAN -- Port Purvis, Guadalcanal, Solomon Islands. WW-II.

PENNSYLVANIA -- Noinletina, New Britain. WW-II.

PENNY -- An industry proposal for an expendable supersonic ramjet target drone. Not adopted for development.

PENRYN -- Code name for Tunisia. WW-II.

PENSACOLA CONVOY -- U.S. convoy, escorted by heavy cruiser, USS Pensacola, enroute to Manila, Philippines, at time of Pearl Harbor; carried air corps and field artillery troops, planes, ammunition and supplies; after high level consultations re-routed to Brisbane, Australia. December 1941. WW-II.

PENSIONER -- Jolo, Philippine Islands. WW-II.

PENTAGON -- Occupation of French Somaliland by Free French Forces. 28 December 1942, WW-II.

PENTHOUSE -- Ulalu Island, Truk Lagoon, Caroline Islands. WW-II.

PENUMBRA -- Oro Bay, New Guinea. WW-II.

PEON -- Samoa Islands. WW-II.

PEOPLE'S FIGHTER -- See VOLKSJAGER

PEPPER -- Lunga Signal Tower, Guadalcanal, Solomon Islands. WW-II.

PEPPER BOX RECEIVER -- See ASPEN

PEPPER POT -- Allied term for coordinated fire, sweeping enemy front lines at relatively short range, of all available tank guns, anti-tank guns, light anti-aircraft guns, medium machine-guns and heavy mortars. WW-II.

PEPPERCORN -- Bizerta, Tunisia, North Africa. WW-II.

PEPSODENT -- Ania River, New Britain. WW-II.

PEPYS COLUMN -- Name for small British unit during action around Bengasi, Libya. December 1941, WW-II.

PEQUE -- Spanish AISA I-II monoplane. First flew 1950.

PERAFEX -- Allied mechanical deception device dropped from air; on hitting ground imitated sound of rifle fire and explosion of hand grenades. WW-II.

PERCUSSION -- Allied code name for air patrol seeking out German submarines in Bay of Biscay. Began in 1943, WW-II.

PEREGRINE FALCON -- Japanese Nakajima KI.43 HAYABUSA fighter. See OSCAR.

PERFECT -- Amchitka Island, Aleutian Islands. WW-II.

PEFECTO -- Anwek Peninsula, New Britain. WW-II.

PERFUME -- Freetown, Sierra Leone, Africa. WW-II.

PERHAPSATRON -- A Torus, or doughnut-shaped, tube in which ionized gas reactions are performed. First built at Los Alamos Scientific Laboratory, New Mexico, in 1952. Now generic term for Los Alamos toroidal devices.

PERIMETER, THE -- U.S. beachhead at Cape Torokina on Empress Augusta Bay, Bougainville. 1943-44. WW-II.

PERIMETER, BATTLE OF THE -- See TA OPERATION

PERPETUAL -- Allied Eastern Task Force reserve landing at Bougie, Algeria. 11 November 1942. WW-II.

PERSECUTION -- Allied task force under ALAMO which carried out operation against Aitape area, New Guinea, to seize and rehabilitate Japanese airstrips. See also TED. 22 April-25 August 1944, WW-II.

PERSHING -- U.S. Army solid propellant tactical ballistic missile for support of the Field Army. Inertially guided, the 10,000-pound missile is transportable by four tracked vehicles, helicopters or troop transports. Carrying a nuclear warhead, it was developed as a replacement for the cumbersome liquid fueled REDSTONE. Range is about 400 miles for the two-stage missile. West Germany is also procuring the system for its army.

PERT -- Acronym for Program Evaluation and Review Technique.

PERTH -- Blackburn trimotor biplane flying boat first built in 1932 in Great Britain.

PERUKE -- Code name for Eastern Africa. WW-II.

PESTER -- Muniai River, Woodlark Island. WW-II.

PET -- An industry development of a small control rocket to be used to instantaneously close a valve or initiate some other critical action.

PETE -- Name for Japanese Navy Sasebo, Zero-0 float plane. WW-II.

PETER -- Code word for letter "P" in a phonetic alphabet, used to avoid possibility of a misunderstanding in transmitting messages. See also PAPA.

PETER RABBIT -- Project of U.S. Air Force Air Material Command to buy on a crash basis a one-year supply of replacement parts for Sabre jet aircraft in Korea. Early 1951, Korean Conflict.

PETERSBURG -- Plan prepared by General Douglas MacArthur for evacuation of New Guinea should Guadalcanal fall to the Japanese. Published 31 October 1942, WW-II.

PETIE -- Typhoon. 19-23 October 1950. First detected east of Iwo Jima, Volcano Islands. Moved northwestward briefly, then northeastward over Chichi Jima, and out over North Pacific.

PETREL -- (1) Percival Q-6, one of Britain's most popular pre-World War II private and commercial aircraft, which was adapted for wartime military use.

(2) U.S. Navy air-to-underwater turbojet missile for use against submarines and surface ships. With a limited 20-mile range, the missile homes on its target by radar, and once in the water, is essentially a torpedo. System was declared operational in 1956 and was cancelled by the Navy in July 1957. See also DIVER.

PETWORTH -- Lampedusa Island, Mediterranean Sea. WW-II.

PEWTER -- Code name for Iceland. WW-II.

PFIEL -- (English translation: Arrow) Dornier Do.335 fighter-bomber of unconventional design. First flown in 1943.

PHAETON -- (1) French satellite for magnetic and radiation measurements in space. Electrically propelled, the satellite will weigh between 660 and 2420 pounds. Acknowledged as the first laboratory developed satellite design in Europe. A candidate for the European Space Research Organization satellite development and launch.

(2) Code name for Alaska. WW-II.

PHALENE VI -- Caudron light cabin monoplane built in the early 1930's in France.

PHANTOM -- U.S. Air Force technique employing ground-radar direction for night-bombing attacks on ground targets in Korea. Initially called X-Ray. Korean Conflict.

PHANTON II -- Mach 2 McDonnell F4 aircraft which entered U.S. Navy service in 1961 and joined the U.S. Air Force in 1962.

PHANTOM RIDGE -- Military name for topographic feature in Cassino area, Italy. Spring 1944, WW-II.

PHANTON SERVICE -- British monitoring of friendly radio nets to provide commanders with immediate and accurate information upon progress of their own troops. Also known as J SERVICE. WW-II.

PHARISEE -- Stephenville, Newfoundland, WW-II.

PHARMACY -- Vila, Kolumbangara Island, Solomon Islands. WW-II.

PHENOMENON --Omsk, Siberia. WW-II.

PHILIP MORRIS -- One of five camps of RED HORSE STAGING AREA in region of Le Havre-Rouen, France. Established April 1945, WW-II.

PHILIPPINE DIVISION -- U.S. military unit composed of regular army men stationed in Philippine Islands. Ceased to exist after Japanese occupation of Philippines at beginning of World War II.

PHILIPPINE SEA, BATTLE OF -- See A-GO OPERATION

PHILISTINE -- Nanomea Island, Ellice Islands. WW-II.

PHILLIE -- Meto Plantation, Vitu Islands, Bismarck Archipelago. WW-II.

PHLOX -- Clark Field, Philippine Islands. WW-II.

PHOENIX -- (1) Japanese World War II bomber. See OTORI.

(2) Two-stage, solid-propelled sounding rocket capable of carrying 10-pound payload to altitude of 200 miles. Has been used by National Aeronautics and Space Administration and U.S. Air Force. First fired from Point Mugu, California, 23 August 1960.

(3) Long-range studies by both Air Force and non-profit industry organizations to determine future Air Force large space booster requirements and the optimum combinations for development through 1975. Solid propellants, in particular were studied, but other propulsion systems were not neglected. The most immediate result, and certainly the most spectacular to date, was the definition and subsequent approval for development of the TITAN III standardized space launch vehicle.

PHOENIXES -- Allied code name for concrete caissons or barges towed across the English Channel to Continent after Normandy landings and sunk to form main breakwaters for artificial harbors, MULBERRIES. 1944, WW-II.

PHOSPHATE -- Code name for Ebon (Boston) Atoll, Marshall Islands. WW-II.

PHOSPHORUS -- New Guinea Task Force. WW-II.

PHOTO JOE -- Nickname for Japanese scout plane operating over Bataan Peninsula, Philippines. Early 1942, WW-II.

PHYLLIS -- (1) Typhoon. 16-20 August 1953.. Formed near Guam. Moved northwestward across Philippine Sea and Taiwan and entered China mainland.

(2) Thphoon. 25 May - 1 June 1958. Formed southwest of Ponape in Caroline Islands. Moved west-northwestward at first and then turned northward through the Philippine Sea. Dissipated southeast of Japan. Caused one death, and damage on Namoluk and Pulusuk Atolls.

(3) Typhoon. 11-20 December 1960. Formed west of Truk Island. Moved west-northwestward into Philippine Sea, then turned northeastward briefly and dissipated.

(4) Name also applied to tropical cyclones in western North Pacific which occurred prior to (1) through (3) above.

PI -- See SIGMA

PIANO -- Onslow, Australia. WW-II.

PIANORO -- Plan for U.S. 5th Army offensive south of Bologna, Italy. See also BIG GAME. 1944-45, WW-II.

PIAT -- Acronym for Projector Infantry, Anti-Tank British shoulder-controlled weapon firing hollow-charge bomb designed to penetrate armor. See also U.S. counterpart, BAZOOKA. Came into use in 1943, WW-II.

PICADOR -- (1) Plan for transporting U.S. Marine regiments to Samoa. WW-II.

(2) See BARRISTER

PICAROON -- Nukufetau Island, Ellice Islands. WW-II.

PICCADILLY -- Code word for jungle clearing behind Japanese lines in northeast

Burma; proposed site of airstrip during Allied OPERATION THURSDAY; not used because occupied by Japanese. March 1944, WW-II.

PICCADILLY HOPE A -- Allied aircraft landing strip at Griblje, Yugoslavia. See also OPERATION DUNN. Spring 1945, WW-II.

PICCHIO -- (English translation: Woodpecker) Italian monoplane, the Procaer F.15. First flown 7 May 1959.

PICCOLO -- (1) Code name for jammer which used series of high-power magnetrons.

(2) Malakal Harbor, Malakal Island, Palau Islands. WW-II.

PICKET-FENCE -- General term for U.S. plasma-trapping device using mirror coils connected in opposition.

PICKLE -- Gulf of Boni, Celebes, Netherlands East Indies. WW-II.

PICK'S PIKE -- Name given by U.S. troops in Burma to LEDO ROAD, referring to Major General Lewis A. Pick, who commanded construction operations. Later called STILWELL ROAD. WW-II.

PICKUP -- (1) Anchorage, Alaska. WW-II.

(2) Cape Hoskins Airdrome, New Britain. WW-II.

(3) Lae Airdrome, New Guinea. WW-II.

(4) General term used by Allies for landing operation by aircraft behind enemy lines to bring out friendly agents. WW-II.

PICKWICK -- Saint George Island, Pribilof Islands. WW-II.

PIECRUST -- Code name for India. WW-II.

PIED PIPER -- See SAMOS

PIGEON -- Japanese photo plane. See HATO.

PIGEON FRASER SCOUT -- See ALBREE MONOPLANE

PIGGY BACK -- U.S. Air Force project designed to carry environment-measuring packages in satellites. See also SPACER.

PIGHEADED -- Namoi Island, Caroline Islands. WW-II.

PIGIRON -- Agadir, French Morocco. WW-II.

PIGSTICK -- Allied plan for assault on Mayu peninsula aimed at Akyab, Burma. Also called Pigsticking. Cancelled 6 January 1944, WW-II.

PIGSTICKING -- See PIGSTICK

PIKE -- See HECHT

PILE DRIVER -- U.N. operation in the area of the IRON TRIANGLE, Korea. June 1951, Korean Conflict.

PILGRIM -- (1) General Electric proposal for a gigantic space vehicle with a closed life support system for journeys to other solar systems. Included in the proposal would be provisions for several generations of human beings. Not under serious consideration.

(2) See TONIC

PILICAN -- Singapore. WW-II.

PILLAR BOX -- British rocket launcher mounted on ships to fire two-inch surface-to-air barrage rockets. The 20-rocket launcher was used extensively in World War II.

PILLBOX -- A not commonly used nickname for TIROS.

PILLION -- Trinidad, British West Indies. WW-II.

PILLORY -- Dutch Harbor, Alaska. WW-II.

PILLOWCASE -- Island of Crete, Mediterranean Sea. WW-II.

PILOT -- U.S. Navy solid propellant research vehicle to determine the feasibility of launching small payloads into orbit from a high flying airplane. Some tests have been conducted in 1958 by the Naval Ordnance Test Station. Effort is continuing at a low level of funding.

PIMA -- Name for a solid propellant jet assisted take-off unit used for launching the U.S. Army surveillance drone, SD-2XAE-1. Two of the units are used to launch the drone from its zero-length launcher. It can also be used for chemical missions. Operational.

PIMENTO -- Lamotrek Island, Caroline Islands. WW-II.

PIMPLE HILL -- Military name for topographic feature near crest of Mount Myoko, Luzon, Philippines. Spring 1945, WW-II.

PIMPLE, THE -- Military name for topographic feature near Mubo, northeastern New Guinea, inland from Huon Gulf. 1943, WW-II.

PIMPLES, THE -- Military name for four small hills on Saipan Island. June 1944, WW-II.

PINAFORE -- Freemantle, West Australia. WW-II.

PINCHER CREEK -- Allied code name for road junction south Ortona, Italy, in area to be defended by British Indian troops. May 1944, WW-II.

PINE CONE -- Name for U.S. peacetime military exercise. 1956.

PINE CONE III, EXERCISE -- See BRIGHT STAR

PINE RIDGE -- Name for U.S. peacetime mountain training exercise.

PINEAPPLE -- Nakambo Island, Solomon Islands. WW-II.

PINETREE -- Code name for headquarters U.S. VIII Bomber Command at High Wycombe, England. Set up, Spring 1942, WW-II.

PINETREE LINE -- Canadian-American radar station chain built along border between the two countries. See also McGILL FENCE, DEW LINE.

PINK HILL -- Military name for topographic feature near Canea, Crete. May 1941, WW-II.

PINK PANSIES -- Allied incendiary bombs used by PATHFINDERS.   So named because of characteristic color and shape. WW-II.

PINKHAM -- Lue Passage, New Britain. WW-II.

PINMONEY -- Port Purvis, Guadalcanal, Solomon Islands. WW-II.

PINNACLE, THE -- (1) U.S. military name for Iegusugu Mountain on Ie Shima, Ryukyu Islands. 1945, WW-II.

(2) U.S. military name for topographic feature on east coast of Okinawa. 1945, WW-II.

PINPOINT -- U.S. Air Force program intended to improve the capability of the Automatic Terrain Radar and Navigation system used on the MACE. ATRAN system uses map-matching techniques to guide the air-breathing missile to its target.

PINPOINT, PROJECT -- Evaluation made by U.S. 5th Air Force in Korea of accuracy of bombing on pinpoint targets of ground-radar directed B-26 aircraft. Korean Conflict.

PINTO -- (1) Temco TT-1 turbojet trainer first delivered to the U.S. Navy in 1957.

(2) El Geneina, Suda. WW-II.

PIONEER -- (1) Scottish Aviation C.C.I. in service with British Royal Air Force and other air arms.   First flown 1950.

(2) Series of five space vehicles authorized by the Defense Department as a contribution to the International Geophysical Year. Launched by THOR-ABLE and JUNO II boosters between 11 October 1958 and 11 March 1960, the series was designed to explore the cislunar, lunar and space environment. Pioneet I made first measurements of interplanetary magnetic fields and micro-meteorites. Pioneer III discovered outer Van Allen radiation belt. Pioneer IV provided first radio communications from beyond the moon. Pioneer V proved feasibility of interplanetary communications by sending back data from 20 million miles in space.

(3) Three-stage ATLAS-ABLE space vehicle powered by hydrazine engine. Launched 25 September 1960. Did not orbit.

PIPISTRELLO -- (English translation: Bat) Tri-motor Italian Savoia-Marchetti SM.81 aircraft. First flown in 1935.

PIPS, BATTLE OF THE -- Name for shelling by U.S. naval force composed of battleships and cruisers on targets, believed to be ships of Japanese reinforcement convoy to Kiska, Aleutian Islands, but which turned out to be radar phantoms caused by return echoes from mountains 100-150 miles away. July 1943, WW-II.

PIPSQUEAK -- Wewak, New Guinea. WW-II.

PIPSQUEAK VALLEY -- Name for wadi near Giarabub, eastern Libya. So named because it was commanded by Italian 44-mm. gun which Austrailians nicknamed pipsqueak. 1940-41, WW-II.

PIPSQUEAK X-1 -- Missile, composed of three helium-filled ballons carrying a china mouse in a plastic gondola. Launched from site in Detroit, Michigan, by nine-year-old Larry Schoenholtz on 4 January 1958. Recovered 23 days later in Monroe County, Ohio, over 200 air miles away.

PIQUANT -- Brest, France. WW-II.

PIRAT -- Convertible land or seaplane built in Sweden in 1933 by Svenska.

PIRATE -- (1) Haiphong, China. WW-II.

(2) Anglo-Canadian exercise in assault against a heavily defended beach, held in Studland Bay, Dorset, England, involving combined operations of army, air force and naval units. 16-19 October 1943, WW-II.

PIREP -- Aviation communications code word and commonly used contraction for pilot report. Usually contains position and weather information.

PISA-RIMINI LINE -- See GOTHIC LINE

PISTOL PETE -- (1) Nickname for Japanese artillery which fired on Henderson Field, Guadalcanal. October 1942, WW-II.

(2) U.S. nickname for two 120-mm. Japanese naval guns which shelled Munda airfield, New Georgia, from nearby islet of Baanga. 16-19 August 1943, WW-II.

PITAPAT -- Cherbourg, France. WW-II.

PITCH -- Aircraft for Russians from U.S. March 1945, WW-II.

PIVA UNCLE -- U.S. bomber airstrip at Cape Torokina on Empress Augusta Bay, Bougainville. Completed Christmas 1943, WW-II.

PIVA YOKE -- U.S. fighter airstrip at Cape Torokina on Empress Augusta Bay, Bougainville. Completed January 1944, WW-II.

PLAINTIFF -- Fouseca, Nicaragua. WW-II.

PLANET I-II -- U.S. critical configuration safety lists at Los Alamos Scientific Laboratory, New Mexico.

PLANISH -- Le Havre, France. WW-II.

PLASTIC MAN -- Plastic U.S. anti-radiation contamination suit. Inflated, it creates a positive pressure of air and prevents infiltration by contamination.

PLATO -- (1) Army project for a mobile anti-missile missile system studied by Cornell Aeronautical Laboratory and Sylvania Electric Company from 1955 to February 1959. Program was terminated and then revived as FABMIDS.

(2) Acronym for Programmed Logic for Automatic Teaching Operations.

PLATTE -- American Mission, Bogota, Columbia. WW-II.

PLATTSBURG -- Rendova, Solomon Islands. WW-II.

PLAY BALL -- Signal in reply to BATTER UP ordering units of Allied Western Naval Task Force to return fire from local French forces, encountered during Morocco landings. November 1942, WW-II.

PLAYFUL -- Makin Island, Gilbert Islands. WW-II.

PLAZA -- Melinglo, New Britain. WW-II.

PLEBIAN -- Salinas, Ecuador. WW-II.

PLEDGE -- German surrender of U-Boats at sea. 9 May-6 June 1945, WW-II.

PLENAPS -- Acronym for Plans for the Employment of Naval and Air Forces of the Associated Powers in the Eastern Theatre in the Event of War with Japan; drawn up at American-Dutch-British conference in Singapore on 21-27 April 1941. WW-II.

PLETHORA -- Ceram Island, Netherlands East Indies. WW-II.

PLEXUS -- Bethel, Alaska. WW-II.

PLICATE -- Kurile Islands, Japan. WW-II.

PLIGHT -- Boulogne, France. WW-II.

PLIMSOLL -- Great Sitkin Island, Alaska. WW-II.

PLOUGH FORCE -- 1st Special Service Force, unique international military organization made up of volunteer personnel from U.S. and Canadian armies; created originally in 1942 for action on snow in PLOUGH, OPERATION; after cancellation of this, saw service at Kiska in Aleutians, Italy, and south of France under commands of Colonel Robert T. Frederick and Colonel Edwin A. Walker.

Disbanded December 1944, WW-II.

PLOUGH, OPERATION -- Project, credited to Englishman, Geoffrey Pyke, for development of special force with special equipment to be air dropped for diversionary sabotage activities on snow against Rumanian oil fields and hydroelectric plants in Norway and northern Italy during winter 1942-43; turned over by British to Canadian and U.S. joint control. Canceled October 1942, but resulted in development of PLOUGH FORCE and vehicles, PENGUIN and WEASEL. WW-II.

PLOVER -- (1) Nickname for the GORGON (KDN-1) DRONE, air launched from a host aircraft. Parachute-recoverable, it had a radio command guidance system. Although 19 were built and eight used in flight and parachute recovery tests, it never became operational. WW-II.

(2) Warup River, New Guinea. WW-II.

PLOWSHARE -- U.S. program to develop non-military applications of nuclear explosive devices. Initiated at University of California Laboratory, Livermore, California. See also GNOME PROJECT. 1957.

PLUGHOLE -- Code name for Iraq. WW-II.

PLUM -- Koli Point, Guadalcanal, Solomon Islands. WW-II.

(2) Code name for Philippine Army (Regular). WW-II.

PLUM PUDDING HILL -- U.N. military name for topographic feature near Songju, Korea. Korean Conflict.

PLUMBBOB -- U.S. nuclear weapons test at Nevada Test Site. See also RAINIER and GENIE. Summer 1957.

PLUMBLINE -- Kolumbangara Island, Solomon Islands. WW-II.

PLUNDER -- Allied 21st Army Group crossing of the Rhine River, north of the Ruhr, Germany. See also FLASHPOINT, VARSITY. Began 23 March 1945, WW-II.

PLUTO -- (1) Acronym for Pipe Line Under The Ocean, referring to British project to have small flexible, armored pipe rapidly laid by ship under Channel from England to France for supplying invading Allied armies in Operation OVERLORD with petroleum products. 1944, WW-II.

(2) Name for the nuclear-powered ramjet engine to be developed for SLAM. Goal is to develop a flight weight reactor to power the missile. The TORY series of tests now underway are expected to provide inputs to this development. In fact, success of the tests will probably determine the fate of Pluto and SLAM.

PLUTOCRAT -- French Frigate Shoals, Territory of Hawaii. WW-II.

PLYMOUTH BRIDGE -- Bailey bridge built across Gari River south of Sant'Angelo, Italy, by Allied army engineers. May 1944, WW-II.

PLYMOUTH ROCK -- Name for peacetime military project.

POGO -- (1) U.S. parachute test vehicle and radar target developed by New Mexico A. and M. College and fired from White Sands, New Mexico, missile range for the Navy. Fired to maximum altitude where the parachute would open, and during the descent, provided a radar target for ground trackers. Program was conducted in the early 1950's.

   (2) Convair XFY-1, Vertical-Take-Off and Landing (VTOL) experimental fighter for the U.S. Navy. First flown 1954.

   (3) Acronym for Polar Orbiting Geophysical Observatory, a specilized mission for OGO, in which it will be placed in a polar orbit for studies of both the earth's atmosphere and ionosphere. First launch expected in 1964.

POGO-HI -- U.S. Army mach 4 missile target drone. See also UPSTART.

POINT -- Allied occupation of Bonin and Volcano Islands. See also DETACHMENT. Early 1945, WW-II.

POINT ICEBERG -- Allied occupation of positions in the Ryukyus. WW-II.

POINTBLANK -- Combined Bomber Offensive by strategic air forces of British Royal Air Force and U.S. Army Air Forces, each operating against sources of Germany's war power according to its own peculiar capabilities and concepts in preparation for Operation OVERLORD. June 1943-Spring 1944, WW-II.

POISON -- Code name for Indian Ocean. WW-II.

POL-1 -- Russian two-stage research vehicle to obtain meteorological data and investigate thermal heating. Can carry a nine-pound payload to altitudes over 100 miles. Used during the International Geophysical Year.

POL-2 -- Russian single-stage solid propellant research rocket capable of carrying 90-pound scientific payload to an altitude of about 100 miles and recovering them by parachute. The inertially guided rocket is propelled by cluster of four solid motors. It was used extensively during the International Geophysical Year for upper atmospheric research.

POLAR BEAR -- Joint U.S.-Canadian training exercise, involving move by composite force across coastal mountains in British Columbia from interior dry cold to coastal wet cold. Winter 1944-45, WW-II.

POLAR PASS -- U.S. peacetime military exercise in Alaska, 1962.

POLARFUCHS -- (1) Operations of German XXXVI Corps in 1941. WW-II.

   (2) Russian name for alleged German plan to invade Sweden in 1943. WW-II.

POLARIS -- U.S. Navy submarine-launched ballistic missile which, along with the Air Force MINUTEMAN, is expected to provide the backbone of the U.S. strategic retaliatory force for the rest of this decade. Sixteen missles are carried

aboard specially-built nuclear powered submarines. The presently-authorized program will give the U.S. 656 operational Polaris missiles in 41 nuclear submarines.
Already operational are the 1200 nautical-mile A-1 model and the 1500 nautical-
mile A-2. The A-3 with a range of 2500 nautical-miles is undergoing flight
testing and a 5000 nautical-mile A-4 missile is under consideration for development.
At present, nine Polaris submarines are operational.

POLECAT -- (1) U.S. Army study of a small, simple missile able to be fired from a
recoilless rifle. At least one contract to study simple guidance has been let.
See also DAVY CROCKETT.

(2) U.S. Army two-weasel chassis for personnel transportation.

(3) Sirik Island, New Britain. WW-II.

POLLARD -- Waller Field, Trinidad, British West Indies. WW-II.

POLLY -- (1) Typhoon. 27 September - 1 October 1952. Formed in eastern Caroline Islands. Moved northwestward through Marianas, then turned northward and
finally northeastward off Japan, and out over North Pacific.

(2) Typhoon. 7-10 December 1956. Formed in southern Philippine Sea. Moved
westward across central Philippines and dissipated, causing 76 deaths and great
property damage.

(2) Typhoon. 17-29 July 1960. Formed in Yap - Koror Island area. Moved
westward south of Guam, then north-northwestward, passed west of Okinawa
into northern China. Caused minor damage.

(4) Name also applied to tropical cyclones in western North Pacific which
occurred prior to (1) through (3) above.

POLYGLOT -- Palmyra, Syria. WW-II.

POLYGON -- British diversionary operation during capture of Termoli, Italy, giving
the enemy cause to believe a landing was being made behind his line. 3-4
October 1939, WW-II.

POMAR -- Acronym for Position Operational, Meteorological Aircraft Report, a code
in which certain meteorological elements and aircraft data are encoded and transmitted from transport aircraft.

POMEGRANATE -- Operation by British XXX Corps to capture heights around Noyers,
near Caen, France. Preliminary to Operation GOODWOOD. 16 July 1944,
WW-II.

POMILIO -- Italian-designed, American-built, Liberty-engine biplane designated
the FVL-8. First appeared in 1919 at the U.S. Air Service's McCook Field.

PONTIAC -- (1) Noru Island, Admiralty Islands. WW-II.

(2) Taivo, Guadalcanal, Solomon Islands. WW-II.

PONTUS -- Name for the Advanced Research Project Agency's program to develop better materials and improve present materials. Representative areas of interest include metallurgy, ceramics, inorganic chemistry, solid state physics and polymer chemistry. Funded annually at about 15 million dollars, the program is not aimed at a particular system, but at improving the state-of-the-art.

POOH -- See WINNIE and POOH

POONA -- Code name for Canadian 1st Infantry Divison; used in deception oper- ation PENKNIFE, during movement of Canadian troops from Italy to northwestern Europe. February-March 1945, WW-II.

POPBOTTLE -- Matutana, New Britain. WW-II.

POPEYE -- Nesup Island, New Britain. WW-II.

POPI -- Acronym for Post-Office Position Indicator, a long-distance, low-frequency navigation system which provides bearing information. System developed by British post office.

POPLIN -- Dieppe, France. WW-II.

POPPY -- U.S. task force sent from New York by way of Australia to garrison New Caledonia. Early 1942, WW-II.

POPSKI'S PRIVATE ARMY - - Small special scout force of British 8th Army, founded by Russo-Belgian officer, Major Vladimir Peniakoff. Originally designated No. 1 Long Range Demolition Squadron. WW-II.

POP-UP, OPERATION -- U.S. Navy program which carried OPERATION PEASHOOTER one step further by testing ejection methods from submerged launch containers. These tests, using a special tethered test vehicle, were conducted at San Clemente Island off the California coast in 1958 and 1959.

PORCELAIN -- Kwajalein Island, Marshall Islands. WW-II.

PORCUPINE -- (1) Samar, Philippine Islands. WW-II.

(2) Name for Royal Canadian Air Force Squadron Number 433.

PORK CHOP HILL -- Military name for topographic feature in Yokkokchon Valley, Korea. Military action which took place here, Spring 1953, subject of book, Pork Chop Hill, by Brigadier General S.L.A. Marshall. Korean Conflict.

PORK SAUSAGE -- Code word signaling favorable conditions for landing of second wave of Allied airborne troops in jungle clearing, called BROADWAY, behind Japanese lines in northeast Burma. March 1944, WW-II.

PORKPIE -- Code name for Iran. WW-II.

PORPOISE -- Cape Schirltz, New Britain. WW-II.

PORRIDGE -- Adak Island, Aleutian Islands. WW-II.

PORTCULLIS -- Allied convoy from Egypt to Malta. December 1942, WW-II.

PORTER -- Swiss Pilatus P.C.6 single-engine utility aircraft. First flown in 1959.

PORTERFORCE -- Special formation of British and Canadian armored and artillery units active around Ravenna, Italy. Commanded by British Lieutenant-Colonel Sir Andrew Marshall Horsbrugh-Porter. Later 1944, WW-II.

PORTERHOUSE -- Bola, New Britain. WW-II.

PORTFOLIO -- Tol Island, Truk Lagoon, Caroline Islands. WW-II.

PORTIA -- Name reserved for meteorologists for tropical cyclone in North Atlantic area.

PORTICO -- Morobe, New Guinea. WW-II.

PORTREX -- U.S. Army-Navy exercise held in Caribbean. 1950.

POSITIVE CONTROL -- See FAIL-SAFE

POST-ARCADIA -- Combined Chiefs of Staff Conference, Washington. Participants were United States, Great Britain, Australia, New Zealand, the Netherlands. See also ARCADIA. January-February 1942, WW-II.

POSTERN -- Allied operations in Lae-Salamaua-Finschhafen-Madang area of New Guinea. Part of ELKTON III plan. Summer 1943, WW-II.

POSTFREE -- Bathurst, British Gambia, Africa. WW-II.

POSTILLION -- Onamue Island, Truk Lagoon, Caroline Islands. WW-II.

POSTSCRIPT -- Majuro Atoll, Marshall Islands. WW-II.

POSY -- U.S. code name for Rigili Island, Eniwetok Atoll, Marshall Group. WW-II.

POT OF GOLD -- Plan to send large U.S. expeditionary force to Brazil in event of Axis threat there. 1940, WW-II.

POSTASSIUM -- Code name for Northern Ireland. WW-II.

POTEEN -- Haifa, Palestine. WW-II.

POTHOOK -- Kuibyshev, U.S.S.R. WW-II.

POTOMAC -- Military Attaché, Lima, Peru. WW-II.

POTSHOT -- Exmouth Gulf, West Coast, Australia. WW-II.

POTTAGE -- Cagliari, Sicily. WW-II.

POTTER'S RIDGE -- U.S. military name for topographic feature north of Gusukuma, Okinawa. 1945, WW-II.

POULTICE -- Code name for Turkey. WW-II.

POWERBOX -- U.S. Air Force airborne very low frequency communication network which uses KC-135 aircraft.

POWER PACK -- Name for series of peacetime military exercises.

PRAIRIE DIVISION -- Nickname for U.S. 33rd Infantry Division. Also called MONEY DIVISION.

PRECEDENT -- Shemya Island, Aleutian Islands. WW-II.

PRECEPT -- Falo Island, Truk Lagoon, Caroline Islands. WW-II.

PREFECT -- Amchitka Island, Aleutian Islands. WW-II.

PREJUDICE -- Allied operations for control of Celebes-Sulu Seas. WW-II.

PRENTICE -- British Aviation Traders Limited conversion of the former Percival Royal Air Force trainer.

PRESIDENT -- British commercial airline version of the Hunting PEMBROKE.

PRESIDENT ROOSEVELT BRIDGE -- Railway bridge erected by U.S. Army across Rhine River at Mainz, Germany. Completed 14 April 1945, WW-II.

PRESSBOX -- Roebuck Point, New Britain. WW-II.

PRESSMAN -- Code word for Soviet. WW-II.

PRESSURE PUMP, OPERATION -- Air assault against 30 targets in Pyongyang, capital of North Korea, involving almost every operational U.N. air unit in Far East. 11 July 1952, Korean Conflict.

PRESTONE -- Nakarp, New Britain. WW-II.

PRICE ROAD -- Military name for northern branch of Agana-Pago Bay road on Guam. Summer 1944, WW-II.

PRICELESS -- Code name for possible Post-HUSKY Operations in Mediterranean. First used in August 1943, WW-II.

PRIEST -- Nickname for U.S. self-propelled weapon consisting of 105-mm. howitzer mounted on medium tank chassis. See also UNFROCKED PRIEST. WW-II.

PRIM -- Lae, New Guinea. WW-II.

PRIMITIVE -- Argentia, Newfoundland. WW-II.

PRIMROSE -- British exercise held at Kilbride Bay to experiment with employment of self-propelled army artillery firing from tank landing craft in assault. March–April 1943, WW-II.

PRINCE III -- Light, twin-engine Hunting-Percival P.50 transport. Prototype flew in 1948. Other versions and modifications are the PEMBROKE, PRESIDENT, SEA PRINCE.

PRINCETON HILL -- Military name for Yokkokchon Valley, Korea, near PORK CHOP HILL. Spring 1953, Korean Conflict.

PRINCIPAL -- Simultaneous attack by British human torpedoes, known as CHARIOTS, on Italian ports of Palermo, Cagliari and Meddelina, with objective of destroying Italian naval and merchant shipping. 2 January 1943, WW-II.

PRINCIPIA -- Name for the Advanced Research Projects Agency program for the improvement of propellants of all types. Also of interest is the improvement of propellant chemistry, synthetic chemistry and propellant formulation and evaluation, as well as the general areas of the thermodynamics and thermochemistry. Annually funded at about 20 million dollars.

PRINT -- (1) Acronym for Pre-edited Interpretive System, used in data processing.

(2) Bomatu Point, Trobriand Islands. WW-II.

PRISCILLA -- (1) Typhoon. 8-13 September 1946. First detected near Eniwetok Atoll, the Pacific. Moved northwestward to vicinity of Marcus Island, then turned northeastward out over the Pacific.

(2) Name also included in sequence prepared by meteorologists for future tropical cyclones in eastern North Pacific.

PRIVATE -- U.S. Army special test vehicle used to provide experimental data on the effect of sustained thrust on a fixed fin-stabilized rocket, and to learn how to use booster rockets to launch missiles. Information was to be used in the development of the CORPORAL missile. Between 1-16 December 1944, 24 test vehicles were successfully fired at Barstow, California, to ranges of 10 miles. The Private F was almost exactly the same as the A model except the fins were replaced with two horizontal lifting surfaces to determine the effect that this would have on the missile. 17 firings were conducted on 1-13 April 1945 at Fort Bliss, Texas.

PRIVATEER -- World War II variant of the Consolidated B-24 U.S. Navy PB4Y differed by having a single fin and rudder.

PRIVILEGE -- Eniwetok Island, Marshall Islands. WW-II.

PRIZE -- Allied over-all campaign for the clearance of Burma. WW-II.

PROCTOR -- British Percival P.44 single-engine monoplane. First flown in 1939.

PROCURATOR -- Dunkirk, France. WW-II.

PROP -- Acronym for an industry proposal for Planetary Rocket Ocean Platform, a scheme in which extremely large space boosters would be launched from ocean platforms to reduce the hazards from chemical booster explosions or nuclear engine contamination.

PROPULSION -- Nagasaki, Japan. WW-II.

PROSERPINE -- Operable French aqueous homogeneous plutonium and uranium nuclear reactor in Saclay, France.

PROSPECT -- Oroluk Lagoon, Caroline Islands. WW-II.

PROSPECTOR -- (1) Lancashire-built monoplane derived from the British Edgar-Percival E.P.6 which first flew in 1955. Now in production.

(2) National Aeronautics and Space Administration mobile, soft-landing lunar vehicle designed to rove the lunar surface, collect data and television pictures and transmit them back to the earth. Concept was valid prior to acceleration of APOLLO program; since then Congress has refused to appropriate funds for the program on the grounds that it would not fly until the same time period as Apollo and, therefore, was unnecessary. Concept has been revived in a post-Apollo Lunar Logistic Vehicle.

PROTHERO 1-2 -- Military name for twin mountain features in SHAGGY RIDGE area, northeastern New Guinea; objectives of Australian attacks against Japanese. January 1944, WW-II.

PROUDLY -- Calais, France. WW-II.

PROVENCE -- Breguet 763 four-engine transport in service with Air France. First flight in 1951. Popularly known as the Duex Ponts.

PROVIDENCE -- Allied plan for occupation of Buna, New Guinea, to set up airfield; forestalled by Japanese occupation of Buna. Summer 1942, WW-II.

PROVIDER -- C-123 originally designed by Chase Aircraft and called the Avitruc. Made its first flight in 1949. The Fairchild-built craft also appeared in a version called PANTOBASE.

PROVOST -- After its first flight in 1950, the Hunting-Percival T.1 entered service with Royal Air Force Flying Training schools. The British aircraft also serves other air arms.

PRUDENCE -- Name reserved by meteorologists for tropical cyclone in eastern North Pacific.

PRUDENTIAL -- Pis Island, Truk Lagoon Caroline Islands. WW-II.

PRUNE BARGE -- Nickname for battleship, USS California. WW-II.

PTARMIGAN FLIGHT -- Any regular weather reconnaissance flight between Alaska and North Pole.

PTERODACTYL -- Unusual, tailless, single-engine pusher cabin monoplane built by by Great Britain's Westland-Hill in 1933.

PUDDING -- Ujae Atoll, Marshall Islands. WW-II.

PUEPPCHEN -- (English translation: Dolly) German air force slang name for a single-seater fighter aircraft. WW-II.

PUERTO PINE, OPERATION -- See BIG SLAM

PUFFIN -- U.S. Navy winged and fin-stabilized flying torpedo propelled by a gasoline and air engine. Developed as part of the KINGFISHER program, the missile had a range of 10-20 miles with a 500-pound bomb. Air launched, it had an active radar seeker which guided it to its target. WW-II.

PUGILIST GALLOP -- British Eighth Army attack on German-held Mareth Position, southern Tunisia. Began 20 March 1943, but abandoned in favor of SUPERCHARGE II. WW-II.

PUJA -- Nandi, Viti Levu, Fiji Islands. WW-II.

PUMA, OPERATION -- British plan to occupy the Spanish Canary Islands involving large commitment of ships and troops. First half of 1941, WW-II.

PUMP HANDLE -- U.S. Air Force high-altitude air refueling area over Alabama-Florida-Georgia.

PUNCHBOWL -- Military name for circular mountain-rimmed valley northeast of Yangu, Korea. Korean Conflict.

PUNCHER -- Project for establishment of Amphibious Force, Mediterranean, U.S. Atlantic Fleet. WW-II.

PUNKAH -- Tel Litvinsky, Palestine. WW-II.

PURIFICATOR -- Saigon-Camrank Bay, French Indo-China. WW-II.

PURPLE -- Code name for Central America. WW-II.

PURPLE HEART PLAIN -- U.S. 12th Armored Division name for area in Alsace, France. WW-II.

PURPLE HEART RIDGE -- Military name for hill system east of DEATH VALLEY on Saipan. From south to north hills designated QUEEN, LOVE, GEORGE-HOW, X RAY-YOKE, OBOE, KING and ABLE. 1944, WW-II.

PURPLE PROJECT -- Project to shift about 95 C-54 aircraft from U.S. Air Transport Command's North Atlantic and North African services and Ferrying Division to Pacific routes. Early August 1945, WW-II.

PURPLE TASK FORCE -- Task force composed around Chinese 149th Regiment, 50th Division, sent into small valley of the Lasi Hka, northern Burma, from Mogaung Valley. Mission not completed. Early 1944, WW-II.

PURR-KEE -- U.S. Navy unguided sounding rocket designed to gather meteorological data at altitudes from one half mile to 3.5 miles. Essentially a boosted dart, it can be launched by a variety of boosters, including DEACON, CAJUN and NIKE. After boost to altitude, the dart is separated from the booster, a parachute opens, and the instruments measure atmospheric conditions during the descent. In operational use.

PUSHA MARU BOAT LINE -- U.S. nickname for improvised transportation on Matanikau River in Guadalcanal carrying supplies in to front lines and evacuees out; used captured Japanese assault boats and pole and motor barges, some of which were constructed from gasoline drums. 1943, WW-II.

PUSHOVER -- U.S. Navy test program in which a fully-fueled V-2 was deliberately exploded to determine its effects on ships which might be used for launching missiles. Test conducted in early 1947.

PUSHPAK -- Hindustan single-engine monoplane which first flew in 1958. In production for Indian flying clubs.

PUSSYFOOT -- Au, New Britain. WW-II.

PUTT-PUTT -- A series of tests conducted by the U.S. Air Force and its contractor General Atomics to determine the feasibility of propelling 1000-ton space vehicles by small nuclear explosions. A three-foot diameter scale model of the ORION vehicle was used with three-pound high explosive charges simulating the nuclear explosions. The 1960 tests were reportedly extremely successful. Early name was Gasp.

PUTTER -- Arara, New Britain. WW-II.

PYE -- British solid propellant anti-tank missile developed by Pye Limited. Two motors power the 80-pound wire-guided missile, and the gunner controls it by watching it through binoculars and manuevering a toggle stick. Company-funded effort, but not procured by the British Army.

PYORREMYRSKY -- (English translation: Whirlwind) Finnish fighter designed in 1943 and first flown in 1945.

PYRAMID -- Plan for transporting personnel to Auckland, New Zealand. WW-II.

PYRAMIDERS -- Nickname for U.S. Army Air Forces 98th Heavy Bombardment Group. WW-II.

PYRITES -- Enogai Area, New Georgia, Solomon Islands. WW-II.

PYRRHUS -- Formosa Strait, Formosa. WW-II.

PYTHON -- (1) U.S. Air Force two-stage solid propellant sounding rocket capable of carrying a 400-pound payload to an altitude of 25 miles. Both stages are NIKE motors. Under development.

(2) British scheme to repatriate men and women of the armed forces who had

served for long periods in theaters overseas.   1945, WW-II.

(3) See PYE

Q

Q, ADMIRAL -- Code name for U.S. President Franklin D. Roosevelt. WW-II.

Q BOATS -- Small Japanese plywood boats, powered by 6-cylinder Chevrolet engines; carried two depth charges which were released close to Allied ships, generally causing death of Japanese pilot. See also MARU BOATS. WW-II.

Q TRAIN -- German devised FLAK train consisting of freight wagons which contained dozens of anti-aircraft guns concealed in collapsible car bodies; used to fire on aircraft following railway to targets in TIDALWAVE raid against Ploesti, Rumania. August 1943, WW-II.

QUADRANGLE, OPERATIONS -- Allied convoys to Malta from the east. December 1942 - January 1943, WW-II.

QUADRANT -- First Anglo-American conference at Quebec, Canada, attended by President Roosevelt and Prime Minister Churchill. See also OCTAGON. 14-24 August 1943, WW-II.

QUAIL -- U.S. Air Force air-launched decoy missile carried aboard B-52 bombers to confuse and divert enemy warning networks and interceptors. Duplicating the speed and altitude of the B-52, the missile has a range of more than 200 nautical miles, and carries electronic countermeasures and B-52 simulation equipment. Each jet bomber carries several of the decoys and releases them as it comes within range of enemy air defenses. Operational in 1960. Also known as Green Quail early in development. Official designation: GAM-72.

QUANDRY -- Urin, New Britain. WW-II.

QUANTUM -- Alu-U, New Britain. WW-II.

QUARTERBACK -- Code name used in U.S. radio messages for General Joseph W. Stilwell. WW-II.

QUARTZ -- Kiep Plantation, New Britain. WW-II.

QUEASY -- An automatic coding system used in data processing.

QUEBEC -- Code word for letter "Q" in a phonetic alphabet, used to avoid possibility of a misunderstanding in transmitting messages. See also QUEEN.

QUEEN -- (1) Code word for letter "Q" in a phonetic alphabet, used to avoid possibility of a misunderstanding in transmitting messages. See also QUEBEC.

(2) Co-ordinated Allied air-ground offensive to clear Roer plain between Roer and Wurm Rivers. Began 16 November 1944, WW-II.

QUEEN, THE -- Nickname for battleship, USS New Mexico. WW-II.

QUEEN AIR -- Beechcraft Model 65 executive transport civilian counterpart of the U.S. Army L-23. Introduced in 1960.

QUEEN BEE -- (1) British radio-controlled target bi-plane developed about 1935 and tested from both ships and land launchers. One of the earliest target drones developed. See also QUEEN WASP.

(2) Yugoslav trainer. See MATICA.

QUEEN COBRA -- U.S. four-stage solid propellant sounding rocket designed to carry large diameter payloads to altitudes of 200 miles or a 800-pound payload to 75 miles. Launched from a standard zero-length launcher, the rocket is 44 inches in diameter and consists of an HONEST JOHN first stage, NIKE second and third stages and a cluster of five solid motors in the fourth stage. Under development.

QUEEN, HILL -- (1) Military name for topographic feature in PURPLE HEART RIDGE on Saipan. 1944, WW-II.

(2) U.S. military name for topographic feature near Naha, Okinawa. 1945, WW-II.

QUEEN KNOB -- See KING-QUEEN-JACK FINGER

QUEEN MARY -- Royal Canadian Air Force term for long low loading vehicle designed to transport airframes. WW-II.

QUEEN WASP -- Essentially the same as the QUEEN BEE, it was also a radio-controlled target drone biplane. Developed in the 1930's; tested at sea by the British.

QUEENIE -- Typhoon. 3-8 August 1945. First detected in western Caroline Islands. Moved northwestward over Philippine Sea, the Island of Luzon, and the South China Sea and into China west of Hong Kong.

QUERANDI -- Argentinian I.A. 45 twin-pusher light transport. First flight in 1957.

QUERIDA -- Typhoon. 18-22 September 1946. First detected near Eniwetok Atoll, the Pacific. Moved west-northwestward passing just north of Guam and across Taiwan into China mainland.

QUERPO -- Tablas Strait, Mindoro Island, Philippine Islands. WW-II.

QUEST -- Didi, New Britain. WW-II.

QUESTION MARK HILL -- Military name for topographic feature northeast of Sison, Luzon, Philippines. February 1945, WW-II.

QUEUE -- Monglo (Manglo) River, New Britain. WW-II.

QUIBBLE -- Crocodile Point, New Britain. WW-II.

QUICK -- An automatic coding system used in data processing.

QUICK ANGER -- See ANGER

QUICK KICK, OPERATION -- Coordinated land-sea-air triphibious assault on a beachhead by Army, Navy, Air Force and Marine units. 7 May 1962.

QUICK SILVER -- Kubua River, New Britain. WW-II.

QUICK SILVER, EXERCISE -- Radio deception scheme conducted by Allies to mislead Germans about size and location of units in Operation OVERLORD and lead them to believe attack on Pas de Calais, France, was being mounted. 24 April-14 June 1944, WW-II.

QUICK STRIKE -- Name for U.S. peacetime military exercise at Fort Bragg, North Carolina, 1960.

QUINCE -- St. Lucia, Windward Islands, Caribbean Sea. WW-II.

QUININE -- Arawe Island, New Britain. WW-II.

QUISLING COVE -- Name for southern beach on Kiska Island, Aleutians; site of unopposed Allied landing. 15 August 1943, WW-II.

QUITCLAIM -- Luwang Island, Chusan Archipelago, China. WW-II.

QUIVER -- Juneau, Alaska. WW-II.

QUIXOTE -- Samudo Island, New Britain. WW-II.

QUORUM -- Laut Island, Java, Netherlands East Indies. WW-II.

R

R DAY -- Initial U.S. landings on island of Mindanao, Philippines, in VICTOR V. 17 April 1945, WW-II.

R4 -- British Army project for landing in Norway. Abandoned before German occupation. Spring 1940. WW-II.

R.M. OPERATION -- See ROYAL MARINE

R, PLAN -- See X, Plan

RABBIT -- (1) Alsega Bay, New Britain. WW-II.

(2) Ma Asin, Leyte, Philippine Islands. WW-II.

RACCOON -- (1) Maitbog, Leyte, Philippine Islands. WW-II.

(2) Thilenius Harbor, New Britain. WW-II.

RACER'S STORM -- Hurricane. 27 September - 10 October 1837. Named after British sloop of war, Racer, which encountered it in the Yucatan Channel, 1 October 1837. Formed in Caribbean Sea, moved into Gulf of Mexico, recurved along the northern Gulf coast and moved northeastward over the Atlantic.

RACHEL -- (1) Name given to Mannheim, Germany, as one of three possible objectives proposed for a concentrated British bombing; was eventually target selected. See also ABIGAIL, JEZEBEL, DELILAH. Night of 16 December 1940, WW-II.

(2) Name reserved by meteorologists for tropical cyclone in North Atlantic area.

RACKET -- Adi River, New Britain. WW-II.

RACKETEER -- Fanning Island, Line Islands. WW-II.

RACKLE -- Rotterdam, Neth rlands. WW-II.

RADAR -- Acronym for Radio Detection and Ranging.

RADAR HILL -- (1) Military name for topographic feature on Saipan Island. Summer 1944, WW-II.

(2) Military name for topographic feature on Peleliu Island; contained Japanese radar installations. Fall 1944, WW-II.

RADIATOR -- Kanaga Island, Choiseul Island, Solomon Islands. WW-II.

RADIO ROAD -- Military name for topographic feature on central Saipan. June 1944, WW-II.

RADIST -- Radio-navigation system which uses three or more ground stations to determine position of vehicle. Similar to LORAC.

RADSAFE -- U.S. task force at central office at Eniwetok Proving Ground, Marshall Islands. Prepared for possible, significant fallout in inhabited areas during U.S. nuclear tests. 1956.

RAFCHIN -- About 350 ground staff of BURWING who retreated from Burma to Chungtu, China, where they assisted Chinese at main air bases and in training. 1942, WW-II.

RAFFICA -- (English translation; Squall) Twin-engine Caproni Ca. 331. First flew in 1940.

RAFFLING -- Nobeoka, Japan. WW-II.

RAFT -- Acronym for Recomp Algebraic Formula Translator, used in data processing.

RAGAMUFFIN -- Karai Ai, New Britain. WW-II.

RAGGED. -- Birik, New Britain. WW-II.

RAGTIME -- Spratly Island, China Sea. WW-II.

RAGWEED -- Jacquinot Bay, New Britain. WW-II.

RAIDEN -- (English translation: Thunderbolt) Japanese World War II interceptor. See JACK.

RAIDER -- Name for U.S. Army patrol, made up of volunteers, active during fighting at OUTPOST EERIE. March 1952, Korean Conflict.

RAIDER'S RIDGE -- See BLOODY NOSE RIDGE

RAIL ROOTER -- German device to pull up railroad tracks. See also BIG HOOK. WW-II.

RAILING -- Kawasaki, Japan. WW-II.

RAILSPLITTERS -- Nickname for U.S. 84th Infantry Division; taken from design on shoulder patch. Also called LINCOLN DIVISION, HATCHET MEN.

RAINBOW -- (1) Code name for Rome-Berlin-Tokyo Axis. WW-II.

(2) Nickname for U.S. 42nd Infantry Division. Name taken from statement during World War One by General of the Army Douglas MacArthur (then a major), "This division will stretch over the land like a rainbow." This was in reference to fact that it was composed of men from many states.

(3) Five U.S. plans prepared between 1939 and 1941 to meet Axis aggression involving more than one enemy. Replaced war plans developed in 1920's which used single-color code names.

(4) Landing exercise held in Algeria for U.S. troops to test invasion training in preparation for HUSKY, invasion of Sicily. Spring 1943, WW-II.

(5) Allied plan for Salween offensive in Burma. 1943-44, WW-II.

(6) Name for military exercise.

(7) See REGENBOGEN

RAINBOW CORNER -- Club for Allied enlisted men operated by American Red Cross in Hotel de Paris in Paris, France. WW-II.

RAINBOW VILLAGE -- Site near Panmunjom, Korea, where exchanged prisoners were processed during OPERATION LITTLE SWITCH. April 1953, Korean Conflict.

RAINCOAT -- First phase of U.S. 5th Army assault against German WINTER LINE in Italy aimed at capture of Camino hill mass. Began 3 December 1943, WW-II.

RAINDROP -- Name for series of peacetime military exercises.

RAINIER -- The detonation of a US 1.7 kiloton nuclear device in an underground tunnel at Nevada Test Site. See also PLUMBBOB. 19 September 1957.

RAKEOFF -- Ust-Bolshervetski, Kamchatka, U.S.S.R. WW-II.

RALLYE-CLUB -- French Morane-Saulnier 880 monoplane. In production in 1961. See also SUPER-RALLYE.

RAM -- (1) Canadian cruiser tank. Came into use in 1942, WW-II.

(2) Italian World War II fighter-bomber. See ARIETE.

(3) Three stage solid propellant booster of the scout class. National Aeronautics and Space Administration considered the vehicle as scout replacement, but shelved it in favor of improving payload capability of the Scout.

(4) U.S. air-to-air rocket developed in 1950 and fired from F4U Corsairs during the Korean War. Using a-shaped charge warhead, the solid propellant rocket was a larger version of the HOLY MOSES.

(5) Acronym for Radio Attenuation Measurement National Aeronautics and Space Administration project to investigate the interference of the ionized flow field with communications between earth and manned re-entry vehicles. ARGO D-8 and BLUE SCOUT, JUNIOR are being used to launch payloads to velocities of 20,000 feet per second.

(6) Acronym for Research Aviation Medicine, a continuing U.S. Navy program of research into aerospace medical techniques, including instrumentation for manned space flights.

(7) Name for Royal Canadian Air Force Squadron Number 401.

RAMARK -- Radar Beacon that provides bearing information to radar-equipped ships and aircraft by continuously emitting radar waves.

RAMBLER - Sounding rocket under development for National Aeronautics and Space Administration. Essentially, a SCOUT class vehicle having the capability of launching small satellite payloads.

RAMGARH FORCE -- See X FORCE

RAMIER -- Military version of the Nord 1101 aircraft. See NORALPHA.

RAMONA -- Name reserved by meteorologists for tropical cyclone in eastern North Pacific.

RAMPS -- Acronym for Recovered Allied Military Personnel. WW-II.

RAMROD -- British code name for a type of air operation in which bombers, fighter-bombers, or, sometimes, cannon fighters attacked an enemy target. WW-II.

RAMSHACKLE -- Monga Monga Point, New Britain. WW-II.

RANCID -- Code name for Greenland. WW-II.

RAND -- Acronym for Research and Development Corporation, a U.S. non-profit research organization.

RANDEM -- Tai Shei Sha Island, Chusan Archipelago, China. WW-II.

RANDY -- Japanese World War II Kawasaki KI. 102 attack fighter. First flight in 1944, but production minimal due to B-29 bombings.

RANGEMASTER -- A refinement of the original North American Navion, now being built by Navion Aircraft Company.

RANGER I-V -- (1) Bell 47J-2 helicopter which set two world's records in 1961. Department of Defense H-13 series.

(2) National Aeronautics and Space Administration lunar exploration vehicle to rough-land instruments on the moon's surface and take high-resolution pictures

of the lunar surface prior to impact. Five vehicles have been launched by ATLAS-AGENAS and all have failed in one way or another to perform their missions. Ranger V, according to NASA, impacted the back side of the moon, but a power failure robbed it of any usefulness. Nine more shots are planned and will carry the program through 1964.

(3) U.S. nuclear weapons test at Nevada Test Site. Early 1951.

RANGER STRIKE -- U.S. peacetime military exercise.

RANGERS -- See AMERICAN RANGERS

RANGOON -- Royal Air Force trimotor biplane flying boat used for long-range reconnaissance. Military version of Short Brothers Company. See also CALCUTTA.

RANKIN -- Allied plans for emergency return to European Continent in event of deterioration of German position. See also RANKIN CASE A-C, OVERLORD. WW-II.

RANKIN CASE A -- Plan for Allied action in case of substantial weakening of strength and morale of German armed forces to extent that a successful assault could be made by Anglo-American forces before OVERLORD. WW-II.

RANKIN CASE B -- Plan for Allied action in case of German withdrawal from occupied countries. WW-II.

RANKIN CASE C -- Plan for Allied action in case of German unconditional surrender and cessation of organized resistance. WW-II.

RANQUEL -- Argentinian I.A.46 agricultural aircraft. First flight 1957.

RAPHAEL -- Cape Schellong, New Britain. WW-II.

RAPIER -- Name assigned to North American F-108 twin-jet, stainless steel interceptor, under development in 1957, but cancelled before prototype built.

RAPSCALLION -- Aguijan Island, Marianas Islands. WW-II.

RAPTUROUS -- Amsterdam, Netherlands. WW-II.

RAREP -- Report of radar meteorological observation.

RASCAL -- (1) U.S. Air Force air-to-surface missile with a range of 100 miles. Developed as a stand-off weapon for the B-47 jet bomber, the missile was liquid propelled and guided by radio command. Program began in 1946 as part of the SHRIKE test program and the testing of the Rascal itself began in 1951. Program was cancelled in November 1958.

(2) Manipa Strait, Waspimat Bay, Netherlands East Indies. WW-II.

RASHNESS -- See CARBONADO

RASPBERRY -- (1) Linga Linga, New Britain. WW-II.

    (2) Wilson Island, Treasury Islands. WW-II.

    (3) Military name for house in Kapelsche Veer, Netherlands, during OPERATION ELEPHANT. January 1945, WW-II.

    (4) British method of protecting convoys against U-Boat attacks. WW-II.

RAT -- (1) Translation of Rata, Russian I-16 aircraft. See MOSCA.

    (2) Acronym for the U.S. Navy's Rocket Assisted Torpedo, an anti-submarine solid propellant rocket assisted torpedo with an acoustical homing device. Launched from destroyers, it has a range of five miles. Prior to the program's cancellation in 1959 some work had been done to adapt the missile to air launching.

RATA -- (English translation: Rat) Spanish Fascist name for Russian I-16 aircraft. See MOSCA and SUPER RATA.

RATCATCHER -- Cyprus, Mediterranean Sea. WW-II.

RATION -- Allied interception of Vichy French ships. WW-II.

RATS OF TOBRUK -- Allied nickname for 9th Australian Division. WW-II.

RATSBANE -- Southern Kyushu, Japan. WW-II.

RATTLE -- Allied conference held at Combined Training Centre, Largs, Scotland, to consider problems of cross-Channel invasion. 28 June - 1 July 1943, WW-II.

RATTLESNAKE DIVISION -- Nickname for U.S. 40th Infantry Division. Also called SUNBURST DIVISION.

RATTLING BRIDGE -- Military name for topographic feature near Heraklion, Crete. May 1941, WW-II.

RATTRAP -- Bismarck Archipelago. WW-II.

RATWEEK -- Harrassment of German retreat in Yugoslavia through co-ordinated attacks on communications by Partisans and Allied Balkans Air Forces. Began 1 September 1944, WW-II.

RAVEN -- (1) Hiller OH-23 U.S. Army standard light observation helicopter. First flew in 1956.

    (2) U.S. Navy studies of a long-range air-to-surface missile for fighter-bombers. The missile would be able to stand-off from its target, thus reducing its vulnerability, while launching its warhead to the target. No contracts have

been announced and no approval appears to have been given for development.

RAVENOUS -- Limited operation in north Burma to be conducted by General Joseph W. Stilwell as part of Operation ANAKIM. Planned for fall 1943, but abandoned. WW-II.

RAVEN'S NEST -- English translation of Nido del Corvo, name of crag on long ridge behind San Pietro, Italy, where Allies established an observation post. November 1943, WW-II.

RAVIOLI -- Tarawe, New Britain. WW-II.

RAWBONE -- Cape Knorr, New Britain. WW-II.

RAWHIDE -- Anu River, New Britain. WW-II.

RAWINSONDE -- Acronym for Radiosonde and Radar Wind Sounding, an upper air observation consisting of evaluation of wind speed and direction, temperature, pressure and relative humidity, by means of balloon-borne radiosonde tracked by a radar or radio direction-finder.

RAWLINSON -- Proposed operation by Third British Division to enlarge bridgehead across Orne River, south of Bois de Bavent, France. Not carried out. See also BYNG. August 1944, WW-II.

RAYBAN -- Cape Tawop, New Britain. WW-II.

RAZON -- Bomb with remotely-controlled tail fins which responded to bombardier's radio signals permitting guidance to target with range and azimuth corrections. See also TARZON, TRIZON, AZON. Developed during World War II.

RAZOR -- Kosesikwa Point, Lusancay Island, Trobriand Islands. WW-II.

RAZORBACK HILL -- U.S. military name for topographic feature on New Britain Island; called by Japanese Eboshi Yama. December 1943. WW-II.

RAZZLE -- Code name for the smaller of two versions of an American incendiary weapon designed to be dropped from planes on crops and forests. See also DECKER. WW-II.

REAR LINK -- Radio detachment sent by Royal Canadian Army Service Corps to transmit calls for Royal Canadian Air Force air support. WW-II.

REBATE -- Plaines de Gaiacs Aerodrome, New Caledonia. WW-II.

REBECCA -- Tropical storm. 3-4 October 1961. Formed over Pacific Ocean about midway between Central America and Hawaii. Moved west-northwestward and dissipated over the ocean.

REBECCA-EUREKA -- British radar combination consisting of Rebecca, in the aircraft, which transmitted pulses, received and retransmitted by the ground-beacon, Eureka, carried in a suitcase, and thus directing aircraft to destination. Used for both dropping and landing operations behind enemy lines. WW-II.

REBELLIOUS -- Malabang, Mindanao, Philippine Islands. WW-II.

REBOUND -- National Aeronautics and Space Adminisitration passive communications satellite program consisting of several multiple-launched low-orbit inflatable satellites. ATLAS-AGENA booster will be used. Program may be cut-back or eliminated for lack of funds. First orbital flight scheduled for 1963, and experiments will be conducted jointly with the U.S. Air Force.

REBUILD, OPERATION -- Repair and reclamation of ordnance materiel by U.S. Far Eastern Command for use in Korean Conflict. See also OPERATION ROLL-UP.

RECCO -- Maug Island, Marianas Islands. WW-II.

RECCO CODE -- International Form of message for encoding meteorological observations made in reconnaissance aircraft.

RECEPTACLE -- Wotje Island, Marshall Islands. WW-II.

RECKLESS -- Allied task force under ALAMO which carried out OPERATION G in Hollandia area, New Guinea. See also LETTERPRESS and NOISELESS Landing Forces. 22 April - 25 August 1944, WW-II.

RECLAIM -- Jerusalem, Palestine. WW-II.

RECON -- Proposal to use helicopters to relay information from reconnaissance satellites equipped with television cameras to ground stations. Never actively developed.

RECOVER -- Nama Island, Caroline Islands. WW-II.

RECRUIT -- (1) Early World War II Ryan low-wing PT-21,-22 primary trainer plane for the U.S. Army Air Forces.

(2) A scaled down version of the Sergeant solid propellant motor used in clusters of eleven for the second stage of the JUPITER C. A single recruit is used as the third stage. Thrust of the motor was 4800 pounds. It was also used in the X-17 test vehicle. Also known as Scaled Sergeant.

RECUPERATE -- Ellice Islands. WW-II.

RED ARROW -- Nickname for U.S. 32nd Infantry Division. Also called LES TERRIBLES.

RED BALL EXPRESS -- (1) Allied military trucking service from St. Lo, France, eastward to supply advancing armies. 25 August - 16 November 1944, WW-II.

(2) U.N. military trucking service from Han River in Korea to I Corps. 1950, WW-II.

(3) U.N. combined rail and sea military transportation service for supplies needed in Korea. Went from Yokohama to Sasebo, Japan, by train, and from Sasebo to Pusan, Korea, by ship. Began 23 July 1950, Korean Conflict.

RED BALL EXPRESS SYSTEM -- Allied shipment of high-priority freight, such as blood, medical supplies, radio sets and parts, from Southampton, England, to Continent after Normandy landings. Not to be confused with later RED BALL EXPRESS trucking service. 1944, WW-II.

RED BANNER -- British Royal Air Force-Army peacetime military exercise.

RED BERRY -- Name for peacetime military operation held in the Arctic.

RED BULL -- Nickname for U.S. 34th Infantry Division.

RED COW, OPERATION -- 105 fighter-bomber sorties by U.S. 5th Air Force against 24 enemy troop and artillery targets on front lines. 8-25 October 1952, Korean Conflict.

RED DEAN -- British air-to-air missile powered by a liquid propellant motor with a range of up to 5 miles. An active radar homing device guided the missile to its target. Program was cancelled in 1957 before it was ever placed in production.

RED DEVILS -- Nickname reputedly given by Germans to U.S. 5th Infantry Division during Wold War II. Also called RED DIAMOND DIVISION.

RED DIAMOND DIVISION -- Nickname for U.S. 5th Infantry Division; taken from shape and color of shoulder insignia. Also called RED DEVILS.

RED DIAMOND ROUTE -- U.N. military transportation route through western mountains from Pusan to Taegu, Korea. See also GREEN DIAMOND ROUTE. Korean Conflict.

RED HERRING -- Finschhafen, New Guinea. WW-II.

RED HILL -- U.S. military name for topographic feature west of Minami-Uebaru, Okinawa. So named because of its color. April 1945, WW-II.

RED HILLS -- Name for U.S. peacetime military exercise at Fort Bragg, North Carolina, 1962.

RED HORSE STAGING AREA -- Tract of land in region of Le Havre-Rouen, France, divided into five camps, named after popular brands of cigarettes, which were used by U.S. Army as staging areas; at first, for troops arriving from U.S. and, later, for troops returning to U.S. or going to Far East. Organized November 1944 and expanded April 1945, WW-II.

RED INDIAN -- Name for Royal Canadian Air Force Squadron Number 421.

RED LINE -- German defense line in Italy about three miles in front of GOTHIC LINE. August 1944, WW-II.

RED LION EXPRESS ROUTE -- Allied military trucking route from Bayeux, France, to Brussels, Belgium, to carry supplies, largely petroleum, for airborne operation by 21 Army Group in Holland. Also called B.B. (Bayeux to Brussels) Route. 16 September - 12 October 1944, WW-II.

RED ONE, THE -- Nickname first used by Germans during World War II for U.S. 1st Infantry Division. So named for color and numeral on shoulder patch. Also called THE FIRST, THE FIGHTING FIRST.

RED PATCH -- Name for peacetime military exercise.

RED SHIELD CLUB -- British and Canadian rest and recreation facility for war-weary troops in Opera House, Ortona, Italy. WW-II.

RED SLASH HILL -- U.N. name for ridge near Obong-ni and Naktong River, Korea. So named because of eroded area of red clay and shale. Also called by newspaper correspondents No Name Ridge. 1950, Korean Conflict.

RED STOCKING -- Series of flights by Allied Mosquito aircraft, equipped with recording devices, over pinpoints behind enemy lines in Europe to pick up and record messages from agents on ground. 1945, WW-II.

RED, TASK FORCE -- Armored force, part of CENTER TASK FORCE, which was among units that landed at Z BEACH near Oran Algeria. See also TASK FORCE GREEN. November 1942, WW-II.

RED TOP -- British air-to-air missile with a range of nine miles. Infrared guidance and solid propellants are used on the missile which is replacing the FIRESTREAK on British Lightning aircraft. In the final stages of development.

REDDY FOX -- A U.S. Navy version of bangalore torpedo consisting of long pipe filled with explosives which was towed or pushed into position over obstacles and exploded during landing operations. WW-II.

REDEYE -- U.S. Army surface-to-air missile for individual protection against low-flying aircraft. Bazooka-launched, the 22 pound missile uses an infrared guidance system and a high explosive warhead. Limited procurement of the system has been authorized in fiscal year 1963 in spite of disappointing system tests. Marine Corps will also procure the weapon. See also HARPY.

REDHEAD -- See REDHEAD ROADRUNNER

REDHEAD ROADRUNNER -- U.S. Army supersonic target missile with a speed of Mach 2 and a ceiling of 50,000 feet. Boosted by solid propellant motor and sustained by a ramjet engine; system is designed for both low-altitude and high-level missions. For the former, it is flown without the wings. Radio command guidance. Parachute recoverable, the system is in final stages of development.

REDLEAD -- Lindenhafen Plantation, New Britain. WW-II.

REDLINE -- Name given to several radio circuits exclusively for messages to and from Supreme Commander in France. Set up in September 1944, WW-II.

REDSTART -- Kagoshima, Kyushu Island, Japan. WW-II.

REDSTONE --U.S. Army surface-to-surface missile with a range of 200 miles. Liquid propelled and inertially-guided, Redstone units have been deployed in Europe since 1958, and are designed to provide fire support for the Field Army. A modified Redstone, re-named JUPITER C, was used to put the first U.S. satellite EXPLORER I into orbit. Also modified Redstones were used for the Project MERCURY sub-orbital flights of Commander Shepherd and Captain Grissom in 1961. Redstone will be replaced by PERSHING beginning in 1963.

REDWING -- Nuclear test series conducted in the Pacific in May 1956. Consisted of two nuclear tests, the first in the kiloton range was detonated at the earth's surface at Eniwetok and was known as LaCrosse; the second was an air burst at Bikini of several megatons. The latter was the first air drop by U.S. of a thermonuclear weapon and was called Cherokee.

REDWOOD -- Lunga Signal Tower, Guadalcanal, Solomon Islands. WW-II.

REEDBIRD -- Yokohama, Japan. WW-II.

REEFER -- Verde Island Passage, Philippine Islands. WW-II.

REFEREE -- South Seymour Island, Galapagos Islands. WW-II.

REFUGE POINT -- Military name for topographic feature near Retimo, Crete. May 1941, WW-II.

REGENBOGEN -- (English translation: Rainbow) German operation against Allied convoy, JW51, bound for Russia. December 1942 - January 1943, WW-II.

REGEX 62 -- NATO peacetime exercise in Mediterranean, 1962.

REGULUS -- Name for two Navy surface-to-surface turbojet-powered missiles designed to be deck-fired from submarines or cruisers. REGULUS I has a range of 500 nautical miles, a ceiling of 40,000 feet and an inertial guidance system. Solid propellant booster also used. REGULUS II was to have had twice the range and speed of the I model but, because of obsolesence and budgetary difficulties, the Navy cancelled the program in December 1958. Regulus I is deployed on five submarines including one nuclear submarine and two cruisers. Initially operational in 1954.

REGULUS I -- U.S. Navy surface-to-surface subsonic turbojet winged missile. See also REGULUS.

REGULUS II -- U.S. Navy surface-to-surface supersonic turbojet winged missile. See also REGULUS.

REICH, DAS -- Name of German Schutzstaffel (S.S.) division. WW-II.

REINDEER -- Anato, New Britain. WW-II.

RELAX, OPERATION -- U.S. 8th Army program for sending about ˙200 battle-fatigued men daily from Korea to Japan on five-day passes; began on 30 December 1950. Standardized throughout Far East Command as R&R (Rest and Recreation) program in September 1951. Korean Conflict.

RELAY -- National Aeronautics and Space Administration experimental active re-peater communications satellite program capable of handling a standard television channel or 12-two-way voice channels on each of its two communications trans-ponders. First satellite launched by a THOR-DELTA in December 1962, but power supply difficulties decreased its effectiveness. Three more launches planned for 1963. Britain, France, Brazil and Germany have built ground stations to participate in program. Relay is same type of satellite as TELSTAR. See also ADVANCED RELAY.

RELEVANT -- Postwar Base Development Plan for Philippine Islands and Okinawa. WW-II.

RELIANT -- Monoplane built in Wayne, Michigan by the Stinson Aircraft Company, 1933.

RELUCTANT -- Name for peacetime military exercise.

RENA -- (1) Tropical storm. 7-16 November 1949. Formed in Caroline Islands, the Pacific. Moved northwestward through the Philippines and over South China Sea, then recurved northeastward and weakened over north portion of South China Sea.

(2) Name also included in sequence prepared by meteorologists for future tropical cyclones in North Atlantic.

RENAE -- U.S. Navy proposal for a meteorological satellite designed to gather tactical weather data for fleet operations. Not under active development.

RENNTIER -- German Standing plan for occupation of Pechenga, U.S.S.R. August 1940 - June 1941, WW-II.

RENO -- Military name for outpost in Korea. Spring 1953, Korean Conflict.

RENO I-V -- Allied strategic plans for movement westward by successive stages along northern coast of New Guinea, into islands lying west of New Guinea, and final assault on Philippines. Developed and revised by General MacArthur's Southwest Pacific Area, General Headquarters, February 1943 - 15 June 1944. WW-II.

RENOVATION -- Karkar Island, New Guinea. WW-II.

REPEATEDLY -- Mining of Singapore. WW-II.

REPENT -- Boela, Ceram, Netherlands East Indies. WW-II.

REPPU -- (English translation: Hurricane) World War II Japanese Mitsubishi A7M1 shipboard fighter. See SAM.

REPREHEND -- Kagoshima Bay, Kyushu Island, Japan. WW-II.

REPROBATE -- Rongelap Atoll, Marshall Islands. WW-II.

REPROVE -- Palams Island, Mindanao, Philippine Islands. WW-II.

RESCU -- Acronym for Rocket-Ejection Seat Catapult Upward, used in aviation.

RESCUER -- Nickname for the SH-21 version of the Vertol Model 43 as used by the U.S. Air Force Air Rescue Service. See WORKHORSE.

RESERVIST -- Seizure of vital points in harbor at Oran, Algeria, and landing of British and U.S. forces to prevent sabotage. A phase of Operation TORCH. See also TERMINAL. 8 November 1942, WW-II.

RESPLENDENT -- Code word for China-Burma-India Theatre. WW-II.

RETICULE -- Velkal, Siberia. WW-II.

RETRIBUTION -- Code name for Allied counter-measures to be taken against expected Axis evacuation from Tunisia. May 1943, WW-II.

RETRIEVER -- Vertol light cargo helicopter developed for the U.S. Navy and designated HUP-1 when delivered in 1950. New Department of Defense designation is UH-25. Army version is called Army Mule.

RETROSPECT OPERATION -- Allied occupation of coastal village of Madang, Northeast New Guinea. 24 April 1944, WW-II.

REUNION, OPERATION -- Mass aerial evacuation of more than 1100 American prisoners of war from Rumania to Italy. 1944, WW-II.

REVERE -- Tambiu Island, New Britain. WW-II.

REVERSE BOLERO -- See RHUMBA

REX -- Rapid Allied express shipping service between New York and ports in Europe. Began January 1945, WW-II.

RHEINBOTE -- (English translation: Rhine Maiden) German four-stage fin-stabilized surface-to-surface missile with a maximum range of 135 miles. A highly mobile solid propellant missile, it was fired against Antwerp in November 1944, with little effect. Over 60 missiles were launched against the city, each carrying only 88 pounds of high explosives.

RHEINTOCHTER -- German surface-to-air, anti-aircraft missile with a range of 7.5 miles; able to reach altitudes of 3.7 miles. Solid boosted and sustained, over 80 of the radio-controlled missiles were test fired by the beginning of 1945. However, the missile was never placed into production. A more advanced version was also developed with a range of 22 miles, and ability to reach an altitude of 22 miles. It used a solid booster and either a hypergolic liquid propellant engine or a solid motor. Both versions were tested in 1944-45, but were never placed in production.

RHEINUEBUNG -- (English: Rhine Exercise) German operation by battleship, Bismarck, and cruiser, Prinz Eugen, against merchant shipping in North and Middle Atlantic. May 1941, WW-II.

RHEUMATISM -- Laughlan Island, Louisiade Archipelago. WW-II.

RHINE MAIDEN -- See RHEINBOTE

RHINO FERRY -- Barge constructed of bolted ponton units and propelled by outboard motor. Used by Allies in invasion of Normandy, Operation OVERLORD. WW-II.

RHO-THETA -- Radio navigational system using polar-coordinate and omnibearing-distance facilities.

RHODA -- Name reserved by meteorologists for tropical cyclone in the North Atlantic area.

RHODODENDRON -- Rua Sura, Guadalcanal, Solomon Islands. WW-II.

RHUBARB -- (1) Bilomi River, New Britain. WW-II.

(2) Inagau, Guadalcanal, Solomon Islands. WW-II.

RHUBARBS -- (1) British code name for offensive operations by fighter aircraft designed to make enemy retain strong air forces in western Europe. Originally called Mosquitoes, but changed to avoid confusion with aircraft of that name. Known as CIRCUS when bombers were included in mission. Began 20 December 1940, WW-II.

(2) British Royal Air Force joint operations in support of army in Burma; included setting fire to bamboo huts of Japanese-held villages and attacks on Japanese communications. WW-II.

RHUMB -- Mindoro Strait, Philippine Islands. WW-II.

RHUMBA -- Plan for transferring U.S. logistic machinery to Continent, so that American troops and supplies could enter France directly from U.S. after launching of OVERLORD. Originally called Reverse BOLERO or OreloB. WW-II.

RIBBON OFFENSIVE -- Allied name for air patrol of strips of water on transit routes in Bay of Biscay to seek out German submarines. Began March 1943, WW-II.

RICHARD, CASE -- See CASE RICHARD

RIDDANCE -- Code word for Japanese home islands. WW-II.

RIFFLER -- Ariake Wan, Kyushu, Japan. WW-II.

RIFLERANGE -- Kiska Island, Aleutian Islands. WW-II.

RIFT -- National Aeronautics and Space Administration acronym for Reactor In-Flight Test system, an upper stage vehicle designed to flight-test the NERVA nuclear rocket engine. Launched as an upper stage on the ADVANCED SATURN; will provide first actual flight test data on the operation, recovery and safety of nuclear rockets. First flight test expected in early 1967 from Cape Canaveral. See also ROVER.

RIGEL -- U.S. Navy submarine-launched shore bombardment missile fired from a submarine hanger. Launched by four high-acceleration wrap-around solid boosters and sustained by ramjet engines, the missile was to have a range of 550 miles. Twelve test vehicles were built and fired from Point Mugu, California, before the development was cancelled in 1953. One of the earliest applications of the concept of submarine launching of ballistic missiles. Program began in 1946, with flight testing starting in 1950.

RIGHTHOOK -- Solomon Sea. WW-II.

RIGOROUS SWORD -- World War II Japanese Mitsubishi J8M1 rocket-powered interceptor. See SHUSUI.

RINGBOLT -- Tulagi Island, Solomon Islands. WW-II.

RINGER -- Basra, Iraq. WW-II.

RIP TIDE IV -- Name for U.S. Navy peacetime military exercise, 1961.

RIPPER -- U.N. operation in Korea with double mission of retaking Seoul and destroying enemy troops and equipment as rapidly, and in as great numbers, as possible. Began 7 March 1951, Korean Conflict.

RIPVANWINKLE -- Cape Archway, New Britain. WW-II.

RISE -- Acronym for Research in Supersonic Environment, a program in which a NAVAHO missile was used to obtain temperature and pressure data for the HOUND DOG missile, the B-70 and the F-108 aircraft. Flights took place in 1958.

RISING STAR -- Name for peacetime military exercise.

CODE NAMES DICTIONARY

RITA -- (1) U.S. code name for Darrit Island, Majuro Atoll, Marshall Group. WW-II.

(2) Typhoon. 3-10 November 1948. First detected in western Caroline Islands. Moved northwestward across Philippine Sea, skirted north coast of Luzon, and continued westward across South China Sea toward China mainland.

(3) Typhoon. 27 August - 1 September 1953. Formed in eastern Carolines. Moved westward through northern Mariana Islands, across Philippine Sea, and between Luzon and Taiwan toward China mainland.

(4) Typhoon. 9-12 June 1958. Formed in western Caroline Islands. Moved northwestward through the Philippine Sea, then recurved northeastward and dissipated southeast of Japan.

(5) Tropical storm. 14-20 January 1961. Formed near Koror Island, western Caroline Islands. Moved northwestward at first, then east-northeastward and dissipated west of Saipan, Mariana Islands.

(6) Name also applied to tropical cyclones in western North Pacific which occurred prior to (2) through (5) above.

RITA LAKE -- Military name for topographic feature on Butaritari Island, Makin Atoll. November 1943, WW-II.

RIVIERA -- Italian SIAI-Marchetti FN-333 commercial amphibian flying boat in production. Basic version first flew in 1952.

RIVIERE 1, LA -- 75-mm. German casemate, north of Vaux at western limit of Canadian beaches in Operation OVERLORD. June 1944, WW-II.

RO, OPERATION -- Japanese reinforcement of Rabaul, New Britain, with 173 carrier aircraft from Truk in order to raid Allied supply routes and crush forthcoming offensives. 28 October - 1 November 1943, WW-II.

ROADMAKER -- See GYMKHANA-ROADMAKER

ROADSTEAD -- British code name for air operation to escort bombers and, sometimes, fighters in diving or low-level attacks on ships, at sea or in port. WW-II.

ROARING -- Hawaii Island, Territory of Hawaii. WW-II.

ROAST -- British operation to clear Comacchio Spit between Lake Comacchio and sea in northern Italy. See also FRY, LEVER. April 1945, WW-II.

ROB -- Unusual Japanese experimental Kawasaki KI.64 fighter conceived in 1939. First flight in 1943, but did not become operational.

ROBCOL -- Name of column from 10th Indian Division during action near El Alamein, Egypt. July 1942, WW-II.

419

ROBERT ARRIVE -- Signal broadcast by British Broadcasting Corporation warning that Allied landings in North Africa were about to commence. 7 November 1942, WW-II.

ROBIN -- U.S. Air Force sounding rocket designed to obtain information on wind and air density at high altitude; a modified ARCAS carrying an inflatable 4-ounce, 3-foot diameter balloon, is launched to maximum altitude, the balloon is ejected and inflated and tracked by radar to obtain the meteorological data. In operational use.

ROBOT 304 -- See JAKTROBOT

ROBOT 315 -- Swedish surface-to-surface tactical missile specifically designed for launch from surface ships. Four solid propellant boosters, usually located forward of the sustainer, are used to launch the missile and a pulsejet engine is employed as the sustainer. Development began in 1949, and, in 1955, a successful shipboard launch took place. The weapon is currently deployed aboard several Swedish destroyers.

ROBOT 322 -- Swedish surface-to-air missile under development. Using a solid propellant booster, the missile is sustained by twin ramjet engines and radio-command guided. Several earlier versions are in operation.

ROBOTTI -- Name of an Italian liquid propelled test rocket, as well as that of a family of supersonic unguided missiles under development.

ROC -- Standard fighter of Great Britain's Fleet Air Arm in early World War II. The Blackburn-produced craft first flew in 1938 and first deliveries were made in 1940.

ROCHE -- Radio code word ordering withdrawal of British troops from HANGMAN'S HILL, near Monte Cassino, Italy. 24 March 1944, WW-II.

ROCHEN -- German experimental rocket developed by the Torpedo Research Center and tested there for ship-to-ship, ship-to-shore and surface-to-surface applications. Wire-guided, the missile had a range of 4 miles and carried a 220-pound payload. World War II development, it never reached the production stage.

ROCK, THE -- Name for island of Corregidor in Manila Bay, Philippines. WW-II.

ROCK FORCE -- Name for U.S. 503rd Parachute Infantry Regiment during airborne attack on island of Corregidor, Philippines. 16 February 1945, WW-II.

ROCK OF THE MARNE -- Nickname for U.S. 3rd Infantry Division; earned during stand against Germany's last great counteroffensive of World War One. Also called THE FIGHTING THIRD.

ROCKAIRE -- U.S. Air Force research rocket launched from a high flying aircraft. A single stage solid propellant DEACON rocket, it was to carry an atmospheric measurement payload of 40 pounds to an altitude of 28 miles. Four flight tests were conducted in December 1956, using a F-86D airplane as the launch plat-form. None were successful. Program discontinued.

ROCKALONG -- Maiduguri, Africa. WW-II.

ROCKBOTTOM -- Allied China-Burma-India Theater plan for Hump deliveries. Fall 1943, WW-II.

ROCKCRUSHER -- Iwo Jima, Bonin Islands, Japan. WW-II.

ROCKET RUN -- Nickname for U.S. Air Transport Command's operations in North Africa. Late World War II.

ROCKEYE -- U.S. Navy air-to-surface missile for close support of ground troops. Launched from carrier aircraft, the missile is a free-fall weapon. Several proto-types have been tested but the weapon is not under development.

ROCKOON -- U.S. Navy acronym for Rocket Balloon, a program in which 20-pound payloads are carried to alitudes of 80,000 feet by a balloon and then to altitudes of 60-70 miles by a rocket fired through the balloon. Fired from various parts of the world during the late 1950's, the most common experiments were studies of solar flares. DEACON rocket was used. See also HARP.

ROCKY CRAGS -- (1) U.S. military name for topographic feature on Okinawa. 1945, WW-II.

(2) See KING I

ROCKY POINT -- Military name for northern part of LONE TREE HILL which ex-tended into Maffin Bay, Netherlands New Guinea. Spring 1944, WW-II.

ROCKY SHOALS -- Name for U.S. peacetime military exercise held on West Coast.

ROCOCO -- Maug Island, Marianas Islands. WW-II.

RODENT -- Akureyri, Iceland. WW-II.

RODEO -- British code name for fighter sweeps over enemy territory without bombers. WW-II.

ROESSELSPRUNG -- (English translation: Knight's Move) German operation which inflicted heavy damage on Allied convoy, PQ 17, bound for Russia; used all submarine, air and surface forces available including battleship, Tirpitz, two pocket battleships and one heavy cruiser. July 1942, WW-II.

ROFOR -- International code word used to indicate a meteorological air route forecast.

ROFOT -- An international code word denoting route forecast, units in metric system.

ROGER -- (1) Code word for letter "R" in a phonetic alphabet, used to avoid possibility of a misunderstanding in transmitting messages. See also ROMEO.

(2) British plan to occupy Phuket Island, off Kra Isthumus, Burma. Canceled May 1945, WW-II.

ROGER HILL -- U.S. military name for topographic feature near Yonabaru, Okinawa. 1945, WW-II.

ROGER WHITE -- Strip of land on UTAH beach opened after Normandy landing. June 1944. WW-II.

ROISTERER -- Legaspi, Philippine Islands. WW-II.

ROITAN -- Siassi Island, New Britain. WW-II.

ROKEBY -- Name of Australian training center near Seymour in Victoria, Australia. WW-II.

ROKSONDE 100 -- U.S. single-stage meteorological rocket designed to carry a 5-10-pound separate low drag free-flight dart with desired instrumentation to altitudes of 125,000 feet. At burnout, the dart coasts to peak altitude before ejecting chaff for radar tracking or taking measurements with its own instruments. In operational use.

ROKSONDE 200 -- U.S. single-stage meteorological rocket designed to propel payload to 200,000 feet. Payload contained in free-flight, low-drag dart.

ROLL-UP, OPERATION -- U.S. Far East Command reclamation of ordnance items from World War II remaining on Pacific island outposts and their repair or reconstruction in Japan. Started in 1948; especially active during Korean Conflict. See also OPERATION REBUILD.

ROLLING W DIVISION -- Nickname for U.S. 89th Infantry Division. Named after shoulder patch, an inverted M, for its other name, MIDDLE WEST DIVISION.

ROLLITRAILER -- U.S. Army 12-ton, 2000-gallon cargo or petroleum, oil and lubricants trailer.

ROMA -- U.S. Air Service semi-rigid airship which crashed in 1922.

ROMANCE -- Code name for Brazil. WW-II.

ROMANCER -- Sepik River, New Guinea. WW-II.

ROME LINE -- German defense line in Italy which crossed peninsula through Avezzano and Popoli. Fall 1943, WW-II.

ROMEO -- (1) Code word for letter "R" in a phonetic alphabet, used to avoid possibility of a misunderstanding in transmitting messages. See also ROGER.

(2) Marli, New Britain. WW-II.

(3) Force of French commandos which landed in Cap Negre area of southern France, clearing coastal defenses and blocking coastal highway during Operation DRAGOON. 15 August 1944, WW-II.

ROMET -- International code word denoting route forecast, units in metric system.

ROMNEY -- Cape Balangori, New Britain. WW-II.

ROMULUS -- Allied operation for the clearance of Arakan down to and including Akyab, Burma. See also TALON. Began 12 December 1944, WW-II.

RONDONE -- Post World War II Italian Ambrosini F.4,-7, single-engine monoplane.

RONSON -- Flame thrower weapon, mounted on carrier; developed in United Kingdom. Came into use in 1942, WW-II.

ROOFTREE -- Joint U.S. Army and Navy plan for participation in TORCH, WW-II.

ROOK -- Polish PZL.101 aircraft. See GAWRON.

ROOKERY -- Corinto, Nicaragua. WW-II.

ROORKEE ROAD -- Maintenance route near Cassino, Italy, used by British Indian troops. Early 1944, WW-II.

ROOSEVELT BRIDGE -- See PRESIDENT ROOSEVELT BRIDGE

ROOSTER -- (1) Airborne radar homing beacon.

(2) Batavia, Java, Netherlands East Indies. WW-II.

(3) Gasmata, New Britain (Canceled). WW-II.

(4) Allied operation to transport by air Chinese 22nd Division to Chihchiang, China, to assist in defense of U.S. 14th Air Force base. 21 April - 11 May 1945, WW-II.

ROOTER PLOW -- See BIG HOOK

ROPE -- Electronic energy reflectors made from long strips of metal foil or other metalized material. Used to confuse enemy radar. See also ANGEL, WINDOW.

ROR -- Abbreviation for Rocket-on-Rotor a mechanism attached to the end of helicopter rotor blades to assist in takeoffs. Hydrogen peroxide fueled, the small one pound rockets could be used for six takeoffs. In use during 1954-55; now obsolete.

ROSALIE -- (1) U.S. code name for Uliga Island, Majuro Atoll, Marshall Group. WW-II.

(2) Name reserved by meteorologists for tropical cyclone in eastern North Pacific.

ROSALIND -- Typhoon. 6-11 October 1947. First detected north of Mariana Islands, the Pacific. Moved erratically northward, then turned northeastward, out over the Pacific well, east of Japan.

ROSE -- (1) Allied code name for Ruhr pocket, Germany. April 1945, WW-II.

(2) Typhoon. 5-9 October 1952. Formed east of Philippines. Moved northeastward through Bonin and Volcano Islands and southeast of Japan out over Pacific.

(3) Typhoon. 22-27 January 1957. Formed near Truk, Caroline Islands. Moved west-northwestward and dissipated over northern Philippine Sea.

(4) Allied landing at Tuleer, Madagascar. 29 September 1942, WW-II.

ROSEBUD -- (1) Airborne radar beacon used in radar control and Identification, Friend or Foe (IFF) messages.

(2) Samar, Philippine Islands. WW-II.

ROSEBUSH -- Name for NATO peacetime military exercise.

ROSELIN -- Stettin Bay, New Britain. WW-II.

ROSEMONT -- Rein Bay, New Britain. WW-II.

ROSES -- Efate, New Hebrides Islands. WW-II.

ROSEWOOD -- Alokun Island, Solomon Islands. WW-II.

ROSIE -- Unsuccessful French operation in which small Groupe Navale d'Assaut de Corse, simulating big task force, attempted to land commandos near Cannes, southern France, during Operation DRAGOON: heavy casualties suffered. 15 August 1944, WW-II.

ROSLYN -- Name reserved by meteorologists for tropical cyclone in eastern North Pacific.

ROTODYNE -- 1960 Westland VTOL transport, powered by two British Rolls-Royce two-spool turboprops. Capable of carrying 65 passengers.

ROULETTE WHEEL -- U.S. military name for topographic feature in ridge near Kuhazu, Okinawa. 1945, WW-II.

ROULEUR -- French-built Morane trainer used at French training schools by American students during World War One.

ROUND TOP -- Name for Hill 181 near Yongdok, Korea. Korean Conflict.

ROUNDHAMMER -- Code name used at Washington TRIDENT Conference for cross-Channel invasion of European Continent. Conceived as operation midway in size between ROUNDUP AND SLEDGE HAMMER, it borrowed part of each code name. See also OVERLORD. May 1943, WW-II.

ROUNDUP -- Various 1941-43 plans for cross-Channel attack on European Continent. Alternative to SLEDGEHAMMER. See also ROUNDHAMMER, OVERLORD.

ROUNDUP, OPERATION -- U.N. advance toward Hongchon, Korea. Began 5 February 1951, Korean Conflict.

ROVER -- U.S. Atomic Energy Commission - National Aeronautics and Space Administration overall designation for the program to develop a nuclear rocket for space use. Various sub-divisions of the program are KIWI (non-flying reactor tests), NERVA (development of flyable nuclear engine) and RIFT (nuclear stage for flight tests). Program began in 1955. Expected to yield operational nuclear stage for space missions in the early 1970's. See also HONEYCOMB and ZEPPO.

ROVER BOYS -- Name given to U.S. fliers by ground troops in Marshall Islands campaign. WW-II.

ROVER DAVID -- British system of target location for patrolling fighters and fighter bombers engaged in close tactical support of ground troops; conducted by mobile observation posts situated with forward troops and equipped with radio transmitters; included armored cars, trucks, jeeps. Originated by and named after Royal Air Force Wing Commander David Haysom. See also CAB-RANK, ROVER JOE. WW-II.

ROVER JOE -- U.S. system of target location for patrolling aircraft engaged in close tactical support of ground troops; conducted by mobile observation posts, such as jeeps, situated with forward troops and equipped with radio transmitters. Came into use after British ROVER DAVID. WW-II.

ROWAN WADI -- Military name for topographic feature near Bardia, Libya. Named after Australian Lieutenant Colonel J.G. Rowan. 1941, WW-II.

ROWBOAT -- Cratering study conducted at Playa Lake Bed at the Nevada Test Site by University of California's Lawrence Radiation Laboratory, Livermore, California.

ROWLEY -- Manfredonia, Italy. WW-II.

ROWLOCK -- Kwajalein Island, Marshall Islands. WW-II.

ROXIE -- Name reserved by meteorologists for tropical cyclone in North Atlantic area.

ROYAL CANADIAN AVENUE -- Canadian nickname for narrow road, unnamed on maps, from Adriatic coast south of Ortona, Italy, to San Leonardo. December 1943, WW-II.

ROYAL FLUSH -- Allied air operation by fighter planes designed to interfere with enemy air and land movement in France during Normandy invasion. Similar to STUD and FULL HOUSE. June 1944, WW-II.

ROYAL MARINE -- British operation to lay fluvial mines in German waterways, particularly the Rhine River; mines were designed to become harmless before reaching neutral waters. Also called R.M. Operation. Early 1940, WW-II.

ROYAL PERIVOLIANS -- Name given to New Zealand Composite Battalion by Lieutenant General E.C. Weston, British commander on Crete, for action in dealing with German paratroops in woods near Perivolia, Crete, while King of Greece was staying in vicinity. May 1941, WW-II.

RUBE -- Name given to destroyer, USS Reuben James, by her crew; sunk in Atlantic by German submarine on 31 October 1941. WW-II.

RUBEN THE CUBAN -- U.S. Marine Corps nickname for a Castro militiaman in Cuba. 1960's.

RUBICON -- Code name for Bolivia. WW-II.

RUBY -- (1) Typhoon. 28-31 October 1950. First detected in central Philippine Sea. Moved northeastward past Japan, and dissipated over northern Pacific.

    (2) Typhoon. 3-11 November 1954. Formed in central Caroline Islands. Moved northwestward across Philippine Sea and central Luzon and entered China mainland east of Hong Kong. Caused heavy damage and two deaths in Luzon.

    (3) Tropical storm. 27-29 February 1959. Formed south of Guam, Mariana Islands, Pacific. Moved westward, and dissipated near Koror Island.

    (4) Tropical storm. 21-24 September 1961. Formed in western Philippine Sea. Moved westward across Luzon and the South China Sea into Central Viet Nam.

    (5) Name also applied to tropical cyclones in western North Pacific which occurred prior to (1) through (4) above.

    (6) A study being conducted by Cornell University for the U.S. Air Force. Investigates factors affecting the return of radar echoes from objects in space.

RUDDINESS -- Shibushi, Japan. WW-II.

RUDGE -- Code word for early Allied plan to invade European continent. See also OVERLORD. WW-II.

RUDIMENTARY -- Freemantle, Australia. WW-II.

RUGBY -- (1) Boli Point, Lusancay Island, Trobriand Islands. WW-II.

(2) U.S. 1st Airborne Task Force, which dropped in rear of assault beaches in area of Le Muy-Le Luc, southern France, to block off coast from interior prior to DRAGOON. 15 August 1944, WW-II.

RULER -- Sulu Sea, Philippine Islands. WW-II.

RUM JUNGLE -- Australian mine which provided uranium concentrates for the Combined Development Agency.

RUMPELKAMMER -- German operation to bombard England by flying bombs. Began 12 June 1944, WW-II.

RUMPLER -- German World War One fighter/observation biplane.

RUNCIBLE -- Acronym for Revised Unified New Compiler with its Basic Language Extended, used in data processing.

RUNDSTEDT COUNTER-OFFENSIVE -- Name for German Ardennes offensive. Named after General Field Marschall Gerd von Rundstedt. December 1944, WW-II.

RUNT -- Samarai Island, New Guinea. WW-II.

RUNYON -- Bola Bola, New Britain. WW-II.

RUPERT -- Planned Allied expedition to Narwik, Norway. Succeeded by OPERATION MAURICE. April 1940, WW-II.

RUSTY -- (1) Anambas Islands, Netherlands East Indies. WW-II.

(2) Photo reconnaissance in Africa. WW-II.

RUTH -- (1) U.S. Navy designation of zone in Manila Bay, Philippines, for mine sweeping operations. February 1945, WW-II.

(2) Typhoon. 22-27 August 1945. First detected in central Philippine Sea. Moved northeastward at first, then northward across Honshu, Japan, and over Sea of Japan.

(3) Typhoon. 7-14 October 1951. Formed southeast of Guam. Moved west-northwestward, passed south of Guam into Philippine Sea, gradually turned northeastward, passed near Okinawa and entered Japan, gradually lost force.

(4) Typhoon. 12-17 December 1955. Formed in central Caroline Islands. Moved northwestward over Philippine Sea, recurved northeastward and lost force over the Pacific southeast of Japan.

(5) Tropical depression. 9-11 September 1959. Formed in northeastern Philippine Sea. Moved southwestward 300 miles and dissipated.

(6) Typhoon. 13–23 August 1962. Formed east of Guam. Moved northward along the Mariana Islands, then north-northwestward toward Japan. Recurved northeastward just short of Honshu, Japan, and out over the North Pacific.

(7) Name also applied to tropical cyclones in western North Pacific which occurred prior to (2) through (6) above.

RUTTER -- See JUBILEE

RYAN RIDGE -- Military name for topographic feature on west coast of Okinawa; captured by U.S. Captain Bernard Ryan. April 1945, WW-II.

RYAN'S RIDGE -- Military name for topographic feature on Saipan Island. Named for U.S. Army Captain Paul Ryan, killed in action on ridge, 17 June 1944, WW-II.

RYE -- Three Island, Treasury Islands. WW-II.

S

S-BOOT -- Small German torpedo boat. WW-II.

S DAY -- Day when U.S. invasion of Lingayen Gulf, Luzon, Philippines, commenced. 9 January 1945, WW-II.

S MINE -- German antipersonnel Schrapnellmine. Nicknamed BOUNCING BETTY. See also T MINE, SCHÜ-MINE 42. WW-II.

S PHONE -- Radio telephone used for talking an aircraft down to the right place. Used by Resistance forces. WW-II.

SAAR HEIGHTS POSITION -- See SAAR-HOEHEN STELLUNG.

SAAR-HOEHEN STELLUNG -- (English translation: Saar Heights Position) German military name for area of high ground west of Saar River, just across German border. Late 1944, WW-II.

SABER -- Solid propellant improved version of the VIPER. Designed primarily for sled propulsion and application to sounding rockets. Not presently being used.

SABRE -- The most famous fighter since World War II, the North American F-86 was especially successful in Korean combat. First production model delivered to U.S. Air Force in 1948. See SILVER CHARGER and FURY.

SABRE HAWK -- Name for peacetime military exercise.

SABRE MARK 6 -- Canadair CL-13B version of F-86. In service with Royal Canadian Air Force in Europe, and with Germany, Colombia, and South Africa.

SABRE MARK 32 -- Australian version of the F-86. Built by Commonwealth as the CA-27. Prototype first flew in 1953. In service with Royal Australian Air Force.

SABREJET -- Name sometimes used to describe the North American F-86 aircraft series.

SABRELINER -- North American twin-jet utility transport. Operational with the U.S. Air Force as the T-39. Also offered in civilian version. First flew 1958.

SACKTIME LINE -- Special shuttle of C-47 aircraft to transport combat personnel of U.S. 5th Air Force, on leave from New Guinea, to rest and recreational facilities in Sydney, Australia. So named because job was somewhat oversupplied with crews, who thus did a minimum of flying and a maximum of resting. Started July 1943, WW-II.

SACO -- Acronym for Sino-American Cooperative Organization, which conducted guerrilla and intelligence activities behind Japanese lines. See also PACT DOG. Established 15 April 1943, WW-II.

SAD SACK -- Code name for Hwangto Do, island occupied by U.N. forces during naval siege of Wonsan harbor, North Korea. Name taken from U.S. slang term for a person, especially a soldier, with good intentions who is nevertheless ineffective. 16 February 1951-27 July 1953, Korean Conflict.

SADDLEHORSE -- Meselia, New Britain. WW-II.

SADIE -- Name reserved by meteorologists for tropical cyclone in North Atlantic area.

SADSACK -- Pulie River, New Britain. WW-II.

SAETA -- (English translation: Lightning) First turbojet aircraft of Spanish origin, the Hispano HA-200 trainer; first flew in 1955, and is being built for the Spanish Air Force as well as in Egypt as The Cairo.

SAETTA -- (English translation: Lightning) Italian Macchi C.200 fighter plane. First flew in 1937.

SAFARI -- German operation for full military occupation of Denmark to reduce activities of underground movements. August 1943, WW-II.

SAFARI, OPERATION -- U.S. Air Force Congo Airlift of United Nations troops. Started from Evereaux, France, 14 July 1960.

SAFCADIO -- Wabmete, New Britain. WW-II.

SAFE HAVEN, OPERATION -- Airlift of Hungarian refugees by U.S. Air Force Military Air Transport Service aircraft in late 1956. Also called the Air Bridge to Freedom.

SAFEGUARD -- Alexisbafen Airdrome, New Guinea. WW-II.

SAFIR -- Swedish monoplane. First flew in 1951.

SAGE -- Acronym for Semiautomatic Ground Environment; a U.S. defense system providing instantaneous information needed for waging air battles; built around a type of electronic digital computer. Originally called LINCOLN.

SAGEBRUSH -- (1) U.S. code for Elugelab Island, Eniwetok Atoll, Marshall Group. WW-II.

(2) U.S. Army-Air Force peacetime exercises held in Louisiana in 1955, the biggest such maneuvers since World War II.

SAGITTARIO -- (English translation: Archer) Reggiane Re.2005 interceptor which first flew in 1942. Delivered to Italian air arm in 1943.

SAHARA -- French military development of the Brequet Type 763, Provence. The 765 flew in 1958. Only four were built. Still operational.

SAIL -- An automatic coding system used in data processing.

SAILFISH -- Cape Peiho, New Britain. WW-II.

SAILMAKER -- Plan for troops under Canadian 1st Army command to capture island of Schouwen, north of the Bevelands, Netherlands, and establish radar station there. Postponed indefinitely, 20 November 1944, WW-II.

SAINT -- Acronym for both Satellite Inspector and Satellite Interceptor, a U.S. Air Force program to develop a spacecraft capable of rendezvousing with an unidentified satellite and inspecting it with television. Infrared, optical and radiation sensors. In the more advanced interceptor, if the satellite was determined to be hostile it would be destroyed. Development was initiated in 1959, but in December 1962 the program was "re-oriented" (in effect cancelled) because of technological advances and development difficulties. Studies now underway to determine characteristics of a Saint. Name was dropped by the Air Force because of objections of religious groups. Called Hawkeye in earlier phase. Sometimes called Satin.

SAINT FORCE -- Battle group of Canadian 6th Brigade active in southeast Netherlands. Fall 1944, WW-II.

ST. POLYCARP -- Allied code name for road junction south of Ortona, Italy, in area to be defended by British Indian troops. May 1944, WW-II.

SALAMANDER -- (1) German World War II He-162A aircraft. See SPATZ.

(2) Kainau-A, New Britain. WW-II.

(3) See MOLCH

SALE -- Acronym for Simple Algebraic Language for Engineers.

SALINE -- Nepui, New Caledonia. WW-II.

SALLY -- (1) Mitsubishi twin-engine bomber first used by the Japanese in 1937 to bomb China. Used throughout World War II.

(2) Verde Island Passage, Philippine Islands. WW-II.

(3) Typhoon. 12-20 November 1954. Formed in southeastern Philippine Sea. Moved westward at first, then northwestward, approached east coast of Luzon, then turned northeastward and dissipated over northern Philippine Sea.

(4) Tropical storm. 4-12 March 1959. Formed south of Kwajelein Atoll, Marshall Islands, Pacific. Moved westward through Caroline Islands and dissipated in southern Philippine Sea.

(5) Typhoon. 21-29 September 1961. Began forming near Eniwetok Atoll, Pacific. Moved west-northwestward over Guam and reached typhoon intensity over Philippine Sea. Moved across southern Taiwan and entered Asiatic mainland northeast of Hong Kong.

(6) Name also applied to tropical cyclones in western North Pacific which occurred prior to (3) through (5) above.

SALMON -- Allied search for U-Boats in North Atlantic. WW-II.

SALOME -- (1) U.S. code name for Dalap Island, Majuro Atoll, Marshall Group. WW-II.

(2) Tropical storm. 18-26 August 1950. First detected northwest of island of Kauai, Hawaii. Moved west-northwestward over the open ocean and eventually dissipated.

SALTPETER -- Via River, New Britain. WW-II.

SALUBRIOUS -- Tayabas Bay, Luzon, Philippine Islands. WW-II.

SALUTATION -- Nizki Island, Aleutian Islands. WW-II.

SAM -- (1) Mitsubishi A7M1 shipboard fighter first flown in 1944. Did not become operational due to wartime production difficulties. Called Reppu (Hurricane) by Japanese.

(2) Tabian Village, Gilbert Islands. WW-II.

SAMARITAN -- (1) Military version of the Convair CV-x40 series. Used by the U.S. Air Force for aeromedical evacuation and transport duties as the C-131. Also see FLYING SCHOOLROOM and METROPOLITAN.

(2) Tamari River, New Britain. WW-II.

SAMOS -- Acronym for Satellite-Missile Observation System. Highly classified U.S. photo reconnaissance satellite system designed to gather intelligence from 100-330-mile orbits and transmit it by television data links or capsule recovery to the ground. Replacement for U-2 reconnaisance over Russia. Launched by an ATLAS-AGENA into a circular polar orbit, the system is said to have about 20 days of useful life. Reported to be operational, although government officials refuse to admit its existence. Early name was Sentry, Pied Piper. See also PEGASUS.

SAMOS I -- U.S. two-stage satellite launched by ATLAS-AGENA. See SAMOS.

SAMOS II (1961 ALPHA) -- U.S. satellite used to test feasibility of earth, space, and atmosphere observations from satellites. See SAMOS.

SAMOS III - U.S. satellite launched by ATLAS-AGENA. Launch vehicle exploded on launch pad. See SAMOS.

SAMPAN -- Basilan Strait, Philippine Islands. WW-II.

SAMPSON -- Allied code name for blind GEE bombing attack. WW-II.

SAMS -- Acronym for Satellite Automonitor System.

SAN ANTONIO I -- First B-29 bomber raid on Tokyo, Japan, from Isley Field, Saipan, Marianas; specific target was Nakajima aircraft engine plant. 24 November 1944, WW-II.

SAN ANTONIO II -- Second B-29 bomber raid on Tokyo, Japan, from Saipan, Marianas, with specific target, Nakajima aircraft engine plant. 27 November 1944, WW-II.

SAN CIRIACO -- Hurricane which struck Puerto Rico, 8 August 1899. Named after saint's day on which it occurred. Caused more than 3000 deaths and 20 million dollars damage.

SAN FELIPE (THE FIRST) -- Hurricane which struck Puerto Rico, 13 September 1876. Named after saint's day on which it occurred.

SAN FELIPE (THE SECOND) -- Hurricane which struck Puerto Rico, 13 September 1928. Named after saint's day on which it occurred. Caused 300 deaths and 50 million dollars damage. Same hurricane moved into Florida and caused 1836 deaths and 25 million dollars damage.

SAN NARCISO -- Hurricane which struck Puerto Rico on 29 October 1867. Named after saint's day on which it occurred.

SANATOGEN -- Long Island, New Guinea. WW-II.

SANATOGEN MISSION -- Code name for landing by U.S. Army 2nd Engineer Special Brigade on Long Island, west of New Britain. 26 December 1943, WW-II.

SANCHO -- Simiutak, Greenland. WW-II.

SANCY -- Version of French Wassmer Super IV. See PARIOU.

SANDBAG -- Djailolo Airdrome, New Guinea. WW-II.

SANDBORN -- Sakar Island, New Britain. WW-II.

SANDRA -- Name reserved by meteorologists for tropical cyclone in North Atlantic area.

SANDRINGHAM -- Civilian conversion of the World War II Short Sunderland flying boat.

SANDSTONE -- U.S. nuclear weapons test at Eniwetok Proving Ground, Marshall Islands. Spring 1948.

SANDTRAP -- Montagu Harbor, New Britain. WW-II.

SANDWAY -- Alghero, Sicily. WW-II.

SANDWICH -- Proposed protective invasion by British of southern Thailand against Japanese. 11 August 1941, WW-II.

SANDY OPERATION -- U.S. Navy code name for the launching of a V-2 at sea from the deck of the aircraft carrier, USS Midway. Test was conducted on 6 September 1947.

SANDY SPOT -- U.S. Air Force high-altitude air refueling area over Arkansas-Missouri-Illinois-Kentucky.

SANITAIRE -- Liore-et-Olivier LeO-21 French twin-engine biplane modified as an ambulance aircraft in 1932-33.

SANTA ANA -- Hurricane which struck Puerto Rico 26 July 1825, causing 374 deaths and severe damage. Named after saint's day on which it occurred.

SANTA MARIA -- Macchi-built Lockheed LASA-60, produced in Italy. Another version is built in Mexico. Flew in 1959.

SAPHIRE -- Operable Swiss pool nuclear reactor at Wurenlingen, Switzerland.

SAPLING -- Name for peacetime military exercise.

SAPO -- Isle of Pines, Cuba. WW-II.

SAPPHIRE -- (1) French space research and intermediate range ballistic missile development test vehicle, the second in the precious stone series. It is designed to determine the characteristics and technology necessary for both a space launch vehicle and a military weapons system. A liquid propellant first stage is used with a solid second stage and a dummy third stage. Inertially guided, the vehicle is to be tested during 1963.

(2) Kadai Island, New Guinea. WW-II.

SAPSUCKER -- Kobe, Japan. WW-II.

SARAH -- (1) U.S. Air Force acronym for Search And Rescue And Homing.

(2) An early name for the Sidewinder I-C. See SIDEWINDER.

(3) Buariki Island, Gilbert Islands. WW-II.

(4) Typhoon. 21 March - 4 April 1956. Formed near equator in Caroline Islands, the Pacific. Moved west-northwestward over Philippine Sea and dissipated east of Philippines.

(5) Typhoon. 12–18 September 1959. Developed near Guam. Moved northwest-ward through Philippine Sea, turned northward through East China Sea, passed near Pusan, Korea, across Sea of Japan to Hokkaido. Caused over 600 deaths and over 100 million dollars damage, mostly in Korea.

(6) Typhoon. 15–23 August 1962. Formed about 300 miles east of Taiwan. Moved northward into East China Sea, then turned northeastward into Japan.

(7) Name also applied to tropical cyclones in western North Pacific which occurred prior to (3) through (5) above.

SAROTOGEN -- Long Island, New Guinea. WW-II.

SARTORIAL -- Lingayan Gulf, Philippine Islands. WW-II.

SASSAFRAS -- Walanguo Island, New Britain. WW-II.

SATAN -- (1) Acronym for Satellite Active Nullifier, a proposal for an anti-satellite weapon which would be put into orbit with missiles or some other kill mechanism to destroy hostile satellites. Reportedly under study by the Defense Department.

(2) Gongo, New Britain. WW-II.

SATANIC -- Luzon, Philippine Islands. WW-II.

SATIN -- (1) Acronym for SAGE Air Traffic Integration.

(2) An uncommon name for the Air Force's SAINT.

(3) Plan for U.S. II Corps operation against Sfax, Tunisia. Canceled. January 1943, WW-II.

SATINWOOD -- Allied operations to occupy remaining enemy held areas in the Southwest Pacific area upon collapse or surrender of Japan. WW-II.

SATURN -- (1) National Aeronautics and Space Administration launch vehicle developing 1.5 million-pound thrust in its first stage, and 90,000-pound thrust in the second. It will be capable of putting 20,000 pounds in a 345-mile orbit. Eight H-1, kerosene/liquid oxygen engines are clustered in the first stage and six RL-10A3 engines are used in the second. Three successful tests of the first stage have been conducted. To be operational in 1964. Another version, Saturn C-1B, using a single J-2 engine in the second stage, is also being developed. Will be used in the APOLLO program and in unmanned planetary probes.

(2) Paris, France. WW-II.

(3) Vavosi, New Britain. WW-II.

(4) British plan to reduce amount of aid to Turkey as specified in HARDIHOOD AGREEMENT. December 1943, WW-II.

SATURN, ADVANCED -- Largest U.S. space launch vehicle under development by National Aeronautics and Space Administration for the APOLLO program. First stage, 5 RP1/LOX F-1 engines clustered to develop 7.5 million-pound thrust; second stage, 5 liquid hydrogen/LOX J-2 engines developing million-pound thrust; and third stage, 1 J-2 engine developing 200,000-pound thrust. Capable of placing 200,000 pounds in earth orbit, 85,000 pounds to escape and 60,000 pounds to planetary missions. First flight scheduled for 1965.

SATURN C-1 -- National Aeronautics and Space Administration two-stage space booster, largest developed by U.S. First flight 27 October 1961 from Cape Canaveral. Will be used to orbit three-man APOLLO spacecraft.

SATURN - C-1B -- U.S. million-pound thrust launch vehicle. See also SATURN.

SAUCER -- Fuiloro, Timor, Netherlands East Indies. WW-II.

SAUCY -- Limited Allied offensive to reopen land route from Burma to China. Modified version of ANAKIM, adopted at TRIDENT Conference. 1943, WW-II.

SAVAGE -- North American AJ attack aircraft for the U.S. Navy, 1946 to 1951.

SAVORY -- Vigan, Philippine Islands. WW-II.

SAVOY -- Serr Island, New Britain. WW-II.

SAVOYARD -- Code name for Albania. WW-II.

SAVVY -- Allied exercise, held in England, to determine usefulness of assault fire by seaborne army artillery. 12 February 1944, WW-II.

SAWDUST -- Catania, Sicily. WW-II.

SAXOPHONE -- (1) Leghorn, Italy. WW-II.

(2) Lolatola, New Britain. WW-II.

SAXTON AND COMPANY -- Fictitious fish cannery construction company, in whose name equipment and supplies were purchased and personnel hired for building air base at Cold Bay, Alaska, early 1942. Directed by U.S. Alaska Defense Command through dummy CONSOLIDATED PACKING COMPANY. WW-II.

SCALDED-CAT RAID -- Nickname for air raid by heckler aircraft of North Korean Peoples Army. Korean Conflict.

SCALE SERGEANT -- See RECRUIT

SCALLYWAG -- Code name for Egypt. WW-II.

SCALPER -- Anwek River, New Britain. WW-II.

SCAMP GOER -- U.S. Army five-ton sectionalized cargo truck.

SCAMPER -- Garua Island, New Britain. WW-II.

SCANDIA -- Swedish SAAB-90 twin-engine transport plane.

SCANTLING -- Gulf of Naples, Italy. WW-II.

SCAPA -- Supermarine 1933 development of the Southampton flying boat. See SOUTHAMPTON.

SCAPEGRACE -- Jaluit Island, Marshall Islands. WW-II.

SCAR -- U.S. Navy sub-caliber aircraft rocket for training pilots in rocket-firing techniques. Resembling the 3.5-inch and 5-inch folding fin aircraft rockets, it used a solid propellant 2.25-inch motor to approximate the characteristics of the larger rockets. A World War II development.

SCARAMOUCH -- Port Moresby, New Guinea. WW-II.

SCARECROW -- North Borneo, Netherlands East Indies. WW-II.

SCATTERBRAIN -- Allied operations in the Arafura Sea, Australia. WW-II.

SCATTERED TREES RIDGE -- Military name for topographic feature on Luzon, Philippines. 1945, WW-II.

SCATTERING -- Okinawa, Ryukyu Island, Japan. WW-II.

SCAVENGER -- U.S. Navy operation to attack Japanese aircraft, shipping, and shore installations in Bonin Islands and Iwo Jima, as adjunct of Marianas campaign. August 1944, WW-II.

SCHELDT FORTRESS FOUTH -- Name used by Germans for Breskens Pocket during Operation SWITCHBACK. Fall 1944, WW-II.

SCHILL LINE -- Second defense belt of German WESTWALL. WW-II.

SCHLEMIEL -- Gasma, New Britain. WW-II.

SCHMETTERLING -- (English translation: Butterfly) German surface-to-air missile with an effective range of 10 miles up to altitudes of six-seven miles. Boosted by two solid propellant motors and sustained by liquid hypergolic fuels, the missile was radio-command guided. Although some 60 test firings were conducted, missile never became operational. Development began in 1941 and ended in 1945. Officially known as the Hs 117.

SCHOOLBOY -- Lae, New Guinea. WW-II.

SCHOOLGIRL -- Palau Islands. WW-II.

SCHULTZ, OPERATION -- Canadian raid on village across Maas River, near 's-Hertogenbosch, Netherlands, to capture German prisoners for intelligence purposes. 17 January 1945, WW-II.

SCHÜ-MINE 42 -- German anti-personnel mine. See also S MINE. WW-II.

SCHWALBE -- (English translation: Swallow) Messerschmitt Me-262, world's first jet fighter. First flew in 1942. Hitler insisted it be developed into a bomber, thus slowing production. Bomber version: STURMVOGEL (Stormbird).

SCHWARZ -- German Operational plan for the capture of the Italian Fleet and military occupation of Italy by German Army after Italian armistice with Allies. September 1943, WW-II.

SCIMITAR -- Large swept-wing fighter plane developed by Vickers of Great Britain in 1956, and still operational.

SCIPIO -- (1) Short Aircraft of British four-engine flying boat of early 1930's.

(2) British Eighth Army attack on German-held Chott Position, southern Tunisia, at Akarit wadi. Began 6 April 1943, WW-II.

(3) See MENACE

SCOOP -- U.S. Air Force acronym for Scientific Computation Of Optimum Procurement.

SCOOTER -- (1) Baghdad, Iraq. WW-II.

(2) U.S. high-explosive project intended to prepare for peaceful nuclear excavations. Million tons of TNT buried at depth of 125 feet in desert alluvium. Resulted in crate, 307 feet in diameter and 75 feet deep. Conducted by Lawrence Radiation Laboratory, Livermore, California. Fall 1960.

SCORCHER -- Occupation and evacuation of Crete by British. May-June 1941, WW-II.

SCORE, PROJECT -- Acronym for Signal, Communications, Orbit, Relay Experiment. U.S. Air Force project under auspices of Advanced Research Projects Agency. Designed to develop capability for recording messages by satellite, and for subsequent readout. Launched with ATLAS, 18 December 1958. Marked first time human voice (President Dwight D. Eisenhower's) was beamed from outer space. See also ATLAS-SCORE, ATLAS-BOOSTER.

SCORPION -- (1) Allied attachment for front of tanks, consisting of flailing chains on revolving drums to detonate enemy mines. WW-II.

(2) Northrop F-89 twin-jet all-weather interceptor; first contracted for by U.S. Army Air Forces in 1946. First flew in 1948.

SCOUT -- (1) Heinrich-designed biplane built by Victor and delivered to the U.S. Air Service in November 1917.

(2) Civil version of the Westland P.531-2 light helicopter. First flew in 1958 as the Saunders-Roe P.531. Military version is the Wasp.

(3) Pigeon Fraser. See ALBREE MONOPLANE.

(4) National Aeronautics and Space Administration four-stage, solid propellant launch vehicle designed to launch space probes and small scientific satellites. First stage, called ALGOL, develops 103,000-pound thrust; second stage, CASTOR, develops 62,000-pound thrust; third stage, ANTARES, develops 13,600-pound thrust, and the fourth, ALTAIR, develops 2800-pound thrust. Capable of placing 200 pounds in a 300-mile orbit. Flight tests completed in 1961. See also BLUE SCOUT and SEA SCOUT.

SCRAM -- Handing over of German warships to Russians. December 1945-June 1946, WW-II.

SCREAMING EAGLES -- Nickname for U.S. 101st Airborne Division; taken from design on shoulder patch. Famous for its resistance to Germans when besieged in Bastogne, Belgium, in December 1944, WW-II.

SCREECH OWL II -- German Do.17Z aircraft. See KAUZ II.

SCREWDRIVER I -- Proposed Allied landings on Arakan coast, Burma. 12 March 1944, WW-II.

SCREWDRIVER II -- British landing on Arakan Coast, Burma. 14 March 1944, WW-II.

SCRICCIOLO -- Aviamilano P.19 two-seat trainer. First flew 1959. In use by Italian flying clubs.

SCRIPT -- Acronym for Scientific and Commercial Subroutine Interpreter and Program Translator.

SCROUNGER -- Rekata Bay, Santa Isabel Islands. WW-II.

SCULPTOR -- Advanced Research Projects Agency program to study optimum payload techniques for ballistic missiles. Studies are also conducted on space payload integration.

SCYLLA -- Landplane version of Short Aircraft flying boat. See SCIPIO.

SCYLLA I -- U.S. thermonuclear device which uses magnetically-driven shock waves to raise plasma temperatures. Made by Los Alamos Scientific Laboratory, New Mexico. First demonstrated, Geneva, Switzerland, 1958.

SCYLLA II -- U.S. thermonclear device which uses magnetically-driven shock waves to raise plasma temperatures and then subjects plasma to a second compression designed ultimately to reach 200,000 gauss. Made by Los Alamos Scientific Laboratory, New Mexico. Completed 1959.

SEA BIRD -- Single-engine amphibian flying boat built of stainless-steel by Fleetwings Incorporated of Pennsylvania, in 1939.

SEA DEVON -- See DEVON and DOVE

SEA FURY -- British Hawker fighter-bomber built by Boulton-Paul during World War II; used by Fleet Air Arm until 1954. See FURY.

SEA GLADIATOR -- British Gloster shipboard version of the GLADIATOR aircraft.

SEA GULL -- (1) Curtiss-Wright SO3C light observation aircraft used by U.S. Navy during World War II. Great Britain also used it as the Seamew.

    (2) German Focke-Wulf A-38 aircraft. See MOWE.

    (3) Name used by Russian cosmonaut Lieutenant Valentina Vladimirovna Chereshkova during her orbital flight in VOSTOK VI. 16-19 June 1963.

SEA GULL V -- Single-engine amphibian developed in Great Britain in 1932-33 by Supermarine Aviation Works Limited.

SEA HAWK -- (1) Curtiss Export Hawk, a version of the F11C Goshawk, fitted as a seaplane and supplied to various foreign governments in 1933. Also see GOSHAWK.

    (2) Hawker shipboard jet fighter. First flown in 1948. Used by Great Britain's Fleet Air Arm until 1960.

SEA HORNET -- 1945 shipboard version of the DeHavilland D.H.103. See HORNET.

SEA HORSE -- (1) U.S. Navy-Coast Guard utility helicopter similar to SEABAT and CHOCTAW.

    (2) Group of hills located between two tributaries of Matanikau River on Guadalcanal. Named after resemblance in aerial photographs. January 1943, WW-II.

SEA HURRICANE -- Folding-wing version of the World War II British Hawker HURRICANE.

SEA JUMP -- Name for peacetime military operation.

SEA KING -- U.S. Navy all-weather anti-submarine warfare helicopter.

SEA KNIGHT -- U.S. Navy-Marine Corps medium assault helicopter similar to Army's CHINOOK.

SEA LION -- See SEELOEWE

SEA PRINCE -- Twin-engine light transport used by the Royal Navy for crew training. Other versions are the PEMBROKE, PRINCE, and PRESIDENT.

SEA RANGER -- Boeing flying boat accepted during the early days of World War II by the U.S. Navy, but soon abandoned in favor of other models.

SEA SCAPE -- Name for military operation.

SEA SCOUT -- U.S. Navy proposal for a four-stage solid propellant launch vehicle for satellite payloads up to 300 pounds. It differs from either SCOUT or BLUE SCOUT in that the first two stages are the same as the POLARIS first and second stages. The upper two stages do not differ from the National Aeronautics and Space Administration and Air Force vehicles. Not approved for development because of the critical importance of Polaris in the Nation's defense. Navy is still pushing the idea because it would give them an economical space booster, but more importantly because surface ships could be adapted to launch the Sea Scout, giving the Navy a mobile launch platform for tactical satellite payloads.

SEA SLUG -- British ship-to-air anti-aircraft missile deployed aboard Royal Navy destroyers. Boosted by four solid propellant motors and sustained by a solid engine; has a range of about 15 miles and can reach altitudes of 10 miles. Uses a beam rider guidance system. Became operational in 1958. A more advanced version with greater range and speed, and possibly a nuclear warhead, is being developed.

SEA VENOM -- Shipboard version of the DeHavilland VENOM aircraft. Operational with Australian Navy.

SEA VIXEN -- Twin-jet fighter delivered to the British Fleet Air Arm in 1959 by DeHavilland.

SEA WALL -- U.S. Strategic Army Command peacetime military test.

SEA WATCH -- Name for NATO peacetime military exercise.

SEABAT -- U.S. Navy anti-submarine warfare helicopter similar to SEAHORSE and CHOCTAW.

SEABEE -- (1) Acronym for member of a Construction Battalion (C.B.), U.S. Navy.

(2) Single-engine pusher amphibian by Republic. First flight in 1944. Many still active in U.S. and overseas.

(3) U.S. Navy liquid propelled test vehicle used to determine the techniques of launching such missiles from underwater. First test took place in October 1961, four miles offshore from Point Mugu, California.

SEACAT -- British Navy ship-to-air missile with a range of four miles for short-range defense of surface ships. Deployed aboard cruisers and destroyers, the solid propellant missile replaces the standard 40 mm. anti-aircraft guns. It uses and infrared scanning and radio command guidance system. West Germany, Sweden, Australia, and New Zealand have ordered the missile. Operational in 1960.

SEACOL -- One of two South African columns guarding coastal plain west of Tobruk, Libya, from seaborne or airborne landings. See also STOPCOL. May 1942, WW-II.

SEAFIRE -- British shipboard version of the famous World War II SPITFIRE aircraft.

SEAFOX -- Fairey catapult-launched reconnaissance biplane. In service with British Fleet prior to World War II.

SEAGRAM -- Meibun Island, New Britain. WW-II.

SEAL -- (1) Great Britain's Fleet Air Arm version of the Fairey IIIF. See GORDON.

(2) Madagascar. WW-II.

(3) See SEEHUND

SEALS -- Acronym for Sea, Air, and Land capability. Used by U.S. Navy for their personnel trained in unconventional or guerrilla warfare after World War II.

SEALSKIN -- Haroekoe Airdrome, Ceram Island, Netherlands East Indies. WW-II.

SEAMASTER -- Early jet-age seaplane built by Martin for the U.S. Navy as the P6M.

SEAMEW -- See SEAGULL

SEAMLESS -- Elmore (Ailinglaplap) Island, Marshall Islands. WW-II.

SEARCHLIGHT -- Name for peacetime military project.

SEASHELL -- Montamalua Island, New Britain. WW-II.

SEASLUG I -- British ship-to-air antiaircraft missile which carries high explosive payload. Operational.

SEASLUG II -- British ship-to-air antiaircraft missile. In development.

SEASPRAY -- Name for peacetime military exercise.

SEASPRITE -- Kaman turbine-powered helicopter in production for the U.S. Navy. First flight in 1959.

SEA STAR -- Navy version of the U.S. Air Force T-33 jet trainer. See also TEE BIRD.

SEATO -- Acronym for Southeast Asia Treaty Organization.

SEATTLE -- One of the Douglas World Cruisers of 1924. This plane did not complete the trip--crashing into an Alaskan mountain side at start of trip. See also WORLD CRUISER.

SEAWASP -- Cold Bay, Alaska. WW-II.

SECLUSION -- Bonin Islands. WW-II.

SECOR -- Acronym for Sequential Collation Of Range, a U.S. Army program to use a small radio-ranging device in a satellite, tying the existing datum planes of the world together and thereby reducing the position error between two points to about 100 feet in a 1000 miles. One of the three experiments in the ANNA satellite. Also flown separately on the unsuccessful Composite I payload. Program expected to continue for three to five years.

SEDIMENT -- Tanaga Island, New Britain. WW-II.

SEEHUND -- (1) (English translation: Seal) German two-man midget submarine. First used in January 1945, WW-II.

(2) German air-to-surface glide bomb without propulsion. Weighing 2000 pounds with a 1000-pound payload, the bomb was flight stabilized and equipped with a homing device. WW-II.

SEELOEWE -- (English translation: Sea Lion) Code name for German plan to invade the United Kingdom after fall of France. Not carried out. 1940-41, WW-II.

SEESAW -- An automatic coding system used in data processing.

SEEWOLF -- Group of six German 740-ton snorkel U-boats dispatched in March 1945 to harass shipping on U.S. East Coast; mission broken up by U.S. TEARDROP operation. WW-II.

SEIZURE -- Bikini Atoll, Marshall Islands. WW-II.

SELFRIDGE -- Anglo-American bombing operation against ball bearing factories at Schweinfurt, Germany. Partially carried out on 17 August 1943, WW-II.

SELMA -- Name reserved by meteorologists for tropical cyclone in eastern North Pacific.

SEMAPHORE HILL -- Military name for topographic feature on Italian Pantelleria Island where white flag was flown during Allied landing. June 1943, WW-II.

SEMICIRCLE -- Samate, New Guinea. WW-II.

SEMICONIC -- Izuki (Izaku), Japan. WW-II.

SEMINOLE -- Beech Model 50. First flew in 1958. In use by U.S. Army as the L-23. Now designated U-8.

SEMOLINA -- Rome, Italy. WW-II.

SENECA -- (1) Cessna helicopter. See SKYHOOK.

(2) Tamgass Harbor, Alaska. WW-II.

SENECA SPEAR -- Name for U.S. peacetime military exercise at Camp Drum, New York, 1962.

SENGER RIEGEL -- See ADOLF HITLER LINE

SENGER SWITCHLINE -- See ADOLF HITLER LINE

SENIOR PACEMAKER -- Bellanca cabin monoplane built in the U.S. in the early 1930's. Also see SKYROCKET SENIOR.

SENTINEL -- Stinson L-5 liaison aircraft first flown in 1942. Also called Flying Jeep.

SENTRY -- Early name for SAMOS.

SEOUL CITY SUE -- Nickname for North Korean woman radio propagandist broadcasting to U.N. troops in Korea. First heard in August 1950.

SEPARATE -- Arno Atoll, Marshall Islands. WW-II.

SERENE -- Lifumatola Island, Netherlands East Indies. WW-II.

SERF -- Acronym for Sandia Engineering Reactor Facility at Sandia Base, New Mexico.

SERGEANT -- U.S. Army surface-to-surface tactical ballistic missile with a range of 75 nautical miles for support of Field Army Corps. The inertially guided solid propellant missile is a highly mobile, air-transportable system which carries a nuclear warhead. Just becoming operational; to be deployed to Europe early in 1963. See also CORPORAL.

SERGEANT-DELTA -- National Aeronautics and Space Administration two-stage solid propellant test vehicle used to lift a 100-foot diameter inflatable sphere to suborbital speeds of about 7000 miles per hour and an altitude of 200-250 miles. Sphere is then ejected and inflated to check out the techniques to be used in the ECHO passive communications satellite program. Four tests were successfully conducted from Wallops Island, Virginia, between 28 October 1959 and 1 April 1960.

SERIAL 1-4 -- Four serials or echelons of U.S.-Australian force which were to proceed in stages in planned occupation of Buna, New Guinea, PROVIDENCE operation, to set up air field; forestalled by Japanese occupation of Buna. Summer 1942, WW-II.

SERRATE -- Allied radar device enabling fighters to home on radar transmission of enemy aircraft. WW-II.

SERT -- National Aeronautics and Space Administration satellite program in which two ion engines will be put in orbit to test their effectiveness. SCOUT booster will be used. The two electrical propulsion engines will be mounted so that their thrust will cause the satellite to spin on its axis in orbit. Scheduled for launch in 1963.

SESAME -- Acronym for Service, Sort and Merge, a data processing term.

SESSION -- Name for peacetime military exercise.

SET -- Acronym for Sensory Evaluation Test program to determine the effectiveness of various surveillance and combat intelligence gathering sensors at supersonic speeds. Used the Q-5 drone version of the X-7. Results encouraged the U.S. Army to go ahead with the AN/USD-5 drone. Latter has since been cancelled because of mounting costs.

SETTING SUN -- Early U.S. plan to bomb Japan by B-29 aircraft flying from chain of airfields along 400-mile axis north and south of Changsha, China, with logistical support coming from India. See also DRAKE. Fall 1944, WW-II.

7, PROJECT -- Movement by U.S. Air Transport Command of personnel, aircraft and materiel from Florida to India as part of operation to increase supply tonnage flown over the Hump to China. Summer 1943, WW-II.

SEVENTEEN, MISSION -- U.S. Air Transport Command transportation of President Roosevelt and American delegation to and from Yalta conference (ARGONAUT). Early 1945, WW-II.

75, MISSION -- U.S. Air Transport Command's part of BAKER-SIXTY Plan; involved assemblying of over 200 C-54 transport aircraft at Kadena Airfield, Okinawa, and their use in transporting military forces to Atsugi Airport near Tokyo, Japan, after Japanese surrender. August-September 1945, WW-II.

SEVERITY -- Takao, Japan. WW-II.

SEXTANT -- International conference at Cairo, Egypt, attended by President Roosevelt, Prime Minister Churchill, and Generalissimo Chiang Kai-shek. Held before and after EUREKA Conference at Teheran, Iran. 22-26 November and 2-7 December 1943, WW-II.

SEXTON -- Nickname for Canadian self-propelled weapon consisting of 25-pounder mounted on RAM Tank chassis. WW-II.

SFAZI CODE -- International code used to report direction of sferics azimuth in terms of bearings from the observing station.

SFAZU CODE -- International code used to report direction of sferics azimuth for the previous 24 hours in terms of bearings from observing station.

SHACKLETON -- Avro post-World War-II development of the Lancaster/Lincoln aircraft. Used by Royal Air Force Coastal Command for reconnaissance duties.

SHADOW 82 -- Plan for U.S. Army Air Forces to understudy and eventually to relieve British Royal Air Force fighter units in Northern Ireland. Early WW-II.

SHAGGY -- Cape Cretin, New Guinea. WW-II.

SHAGGY RIDGE -- Military name for topographic feature south of Astrolabe Bay in northeastern New Guinea. Scene of fighting between Australians and Japanese. January 1944, WW-II.

SHAKEDOWN -- Arawe Passage, New Britain. WW-II.

SHAKER -- Allied code name for method of illuminating and marking a target with the aid of GEE equipped aircraft. WW-II.

SHAKO -- (1) Banda Sea, Netherlands East Indies. WW-II.

(2) Macclesfield Bank, South China Sea. WW-II.

SHAMBLES -- Milli Island, Marshall Islands. WW-II.

SHAMPOO -- Wakis, New Britain. WW-II.

SHAMROCK -- Dagupan, Philippine Islands. WW-II.

SHARECROPPER -- Willaumez Peninsula, New Britain. WW-II.

SHAREPUSHER -- Kabarei Bay, New Guinea. WW-II.

SHARK -- (1) U.S. Army II Corps force in the invasion of Sicily. 1943, WW-II.

(2) One of four flights in U.S. KIT PROJECT to send A-20 aircraft from Florida to Oran, Algeria, for use in North African campaign. November 1942, WW-II.

SHARON -- Name reserved by meteorologists for tropical cyclone in eastern North Pacific.

SHARP EDGE -- Joint U.S. Army-Navy and Korean Air Force peacetime amphibious landing exercise in South Korea, 1961.

SHARPENER -- Code name for small advance command post of Supreme Headquarters, Allied Expeditionary Force (SHAEF) at Portsmouth, England, opened early May 1944; later enlarged and called SHIPMATE. WW-II.

SHAWNEE -- U.S. Army medium transport helicopter.

SHEEP DOGS -- U.S. Navy combat air patrol aircraft which flew over picket destroyers, TOM CATS, in order to weed out and destroy Japanese KAMIKAZE aircraft which were apt to joint American aircraft formations returning from missions in order to attack their carriers. Name came from idea of separating sheep from goats. See also DELOUSING. WW-II.

SHELLBURST -- Code name for small advance headquarters of Supreme Headquarters, Allied Expeditionary Force (SHAEF) opened in August 1944 near Tournières, France. WW-II.

SHELLPROOF -- Yamakawa (Zamakawa), Japan. WW-II.

SHENANDOAH -- U.S. Navy rigid airship lost in a line squall over Ohio in September 1925 after two years of service.

SHEPHERD -- (1) Cape Pedder, New Britain. WW-II.

(2) Advanced Research Projects Agency-U.S. Air Force program to improve the capabilities of the U.S. space tracking system. Of particular emphasis is the updating of SPADATS to detect, track, and display information on dark or silent satellites. Improvements are introduced progressively, rather than developing a completely new system.

SHERIDAN -- U.S. Army-Marine Corps armored reconnaissance airborne assault vehicle.

SHERRY -- (1) Wabana Point, Woodlark Island. WW-II.

(2) Name reserved by meteorologists for tropical cyclone in North Atlantic area.

SHERWOOD -- U.S. long-range research program to develop controlled release of energy by atomic fusion. Major efforts carried out at Atomic Energy Commission laboratories operated by University of California at Los Alamos, New Mexico, and Livermore, California; and at Princeton University, New Jersey.

SHIDEN -- (English translation: Violet Lightning) Japanese World War II Kawanishi N1K1 fighter plane. See GEORGE.

SHILLELAGH -- U.S. Army surface-to-surface missile for close support of combat troops against armor and field fortifications. Using a command guidance system and a solid propellant motor, the missile is to be mounted on the M-60 main battle tank. Under development, the system should be operational in 1964 or 1965.

SHINDEN -- (English translation: Magnificent Lightning) One of the very few aircraft of "canard" (tail-first) design to be developed during World War II. The Japanese Kyushu J7W1 first flew in 1945.

SHINGLE -- Allied amphibious operations at Anzio, Italy, planned as end run around right flank of German WINTER and GUSTAV LINES and advance to Rome. Began 22 January 1944, WW-II.

SHINPLASTER -- Makurazaki, Japan. WW-II.

SHIP HILL -- Military name for topographic feature near Giarabub, eastern Libya. 1940-41, WW-II.

SHIPMATE -- Code name for enlarged SHAEF forward headquarters near Portsmouth, England; replaced SHARPENER. Opened 1 July 1944, WW-II.

SHIRLEY -- (1) Typhoon. 10-18 April 1957. Formed near Koror, western Caroline Islands. Moved northwestward across Philippine Sea and dissipated near northern Luzon.

(2) Typhoon. 29 July - 6 August 1960. Formed near Yap Island. Moved northwestward across Philippine Sea, northern Taiwan, and China coast. Turned northeastward over Yellow Sea and then back into mainland. Killed 104 people and caused considerable damage on Taiwan.

(3) Name also applied to tropical cyclones in western North Pacific which occurred prior to (1) and (2) above.

SHIRT -- Hong Kong, China. WW-II.

SHO GO -- See SHO OPERATIONS

SHO ICHI GO -- See SHO I

SHO OPERATIONS -- (English translation: Victory Operations) Japanese plans for great counterattack by sea, land, and air against Allied forces attempting to establish themselves within her inner western Pacific defense zone, the area Philippines-Formosa-Ryukus-Japan-Kuriles. See individual plans SHO I-IV. 1944, WW-II.

SHO I -- Japanese plan for defense of Philippines. Also called SHO ICHI GO. 1944, WW-II.

SHO II -- Japanese plan for defense of Formosa, Nansei Shoto, and south Kyushu. 1944, WW-II.

SHO III -- Japanese plan for defense of Kyushu-Shikoku-Honshu. 1944, WW-II.

SHO IV -- Japanese plan for defense of Hokkaido. 1944, WW-II.

SHOESTRING, OPERATION -- Nickname given by U.S. sailors in South Pacific to Operation WATCHTOWER, landing on Tulagi and Guadalcanal, because time was short for planning it and materiel was sparse. July-August 1942, WW-II.

SHOESTRING RIDGE -- Military name for topographic feature on Leyte, Philippine Islands. November 1944, WW-II.

SHOKI -- (English translation: Demon) Nakajima KI.44 World War II Japanese fighter plane. See TOJO.

SHOOTING GALLERY -- Military name for hill area behind Wonsan, North Korea. Korean Conflict.

SHOOTING STAR -- Second U.S. jet aircraft, and first in combat, the U.S. Army Air Forces P-80 was a Lockheed Model L-14 designed around a British Goblin engine and first flew 8 January 1944.

SHORAN -- Radar beacon system operating on transponder-responder principle. Used for photomapping, reconnaissance, and geodetic survey.

SHOREHAM -- Sekul, New Britain. WW-II.

SHORTNIN' BREAD -- Name for peacetime military project involving a supply lift.

SHORTSTOP -- Habbaniya, Iraq. WW-II.

SHOT PUT -- National Aeronautics and Space Administration project in which a 100-foot mylar inflatable balloon is launched to suborbital speeds, ejected and inflated. The experiment's purpose is to check out the techniques of ejecting and inflating passive communications satellites. Four launches were made from Wallops Station, Virginia, during 1959-60. All were successful. See also ECHO.

SHOVELNOSE -- Taveliaio, New Britain. WW-II.

SHOW HORSE DIVISION -- Nickname for U.S. 8th Armored Division. Also called IRON SNAKE.

SHOWDOWN, OPERATION -- U.S. IX Corps limited-objective attack to capture TRIANGLE HILL and SNIPER RIDGE, northeast of Kumhwa, Korea. Began October 1952, Korean Conflict.

SHOW-OFF -- Name for peacetime military exercise.

SHRIKE -- (1) U.S. Army Air Corps A-8 to -12 attack monoplane delivered by Curtiss in 1932.

(2) U.S. Navy air-to-surface anti-radar missile for fleet carrier and attack aircraft. The solid propellant missile formerly known as Arm, homes on electromagnetic radiations from the ground. No other details are available on the system. Naval aircraft are to be equipped with the missile during fiscal year 1963.

SHRIMP -- (1) Saigon, Cochin-China. WW-II.

(2) U.S. Air Force study of small mobile intercontinental ballistic missiles that would be able to be deployed on trucks, trains, ships, barges, or just planted until ready for use. The main idea is a reduction in weight through the use of improved propellants and lighter materials without a reduction in range, payload or accuracy. No such studies have borne fruit as yet, although medium range ballistic missiles might be applied to this class.

SHRINE HILL -- Military name for topographic feature on western Angaur Island, Palau Group. Fall 1944, WW-II.

SHTURMOVIK -- Russian World War II IL-2 aircraft. See STORMOVIK.

SHUSUI -- (English translation: Rigorous Sword) World War II Japanese Mitsubishi J8M1 rocket interceptor aircraft. First, and last, flight 7 July 1945. Crashed after takeoff. Trainer version, a wooden glider, flew in 1944 as the Akigusa.

SIAM -- Acronym for Signal Information And Monitoring service; American monitoring of friendly radio nets to provide commanders with immediate and accurate information upon progress of their own troops. WW-II.

SIBERIA -- Military name for hill outpost in Korea. Summer 1952, Korean Conflict.

SICKLE -- Build-up of U.S. Eighth Air Force in United Kingdom for bomber offensive against Germany. Separate from ground and service force build-up, known as BOLERO. WW-II.

SICKLE, OPERATION -- Landing of Allied troops at small ports of Molde and Aandalsnes on Romsdal Fiord, Norway, and their subsequent evacuation. Late April-early May 1940, WW-II.

SIDCOT SUIT -- British one-piece flying suit, now outmoded, made of padded fabric; used in unheated aircraft. Named for its inventor, Sidney Cotton.

SIDELINE -- Oroport, New Britain. WW-II.

SIDESTRAND III -- Twin-engine biplane bomber of 1932 made by Great Britain's Boulton-Paul Limited.

SIDEWINDER -- U.S. Navy-Air Force air-to-air infrared homing missile in use by carrier-based aircraft, Air Force Century series fighters, NATO and Nationalist Chinese forces. With a range of 6-8 miles, the solid propellant missile can operate at altitudes up to 50,000 feet. The more advanced (I-C) model has switchable infrared and radar homing warheads. Operational since 1956, the missile was successfully used by the Nationalist Chinese during the 1958 Quemoy crisis. Early name of I-C was Sarah. See also DIAMONDBACK.

SIDNEY -- Binoinano Village, Gilbert Islands. WW-II.

SIEGFRIED LINE -- See WESTWALL

SIEGFRIED SWITCH -- See ORSCHOLZ SWITCH LINE

SIERRA -- Code word for letter "S" in a phonetic alphabet, used to avoid possibility of a misunderstanding in transmitting messages. See also SUGAR.

SIESTA -- Projected operation to clear Germans from the "island" between Waal and Neder Rijn Rivers, Netherlands, eastward to Pannerdensch Canal. Carried out as Operation DESTROYER. November 1944, WW-II.

SIGHT-SEEING SIXTH -- Nickname for U.S. 6th Infantry Division. So named for many engagements and long marches in France during World War One.

SIGMA -- Surinam, Netherlands East Indies. WW-II.

SIGMA and PI -- Two Japanese sounding rockets developed for the country's participation in the International Geophysical Year. Both were designed to be launched from balloons at altitudes of 12.5 and 18.6 miles, respectively. Both were solid-propelled and were used primarily for vehicle performance and cosmic ray studies. Payload of Sigma was 9 pounds and of Pi 6.6 pounds. Preliminary flight testing was conducted in September 1956.

SIGMA 7 -- Name selected by U.S. Commander Walter M. Schirra Jr. for the MERCURY capsule in which he achieved six orbits, 3 October 1962.

SIGNAL HILL -- Allied military name for topographic feature near Balikpapan, Netherlands Borneo. July 1945, WW-II.

SILAS -- Baretoa Village, Gilbert Islands. WW-II.

SILBERFUCHS -- Operations of German Army of Norway and attached Finnish units out of northern Finland. 1941, WW-II.

SILENCER -- Polillo Island, Philippine Islands. WW-II.

SILICON -- Aswan, Egypt. WW-II.

SILK HAT, OPERATION -- Military aviation show conducted by U.S. Air Force for President John F. Kennedy. Spring 1962.

SILVAIRE -- Luscombe single-engine cabin monoplane built in New Jersey in the 1930's.

SILVER -- Code name for Puerto Rico. WW-II.

SILVER CHARGER -- North American XP-86 aircraft ordered by the U.S. Army Air Forces in May 1945 at which time the design did not include swept-wings. However, by the time of the first flight, 1 October 1947, a swept-wing had been developed. See SABRE.

SILVER FOX -- Name for Royal Canadian Air Force Squadron Number 441.

SILVER SIXTY -- Rhodes Berry conversion of the popular Douglas B-26 aircraft into an executive transport.

SILVER STAR -- T-33 in Royal Canadian Air Force service.

SILVERSAND -- Mindanao Island, Philippine Islands. WW-II.

SILVERSTICK -- Corsica. WW-II.

SILVERTOWN -- Duaga Harbor, New Britain. WW-II.

SILVERWARE -- Mindanao Island, Philippine Islands. WW-II.

SIMLA -- Code name for Canadian 1st Armoured Brigade, used in deception operation PENKNIFE, during movement of Canadian troops from Italy to northwestern Europe. February-March 1945, WW-II.

SIMMER -- Special training exercises for Allied JUBILEE raid on Dieppe, France. Summer 1942, WW-II.

SIMONE -- Tropical storm. 1-2 November 1961. Formed off west coast of Guatemala. Moved toward the northwest at first, then northward into Mexico near Salina Cruz.

SIMPLE -- An automatic coding system used in data processing.

SINGAPORE I -- Twin-engine flying boat produced by Great Britain's Short Aircraft in 1926.

SINGAPORE II -- Short Aircraft 1933 four-engine development of the -I, with engines arranged in two tandem pairs.

SINGAPORE III -- Four-engine biplane developed by Short Aircraft in Great Britain in the mid-1930's.

SINGLETREE -- Ningpo Peninsula, China. WW-II.

SINS -- Self-contained, inertial marine navigation system, especially applicable to submarine use.

SIOUX -- (1) Bell 47G-2, most widely-used commercial helicopter in the world. Army designation H-13H.

    (2) Reportedly, the name of a sounding rocket designed to test recovery techniques. Under development.

SIR -- An automatic coding system used in data processing.

SIRIUS -- First low-wing Lockheed. Designed for Lindbergh and flown in 1929. See also ALTAIR.

SISKINS, THE -- Royal Canadian Air Force aerobatics team formed during the 1930's; flew Armstrong-Whitworth Siskin Fighters.

SITKA -- U.S. Special Service Force which invaded small islands of Levant and Port Cros to secure left flank of assault area in DRAGOON invasion of southern France. 15 August 1944, WW-II.

SITUATION INNOCUOUS -- Code word, broadcast by General Maxwell D. Taylor from Rome to Allied headquarters in North Africa, indicating that situation made it hazardous for U.S. 82nd Airborne Division to land at Rome after armistice was announced. 8 September 1943, WW-II.

SIXTEEN TONS -- Name for largest airlift in U.S. Air Force Reserve history. 1950's.

SKATE -- Rutba, Iraq. WW-II.

SKEET -- U.S. Air Force anti-missile missile study. Not under development. No other details available.

SKEETER -- Saunders-Roe two-seat helicopter. Production terminated in 1960 in Great Britain.

SKEEZIX -- Graah Point, New Britain. WW-II.

SKI JUMP -- Name for peacetime military exercise.

SKI-SITE -- One type of site for launching German V-weapons. So named by Allies because it looked from the air like a pair of skis or hockey sticks. WW-II.

SKIMMER -- Single-engine flying boat originally known as the Colonial C-2. Now built as the Lake Model C-2. First flight in 1960 in latter version.

SKIPPER -- U.S. Navy study of the feasibility of launching an anti-satellite rocket into the path of a hostile satellite. The vehicle would dispense steel pellets or be detonated in the path of the enemy space vehicle. Essentially, the same proposal as EARLY SPRING. Not under development.

SKITTLEALLEY -- Snake Bay, Melville Island, Australia. WW-II.

SKOKIE 1 and 2 -- U.S. rocket-powered parachute test vehicle developed for test-ing recovery systems for missiles and target aircraft. Air-launched from a B-29 at an altitude of six miles, the vehicle would fall to earth with instruments measuring such things as parachute drag and rate of descent, and cameras record-ing the functioning of parachute system. A pointed landing spike was provided to minimize damage of impact. Skokie 2 was propelled to velocities just under Mach 2 by a solid motor and then allowed to begin its descent. A post-World War II development.

SKUA -- Two-seat fleet fighter dive-bomber produced in 1937 by Blackburn Aircraft of England and used in World War II.

SKUNK -- Pidu, New Britain. WW-II.

SKUNKS -- U.S. Navy sea term for suspicious objects on water. WW-II.

SKY AFT -- Name for antiaircraft control center on U.S. battleships.

SKY DROP -- U.S. peacetime military exercise.

SKY RAID -- Name for peacetime military exercise.

SKY SCORPIONS -- Nickname for U.S. Army Air Forces 389th Heavy Bombardment Group. WW-II.

SKY SHIELD II, OPERATION -- Largest air defense maneuver ever held in the Western World. More than 6000 sorties flown by over 2000 aircraft in October 1961.

SKYBOLT -- U.S. Air Force solid propellant air-launched ballistic missile designed to be carried by B-52G & H bombers and the British VULCAN bomber. With a design range of 1000 miles, the stellar-inertially guided missile was expected to extend the life of manned bombers into the 1970's by providing an anti-aircraft suppressive fire weapon. Program was officially cancelled in January 1963 after it had failed in all six of its flight tests. See also HOUND DOG.

SKYCRANE -- Sikorsky S-60 crane helicopter of the 1950's.

SKYDART 1 -- U.S. Air Force expendable rocket-powered target drone designed to serve as a high altitude target for fighter-interceptors, aerial gunnery crews and radar training stations. Capable of reaching altitudes from 8-12 miles, at speeds from 0.8-2 Mach, the drone is air-launched from fighter aircraft. Not under active development, although successfully test-fired in 1959.

SKYFIRE, PROJECT -- A research program conducted by U.S. Forest Service in cooperation with other agencies to protect trees against lightning-caused fires.

SKYHAWK -- (1) Douglas A4D jet attack bomber for U.S. Navy. First flown in 1954.

(2) Deluxe Cessna single-engine monoplane now in production.

SKYHOOK -- (1) Early retardation device for use in airdropping, with principle of operation based upon floating movement of winged maple tree seed. Developed by U.S. Army Quartermaster Corps during World War II.

(2) Cessna development of the Seibel S-4 helicopter which first flew in 1954. Being evaluated by the U.S. Army as the YH-41 Seneca.

(3) Exercise to test H-19C Sikorski light-cargo helicopters in combat during which U.S. Army 6th Transportation Company (Helicopter) used them to supply three front-line infantry regiments for three days. May 1953, Korean Conflict.

(4) U.S. Navy project to launch research balloons.

SKYLANCER -- Douglas F5D which is similar to the U.S. Navy -4D Skyray, but has a thinner wing and longer fuselage. Development of mid-1950's.

SKYLANE -- Cessna 1962 Anniversary Fleet U.S. business plane.

SKYLARK -- (1) Light biplane built in the U.S. by Driggs Aircraft in the late 1920's.

(2) Light cabin monoplane built in 1939 by Pasped Aircraft Corporation of Burbank, California.

(3) Six-passenger Cessna aircraft currently in production in the U.S.

(4) British, single stage, solid propellant sounding rocket designed to carry a 100-150-pound payload of atmospheric instruments to an altitude of 100 miles. First fired in 1957. U.S. Space Agency uses rocket for atmospheric experiments in the southern hemisphere, principally at Australia's Woomera Test Range.

SKYLINE DRIVE -- Military name for ridge road in Luxembourg and Belgium. 1945, WW-II.

SKYLINE RIDGE -- U.S. military name for topographic feature on east coast of Okinawa. 1945, WW-II.

SKYLINER -- An industry term suggested for space vehicles used in future space travel.

SKYMASTER -- Military version of the Douglas DC-4, which made its first flight in 1942. Designated the C-54 by the U.S. Air Force and still operational. Workhorse of the Berlin Airlift.

SKYMASTER -- 1962 Cessna Model 336, unusual-design twin-engine, twin-boom commercial aircraft.

SKYNET -- Name for peacetime military operation.

SKYNIGHT -- (1) U.S. Navy F3D twin-jet, straight-wing fighter developed by Douglas after World War II.

(2) A new 265 mph executive twin aircraft in production in the U.S. by Cessna.

SKYRAIDER -- Pre-Korea Douglas ground support aircraft covering the U.S. Navy AD-1 through -7 series. Recently phased out of first-line service.

SKYRAY -- Douglas carrier jet fighter with a "manta-ray" wing, designated the F4D by the U.S. Navy and first flown in 1951.

SKYROCKET -- Grumman XF5F twin-engine fleet fighter produced in early 1940 for U.S. Navy testing.

SKYROCKET SENIOR -- Standard Bellanca Senior Pacemaker with a larger engine. See SENIOR PACEMAKER.

SKYSCRAPER -- Early Allied cross-Channel attack plan which bore close resemblance to OVERLORD. Produced in spring 1943, WW-II.

SKYSWEEPER -- U.S. radar-directed, automatic-firing, 75-mm. antiaircraft gun.

SKYTRAIN -- The venerable aerial workhorse of the world. The Douglas DC-3 made its first flight in 1932 and is still flying every day as the U.S. Air Force-U.S. Navy C-47, Canadian Dakota, or under a dozen other familiar names throughout the world. Also called Gooney Bird, Skytrooper, Grand Old Lady, and the C-48, -49, -50, -51, -52, -53.

SKYTROOPER -- See SKYTRAIN

SKYWAGON -- Cessna 185 single-engine monoplane introduced in 1962.

SKYWARRIOR -- Douglas twin-jet attack bomber designated A3D by the U.S. Navy. Entered service in the mid-1950's. Another version is the U.S. Air Force B-66 Destroyer.

SKYWISE -- Name for military exercise.

SLAM -- Acronym for the Air Force's Supersonic Low Altitude Missile, a nuclear ramjet-powered vehicle which would have an extremely long endurance and a very high range payload ratio. Because of its low-altitude capability, it would have greater penetrability by flying under the enemy's air defenses. A series of tests on a non-flyable nuclear reactor are being conducted under the TORY program and the overall propulsion system is being developed under Project PLUTO. Program has been funded at about 20 million dollars annually, essentially at a component development level. Future development hinges on success of Tory tests in 1963. See also BIG STICK, CLAM.

SLANESVILLE -- Anusnus Point, New Britain. WW-II.

SLANG -- Acronym for Systems Language.

SLAPSIE -- Put Put, New Britain. WW-II.

SLAPSTICK -- See GIBBON-SLAPSTICK

SLAVE STATIONS -- Two stations of GEE medium-range radar system, situated on east coast of Great Britain; time-lag in reception of signals transmitted by them and MASTER STATION in center enabled navigator to plot position of his aircraft. WW-II.

SLED -- Plaines des Gaiacs, New Caledonia. WW-II.

SLEDDING -- Aburatsu, Japan. WW-II.

SLEDGE -- Allied bombardment of enemy batteries near Reggio, Italy. 2 September 1943, WW-II.

SLEDGE HAMMER -- Name for peacetime military exercise held in Louisiana.

SLEDGEHAMMER -- Allied plan for limited cross-Channel attack on European Continent in 1942, contingent on condition of Russian front and German morale in West. Alternative to ROUNDUP. See also ROUNDHAMMER, OVERLORD. Canceled 8 July 1942, WW-II.

SLICK CHICK -- Code name for Ung Do, island occupied by U.N. forces during naval siege of Wonsan harbor, North Korea. 16 February 1951-27 July 1953, Korean Conflict.

SLIM JOHN -- Advanced model of HONEST JOHN.

SLIPSTREAM -- Nabire, New Guinea. WW-II.

SLOANE -- See ABBEY AND SLOANE

SLOMAR -- Acronym for Space Logistics, Maintenance and Rescue spacecraft. A U.S. Air Force study program of a manned logistics spacecraft to serve as an earth-space station ferry and as an orbital assembly operations and rescue station. Study contracts were awarded in 1960 to six industrial firms. The studies were submitted in 1961. No development has been authorized.

SLOPE HEAD -- Code name for Tae Do, island occupied by U.N. forces during naval siege of Wonsan harbor, North Korea. 16 February 1951-27 July 1953, Korean Conflict.

SLOT, THE -- Japanese shipping lane between Bougainville and Guadalcanal Islands. WW-II.

SLUMBERLAND -- Bosnek, Biak Island, New Guinea. WW-II.

SMACK, OPERATION -- Experimental operation observed by troops, staff officers and journalists; involved actual daylight raid on T-BONE HILL, Korea, by units of U.S. 7th Infantry Division, supported by tanks and tactical air strikes. 25 January 1953, Korean Conflict.

SMALLPOX -- Alice Channel, British North Borneo. WW-II.

SMART -- Acronym for Satellite Maintenance and Repair Techniques and U.S. Air Force program to study the feasibility of in-orbit repair of space vehicles by rendezvous of manned vehicles. An in-house study it is reportedly to be merged with SLOMAR and other manned space vehicle programs.

SMOKEY -- Name for military fire-fighting exercise.

SNAKE -- (1) Allied device consisting of long pipe or tube filled with explosive, designed to be pushed through barbed wire or mine fields and there exploded, somewhat in manner of bangalore torpedo. WW-II.

(2) U.S. anti-mine missile propelled along the ground by a 4.5-inch rocket. It drags a 100-foot long rail-like structure on which are mounted high explosives. The explosives are then detonated clearing a path through the mine field. Post-World War II development.

SNAKE HILL NORTH -- Military name for topographic feature on Luzon, Philippines. 1945, WW-II.

SNAKE HILL WEST -- Military name for topographic feature on Luzon, Philippines. 1945, WW-II.

SNAKE RIDGE -- Military name for topographic feature on Guadalcanal, southwest of Hill 66. January 1943, WW-II.

SNAKEBIRD -- Fukushima, Japan. WW-II.

SNAKE'S HEAD -- Military name for topographic feature near Cassino, Italy. Early 1944, WW-II.

SNAKY RIVER -- Name given by U.S. 158th Infantry Regiment to short, violently twisting stream which ran down LONE TREE HILL into Maffin Bay, Netherlands New Guinea. Spring 1944, WW-II.

SNAP -- Acronym for Systems for Nuclear Auxiliary Power. Development of small, lightweight nuclear-power sources for satellites, space craft, and other special applications. Odd-numbered projects developed by Martin-Marietta Company, Baltimore, Maryland; even-numbered projects developed by Atomics International. See also SNAPSHOT and SURVEYOR.

SNAPDRAGON -- Allied landing on Island of Pantelleria, Mediterranean. May 1943, WW-II.

SNAPSHOT -- (1) U.S. joint Atomic Energy Commission and Air Force project designed to demonstrate feasibility of small compact reactors in space. See also SNAP.

(2) U.S. Navy operation in western Caroline Islands to obtain photographic coverage and attack Japanese shipping. July 1944, WW-II.

SNARE -- Surface-to-air anti-aircraft missiles used with some success by both the British and Russians during World War II. Worked on the simple principle of using rockets trailing wire to foul airplane propellers. One of the first applications of rocketry to modern warfare.

SNARK -- U.S. Air Force winged air-breathing intercontinental ballistic missile with a range of 6000 miles. Solid booster is used to launch the missile and turbojet engine acts as the sustainer. System incorporates an inertial guidance system with a star tracking device. Operates at an altitude of 10 miles and a speed of Mach 0.94. First operational in 1958. Snark was the first surface-launched intercontinental ballistic missile to become operational in the U.S. Arsenal. Now obsolete.

SNIFFER -- Radar system designed for use on semi-isolated targets over water, as well as for skip bombing. Frequency-modulated and designed for automatic bomb release at altitudes from 40 to 400 feet.

SNIPE -- Allied loading exercise in United Kingdom in preparation for OVERLORD. See also NUDGER, GULL. February 1944, WW-II.

SNIPER RIDGE -- Military name for topographic feature northeast of Kumhwa, Korea. Also called Sniper's Ridge. Fall 1952, Korean Conflict.

SNIPER'S RIDGE -- See SNIPER RIDGE

SNIPERSCOPE -- U.S. device for seeing in dark by means of infrared radiation, which was mounted on carbines and permitted accurate night firing. See also SNOOPERSCOPE. Late WW-II.

SNOOK -- Name for military outpost in Yokkokchon Valley, northeast of PORK CHOP HILL. Spring 1953, Korean Conflict.

SNOOPER -- (1) Nickname for the winged all-weather SD-3 surveillance drone used for collection of tactical intelligence by the Army. Propeller-driven, the drone has a range of 100 miles and is parachute-recoverable. Interchangeable nose sections allow collection of various types of intelligence, including: photographic, infrared, radar or television. In limited use. Also called PEEPING TOM.

(2) Proposal by Rocketdyne Division of North American Aviation to develop an ion propulsion space vehicle which would be launched by SATURN class vehicles. Thrust would be 1 to 2 tons. Not under active development.

SNOOPERSCOPE -- U.S. device for seeing in dark by means of infrared radiation, used on hand-held mounts for night observation and signaling. See also SNIPERSCOPES. Late WW-II.

SNORT -- Acronym for Supersonic Naval Ordnance Research Track located at the Naval Ordnance Test Station, China Lake, California.

SNOW BIRD -- Joint U.S. Air Force-Army peacetime military exercise held in sub-Arctic regions. 1955.

SNOW DROP -- U.S. peacetime airborne maneuver conducted at Pine Camp, New York. November 1947-February 1948.

SNOW FALL -- Largest winter military maneuver ever held in United States to its date; conducted at Camp Drum, New York. Winter 1952.

SNOW GOOSE -- Early name for the BLACK BRANT series of sounding rockets. Developed by the Canadian Armament Research and Development Establishment, the solid fueled, two-stage vehicle can carry a 40-pound payload to an altitude of 600 miles.

SNOW STORM -- U.S. peacetime military exercise to indoctrinate individuals and units in ground and airborne operations under conditions of cold temperatures, snow-covered terrain, and high wind chill. Held at Camp Drum, New York. January-March 1953.

SNOW TIGER -- Name for peacetime military training exercise.

SNOW WHITE -- Code name used in U.S. radio messages for Madame Chiang Kai-shek. WW-II.

SNOWBALL -- (1) Nickname for a series of DISCOVERER satellite launchings preparatory to the BOSS program. Basic purpose was to develop recovery techniques and operational procedures for capsule recovery. Some launchings were conducted in 1961, but the program was cut back when BOSS was not approved.

(2) Reykyavik, Iceland. WW-II.

(3) U.S. military air transport service from Presque Isle, Maine, over North Atlantic route to Valley, Wales. Began July 1944, WW-II.

SNOWEY OWL -- Name for Royal Canadian Air Force Squadron Number 420.

SNOWFLAKE -- Name for type of flare used by Allies in anti-submarine warfare. WW-II.

SNOWMAN -- Melbourne, Australia. WW-II.

SOAP -- Acronym for Symbolic Optimum Assembly Programming.

SOAPSUD -- Melebo, New Britain. WW-II.

SOAPSUDS -- See TIDALWAVE

SOCOM -- U.S. Air Force acronym for Solar Communications, a system by which the sun's rays are collected by a mirror, cooled and then reflected to another receiver. Intensity modulation would be used to transmit information. Under development.

SOFAR -- Acronym for Sound Fixing And Ranging, a means of locating shipwrecked personnel by the transmission of the sound of a bomb exploded by those shipwrecked.

SOLAR -- U.S. Air Force research vehicle designed to study applications of solar energy. Under development.

SOLICITOR -- Seroci, Japen Island, New Guinea. WW-II.

SOLIDARITY, OPERATION -- See BANYAN TREE III

SOLO -- Acronym for Selective Optical Lock-On, a sighting and aiming device under consideration by U.S. Army for guidance of tactical missiles. The idea would be to have the missile home on a target selected and held by the optical sight. Particularly applicable to tanks and hard point targets. Under study.

SOLOIST -- Vivi ai Island, Solomon Sea. WW-II.

SOMNAMBULIST -- (1) Manus, Admiralty Islands. WW-II.

(2) Rabaul, New Britain. WW-II.

SOMNIUM -- U.S. Navy project at the Pacific Missile Range in 1960. Since cancelled.

SONAR -- Acronym for Sound Navigation and Ranging; used as name for device to determine the presence and location of objects under water by measuring the direction and return of sound echo. See also ASDIC.

SONNE -- German modification of ELECTRA. Consists of linearly varying radio-frequency phases of two of the three antennas.

SONNENBLUME -- (English translation: Sunflower) German code word for movement of German forces under Field Marshal Erwin Rommel to North Africa; beginning of Deutsches Afrika Korps. February 1941, WW-II.

SONNIE -- U.S. project to transport from Sweden to Great Britain Norwegian aircrew trainees and American aircrew internees released by Swedish government; conducted on nominally civilian basis by organization called American Air Transport Service. Began early 1944, WW-II.

SONO BUOY -- Buoy used by Allies in anti-submarine operations; contained apparatus for detecting noises made by submerged submarine's propellers. WW-II.

SONS OF SATAN -- Nickname for U.S. Marine Corps dive bombing squadron operating from air bases on Lingayen Gulf, Philippines. 1945, WW-II.

SOP 10 -- U.S. plan for local procurement of supplies and services in European Theater of Operations. Published 1 April 1944, WW-II.

SOP 29 -- U.S. plan for procurement, utilization and administration of civilian labor in liberated and occupied areas of European Theater of Operations. Published 26 May 1944, WW-II.

SOPHIA -- See TUNGSTEN and SOPHIA.

SOPHISTER -- Taniyama, Japan. WW-II.

SORDID -- Buka Island, Solomon Islands. WW-II.

SOS PLAN -- U.S. Army plan concerned with operation of communication and transportation facilities in Iran between Persian Gulf ports and Tehran. WW-II.

SOUFFLE -- Sendai Gawa Gawa, Japan. WW-II.

SOUPCON -- Ujeland Atoll, Marshall Islands. WW-II.

SOURCE -- British attack on German battleship Tirpitz by midget submarines, X-CRAFT. 22 September 1943, WW-II.

SOUTH DAUGHTER -- Military name for mountain height near Rabaul, New Britain. WW-II.

SOUTH KNOB -- Part of hill 260 outside THE PERIMETER on Bougainville. WW-II.

SOUTHAMPTON -- Supermarine twin-engine flying boat for Great Britain's Royal Air Force. First appeared in 1925. See also SCAPA.

SOUTHERN PINE -- U.S. peacetime military maneuver to drill 110,000-strong Army-Air Force Team in established tactics and techniques. July-August 1951.

SOUTHWIND -- Name for U.S. peacetime military exercise at Fort Bragg, North Carolina. 1960.

SOUVENIR -- Opai, New Britain. WW-II.

SOXO -- Shipping designator used in World War II for cargo to be received in Zone I of United Kingdom, comprising area north of line of county boundaries drawn through London and Banbury, excluding Northern Ireland. See also GLUE, BANG, UGLY. Instituted 1943.

SOYABEAN -- Tawi Tawi Islands, Philippine Islands. WW-II.

SOYOKAZE -- (English translation: Freight Carrier) Mitsubishi OB-96 pre-World War II Japanese transport converted to a twin-engine military bomber.

SPACE -- Acronym for Symbolic Programming Anyone Can Enjoy.

SPACER -- U.S. Air Force program to measure the space environment with instrumentation carried aboard various Air Force satellites such as DISCOVERER.

SPACETRACK -- One of the earliest elements of the U.S. space object detection "fence." Originally consisting of six minitrack stations and one Army doppler locating device along the 32nd parallel in the U.S., it is now one of the elements of the North American Air Defense Command SPADATS system. Built for the VANGUARD program in 1958, it can detect satellites in orbits greater than 32-degree inclination and at altitudes less than 500 miles.

SPADATS -- Acronym for Space Detection and Tracking System, the overall designation for the North American Air Defense Command's program for tracking and cataloguing all objects in space. Inputs are received and processed from a myriad of military and non-military sources including SPASUR, SPACETRACK, National Aeronautics and Space Administration tracking stations, Moon Watch teams, the Smithsonian Institute Baker-Nunn camera system, the DISCOVERER tracking network. Major improvements to cover all objects out to lunar distances are being developed.

SPAEROBEE -- U.S. two-stage sounding rocket which uses a solid propellant AEROBEE 100 as a first stage and a solid SPARROW I as the second. It can carry a 50-pound payload to an altitude of 300 miles. Vehicle is used by both National Aeronautics and Space Administration and the Air Force. Also known as the AEROBEE-300 or 300A (300 with fins).

SPAN -- Allied feint from Corsica against the flank of the enemy's position in Italy; carried out in connection with DRAGOON. 14 August 1944, WW-II.

SPAR -- (1) Acronym for Symbolic Program Assembly Routine.

(2) Acronym for Super-Precision Approach Radar, an easily transportable radar system designed for small civil airports and for certain military applications.

(3) An automatic coding system used in data processing.

(4) Acronym taken from "Semper Paratus--Always Ready." Latin motto (and its translation) of U.S. Coast Guard. Used to refer to member of Coast Guard Women's Reserve. Established during World War II.

SPARK -- (1) Polish trainer plane. See ISKRA.

(2) Mia Island, New Britain. WW-II.

SPARROW -- (1) World War II German He 162A aircraft. See SPATZ.

(2) German monoplane. See SPERLING.

(3) Three Navy air-to-air rocket missiles. See SPARROW I, II, III. See also ORIOLE.

(4) Buton Pass, Halmahera Island, Netherlands East Indies. WW-II.

SPARROW I -- U.S. Navy air-to-air missile for defense against both fighter and bomber aircraft. Using a radar beam-riding guidance system, it has a range of three to six miles and can operate at altitudes up to 10 miles. Solid propellant. First such missile developed and mass-produced in the U.S. Development began in 1946, production in 1951, and deployment with carrier-based aircraft in 1956. Now obsolete, it has been replaced by SPARROW III.

SPARROW II -- Advanced version of the U.S. Navy's SPARROW I, with a more effective guidance system. System was developed and flight tested from 1950 to 1958, but the program was discontinued in favor of the more advanced SPARROW III.

SPARROW III -- U.S. Navy air-to-air missile for fleet air defense. An outgrowth of the SPARROW I and II, it has a range of five nautical miles, and is effective at altitudes up to 10 miles. A radar beam-riding missile, it gives Navy carrier-based fighter-interceptors a truly all-weather weapon system which can attack enemy aircraft from any aspect, including head-on. Operational.

SPARROW FORCE -- Australian troops sent to Koepang, Netherlands Timor. December 1941, WW-II.

SPARROWHAWK -- Curtiss F9C single-seat airship fighter designed for U.S. Navy dirigibles in the early 1930's.

SPARTAN -- (1) Cape Ndoll, New Britain. WW-II.

(2) Large-scale Allied exercise, held on south coast of England, invloving ten divisions in breakout from bridgehead. March 1943, WW-II.

SPARVIERO -- (English translation: Hawk) Savoia-Marchetti SM.79. Italy's standard bomber prior to World War II. Commercial prototype was the SM.75. See also MARSUPIALE.

SPASMODIC -- Tigalda, Alaska. WW-II.

SPASTIC -- Miyakenojo, Japan. WW-II.

SPASUR -- Acronym for the U.S. Navy-operated Space Surveillance system. An important part of SPADATS system, it consists of two stations, one located at San Diego, California, and the other at Fort Stewart, Georgia, with a central command complex at Dahlgren, Virginia. System can accurately track satellites out to at least 1000 miles, and indicate the past, present, and future orbital elements of a space vehicle. By using two transmitter-recievers, orbital data is computed by doppler-triangulation techniques.

SPATZ -- (English translation: Sparrow) German Heinkel He.162A jet interceptor which first flew in 1944 and became operational with the Luftwaffe in 1945. Also called Salamander and Volksjager.

SPAVEN -- Code name for Australia. WW-II.

SPEAKEASY -- Dodecanese Islands, Mediterranean Sea. WW-II.

SPEAR -- Solid propellant rocket motor developed and fired to test the ability of a solid propellant to function under poor environmental conditions. Has thrust of 53,000 pounds. Results applicable to rocket motors for mobile operations such as POLARIS or PERSHING.

SPEAR HEAD -- Name for peacetime military exercise held in Europe.

SPEARHEAD DIVISION -- Nickname for U.S. 3rd Armored Division.

SPEARMINT -- Lunga Signal Tower, Guadalcanal, Solomon Islands. WW-II.

SPEED -- Acronym for Self Programmed Electronic Equation Delineator.

SPEEDBALL -- U.S. Army target rocket used in preliminary testing of the NIKE-ZEUS at Kwajelein Island. Used primarily to checkout the electronic components of the system such as the detection and discrimination radars.

SPEEDWING -- (1) Laird open-cockpit biplane built in the U.S. in the early 1930's.

(2) Curtiss-Wright A14D 1933 version of the 16E aircraft, with a more powerful engine.

SPEEDY -- Code word for U.S. II Corps in Tunisia and Sicily. WW-II.

SPENCER -- Senta Bay, Bismarck Archipelago. WW-II.

SPERLING -- (English translation: Sparrow) German Scheibe SF-23C monoplane first flown in 1955.

SPERT -- Acronym for Special Power Excursion Reactor Test facility, heterogeneous U.S. reactor facilities operated by Phillips Petroleum Company at reactor testing station in Idaho. See also SPERT I-IV.

SPERT-I -- Heterogeneous unpressurized reactor using water as moderator and reflector. Completed July 1955. See also SPERT.

SPERT-II -- Pressurized water reactor of medium pressure and temperature, designed to supply test technology in the intermediate zone between unpressurized SPERT I and high-pressure SPERT III. Completed 1958. See also SPERT.

SPERT-III -- Light water-moderated reactor for conducting safety tests applicable to boiling water and fully pressurized water reactors. Completed 19 December 1958. See also SPERT.

SPERT-IV -- Pool facility permitting detailed study of reactor stability based on varying conditions. Completed September 1961. See also SPERT.

SPHINX -- (1) Nuvaregi Island, New Britain. WW-II.

(2) An over-all Army project concerned with testing of equipment and tactics for detecting and reducing Japanese field fortifications. WW-II.

SPIDER -- Sasebo, Japan. WW-II.

SPIDER WEB -- Name for British Royal Navy Air Service patrols over North Sea during World War One.

SPIN -- U.S. Army program designed to improve the accuracy of missile gyros by an order of magnitude. Industrial contract has been let.

SPIRALE -- French GAM Dassault 410, military version of the M.D.415, this twin-turboprop monoplane is used in a close-support role primarily. See also COMMUNAUTE.

SPIRE -- Prototype inertial guidance system developed by Massachusetts Institute of Technology.

SPIRIT -- Evacuation of Polish troops from southern France. February-April 1941, WW-II.

SPIRIT OF ST. LOUIS -- Single-engine Ryan Aircraft Special which Charles Lindbergh flew solo, non-stop to Paris, 20-21 May 1927.

SPIRITED -- Ivigtut, Greenland. WW-II.

SPIRITOUS -- Miyazaki, Japan. WW-II.

SPITEFUL -- Laminar-wing development of the SPITFIRE. First flown in 1944.

SPITFIRE -- One of the few planes produced before World War II which retained its reputation as a first-line fighter throughout the war, due to continual power plant changes by Vickers-Supermarine. Its power increased 100% in six years of war. The British built over 21,000.

SPITKITS -- Nickname for larger type of Allied landing craft; named after tin can ash trays secured to ships' life rails. WW-II.

SPLICE -- Arrival by air of British Hurricane fighter planes on island of Malta. May 1941, WW-II.

SPLINTER FLEET -- Name for converted civilian boats which patroled for German U-boats off Atlantic and Gulf coasts of U.S. June 1942 - December 1944, WW-II.

SPOILSMAN -- Kaimondake, Japan. WW-II.

SPOILSPORT -- Kamiri, Noemfoor Island, New Guinea. WW-II.

SPOOK -- Acronym for Supervisor Program Over Other Kinds.

SPOOKY -- Novo Sibirsk, Siberia, U.S.S.R. WW-II.

SPOONER -- Code name for New Zealand. WW-II.

SPOONFUL -- Ngulu Island, Caroline Islands. WW-II.

SPORT -- Curtiss-Wright 16E three-seat biplane built in the U.S. in 1933.

SPOTLIGHT -- U.S. 5th Air Force cooperative night attacks by flare-dropping and intruder aircraft against rail traffic and trains in North Korea. Late 1952 - early 1953, Korean Conflict.

SPOTTED DOG -- Nickname for set of altitude contours resulting from screening and showing radar coverage of a site.

SPOUSE -- British term describing weather condition, when visibility was very bad, which called for use of anti-aircraft guns only in defense against German V-weapon attacks. See also FLABBY, FICKLE. WW-II.

SPREADEAGLE -- Sorol Island, Caroline Islands. WW-II.

SPRIGHTLY -- Mindanao, Philippine Islands. WW-II.

SPRING -- Canadian attack from positions in vicinity of Caen, France; coincided with American Operation COBRA. Followed by TOTALIZE. Began 25 July 1944, WW-II.

SPRING BREEZE -- See FRUEHLINGSWIND

SPRING THAW -- U.S. Far Eastern Air Force short, intensive aerial indication attacks on supply lines and transportation in North Korea to force enemy to consume supplies stored in forward areas. Began 21 March 1953, Korean Conflict.

SPRINGBOARD -- Name for U.S. Navy peacetime exercise in Caribbean.

SPRINGFIELD -- Ring Ring Plantation, New Britain. WW-II.

SPRINT -- (1) U.S. Army-Advanced Research Projects Agency surface-to-air anti-missile missile. See also NIKE-ZEUS.

(2) Acronym for Selective Printing, used in data processing.

SPRITSAIL -- Owi Island, New Guinea. WW-II.

SPRUCE -- Kukum Signal Tower, Guadalcanal, Solomon Islands. WW-II.

SPRUCE HILL -- U.S. military name for topographic feature near Yonabaru, Okinawa. 1945, WW-II.

SPRUCE UP -- Name for peacetime emergency disaster control exercise.

SPUD-1 -- Solar power unit under development by an aerospace firm.

SPUR -- Acronym for Space Power Unit Reactor, a 300-kilowatt nuclear turbo-generator under development for the U.S. Air Force. Using a liquid metal as the working fluid, the power system is to have an operational life of three years and is designed to meet space power requirements in the later 1960's.

SPUTNIK -- Name given to the initial Soviet series of earth satellites which, begun under the auspices of the International Geophysical Year, gave the Russians a research program leading to the first manned orbital flight. Sputnik I (184 pounds) was first earth satellite, launched on October 4, 1957. Sputniks II, IV, V, VI, IX, and X carried dogs and other biological instruments. Sputnik IV carried a "dummy" astronaut. Sputnik VIII launched a Soviet Venus probe from a parking orbit. Satellite weights ranged from 184 to 14,293 pounds. Program lasted from October 1957 to March 1961 with 10 satellites launched preparatory to VOSTOK.

SPYGLASS -- Wisil Island, New Britain. WW-II.

SQUALL -- Italian Caproni Ca.331 aircraft of 1940. See RAFFICA.

SQUARE HEAD -- U.N. code name for Kalma Gak on Wonsan harbor, North Korea. See also HAIRLESS JOE. Korean Conflict.

SQUAREPEG -- Nissan Island, Green Islands. WW-II.

SQUAWK -- Radiophone terminology when referring to turning the IFF (Identification, Friend or Foe) radar beacon on.

SQUAWK FLASH -- Radar beacon phraseology for actuating the identification button on the IFF (Identification, Friend or Foe). See PARROT.

SQUAWK MAYDAY -- Radar beacon code word phraseology for following appropriate emergency procedure with IFF (Identification, Friend or Foe).

SQUAWK ONE, TWO, THREE -- Refers to various positions on control panel of IFF (Identification, Friend or Foe) radar beacon.

SQUID -- (1) British Royal Navy ahead-thrown anti-submarine weapon. Developed in 1945, WW-II.

(2) U.S. Navy research project in aircraft, missile and space propulsion, with emphasis on the investigation of physical and chemical processes associated with the conversion of energy into thrust. Originally under auspices of Princeton University; transferred to University of Virginia in 1962. Began 1946.

(3) Cuyo Pass (East), Philippine Islands. WW-II.

SQUIRREL -- Mia Passage, New Britain. WW-II.

SQUITTER -- Random transmission of a transponder in the absence of interrogation by the "Identification, Friend or Foe" system (IFF).

STADIUM -- (1) Agusan, Philippine Islands. WW-II.

(2) Tavalo, New Britain. WW-II.

STAFF-GOGGLES -- See GENERALSTABBRILLE

STAGHOUND -- Name for a U.S. armored vehicle. WW-II.

STAGNATE -- Rongelap, Marshall Islands. WW-II.

STALAG -- Acronym for Stammlager, German prisoner of war camp.

STALEMATE -- U.S. invasion of Palau Islands. Part of GRANITE and GRANITE II. Began 15 September 1944, WW-II.

STALIN ORGAN -- Russian World War II mobile rocket launcher capable of firing 30-48 rockets with a range of three miles. Used operationally.

STAMINA -- Maintenance operation to supply by airlift British IV Corps and Royal Air Force squadrons on Imphal plain, Burma. Began 18 April 1944, WW-II.

STAMP -- Basilan Strait, Philippine Islands. WW-II.

STAMPEDE -- Ras Heilf, Oman. WW-II.

STAND OR DIE ORDER -- Name given by press to order issued on 29 July 1950 by Lieutenant General Walton H. Walker, commander of U.S. 8th Army, to check enemy advance in Taegu area of Korea. Korean Conflict.

STAR -- (1) Acronym for Shield Test Air Facility Reactor. Planned U.S. Atomic Energy Commission nuclear reactor at Nuclear Reactor Testing Station, Idaho.

(2) An automatic coding system used in data processing.

(3) Allied code name for route to GOTHIC LINE in British XII Corps sector, central Italy. Summer 1944, WW-II.

STAR GAZER, PROJECT -- U.S. Air Force research program for manned, stabilized balloon flights to the fringes of the atmosphere (above 90,000 feet) to study the stars and planets without the obscuration of the air. Flight to be made by two men in the latter part of 1963.

STAR SERIES -- Reference to practice of Lockheed Aircraft assigning "heavenly body" nicknames to their planes. For example--LODESTAR, SHOOTING STAR, CONSTELLATION.

STAR SHELL -- Name for type of flare.

STARDUST -- Geographical location in connection with ARGONAUT. WW-II.

STARFIGHTER -- Interceptor aircraft developed by Lockheed and designated the F-104 by the U.S. Air Force. First flight of prototype was on 9 February 1954. Also in use by Allied air arms.

STARFIRE -- Lockheed F-94 all-weather interceptor for the U.S. Air Force. First flew in July 1949; no longer used.

STARFISH -- Name for decoy fires set up on German bombing runs in England to misdirect aircraft from targets. Started January 1941, WW-II.

STARKEY -- Name for the feigned Allied threats directed towards Pas-de-Calais; part of COCKADE operation intended to give impression that an Allied invasion was being planned for the Continent in 1943. WW-II.

STARLIFTER -- Lockheed C-141 jet transport officially designated by the U.S. Air Force 18 April 1962. Aircraft in developmental stage.

STARLIGHT -- Name for peacetime military exercise.

STARLINER -- (1) Light transport monoplane with two engines driving a single propellor. Pre-World War II design by Vega Airplane Company, a subsidiary of Lockheed.

(2) L.1649 commercial transport aircraft, long-range Lockheed derivation of the L.1049, in service with Trans-World Airlines, Air France, and Lufthansa.

STARLIT -- Iwo Jima, Bonin Islands. WW-II.

STARSEEKER -- U.S. four-stage sounding rocket capable of carrying a 100-pound payload to an altitude of 1000 miles or a 20-pound load to 2000 miles. All four stages are solid propellant charged. Three stage version with the same name being developed. Neither as yet is in active use.

START -- Acronym for Space Transport and Re-entry Tests, an industry proposal for a high speed solid propellant booster for nose cone re-entry tests. Not actively developed, although both the U.S. Air Force and National Aeronautics and Space Administration have several re-entry programs utilizing the same concept.

STARVATION I AND II -- Two missions flown by U.S. Army Air Forces B-29 aircraft to lay acoustic and magnetic mines in Shimonoseki Strait, Japan. Late March 1945, WW-II.

STATALTEX -- French experimental surface-to-air missile designed to develop ramjet power-plants for anti-aircraft weapons. Boosted to Mach 3.2 by a solid booster and then to Mach 5 by the ramjet sustainer. In tests, it has reached an altitude of 125,000 feet. Test firings were conducted in 1961.

STATESMAN -- See TIDALWAVE

STATION MASTER -- British Royal Air Force slang name for the commanding officer of an air station. WW-II.

STATION WAGON -- Hiller E-4 helicopter used by the U.S. Army as the OH-23.

STATUE OF LIBERTY DIVISION -- Nickname for U.S. 77th Infantry Division.

STEAMROLLER -- Manila, Philippine Islands. WW-II.

STEER -- Early U.S. Air Force program to use a polar-orbiting, active repeater satellite as a communications relay between Strategic Air Command forces, both airborne and ground-based. Initially believed to have been integrated into the ADVENT program; information from Program 279 indicates that the concept of emergency warning from a satellite-based system has been continued and may be operational.

STELLA -- Name reserved by meteorologists for tropical cyclone in North Atlantic area.

STEM -- Ta Island, Solomon Islands. WW-II.

STENOGRAPHER -- Hyane Harbor, Los Negros Islands, Admiralty Islands. WW-II.

STEP -- (1) Acronym for Space Terminal Evaluation Program, an industry proposal to use intercontinental ballistic missiles to launch an orbiting space station; in effect until the SATURN-class boosters become operational. Not under consideration.

(2) Acronym for Simple Transition to Electronic Processing.

(3) Canadian training exercise emphasizing operations involved in a breakout from a bridgehead. Held in United Kingdom in preparation for OVERLORD. 1-9 April 1944, WW-II.

STEPS -- Acronym for Solar Thermionic Electric Power System, an auxiliary power unit which uses a solar collector to concentrate solar energy on several thermionic elements at the focus. The power levels for the converter will be 3-10 kilowatts at the peak and .5 kilowatts continuously.

STEPSISTER -- Transfer of Australian troops from Middle East to Far East. February-April 1942, WW-II.

STEREOTYPED -- Bathurst Island, Australia. WW-II.

STERLIN CASTLE -- Canadian name for farmhouse on ROYAL CANADIAN AVENUE near San Leonardo, Italy. Named for Lieutenant M. Sterlin. Scene of heavy fighting, 9 December 1943, WW-II.

STERNUM -- Godhavn, Greenland. WW-II.

STERNWALK -- MacKenzie Bay, Greenland. WW-II.

STEVEDORE -- Guam Island, Marianas Islands. WW-II.

STICKATNAUGHT -- Allied operation against Wakde Island-Toem, New Guinea, area, conducted by TORNADO Task Force. Also called Operation H. 17 May-2 September 1944, WW-II.

STIEGLITZ -- Biplane trainer built in Germany by Focke-Wulf in the early 1930's.

STILETTO -- Code name for Turkey. WW-II.

STILO -- Lae, New Guinea. WW-II.

STILWELL RATION -- A popular name for an allotment of crackers, one fruit bar, sugar, peanuts, salt and a vitamin pill received as supplement to diet by Chinese troops. WW-II.

STILWELL ROAD -- Later name of the LEDO ROAD or PICK'S PIKE in North Burma; began at Ledo, in Assam, intersected Burma Road, and ended in Kunming, China. Change of name suggested by Generalissimo Chiang Kai-shek in 1945 to honor Lt. General Joseph W. Stilwell. Also called Stilwell Highway. WW-II.

STIMULATE -- Rota Island, Marianas Islands. WW-II.

STINKER -- Mios Woendi Island, Schouten Islands, New Guinea. WW-II.

STIPPLE -- Allied procedure which stipulated that only convoys considered liable to attack would be given air cover while those thought to be reasonably safe were left to care of their surface escorts. WW-II.

STIRLING -- One of the first four-engine bombers employed by Great Britain in World War II; manufactured by Short.

STIRRUPUMP -- Geelvink Bay, New Guinea. WW-II.

STOCKFORCE -- Formation active in Bodo area, Norway. Commanded by Lieutenant-Colonel H. C. Stockwell. May 1940, WW-II.

STOCKINGFORD -- Code name for Turkey. WW-II.

STOCKWELL -- Ajaccio, Corsica. WW-II.

STOMPING -- Gi (Gie), New Britain. WW-II.

STONEAGE -- Allied convoy from Alexandria, Egypt, to Malta. Marked final and effective relief of that island. November 1942, WW-II.

STONEFACE -- Tawale, New Britain. WW-II.

STOOGE -- British aerodynamic missile developed to provide anti-aircraft defense of ships from Japanese KAMIKAZES. Equipped with large rectangular wings and horizontal and vertical stabilizers; was actually a solid propelled pilotless aircraft. Had a range of eight miles at speeds up to 500 miles per hour. Development began in 1945 and several test firings were conducted but, with the end of the war, the program was discontinued.

STOPCOL -- One of the two South African columns guarding coastal plain west of Tobruk, Libya, from seaborne or airborne landings, May 1942. See also SEACOL. WW-II.

STOPPER -- (1) Coronado Point, Philippine Islands. WW-II.

(2) British Coastal Command air patrol designed to cover exits from port of Brest, France, during hours of darkness. WW-II.

STOPWATCH -- Name for peacetime military operation.

STORCH -- (English translation: Stork) Three-place observation aircraft used extensively by Nazis during World War II. First flown in 1936. Still flying in substantial numbers.

STORK -- (1) German World War II aircraft. See STORCH.

(2) Italian bomber. See CICOGNA.

STORM -- Finnish fighter plane. See MYRSKY.

STORMBIRD -- Bomber version of the World War II German Me-262 Swallow. See STURMVOGEL.

STORMFURY -- Project name of series of scientific experiments in hurricane modification being conducted jointly by the U.S. Weather Bureau, the U.S. Navy, and other agencies. First test conducted in hurricane ESTHER northeast of Puerto Rico in September 1961.

STORMOVIK -- Russian IL-2 aircraft which first entered service on the Eastern Front in 1942 and used, in a variety of roles, throughout World War II. Another spelling: Shturmovik.

STORTEBEKER -- German Junkers Ju.388 aircraft designed to combat the night-flying British Royal Air Force. First flown in 1943.

STOSSER -- Focke-Wulf Fw.56 trainer plane used in Germany by the Luftwaffe before World War II.

STOUT COOTIE -- See COOTIE

STOVEPIPE -- Cape Turane, French Indo China. WW-II.

STRAFGERICHT -- German bombing of Belgrade, Yugoslavia. April 1941, WW-II.

STRAIGHTFLUSH -- Morobe, New Guinea. WW-II.

STRAIGHTLEFT -- Momote, Los Negros Islands, Admiralty Islands. WW-II.

STRAIGHTLINE -- Allied operation under ALAMO against Wakde Island and Sarmi, New Guinea. Changed in late April to operations against Wakde Island-Toem, STICKATNAUGHT, and Biak Island, HORLICKS. WW-II.

STRANGE -- Acronym for SAGE Tracking And Guidance Evaluation system.

STRANGLE, OPERATION -- (1) Allied air operation to interrupt and destroy enemy road, rail, and sea communications in Italy. March-May 1944, WW-II.

(2) Operation for air interdiction of enemy lines of communication in zone between railheads at 39th parallel and front lines in Korea; divided zone into three sections for intensive attack by U.S. 5th Air Force, lst Marine Air Wing, and Navy Task Force 77; initially concerned with highways, later included railroads. Began 31 May ,1951, Korean Conflict.

STRANGLE PARROT -- Radiophone terminology for turning IFF (Identification, Friend or Foe) radar beacon off.

STRANGLEHOLD -- Sandakan, Borneo. WW-II.

STRANRAER -- Vickers-Supermarine biplane flying boat of early 1930's.

STRATFORD, FORCE -- Proposed Allied expeditionary force for Stavanger, Bergen and Trondheim, Norway. Early 1940, WW-II.

STRATOCRUISER -- Boeing 377, civil counterpart of the U.S. Air Force C-97 Stratofreighter transport plane. First delivered in 1949.

STRATOFORTRESS -- Boeing B-52 heavy bomber operational with the U.S. Air Force's Strategic Air Command. First flight of prototype was 15 April 1952.

STRATOFREIGHTER -- U.S. Air Force C-97 transport/tanker plane built by Boeing since the early 1950's.

STRATOJET -- Boeing B-47, U.S. Air Force strategic medium bomber, first flown in 1947. Still operational.

STRATOLIFTER -- Boeing-built U.S. Air Force C-135 aircraft, military counterpart of the commercial 707. See also STRATOTANKER.

STRATOLINER -- Boeing 307 four-engine commercial transport plane designed in 1936. Only ten were built and all still flying in 1962.

STRATOSCOPE I -- A program, developed by Martin Schwarzchild of Princeton University, to balloon-carry a 12-inch telescope above most of the distorting effects of the atmosphere. Six flights were made from 1957-59. One of the flights obtained extremely clear pictures of Mars. See also STRATOSCOPE II.

STRATOSCOPE II -- Follow-on program to STRATOSCOPE I. A 36-inch telescope with a pointing accuracy of 0.1 sec of arc for up to 24 hours is balloon-carried to altitudes above 80,000 feet for astronomical observations. One flight in March 1963.

STRATOTANKER -- U.S. Air Force KC-135 multi-purpose tanker/transport aircraft, version of the Boeing 707. Transport version, without aerial refueling boom, is called STRATOLIFTER.

STRAW -- Code word for Samoan Defense Group. WW-II.

STRAWBERRY HILL -- U.S. military name for topographic feature in southern Okinawa. 1945, WW-II.

STRAWBOARD -- Defense project for Wallis Island, Tonga Islands. WW-II.

STRAWHAT -- Upolu Island, Samoa Islands. WW-II.

STRAWMAN -- Savaii Island, Samoa Islands. WW-II.

STRAWSTACK -- Tutuila Island, Samoa Islands. WW-II.

STREAM -- (1) Surigao Strait, Philippine Islands. WW-II.

    (2) Capture of Majunga, Madagascar, by Allied Forces. 10 September 1942, WW-II.

STREAMING -- Manila, Philippine Islands. WW-II.

STREAMLINE -- (1) Name for a study of the use of the SATURN to boost the DYNA-SOAR space glider. Study was made in 1961, but never accepted.

    (2) Lipari Islands, Philippine Islands. WW-II.

STRICOM -- Acronym for Strike Command, a military planning and operational headquarters established in 1961 for the closer integration of the U.S. Army's Strategic Army Corps and the Air Force's Tactical Air Command. Conventional warfare forces are headquartered at McDill Air Force Base, Florida.

STRIKE -- U.N. psychological warfare plan involving leaflet drops on North Korea warning civilians to stay away from main supply routes and communications centers before impending air attack and telling them after attack that they had been so warned. Similar to BLAST. 1952, Korean Conflict.

STRIKE BACK -- Name for NATO peacetime sea exercise.

STRIKER -- U.S. Navy jargon meaning enlisted man studying for non-commissioned promotion. WW-II.

STRIP POINT -- Military name for topographic feature near Buna, New Guinea. 1942, WW-II.

STRIVE -- Advanced Research Projects Agency nickname for studies and programs to improve the reliability of weapons systems. Continuing.

STRONGARM -- U.S. Army sounding rocket designed to carry a 15-pound payload of atmosphere electron-density detectors to an altitude of 1050 miles. Five-stage solid propellant rocket, it was first launched on 10 November 1959.

STRONGBACK -- Name for peacetime military operation.

STRONGHOLD -- Name for peacetime military exercise.

STRONGPOINT -- Establishment by Major General Claire L. Chennault of East China Air Task Force to operate east of Japanese corridor in China and assist Chinese army of Marshal Hsueh Yo. Halted by Japanese advance. November 1944-February 1945, WW-II.

STRSLJEN -- (English translation: Hornet) Lightweight, twin-jet, close-support aircraft designated the J-451MM by the Yugoslav Air Force. Development of late 1950's.

STRUCTURE -- Liberia, Africa. WW-II.

STUD -- Allied air operation by fighter planes designed to interfere with enemy air and land movement in France during Normandy invasion. Similar to ROYAL FLUSH and FULL HOUSE. June 1944, WW-II.

STUDEBAKER -- Point Cruz, Philippine Islands. WW-II.

STUDENT -- German plan to restore Fascism in Italy after resignation of Mussolini. Summer 1943, WW-II.

STUDENTS -- Nickname for inexperienced Communist pilots of MIG jet fighter aircraft in Korea. See also HONCHOS. Korean Conflict.

STUKA -- Contraction of Sturzkampfflugzeug, German term for dive bomber; used as popular name for Nazi Junker Ju-87, scourge of the early World War II skies; first flown in 1937, and tested with the Condor Legion in Spain. In later World War II actions it was no match for Allied aircraft.

STURMFLUT -- German operation against Kasserine Pass and Sbiba gap, Tunisia. 19-22 February 1943, WW-II.

STURMVOGEL -- (English translation: Stormbird) Attack bomber version of the Me-262 jet interceptor which first flew in this model in 1944. See SCHWALBE (Swallow).

STYLE -- British convoy to Malta of warships carrying soldiers and airmen who were left at Gibraltar after SUBSTANCE convoy. 31 July-2 August 1941, WW-II.

STYMIE, EXERCISE -- Planned large-scale Canadian exercise on section Ayrshire coast, Great Britain, which resembled Sicilian beaches; in preparation for HUSKY. Canceled 22 June 1943 on account of unfavorable weather. WW-II.

STYX -- Caracas, Venezuela. WW-II.

SUBJUNCTION -- Canton-Hong Kong Area, China. WW-II.

SUBLIME -- Code name for China. WW-II.

SUBROC -- Navy underwater-surface-underwater missile for anti-submarine warfare. Solid propelled, it has a range of about 25 nautical miles and carries a nuclear warhead. Nuclear-powered submarine Thresher was the first equipped with the missile. Operational in 1961 and reportedly tested in the Pacific in the DOMINIC series of nuclear tests.

SUBSTANCE -- British operation to pass supply convoy from Gibraltar to Malta and at same time run ships from Malta to Gibraltar. July 1941, WW-II.

SUCROSE -- Moulmein, Burma. WW-II.

SUDBURY, CITY OF -- Name for Royal Canadian Air Force Squadron Number 430.

SUGAR -- Code word for letter "S" in a phonetic alphabet, used to avoid possibility of a misunderstanding in transmitting messages. See also SIERRA.

SUGAR CHARLIE -- Code name for Japanese 300 to 1000-ton supply vessel, with two hatches. WW-II.

SUGAR DOG -- Code name for small Japanese 150 to 300-ton supply vessel, with one hatch. WW-II.

SUGAR HILL -- U.S. military name for topographic feature near Yonabaru, Okinawa. 1945, WW-II.

SUGAR LOAF -- (1) Military name for topographic feature on island of Hong Kong. December 1941, WW-II.

(2) Military name for small hill near Wonsan, North Korea, during U.N. naval siege. 16 February 1951-27 July 1953, Korean Conflict.

SUGAR LOAF HILL -- U.S. military name for topographic feature near Naha, Okinawa. 1945, WW-II.

SUGAR RED -- Strip of land on UTAH Beach, Normandy. June 1944. WW-II.

SUICIDE CREEK -- U.S. military name for topographic feature on New Britain Island. 1943-44, WW-II.

SUICIDE POINT -- U.S. military name for topographic feature on Rendova Island, New Georgia group. 1943. WW-II.

SUITCASE -- Operations by four divisions, each from a different Allied country, near Scheldt estuary, Netherlands, to prevent Germans from interfering with 2nd Canadian Infantry Division during its capture of South Beveland in Operation VITALITY. Began 20 October 1944, WW-II.

SULTAN -- Karimata Strait, Japan. WW-II.

SUMAC -- Code name for Australia. WW-II.

SUMMER HOUSE HILL -- Name of topographic feature in Naga Hills near Kohima, Assam; site of heavy fighting between British and Japanese troops. April 1944, WW-II.

SUMMIT, OPERATION -- Movement of troops in combat by U.S. Marine Corps helicopters in area of PUNCHBOWL, Korea. September 1951, Korean Conflict.

SUN -- Allied code name for route to GOTHIC LINE in British XIII Corps sector, central Italy. Summer 1944, WW-II.

SUN DOG TWO -- Name for military exercise.

SUN SHOT I -- Canadian peacetime military exercise.

SUNBATH -- Nizki Island, Aleutian Islands. WW-II.

SUNBEAM -- Name for peacetime air defense exercise.

SUNBURN -- Search off Levant by British Royal Air Force for ships carrying illegal immigrants to Palestine. December 1945, WW-II.

SUNBURST DIVISION -- Nickname for U.S. 40th Infantry Division. See also RATTLESNAKE DIVISION.

SUNDANCE -- Majuro Atoll, Marshall Islands. WW-II.

SUNDERLAND -- British four-engine flying boat of World War II, built by Short. Called the Flying Porcupine by the Germans due to its extensive armament.

SUNFLARE -- National Aeronautics and Space Administration program to gather data on solar flares and particles using NIKE-CAJUN and AEROBEE rockets launched from Wallops Island, Virginia. A continuing program.

SUNFLOWER -- (1) National Aeronautics and Space Administration solar power system designed to develop three kilowatts of electrical power as a power source for satellites and space probes. To be tested in 1964.

(2) Talisi Anchorage, Guadalcanal, Solomon Islands. WW-II.

(3) See SONNENBLUME

SUNFLOWER SEED -- Code name for British-developed rocket launcher installed in B-17 aircraft for use against enemy attacks on bomber formations from above. WW-II.

SUNKIST -- Tomo, New Britain. WW-II.

SUNRAY -- Nickname for the U.S. Navy's GREB satellite.

SUNRISE -- Advanced Research Projects Agency code name for studies of advanced weapons concepts not currently under contract. Unsolicited proposals would initially fall in this category. See also ARCADE.

SUNSET PROJECT -- Return to United States from Pacific Theater of B-29 aircraft of 8th and 20th Air Forces, B-24 aircraft of Far East Air Force as well as other planes not required by occupation forces. Began September 1945, WW-II.

SUNSHINE -- Ombai Strait, New Guinea. WW-II.

SUNSHINE PROJECT -- U.S. Atomic Energy Commission's long-term study of effects at radiostrontium in fall-out material from nuclear weapons tests.

SUPER -- Czech-built development of the Russian IL-14 aircraft. See CRATE.

SUPER AERO -- Twin-engine light transport first flown in 1947. The Czech aircraft is serving with various nations.

SUPER BIDON -- Spanish CASA Breguet single-engine biplane which flew nonstop from Spain to Cuba, 4906 miles in June 1933.

SUPER BROUSSARD -- Twin-turboprop transport, the M.H.260, currently being manufactured by Nord-Aviation.

SUPER CAB -- French GY-30 monoplane of the 1950's.

SUPER CHIEF -- Aeronca light monoplane built in the U.S. in the late 1930's.

SUPER CONNIE -- See SUPER CONSTELLATION

SUPER CONSTELLATION -- Lockheed Model L.1049G commercial transport which first flew in the mid-1950's. Also in use with the U.S. Air Force as the C-121.

SUPER CONVAIR -- Standard Convair 340/440's modified with Allison turboprops. First delivered in 1960.

SUPER COURIER -- High performance, Helio Aircraft Model H-395 STOL-type airplane. A version in service with the U.S. Air Force as the U-10A. First flown in 1958.

SUPER CUB -- Piper PA-18 "150", 1950 development of the Cub. Used by U.S. armed forces as the L-21.

SUPER ELECTRA -- Lockheed Model 14 commercial transport which first flew in 1937. Basis for the many World War II modifications and designations which followed.

SUPER FALCON -- Distinction usually applied to the 3A, 4A and 9 versions of the FALCON air-to-air missile.

SUPER FURY -- 1933 development of Great Britain's Hawker single-engine biplane fighter. See FURY.

SUPER G18S -- Twin-engine U.S. executive transport plane under production by Beech Aircraft.

SUPER-GYMNAST -- Plan for Anglo-American invasion of French North Africa, combining U.S. and British plans. Often used interchangeably with GYMNAST. See also TORCH. 1941-42, WW-II.

SUPER LODESTAR -- Recent Minnesota Air Motive modification of the Lockheed Model 18 aircraft. See also LODESTAR.

SUPER MYSTERE -- Improved version of the M.D.452, in service with French and Israel air arms. See MYSTERE.

SUPER PHALENE -- Avions Caudron, France, 1933-development of the Phalene monoplane.

SUPER-RALLYE -- Updated version of French M.S.880 aircraft. See RALLYE-CLUB.

SUPER RATA -- A larger and more powerful version of the Russian I-16 aircraft. See RATA.

SUPER-ROUNDUP -- Code name for early Allied plan to invade European Continent. See also OVERLORD. WW-II.

SUPER SABRE -- North American F-100, first of the Century Series fighters, completed its first flight in 1953, and has been delivered to the U.S. Air Force in quantity.

SUPER 6TH -- Nickname for U.S. 6th Armored Division. Also called BRASSIERE BOYS.

SUPER SOAP -- An improved SOAP.

SUPER SOLUTION -- Special racing airplane built by Laird Airplane Company of Illinois in 1931. Jimmy Doolittle set a West-to-East transcontinental record in it, 1931.

SUPER SPORTSTER -- 1933 modification of Gee-Bee, Granville Aircraft of Massachusetts, of the plane in which Jimmy Doolittle won the 1932 Thompson Trophy Race.

SUPER-TALOS -- See TYPHON

SUPER-TARTAR -- See TYPHON

SUPER THUNDERSTREAK -- Essentially the same as the F-84F, the -J model of this popular Republic series, made its first flight in 1954.

SUPER TIGER -- Fighter-bomber-interceptor version of the Grumman F11F aircraft. See TIGER.

SUPER 26 -- One of the many high-speed executive transport versions of the Douglas B-26 aircraft, this one by Lockheed Air Service.

SUPER WAL -- Dornier flying boat with two pairs of engines mounted in tandem. 1933 development of the WAL.

SUPERBOMBER -- Little-used, unofficial nickname for the Boeing/U.S. Air Force B-50 aircraft series.

SUPERCHARGE -- Breakout by British 8th Army, 30 Corps, at El Alamein, Egypt. Began 2 November 1942, WW-II.

SUPERCHARGE II -- British 8th Army breakthrough German-held Mareth Position, southern Tunisia, at El Hamma gap. Conducted in manner of El Alamein SUPERCHARGE. See also PUGILIST GALLOP. March 1943, WW-II.

SUPERFORTRESS -- (1) Boeing B-29, very heavy U.S. Army Air Forces bomber of World War II. Dropped the first atomic bombs. Used after the war as a medium bomber, aerial tanker, rescue craft and hurricane hunter. Also used in Korea as a bomber.

(2) Nickname shared by the B-29 replacement, the Boeing B-50. U.S. Air Force bomber operational with the Strategic Air Command in 1948 and presently used as an aerial tanker by the Tactical Air Command.

SUPERSNIFFER -- Airborne, 73-centimeter, frequency-modulated, bomb-release radar. Can automatically track an isolated target.

SUPERSONIC III -- U.S. solid propellant research vehicle capable of carrying a 2000-pound payload to an altitude of 70,000 feet. Under development.

SUPERVISOR -- Accra, Gold Coast, Africa. WW-II.

SURA -- Swiss surface-to-air missile for tactical air defense of combat troops. Solid propellant motor develops 2640-pound thrust. Also tested from aircraft with highly successful results. In operational use.

SURFBOARD -- Name for joint U.S. Army-Navy peacetime military exercise.

SURGE -- Acronym for Sorting, Updating, Report Generating, Etc., used in data processing.

SURVEYOR -- National Aeronautics and Space Administration program to soft-land a 750-pound spacecraft on the moon, including 100-300 pounds of instrumentation. Payload will include: Stereo-color television cameras, spectrometer, lunar surface drill, X-ray spectrometer, gas chromatograph and other analytical instruments. Booster was the ATLAS-CENTAUR. However, delays in that program may force use of ATLAS-AGENA, with consequent reduction in payload. First moon flights expected by mid-1964, with seven vehicles planned for soft-landing, and five for lunar orbiting missions. See also MOONSHOT, SNAP.

SUSAN -- (1) Port Harvey, New Guinea. WW-II.

(2) Solomon Islands. WW-II.

(3) Typhoon. 23-28 August 1945. First detected east of Taiwan. Moved northeastward at first, then turned northward across southwestern Honshu, Japan, and over Sea of Japan.

(4) Typhoon. 13-19 September 1953. Formed east of Luzon, Philippines. Moved northwestward through Balintang Channel and entered China mainland near Hong Kong.

(5) Typhoon. 14-16 June 1958. Formed between Truk and Ponape Islands, the Pacific. Moved northwestward across Guam as a weak storm, but intensified over Philippine Sea. Recurved northeastward and dissipated near Iwo Jima.

(6) Tropical storm. 27 February - 1 March 1961. Formed west of Koror Island, Western Caroline Islands. Moved northward a short distance and dissipated in the southern Philippine sea.

(7) Name also applied to tropical cyclones in western North Pacific which occurred prior to (1) through (4) above.

SUSCRIBE -- Karakelong Island, Netherlands East Indies. WW-II.

SUSIE -- (1) U.S. shield test pool facility nuclear reactor at Nuclear Reactor Testing Station, Idaho. Startup 1959.

(2) U.S. Navy designation of channel in Manila Bay just south of Corregidor, Philippines, for mine sweeping operations. February 1945, WW-II.

SUSPECT -- Bwoi Bwoi, Woodlark Island. WW-II.

SUSPENDER -- Yangla, New Britain. WW-II.

SUSPICION -- Southampton Island, Canada. WW-II.

SUXE -- Efate, New Hebrides. WW-II.

SUZANO -- Study program of the U.S. Defense Department's Advanced Research Projects Agency directed at the development of military and scientific space station. Study was conducted in 1960. Program not approved for development.

SUZU PLAN -- Orders issued on 17 August 1944 by Lieutenant General Sosaku Suzyki for the defense of Visayan Islands and Mindanao in the Philippines by Japanese 35th Army. WW-II.

SWAGGERCANE -- Big Delta, Alaska. WW-II.

SWALLOW -- (1) Japanese World War II Kawasaki KI.61 HIEN fighter.

(2) Messerschmitt Me-262 aircraft. See SCHWALBE.

(3) U.S. Army nickname for the SD-4 combat surveillance drone. Designed to carry variety of intelligence-gathering sensors (infra-red, radar etc.), the jet assisted take-off turbojet drone was to have a weight of about 3000 pounds and a range of 200 miles. Program cancelled after 30 million dollars had been spent on prototype vehicles.

SWAMP -- Namoluk Island, Caroline Islands. WW-II.

SWAMP FOX, PROJECT -- U.S. Army peacetime military exercise in Panama jungles; aimed at improving transportation and communication techniques in tropics. 1961.

SWAMP HUNT -- See SWAMP OPERATIONS

SWAMP OPERATIONS -- Tactics devised by Allies in Mediterranean in 1943 to keep enemy submarines submerged to point of exhaustion and overwhelm them when they surfaced. Also called SWAMP HUNT. WW-II.

SWAMPRAT -- Name for military operation.

SWAP -- An automatic coding system used in data processing.

SWARMER -- Major U.S. Army-Air Force peacetime combat exercise involving airborne-mounted attack completely supplied by airdropped and airlanded supplies. Based at Camp Mackall and Fort Bragg, North Carolina. April-May 1950.

SWASHING -- Kintang Island, Chusan Archipelago, China. WW-II.

SWAYBACK MARU -- Nickname for heavy cruiser, USS Salt Lake City. WW-II.

SWEET BRIAR -- Joint U.S.-Canadian peacetime military exercise. Fiscal year 1950.

SWEETACRES -- Mokmer Airdrome, Biak Island, New Guinea. WW-II.

SWEETPEA --Code name for United States Eight Military District. WW-II.

SWIFT -- (1) British light monoplane produced by Comper Aircraft after its formation in March 1929.

(2) Monoplane built in 1939 by the Wendt Aircraft Corporation of New York.

(3) Vickers-Supermarine British jet fighter which set a world speed record in 1953.

SWIFT, OPERATION -- Code name for transfer of operational roles from 3rd British Division to Canadian 1st Infantry Division in preparation for Allied invasion of Sicily. April 1943, WW-II.

SWIFT STRIKE, OPERATION -- Joint U.S. Army-Air Force exercise began 8 August 1961 with the parachuting of 7500 troops of the 82nd Airborn Division from Air Force planes, near Fort Bragg, North Carolina.

SWIFT STRIKE II -- Joint U.S. Army-Air Force peacetime military exercise in North and South Carolina. 1962.

SWIFTLIFT -- U.S. peacetime military operation. 1957-60.

SWITCH, OPERATION BIG -- See BIG SWITCH, OPERATION

SWITCH, OPERATION LITTLE -- See LITTLE SWITCH, OPERATION

SWITCHBACK -- Canadian 3rd Division operation to attack and destroy, or capture, all Germans remaining in Breskens Pocket (SCHELDT FORTRESS SOUTH), the area of Belgium and Holland, south of West Scheldt estuary. October - early November 1944, WW-II.

SWIVELPIN -- Ascension Island, Atlantic Ocean. WW-II.

SWORD -- (1) Beach assaulted by troops of British 3rd Infantry Division on D DAY, 6 June 1944, in Operation OVERLORD: located between Lion-sur-Mer and Ouistre-ham, Normandy, France. See also ASSAULT FORCE S.

   (2) Allied code name for route to GOTHIC LINE in British XIII Corps sector, central Italy. Summer 1944, WW-II.

SWORD AND DRUM -- British and Canadian rest and recreation facility for war-weary troops in San Vito, Italy. WW-II.

SWORD THRUST -- Name for NATO peacetime military exercise. 1960.

SWORDFISH -- Fairey carrier-based torpedo bomber used by Great Britain early in World War II.

   (2) Name for Royal Canadian Air Force Squadron Number 415.

SWORDHILT -- Allied plan to capture port of Brest, France, by combined airborne and amphibious operation if complete stalemate occurred in Normandy bridgehead area in summer 1944. WW-II.

SYCAMORE -- (1) General purpose helicopter developed by Bristol Aircraft in Great Britain; in use by the military at the present time.

   (2) Kokubona, Guadalcanal, Solomon Islands. WW-II.

SYLLABLE -- Tonelik Island, Caroline Islands. WW-II.

SYLVIA -- Name reserved by meteorologists for tropical cyclone in eastern North Pacific.

SYMBOL -- Code name for international conference at Casablanca, Morocco, attended by U.S. President Roosevelt, British Prime Minister Churchill, and French Generals de Gaulle and Giraud. Because held at Anfa Hotel, sometimes given code name Anfa. 14-23 January 1943, WW-II.

SYNCOM -- National Aeronautics and Space Administration instanteous, active repeater communications satellite to be launched in the 24-hour stationary earth orbit. It weighs 55 pounds, and is capable of carrying one full duplex radio-telephone channel. THOR-DELTA launch vehicle will be used for inclined orbits of about 30 degrees, and an ATLAS-AGENA for equatorial orbits. An experimental system, it will be supplanted by ADVANCED SYNCOM. Three flights are planned in the next six months, with the first expected in January 1963.

SYRACUSE -- Penguin Point, Solomon Islands. WW-II.

T

T-BIRD -- See TEE BIRD

T-BONE HILL -- Military name for topographic feature in Yokkokchon Valley, Korean, north of PORK CHOP HILL. Korean Conflict.

T MINE -- German anti-tank Tellermine. WW-II.

T.T. -- Martin biplane trainer of World War One. Notable because it marked the first time one company supplied the airframe and another, Curtiss, supplied the engine.

TA OPERATION - (1) Japanese attack on U.S. beachhead at Cape Torokina on Empress August Bay, Bougainville. Called by U.S. Battle of THE PERIMETER. March 1944, WW-II.

(2) Japanese landing of reinforcements of estimated 45,000 troops and 10,000 tons of supplies on west coast of Leyte, Philippines. Fall 1944, WW-II.

TABLETALK -- Lorungau, Manus Island, Bismarck Archipelago. WW-II.

TABLETENNIS -- Allied operation against Noemfoor Island, off north coast of Netherlands New Guinea, carried out by CYCLONE Task Force. 2 July - 31 August 1944, WW-II.

TABLOID -- Code name for Sardinia. WW-II.

TABSTONE -- Advanced Research Projects Agency program being conducted in conjunction with the U.S. Army's NIKE-ZEUS Kwajelein Island test program designed to study sensors to detect re-entry vehicles from infra-red and ultra-violet emanations. Program was accelerated during Fiscal year 1963, and is said to have been highly promising.

TACAIR -- Name for series of peacetime military air exercise.

TACAN -- Acronym for Tactical Air Navigation, a pulse-modulated, phase-comparison, short-range navigation system.

TACK, OPERATION -- Name given to airdrop by C-47 aircraft of U.S. 3rd Bombardment Wing of eight tons of roofing nails on highways south of Pyongyong,

Korea. 4 February 1951, Korean Conflict.

TACKLE -- Early U.S. Air Force program for a polar-orbiting communications satellite. Program integrated into objectives of the ADVENT program. No active development.

TADPOLE -- Name for peacetime military exercise.

TADPOLE ISLAND -- Ubrantakoto Island, Marshall Islands. WW-II.

TAF -- International meteorological code word used to indicate abbreviated terminal airport weather forecast. Abbreviated form of TAFOR.

TAFFY 1-3 -- Three task units of U.S. Escort Carrier Group (Task Group 77.4), commanded by Rear Admiral Thomas L. Sprague, during naval battle with Japanese off Samar, Philippines. Named after voice radio call sign used by each unit commander. October 1944, WW-II.

TAFOR -- International code word used to indicate a complete airport weather forecast.

TAFOT -- International code word denoting terminal airport weather forecast, units in English system.

TAG -- Acronym for The Acronym Generator.

TAIFUN -- (1) Messerschmitt Me. 108B aircraft, forerunner of the Me.109. Used for liaison prior to World War II by Germany. Also used in England where it was called Aldon.

(2) German anti-aircraft, unguided barrage rocket. Spin-stabilized, was launched in salvo from a special rack. It had a range of seven and one half miles, and could reach an altitude of five miles. WW-II development.

TAILLIGHT -- Portion of naval blockade of Korean east coast by units of U.N. Task 95 between front lines and Wonsan. Began early 1951, Korean Conflict.

TALISMAN -- See ECLIPSE

TALKING BIRD -- Communications package for various U.S. Air Force aircraft which permits them to become airborne command posts.

TALL BOY -- Allied 12,000-pound earthquake bomb. Scaled down version of GRAND SLAM. Made possible destruction of German battleship Tirpitz. WW-II.

TALLULAH -- See TRACTABLE

TALON -- (1) Northrop T-38, first supersonic aircraft designed from the outset for training role; entered service with the U.S. Air Force in 1961. First flown 1959.

(2) Allied seaborne invasion of Akyab, Burma; met with no opposition. 3 January 1945, WW-II.

TALOS -- U.S. Navy surface-to-air ship-mounted missile for use against high-speed aircraft. The two-stage vehicle has a range of more than 65 nautical miles, and can reach extreme altitudes. Boosted by a solid propellant motor, it is sustained in flight by a ramjet engine. An outgrowth of the BUMBLEBEE PROJECT, it was first fired in May 1954, and became operational in 1959. Deployed aboard guided missile cruisers.

TAMET -- International code word denoting terminal airport weather forecast, units in the metric system.

TAMPER -- Diversionary landing by British at Morondava, Madagascar. 10 September 1942, WW-II.

TAN -- Code name for Cuba. WW-II.

TANBARK -- Mt. Welcker, New Britain. WW-II.

TANGENT -- Kangean Island, Netherlands East Indies. WW-II.

TANGERINE -- Nugu Point, Guadalcanal, Solomon Islands. WW-II.

TANGO -- Code word for letter "T" in a phonetic alphabet, used to avoid possibility of a misunderstanding in transmitting messages. See also TARE.

TANNE -- Proposed occupation of Suursaari (Tanne Ost) and Aland Islands (Tanne West) in Gulf of Finland. 1944, WW-II.

TANYA -- Name reserved by meteorologists for tropical cyclone in North Atlantic area.

TAPE WORM I -- Natata Island, Marshall Islands. WW-II.

TAR HEEL -- U.S. peacetime maneuvers held at Fort Bragg in the spring and summer of 1949.

TARA -- Hurricane. 11-12 November 1961. Formed over Pacific off Acapulco, Mexico. Moved northward and inland between Acapulco and Zihuantanejo, causing floods, landslides, and over 436 deaths.

TARE -- Code word for letter "T" in a phonetic alphabet, used to avoid possibility of a misunderstanding in transmitting messages. See also TANGO.

TARE GREEN -- Strip of land, 1000 yards in width, on UTAH Beach, Normandy. June 1944. WW-II.

TARE HILL -- U.S. military name for topographic feature on Okinawa. 1945, WW-II.

TARGET HILL -- Military name for topographic feature on New Britain Island. December 1943, WW-II.

TARGETEER -- U.S. Navy target missile designed for testing surface-to-air missiles at altitudes up to 60,000 feet. Propelled by DEACON solid propellant motor, it has optical tracking flares attached to motor and a radar reflective parachute system for recovery. In operational use.

TART -- U.S. Air Force-Navy countermeasures rocket which uses a small solid propellant rocket. Produced in 1960.

TARTAN -- Name for peacetime military exercise.

TARTAR -- U.S. Navy surface-to-air ship-mounted missile for defense against both high and low flying aircraft. The two-stage solid propellant missile is designed as the primary anti-aircraft armament for destroyers and secondary armament for cruisers. It replaces the 5-inch naval gun. First firing took place in December 1956. Operational. See also BUMBLEBEE PROJECT.

TARZAN -- (1) U.S. radio-controlled bomb developed in 1945 and continued experimentally after World War II. Weighing about six tons, it was to have been carried by B-29 or B-36 aircraft.

(2) Allied plan for airborne capture of Indaw-Katha area, Burma, in conjunction with a major land advance. Modified into GRIPFAST. Late 1943, WW-II.

TARZON -- Six-ton RAZON bomb; used briefly during Korean Conflict, but withdrawn on account of faulty safe-salvo feature. See also TRIZON, AZON.

TATTERSALLS -- Tinian Island, Marianas Islands. WW-II.

TATTLETALE -- U.S. Air Force program to test the feasibility of employing radio transmitters in rockets to establish an emergency communications net. Tests were made in 1960 with SPAEROBEE rockets in which a 47-pound payload was launched to a 300-mile altitude. Results were favorable, but program is not being actively pursued.

TAUNUS -- Code name for anti-jamming device that differentiates blip of genuine target from that of WINDOW.

TAURUS -- Allahabad, India. WW-II.

TAVERN -- Susua Point, Trobriand Island. WW-II.

TAXABLE -- British deception operation, using 16 planes and 18 small ships; intended to induce Germans to believe that large convoy was proceeding across narrowest part of English Channel, to the north of Operation OVERLORD. 5-6 June 1944, WW-II.

TAXI NUMBERS -- Part of ordnance classification system used by U.S. Army in which subdivision for standard articles, such as automotive parts, hardware, or tools, consisted of a number prefixed by four letters, the last of which was always X. Named after first number of this type, TAAX1. Used until adoption of IBM cards in 1941.

TAXPAYER -- Angaur, Palau Islands. WW-II.

TAYLOR SUIT -- Electrically heated flying suit used by British during WW-II.

TEACUP -- Manus Island, Bismarck Archipelago. WW-II.

TEAK -- Port Moresby, New Guinea. WW-II.

TEAL -- U.S. Navy air-launched target drone equipped with corner radar reflectors and flares for pilot training in firing air-to-air missiles. Solid propelled, it indicates the accuracy of the attacking missile by firing marker flares when a missile comes within lethal distance. Initially tested in September 1957. Official designation: XKDT-1.

TEAMMATE -- Name for peacetime military operation.

TEAPOT -- Cape Goltz, New Britain. WW-II.

TEAPOT, OPERATION -- U.S. nuclear weapons test at Nevada Test Site. Spring 1955.

TEARAWAY -- Saipan, Marianas Islands. WW-II.

TEARDROP -- Operation by two U.S. Navy air and sea Barrier Forces against German submarines mistakenly believed to be attempting to launch robot rocket attacks on East Coast cities; broke up mission of SEEWOLF group of U-boats, March-May 1945. WW-II.

TEARDROP, THE -- Military name for Japanese position on Biak, island off north coast of Netherlands New Guinea. Captured by U.S. 186th Infantry Regiment, 25 June 1944, WW-II.

TEAS -- Acronym for U.S. Air Force study of a Threat Evaluation and Action Selection program. Part of a program to determine the requirements of a command and control center for defense and civilian use during the 1970's. Program is being emphasized by top Department of Defense officials.

TECHNICOLOR -- Kalagen, New Britain. WW-II.

TED -- Force under PERSECUTION Task Force consisting of U.S. 124th Infantry Regiment reinforced; active in counteroffensive against Japanese in Driniumor River area, near Aitape, New Guinea. Code name taken from nickname of commanding officer, Colonel Edward M. Starr. 31 July-10 August 1944, WW-II.

TEDDER CARPET -- Method of fast, low-level strafing developed by Royal Air Force Chief Marshal Sir Arthur Tedder. WW-II.

TED'S TRAVELING CIRCUS -- Nickname for U.S. Army Air Forces 93rd Heavy
Bombardment Group. Named after its commander, Colonel Edward J. Timberlake.
WW-II.

TEE BIRD -- Lockheed T-33, trainer version of the P/F-80; first flew in 1948.
Widely used throughout the U.S. Air Force and U.S. Navy. Called Sea Star
by Navy.

TEEPEE -- U.S. Navy program designed to reflect radar beams off the ionosphere
and to detect exhaust gases of missile launchings at vast distances. Preliminary
tests have been successful and program is to get increased emphasis in Fiscal year
1963-64. Technique is said to be able to detect missile launches at distances of
4000 miles.

TEETH TO TAIL -- British term to describe proportion of administrative and supply
units to fighting troops. WW-II.

TELEGRAPH HILL -- U.S. military name for topographic feature in east Naha,
Okinawa. 1945, WW-II.

TELERAN -- Navigation system using ground radar and television transmitting equipment and airborne television receiving equipment.

TELLEBOMB -- Italian guided bomb developed in the 1920's. Weighs 175 pounds
with a payload of 130 pounds. The air-to-surface weapon had a range of six
miles and a speed of 250 miles per hour.

TELSTAR -- U.S. experimental, active repeater communications satellite used to
provide information on the feasibility of this type of satellite, and to measure
radiation effects on the satellite and its lifetime. Weighing 170 pounds, it was
launched into a medium altitude orbit (apogee 5603 miles), July 1962; successfully received and transmitted television, telephone and radio signals from Europe
and the U.S. First U.S. communications satellite; developed by American Telephone and Telegraph Company and launched on a cost-reimbursable basis by
National Aeronautics and Space Administration. Several more launches planned
in 1963. See also RELAY.

TEMPEST -- Hawker series of interceptors/fighter-bombers which first flew in 1942.
Final version was the last single-seat, single-piston-engine fighter-bomber to
fly with the British Royal Air Force.

TEMPO -- Acronym for Technical Military Planning Operation.

TEMPO II -- Smith Aircraft conversion of the Douglas B-26 INVADER aircraft.

TEMPTATION -- Little Malumalu Island, New Britain. WW-II.

TEN -- Avro 8-passenger British-built version of the Fokker F-VII trimotor aircraft
of the early 1930's.

TEN-ICHI, OPERATION -- Planned Japanese surface attack by naval force against U.S. forces at Okinawa; intercepted by U.S. aircraft and ships destroyed (including Yamato, biggest warship ever built) or dispersed. April 1945, WW-II.

TEN, MISSION -- Initial movement of equipment and ground personnel of U.S. XX Bomber Command to India. April 1944, WW-II.

TEN 99 -- Six-place, all-purpose Hiller helicopter. First flown in 1961.

TENRAI -- (English translation: Heavenly Thunder) World War II Japanese Nakajima J5N1 twin-engine heavy interceptor first flown in 1944. Did not advance beyond prototype.

TENSTRIKE -- Chilkoot Barracks, Alaska. WW-II.

TENTERHOOK -- Horta, Azores. WW-II.

TERESE -- Name reserved by meteorologists for tropical cyclone in North Atlantic area.

TERMINAL -- (1) Seizure of vital points in harbor at Algiers, North Africa, and landing of British and U.S. forces to prevent sabotage. A phase of Operation TORCH. Similar to RESERVIST at Oran. 8 November 1942.

(2) Code name for international conference at Potsdam, Germany, attended by U.S. President Truman, Soviet Premier Stalin, old and new British Prime Ministers Churchill and Attlee. 16 July - 2 August 1945, WW-II.

TERMITE -- (1) Kapoli Lake, New Britain. WW-II.

(2) Taiagina Bay, Solomon Islands. WW-II.

TERNE -- Norwegian ship-to-underwater unguided missile for use in anti-submarine warfare. Solid propelled with an high explosive depth charge warhead, it has a range of more than three and one half miles. Operational aboard Norwegian ships; also being evaluated by the U.S. for use on destroyer escorts.

TERRACE -- Apo Pass, Philippine Islands. WW-II.

TERRAPIN -- (1) Nickname for Allied amphibious vehicle. WW-II.

(2) U.S. upper-atmosphere research rocket capable of carrying 4-20 pound payloads to altitudes of 88 miles. Two-stage solid propellant rocket. No longer in use.

TERRIBLES, LES -- Nickname given by French during World War One to U.S. 32nd Infantry Division.

TERRIER -- (1) U.S. Navy surface-to-air ship-mounted missile for use aboard guided missile cruisers, destroyers, aircraft carriers, frigates and for shore-use by Marine Corps. The first Navy operational missile system, Terrier I had a range of 10-

12 miles and could reach altitudes of more than eight miles. Terrier 2 has a range of up to 20 miles and can reach altitudes of 10 miles. Both are two-stage solid propellant vehicles differing essentially in the improved guidance system of Terrier 2. Terrier 1 first fired in 1954 from the USS Mississippi and became operational in 1956. Terrier 2 is also operational. Both are being replaced by the TERRIER, ADVANCED. See also BUMBLEBEE PROJECT.

(2) U.S. Army land version of Navy's surface-to-air TERRIER. Program cancelled in 1956.

TERRIER 1 -- See TERRIER

TERRIER 2 -- See TERRIER

TERRIER, ADVANCED -- Improved version of TERRIER; has almost double the range (about 22 miles) of the earlier missiles. Also has an improved guidance system, with both terminal homing and mid-course guidance. Improved version became operational in 1961 aboard the USS Dewey, a guided missile frigate. Planned to replace earlier Terrier models aboard naval vessels.

TERRIGAL, BATTLE OF -- Depth charge attack against submarine claimed to have been sighted by two boys at Terrigal, 20 miles north of Sydney, Australia; conducted by Australian destroyer, Stuart, against object, picked up on detection gear, which later proved to be underwater rock outcrops. 9 September 1939, WW-II.

TERRY -- Name reserved by meteorologists for tropical cyclone in eastern North Pacific.

TERRY AND THE PIRATES -- Special air force, officially known as Air Commandos, which flew out wounded men of long range penetration groups from behind Japanese lines in Burma; commanded by U.S. Colonel Philip Cochran. Nickname taken from comic strip, created by Milton A. Caniff, who had been a friend of Cochran at Ohio State University, and who based character, Flip Corkin, on him. Also called Cochran's Young Ladies. See also BLOOD CHARIOTS. WW-II.

TERZI POINT -- Military name for topographic feature on New Britain Island; named in honor of U.S. Marine Corps Captain Joseph A. Terzi, who was killed in action during landings on island; initially called HELL'S POINT. December 1943. WW-II.

TESS -- (1) Typhoon. 24-25 August 1945. First detected in northern part of South China Sea. Moved northward into China mainland east of Hong Kong.

(2) Typhoon. 17-23 September 1953. Formed in central Caroline Islands. Moved west-northwestward at first, then turned northward over Philippine Sea and northeastward over Pacific.

(3) Typhoon. 2-4 July 1958. Formed near Ponape in Caroline Islands, the Pacific. Moved northwestward, passed north of Guam, and dissipated east of Taiwan.

(4) Typhoon. 24–31 March 1961. Formed near Caroline Islands. Moved west-ward south of Guam, turned northward through Philippine Sea, then north-eastward, but dissipated before reaching Volcano Islands. Caused damage on Yap and Ulithi, West Caroline Islands.

(5) Name also applied to tropical cyclones in western North Pacific which occur-red prior to (1) through (4) above.

TEST RIG -- U.S. Army one-ton utility truck.

TEST-DROP -- Name for military exercise.

TESTAMENT -- Legom River, New Britain. WW-II.

TETRAHEDRA -- Pyramid-shaped obstacles in German beach defences formed of three concrete, steel or wooden bars. WW-II.

TEXAN -- North American trainer, first produced in 1938; in service with the U.S. Air Force as the T-6 until 1955. Called the SNJ by the U.S. Navy and Harvard by the British.

TEXAS -- Military name for outpost in Korea. 1953, Korean Conflict.

TEXAS DIVISION -- Nickname for U.S. 36th Infantry Division.

TEXAS TOWER -- Off-shore, platform-based radar installation.

TEZUITLAN -- Antonio Sea model trainer plane built of plywood for the Mexican air arm during World War II.

THELMA -- (1) Typhoon. 16–25 April 1956. Formed in central Caroline Islands. Moved west-northwestward across Philippine Sea and island of Luzon, then re-curved northeastward and dissipated over the Ryukyu Islands.

(2) Tropical Depression. 18–20 September 1959. Formed south of Guam. Mov-ed northwestward over Philippine Sea and dissipated.

(3) Typhoon. 21–28 August 1962. Formed over northern Mariana Islands. Mov-ed northwestward toward Japan and turned northward across Honshu, Japan. Entered Sea of Japan and joined another storm system south of Kamchatka.

(4) Name also applied to tropical cyclones in western North Pacific which oc-curred prior to (1) through (3) above.

THEASAURUS -- Kirensk, Siberia. WW-II.

THESEUS -- Axis plan to occupy all of Cyrenaica, North Africa. Spring 1942, WW-II.

THESIS -- Mass strafing raid by British on aerodrome and military targets on Crete. 23 July 1943, WW-II.

THETIS -- German code-name for spar-buoys supporting reflecting material, released by submarines to confuse Allied radar operators.   WW-II.

THIMBLE -- Sibuyan Sea, Philippine Islands.   WW-II.

THING, THE -- U.S. Marine Corps nickname for U.S. anti-tank vehicle, carrying six 106-mm. recoilless rifles, used in Cuba in 1960's.

THINGLESS -- Avach Bay, U.S.S.R. WW-II.

THIRSTY -- Broome, Australia.   WW-II.

31-KNOT BURKE -- Nickname for Admiral Arleigh A. Burke given for actions in Pacific during World War II.

32, PROJECT -- First program undertaken by U.S. Air Corps Ferrying Command (predecessor to Air Transport Command) to train its own officers and enlisted personnel for overseas ferrying operations.   So named because number of crews originally trained was 32 a month.   February-June 1942, WW-II.

THOR -- U.S. Air Force intermediate range ballistic missile with a range of 1500 nautical miles.   One of the earliest operational long-range ballistic missiles, the liquid propelled vehicle was first flight tested in January 1957, and became operational in fall 1958.   Four squadrons of 15 missiles each have been deployed, but will be phased out over the next couple of years.   Widely used in the U.S. space program as the first stage for a space booster; has proven to be one of the most reliable of U.S. launch vehicles.   Official Air Force designation: SM-75.

THOR-ABLE -- U.S. space launch vehicle with an adapted THOR first stage and Able upper stages.   First stage develops 150,000-pound thrust from its liquid propellant engines; second stage 7500-pound thrust; third, 3000-pound thrust, fourth (a solid motor) 2200-pound thrust.   Payload capability of the vehicle was about 250 pounds.   Used in the PIONEER and EXPLORER programs.   No longer in use.

THOR-ABLE-STAR -- U.S. space launch vehicle with a modified THOR first stage and Able-Star upper stages.   First stage thrust: 150,000 pounds; second stage thrust: 7900 pounds.   Payload capability in a 300-mile orbit is 900 pounds. Able-Star has a restart capability.   Used in GREB, TRANSIT, COMPOSITE, ANNA and COURIER satellite programs; only ANNA is still launched by the Thor-Able-Star.   Early name was Thor-Epsilon.

THOR-AGENA -- U.S. space launch vehicle with a modified THOR first stage and an AGENA upper stage.   First stage thrust: 150,000 pounds, second stage thrust 16,000 pounds.   Payload capability 1600 pounds in a 300-mile orbit.   Vehicle is used in the DISCOVERER, NIMBUS, ECHO, OGO, Topside Sounder and other satellite programs.   Agena has a restart capability.   First used in February 1959 to launch Discoverer I.   Early name was THOR-HUSTLER.   See also ALOUETTE.

THOR-AGENA B -- U.S. space launch vehicle with adapted THOR first stage and Agena B second stage. See AGENA.

THOR-DELTA -- U.S. space launch vehicle with a modified THOR first stage and DELTA upper stages. First stage thrust: 150,000 pounds, second stage thrust: 7500 pounds, and third stage thrust; 3000 pounds (solid motor). Capable of putting 500-pound payload into a 345-mile orbit, with 60 pounds to escape velocity. One of the most reliable of U.S. launch vehicles, it is used in the TIROS, ECHO, EXPLORER, TELESTAR and other satellite programs. First used in an unsuccessful launch of Echo.

THOR-EPSILON -- Early name for the THOR-ABLE-STAR.

THOR-HUSTLER -- Early name for the THOR-AGENA.

THOR-VANGUARD -- Early name for the THOR-ABLE.

THORA -- Name reserved by meteorologists for tropical cyclone in North Atlantic area.

THORITE -- Koskiki, Japan. WW-II.

THORN -- Rabaul, New Britain. WW-II.

THREADWORN -- Okino Daito Jima, Japan. WW-II.

THREE SISTERS -- See JANE HILL

THREE SPEARHEADS, THE -- Nickname for Company E, U.S. 126th Regiment, which on landing at Fort Moresby on 15 September 1942 became first U.S. infantry unit in New Guinea. Taken from reference in departure talk by Major General Edwin F. Harding to "the spearhead of the spearhead of the spearhead," meaning that the company was the spearhead of the regiment which in turn was the spearhead of the division and corps. WW-II.

THREE SPURS -- Australian military name for topographic feature on Portuguese Timor. Early 1942, WW-II.

THREE WAYS -- Name for road junction near Rabaul, New Britain. WW-II.

THROAT -- British capture of Mayotte Isle near Madagascar. 2 July 1942, WW-II.

THUD -- Acronym for Thorium, Uranium, Deuterium criticals used in zero-power reactor facilities.

THUMPER -- U.S. surface-to-air command-guided rocket with a range of 35 miles. No longer under development.

THUNDER -- Zamboanga, Philippine Islands. WW-II.

THUNDERBIRD -- (1) British surface-to-air, solid propellant missile with a range of 25 miles at altitudes of 12 miles. Four wrap-around boosters are used to accelerate the missile to Mach 2, and one solid motor isused as a sustainer. A mobile system, the missile has been operational since 1959. A more advanced version is undergoing evaluation tests. It will be capable of destroying low-flying aircraft at greater ranges than the earlier version.

(2) Name for Royal Canadian Air Force Squadron Number 426.

THUNDERBIRD DIVISION -- Nickname for U.S. 45th Infantry Division.

THUNDERBOLT -- (1) Developed from the Seversky/Republic P-35, and the P-43/P-44, the Republic P-47 aircraft achieved great success in World War II. First flight in 1942. Also called the Jug.

(2) Allied air-ground offensive in Metz area, France. Fall 1944, WW-II.

(3) Conference held in London to examine effectiveness of air operations in OVERLORD. Summer 1947

(4) Name for U.S. peacetime military exercise at Fort Hood, Texas; designed to provide combined unit training for armored division combat command. 1961.

(5) See RAIDEN

THUNDERBOLT DIVISION -- Nickname for U.S. 83rd Infantry Division.

THUNDERBOLT, OPERATION -- Limited objective attack, mounted by U.S. I and IX Corps, designed to clear enemy out of area south of Han River, Korea. Began 25 January 1951, Korean Conflict.

THUNDERBOLTS -- Nickname for U.S. 11th Armored Division.

THUNDERCEPTOR -- Republic XF-91 aircraft which underwent three years of developmental testing starting in May 1948, but did not get past the prototype stage.

THUNDERCHIEF -- All-weather Republic F-105 fighter-bomber. This U.S. Air Force tactical workhorse did not enter the inventory in large numbers until 1959, even though its first flight was made in 1955.

THUNDERCLAP -- (1) A Allied higher command staff exercise during April and May 1944. WW-II.

(2) Projected operation by all available U.S. and British heavy bomber aircraft for joint daylight assault on Berlin, Germany, the object being to destroy as much of city as possible. First proposed in August 1944; abandoned. WW-II.

THUNDERFLASH -- RF-84 reconnasissance version of the Republic F-84; first flew in U.S. Air Force tests in February 1952. Modified in the mid-1950's as the GRF-84F, a parasitic, long-range, strategic reconnaissance aircraft, mated to an RB-36.

THUNDERJET -- Nickname for the Republic XP-84 jet interceptor which first flew in 1946. Still operational in many of the Free World's air arms.

THUNDERMUG -- (1) Nickname for improvised anti-aircraft weapon; consisted of iron pipe set in concrete block and filled with explosives and rocks; charge was set off by low-flying planes and rocks were sprayed in air. WW-II.

    (2) Name of flagship of squadron of U.S. Navy Liberator aircraft, commanded by Commander Norman H. Miller, active in Pacific against Japanese ships and planes. WW-II.

    (3) Mt. Lollo, New Britain. WW-II.

THUNDERSTORM, OPERATION -- Dragnet operated by German GESTAPO after assassination attempt on Hitler, 20 July 1944, in which thousands of people were arrested. WW-II.

THUNDERSTREAK -- Sweptwing version of the world-famous Republic F-84 aircraft series. This was the F model which made its first flight in 1950 and is still operational.

THUNDERSTRUCK -- Port Darwin, Australia. WW-II.

THURSDAY, OPERATION -- Airborne and land advance by Major General Orde Wingate's Chindits to positions behind Japanese lines in northeast Burma; General Wingate was killed in air crash during operation. Began 5 March 1944, WW-II.

THYME -- Nogokiki, Guadalcanal, Solomon Islands. WW-II.

TIAMAT -- U.S. Army Air Force air-to-air missile designed as an experimental test vehicle and often ground-launched during the test program. Solid propelled and radar-guided, it got its name from an earlier two-stage National Advisory Committee for Aeronautics test vehicle which underwent testing at Wallops Island, Virginia, in late 1944. Air Force program terminated in 1946. Official designations: JB-3 (Air Force), MX-570 (NACA).

TICONDEROGA -- Allied code name for road junction south of Ortona, Italy, in area to be defended by British Indian troops. May 1944, WW-II.

TIDALWAVE -- (1) U.S. low-level attack on oil refineries at Ploesti, Rumania, by B-24 heavy bombers based in Libya. Previously called Statesman, and Soapsuds; change from Soapsuds to more impressive final name appreciated by both Prime Minister Churchill and President Roosevelt. Considered one of outstanding air operations of war, with five Medals of Honor awarded to participants. 1 August 1943, WW-II.

    (2) Name for U.S. peacetime military exercise in Far East-Pacific area.

TIDEMARSH -- Amalfi, Italy. WW-II.

TIGAR 1C -- U.S. Ledo-Myitkyina-Kunming Road project. Also called TIG-1C. WW-II.

CODE NAMES DICTIONARY

TIGAR 26A -- Project to move supplies for U.S. 14th Air Force over line of communications Kunming-Chanyi-Kweiyang-Tushan-Liuchow-Kweilin to be distributed
around east China airfields. Also called TIG-26A. 1944-45, WW-II.

TIGAR 26 B -- U.S. project to bring 500 five-ton truck-trailer combinations from
Persian Gulf to China by way of Soviet Union. See also LUX Convoy. 1944-45
WW-II.

TIGER -- (1) German Mark VI heavy tank equipped with 88-mm. gun. See also
PANTHER. WW-II.

(2) Fieseler F.2 acrobatic biplane built in 1932 by the firm of the famous German
acrobatic pilot, Gerhard Fieseler.

(3) Grumman F11F midwing, supersonic fighter plane, originally designated F9F.
Entered U.S. Navy service in 1958. See also SUPER TIGER.

(4) Name for Axis-defended locality near Tobruk, Libya. Scene of action in
Operation CRUSADER. November 1941, WW-II.

(5) Canadian military name for ridge east of Nissoria, Sicily. July 1943, WW-II.

(6) Amerer River, New Britain. WW-II.

(7) Projected force of British long-range bombers to be used in Pacific against
Japan. 1944-45, WW-II.

(8) Name for Royal Canadian Air Force Squadron Number 424.

(9) British naval operation; included fast convoy of tanks and Hurrican fighter
aircraft from United Kingdom by way of Gibraltar to Egypt, slow and fast
convoys from Alexandria, Egypt, to Malta, and bombardment of Bengasi,
Libya. May 1941, WW-II.

(10) Large-scale Canadian and British training exercise in England involving six
divisions; counties of Kent and Sussex were assumed to be independent hostile
nations, with Surrey independent. 19-30 May 1942, WW-II.

(11) One of four flights in U.S. KIT PROJECT to send A-20 aircraft from Florida
to Oran, Algeria, for use in North African campaign. November 1942,
WW-II.

(12) Full-dress rehearsal invasion exercise, held in Slapton Sands area, England,
by U.S. VII Corps in preparation for landing on UTAH Beach, Normandy,
in Operation OVERLORD. Before exercise's H HOUR some of its Landing
Ships, Tanks (LST's) unexpectedly encountered German warships and suffered
loss of life greater than that in initial UTAH assault. 22-30 April 1944,
WW-II.

TIGER GROUP -- Strong Canadian armored force active northeast of Udem, Germany,
during Operation BLOCKBUSTER. See also LION GROUP. Late February 1945,
WW-II.

TIGER MOTH -- D.H. 82 single-engine biplane which first appeared in 1931, and was built in large numbers, by DeHavilland, during World War II as a British trainer.

TIGERCAT -- Grumman F7F twin-engine fighter aircraft developed for the U.S. Navy-Marine Corps during World War II.

TIGERS -- Nickname for U.S. 10th Armored Division.

TIGERSCHWALBE -- Early-1930's Svenska biplane trainer for the Swedish Air Force.

TIGRESS -- Samarinda, Borneo. WW-II.

TILDA -- (1) Typhoon. 25-30 November 1954. First detected southeast of Guam. Moved westward past Guam, across the Philippine Sea, through central Philippines and out over South China Sea. Caused considerable damage in Philippines.

(2) Typhoon. 15-21 April 1959. Formed south of Truk Island. Moved northwestward past Guam, then turned northward through eastern Philippine Sea and dissipated southwest of Iwo Jima.

(3) Typhoon. 27 September - 5 October 1961. Formed east of Guam. Moved west-northwestward across northern Mariana Islands and Okinawa and dissipated near Shanghai, China. Caused 11 deaths and over six million dollars damage.

(4) Name also applied to tropical cyclones in western North Pacific which occurred prior to (1) through (3) above.

TILFORD -- Code name for "toe" of Italy. WW-II.

TILLIE -- Name reserved by meteorologists for tropical cyclone in eastern North Pacific.

TILTING -- Palm (Revirevi) Island, Solomon Islands. WW-II.

TIMBERLINE -- Joint U.S. Army-Air Force maneuvers.

TIMBERWOLF -- Movement of additional Canadian units, including 5th Armoured Division, from United Kingdom to Mediterranean in order to bring Canadian strength there up to corps level. October-November 1943, WW-II.

TIMBERWOLF DIVISION -- Nickname for U.S. 104th Infantry Division.

TIN HATS -- Canadian concert troupe entertaining military personnel in Italy. WW-II.

TIN PAN ALLEY -- U.N. code name for portion of Wonsan harbor, North Korea. Korean Conflict.

CODE NAMES DICTIONARY

TINDALL -- Name for the simulated preparations of the British in Scotland for an attack on Norway in 1943; part of COCKADE operation which feigned Allied attack on continent. WW-II.

TINDERBOX -- Code name for Dead Sea. WW-II.

TING-A-LING -- One of the early names for GENIE.

TINKERTOY -- Name for peacetime military project.

TINSEL -- British Royal Air Force jamming of German radio telephonic communication by airborne fighters. WW-II.

TINY TIM -- U.S. Navy solid propellant rocket with a range of one mile and a warhead of 150 pounds of TNT. The 1200-pound weapon was developed in the latter stages of World War II and was used in the battle of Okinawa. In Korea, the rocket was employed with great effectiveness by Marine aircraft. No longer in use.

TIROS -- Project name for experimental meteorological satellite system which has been in operation since the first launch from Cape Canaveral on 1 April 1960. Name is a contraction for television infra-red observation satellite. Also called Pillbox. See also NIMBUS.

TIROS V -- U.S. THOR-DELTA - launched satellite for gathering data on ice-break-up and hurricane growth in south Atlantic.

TITAN I -- U.S. Air Force intercontinental ballistic missile with a range of more than 5500 miles. Using a radio-inertial guidance system, the liquid propelled missile develops a first stage thrust of 300,000 pounds, and a second stage thrust of 80,000 pounds. Development began in 1955, as a backup to ATLAS, and the first firing took place in February 1959. Missile stored in hardened silos and raised to the surface for firing. First squadron became operational in April 1962. Six squadrons planned. Official designation: SM-68A.

TITAN II -- U.S. Air Force intercontinental ballistic missile with a range of more than 5500 miles. Greatly improved and simplified version of TITAN I; develops first-stage thrust of 430,000 pounds and a second stage thrust of 100,000 pounds. Has an all-inertial guidance system. Will be stored and fired from underground silos. Flight test program began in 1962; expected to become operational in 1963. Six squadrons planned. National Aeronautics and Space Administration will use a modified, man-rated Titan II for launching its GEMINI space capsule.

TITAN III -- U.S. Air Force standardized space launch vehicle designed as a flexible space booster for all military space vehicles over the next decade. Capable of orbiting 5,000-20,000-pound payload, the Titan III will use the TITAN II first and second stages as a central core with two large, 120-inch diameter solid propellant boosters strapped on as the first stage. A new transition will also be developed as a third stage for the core vehicle. Approved for development in 1962; first flight expected in late 1964 or early 1965. See also PHOENIX.

TITANIC -- Cape Sam Augustin, Philippine Islands. WW-II.

TO OPERATION -- Japanese plan to intercept and annihilate any enemy fleet approaching their homeland; inaugurated during U.S. Navy carrier raid against Marcus and Wake Islands. 20-24 May 1944, WW-II.

TOBOGGAN -- Chemical high explosive project intended to prepare for peaceful nuclear excavation projects. Conducted by Sandia Laboratory, New Mexico, in the Playa Lake Bed at Nevada Test Site.

TOBRUK FERRY SERVICE -- Shuttle service of British and Australian destroyers from Alexandria and Mersa Matruh, Egypt, to carry supplies and troop reinforcements to besieged port of Tobruk, Libya. May-December 1941, WW-II.

TOBRUK WEAPON-PIT -- German underground concrete chamber with circular neck-like opening a few inches above ground; metal track inside neck provided for rotation of either anti-tank turret or machine-gun mount. WW-II.

TODD CITY -- Name for U.S. Navy repair and supply base in central Solomons. Named for Leon E. Todd, Jr., one of first PT boat men killed in area. WW-II.

TOE AND BALL OPERATION -- Project for two-pronged invasion at Gioja and Crotone in Calabria region at foot of Italian peninsula or boot. 1943, WW-II.

TOENAILS -- U.S. Admiral William F. Halsey's operation against New Georgia. Also called Operation A. Began 21 June 1943, WW-II.

TOGGLE -- Laur, Luzon, Philippine Islands. WW-II.

TOGO -- Japanese plan for operations in China in three phases: capture of Heng-yang; capture of Kweilin and Liuchow; capture of Nan-ning, opening of Canton-Hankow railroad and overrunning of U.S. 14th Air Force's fields at Sui-chuan and Nan-hsiung. Second part of ICHIGO. Began 27 May 1944, WW-II.

TOJO -- Allied designation for the Nakajima KI.44 fighter which first flew in 1940. Entered production in 1942 and remained in service throughout World War II. Japanese nickname: Shoki (Demon).

TOKA -- Japanese piloted-bomb project. Not as far advanced as BAKA BOMB. WW-II.

TOKKATAI -- Suicide pilots of Japanese Army Air Force; volunteered to fly aircraft into target and there to perish with it. Called KAMIKAZE in Japanese Naval Air Force. WW-II.

TOKYO EXPRESS -- (1) Nickname for U.S. 27th Infantry Division. Also called EMPIRE DIVISION, NEW YORK DIVISION, GALLA VANTERS.

(2) U.S. nickname for Japanese attempts to supply and reinforce their garrisons in Southern Solomons by fast runs of destroyers and light cruisers down THE SLOT. 1942-43, WW-II.

TOKYO ROSE -- American-born Japanese woman, Mrs. I. Toguri D'Aquino, who broadcast propaganda to Allied troops on radio from Japan. Sentenced to prison for treason, 1949. WW-II.

TOKYO TANK -- Nickname for extra, externally-fitted fuel tank on an airplane. WW-II.

TOLSTOY -- Meeting in Moscow between British Prime Minister Winston S. Churchill and Russian Premier Joseph Stalin. Began 9 October 1944, WW-II.

TOM CATS -- U.S. Navy picket destroyers, equipped with radar and aircraft homing devices, which were stationed about 60 miles out from a naval carrier task force on strike days in order to give advance warning of approaching enemy aircraft, especially Japanese KAMIKAZES. WW-II.

TOM HILL -- U.S. military name for topographic feature on Okinawa. 1945, WW-II.

TOM OBJECTIVE -- Hill objective, one and a half miles north of Arnara, Italy, taken by Canadian troops. May 1944, WW-II.

TOMAHAWK -- (1) British name for the early World War II U.S. export models of the Curtiss P-40/Hawk series. Other versions called: Hawk, Kittyhawk, WARHAWK.

   (2) One of the early industry studies of an anti-tank missile with considerable performance improvement over the ENTAC. Studies of this type, and a U.S. Army requirement for such a system, led to the approval for development of TOW.

   (3) Lolo, Belgian Congo. WW-II.

TOMAHAWK, OPERATION -- Airdrop of U.S. 187th Regiment at Munsan-ni, Korea. 23 March 1951, Korean Conflict.

TOMATO -- Watson Island, Treasury Islands. WW-II.

TOMB HILL -- U.S. military name for topographic feature on Okinawa. Named for numerous burial vaults along its sides. 1945, WW-II.

TOMBOLA -- Flexible six-inch underwater pipeline designed to discharge oil tankers anchored offshore in Normandy, France. WW-II.

TOMBSTONE -- Sinakela, Trobriand Islands. WW-II.

TOMBSTONE RIDGE -- U.S. military name for topographic feature on Okinawa. 1945, WW-II.

TOMMY -- Popular name for the Thomas-Morse biplane, S-4b, which was delivered to the U.S. Air Service in January 1918.

TONI -- Name reserved by meteorologists for tropical cyclone in eastern North Pacific.

TONIC -- Allied plan to occupy Spanish Canary Islands. Originally planned in 1940 under code name, Pilgrim. Abandoned December 1942, WW-II.

TONNAGE -- Exercise held by U.S. engineer special brigades in preparation for OVERLORD; involved handling of supplies over beaches. See also CARGO. WW-II.

TONTO -- Nickname for a 328-pound package to be rough-landed on the moon in order to measure moon-quakes. It consists of a balsa-wood sphere in which a seismometer is housed. After impact, which is absorbed by the balsa wood, the seismometer is righted and is ready to make seismic measurements and transmit them back to earth. RANGER 5, carrying the first package, was launched 18 October 1962. However, the spacecraft failed after injection into its lunar trajectory and the capsule was not ejected. Another attempt to land the package will take place in late 1963.

TONY -- Japanese Kawasaki KI.61 fighter plane which first flew in December 1941. Entered service in August 1942 and was used throughout World War II as a fighter-bomber/escort. Japanese name: Hien (Swallow).

TOOFANI -- Nickname given by the air arm of India to the French OURAGAN jet fighter.

TOOT SWEET EXPRESS -- U.S. military railway service to carry high-priority freight on fast schedule from Cherbourg, France, via Paris to forward areas. Replaced LITTLE RED BALL EXPRESS ROUTE. Began 21 January 1945, WW-II.

TOOTH -- Kamranh Bay, French Indo China. WW-II.

TOOTHBRUSH -- Sulu Archipelago, Philippine Islands. WW-II.

TOP FLIGHT -- Name for peacetime military project.

TOPAZE -- French research rocket based on the AGATE. May be adapted to the space launch vehicle to be developed from the "Precious Stones" series. See DIAMANT, SAPPHIRE and EMERAUDE.

TOPDOG -- Tangier, Spanish Morocco. WW-II.

TOPFLIGHT -- Signal for release of information on Normandy landings by news media. 6 June 1944, WW-II.

TOPHAT -- See AVALANCHE

TOP-HEAVIES -- Nickname for U.S. Navy destroyers of 1630-ton class; new in 1940. WW-II.

TOPHEAVY -- Toem, New Guinea. WW-II.

TOPLINK -- Plan to assist in containing the greatest possible number of enemy troops in northern Italy until ANVIL. WW-II.

TOPSIDE -- High mass of island of Corregidor in Manila Bay, Philippines. See also BOTTOMSIDE, MIDDLESIDE. WW-II.

TOPSIDE SOUNDER -- See ALOUETTE

TOPSIDE SOUNDER, FIXED FREQUENCY -- See FIXED FREQUENCY TOPSIDE SOUNDER

TOPSOIL -- Minda, New Britain. WW-II.

TOPSPEED -- Allied Operations in Norway in the event of continued German resistance in that country. WW-II.

TOPSY -- Name for Japanese twin-engine transport plane. WW-II.

TORA -- Japanese map maneuvers designed to test intentions and capabilities of enemies in the Pacific and China area. Winter 1943, WW-II.

TORBEAU -- Two-place version of the World War II Bristol Beau-fighter equipped with torpedoes. See BEAUFIGHTER.

TORCH -- Code word for Allied landings in French North and Northwest Africa. See also GYMNAST and SUPER-GYMNAST. Began 8 November 1942, WW-II.

TOREADOR -- Projected Allied airborne landing by two divisions in central Burma and advance toward Mandalay. Fall 1943, WW-II.

TORNADO -- (1) First flown in 1939, the British Hawker aircraft met World War II production difficulties and ended up as the prototype for the TEMPEST II.

(2) Allied task force under HURRICANE Task Force which carried out operation against Wake Island-Toem, New Guinea, area. 17 May - 2 September 1944, WW-II.

TORONTO -- Canadian military name for objective on ROYAL CANADIAN AVENUE near San Leonardo, Italy. See also HALIFAX. December 1943, WW-II.

TORONTO, CITY OF -- Name for Royal Canadian Air Force Squadron Number 400.

TORPEDO JUNCTION -- (1) American nickname for Coral Sea area between Espiritu Santo and the Solomons, patrolled by Japanese submarines. WW-II.

(2) Name given by merchant seamen to shipping lane in Atlantic Ocean, southwest of Iceland, which had been marked-off by German government as a zone of destruction by submarines. Early 1941, WW-II.

TORPEX -- High explosive consisting of TNT, cyclonite, aluminum powder and wax; used in torpedoes, mines and depth charges.

TORRENT -- Allied cover operations in the northwest European Theater to conceal Operation OVERLORD, WW-II.

TORRID TURTLES -- Nickname for U.S. Marine Corps dive bombing squadron operating from air bases on Lingayen Gulf, Philippines. 1945. WW-II.

TORTILLA -- Cape Busching, New Britain. WW-II.

TORTOISE, PLAN -- See TORTUE, PLAN

TORTUE, PLAN -- (English translation: Plan Tortoise) Plan for interference with German military road traffic by French Resistance forces to aid Allied Normandy landings; originally called for sabotage, but due to lack of heavy equipment was converted into project for blocking road movements through guerrilla action. 1944, WW-II.

TORY -- U.S. Air Force ground test reactor program for the PLUTO-SLAM project. Some short duration, low thrust tests of the Tory II A-1 have been successfully made. Tests of the Tory II-C nuclear ramjet engine are scheduled for this year. Outcome of these tests will probably determine if the PLUTO-SLAM program is to be continued.

TORY II -- Small-scale nonflyable reactor constructed at Nevada Test Site by University of California Lawrence Radiation Laboratory. For PLUTO. Startup 1960.

TORY II A-1 -- Experimental propulsion test reactor built at Nevada Test Site by University of California Lawrence Radiation Laboratory. Startup 1960. Later dismantled. See also TORY II.

TORY II C -- Experimental propulsion test reactor being built at Nevada Test Site by University of California Lawrence Radiation Laboratory. Startup expected 1963.

TORYU -- (English translation: Dragon Killer) World War II Japanese Kawasaki KI. 45 fighter. See NICK.

TOTALIZE -- Heavy Canadian attack with air support from Caen sector to break through German positions in direction of Falaise, France. Followed SPRING; followed by TRACTABLE. 7-10 August 1944, WW-II.

TOTENKOPF -- (English translation: Death's Head) Name of German Schutzstaffel (S.S.) division. WW-II.

TOUGH 'OMBRES -- Nickname for U.S. 90th Infantry Division. Taken from lettering on shoulder patch T-O, standing for Texas and Oklahoma, home states of most of its original personnel.

TOW -- Acronym for Tube-launched, Optically-tracked, Wire-guided anti-tank weapon under development for the U.S. Army. Little information is available on the program, but it appears that the system employs a unique optical tracking system in conjunction with a high-speed missile and shaped charge warhead for armor penetration. Under development as an infantry weapon. See also TOMA-HAWK.

TOWER OF BABEL, HMS -- Popular name for British destroyer, HMS Wells; so named because of several Allied officers aboard speaking each a different language. WW-II.

TOWER HILL -- Military name for topographic feature east of Regalbuto, Sicily. So named from old stone look-out on its summit. Summer 1943, WW-II.

TOWERS MOON -- Name for peacetime military exercise at Fort Bragg, North Carolina and Fort Campbell, Kentucky, 1960.

TOWPATH -- Plans for operation against Rabaul, New Britain. WW-II.

TOWROPE -- Strait of Bonifacio, Corsica. WW-II.

TRAAC -- Acronym for Transit Research and Attitude Control program, a U.S. Navy satellite launched piggy-back on TRANSIT IVB in November 1961, to test the feasibility of spacecraft stabilization using the earth's gravitational field. Door-knob shaped satellite did not function perfectly, but its performance was suffici-ent to convince the Navy that this form of stabilization could be used on the operational TRANSIT.

TRACE -- High-speed missile checkout system developed for POLARIS. The com-pletely automated system reduces the countdown time from five hours to eight minutes.

TRACER -- Grumman WF-2 aircraft, evolved from the TF-1, first flew in 1958 and entered service with the U.S. Navy Atlantic Fleet in 1960 as a shipboard early warning aircraft.

TRACK DOWN -- Name for U.S. peacetime military exercise at Fort Hood, Texas, 1962.

TRACK RIPPER -- See BIG HOOK

TRACKER -- Twin-engine Grumman S2F anti-submarine aircraft developed for the U.S. Navy. Latest version flew in 1959.

TRACTABLE -- Canadian advance toward Falaise, France; followed TOTALIZE. Originally called Tallulah. 14-16 August 1944, WW-II.

TRACY -- Cape Gauffre, New Britain. WW-II.

TRADER -- Grumman TF-1 utility shipboard trainer and transport in service with the U.S. Navy.

TRADESMAN -- Allied land based air operations against the Netherlands East Indies. WW-II.

TRADEWIND -- (1) Convair R3Y turboprop tanker-transport aircraft in service with U.S. Navy at the present time.

(2) French anti-submarine aircraft. See ALIZE.

(3) Code name for Northwest Africa. WW-II.

(4) Allied task force under ALAMO which carried out Operation INTERLUDE against Morotai Island, Netherlands New Guinea. 15 September - 4 October 1944, WW-II.

TRADIC -- Acronym for Transistor Digital Computer, designed to be used in aircraft flying at supersonic speeds. Capable of performing 60,000 additions or subtractions, or 3000 multiplications or divisions in a second.

TRAFALGAR -- Canadian objective to the left of the Villa Grande-Tollo Road, Italy. January 1944, WW-II.

TRAGEDY -- Iloilo, Panay, Philippine Islands. WW-II.

TRAIL BREAK -- U.S. peacetime exercise at Camp Drum, New York, to test battle group mobility. 1961.

TRAILBLAZER DIVISION -- Nickname for U.S. 70th Infantry Division.

TRAILBLAZER I and II -- U.S. re-entry test vehicles. Trailblazer I is a six-stage solid propellant in which the first three stages boost it to a 200-mile altitude and the final three stages fire the payload back into the atmosphere. Velocities up to 25,000 feet per second have been attained in this manner. Trailblazer II functions in the same manner. However, it only has four solid stages, with two providing boost and two the re-entry speeds of about 17,000 feet per second. First vehicle is used by National Aeronautics and Space Administration for heat shield studies, while second is used by Department of Defense to determine characteristics of re-entering intercontinental ballistic missile warheads.

TRAINBUSTERS CLUB -- "Fraternity" of U.N. Task Force 95 blockade ships whose gunfire destroyed an enemy train in Korea after June 1952. Korean Conflict.

TRAITOR -- Northeast Islands, Truk Group, Caroline Islands. WW-II.

TRAJECTORY -- Dampier Straits, New Britain. WW-II.

TRAK -- Electronic code converter which converts Morse code signals into pulses suitable for a standard teleprinter.

TRAMID -- Name for peacetime military operation. Ended 18 June 1955.

TRANSAC -- Transistor computer that can add, subtract, multiply, divide and compare. Capable of performing 600,000 additions per second.

TRANSCON PROJECT -- Air transport of troops between U.S. East and West coasts to relieve heavy pressure on rail transportation caused by returning troops; Conducted by Air Transport Command and civilian airlines. August 1945 - April 1946, WW-II.

TRANSFIGURE -- Allied plan for airborne operation to capture and control important road nets in Paris-Orleans area, France. August 1944. Canceled. WW-II.

TRANSGRESSOR -- Cape Christian, Canada. WW-II.

TRANSIT -- U.S. Navy nuclear-powered satellite project used to provide ships and aircraft with worldwide means for accurately determining their positions electronically rather than through celestial observations. See also BUMBLEBEE PROJECT.

TRANSIT, OPERATION -- Name for shipments of troops and cargo en route from Europe to Pacific through Panama Canal. Summer 1945, WW-II.

TRANSLATE -- Mor Island, Truk Group, Caroline Islands. WW-II.

TRANSPORTATION PLAN -- Allied bombing of major railway servicing and repair centers in France and Belgium. April - June 1944, WW-II.

TRAP -- Savaii, Samoan Islands. WW-II.

TRAP LINE V -- Name for U.S. peacetime military exercise at Fort Meade, Maryland, 1961.

TRAPEZE -- Code name for Roumania. WW-II.

TRASIMENE LINE -- See ALBERT-FRIEDA LINE

TRAVEL AIR -- Beechcraft Model B95A twin-engine executive aircraft first introduced in 1961. A French version is called the Marquis. See also BADGER.

TRAVELING CIRCUS -- See TED'S TRAVELING CIRCUS

TREASURE -- Suloga Harbor, Woodlark Island. WW-II.

TREASURY HILL -- Name of topographic feature in Naga Hills near Kohima, Assam; site of heavy fighting between British and Japanese troops. April 1944, WW-II.

TREAT -- Acronym for Transient Reactor Test. Facility at National Reactor Testing Station, Idaho Falls, Idaho. Built by Argonne National Laboratory to investigate effect of extreme heat upon fuel elements and other components of fast reactors. Reactor achieved criticality 23 February 1959.

TREMBLE -- Salat Island, Truk Group, Caroline Islands. WW-II.

TRENER -- Czech two-seat basic trainer plane, now operational. See TRENER-MASTER.

TRENER-MASTER -- Flown for the first time in 1957, the Czech Z-326 is a single-engine, two-seat trainer. Another version is the AKROBAT.

TRESPASSER -- Sulu Archipelago, Philippine Islands. WW-II.

TRIANA -- Hispano HA-100 advanced trainer for the Spanish Air Force. First flown in 1954.

TRIANGLE -- Allied plan of action in event of major uprising in Germany or Austria. WW-II.

TRIANGLE HILL -- Military name for topographic feature northeast of Kumhwa, Korea. Fall 1952. Korean Conflict.

TRIANGLE, THE -- (1) Military name for topographic feature near Bardia, Libya. 1941, WW-II.

(2) Military name for junction where trails to Buna Mission and Buna Village converge in eastern New Guinea. Also called Bloody Triangle. Late 1942, WW-II.

TRIANGULAR -- Vladivostok Area, U.S.S.R. WW-II.

TRIANGULATION HILL -- (1) U.S. Military name for topographic feature on Okinawa. 1945, WW-II.

(2) Name for Hill 268 near Waegwan, Korea. Korean Conflict.

TRIBE -- Name given to an Advanced Research Projects Agency study of advance military space vehicles capable of performing specific military missions. Study included not only available and required boosters, but also the guidance, stabilization, communcations and control components that would be required.

TRIBESMAN -- Code name for Celebes Sea. WW-II.

TRICE -- Acronym for Transitorized Realtime Incremetal Computer.

TRICKLE -- Transportation Service, U.S. Army forces in British Isles. WW-II.

TRICKLE MOVEMENT -- Experiment in sending British and American merchantmen individually and unescorted between Reykjavik, Iceland, and North Russia. Late 1942 - early 1943, WW-II.

TRI-CON -- Introduced in 1960 by Champion Aircraft, the Model 7JC aircraft is the latest variant of the Model 7.

TRIDENT -- (1) French rocket airplane with a 1050-7500-pound variable thrust engine first flown in December 1955. Capable of reaching an altitude of 15 miles; designed to carry air-to-air missiles under its fuselage. Six were ordered, but the program was cancelled in 1958.

(2) Nasai Island, Solomon Sea. WW-II.

(3) Anglo-American conference held at Washington; attended by President Roosevelt and Prime Minister Churchill. 12-25 May 1943, WW-II.

TRIDENT DIVISION -- Nickname for U.S. 97th Infantry Division.

TRIGA MARK F -- See FLAIR

TRIGGER -- (1) Oburaka, Trobriand Islands. WW-II.

(2) U.S. Army Air Forces training project in ground control of interception conducted in Florida; used personnel trained at British Royal Air Force schools in England as instructors. 1942, WW-II.

(3) Royal Canadian Air Force patrols to intercept German intruders. WW-II.

TRINITY -- First U.S. nuclear weapons test which demonstrated feasibility of atomic weapon. Held at Alamogordo, New Mexico, 16 July 1945.

TRI-PACER -- Piper PA-22 single-engine monoplane first introduced in 1950. See CARIBBEAN, CLIPPER.

TRIPOD -- U.S. Air Force POLARIS-derived transit launch vehicle.

TRITON -- U.S. Navy surface-to-surface ramjet missile designed to fly at an altitude of 15 miles to ranges of 1500 miles. Solid propellant boosters were to boost the missile to speeds of Mach 2-3 before the ramjet sustainer took over. Was to be capable of operating from both surface ships and submarines. Program was cancelled before flight tests as a result of an economy move in 1957.

TRITON I -- Operable French nuclear pool reactor in Fontenay, France.

TRIUMPHANT -- Reconquest of Burma. WW-II.

TRIX -- (1) Typhoon. 18-23 October 1952. Formed in western Caroline Islands. Moved westward across central Philippines and South China Sea into central Viet Nam.

(2) Typhoon. 2-16 May 1957. Formed south of Truk, Caroline Islands. Moved northward at first, then northwestward over northern Mariana Islands, then northeastward over the north central Pacific, where it dissipated.

(3) Typhoon. 4-10 August 1960. Formed over western Caroline Islands, Pacific. Moved northwestward across Philippine Sea, then westward across northern Taiwan and into China mainland. Caused four deaths and major damage on Taiwan.

(4) Name also applied to tropical cyclones in western North Pacific which occurred prior to (1) through (3) above.

TRIZON -- Three-ton RAZON bomb.

TROCADERO -- Ayuet Bay, New Britain. WW-II.

TROJAN -- North American T-28 originally used by the U.S. Air Force-Navy as a trainer plane. First flown in 1949. Now used as an Air Commando aircraft by the Air Force. Also in foreign use. See also FENNEC.

TROJANI -- Italian Aeronautica Umbra A.U.T.18 pre-World War II single-engine monoplane fighter.

TROOPERS -- Address used in telegrams for Canadian War Office. WW-II.

TROPIC LIGHTNING DIVISION -- Nickname for U.S. 25th Infantry Division.

TROUSERS -- (1) Canadian collective divisional assault training exercise, held at Slapton Sands, Devon, England, in preparation for OVERLORD. 12 April 1944, WW-II.

(2) Canadian occupation of Carpiquet airfield, west of Caen, France, during capture of that city. Postponed from 8 to 9 July 1944 by message, "Trousers off until tomorrow." WW-II.

TRUCK KILLER -- U.S. 5th Air Force plan whereby fighter-bombers made road cuts in North Korea at dusk, and light bombers attacked vehicle concentrations behind them during night. December 1952, Korean Conflict.

TRUCULENCE -- Efate Island, New Hebrides. WW-II.

TRUCULENT TURTLE -- Nickname for the Lockheed U.S. Navy twin-engine landplane which flew nonstop, without refueling, from Australia to Ohio in October 1946.

TRUDY -- Name reserved by meteorologists for tropical cyclone in North Atlantic area.

TRUMP -- Acronym for Target Radiation Measurement Program, a U.S. Air Force study of infra-red measurement problems and sensor capabilities for MIDAS-type satellites which must distinguish between missile launchings and other radiation sources. Program will be considerably expanded in 1963 to attempt to solve problems of present Midas system. See also LOFTER.

TRUNCHEON -- Combined raid on Leghorn, Italy. WW-II.

TRUNK -- See KISTE

TUBA -- Code name for jamming transmitter which operates in the 480-500 megacycle range.

TUBE ALLOYS -- Code name for Allied atomic bomb reasearch. WW-II.

TUBULAR -- British air cover for convoys. WW-II.

TUCKAHOE -- Kolombangara Island, Solomon Islands. WW-II.

TUDOR -- Merauke, New Guinea. WW-II.

TULIP -- Tetero, Guadalcanal, Solomon Islands. WW-II.

TULSA -- Early plans of general headquarters, Southwest Pacific Area, for operations directed at capture of Rabaul, New Britain. 1942, WW-II.

TUMBLER -- Lazy Bay, Alaska. WW-II.

TUMBLEWEED -- Atomic Energy Commission program to collect data on the radiation in the atmosphere after a nuclear test. Instrument package samples air and telemeters the data back to earth. Operational.

TUNA -- Code name for Jamaica. WW-II.

TUNGSTEN and SOPHIA -- British fleet Air Arm attack on German battleship Tirpitz. 3 April 1944, WW-II.

TUNNEL HILL ROAD -- Military name for topographic feature near Rabaul, New Britain. WW-II.

TUPPENCE -- Mt. Wago, New Britain. WW-II.

TURBI -- Two-seat version of the French Druine D.3 aircraft. See TURBULENT.

TURBINLITE -- (1) British name for searchlight fitted to an air interception aircraft to aid it in cooperating with accompanying fighter plane during combat. WW-II.

(2) Plan to provide Army Air Forces night fighter squadron with Royal Air Force equipment and training. WW-II.

TURBO-TRANSPORTER -- Vertol YH-16A turbine-powered helicopter. Made its first flight in 1953, but a U.S. Air Force production contract was cancelled.

TURBULENT -- French Druine D.3 ultra-light monoplane designed for sale in kit form for assembly by amateurs. See also TURBI.

TURKEY HILL -- U.S. military name for topographic feature on Okinawa. 1945, WW-II.

TURKEY SHOOT -- See MARIANAS TURKEY SHOOT

TURNIP -- Mano Island (Money Island), Solomon Islands. WW-II.

TURNOVER -- Baker Island, Pacific Ocean. WW-II.

TURNSTILE -- Abercorn, Northern Rhodesia. WW-II.

TURRET -- High-temperature, gas-cooled reactor experiment at Los Alamos Scientific Laboratory, New Mexico.

TURTLE -- (1) U.S. Army two-ton cargo carrier which transports supplies to front-line.

    (2) One of four plans for U.S. breakout from Anzio beachhead in Italy involving attack in direction Carroceto-Campoleone-Rome. Not used. See also BUFFALO. May 1944, WW-II.

TURTLE HEAD BEND -- Military name for topographic feature on Kuryong River, Korea. Korean Conflict.

TUSKER -- Name for Royal Canadian Air Force Squadron Number 413.

TUTOR -- Training biplane produced by Avro in England and Canada in the early 1930's.

25, UNTERNEHMEN -- (English translation: Operation 25) German code name for invasion of Yugoslavia. Began 6 April 1941, WW-II.

TWENTY GRAND -- One of five camps of RED HORSE STAGING AREA in region of Le Havre-Rouen, France. Established November 1944, WW-II.

TWILFIT -- Balikpapan, Borneo. WW-II.

TWILIGHT -- See DRAKE

TWIN BONANZA -- Twin-engine, six-passenger Beechcraft J50 business plane. First flew in 1949; updated versions are still in production.

TWIN MUSTANG -- Basically two North American P-51's joined by a center wing section, in 1945, as a two-pilot, long-range escort plane. Later developed into an all-weather fighter. Designated the P-82.

TWIN PIONEER SERIES -- British twin-engine light transport plane built in three versions by Scottish Aviation; in operation with the Royal Air Force and civilian operators.

TWIN WADIS -- Military name for topographic feature near Bardia, Libya. 1941, WW-II.

2, BASE -- U.S. naval base, Gore Loch, Scotland. WW-II.

TYPE B -- Second generation Wright airplanes in which early U.S. Army airmen learned the rudiments of powered flight.

TYPEWRITER -- Exmouth Gulf, Australia. WW-II.

TYPHON -- U.S. Navy surface-to-air anti-missile missile being developed to provide Fleet air defense against the anticipated 1970 threat. Two versions, a long-range system and a medium range system, are being developed. Both are based on the TARTAR-TERRIER-TALOS developments and will use similar concepts. Electronic power requirements are so high that system can only be deployed on nuclear-powered surface ships. Formerly known as Super-Talos and Super-Tartar. USS Norton Sound is being converted to test fire the system at sea. See also BUMBLEBEE PROJECT, LOW BLOW.

TYPHOON -- (1) British World War II Hawker fighter plane used as a convoy escort and fighter-bomber by the Royal Air Force. First flown 1940.

(2) Koshun, Formosa. WW-II.

(3) Allied task force under ALAMO which carried out Operation GLOBETROTTER against Sansapor area, Netherlands New Guinea. 20 July - 21 August 1944, WW-II.

TYPHOON CROSSROADS -- Name for Naha, Okinawa. 1945, WW-II.

U

U, ASSAULT FORCE -- Naval unit which carried U.S. troops to UTAH Beach.   6
June 1944, WW-II.

U DAY -- Date for U.S. landing in southwestern Mindoro, Philippines, in LOVE
III operation.   15 December 1944, WW-II.

U GO, OPERATION -- Japanese offensive on Imphal front, Burma.   Began March
1944, WW-II.

U OPERATION -- See U GO, OPERATION

UBIQUE -- Mindoro, Philippine Islands.   WW-II.

UGLY -- Shipping designator for cargo to be received anywhere in United Kingdom
regardless of zone or port.   See also SOXO, GLUE, BANG.   WW-II.

UGUR -- (English translation: Luck) Turkish MKEK-4 primary trainer plane which
recently replaced the Miles Hawk trainer.

UHU -- (English translation: Owl) Heinkel He.219 night fighter.   First flew in 1942.
Operational with the Luftwaffe in the same year.

UKRAINA -- Russian turboprop transport plane.   See CAT.

ULCER GULCH -- U.N. code name for position in Wonsan harbor, North Korea.
Korean Conflict.

ULTIMATUM -- Pagan Island, Marianas Islands.   WW-II.

ULYSSES -- Talasea Harbor, New Britain.   WW-II.

UMBILICAL CORD -- Cable fitted to a missile; provides control over missile equipment
while missile is in the launcher.   Cord is quickly detached at, or just prior to,
lift-off.

UMBRAGE -- Cape Dorset, Canada.   WW-II.

UMBRELLA -- (1) German name for bombing attack on Birmingham, England.
November 1940, WW-II.

(2) Name for military operation.

UMPTEEN -- Howland Island,, Pacific Ocean. WW-II.

UNASSAILABLE -- Manokwari, New Guinea. WW-II.

UNCACK -- Acronym for United Nations Civil Assistance Command, Korea. Korean Conflict.

UNCEASING -- Palawan, Philippine Islands. WW-II.

UNCLE -- Code word for letter "U" in a phonetic alphabet, used to avoid possibility of a misunderstanding in transmitting messages. See also UNIFORM.

UNCLE, OPERATION -- Program of U.S. Marine Corps chaplains to help 3000 Korean orphan boys. Korean Conflict.

UNCLE RED -- Strip of land, 1000 yards in width, on UTAH Beach, Normandy. June 1944, WW-II.

UNCLE SUGAR -- Familiar reference to United States made by military personnel; changed Uncle Sam to complete phonetic alphabet rendition. WW-II.

UNCLE-VICTOR, HILL -- Military name for topographic feature north of PURPLE HEART RIDGE on Saipan. 1944, WW-II.

UNCLOUDED -- Rangoon, Burma. WW-II.

UNDERDOG -- Los Negros Island, Admiralty Islands. WW-II.

UNDERGO, OPERATION -- Canadian capture of Calais, northern France. 25 September -1 October 1944, WW-II.

UNDERGROWTH -- Code name for the Kattegat, North Sea, where sea mines were often laid. WW-II.

UNDERNEATH -- Ujae Atoll, Marshall Islands. WW-II.

UNDERTAKER -- Tacloban, Leyte, Philippine Islands. WW-II.

UNDERTONE -- U.S. 3rd and 7th Army offensive in Germany to break through WESTWALL and clear Saar-Palatinate triangle within Rhine, Mosel, and Saar Rivers. Began 15 March 1945, WW-II.

UNERRING -- San Jose, Mindoro, Philippine Islands. WW-II.

UNFROCKED PRIEST -- Allied nickname for self-propelled PRIEST with gun removed so as to be used as armored personnel carrier. WW-II.

UNICORN -- Cape Bastion, New Britain. WW-II.

UNIFORM -- Code word for letter "U" in a phonetic alphabet, used to avoid possibility of a misunderstanding in transmitting messages. See also UNCLE.

UNIQUE -- Mindoro, Philippine Islands. WW-II.

UNITAS II -- Joint U.S. and South American peacetime anti-submarine warfare exercise, 1961.

UNIVAC -- Acronym for Universal Automatic Computer, manufactured by Sperry Rand Corporation.

UNIVERSAL -- Modified American Fokker single-engine, high-wing monoplane built in Japan in 1932-33 by Nakajima.

UPPER ROCKET -- Military name for Japanese position on Bataan Penisula, Philippine Islands. Early 1942, WW-II.

UPSHOT-KNOTHOLE -- U.S. nuclear weapons test at Nevada Test Site, Spring 1953.

UPSTART -- U.S. vertically-launched, high speed (4000 miles per hour) target missle with a range of over 30 miles. Similar to POGO-HI, the missile is parachute-recovered. First launched in 1961.

UPTOWN -- Caru, Rooke Island, New Britain. WW-II.

URBANA FORCE -- U.S. Army units engaged in military action on New Guinea. WW-II.

URSULA -- Typhoon. 6-14 September 1945. First detected east of Philippines. Moved northwestward across Taiwan into China mainland. Recurved northeastward over Yellow Sea, Korea and Sea of Japan to northern Honshu, Japan.

UTAH -- (1) Beach assaulted by troops of U.S. VII Corps on D DAY, 6 June 1944, in Operation OVERLORD; located on eastern base of Contentin Peninsula, Normandy France. Originally called X, but name changed in March 1944. See also ASSAULT FORCE U. WW-II.

(2) Military name for phase line south of IRON TRIANGLE in Korea. 1951. Korean Conflict.

UTILITY -- Flair FU-24 aircraft designed and built in the U.S. primarily for agricul-tural work in New Zealand. Flew for first time in 1954.

UTOPIA -- Code name for Allied siezure of Andaman Islands when presented at SEXTANT Conference. See also BUCCANEER. Late 1943, WW-II.

UVIS -- Koli Point, Guadalcanal, Solomon Islands. WW-II.

V

V-2 -- Large catapult, made from an inner tube, which could throw a No. 36 grenade fifty yards; improvised by Seaforth Highlanders of Canada during lull on north Italian front. Winter 1945, WW-II.

VACCINE -- Code name for India. WW-II.

VAE -- Typhoon. 17-20 October 1952. Formed east of Philippines. Moved westward across central Philippines as weak storm, intensified in South China Sea, and moved into southern Viet Nam.

VAGABOND -- Marcus Island, Pacific Ocean. WW-II.

VAL -- Japanese Aichi D3A2 Navy dive bomber aircraft which took part in the attack on Pearl Harbor.

VALENTINE -- Type of Allied tank. WW-II.

VALERIE -- Hurricane. 24-25 June 1962. Formed 200 miles west of Acapulco, Mexico. Moved northwestward briefly, then turned northeastward and inland near Mazatlan, Mexico.

VALETTA -- Royal Air Force version of the commercial Viking produced by Vickers-Armstrong and first flown in 1947. See also VARSITY.

VALIANT -- (1) Vultee BT-13 U.S. Army Air Forces trainer of 1940 and World War II basic flying training. Called Vultee Vibrator by students and instructors.

(2) Vickers B.K.1, first of the British Royal Air Force's Vee-class bombers, which flew for the first time in 1951, and entered service in 1955.

VALKYRIE -- Prototype of RS-70 (Reconnaissance-Strike) Mach 3 weapon system for U.S. Air Force, in process of development by North American Aviation.

VAMPIRE -- (1) DeHavilland turbojet, twin-boom fighter plane which first flew in 1943. A considerable number are flying in countries other then Britain.

(2) Emeline Bay, New Britain. WW-II.

VANCOUVER -- Name for Royal Canadian Air Force Squadron Number 405.

VANCOUVER II -- Canadian Vickers twin-engine bi-plane flying boat of 1932.

VANGUARD -- (1) Vultee P-66 single-engine fighter plane delivered in 1942 for shipment to Sweden, but sent, by the U.S., to the Chinese Air Force instead.

(2) Vickers four-engine turboprop which entered service with British European Airways in 1961 as a short- and medium-range commercial transport plane.

(3) First U.S. satellite program, initiated for the International Geophysical Year and developed by Naval Research Laboratory (group was later transferred to National Aeronautics and Space Administration). Series of three environmental satellites were launched: the first 17 March 1958, the second 17 February 1959 and the third 18 September 1959. Vanguard I revealed the pear shape of the earth; Vanguard II, proved the ability of satellites to take cloud cover pictures, and Vanguard III studied magnetic fields and temperatures around the earth, and solar X-rays and micrometeorites. Launched by vehicle with same name. Weighed 3.25, 20.7 and 100 pounds, respectively.

(4) See DRACULA

VANGUARD LAUNCH VEHICLE -- U.S. three stage launch vehicle specifically designed to place VANGUARD satellites into orbit during the International Geophysical Year. First stage used RP-1/Liquid-oxygen explosive combination as propellants, and developed 28,000-pound thrust; the second used unsymmetric dimethylhydrazine and inhibited white fuming nitric acid and developed 7600-pound thrust; the third stage was a solid propellant motor developing 2060-pound thrust. Of the 15-vehicle program, only three successfully orbited satellites. Phased out of use in 1960.

VANQUISHER -- Luzon Strait, Philippine Islands. WW-II.

VARNISH -- Sawar Airfield, New Guinea. WW-II.

VARSITY -- (1) Evolved from the Vickers VALETTA transport, this British Royal Air Force crew trainer first flew in 1949 and is still active. See also VIKING.

(2) Airdrop of two divisions of XVIII Corps of 1st Allied Airborne Army east of Rhine River, north os Wesel, Germany, as part of Operation PLUNDER. 24 March 1945, WW-II.

VARSITY I -- Bikati Island, Marshall Islands. WW-II.

VARSITY DIVISION -- Nickname for U.S. 9th Infantry Division.

VAUDEVILLE -- Tactical air-direction post supporting U.S. IX Corps in Korea. Korean Conflict.

VAULT -- (1) Great Natoena Island, South China Sea. WW-II.

(2) Plan for peaceful occupation of the Azores, cancelled. WW-II.

VAUTOUR -- French Sud-Aviation SO-4050, twin-jet light bomber which made its maiden flight in 1952. Currently in service with French and Israeli air arms.

VAUTOUR INN -- Night fighter variant of the basic French Sud SO-4050.

VEDETTE VI -- Single-engine pusher biplane flying boat built by Canadian Vickers in early 1930's.

VEEP -- (1) Acronym for U.S. Vice President.

(2) A JEEP equipped with very high frequency radio.

VEGA -- (1) The first aircraft manufactured by the Lockheed Company. Built in 1932. Wiley Post's solo round-the-world flight in 1933 was made in this type single-engine monoplane which he nicknamed WINNIE MAE.

(2) National Aeronautics and Space Administration upper stage vehicle for use with the ATLAS BOOSTER. Vehicle as it developed had essentially the same capabilities as the AGENA. Therefore, in December 1959, the program was cancelled. Never flight tested.

(3) French, ramjet-powered surface-to-air anti-aircraft missile capable of Mach 4 speeds at altitudes from 65,000-110,000 feet, and ranges out to 160 nautical miles. Being developed as a prototype for anti-aircraft missile. Some flight tests have been conducted.

VEGA GULL -- Four-seat Percival Aircraft cabin monoplane built in Great Britain before WW-II.

VEGAS -- Military name for outpost in Korea. Spring 1953, Korean Conflict.

VEGETABLES -- Allied sea mines dropped by aircraft. WW-II.

VELA HOTEL, SIERRA AND UNIFORM -- U.S. Advanced Research Projects Agency program for the detection of nuclear explosions in Space by orbiting satellites (Hotel), by ground-based detectors (Sierra) and under ground (Uniform). Satellite-based system employs three, 300-400-pound satelletes in a 60,000-nautical miles orbit and three more in an orbit 90 degrees to the first. Initial launchings were planned for 1962; security prevents confirmation.

VELLUM FORCE -- One battery of U.S. 56th Coast Artillery Regiment sent to Venezuela. February 1942, WW-II.

VELOCIPEDE -- Code name for U.S. Army Air Depots, British Isles. WW-II.

VELTRO -- (English translation: Greyhound) Italian Macchi C.205 fighter which flew alongside Luftwaffe units after Italian capitulation. First flown 1942.

VELVET -- Allied air assistance to Russian southern flank. WW-II.

VELVET GLOVE -- Experimental air-to-air missile designed in Canada.

VENERABLE -- Operation by French Detachment d'Armee de l'Atlantique to open the port of Bordeaux. 14 April 1945, WW-II.

VENETIAN LINE -- German defense line in northern Italy from Adriatic to Alpine rampart behind Lake Garda; designed to guard approaches to passes into Germany. Also called Adige Line. Spring 1945, WW-II.

VENEZIA -- German operation to attack British position at Gazala, Libya, May-June 1942. WW-II.

VENGEANCE -- Vultee single-engine, low-wing dive bomber used by the U.S. Army Air Forces and U.S. Navy during the early part of WW-II.

VENOM -- DeHavilland turbojet fighter-bomber which first flew in 1949. Presently serving with the Swiss and Venezuelan air arms. Naval version is the SEA VENOM.

VENTRILOQUIST -- Adak Island, Aleutian Islands. WW-II.

VENTURA -- Bomber development of the Lockheed Model 18. Served in World War II as the U.S. Army Air Forces B-34 and -37, the U.S. Navy PV-1, and with the British Royal Air Force and South African Air Force. The latter still uses aircraft, as do civil operators.

VENUS -- Mount Lotomgan, New Britain. WW-II.

VENUS PROBE -- Soviet interplanetary spacecraft launched 12 February 1961 from SPUTNIK VIII in earth orbit. Russians predicted that the 1419-pound probe would pass within 62,000 miles of Venus on May 19 or 20, but, early in March, contact was lost with theprobe, and the. mission thereby failed. Experiments included measurements of magnetic fields, cosmic rays, charged particles and instruments for temperature control, telemetry, altitude control and stablilization.

VERA -- (1) Typhoon. 5-8 July 1956. Formed in western Caroline Islands. Moved west-northwestward across central Philippines as weak storm, but reached typhoon force over South China Sea. Passed over Hainan Island and dissipated.

(2) Typhoon. 22-27 September 1959. Formed northeast of Guam. Moved northwestward then northward through central Japan, then northeastward out over North Pacific. Caused over 4500 deaths; worst typhoon disaster in history of Japan. Damage over 26 million dollars.

(3) Typhoon. 25-28 August 1962. Formed in northern Philippine Sea. Moved northward and dissipated near Japanese island of Shikoku.

(4) Name also applied to tropical cyclones in western North Pacific which occurred prior to (1) through (3) above.

VERB -- Midway Island, Pacific Ocean. WW-II.

VERBATIM -- Banda Sea, Netherlands East Indies. WW-II.

VERITABLE -- Attack by Canadian 1st Army employing British XXX Corps south-easterly from Nijmegen area, Netherlands, to clear Germans from region between Maas and Rhine Rivers. Originally called Valediction. See also WYVERN. 8-21 February 1945, WW-II.

VERMILION -- Code name for Bermuda. WW-II.

VERMONT -- Banda Sea, Netherlands East Indies. WW-II.

VERNA -- (1) Tropical storm. 20-21 September 1945. First detected in South China Sea west of Luzon. Moved northwestward across Hainan Island into northern Indo China.

(2) Name also included in sequence prepared by meteorologists for future tropical cyclones in North Atlantic.

VERONICA -- Name reserved by meteorologists for tropical cyclone in North Atlantic area.

VERONIQUE -- French upper-atmospheric research rocket based on German V-2. First launched in 1950; 23 missiles were fired before the program ended in 1954. Using a greatly improved version, the program was revived in 1959. Current version capable of carrying 166-pound payload to an altitude of 140 miles. Liquid propellants are used. Payload can be recovered by parachute.

VERT, PLAN -- (English: Green, Plan) Plan for cutting critical military railroads by French Resistance saboteurs to aid Allied Normandy landings. 1944, WW-II.

VERTIJET -- Vertical takeoff/landing research jet aircraft designated the X-13 by the U.S. Air Force, and built by Ryan in the early 1950's.

VERULAM -- Tongatabu Island, Tonga Islands. WW-II.

VERVILLE -- VCP-1 biplane built by the Engineering Division of McCook Field (U.S. Air Service) in 1919 and modified in 1920 as the R-1 racer.

VESTMENT -- Mesegon Island, Caroline Islands. WW-II.

VESUVIUS -- French operation to liberate Corsica, September-October 1943. WW-II.

VETCH -- Bandoeng, Java. WW-II.

VIASTRA -- Twelve-passenger Vickers twin-engine, high-wing commercial monoplane of 1932-33 in England.

VICARAGE -- Allied project to drop airborne prisoner-of-war contact and reconnaissance teams into Germany under ECLIPSE conditions. WW-II.

VICKERY'S BRIDGE -- Namji-ri Bridge over Naktong River, Korea. Named after a U.S. Lieutenant Vickery, whose platoon had effectively defended it during enemy offensive. 1950, Korean Conflict.

VICKY -- Name reserved by meteorologists for tropical cyclone in North Atlantic area.

VICTOR -- (1) Code word for letter "V" in a phonetic alphabet, used to avoid possibility of a misunderstanding in transmitting messages.

(2) Hadley-Page B.1 four-jet bomber which entered Great Britain's Royal Air Force in 1958.

(3) Cape Verde Islands, Atlantic Ocean. WW-II.

VICTOR, HILL -- Military name for topographic feature east of PURPLE HEART RIDGE on Saipan. 1944, WW-II.

VICTOR OPERATIONS -- U.S. landings in southern Philippines; originally part of MUSKETEER; later part of MONCLAIR. See VICTOR I-V (They did not occur chronologically according to numerical order). February–April 1945, WW-II.

VICTOR I -- U.S. landings on island of Panay, Philippines. 18 March 1945, WW-II.

VICTOR IA -- U.S. landing on island of Negros, Philippines, by same combat and supporting units as in VICTOR I. 29 March 1945, WW-II.

VICTOR II -- U.S. landings on island of Cebu, Philippines, with smaller landings on Negros and Bohol. Began 26 March 1945, WW-II.

VICTOR III -- U.S. Eighth Army landing on island of Palawan, Philippines. 28 February 1945, WW-II.

VICTOR IV -- U.S. Eighth Army landings of Zamboanga, island of Mindanao, Philippines, and in islands of Sulu Archipelago. 10 March-9 April 1945, WW-II.

VICTOR V -- Major U.S. Eighth Army landings on island of Mindanao, Philippines. 17 April-10 May 1945, WW-II.

VICTOR 2 -- B.2 aircraft, greatly modified version of the B.1; flew for the first time in 1959, and is in service with the British Royal Air Force.

VICTORIA -- (1) Twin-engine troop-carrying biplane produced by Great Britain's Vickers Aircraft in the early 1930's.

(2) Name reserved by meteorologists for tropical cyclone in eastern North Pacific.

VICTORY BRIDGE -- Railway bridge erected by U.S. Army across Rhine River at Duisburg, Germany. Completed 8 May 1945, WW-II.

VICTORY DIVISION -- (1) Nickname for U.S. 5th Armored Divison.

(2) Nickname for U.S. 95th Infantry Division.

VICTORY OPERATIONS -- See SHO OPERATIONS

VIDMET -- Project name of U.S. Weather Bureau's experimental closed-circuit television system in Washington, D.C. 1962-63.

VIGILANT -- (1) Liaison and observation single-engine monoplane developed during World War II by Vultee, and used by the U.S. Army Air Forces.

(2) British anti-tank missile with a range of 250 to 1800 yards. The 32-pound missile can be carried and fired by one man or can be mounted on combat vehicles. Shaped charge warhead. Operational.

(3) Name for peacetime military exercise.

VIGILANTE -- North American A3J twin-jet attack bomber developed for the U.S. Navy. Set a climb record in 1960.

VIGILANTE A -- U.S. Army towed anti-aircraft weapon system.

VIGILANTE B -- U.S. Army self-propelled anti-aircraft weapon system.

VIGOR -- Name for U.S. Marine peacetime operation.

VIGOROUS -- British convoy of 11 merchant ships escorted by cruisers and destroyers from Alexandria, Egypt, and other eastern Mediterranean ports for Malta, coinciding with east bound convoy, HARPOON; forced to turn back in BOMB ALLEY when supply of ammunition ran too short to resist further enemy air attacks or possible encounter with nearby strong Italian fleet. June 1942, WW-II.

VIKING -- (1) Three-seat light cabin monoplane. The first built by Aktiebolaget Svenska, and introduced at a Swedish International Aircraft Exhibition in May 1931.

(2) The first British post-World War II commercial transport. This Vickers-Armstrong twin engine monoplane first flew in 1945. Military versions are the VALETTA and VARSITY.

VIKING 1-14 -- U.S. high altitude research rockets which replaced the V-2. A total of 14 of the liquid propelled vehicles were fired from May 1949 until the end of the program in May 1957. Only Number 8 was not successful. Payloads included cameras for photographing the earth, measuring temperatures, densities and pressures and other scientific equipment. No two Vikings were alike; each incorporated improvements based on previous flights. Last two Vikings were launched to gather test data for development of the VANGUARD. Official designation: RTV-N-12. Early names were Marco Polo, Neptune.

VILDEBEEST -- Single-engine biplane developed by Vickers Aircraft at Great Britain as a landplane and seaplane in the early 1930's.

VILLAGE INN -- Nickname for British gun turret on bombers which automatically sighted and fired at enemy aircraft; used on limited scale at time of German surrender. WW-II.

VINDICATOR -- Vought-Sikorsky SB2U single-engine, low-wing monoplane accepted in 1936 by the U.S. Navy and in use during the early days of World War II. British version called Chesapeake.

VINEGAR -- Simiutakstromfjord, Greenland. WW-II.

VINEGAR JOE -- Nickname for U.S. General Jospeh W. Stilwell. WW-II.

VINEYARD -- Hong Kong, China. WW-II.

VINO RIDGE -- Canadian name for topographic feature near Ortona, Italy. December 1943, WW-II.

VINTNER -- Otta Island, Truk, Caroline Islands. WW-II.

VIOLA -- (1) Code name for Kendari, Celebes, Netherlands East Indies. Cancelled; CRUSTACEAN substituted. WW-II.

(2) Malaita Island, Solomon Islands. WW-II.

(3) Typhoon. 9-13 July 1958. Formed southeast of Guam. Moved northwestward, passing just southwest of Guam, turned northward over Philippine Sea, then northeastward. Dissipated east of Japan.

(4) Tropical storm. 9-10 April 1961. Formed in South China Sea. Moved westnorthwestward and inland near Saigon, Viet Nam.

(5) Name also applied to tropical cyclones in western North Pacific which occurred prior to (3) and (4) above.

VIOLET -- (1) Balikpapan, Borneo. WW-II.

(2) Typhoon. 1-6 January 1955. Formed in western Caroline Islands. Moved westward across southern Philippines and dissipated over Sulu Sea.

(3) Tropical depression. 28-29 June 1959. Formed in South China Sea, moved northwestward and inland into central Viet Nam.

(4) Typhoon. Formed southwest of Marcus Island, the Pacific. Moved southwestward through northern Mariana Islands, then northward and northeastward, passing near Tokyo, Japan, and out over Pacific. Caused two deaths and some damage.

(5) Name also applied to tropical cyclones in western Pacific which occurred prior to (2) through (4) above.

VIOLET HILL -- Military name for topographic feature on island of Hong Kong. December 1941. WW-II.

VIOLET LIGHTNING -- Japanese World War II Kawanishi N1K1 Shiden fighter. See GEORGE.

VIOLINS -- Cuyo Pass (West), Philippine Islands. WW-II.

VIPAN -- (English translation: Peewit) Swedish MFI-10 monoplane first flown in 1961. Now on order for Swedish Army.

VIPER -- (1) XP-13 biplane pursuit, the last of the Thomas-Morse firm before it was absorbed by Consolidated. The aircraft was destroyed during tests in 1930.

(2) Solid propellant motor originally used by U.S. Air Force in clusters to propel rocket sleds. Later used as a sounding rocket in conjunction with various upper stages: VIPER-ARROW capable of carrying 20-pound payload to 100-mile altitude; VIPER-FALCON capable of carrying 20-pound payload to 75-mile altitude. VIPER-SCAN was a Navy project in which a Viper rocket was used to carry an infra-red payload to about a 50-mile altitude. Payload was then ejected and commanded to transmit its infrared payload to about a 50-mile altitude. Payload was then ejected and commanded to transmit its infrared pictures to earth. Operational.

(3) See NATTER

VIPER-ARROW -- See VIPER

VIPER-FALCON -- See VIPER

VIPER-SCAN -- See VIPER

VIRAGO -- Code name for Jugoslavia. WW-II.

VIRGINIA -- (1) Obsolete U.S. battleship sunk in September 1923 by U.S. Air Service bombers.

(2) Vickers Aircraft twin-engine night bomber built in England in the later 1920's.

(3) Typhoon. 17-27 June 1957. Formed near Truk, Caroline Islands. Moved northwestward, passed south of Guam, across Philippine Sea, over Batan Island north of Luzon, turned northward across Taiwan, and then turned northeastward and weakened over Japan.

(4) Typhoon. 8-12 August 1960. Formed northwest, passed just west of Iwo Jima, crossed southern Japan into Sea of Japan, turned northeastward across northern Honshu and out over the Pacific. Caused two deaths and minor damage in Japan.

(5) Name also applied to tropical cyclones in western Pacific which occurred prior to (3) and (4) above.

VIRGY -- Name reserved by meteorologists for tropical cyclone in North Atlantic area.

VIRTUOSO -- Code name for Bahama Islands. WW-II.

VIRULENT -- Rongelap Atoll, Marshall Islands. WW-II.

VISAYAN FORCE -- Organization of U.S. and Philippine Army units, numbering about 20,000 men, for prolonged defense of island in Visayan group, Philippines. Created 4 March 1942, WW-II.

VISCOUNT -- First turboprop transport to be flown by a scheduled ariline. This early-1950's Vickers aircraft, and subsequent versions, are in service throughout the world.

VISIONARY -- Chichi Jima, Japan. WW-II.

VITAL CORNER -- Military name for position in upper Burma, strongly held by Japanese. Fall 1944, WW-II.

VITALITY, OPERATION -- Clearing of South Beveland, Netherlands, by Allied troops. See also VITALITY I and II. October 1944, WW-II.

VITALITY I -- Second Canadian Infantry Division's advance in OPERATION VITALITY. October 1944, WW-II.

VITALITY II -- British 52nd (lowland) Division's operation across Scheldt in OPERA- TION VITALITY. October 1944, WW-II.

VITTLES, OPERATION -- See BERLIN AIRLIFT

VIVIAN -- Name reserved by meteorologists for tropical cyclone in eastern North Pacific.

VIVISECTION -- Moosonee, Canada. WW-II.

VIXON -- Series of airborne attenuator assemblies designed to automatically reduce power of airborne radar system as it approaches enemy target, and thereby prevent enemy from discovering the approach.

VOCALIST -- Yap Islands, Caroline Islands. WW-II.

VOIS -- Acronym for Visual Observation Instrumentation Subsystem, a National Aeronautics and Space Administration study program to develop systems capable of photographing and mapping lunar features to a resolution of 100 meters. Systems will probably be used on the lunar orbiter version of the SURVEYOR spacecraft.

VOLCANO -- Losap Island, Caroline Islands. WW-II.

VOLITION -- Faleu Island, Truk, Caroline Islands. WW-II.

VOLKSJAEGER -- (English translation: People's fighter) German Heinkel He.162A aircraft. See SPATZ.

VOLUBLE -- Shemya Island, Aleutian Islands. WW-II.

VOODOO -- Nickname orginally applied to the XF-88 aircraft, but now shared by the F/RF-101, also made by McDonnell. The 101 is a large, twin-jet interceptor or photo reconnaissance aircraft. A product of the mid-1950's.

VORTEX -- Saint Michael, Alaska. WW-II.

VOSTOK -- (English translation: East) Russian manned spacecraft weighing more than than five tons. Six flights have been conducted: Major Yuri Gagarin on 12 April 1961 (first manned orbital flight), Major Gherman Titov on 6 August 1961, Major Andrian G. Nikolayev on 11 August 1962, Lieutenant Colonel Pavel Popovich on 12 August 1962, Lieutenant Colonel Valery Bykovsky on 14 June 1963, Lieutenant

Valentina Chereshkova on 16 June 1963 (first woman in space).

VOTER -- Mindanao, Philippine Islands. WW-II.

VOWEL -- Ollan Island, Truk, Caroline Islands. WW-II.

VOYAGER -- (1) Beech twin-engine monoplane. See EXPEDITOR.

(2) National Aeronautics and Space Administration follow-on program to MARINER. It will be a 2400-pound unmanned spacecraft capable of making interplanetary environmental investigations, as well as investigations of the environment of Mars and Venus. It would orbit these planets, inject a capsule to the planetary surface, and transmit data back to earth. Development to begin in 1963, with the first flight in 1965 and a Mars orbital flight in 1966. Saturn C-1 will be used as the booster.

VULCAN -- (1) U.S. Army-Air Force 20-mm. rapid-fire gun.

(2) The first delta-wing jet bomber, the Avro B.1 has been modified into a -2 which entered Royal Air Force Service in 1960.

(3) Final Allied ground offensive to clear Tunisia. Began 6 May 1943, WW-II.

VULCAN CRATER -- Name for topographic feature near Rabaul, New Britain. WW-II.

VULCAN ROAD -- Military name for topographic feature near Rabaul, New Britain. WW-II.

VULPINE -- Salerno, Italy. WW-II.

VULTEE VIBRATOR -- Name given to Vultee BT-13 by U.S. Army Air Forces cadets and instructors of World War II flying schools. See also VALIANT.

VULTURE -- Range-only, 12-centimeter radar equipment used for airborne fire control against land and waterborne targets.

W DAY -- Date for U.S. landing on Guam. 21 July 1944, WW-II.

W MINES --Small mines for use in shallow fresh water. WW-II.

W, PLAN -- Proposed Allied build-up schedule following Normandy landings, 6 June 1944; depended on a delay in capture of Brest, France; four divisions were to be held in reserve in England until February 1945. Renamed Plan P as it represented the pessimistic view. See also PLANS X, Y and Z

WA OPERATION -- Japanese name for attempted land and airborne attack on U.S. held airfields at Burauen, Leyte, Philippines. December 1944, WW-II.

WAC CORPORAL -- U.S. upper altitude research rocket designed to carry a 25-pound payload to an altitude of 20 miles. In its first test, however, the liquid propellant rocket considerably exceeded its design goal by reaching an altitude of 43 and one half miles, 26 September 1945. Never really used for experiments because, by the time it had been developed, German V-2 had been modified to perform research tasks. Did contribute to the BUMPER program as an upper stage for the V-2. Technology developed contributed to the CORPORAL missile program. See also BABY-WAC.

WACHT AM RHEIN -- See HERBSTNEBEL

WADHAM -- Name for feints made in the direction of Brest peninsula by U.S. Forces; part of COCKADE operation to give impression that an Allied invasion was being planned for the Continent in 1943. WW-II.

WAFFLE -- Kampalab, New Britain. WW-II.

WAGMIGHT -- Proposal by Goodyear Company for an inflatable manned aircraft, missile, or drone for use as submarine armament. Although air-breathing, the vehicle was to have had a verticle take-off capability. Not under development.

WAGON -- (1) Ayuet, New Britain. WW-II.

(2) U.S. low-yield nuclear cratering detonation being planned by Livermore laboratory staff of Atomic Energy Commission. To be conducted in basalt formation at Nevada Test Site.

WAGON WHEELS -- Mobile Tactical Air Communications Central that provides telephone, radio and wire teletype facilities. Components are installed in air-transportable vans and shelters.

WAGTAIL -- Air Force air-to-air and air-to-surface retarded launch family of missiles for use from low-flying, high-speed aircraft. Solid propellant; inertially guided, it reportedly has a range of 25 miles.

WAHOO -- Eliak River, New Britain. WW-II.

WAINFLEET -- The Hook, Netherlands. WW-II.

WAIROPI -- Place about thirty miles southwest of Buna, New Guinea; captured by Japanese in attack on Port Moresby. Name taken from wire-rope bridge over gorge of Kumsi River there. 1942, WW-II.

WAISTBAND -- Semichi Island, Aleutian Islands. WW-II.

WAL -- Dornier twin-engine, tandem-mounted, flying boat produced in Germany in 1933.

WALDORF -- Kabu River, New Guinea. WW-II.

WALKER BULLDOG -- U.S. Army 76-mm. gun tank.

WALKIE TALKIE -- U.S. two-way voice radio sets, SCR 194 and 195; powered by dry batteries with range of one to two miles. Also spelled Walky-Talky. WW-II.

WALKY-TALKY -- See WALKIE TALKIE

WALL GROUP -- Temporary collection of British Army columns during action around El Alamein, Egypt; under command of Brigadier R. B. Waller. July 1942, WW-II.

WALLACE -- (1) Westland Aircraft, England, single-engine general purpose biplane which entered Royal Air Force service in 1933. Developed from the WAPITI.

(2) Widu Reef, Bismarck Archipelago. WW-II.

WALLEYE -- Yaga Island, Solomon Sea. WW-II.

WALLFLOWER -- Talina Island, Solomon Islands. WW-II.

WALLIE -- Name reserved by meteorologists for tropical cyclone in eastern North Pacific.

WALLIS --Name reserved by meteorologists for tropical cyclone in North Atlantic area.

WALLSTREET -- British 49th (West Riding) Division plan to cross Neder Rijn River and capture Arnhem, Netherlands. Later carried out as Operation ANGER. Mid-February 1945, WW-II.

WALNUT -- (1) An information retrieval system.

(2) Rendova Island, Solomon Islands. WW-II.

WALRUS -- (1) British search plane. WW-II.

(2) Bonifacio, Corsica. WW-II.

WALT RIDGE -- Military name for topographic feature on Peleliu Island. Fall 1944, WW-II.

WALTER -- Allied device used by air crews ditched at sea consisting of automatic oscillator which registered on radar of searching aircraft. WW-II.

WALTON -- Murcadha Bay, New Britain. WW-II.

WANDA -- (1) Tropical storm. 21-24 September 1945. First detected east of Philippines. Moved northwestward across central Philippines, South China Sea, and Hainan Island to Asiatic mainland.

(2) Typhoon. 15-25 November 1951. Formed near Truk, Caroline Islands. Moved west-northwestward across Philippine Sea, central Philippines, and South China Sea and lost force near Indo China. Caused 87 casualties in Philippines.

(3) Typhoon. 27 July - 2 August 1956. Formed near Guam. Moved northward along Marianas Chain as weak storm, then turned northwestward, intensified, and moved into China mainland south of Shanghai, where it is reported to have caused 2000 deaths and damaged or destroyed 1.9 million homes.

(4) Typhoon. 27 August - 2 September 1962. Formed in central Philippine Sea. Moved west-northwestward between Luzon and Taiwan, across Hong Kong and into mainland China, where it dissipated. Caused over 100 deaths and heavy damage in Hong Kong.

(5) Name also applied to tropical cyclones in western Pacific which occurred prior to (1) through (4) above.

WANGANUI -- British method of sky marking a target by colored markers dropped blindly from aircraft using H2S radar equipment. See also MUSICAL WAGANUI. WW-II.

WAPITI -- Late-1920's Westland biplane, forerunner of the WALLACE.

WAR -- Call letters of the Washington control station of the War Department Radio Net (ACAN), changed from WVA on November 30, 1928.

WAR DANCE -- U.S. Navy term meaning high speed evasive maneuvering to avoid enemy gunfire.

WARBLE -- Fangger, New Guinea. WW-II.

WARD -- Solomon Islands. WW-II.

WARDEN, COLONEL -- Code name for Prime Minister Winston S. Churchill. WW-II.

WARDER -- Sibutu Passage, Philippine Islands. WW-II.

WARDROBE -- Lelis, New Britain. WW-II.

WARHAWK -- Originally built by Curtiss-Wright for ground support and coastal defense, the P-40 was one of two fighter planes in use by the Air Corps at the outbreak of World War II. Outstanding performance with the Flying Tigers in China and Burma, and with the British Royal Air Force, Soviet and U.S. Army Air Forces in the Pacific. Also called Kittyhawk, TOMAHAWK.

WARLIKE -- Code name for Syria. WW-II.

WARM WIND -- U.S. peacetime military exercise held in Alaska; involved 503rd Airborne Regimental Combat Team in winter air and land movement and employment. November 1952.

WARNING STAR -- U.S. Air Force RC-121 and the U.S. Navy EC-121 aircraft which patrol coasts on an "always-on-station" basis. Developed from Lockheed L.1049 for high-altitude radar picket duties.

WARREN TASK FORCE -- Force composed of U.S. 128th Infantry Regiment and supporting elements; active in New Guinea campaign. WW-II.

WARRIOR -- (1) Republic P-44 fighter aircraft development of 1940. Contract cancelled by U.S. Army Air Forces 1942.

(2) Advanced version of IROQUOIS.

WART AREA -- Military name for depressed area of land on Kwajalein Island where Japanese had set up a radio direction finder. February 1944, WW-II.

WART, THE -- Military name for topographic feature on Luzon, Philippine Islands. Spring 1945, WW-II.

WART HILL -- U.S. military name for topographic feature in southern Okinawa. 1945. WW-II.

WARTIME -- Kaoe (Kau) Bay, Halmahera Island, Netherlands East Indies. WW-II.

WASHING-MACHINE CHARLIE -- Nickname for Japanese plane which made nightly nuisance raids over Henderson Field, Guadalcanal. See also LOUIS THE LOUSE, MAYTAG CHARLIE. October 1942, WW-II.

WASHINGTON EAGLE ONE -- Name for peacetime U.S. Strategic Army Command alert exercise.

WASHSTAND -- Finschhafen, New Guinea. WW-II.

WASP -- (1) Allied flame thrower weapon to be mounted on armored personnel carrier. WW-II.

(2) Curtiss 18T triplane of 1919. Probably the fastest plane of its day; set a

record of 165 miles per hour.

(3) Military version of the Westland P.531-2 helicopter. See SCOUT.

(4) Acronym for Weather-Atmospheric Sounding Projectile, an upper altitude research rocket capable of carrying 6-pound air-sampling and meteorological payloads to altitudes of 22 miles. First fired in February 1956. Also used with LOKI first stage to carry the same payload to 35-mile altitudes. This version also known as HASP.

(5) Acronym for U.S. Women's Air Force Service Pilots.

WASSAIL -- Code name for Dutch New Guinea. WW-II.

WASSERFALL -- German surface-to-air missile designed to break-up bomber formations and destroy individual aircraft at ranges out to 30 miles and altitudes of 8-10 miles. Essentially, a one-third scale version of the V-2. Optical radio control guidance used. First firing 28 February 1945. 35 test firings were conducted in 1944 and 1945 before the war ended. Never reached production stage.

WATCH ON THE RHINE -- See HERBSTNEBEL

WATCHDOG -- Name for peacetime military exercise.

WATCHTOWER -- U.S. landings on Tulagi and Guadalcanal, Solomon Islands. First amphibious operation by U.S. since 1898. Nicknamed by sailors OPERATION SHOESTRING. Began 7 August 1942, WW-II.

WATER BUFFALO -- Name for U.S. Landing Vehicle, Tracked (LVT), unarmored, Mark I. See also ALLIGATOR. WW-II.

WATER BUGS -- Nickname for Landing Craft, Vehicle and Personnel (LCVP) and Landing Craft, Mechanized (LCM). WW-II.

WATERHOLE -- Turitei, New Britain. WW-II.

WATERLOO -- Practice exercise by Canadian Corps and British 8th Armored Division in mobile counter-attack against parachute drops and glider and seaborne landings; held in central coastal region of Sussex, England. June 1941, WW-II.

WATERTOWN -- Renard Entrance, Rendova, Solomon Islands. WW-II.

WATSON -- Cherbourg, France. WW-II.

WATT, MR. -- Assumed name used by Field Marshall Lord Wilson, commander of British troops in Greece, during talks in Athens with a Colonel Peresitch of Yugoslav General Staff, who used name, MR. HOPE. March 1941, WW-II.

WAXBEAN -- Annha Island, Tulagi-Florida Group, Solomon Islands. WW-II.

WAYSIDE SERVICE STATION -- Nickname given by U.S. B-29 aircraft crews to Iwo Jima. 1945, WW-II.

WAYWARD -- North Pass, Truk Lagoon, Caroline Islands. WW-II.

WEAPON ABLE -- See WEAPON ALFA

WEAPON ALFA -- U.S. Navy solid propelled free flight depth charge weighing about 500 pounds. Fired from a deck launcher resembling a gun turret; has a range of approximately 900 yards, and has been deployed aboard destroyers and other comparable vessels since 1952. Also known as Weapon Able, Weapon Alpha, Alpha, Able.

WEAPON ALPHA -- See WEAPON ALFA

WEASEL -- Allied cargo carrier M29, tracked vehicle with low ground pressure designed for use over snow and ice and across fields or poor trails. Carried a crew of two and payload of about 1000 pounds. WW-II.

WEARY-WILLIE -- Code name of experiment, initiated by U.S. General Carl Spaatz, for developing and using worn-out conventional bomber aircraft as guided missiles in CROSSBOW OPERATION against German V-weapon sites. After takeoff, pilot would bail out and another plane would control the craft by radio. Also called APHRODITE, BATTY, CASTOR and ORPHAN. WW-II.

WEATHERBIRD -- U.S. Air Force conversion of B-47 and C-130 aircraft into weather reconnaissance planes.

WEBFOOT -- U.S. rehearsal landing operation held on beaches south of Salerno, Italy, in preparation for assault on Anzio, Operation SHINGLE. 17-19 January 1944, WW-II.

WEDGE -- Acronym for Weapon Development Glide Entry, a Boeing Company study of the application of the DYNA-SOAR research vehicle to the orbital bomber concept. It was not adopted and Dyna-Soar continues as a research project.

WEED -- Loun Island, Solomon Islands. WW-II.

WEEVIL -- Rocket adapted for use on Army helicopters. Various combinations of 2.75-inch and 4.5-inch rockets were tested; and both are now being used. The SS-10/SS-11 are also being adapted to helicopter launch.

WEIHE -- Focke-Wulf Fw.58, twin-engine advanced trainer plane developed from the commercial transport of the 1930's.

WEISS OPERATION -- (English translation: White Operation) German operation for invasion of Poland. Also called Fall Weiss. Began 1 September 1939, WW-II.

WELKIN -- British Westland twin-engine interceptor aircraft first flown in 1942. Did not become operational.

WELCOME -- Commodore Bay, New Britain. WW-II.

WELDER -- Siplawatni, New Britain. WW-II.

WELDFAST -- Name for peacetime military exercise.

WELLBEING -- Cape Lambert, New Britain. WW-II.

WELLESLEY -- Vickers-Armstrong pre-World War II general purpose aircraft used throughout Great Britain.

WELLHIT -- Operation of Canadian 3rd Divison to capture Boulogne, France. 17-22 September 1944, WW-II.

WELLINGTON -- Vickers-Armstrong-built twin-engine aircraft which was the British Royal Air Force's principal heavy bomber during the early days of World War II. Also called Wimpy.

WELLINGTON MINESWEEPER -- Soecialized version of the bomber, distinguished by large, external circular deGaussing belt. The electrically-controlled loop was used to explode mines from an average altitude of sixty feet over the water.

WELMAN CRAFT -- British one-man submarines. Named after their inventor, an Army officer. WW-II.

WELVERT ROAD -- Military name for road, constructed by U.S. Army Engineers, running eastward from Thélepte, Tunisia. March 1943, WW-II.

WEMBLEY -- Cape Ruge, New Britain. WW-II.

WENDA -- Name reserved by meteorologists for tropical cyclone in North Atlantic area.

WENDY -- (1) Typhoon. 10-16 July 1957. Formed in western Caroline Islands. Moved west-northwestward over northern Luzon, causing one of worst floods in Philippine history; moved across South China Sea into China mainland east of Hong Kong.

(2) Typhoon. 10-13 August 1960. Formed west of Iwo Jima. Moved northward across Shikoku, Japan, over Sea of Japan, then northeastward across northern Honshu, Japan, and out over the Pacific. Caused little damage.

(3) Name also applied to tropical cyclones in western North Pacific which occurred prior to (1) and (2) above.

WERFGERAT -- German rocket launcher which fired the 32-centimeter rocket which weighed about 300 pounds and had a range of over a mile. WW-II.

WESER EXERCISE --See WESERÜBUNG

WESERÜBUNG -- (English translation: Weser Exercise) German operation for occupation of Denmark and Norway. Also called Fall Weserübung. 8 April 1940, WW-II.

WESPE -- Tailless, single-engine monoplane, second plane of the Fieseler Aircraft Company to be built. Germany 1932.

WESSEX -- (1) Westland trimotor commercial monoplane built in the early 1930's in England.

(2) Derived from the Sikorsky S-58 aircraft, the Westland H.A.S.1 entered service with the British Royal Air Force in 1961.

WEST CAVES -- Military name for three large depressions on Biak Island off Netherlands New Guinea; connected by underground tunnels and caverns and heavily defended by Japanese. May-June 1944, WW-II.

WEST FORD -- U.S. Air Force program to disperse in orbit some 350 million one-eighth inch tuned dipoles as a means of providing a world-wide passive communications system for use by the Strategic Air Command. Total weight of payload package is 75 pounds. First launch took place 21 October 1961 when, as companion payload to MIDAS IV, it was carried piggy-back into orbit by an ATLAS-AGENA. Needles failed to disperse. Second try in 1962 also unsuccessful. Project has been denounced by scientists throughout the world as potentially harmful to optical astronomy; special White House panel denies this possibility. Further launches may be conducted. Early name was NEEDLES.

WEST PINNACLE -- Military name for topographic feature in Urasoe-Mura Escarpment on Okinawa. See also BATTLE OF THE PINNACLES. April 1943, WW-II.

WEST POINT OF THE AIR -- Randolph Field, San Antonio, Texas, headquarters of the U.S. Air Corps Training Center, and the site of the primary flying school in 1931. Used, basically, for the same purpose to this day.

WEST WADI -- Military name for topographic feature near Heraklion, Crete. May 1941, WW-II.

WESTERN TASK FORCE -- Large Allied force, under command of U.S. Major General George S. Patton, with mission of occupying French Morocco; included landings near Safi, Fedala and Mehdia, west of Port Lyautey, November 1942, WW-II.

WESTMOUNT, CITY OF -- Name for Royal Canadian Air Force Squadron Number 439.

WESTOMP -- Acronym for Western Ocean Meeting Point, south of Newfoundland, where U.S. Navy exchanged responsibility for escorting convoys in Atlantic with British and Canadian naval forces. WW-II.

WESTON -- Canadian military name for woods west of Xanten, Germany. March 1945, WW-II.

WESTVIEW -- Military name for outpost south of PORK CHOP HILL in Korea. Korean Conflict.

WESTWALL -- Official German name for fortified belt along western German frontier. Also known as Siegfried Line. WW-II.

WETBLANKET -- Champagny Island, Australia. WW-II.

WETBOB -- Allied plan to gain permanent foothold on Continent in area of Cherbourg, France, in Fall 1942, in case of urgent political necessity. WW-II.

WEWAK WELTER -- Name of Australian air-raid on Japanese-held Wewak Airfield, New Guinea. 11 September 1944, WW-II.

WHALE -- Cape King, New Guinea. WW-II.

WHALEBONE -- Hinchinbrook, Alaska. WW-II.

WHALES -- Allied code name for flexible steel roadways, made of bridge spans, resting on pontons, BEETLES, and connecting pierheads of artificial harbors, MULBERRIES, with shore. 1944, WW-II.

WHATNOT -- Hafn, Iceland. WW-II.

WHEAT HILL -- Military name for topographic feature near Canea, Crete. May 1941, WW-II.

WHEN AND WHERE -- Project of U.S. Air Transport Command, based in Sweden, to deliver Norwegian military personnel and cargo to various points in northern Norway to fight against German occupying forces. Began January 1945, WW-II.

WHIMSICAL -- Bismarck Sea. WW-II.

WHIP -- Popular name of U.S. Army airborne assault weapon system.

WHIPCORD -- (1) Wongakai, New Britain. WW-II.

(2) Plan for British attack on Sicily. Abandoned Fall 1941, WW-II.

WHIPPED CREAM DIVISION -- Nickname for German 416th Division, which was filled with replacements with average age of 38 years. WW-II.

WHIRL WING -- AGA PA-36 gyroplane built in the U.S. during the 1930's. Formerly known as the Pitcairn -36.

WHIRLAWAY -- Dutch Harbor, Alaska. WW-II.

WHIRLWIND -- (1) Designed in Great Britain in 1936, and first flown in 1938, this Westland aircraft was the British Royal Air Force's first twin-engine, single-seat fighter. Last built 1942.

(2) Finnish fighter plane. See PYORREMYRSKY.

(3) Makasi Island, Philippine Islands. WW-II.

WHIRLWIND SERIES -- Westland developments of the Sikorsky S-55 helicopters. At least eight versions have been built since the mid-1950's.

WHISKY -- Code word for letter "W" in a phonetic alphabet, used to avoid possibility of a misunderstanding in transmitting messages. See also WILLIAM.

WHISPERING GIANT -- Popular nickname for Great Britain's Bristol BRITTANIA.

WHISTLING HILL -- Military name for small ridge southeast of Ragalbuto, Sicily; captured by Canadian troops. August 1943, WW-II.

WHITE ALICE -- U.S. defense communication network in Alaska; employs over-the-horizon radio adapted to arctic environment.

WHITE BALL EXPRESS -- Allied military trucking service to haul supplies from ports of Le Havre and Rouen, France, either directly to armies or to rail transfer points at Paris and Rheims. 6 October 1944-10 January 1945, WW-II.

WHITE CITY -- Name for jungle clearing behind Japanese lines in northeast Burma; used as airstrip during Allied OPERATION THURSDAY. Spring 1944, WW-II.

WHITE HORSE HILL -- Military name for topographic feature in Korea near PORK CHOP HILL. Korean Conflict.

WHITE LANCE -- See LANCE

WHITE, MR. -- See MR. WHITE

WHITE OPERATION -- See WEISS OPERATION

WHITE PATROL -- Task Force of U.S. Atlantic Fleet based on Iceland, which patrolled Denmark Strait for German ships. 1941-42, WW-II.

WHITE POPPY -- Noumea, New Caledonia. WW-II.

WHITE PROJECT -- Project by U.S. Air Transport Command to fly heavy bombers with full combat crews and some passengers to U.S. from European and Mediterranean Theaters for eventual transfer across Pacific. Also called Home Run Project. 20 May - 31 October 1945, WW-II.

WHITE WING -- A powered flying machine developed by Alexander Graham Bell. Lieutenant Thomas E. Selfridge, who had become the first U.S. Army officer to make a solo flight in a powered flying machine--the White Wing--was later killed--the first military aerial casualty.

WHITEFLAT -- Saidor, New Guinea. WW-II.

WHITELEATHER -- Kakumo, New Britain. WW-II.

WHITELINE -- Perth, Australia. WW-II.

WHITEOAK -- Tuwatu Point, New Britain. WW-II.

WHITEWASH -- Luzon Island, Philippine Islands. WW-II.

WHITING -- Kurile Islands, Japan. WW-II.

WHITLEY -- Vickers-Armstrong craft, developed in the early 1930's, and in production until 1943. First British bomber to see combat in World War II.

WHITSTABLE -- Allied code name for Le Harve, France. WW-II.

WHIZ BANG -- U.S. Army 20-tube rocket launcher which fired the 7.2-inch Demolition Rocket. WW-II.

WHOOFUS -- U.S. Army name for landing vessels used by U.S. Navy which were equipped with banks of as many as 1000 rockets capable of being fired in salvos or discharged simultaneously. WW-II.

WICKIE -- Name of mouse carried in the nose cone of THOR-ABLE test vehicle in July 1958. Third in the series of Thor-Able tests, the nose cone was fired down the Atlantic Missile Range and was not recovered.

WIDEAWAKE CONFERENCES -- U.S. staff meetings held in Brisbane, Australia, July-September 1944, to plan operations culminating in establishment of air bases in central Luzon, Philippines. WW-II.

WIDEWING -- Code name for Supreme Headquarters, Allied Expeditionary Force (SHAEF) at Bushy Park, Kingston-on-Thames, England; moved from Norfolk House, London, March 1944. WW-II.

WIDGEON -- (1) Grumman G-44 aircraft which first flew in 1944; built in small numbers during World War II as a light utility-patrol amphibian.

    (2) Westland development of the Dragonfly helicopter which, in turn, was a license-built version of the Sikorsky S-51 of the 1950's.

WIDOW -- Miri, Borneo. WW-II.

WIGMORE -- Allied code name for Ouistreham, France. WW-II.

WIGWAM, OPERATION -- U.S nuclear weapons test held off coast of California, Spring 1955.

WILD CAT -- (1) Variant of the U.S. Monocoupe Zephyr aircraft especially equipped for military transitional flying. See ZEPHYR .

    (2) Name for Royal Canadian Air Force Squadron Number 438.

WILD GOOSE -- See KARIGANE

WILD HARES -- Nickname for U.S. Marine Corps dive bombing squadron operating from air bases on Lingayen Gulf, Philippines. 1945, WW-II.

WILDA -- (1) Typhoon. 22-27 March 1955. Formed in vicinity of Kwajalein Atoll, Pacific. Moved north-northwestward to position east of Marcus Island, then turned east-northeastward out over Pacific.

    (2) Tropical storm. 4-5 July 1959. Formed in South China Sea; moved northward into China mainland northeast of Hong Kong.

CODE NAMES DICTIONARY

(3) Tropical storm. 11-13 October 1961. Formed in South China Sea and moved westward into Viet Nam near Binh Dinh.

(4) Name also applied to tropical cyclones in western Pacific which occurred prior to (1) through (3) above.

WILDCAT -- Standard U.S. Navy fighter plane during the earlier days of World War II, the Grumman F4F also saw service with the Fleet Air Arm and was dubbed Martlet by the British.

WILDCAT BOWL -- Military name for topographic feature on Peleliu Island. Fall 1944, WW-II.

WILDFLOWER -- Code name for Great Britain. WW-II.

WILDHORN III -- PICK-UP operation behind enemy lines in Poland by British airplane to bring out friendly agents. 25 July 1944, WW-II.

WILDROOT -- Tuguho River, New Britain. WW-II.

WILFRED -- British operation to lay mines in the Indreled, or Inner Leads, off coast of Norway; occurred shortly before German invasion of Norway. April 1940, W-WW-II.

WILK -- (English translation: Wolf) Polish PZL P.38 destroyer aircraft designed in 1936, but production priorities for an interceptor forced its abandonment.

WILLA -- Tropical storm. 7-11 July 1962. Formed south of tip of Baja California, Mexico. Moved westward out over Pacific, and dissipated.

WILLIAM -- Code word for letter "W" in a phonetic alphabet, used to avoid possibility of a misunderstanding in transmitting messages. See also WHISKY.

WILLIAM TELL 61 -- Realistic defense exercise conducted by the U.S. Air Defense Command's fighter-interceptor teams in 1961.

WILLIS -- Purvis Bay, Solomon Islands. WW-II.

WILLOW -- (1) U.S. Army tactical missile under development by the Chrysler Corporation in 1960. Indications are that the program has been discontinued.

(2) Baison Island, Solomon Islands. WW-II.

(3) Lilim Island, New Britain. WW-II.

WILLOW FREEZE -- Joint U.S. Air Force-Army peacetime exercise held in Alaska, 1961.

WILLOW RUN -- Nickname for large consolidated officers mess located in Grosvenor House, London. Opened December 1943, WW-II.

WILMA -- Typhoon. 23-26 October 1952. Formed in eastern Caroline Islands.

Moved westward across central Philippines, the South China Sea and Central coast of Viet Nam.

WILNA -- Name reserved by meteorologists for tropical cyclone in North Atlantic area.

WIMPY -- Popular name for the World War II WELLINGTON bomber.

WINCH -- British operation to reinforce Malta. Winter 1940-41, WW-II.

WINCHESTER -- Walawalapua, New Britain. WW-II.

WINDBAG -- Sarangani Bay, Philippine Islands. WW-II.

WINDOW -- Metalized strips dropped by Allied aircraft to confuse enemy radar. Also called Chaff. First used in major attacks on Hamburg, Germany at end of July 1943. WW-II.

WINDOW ROCKET -- U.S. Navy program based on the use of 3.5-inch aircraft rocket to launch over 75,000 small pieces of aluminum foil to confuse enemy radars. World War II development.

WINDOWBOX -- Bogadjim, New Guinea. WW-II.

WINDSHIELD --Portion of naval blockade by units of U.N. Task Force 95 between Chaho and Yang Do off Korean east coast. Began early 1951, Korean Conflict.

WINDSOR, CITY OF -- Name for Royal Canadian Air Force Squadron Number 417.

WINDSOR, OPERATION -- Third Canadian Division attack from west on Carpiquet, near Caen, France. See also OTTAWA. 4 July 1944, WW-II.

WINDY CORNER -- Military name for turn on Merdjayoun-Rasheiya road, Lebanon. Spring 1941, WW-II.

WINGED VICTORY DIVISION -- Nickname for U.S. 43rd Infantry Division.

WINIFRED -- Name reserved by meteorologists for tropical cyclone in eastern North Pacific.

WINJEEL -- (English translation: Eagle) Royal Australian Air Force basic trainer, the CA-25, first flown in 1950 as the CA-22.

WINNIE -- (1) Typhoon. 12-16 July 1958. Formed near Guam. Moved west-northwestward across Taiwan, causing nine deaths and heavy damage, and then entered China mainland.

(2) Tropical storm. 6-9 May 1961. Formed near Andaman Islands, moved north-westward, then northward through Bay of Bengal into East Pakistan.

(3) Name also applied to tropical cyclones in western North Pacific which occurred prior to (1) and (2) above.

WINNIE MAE -- Nickname for the Lockheed VEGA 5C aircraft which Wiley Post flew solo round-the-world in July 1933 in 187 flying hours.

WINNIE and POOH -- Nicknames of two mammoth 14-inch guns on the South Foreland, east of Dover, England, which fired at Continent. WW-II.

WINNIE THE WAR WINNER -- Radio transmitter improvised by Australian troops at Mape, Portuguese Timor, to communicate with Darwin, Australia. April 1942, WW-II.

WINNIPEG BEAR -- Name for Royal Canadian Air Force Squadron Number 402.

WINNY -- Name reserved by meteorologists for tropical cyclone in eastern North Atlantic area.

WINONA -- Name reserved by meteorologists for tropical cyclone in eastern North Pacific.

WINSOME -- Riebeck Bay, New Britain. WW-II.

WINTER BATTLE -- See CRUSADER

WINTER LINE -- German defensive line across Italian peninsula from Ortona to Gaeta. Also known as Bernhard Line. See also GUSTAV LINE, ADOLF HITLER LINE. 1943-44.

WINTER SHIELD I -- Name for peacetime military exercise held in Germany.

WINTER SHIELD II -- Name for NATO peacetime military exercise.

WINTERGREEN -- Nikolski, Alaska. WW-II.

WINTERROSE -- Langemak Bay, New Guinea. WW-II.

WINTERSTELLUNG -- See WINTER LINE

WIPER -- Liquidation of enemy opposition on Isles D'Hyeres. WW-II.

WISTERIA -- Narau Sound, Guadalcanal, Solomon Islands. WW-II.

WITCHCRAFT -- Samar, Philippine Islands. WW-II.

WIZARD -- U.S. Air Force surface-to-air anti-missile missile program. Not actively developed, the program led to the development later of the BOMARC anti-aircraft missile. Wizard were early post-World War II studies by the University of Michigan.

WOLF -- (1) Polish P.38 aircraft design of 1936. See WILK.

(2) Name for Royal Canadian Air Force Squadron Number 403.

WOLFBERRY -- Bonifacio, Corsica. WW-II.

WOLFHOUND RIDGE -- Military name for topographic feature near LONE TREE HILL on Luzon, Philippines. Cleared by U.S. 27th Infantry Regiment on 5 May 1945, WW-II.

WOLFHOUND, TASK FORCE -- U.N. regimental combat team used to feel out enemy strength in area of Osan and Suwon, Korea. Mid-January 1951, Korean Conflict.

WOLFHOUNDS -- Nickname for U.S. Army 27th Infantry Regiment.

WOLFISH -- Code name for Bulgaria. WW-II.

WOLF'S LAIR -- See WOLFSCHANZE

WOLFSCHANZE -- (English translation: Wolf's Lair) Adolf Hitler's headquarters near Rastenburg, East Prussia. WW-II.

WOLVERINE -- U.S. project for ten thousand electric-kilowatt, aqueous homogeneous nuclear powerplant proposed by Wolverine Electric Cooperative for Hersey, Michigan. Project dropped in 1958.

WOLVES -- U.S. code word for destroyers during naval battle with Japanese off Samar, Philippines. See also LITTLE WOLVES. October 1944, WW-II.

WOMANHOOD -- Kapepa Island, New Britain. WW-II.

WOO -- Abbreviation of Western Operations Office, a small group of National Aeronautics and Space Administration personnel situated in southern California to manage and provide liaison with industry doing work for various NASA centers.

WOODBANK -- Paris, France. WW-II.

WOODBURY -- Altavalo, New Britain. WW-II.

WOODCHUCK -- Gazelle Peninsula, New Britain. WW-II.

WOODPECKER -- Italian monoplane. See PICCHIO.

WOODPRINT -- Doroeba, Morotai Island, Netherlands East Indies. WW-II.

WOOD'S HOLE -- One of two groups of beaches in U.S. CENT landing area near Scoglitti, Sicily. Name taken from naval transport at beach, USS Leonard Wood, as well as place in Massachusetts. July 1943, WW-II.

WOOFUS -- U.S. Army 120-tube rocket launcher which fired the 7.2-inch demolition rocket with a 32-pound warhead. World War II weapon used during the attack on Southern France in August 1944.

WOOLAROC -- (Oklahoma Indian for "Good Luck") Single-engine, Travelair monoplane which won the "Pineapple Derby" air race to Hawaii in 1927. See also ALOHA.

WOOLCOAT -- Rada, New Britain. WW-II.

WOOLSACK -- Riyan, Aden Protectorate. WW-II.

WOOLY -- Sagewin Strait, New Guinea. WW-II.

WOOTTEN HOUSE -- Italian outpost near Giarabub in eastern Libya. Named after Australian Major-General C. F. Wootten. March 1941, WW-II.

WOP -- Operation by U.S. Army II Corps to attack Gafsa and Maknassy, Tunisia, in support of British 8th Army moving in from the east. Began 17 March 1943, WW-II.

WORKHORSE -- Vertol H-21 helicopter in U.S. Army-Air Force service. First flown in 1952. The HH-21 (formerly SH-) is sometimes called RESCUER.

WORKHOUSE -- Manasaha, New Britain. WW-II.

WORKMAN -- Iwo Jima, Bonin Islands. WW-II.

WORKMASTER -- British Auster J1U agricultural monoplane. First flown in 1958.

WORKSHOP -- British plan to capture the Italian held island of Pantelleria. Cancelled 20 January 1941, WW-II.

WORLD CRUISER -- Douglas biplanes, equipped with floats, which made the first round-the-world air tour, the first trans-Pacific flight, and the first westbound Atlantic crossing, April-September 1924. See also BOSTON, CHICAGO, NEW ORLEANS, SEATTLE.

WOT -- Ultra-light Currie-designed British biplane of 1937.

WOWSER -- Largest operation of U.S. 15th Air Force in Italy, involving practically every flyable heavy bomber, in tactical air support of ground forces during Bologna breakthrough. April 1945, WW-II.

WRANGLER -- U.N. plan to land at Kojo on eastern coast of Korea, drive southwestward to link up with U.S. 8th Army, thereby cutting North Korean Army from its source of Chinese supply. Proposed mid-1951, Korean Conflict.

WREN -- (1) Small Australian military detachment, installed on Nauru Island in the western Pacific, in February 1941 to serve against attack by German raiders. WW-II.

(2) See ZAUNKÖNIG

WRESTLER -- South Sulu Sea, Philippine Islands. WW-II.

WURGER -- (English translation: Butcher Bird) German Focke-Wulf 190A. First flown in 1939. Over 20,000 delivered to the Luft-waffe before World War II end.

WURZBURGS -- Two types of German radar devices: Giant Wurzburgs, which located positions of Allied bombers and directed fighters to them; small Wurzburgs which aimed radar-predicted anti-aircraft guns. WW-II.

WYOMING -- Military name for U.N. defense line in Korea, north of KANSAS line. 1951, Korean Conflict.

WYVERN -- British XXX Corps plan for offensive between Maas and Rhine Rivers, Netherlands and Germany; turned over to Canadians who carried it out as Operation VERITABLE. October 1944, WW-II.

X

X -- See UTAH

X APPARAT -- See X GERÄT

X, BATTLESHIP -- Nickname for battleship, U.S.S. South Dakota. Also called
OLD NAMELESS, BIG BASTARD. WW-II.

X BEACH -- Area in Bay of Mersa bou Zedjar, Algeria, where TASK FORCE
GREEN landed in assault on Oran. Also called X-Ray Beach. November 1942,
WW-II.

X-CRAFT -- British midget submarines; were towed to distant waters by "parent"
conventional submarines. WW-II.

X DAY -- (1) Date, 8 September 1943, when news of armistice between Italy and
Allies was made public in radio broadcasts by General Dwight D. Eisenhower
and Marshal Pietro Badoglio. WW-II.

    (2) Date for executing MIKE VI invasion of Nasubu-Pagbilao area, Philippines.
31 January 1945, WW-II.

    (3) Allied code name for proposed day of attack on the Japanese home islands.
Planned for November 1945, WW-II.

X-15 -- U.S. National Aeronautics and Space Administration - Air Force - Navy
advanced rocket propelled research aircraft used to investigate flight regimes
up to speeds of 4000 miles per hour and at altitudes up to 50 miles. Both
design goals have been exceeded with a record speed of 4159 miles per hour
on 27 June 1962 and an altitude record of 314,750 feet. Aircraft is air-launched from a B-52 aircraft at about 600 miles per hour. X-15 burns liquid oxygen
and liquid ammonia developing some 57,000 pounds thrust. Program has been
expanded to include space research and spacecraft component tests. Also testing
re-entry and glide maneuvers for the DYNA-SOAR. First powered flight took
place on 17 September 1959.

X FORCE -- (1) About 45,000 Chinese troops training at Ramgarh in northeastern
India for collaboration with Y FORCE from Yunnan Province, China, in pincer
movement against Japanese in northern Burma. Also called Ramgarh Force,
X-Ray Force. WW-II.

(2) See BLACKSTONE SUB-TASK FORCE

X GERÄT -- German radio-aid system for blind-bombing of precision targets; used
fine beam to give aircraft its course and three intersecting beams to signal
arrival over target. Took place of KNICKEBEIN and was superseded by Y GERÄT.
Also called X Apparat. First used November 1940, WW-II.

X, PLAN -- (1) Project worked out by U.S. Army General Staff on 20 December
1941 for building up supplies in Australia, which was to serve as rear base for
logistical support of the Philippine battle front. WW-II.

(2) Proposed Allied build-up schedule following Normandy landings, 6 June 1944
(D Day); called for 21 divisions on Continent by D plus 90 days, 25 divi-
sions by D plus 120 days and 30 divisions by D plus 150 days. Renamed
Plan R since it represented the realistic view. See also PLANS W, Y and
Z. WW-II.

X, PROJECT -- Operation of ferrying heavy bombers to Far East and Australia by
way of Florida, Brazil, Africa and India, early 1942. First major U.S. foreign
ferrying job. WW-II.

X-RAY -- (1) Code word for letter "X" in a phonetic alphabet, used to avoid
possibility of a misunderstanding in transmitting messages.

(2) See PHANTOM

X-RAY BEACH -- See X BEACH

X-RAY FORCE -- See X FORCE

X-RAY RIVER -- Military name for topographic feature in Hollandia-Aitape area,
New Guinea. Summer 1944, WW-II.

X-RAY-YOKE, HILL -- Military name for topographic feature in PURPLE HEART
RIDGE on Saipan. 1944, WW-II.

X, ROUTE -- Central sea route of 55 sea miles used during OPERATION DYNAMO,
the evacuation of Allied troops from Dunkirk, France, to Dover, England. See
also ROUTES Y and Z. May-June, 1940, WW-II.

X-SHIPS -- U.S. transport vessels, mostly old and slow LAKERS, which contained
refrigerator space for carrying perishables in Southwest Pacific Area. WW-II.

X, SQUADRON -- French ships under Admiral Godfrey in North African ports.
April-August 1943, WW-II.

X, TASK FORCE -- See DARBY'S RANGERS

X WING -- See BURWING

XYZ EXPRESS -- Allied military trucking service to supply operations beyond Rhine River in Germany; moved forward as railheads were set up and armies advanced; planned to increase daily tonnage carried in three phases, X,Y,Z. Also called XYZ Operation. 25 March - 31 May 1945, WW-II.

XYZ OPERATION -- See XYZ EXPRESS

XYLOPHONE -- U.S. Army rocket launcher used in World War II. An eight-tube launcher, it fired 4.5-inch rockets at intervals of one-half second. Type classified as M8.

Y

Y -- See OMAHA

Y APPARAT -- See Y GERÄT

Y BEACH -- Area near small village of Les Andalouses, Algeria, where landing was made in assault on Oran. Also called Yorker Beach. November 1942, WW-II.

Y DAY -- (1) Target date for any military operation; specifically, date on which all preparations had to be complete for Normandy landings, OVERLORD. 1 June 1944 (D DAY, the day of attack, was 6 June 1944), WW-II.

(2) Date for U.S. landing on island of Negros, Philippines. 29 March 1945, WW-II.

Y FORCE -- (1) Large number of Chinese troops training in Yunnan Province, China, for action against Japanese in northern Burma. Also called Yunnan Force, YOKE FORCE, WW-II.

(2) See BRUSHWOOD SUB-TASK FORCE

Y GERÄT -- German radio-aid system for blind-bombing of precision targets; used single beam for giving aircraft its course and position. Superseded X GERÄT. Also called Y Apparat. WW-II.

Y-GUN -- U.S. Navy anti-submarine depth-charge projector, Mark-1; replaced by K-GUN. Early WW-II.

Y, PLAN -- (1) Proposed accelerated Allied build-up schedule following Normandy landings, 6 June 1944 (D Day); called for 27 divisions transferred to the Continent by D plus 120 days and 34 divisions by D plus 150 days. Renamed Plan O as it represented optimistic view. See also PLANS W, X and Z. WW-II.

(2) Plan proposed in summer 1944 for capture of Mandalay, Burma, by Allied Southeast Asia Command; proposed three-pronged assault by British troops in west and Chinese troops from Ledo, Assam, in the north and Yunnan, China, in the east. Later called CAPITAL. See also PLAN Z. WW-II.

Y, ROUTE -- Northern sea route used during OPERATION DYNAMO, the evacuation of Allied troops from Dunkirk, France, to Dover, England; longest of three routes (87 sea miles). See also ROUTES X and Z. May-June 1940, WW-II.

YAK -- Acronym for Russian aircraft named for designer Yakovlev.

YAKE I -- Onne Island, Gilbert Islands. WW-II.

YALE -- North American BT-9 single-engine trainer plane first produced in 1936 and in use by the U.S. Army Air Force at the time of Pearl Harbor.

YANGTZE -- Boxlike container with retardation device, similar to wings, used in airdropping of supplies. Developed by Nationalist Chinese government and Yangtze Wood Products Company. First tested at Nanking, January 1949.

YANGTZE RAIDERS -- Popular name for SACO Unit 13, established near Hankow, China, in spring 1944 to conduct guerrilla activities and sabotage against railroads and shipping behind Japanese lines. WW-II.

YANKEE -- (1) Code word for letter "Y" in a phonetic alphabet, used to avoid possibility of a misunderstanding in transmitting messages. See also YOKE.

(2) Pressurized water reactor of Yankee Atomic Electric Company at Rowe, Massachusetts.

(3) Cape San Jacques, French Indo China. WW-II.

YANKEE DOODLE -- Fairchild AT-13 World War II advanced trainer plane constructed of wood for the U.S. Army Air Forces. Resembled a stubby Lockheed Hudson.

YANKEE HURRICANE -- Florida hurricane. 30 October - 8 November 1935. So called because came from north. Formed near Bermuda, moved southwestward across Miami, then turned westward and dissipated in Gulf of Mexico. Caused 19 deaths and 5.5 million dollars damage.

YANKEES -- Nickname for U.S. 26th Infantry Division.

YARDBIRD -- Observation Island, Sumatra. WW-II.

YEARBOOK -- Ringring, New Britain. WW-II.

YEARLING ISLAND -- Kiebu Island, Gilbert Islands. WW-II.

YEAST -- Sumalani, New Britain. WW-II.

YELLOW -- (1) Code name for China. WW-II.

(2) Sagsag Bay, Philippine Islands. WW-II.

YELLOW DIAMOND ROUTE -- Allied military trucking route through southern Germany into Austria. March-May 1945, WW-II.

YELLOW LINE -- Initial Allied objective line in south-central Sicily, running from inter-army boundary at Vizzini to seacoast at Palma di Monechiaro. July 1943, WW-II.

YELLOW OPERATION -- See GELB OPERATION

YELLOW PERIL -- See KADET

YELP -- Auckland, New Zealand. WW-II.

YEW -- First phase beachhead objective of Canadian troops in Normandy landing. See also ELM, OAK. 6 June 1944, WW-II.

YIPPEE -- Lockheed YP-38 aircraft. An XP-38 with a different engine and outward rotating propellors. See LIGHTNING.

YIPPIES -- Nickname derived from abbreviation YP's, U.S. Navy yard-patrol craft. WW-II.

YOGI -- (1) Code name for type of end-fire antenna array.

(2) Nickname for a brown bear successfully ejected from a B-58 flying 1060 mph at 45,000 feet over Edwards Air Force Base, California, 6 April 1962.

YOICKS -- Visayan Sea, Philippine Islands. WW-II.

YOKE -- Code word for letter "Y" in a phonetic alphabet, used to avoid possibility of a misunderstanding in transmitting messages. See also YANKEE.

YOKE FORCE -- See Y FORCE

YOKUM -- Heavy Allied attack to paralyze German coast and beach defenses before landings in southern France. August, 1944, WW-II.

YONDER -- Augitni, New Britain. WW-II.

YONKERS -- Rendova Harbor, New Georgia, Solomon Islands. WW-II.

YORK -- Avro derivation of the British World War II Lancaster bomber; first flew in 1942. Production terminated in 1948.

YORKER BEACH -- See Y BEACH

YOUNG -- Vakan, New Britain. WW-II.

YOUNG CRANE -- Japanese monoplane. See HINAZURU.

YOUTH -- Miri, Borneo. WW-II.

YO-YO -- U.S. Navy program to launch small, one-pass reconnaissance satelloids from carrier-based fleet aircraft; would provide tactical intelligence for fleet operations. Satelloid would relay information by television data-link or physical recovery of the payload. Various tests of aircraft launch for satellite payloads have been made by the Navy but the program has not been approved. Also known as Caleb, NOSTIK, NOTS.

YO-YO, OPERATION -- Derisive name given by U.S. Marines to delay in landing operation at Wonsan, North Korea, during which amphibious shipping, heavily laden with troops, sailed northward and southward off coast at 12-hour intervals, while Wonsan harbor was cleared of mines. 19-25 October 1950, Korean Conflict.

YUKON -- (1) CL-44 long range transport plane in Royal Canadian Air Force Service. Designation is CC-106.

(2) U.S. peacetime military maneuver conducted at Fairbanks, Alaska. November 1947 - January 1948.

YUKON I-II -- Two dress rehearsal exercises for Allied raid on Dieppe, France; held near Bridport, Dorset, England, on stretch of coast resembling Dieppe area. See also JUBILEE. 11-12, 22-23 June 1942, WW-II.

YUNNAN FORCE -- See Y FORCE

YVONNE -- Tropical storm. 14-16 November 1945. First detected over Sulu Sea. Moved west-northwestward across South China Sea to central Indo China.

Z

Z -- Japanese plan to engage American fleet in event of attempted invasion of Carolines or Marianas. WW-II.

Z BATTERY -- British surface-to-air rocket fired in salvoes of 48. With a nine and one-half pound, high explosive warhead, the rocket could reach an altitude of four miles. WW-II.

Z BEACH -- Area on Golfe d'Arzew, east of Oran, Algeria, where landing was made by Allies. November 1942, WW-II.

Z DAY -- (1) Date for beginning Australian 7th Division attack on Japanese in Lae-Nadzab area, New Guinea, 5 September 1943; used to distinguish it from D Day of Australian 9th Division in same operation. WW-II.

(2) Date, 15 December 1943, for invasion by U.S. Task Force DIRECTOR of Arawe, New Britain. Used to distinguish it from main D Day invasion at Cape Glouster later. WW-II.

(3) Date, 27 May 1944, for Allied invasion of Biak Island, north of Netherlands New Guinea. WW-II.

(4) Date for beginning Australian landing in Labuan-Brunei Bay area, British North Borneo. 10 June 1945, WW-II.

Z FORCE -- (1) Band of local volunteers for defense of Hong Kong; trained to work behind Japanese lines. December 1941, WW-II.

(2) British Royal Navy fleet, consisting of battleship, Prince of Wales, and battlecruiser, Repulse (both sunk), with escort of four destroyers; sailed up east coast of Malaya from Singapore until attacked by Japanese aircraft. 8-10 December 1941, WW-II.

(3) Battleship squadron; one of two major forces of British Navy in Mediterranean. Was to block Tyrrhenian Sea to the north and then feint toward western Sicily to divert enemy from invasion corner during HUSKY. See also H, FORCE. July 1943, WW-II.

(4) See GOALPOST SUB-TASK FORCE

Z, PLAN -- (1) Proposed Allied build-up schedule following Normandy landings, 6 June 1944 (D Day); called for 35 divisions on the Continent by D plus 150 days and 41 divisions by D plus 180 days. See also PLANS W, X and Y. WW-II.

(2) See DRACULA

Z, ROUTE -- Southern sea route used during OPERATION DYNAMO, the evacuation of Allied troops from Dunkirk, France, to Dover, England; although shortest of three routes (39 sea miles), because it passed close to enemy held coast of France, considered most vulnerable. See also ROUTES X and Y. May-June 1940, WW-II.

ZAHIR, EL -- See EL ZAHIR

ZAUNKÖNIG -- (English translation: Wren) German acoustic torpedo, officially called T-5, used by submarines against convoy escorts. Called by British Admiralty, Gnat (acronym for German Naval Acoustic Torpedo). WW-II.

ZEALOUS -- Bizerte, Tunisia. WW-II.

ZEBRA -- (1) Code word for letter "Z" in a phonetic alphabet, used to avoid possibility of a misunderstanding in transmitting messages. See also ZULU.

(2) First of mass drops after Normandy landings by U.S. 8th Air Force of supplies to MAQUIS for resistance operations inside France. See also CARPET-BAGGERS, CADILLAC. 25 June 1944, WW-II.

ZEBRA HILL -- U.S. military name for topographic feature south of Kochi, Okinawa. 1945, WW-II.

ZED, CONDITION -- U.S. Navy term meaning maximum condition of readiness for attack or defense aboard ship. WW-II.

ZEKE -- Allied designation for the Japanese A6M1 fighter which first flew in 1939 and first appeared over Chunking in 1940. Popularly known, in one version, as the Zero, its Japanese designation was ZERO-SEN (Type O).

ZENITH -- (1) British graphite-moderated research reactor. Results from experiment interchanged with results from U.S. General Atomic Experiment Facility in San Diego, California.

(2) Another version of the Monocoupe monoplane. See ZEPHYR.

ZENOPHEN -- Wankum, New Guinea. WW-II.

ZEPHYR -- (1) Twin-engine cabin monoplane built before World War II by the Monocoupe Corporation of Missouri. Also produced as the WILD CAT and Zenith.

(2) French trainer plane. See MAGISTER.

(3) Ayuet Island, New Britain. WW-II.

(4) Kukum, Solomon Islands. WW-II.

ZEPO -- Study of cold criticals for ROVER reactors at Los Alamos Scientific Laboratory, New Mexico. Startup 1958. Dismantled 1959.

ZERLIMA -- Operable Indian Critical Assembly in Trombay, India.

ZERO -- Japanese World War II fighter plane. See ZERO-SEN.

ZERO-SEN -- (English translation: Type O) Mitsubishi A6M1 fighter plane which came into prominence before World War II in combat with the American Volunteer Group (Flying Tigers) in China. Used throughout the war as a land plane and carrier-based fighter. See ZEKE.

ZETA -- Miller Aircraft single-engine monoplane built in 1938 in Massachusetts.

ZEUS -- See NIKE-ZEUS

ZIG-ZAG PASS -- Military name for topographic feature west of Dinalupihan, Luzon, Philippines; heavily defended by Japanese. Early 1945, WW-II.

ZIMMERMAN - Cape Dampier, New Britain. WW-II.

ZINNIA -- U.S. code name for Bogon Island, Eniwetok Atoll, Marshall Group. WW-II.

ZIP -- (1) Signal used by Allied Commanders-in-Chief to denote start of an operation. WW-II.

(2) Acronym for Zone Improvement Plan of U.S. Post Office; code numbers are assigned to sectional centers and affiliate post offices in surrounding areas to be used in mailing address; designed to speed sorting and distribution of mail. Inaugurated 1 July 1963.

ZIPPER -- Banu River, New Britain. WW-II.

ZIPPER I -- British operations for the capture of Port Swettenham-Port Dickson area and development of this area preparatory to an advance southward to Singapore. Not carried out. 1945, WW-II.

ZIPPER II -- British exploitation southward as far as the Johore Straits as part of overall ZIPPER. Not carried out, 1945, WW-II.

ZITADELLE -- (English translation: Citadel) German operation against Kursk salient in southern Russia. Began 5 July 1943, WW-II.

ZITRONELLA -- Bombardment and landing operation by large German naval force destroying Allied installations on Spitsbergen Island in Arctic Ocean. September 1943, WW-II.

ZNEZHINKA -- (English translation: Snowflake) Companion dog for OTVAZHNAYA on a Russian space flight launched in July 1959. Both dogs were recovered without apparent harm.

ZOLJA -- Light twin-jet research aircraft designed by Yugoslav Major Beslin and first flown in 1952.

ZOMBIE -- Method used by British to defend a convoy attacked by U-boats at night. WW-II.

ZONITE -- Palembang, Sumatra, Netherlands East Indies. WW-II.

ZOOLOGY -- Prestwick, Scotland. WW-II.

ZOOTSUIT -- Awul, New Britain. WW-II.

ZOUAVE -- White Horse, Yukon Territory, Canada. WW-II.

ZULU -- Code word for letter "Z" in a phonetic alphabet, used to avoid possibility of a misunderstanding in transmitting messages. See also ZEBRA.

ZUNI -- U.S. Navy air-to-air folding wing, 5-inch rocket for use by attack aircraft. One plane can carry as many as 48 rockets. It is solid propelled, unguided, with a conventional warhead. Operational with carrier-based aircraft in 1957. See also CROW.